Special Pedagogic Features

Popular **Model Student Activities** are ready to be used or adapted in the classroom.

STANDARDS

Place: Physical and Human Characteristics
* Discuss seasonal changes in the little town, and how those changes affect people.
* Describe a walk along First or Third Street.

Relationships Within Places: Human-Environment Interaction
* Tell how the snow affects the lives of people in the town.
* Tell what might happen if Katy had not been able to plow out the town.

MODEL STUDENT ACTIVITY
Where Would You Locate Your City?

Overview

The object of this activity is to determine whether students will change their original decision in light of new information.

Procedure

Provide students with a copy of Map 1. Ask where, with just the information they have, they would locate a city if they were prospective settlers. Assume that the area is otherwise uninhabited. Permit students to discuss their choices in small groups, and then have each group present its choice to the entire class. Then provide each group with copies of Maps 2, 3, and 4 (see page 352), one at a time, permitting discussion and explanations (as warranted) after each map is distributed.

Sources/Variation

Making the maps for this activity used to be a major undertaking. However, for any teacher with access to the computer programs referred to earlier (*PC-Globe, PC-USA, USA Atlas, World Atlas,* and *Microsoft Encarta*), it is now a simple process, and the areas that students deal with are real. The computer programs will usually print whichever maps you need. However, it is usually necessary to remove the name of the area manually, using typewriter white-out, tape, or some other method, if you wish it to remain anonymous. After students have decided where to locate their cities, you can provide them with a computer-generated map showing the actual location of major cities.

Map 1
Scale: 1 inch = 50 miles

▭ sea water
▭ rivers
▭ lakes

N

(continues on next page)

MAPS AND GLOBES 351

An end-of-text **Resource Handbook** includes instructional materials, planning aids, instructional resources, and annotated bibliographies of children's literature.

Contents

RESOURCE HANDBOOK

Children and Their World

Their World

Strategies for Teaching Social Studies

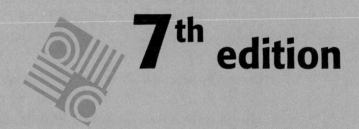

7th **edition**

David A. Welton
Texas Tech University

Houghton Mifflin Company   Boston   New York

To . . .

David Jr., Stephen, Christopher, Lynda, and Shawn

. . . as they encounter their world.

Senior Sponsoring Editor: Sue Pulvermacher-Alt
Senior Development Editor: Lisa Mafrici
Senior Project Editor: Florence Kilgo
Editorial Assistant: Tamara Bhalla
Senior Production/Design Coordinator: Sarah Ambrose
Senior Manufacturing Coordinator: Florence Cadran
Marketing Manager: Jay Hu

Cover image: G&V Chapman, Child Molding Earth From Modeling Clay. © The Image Bank

Printed in the U.S.A.

Library of Congress Control Number: 2001131564

ISBN: 0-618-11646-X

23456789-DC-05 04 03 02 01

Contents

Part 2   Contexts for Teaching Social Studies   95

4.   The Dimensions of Cultural Diversity   96

14. Using Instructional Tools: Print, Multimedia, and Community Resources

 # Preface

Children today are apt to be sitting next to a teacher on the greatest of all roller coasters—a world where change is constant. We know that teaching is future oriented, yet in a constantly changing world, it is challenging to prepare children for a world that none of us can predict with certainty. Each time I prepare a new edition of *Children and Their World* I wonder whether the title should be changed to better reflect the many worlds of childhood—the adult world, the television world, the peer world, the fantasy world, and so forth. Instead of changing the title, I have opted to make clear that the children's world—"their world"—is indeed many worlds.

The teacher's world is changing, too. Teachers dare not ignore the ever-changing technology, the influences of teaching standards, and the increasingly diverse children they greet in their classrooms each day. When I wrote the first edition of this book over twenty-five years ago, the technology was fairly mundane—filmstrips were still "hot stuff"—standards were at least a decade in the future, and whatever diversity there was got little more than a passing glance. In this edition, the focus on diversity has doubled from the previous edition, from one chapter to two. Because of their importance to teachers, technology, standards, and diversity have emerged as themes that reappear at various points throughout the book. These themes are indicated by special marginal icons: a 🔲 for technology, a 🔲 for standards, and a 🔲 for diversity.

In the changing world of teaching there are some constants. The Battle of Hastings, for example, was fought in 1066, and thanks to the nature of history, that's not going to change. What *could* change, however, is whether children will be expected to learn about the Battle of Hastings and many other topics. Also a constant is the often self-imposed belief among beginning teachers that they are expected to know all the content they will be expected to teach before they begin (teaching), yet in reality no one does. Desirable as it might seem to have everything mastered beforehand, beginning teachers will discover that one learns as one teaches. It is among the best of all fringe benefits.

Underlying Assumptions of This Book

Every edition of this book reflects some underlying premises about social studies, about teaching, and about social studies methods books. Here, in summary form, are some of the fundamental ideas that are basic to this edition.

★ The world of teaching elementary- and middle-school social studies is not a world of gimmicks and recipes for teaching activities. Neither is it a chaotic world that somehow becomes clear and understandable if only students are given predetermined bits of information—that Robert E. Lee's horse was named Traveler—or given sets of prescriptive ideas.

* Children come in many different sizes, shapes, forms, and cultural packages. From birth onward, they live in a number of competing worlds and learn countless lessons not taught in classrooms. A fundamental part of the activities that occur in classrooms involves the social and cultural contexts that children bring to school.

* Social studies is complex partly because of the nature of its field of knowledge, and partly because some of its purposes may be in conflict. Consider that social studies is the only subject area in the school curriculum that publicly ascribes to citizenship education an educational goal.

* Teaching elementary- and middle-school social studies sometimes demands a willingness to live with a degree of bewilderment, even confusion.

Audience and Purpose

Children and Their World: Strategies for Teaching Social Studies, seventh edition, is intended for preservice and in-service students taking a first course in teaching elementary- and middle-school social studies. The goal was to make this edition compatible with the growing number of field-based courses where students' time is often at a premium. At the same time, in-service and graduate students should continue to find this edition as useful, or even more so, than previous editions.

A continuing purpose of this book is to help prospective and in-service teachers understand the complex nature of elementary- and middle-school social studies. I, like others, take exception to the conventional contention that "anyone can teach social studies." That contention too often ignores the complexities of a subject area that bridges the social sciences and the humanities. I also advocate a hands-on approach to teaching social studies, but only up to a point. Teachers who adopt a hands-on approach simplistically, and who, for example, have their students spend two weeks building igloos out of sugar cubes, may need to reexamine their priorities. My intent is to help prospective teachers build a perspective for judging the appropriateness of social studies teaching activities, a perspective that recognizes the uniqueness and potential of the underlying subject matter.

This book also is based on the premise that learning is an active, constructivist process. That premise is hardly new or earthshaking, yet it applies equally to students in elementary- or middle-school classrooms and to the preservice students who read this book. For prospective teachers especially, teaching social studies successfully depends primarily on the individual's ability to manage the triumvirate of teaching: the ability to correlate (1) social studies content, (2) teaching methods, and (3) the application of content and methods in classrooms. Content and methods are certainly essential, but the key to effective instruction lies in *application*, in being able to relate subject-matter content with teaching methods, and teaching theory with classroom practice.

The entire text has been extensively revised and updated to incorporate the most recent research in social studies education and to reflect emerging practices and emphases in the field.

New Part Organization and Coverage

This edition still has the same number of parts and chapters as the last edition, but the contents have been thoroughly updated, reorganized and, in some cases, expanded. Part 1, "Building a Framework for Social Studies," focuses on the "what is" of social studies. It explores (1) the dynamic nature of social studies teaching, (2) how social studies reflects the scholarly disciplines that it derives from, and (3) how traditional and alternative social studies programs are organized.

Part 2, "Contexts for Teaching Social Studies," considers factors that impinge on teaching social studies and constitute a context in which it is taught. Consistent with the increased emphasis on diversity in this edition, the single chapter from the prior edition has been expanded into two chapters, one dealing with cultural/multicultural diversity, and the other with educational/instructional diversity. Other chapters in this section focus on developing character and using social studies to enhance students' literacy skills.

The last section, Part 3, "Instruction," which is also the largest, focuses on the nuts and bolts of teaching social studies. Chapters in this section examine planning, assessment, teaching strategies for hands-on learning, teaching critical and reflective thinking, helping students use maps and globes, and, finally, a chapter on instructional tools and resources.

Significant Changes and New Coverage

New and expanded coverage in this edition include the following:

* *Refocused Chapter 1.* A significant portion of Chapter 1, "The Dynamics of Social Studies," is new to this edition and presents case studies on teaching social studies in a technological age.
* *New (and expanded) chapter on cultural diversity.* The new Chapter 4, "The Dimensions of Cultural Diversity," examines multicultural education, as well as the differing expectations and behaviors that can characterize divergent cultural groups.
* *New (and expanded) chapter on educational/instructional diversity.* New to this edition, Chapter 5, "The Dimensions of Instructional Diversity," includes expanded sections on educationally disabled students and multiple intelligences.
* Consistent with the increased coverage on technology in this edition, each chapter has *a new, end-of-chapter feature titled, "Suggested Readings and Resources."* It includes an annotated listing of Internet sources relevant to the content of each chapter.

* *New Technology Updates* have been created for many chapters. The Updates show how teachers can use technology to enhance their teaching.
* *A newly reorganized and expanded section of the literacy chapter* (Chapter 7) is intended to help teachers distinguish between strategies that help children to learn new ideas and techniques for determining whether children comprehend or understand new ideas.
* *The Resource Handbook* at the end of the book has been significantly updated. Additions to this edition include: (1) a sample cooperative bibliography of Abraham Lincoln written by fifth graders, (2) a detailed annotated bibliography of nonfiction and fictional children's books for periods throughout history, and (3) an annotated bibliography of women of achievement in different historical periods.
* Coverage related to the *key themes of technology, standards, and diversity* are highlighted by new icons in the margins of relevant sections of all chapters.
* *A new Web site* at **http://college.hmco.com** (then select "Education") that features pretest and posttest questions for each chapter, additional examples of social studies teaching activities, such as a WebQuest, and links to other resources.

Other Current Features

Several major emphases from previous editions also appear in this edition. These include the following:

* *Exemplary Classroom Practices.* Vignettes of exemplary classroom practices are, in effect, mini-case studies of how real (or composite) teachers elect to approach social studies in their classrooms. For example, the literacy chapter (Chapter 7) begins with a vignette of how a second-grade teacher in Arizona integrates social studies and language experiences with her students, for many of whom English is their second language. Other vignettes illustrate how teachers can use historical documents as a springboard, how they use technology, and how they use a K-W-L chart with their students.
* *Integrating Children's Literature.* Opportunities for integrating children's literature into social studies have been expanded throughout this edition. The same is true for the bibliography of children's fiction and nonfiction books presented in the Resource Handbook, as noted earlier.

Special Pedagogical Aids

To make this text easy to study, appealing to use, and a valuable teaching resource, the following features are included:

* *Key Questions and Key Ideas* at the beginning of each chapter that serve as advance organizers for the content to be covered.
* *Introductions* that provide an overview of what is to come.
* *Technology Updates* that provide technological resources for contemporary social studies programs.
* *Model Student Activities* that illustrate model lesson formats that can be adapted to other social studies topics or content.

* *Commentaries* in which I offer a point of view on various problems and issues.
* *Vignettes of exemplary practice* that demonstrate how various teachers approach social studies with their students.
* *Marginal notes* that highlight (1) key ideas within the text and (2) key themes of diversity, technology, and standards.
* *Summaries* that synthesize the major concepts presented in each chapter.
* *Suggested Activities* that are designed to stimulate further thought or provide opportunities for students to apply the concepts treated within the chapter.
* *Suggested Readings and Resources* that list, with annotations, additional print and Internet sources for students to locate detailed information on topics considered with the chapter.
* A *Resource Handbook* that provides additional sources and materials related to social studies teaching. The four parts of the Handbook include: (1) instructional materials relating to text activities, (2) planning aids, (3) additional instructional resources, and (4) annotated bibliographies of children's books that are keyed to common social studies topics.
* *Web site support* that provides additional resources for students and instructors alike.

Acknowledgments

I am keenly aware of my indebtedness to the many people who helped to make this book possible. This is especially true for John Mallan, my coauthor, mentor, and confidant for the first six editions of this book. After twenty years Dr. Mallan has decided to pursue other opportunities. His advice, counsel, and contributions to shaping this book are simply beyond measure. He will be missed.

I am also indebted to countless elementary- and middle-school students for helping me understand what it means to teach a subject like social studies. Equally important are the college students and in-service teachers with whom I have been privileged to work, and whose questions (and responses to our answers) have indicated directions in which I needed to go and areas where I needed to be clearer than I was.

I gratefully acknowledge the contributions of the following reviewers for the thoughtful advice and criticism they offered at various stages in the development of this book: Carol Adkins, Northern Arizona University; Michael J. Berson, University of South Florida; Dean Cristol, Old Dominion University; Kristi Fragnoli, State University of New York, Cortland; Melaney Kay Gillaspie, Old Dominion University; Karen Moore, California State University, Sacramento; Charles S. White, Boston University.

I also extend special thanks to my talented developmental editors, Sandra Evans and Lisa Mafrici; to a wonderful production editor, Florence Kilgo; and to the rest of the editorial staff at Houghton Mifflin who were my partners in this endeavor.

Finally, I continue to owe special acknowledgment to Kathy Welton, who, after thirty some years, has come to understand the trials and joys associated with producing a book such as this.

DAVID A. WELTON

Prologue: Reflecting on What's Ahead

Remember when you

- couldn't understand why Australia was a continent but Greenland wasn't?
- thought Paris, Boston, and Chicago were states?
- spent countless hours answering the questions at the end of the chapter of your textbook?
- had current events every Friday?
- memorized the Preamble to the Constitution, the Gettysburg Address, or the presidents of the United States, in order?
- were taught that "milk trucks carry milk" when you already knew it?
- made the outline for your report—on Greece, "the South," Andrew Jackson, or whatever—*after* you had written the report?
- realized that when teachers said, "You're not thinking" they were really saying "wrong!" but nicely?

Introduction

Some things about social studies you may remember fondly, and others you've long since forgotten. From time to time you may have asked yourself why you needed to learn certain things, like the states and capitals (assuming you know them), when that kind of information is readily available elsewhere. There are a variety of reasons, some valid and others questionable, why things like the states and capitals are often taught in social studies, reasons we will explore throughout this book.

The Joan of Arc Syndrome

You may be aware that portions of the social studies you studied might not have been taught at all were it not for the "Joan of Arc" syndrome. In this phenomenon, which is illustrated in the following conversation, the most important qualification is that at least one of the speakers has spent time studying about Joan of Arc, the national heroine of France.

"I've heard they're taking Joan of Arc out of social studies. Children won't be studying her anymore."
"What! What are they doing that for?"

"I guess it's because they can't figure out why they should keep her in."

"You gotta be kidding! Why they should keep her in? I mean isn't it obvious?

I learned about Joan of Arc—you did too. She's someone everyone should know about. . . . I mean, well. . . look what it's done for us! We'd never be where we are today if we hadn't learned the stuff that everybody needs to know—including Joan of Arc."

"You're saying that because *we* learned it when we were in school, students today should learn it too."

"Exactly! We learned it, they should learn it too!"

There's probably a little Joan of Arc in each of us—a reluctance to reflect on some of the things we have done in the past. This is not to suggest that everything about the past is "bad" or outdated, or that every new idea that comes along is worthwhile and is the kind of thing that schools should move toward immediately. The point is that tradition, which is what the Joan of Arc syndrome represents, is such a potent force that trying to remove almost any topic from the school curriculum can elicit howls of protest. In many cases, the protestors may not remember much about the topic—whether it's Joan of Arc or whatever—all they must remember is having studied it. As long as people perceive certain topics as useful, those topics tend to remain in the curriculum, which then grows larger with every passing day.

Tradition plays a role in keeping the curriculum as large as it is, but there is another side to this coin: that is, there are some things that could be included in the curriculum but usually are not. For example, you may recall some questions that arose during your school experience that you thought were important, but that were almost never considered at school. These may have included questions like the following:

The questions kids ask

Is it O.K. to lie sometimes? If so, when?
How do other people feel about me, and how can I know for sure?
If cooperation is so important, why don't you get graded on it?
Why are the best movies almost always rated "R"?
Must I like everybody? What happens if I don't?
Why doesn't everyone have all the money he or she needs?

Underlying questions like these are genuine human and social concerns. Some people argue that such questions involve things that students will learn—or should learn—from their parents or from everyday life. They also argue that for schools to get involved in such matters, is either unnecessary or an invasion of parental rights and responsibilities, sometimes both. Although questions and concerns cannot and indeed should not be the sole basis for elementary and middle-school social studies programs, we will explore some legitimate roles they can play.

An Inquiry

After spending a dozen or so years watching social studies teachers in action, you already have some beliefs, assumptions, and impressions about what social studies is and about why it is taught. In the next section, you have the opportunity to clarify what you believe about elementary and middle-school social studies and then compare your beliefs with ours. It is not important that we agree on everything, because the purpose is simply to establish a point of departure.

● A Social Studies Inventory

Select the response that best reflects your impressions of your elementary and middle-school social studies experience by circling the appropriate number.

Comparing beliefs
about social studies

		Agree	*Uncertain*	*Disagree*
1.	Social studies is too often dull and boring.	1	2	3
2.	What children learn in social studies is useful in their everyday lives.	1	2	3
3.	Teaching social studies is not as important as teaching reading or mathematics.	1	2	3
4.	The main purpose of social studies is teaching history and geography.	1	2	3
5.	Most social studies teachers put about the right emphasis on teaching thinking skills.	1	2	3
6.	Many social studies teachers place too much emphasis on textbooks.	1	2	3
7.	Social studies involves everyday classroom behaviors, such as lining up properly to walk through the hall or learning to obey classroom rules.	1	2	3
8.	Small-group work in social studies often uses time that could be better spent learning things that are really important.	1	2	3

● Responses

The responses in this section are geared to traditional social studies programs, and not to one-of-a-kind programs you rarely encounter.

1. *Social studies is too often dull and boring.* Response: Agree.

The coverage problem

Content that deals with people—which is what social studies focuses on—should never be dull and boring, yet too often that's what seems to happen. For example, as Alter and Denworth noted in 1990 (p. 3), "History itself isn't boring; it's just taught that way." As much as one may be inclined to agree with Alter and Denworth, some related problems play a role here. First, many textbooks present materials in ways that are—well—less than thrilling. Second, the vast amounts of material that teachers (and textbooks) are expected to cover during a year can be almost overwhelming. One could argue that a major part of the problem here is the so-called survey course. Sixth-grade teachers, for example, are often expected to teach history that covers prehistoric times to the atomic age—roughly five thousand years. The scope is so broad that they and their students are forced to rush through historic eras so quickly that students often have difficulty differentiating one era from another. Trying to cover so much material in a 180-day school year inevitably results in superficial exposure, not in-depth understanding (see Newmann, 1988). The paradox here is that teachers at other grade levels may spend the entire year on social studies topics that may not require that much time. For example, the traditional curriculum focus for second grade is the neighborhood. Spending 180 days on the neighborhood is more than some second-grade teachers want or need and often leads to situations where they teach social studies only once a week, and that is only *if* they get to it.

"Less is more"

More and more teachers and even some states have begun to address the problems associated with survey courses by adopting an approach that is sometimes referred to as "less is more." The premise is that by studying fewer ("less") topics in greater depth, teachers can spend the time necessary to develop ("more") in-depth understanding. This approach may help reduce the extent to which social studies may have been dull and boring in the past.

2. *What children learn in social studies is useful in their everyday lives.* Response: Uncertain.

Relevance

Because the relevance of social studies often hinges on how teachers approach it, it is difficult to generalize here. Some portions of social studies—especially history—are taught because they represent bodies of knowledge that children are expected to learn and know, regardless of any direct relevance to their day-to-day lives. Still other segments of social studies can be taught in ways that have immediate relevance to children and to their actions as future citizens.

3. *Teaching social studies is not as important as teaching reading or mathematics.* Response: Disagree.

Priorities

The conventional wisdom in many elementary and middle schools holds that teaching reading and mathematics is more important than almost everything else. This book reflects the position that thought-provoking social studies programs will incorporate elements that are just as important as reading and mathematics, possibly more so.

4. *The main purpose of social studies is teaching history and geography.* Response: Disagree.

History and geography are so prominent in many social studies programs that the other social sciences, like anthropology, often fade into the background. Then, too, many people think that social studies is simply another name for history and geography. Common as such thinking is, it is much too limited. Social studies deals with the human experience, with human beings and human behavior in every sense of those terms.

Goal: To produce good citizens

The main purpose for teaching social studies is to produce thoughtful, competent, well-informed, and responsible citizens. In other words, the purpose for teaching social studies parallels the purpose for which schools exist—to produce good citizens. Not every child will become an engineer, a doctor, or a scientist, but everyone will be a citizen; it's an office that every one of us occupies. Walter Parker (1990, p. 17) probably put it best when he stated that social studies

is where, if anywhere, the core knowledge base for citizenship will be developed. The knowledge base for social studies is the only place in the school curriculum

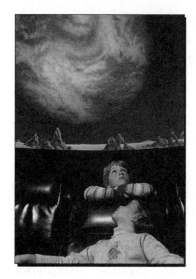

where focused inquiry on democratic ideals and practices might be located. It is where the tragedies and victories of "liberty and justice for all" can be laid out for study. It is where students encounter models of civic courage—Abraham Lincoln and Sojourner Truth [a freed slave who lived in the same era as Lincoln], for example. *And* it is where students stand the best chance of being introduced systematically to popular sovereignty—participating in decision making and grappling with enduring public issues.

5. *Most social studies teachers put about the right emphasis on teaching thinking skills.* Response: Disagree.

Many traditional social studies programs place too much emphasis on learning names, dates, and other information and too little emphasis on using social studies as a vehicle for teaching critical thinking and problem solving. Throughout this book the emphasis is on *using* social studies content—the stuff of which history, geography, and other social sciences are made—for a variety of teaching purposes. Among the most important of those purposes is helping students to become skillful thinkers.

6. *Many social studies teachers place too much emphasis on textbooks.* Response: Agree.

Some teachers apparently feel that skipping one or more chapters in a textbook will leave irreparable gaps in their students' education. Such teachers may rely on textbooks exclusively, perhaps because they are not aware of how to use alternative data sources. Still other teachers feel compelled to emphasize the textbook because of state or school board mandates or other forces beyond their control. All of this notwithstanding, we endorse an approach to social studies in which textbooks serve as teaching tools but do not become the program itself.

Text as tools

7. *Social studies involves everyday classroom behaviors, such as lining up properly to walk through the hall or learning to obey classroom rules.* Response: Uncertain.

This response is not weaseling out or avoiding the issue here because everything depends on the context in which the behaviors take place. In schools and classrooms that employ "developmental discipline" (see Schaps and Solomon, 1990), where students are treated as valued and participating members of a learning community, behaviors such as lining up to go to the cafeteria can be an integral part of social studies. However, this occurs only when students play an active role in classroom governance and decision making. That role includes participating in the development of classroom rules—through which students begin to understand what rules are for—and working collaboratively with teachers to solve problems. Classrooms and schools that function as caring democratic communities—as microcosms of the larger society in which students actually "do" democracy—can provide a vital part of citizenship education. We disagree with people who claim that training children to walk down the hall properly is necessarily a vital part of social studies. Training students to conform to expected behaviors through the imposition of adult authority is obviously one approach to classroom management—and classroom management is clearly something that every teacher must be concerned with. Nevertheless, we question whether teachers who adopt this approach are actually teaching social studies.

Classrooms as caring communities

8. *Small-group work in social studies often uses time that could be better spent learning things that are really important.* Response: Agree.

Group work

Small-group work in many social studies programs sometimes seems to be included as a respite from normal classroom routines, almost as a way to make the regular work more palatable. At the same time, the most common reason that people are fired from their jobs is their inability to get along with others in the workplace. Social studies can provide a context for small-group work, which helps children learn to work effectively with one another.

The key to small-group work and most of the other items on this inventory is how teachers use them. Small-group work can be a raging success, a disaster, or something in between. Likewise, you've had teachers who could somehow make the dullest, most lifeless material become interesting and worthwhile. Clearly, teachers hold the key to vibrant and appealing social studies programs.

Building on what children already know

The other key ingredient is the children. Some of the problems that children experience with social studies—like confusing cities, states, and countries—are simply a result of their lack of experience with the world as we know it. Young children are prone to view their world from a highly personal perspective that, even in this age of advanced technology, may not extend beyond their immediate neighborhood. At the same time, young children are often fascinated with our world and the people who inhabit it. The purpose throughout this book is to provide the basis for developing elementary and middle-school social studies programs that can capitalize on children's inherent interest in their world and that will add depth and richness to what they already know.

Building a Framework
for Social Studies

Part 1 examines three elements that make up the framework for teaching
social studies. The first of these is the nature of social studies itself and the purposes for which it is taught, both of which are the focus of Chapter 1, The Dynamics of Social Studies. The second element of that framework is the knowledge base from which social studies is drawn—history and the social sciences—which is the focus in Chapter 2, History and the Social Sciences: The Knowledge Base for Social Studies. The third element of the framework in Chapter 3, How Social Studies Programs Are Organized, explores how social studies is organized for teaching purposes.

The overarching purpose for teaching social studies, which we address in
Chapter 1, can be captured in two words: citizenship education. That purpose has remained constant for almost one hundred years, but as our society has changed and continues to change, the demands of contemporary citizenship education have also changed. In a society made up of overlapping cultures—national, regional, ethnic, and so forth—citizens are apt to face conflicting demands and allegiances. In addition to the ability to read and write, everyone in our society needs to become conversant in a least three complementary literacies of citizenship: multicultural literacy, civic literacy, and community literacy.

Chapter 2, History and the Social Sciences: The Knowledge Base for Social
Studies, surveys the disciplines from which social studies is drawn. Because history often plays a major role in social studies programs, special attention focuses on the demands that teaching history imposes on teachers.

There are literally hundreds of ways in which you could organize and teach
social studies, but as we explain in Chapter 3, How Social Studies Programs Are Organized, this variety is seldom evident in most textbook-based programs. Chapter 3 focuses on the most common social studies programs—especially the expanding-environments approach, the most common program of all. For balance, several alternative program formats, both past and present, are examined.

1

The Dynamics of Social Studies

Key Questions

* What is social studies, and why is it an integral part of elementary and middle-school programs?
* What is citizenship education?
* How does social studies lend itself to multiple objectives?

Key Ideas

* Social studies is a multidisciplinary school subject based primarily on history and the social science disciplines.
* Social studies is characterized by multiple goals and purposes, some of which it shares with other subject areas.
* The overarching aim of social studies is citizenship education, but how this relates to the selection and use of content in instruction has not been settled.
* The purpose of social studies is to provide children and youth with the knowledge, skills, and dispositions that permit them to participate actively in a democratic society.

Introduction: Teaching Social Studies in a Technological Age

An old adage holds that you need only three things to teach social studies: an atlas, a globe, and a map—preferably one mounted on a roller. Textbooks might be useful, too, but according to the adage, they are not essential.

Ramirez Elementary, one of several schools we will visit from time to time throughout this book, was built in the 1970s and has been around long enough that it still has some atlases, wall maps, and globes. But in many classrooms today, these items are often used as room decorations. Most classrooms have textbooks, too, but for much of the year they sit largely unused on their shelf under the globe. It's not that Ramirez's teachers necessarily dispute the adage, it's just that many of them believe they've identified some better ways to teach social studies— which is why they are featured here.

DIVERSITY

Ramirez Elementary is a predominantly (90%+) Hispanic inner-city school located in a midsize city in the Southwest. Over 95 percent of Ramirez's students are eligible for free breakfast and lunch, the commonly used indicator for the socioeconomic status of the neighborhoods the school serves. The mobility rate at Ramirez is more than 50 percent, which means that over half its student population will either enter or leave the school during a given year. This also means that at the end of the year some teachers' classes are almost completely different from the classes they began with. Note, however, that this is not a unique school; many inner-city schools share similar demographic profiles.

TECHNOLOGY

Putting new computers in regular classrooms

What sets Ramirez Elementary apart from most of its counterparts is not its demographics, but the technology available to its teachers and students. *Every* classroom (including kindergarten) has five computers, each networked to a color printer and equipped with CD-ROM, modem, sound system, and the capability to import images from digital cameras or camcorders. With this kind of hardware, you are correct to assume that these are neither bargain-basement computers nor the ancient Apple 2e machines popular in the 1980s. As Ramirez's principal, Lucy Guiterrez Brown, says, "We put the new computers in classrooms where teachers can use them, and put the old computers in the computer lab where we teach keyboarding skills." For a detailed description of how an inner-city school is able to purchase so many new computers, see Welton (1998). In addition, a description of how second graders at Ramirez use authoring software to produce an animated book of "Colonial Occupations" appears in the Technology Update on page 183 in Chapter 7.

It is incorrect to say that Ramirez's teachers do not use atlases and maps (or textbooks), because with their computer-based atlas and encyclopedia programs they can access an almost infinite range of information, including maps. The key components, of course, are having the hardware and software to accomplish this. Using technology, Ramirez students do some remarkable activities. For example, one group of sixth graders uses information from the Internet to plot the locations of the day's earthquakes on an oversize world map. A detailed description of how they do this appears in the Technology Update, pages 344–345.

TECHNOLOGY

Almost all the fifth-grade students at Ramirez correspond via E-mail with fifth graders elsewhere around the world. At the beginning of the year, neither the Ramirez nor the "foreign" fifth graders know where the others are—although teachers know this, of course. The first tasks for both groups include determining who their correspondents are, which is easy enough, and determining where they live, which is somewhat more difficult. During their first month of E-mailing, both groups of students are restricted to asking questions that can be answered by either yes or no—explanations are not permitted. This means that students must learn to phrase their questions very precisely. Yet in less time than you might imagine, students in both nations will have identified their correspondents' school and its location—maybe not exactly, but close. Thereafter, they are free to interact without restrictions—and interact they do!

Capitalizing on "the need to know"

One clue the students used to identify their partner school's location occurred when they noticed that their correspondents' E-mail messages were dated "Tuesday," for example, when it was still "Monday" here—and vice versa. Even very young students know you cannot jump ahead in time, so their first conclusion was that there was a glitch in the E-mail program. However, after teachers assured them the dates were correct, the situation created the "need to know"—the desire for an explanation—among many students. Teachers from both countries indicated that

Even young students can master elements of computer technology. (© Susie Fitzhugh)

their students *insisted* that they teach them how time zones "work"—and let's do it right now, not sometime later in the year!

Teaching about time zones, which necessarily means that students need to understand latitude and longitude, especially longitude, is a common challenge for most elementary and middle-school teachers; it's part of most fifth- or sixth-grade programs. But having their students ask them to explain time zones is something most teachers seldom encounter and is what is sometimes referred to as having reached "a teachable moment."

TECHNOLOGY

Several clarifications to this illustration are in order. First, the "foreign" students are located in New Zealand, where, because they too speak English, both student groups can use E-mail without translators. Second, with the cooperation of nearby universities that had the necessary hardware, the teachers here and in New Zealand arranged an interactive video conference as a capstone experience for their students. Interactive video is a two-way video system that permits participants to view and hear each other simultaneously. Unfortunately, interactive video conferences (which usually include satellite charges) are frightfully expensive. To pay for them, and with the blessing of their respective school administrations, the American and New Zealand teachers solicited contributions from service groups (e.g., Rotary clubs, etc.) and local foundations.

The time difference between New Zealand and the United States (here are those time zones again) meant that the New Zealand students had to be at their TV studio at 6:30 A.M. and the American students had to be in their studio at 7:30 P.M. Despite this, no student on either continent was absent.

Locating schools elsewhere

Locating another class or school somewhere around the globe to partner with is seldom the problem it might seem. You simply make Internet contact with one of the organizations, such as the Global Schools Network (**http://www.mdc.com.my/ smart/gsn/pages/fullframe.htm**), which specializes in matching schools. The final decision is always up to the participating schools, of course. Details are in the "Suggested Readings and Resources" section at the end of the chapter. There's no guarantee that your experience will be as successful or elaborate as the one described here, but then there should also be no question that what the Ramirez students experienced is a far cry from answering those questions at the end of the chapter in the textbook.

Before personal computers and the Internet became such an integral part of our lives, the Canadian media scholar Marshall McLuhan predicted that the world would become a global village—a place of almost instantaneous communication. Accurate as McLuhan's prediction has proven to be, we doubt that even he anticipated all the effects the Information Age would have on our lives. As suggested in this introduction, technology has had a profound effect on how some teachers approach teaching social studies. Yet technology is not the only element that teachers must address. You are surely aware of the movement, at the state level especially, that focuses on the question "How well are schools performing?" During the 1990s, state-mandated tests designed to determine how well students can perform in reading, mathematics, and other subject areas proliferated, seemingly faster even than technology. If this were not enough, teachers also are confronted with performance standards that identify what students should be expected to know in the various subject areas. The Ramirez teachers were caught up in these expectations as much as teachers elsewhere, especially because the school would become eligible for additional state funds if students did well on the state-mandated tests but could face a variety of sanctions if students performed poorly.

STANDARDS

Are these switched?

The skill of writing E-mail messages (to students in another nation) is not on most state-mandated tests, so you can be sure the Ramirez teachers had to wrestle with the question of whether the activity was worth the time it takes. Ultimately they decided that in addition to the interest the activity aroused in students, the E-mail correspondence involved creating "real" messages as opposed to yet another "out-of-the-book" assignment. And as some teachers told their students, "You've got to write clear E-mail messages that have good grammar and correct spelling. You're gonna look dumb if you make lots of errors." So the Ramirez teachers justified the E-mail activity in terms of the opportunities it provided to teach composing skills, including grammar and spelling, all of which are covered on the state tests.

Does the activity address the standards?

Technology, subject-matter standards, and mandated testing are three elements that teachers today cannot ignore. These elements also have become part of the dynamics of teaching social studies, which is the focus of the balance of this chapter (and throughout this book).

Students in democratic classrooms share responsibility for maintaining safe and caring learning environments.
(© Susie Fitzhugh)

Dynamic Social Studies: The Continuing Debates

The next section of a chapter usually doesn't begin with another teaching vignette after such a lengthy example as this chapter's introduction. Notice that I said "usually." Instead of presenting a list of the emerging practices in teaching social studies, it is better practice to provide students (and readers) with one or more concrete examples that provide a context for the summary list of generalizations that will follow later. In other words, the premise here is that "experience should precede abstraction"—an instructional tactic that we will come back to from time to time.

Experiences should precede abstraction

● Teaching Vignette: Using Cooperative Biographies with Jigsaw Grouping

Tarry Lindquist teaches fifth grade at the Lakeridge Elementary School, which is located in the San Juan Islands immediately across Puget Sound from Seattle, Washington. Although we have not visited Tarry's classroom in person, we made Ms. Lindquist the Focus of a Vignette in this book because she writes (or coauthors) wonderful books about her teaching experiences. These include *Seeing the Whole Through Social Studies* (1995), *Ways That Work: Putting Social Studies Standards into Practice* (1997), and *Social Studies at the Center* (with Douglas Selwyn, 2000), all of which are outstanding.

Writing books cooperatively

What Ms. Lindquist does to warrant our attention here is devote five weeks of class time to having her fifth graders write cooperative biographies of Abraham Lincoln. Cooperative biographies are books that students write together—that is, cooperatively. Having said this, back up for a moment and consider how much time this activity consumes. There are thirty-six weeks in a typical school year, and Ms. Lindquist has elected to devote at least five of them to a cooperative writing project on just one aspect of American history. By devoting so much time to one historical personage, imagine all the history that Ms. Lindquist doesn't have time to cover! Thus, a basic question here is: How can she justify spending so much classroom time on just one activity/person? Before addressing that question directly, you need to understand some of the activities the children engage in as they produce those biographies.

Getting Started. Writing cooperative biographies is such a time-consuming project that students write only one of them during the year. And, because most students have never experienced a writing project of this magnitude, Ms. Lindquist predetermines some elements that make it less overwhelming. One restriction—that all biographies are on the same person, Abraham Lincoln—enables groups of students to work together as they encounter problems. It also simplifies the background information that Ms. Lindquist must provide. In addition, from the outset, Ms. Lindquist predetermines that (1) each writing group will have five members and (2) each biography will have five chapters (the number of chapters or the size of groups can vary depending on the number of students in the class each year). This procedure means that one student in each group will be responsible for one chapter of the final biography. A third ground rule is that there must be a balance among the chapters—no fifty-page chapters on Lincoln's early life, for example. This limitation may not seem important at first, but its importance often grows as the project progresses.

Laying the ground work

You may be asking yourself how Ms. Lindquist knew what to predetermine and what decisions she should leave up to the children. Ms. Lindquist credits Myra Zarnowski's (1990) book, *Learning About Biographies: A Reading and Writing Approach for Children,* a joint publication of the National Council for Teachers of English and the National Council for the Social Studies, as an invaluable resource. If you are thinking that a five-week cooperative biography project might be too ambitious for you or your students, read Zarnowski before you decide.

One of the first questions the writing groups must decide is: what will each chapter be about? Students cannot make this decision until they know something about their subject, of course, and it is also useful to see how previous Lincoln biographers organized their work. At this point, Ms. Lindquist spends several days providing background information—some as read-alouds and others as minilectures—which highlight different aspects of Lincoln's life. Meanwhile, students are doing independent research. The students and Ms. Lindquist then brainstorm significant

Background information after the task is clear

FIGURE 1.1 Jigsaw Grouping

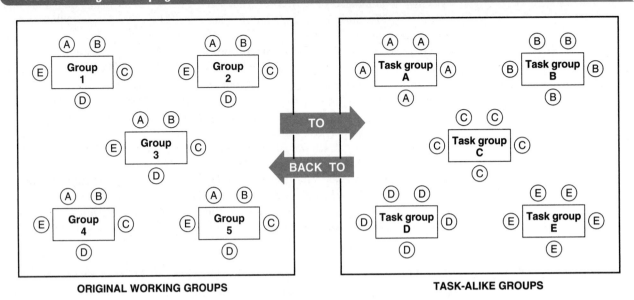

ORIGINAL WORKING GROUPS   TASK-ALIKE GROUPS

events in Lincoln's life, after which they try to categorize and organize their brainstorming ideas into chapter topics—Lincoln's early life, his presidency, and so on. Eventually they decide on the focus for each of the five chapters.

Jigsaw Technique.   Ms. Lindquist also uses a *jigsaw* technique where the students from each writing group who are responsible for Chapter 1 (or 2, or 3) meet together as task-alike groups to share what they should include in their chapter. This technique is reflected in Figure 1.1. After the Chapter 1 (and Chapters 2 and 3) people have returned to their original working group, they spend at least one class discussing how they will organize their respective biographies.

Once the chapter topics have been determined, students engage in more independent research. But this time, and because they know that Chapter 1, for example, will be about Lincoln's early life, their research is more focused. This is where students may encounter another problem—having too much information. To maintain a balance between their chapters (ground rule 3), some students find they need to cut some "really good stuff" from their chapter. Less often, authors may need to beef up their chapters. The overly long chapters may lead to lengthy meetings as group members help the author wrestle with deciding what to cut. The recognition that real-world authors are sometimes forced to omit perfectly good but excessively lengthy materials is one that many fifth graders accept reluctantly—usually very reluctantly.

Fine tuning

Before each cooperative biography is printed, students compose a brief dedication page and an equally brief biography of each author, along with an introduction and a table of contents. These elements are not essential, of course, but when students discover that many biographies of Lincoln contain them, they see no reason theirs should not have them, too.

TECHNOLOGY

Completing the Biographies. Word processing programs greatly simplify the final production of the completed biographies. Usually the writing group goes over the rough draft very carefully, in part because things sometimes look different on paper than they do on a computer screen. Spelling checkers and grammar programs also get a workout, but the finished product invariably looks good. Some tasks still remain however, such as (1) making covers, and then (2) printing extra copies for parents, grandparents, other family members, and (3) finally, making and autographing one copy that will go into the school library. An original cooperative biography written by Ms. Lindquist's students appears on pages 114–131 in her book, *Ways That Work* (Heinemann, 1997; reprinted from *Ways That Work: Putting Social Studies Strategies into Practice,* by Tarry Lindquist; copyright © 1997 by Tarry Lindquist; published by Heinemann, a division of Reed Elsevier, Inc., Portsmouth, NH; used by permission of the publisher).

Adding the finishing touches

Ms. Lindquist's "To Do" list and her time allotments for the cooperative biography project include the following (1997):

Time allotments

1. Content packing (5 periods). Ms. Lindquist reads aloud from various works on Lincoln while students take notes.
2. Content stacking (5 periods). Students read and research independently.
3. Brainstorming key events in Lincoln's life (1 period). A whole-class activity.
4. Categorizing the events identified during brainstorming (1 period). A whole-class activity.
5. Independent writing (3–5 periods). An individual activity.
6. Creating jigsaw groups for sharing by chapter (1–3 periods). Small-group work.
7. Rewriting and refining (1–2 periods). An individual or small-group activity.
8. Book groups meet together and share (1–2 periods). A small-group activity.
9. Revising and refining (1–3 periods). A small-group activity.
10. Creating and adding dedications, the introduction, the table of contents, the bibliography, a cover, and other related elements (3–4 periods). A small-group activity.
11. Publishing and distributing (1–2 periods). A small-group activity.
12. Reading, evaluating, and sharing (1–2 periods). An individual and whole-class activity.
(13.) Phew!

Analysis. Consider for a moment the variety of activities that Tarry Lindquist's students engaged in as they produced their cooperative biographies.

Activities associated with cooperative biographies

★ Based on their independent *research* (along with some help from Ms. Lindquist), they worked *actively* and *cooperatively* with their groups to produce an original (*authentic*) *document* they would share with others.
★ They engaged in realistic *decision-making* activities, such as making choices about what their chapters would focus on, and what materials they would include or need to cut.

* They engaged in *critical thinking* activities, such as comparing how other authors organized their biographies.
* They worked on a single topic—Abraham Lincoln—for five weeks. Clearly this was an *in-depth* effort, not a superficial survey.

Certain terms in the preceding list are highlighted because they appear frequently in at least two places: (1) the National Council for Social Studies (NCSS) publication *Expectations of Excellence: Curriculum Standards for Social Studies* (1994), which is often referred to as the NCSS standards document, and (2) throughout this book. This is not sheer coincidence!

Relationship of Cooperative Biographies to the NCSS Standards

The NCSS standards are one of several sets of standards that apply to social studies. Additional standards have been established by professional organizations associated with social studies—including the history standards, the geography standards, and so forth. In this section we examine how Ms. Lindquist's cooperative biography activity meshes with the NCSS standards.

STANDARDS

The introduction to the NCSS standards publication (*Expectations of Excellence*) identifies four skills that students should gain from an effective social studies program. The following material maintains the language of the NCSS standards but their form has been modified to create a checklist for assessing the cooperative biography project. On the following form, check the appropriate space ("Yes", "No," or "Possibly") to reflect the extent to which you think that the cooperative biography activity addresses each element.

Does the cooperative biography project reflect the following learning skills?

Yes	*No*	*Possibly*	*Did the cooperative biography project enable students to*
___	___	___	1. acquire information and manipulate data?
___	___	___	2. develop and present policies, arguments, and stories?
___	___	___	3. construct new knowledge?
___	___	___	4. participate in groups?

Learning skills

The cooperative biography activity clearly involved students in the acquisition and manipulation of information as well as in participation in group activities. Thus the answers to numbers 1 and 4 are yes. In addition, because the finished biography reflected information that had never existed in that form previously, it probably qualifies for another yes for number 3, "constructing new knowledge." It's true that the knowledge students created was not new to the world—as it might be for scientists who unlock the secrets of DNA, for example. Yet very few professionals, to say nothing of eleven-year-olds, will ever have that opportunity. Thus, it seems appropriate to interpret this item in its narrower sense, that the knowledge Ms. Lindquist's students gained about Abraham Lincoln was new to them.

One criterion that could be a little "iffy" relates to number 2, "developing and presenting policies, arguments, and stories." Because this expectation indicates three formats that students should be able to deal with, it is necessarily more global than the others. However, the standard does not say that all three elements must be dealt with simultaneously. Over a school year or possibly even a school career, it's reasonable to expect teachers to provide activities in which students "develop and present policies, arguments, and stories," but not necessarily in a single activity. In summary, the cooperative biography project incorporates the four NCSS skill criteria, although with some limitations for number 2.

In addition to the skill areas just noted, the NCSS standards also identify characteristics that "powerful" social studies activities should reflect. As we did with the preceding skill areas, decide whether the cooperative biography activity reflects these characteristics.

Does the cooperative biography activity reflect the following characteristics of powerful social studies lessons and activities?

<table>
<tr><td>Characteristics of powerful social studies activities</td><td>*Yes*</td><td>*No*</td><td>*Possibly*</td><td></td></tr>
<tr><td></td><td>___</td><td>___</td><td>___</td><td>meaningful</td></tr>
<tr><td></td><td>___</td><td>___</td><td>___</td><td>integrative (involving multiple disciplines or subject areas)</td></tr>
<tr><td></td><td>___</td><td>___</td><td>___</td><td>value-based (where students must make judgments about what is or is not important, useful, etc.)</td></tr>
<tr><td></td><td>___</td><td>___</td><td>___</td><td>challenging</td></tr>
<tr><td></td><td>___</td><td>___</td><td>___</td><td>active (*Note:* This characteristic relates to students' hands and minds, to their interest and involvement, not simply a manipulative activity.)</td></tr>
</table>

Analysis

The cooperative biography project rates as high or even higher on these "powerful" characteristics than it did on the previous criteria. The activity clearly had meaning for students, even if not at first. It was also integrative in that students had to apply skills from other subject areas, primarily writing and composing. There was also a value base as, for example, when students had to decide what should or should not be included in their chapters. Likewise, producing a historically accurate biography was certainly challenging for fifth graders, as it would be for many adults. Finally, the activity involved students actively as opposed to passively. For example, students were not simply listening to Ms. Lindquist as she provided background information on Lincoln, but were also involved in taking notes and determining what they would or would not use in their chapter.

● The Question of Time

Justifying such a lengthy activity

Regardless of how well the cooperative biography project meets the NCSS standards, we need to address the question of how a teacher can justify spending five weeks on this kind of activity. Consider first that no teacher can hope to cover the entire range of American history, or world history, or whatever, especially if he or she commits five weeks to an activity like this. Consider second that no teacher can cover the entire range of American history, or world history, or whatever, even if he or she does *not* commit five weeks to a cooperative biography project. In almost any traditional social studies program, there is simply more history, more geography, more economics, and so on, than it is possible to teach effectively in any

Is the Abraham Lincoln cooperative biography activity a social studies project that draws heavily on language arts? Or is it a language arts activity that draws on social studies content? Or does its subject classification really matter?

Most students are not much beyond kindergarten before they learn there are apparently clear demarcations between subject areas. It begins with "O.K., children, put away your science books, it's time for social studies," and continues on from there. Perhaps most people don't realize (or necessarily care) that when scholars created separate disciplines of knowledge, they did so for convenience, clarity, and perhaps even a little self-interest. In other words, to be considered an expert (or scholar) in something, it was necessary to have a defined area of knowledge—a discipline—in which to demonstrate one's expertise. It's the phenomenon that practitioners in medicine have made into an art form.

Dividing the immense body of knowledge into smaller chunks, called disciplines, makes it more manageable and, in some instances, easier to understand. But in everyday life, most of the problems we deal with—like deciding what to have for lunch—resist easy classification. For example, suggesting that the decision about what to have for lunch is a sociobiological question seems to border on the absurd.

The point is that in the compartmentalized world we live in today, classification dilemmas sometimes arise. So whether the cooperative biography project is a social studies or a language arts activity is the kind of question that some people ponder. Actually, it's an activity that integrates both language arts and social studies. Pursuing the classification matter further—as in "Well, it's mainly a language arts activity"—is probably not very fruitful. The more significant questions concern whether the teaching activities are authentic and useful to children.

given year. There are occasional exceptions, however. In California, for example, the sixth-grade curriculum does not cover all of world history, as is common in most social studies programs. Rather, the California curriculum for Grade 6 focuses on ancient civilizations through A.D. 500; the Grade 7 program begins at A.D. 500 and carries through to the Middle Ages.

The California program reflects one state's effort to reduce to more manageable proportions the tremendous time periods that most teachers are expected to cover—a topic examined in more detail in Chapter 3. At the same time, consider that although the 180-day school year has remained largely unchanged over the past century, over the same period we have acquired another one hundred years of history. As one wit put it, "history just keeps rollin' along." As a result, teachers face the prospect of squeezing an ever-growing body of historical knowledge into a relatively fixed time period.

The coverage problem   The underlying issue here is one of *coverage*. Even if teachers try to cover only the "really important" parts of American or world history, they still face an almost impossible task. In some instances, they may be faulted for not teaching about Joan of Arc or another topic that someone remembers studying, but the main point is that the survey course format of social studies courses from Grade 4 upward usually asks that teachers cover at least five centuries and often more (sometimes many more). One option here is for a teacher to take a traditional textbook, divide the number of its pages (about 450) by the number of days in a school year (180) and arrive at how many pages you need to cover each day

(2–3)—a procedure some teachers try to use. Recognize, however, that teachers seldom have the entire school year at their disposal; they usually need to subtract days for testing, special programs, in-service activities, parent-teacher conferences, and the like. If you allow time for the miscellaneous activities that can intervene on instructional time, this can effectively double the number of pages you would need to cover on the available "teaching" days—from 2–3 pages to perhaps 5–6 pages. And assuming that you were successful in your effort, you would have "covered" the book. But to what result? Would you have time for hands-on activities? Or studying one or more topics in depth? Probably not.

The trade offs

Dealing with the expectation that they will somehow "cover" social studies is something all teachers must face. And, yes, it's possible to achieve coverage. But there is a price to be paid in trying to do so. It is not surprising to hear students say things like "Oh, yeah, I've heard of the Redcoats . . . they were British, I think. . . . Or were they French? We didn't have much time to talk about them." Zemelman, Daniels, and Hyde (1998) suggest that trying to achieve coverage in social studies typically yields superficiality and is like "painting a room—covering plenty of square feet but only one-thousandth of an inch thick" (p. 139).

As you might expect from a teacher who devotes five weeks to the cooperative biography project, Tarry Lindquist rejects the expectation that she try to "cover" everything. As Ms. Lindquist (2000) says, "Social studies is an enormous discipline. . . . It is not possible to teach everything that has ever happened, so it becomes of paramount importance for us to identify themes and concepts that allow the students to at least begin to understand how to learn about the world" (p. 4).

"Less is more"

Ms. Lindquist ranks among the growing number of teachers who have adopted the "less is more" concept that we noted in the prologue. In practice, this idea means going into detail on selected topics so that students can build in-depth understandings—a practice also called *postholing*, or as Zemelman, Daniels, and Hyde (1998) suggest, "post-holing." Whichever way you spell it, postholing reflects the notion that if you elect to dig one hundred postholes, each one inch deep, your fence is likely to fall over. But if you dig just ten postholes, each ten inches deep, your fence could remain standing for a long time. The basic question concerns whether you will settle for an essentially useless fence that is really long but so shallow that it falls over, or one that is planted deep enough to remain standing for years—but may be just a little short. In other words, it's a tradeoff.

Options

One dynamic of teaching social studies involves deciding how you will deal with the problem of coverage and the superficiality that too often goes with it. This is not entirely an either-or matter because there are some intermediate positions. For example, you could try for a balance between the two positions by spending parts of the year knowing that you are simply "covering" the subject, and the balance of the year going into greater depth. Whatever you elect to do, know that there is not one "approved" way of proceeding.

The next section examines how social studies has evolved as a subject area, and the characteristics that have led to the continuing debates about how it should be organized and taught.

────● **A Social Studies Parable**

In the beginning there was history. People had to be around before there could be history, of course, and the stories of the past that those individuals created were much more personal than the formalized record most of us know today. Nevertheless, history began soon after our ancestors became aware of their past.

How social studies evolved

History was followed almost immediately by geography. It wasn't called "geography" until much later, and it was really rudimentary, focusing on things like locating good hunting and fishing areas, and avoiding places where the water sources dried up in hot weather. Yet knowing the geography of the area—what resources were available and where in the immediate environment—was often essential to survival.

The history and geography that our ancestors dealt with were basic and important. Their history helped them identify who they were, individually and collectively, and where they had come from. Their geography helped them survive what otherwise had to have been a harrowing existence. Yet an equally important aspect of our ancestors' lives dealt with determining how they would conduct relationships between and among themselves. They had to decide things like whether it was O.K. to take another family's food or belongings against their wishes, simply because someone felt the urge to do so. Safe and orderly societies cannot exist when everyone is free to "do his or her own thing," so they also had to decide what would happen to those who violated the "rules." Without clear moral and ethical standards, daily life would be chaotic, and the survival of individuals and the society itself would be questionable. In almost every respect, creating a moral code to live by was as important to our ancestors' survival as was their knowledge of geography—sometimes more so.

Creating a code of moral conduct

Our ancestors obviously learned to cope with their physical and social environments, or we wouldn't be here today. Likewise, when some of our ancestors grew skilled enough that they no longer needed to spend every waking minute worrying about their survival, they were able to formalize their history, expand their geographical horizons, and codify their moral and ethical principles as laws. And so it went through various civilizations—the ancient Egyptians, the Greeks, the Romans, and so forth. Adults in these societies passed on their histories, their geographies, and their codes of ethics to their children so that they too would become aware of their heritage and their responsibilities to others—a challenge that remains to this day.

The emergence of the social sciences

Once they had satisfied their survival needs, some of our ancestors began to examine specialized aspects of human behavior. For example, some individuals began to explore why corn and wheat were more costly when rainfall was scarce, and cheaper when rainfall was plentiful. Investigations such as these marked the beginning of what eventually became the discipline of economics. Other specialized studies followed. Some people began to study cultures, both past and present, thus providing the beginnings of anthropology. Others began to explore how societies govern themselves, which provided the basis for political science (or government).

Still others investigated how groups of people interact, which ultimately led to the discipline of sociology. Even more recently, individuals began to examine everyday human behaviors, such as how we learn and how we develop our beliefs and attitudes, which are part of the discipline of psychology.

From these beginnings, the school subject called social studies was created. History is a major component of social studies, as are the social science disciplines of geography, economics, political science, anthropology, sociology, and psychology. Morals and ethics, which we include as part of philosophy, also play a role in social studies, as do elements from the humanities and the fine arts. These components and others are reflected in the National Council for the Social Studies's (NCSS, 1994) definition of social studies. It states:

Social studies defined

> Social studies is the *integrated study* of the social sciences and humanities to promote civic competence. Within the social program, social studies provides coordinated, systematic study drawing upon such disciplines as anthropology, archaeology, economics, geography, history, philosophy, political science, psychology, religion, and sociology, as well as appropriate content from the humanities, mathematics, and natural sciences. [Emphasis added]

The common focus of social studies is human behavior. In one form or another, the components of social studies deal with how we humans interact with each other, both past and present, how we interact with our environment, and on the myriad ways in which we organize, govern, and trade among ourselves. That focus on human (social) behavior led John Dewey (1938) to suggest the shortest definition for social studies that we know of. He said: "Social studies is the study of things social."

● The Continuing Debates

You may have asked yourself why the subject was called "social studies" when you were in elementary and middle school, but after you got to high school and college, you almost never heard the term? Secondary schools and colleges almost always teach discipline-based courses. In the sciences, for example, you studied subjects like botany, biology, physics, and so forth, and in the social sciences you studied history, geography, political science, and so on. Each course focused on a recognized discipline in its respective field. In all likelihood, your high school and college courses were taught by individuals who identified themselves with discipline-based titles such as historian, botanist, and geographer. Be advised that there are any number of people who go the next step and say that how high schools and colleges organize their courses is the way they should be organized in elementary and middle schools. And this contention has remained at the crux of an ongoing debate almost since social studies was created in the early years of the twentieth century.

Multidiscipline vs. single-discipline subjects

The following Model Student Activity is the first of many model activities in this book. In this instance the activity shows how historically accurate materials can serve as the basis for realistic decision making. Note also that all the model activities in this book are presented as models, that is, as exemplary lesson formats that can be adapted for other topics or content areas.

Who Is Qualified for the Presidency?

Overview

In this activity you are asked to identify which one of seven potential candidates is the best qualified and which is the least qualified to be president of the United States. The biographical data on the candidates are presented on separate cards—a procedure usually referred to as a Q-sort. All the candidates are (or were) real people who meet (or met) the three constitutional qualifications for the presidency; that is, they (1) are natural-born citizens, (2) are at least thirty-five years old, and (3) have resided in the United States for at least fourteen years prior to a presidential election. To ensure that the candidates are judged on their qualifications—and not your prior knowledge of them—their names and gender have been omitted. The candidates' identities appear in the Resource Handbook.

Recommended Procedure

Phases One and Two of this activity should be done in small groups. The discussion questions in Phase Three can also be considered in small groups and then summarized in a large-group discussion.

Phase One—Additional Qualifications

Before considering the candidates, identify any additional qualifications (beyond those identified in the Constitution) that you think a president of the United States should possess. For example, should a president be a college graduate? Should he or she have had prior political experience?

Phase Two—Selection

Use the data cards to select the two individuals, one of whom you feel would be (1) best qualified and the other (2) least qualified to be president of the United States.

[Note: "Age as of this date" on the data cards refers to the point in each candidate's career at which he or she had accomplished all the activities listed on the card. For the candidates who actually served as president, the date used was just prior to their election to office.]

CARD 1

    College Attended: None

    Religion: Protestant

    Career (Major Occupations): Investor, Druggist, Bookseller, Brigadier General in U.S. Army

    Married: 1st spouse: 5 years until spouse's death, 2nd spouse: 1 year   **Children:** 3 by first marriage

    Age as of This Date: 38

    Source: Dictionary of American Biography, Charles Scribner's Sons, 1928, pp. 362–67.

CARD 2

Colleges Attended: Harvard University, Columbia University

Religion: Protestant

Career (Major Occupations): Farmer, Lawyer, State senator, Assistant Secretary of Navy, Governor, Vice-Presidential candidate

Married: 27 years   **Children:** 6

Age as of This Date: 50

Source: The National Cyclopaedia of American Biography, XXXVII, University Microfilms, A Xerox Company, 1967, pp. 1–3.

CARD 3

Colleges Attended: Morehouse College, A.B. and L.H.D.; Crozer Theological Seminary, B.D.; University of Pennsylvania; Boston University, Ph.D., D.D.; Harvard University, L.L.D.; Central State College; Morgan State College

Religion: Protestant

Career (Major Occupations): Protestant minister, Teacher of Philosophy at Harvard, President of a civil rights organization, 1 of 10 outstanding men for the year according to *Time* magazine, Nobel Prize winner, Noted public speaker

Married: 15 years   **Children:** 4

Age as of This Date: 37

Source: Current Biography Yearbook 1965, H. W. Wilson Co., 1966, pp. 220–23; *Current Biography Yearbook 1968,* H. W. Wilson Co., 1969, p. 457.

CARD 4

College Attended: Columbia University

Religion: No specific denomination

Career (Major Occupations): Writer, Served as Lieutenant Colonel in Army, Lawyer, Member of a congress, Member to a constitutional convention, Secretary of the Treasury

Married: 24 years   **Children:** 8

Age as of This Date: 47

Source: Dictionary of American Biography, VII, Charles Scribner's Sons, 1932, pp. 171–79.

CARD 5

College Attended: None (private secondary school in England)

Religion: Protestant

Career (Major Occupations): Teacher, Journalist, Member of a labor union (trade union league), United States delegate to the United Nations Commission on Human Rights, Endorsed by a President for the Nobel Peace Prize, Noted public speaker

Married: 27 years   **Children:** 6

Age as of This Date: 65

Source: Current Biography, Who's News and Why, 1949, H. W. Wilson Co., 1950, pp. 528–32.

CARD 6

College Attended: None

Religion: Roman Catholic

Career (Major Occupations): Director for a community service organization, Founder and director of a farm worker's organization, Served in the United States Navy, Honored for distinguished public service by the American Institute for Public Service, Second recipient of the Martin Luther King Jr. Nonviolent Peace Prize

Married: 29 years   **Children:** 8

Age as of This Date: 47

Source: Who's Who in America, Marquis Who's Who, Inc., 1972, p. 550; *Current Biography Yearbook 1969,* H. W. Wilson Co., 1970, pp. 86–89.

CARD 7

College Attended: None

Religion: No specific denomination

Career (Major Occupations): Postmaster, Lawyer, U.S. Representative, Store owner, State congressman, Served as Captain in U.S. Army, Noted public speaker

Married: 19 years   **Children:** 4

Age as of This Date: 51

Source: Dictionary of American Biography, XI, Charles Scribner's Sons, 1933, pp. 242–49.

Phase Three—Summary

Questions:

1. To what extent did your choices reflect the qualifications you listed in Phase One? Would you modify your list in any way?

2. Determine whether any of the following factors should be considered in selecting a presidential candidate.

2.1. Age	2.7. Previous occupation
2.2. Religion	2.8. Personal appearance
2.3. Gender	2.9. Personality
2.4. Educational background	2.10. Ethnic background
2.5. Number of children	2.11. Marital status
2.6. Character	2.12. Physical health

3. Should any other factors be considered?

4. How did your group decide what qualifications were most important? Least important?

Optional Extending Activities

1. Examine the candidate's identities as shown in the Resource Handbook. Would you change your selection? Why or why not? Does the new information influence your conclusions about the necessary qualifications?

2. Do your qualifications reflect the beliefs of most individuals in your community? in your class? Identify a plan for determining how you could find out.

Source: Adapted from Marsha Hobin, "Clarifying What Is Important," in Allan O. Kownslar, Ed., *Teaching American History: The Quest for Relevancy.* Copyright 1974 by National Council for the Social Studies. Reprinted by permission of Allan O. Kownslar and NCSS.

• •

Studying the disciplines separately or as a unified subject

It is easy to skim over the term "integrated study" in NCSS's definition for social studies without recognizing that some people object—sometimes strongly—to that idea. Their concerns often reflect the following: "What do you mean you select things from several disciplines and then unify them in something called 'social studies'? By doing that you're destroying the purity of these time-honored disciplines." Enter then a social studies advocate who is likely to argue that "teaching the so-called pure academic disciplines to young children is a form of academic arrogance, because all the disciplines focus on the same thing—different aspects of social behavior. By teaching these elements in unified courses we can help children focus on the world they really live in, and everybody knows the world is not neatly divided into the history section, the geography section, the political science section, and so on. Besides, we need to help children understand interrelationships between and among the various disciplines that they would not see if they were taught separately."

Multidisciplinary studies

In many parts of the world, there is no debate about whether schools should teach the social science disciplines separately or as unified social studies. This is because the notion of unified or *multidisciplinary* social studies is limited to three nations primarily: the United States, Canada, and Australia. People almost everywhere study history, geography, and the other social sciences, of course, but in most parts of the world these are taught as separate subjects. This is why students in England, for example, usually study English history and English geography separately.

The practice of intermingling separate disciplines into a single course of study, which is usually referred to as a unified or *multidisciplinary studies* approach to curriculum, is common in American (and Canadian and Australian) elementary- and

A key question for "Who Is Qualified for the Presidency?" or any instructional activity is: "What should students learn from having done it?" It's doubtful, for example, that students will remember much about the constitutional qualifications for the presidency, primarily because that information is almost incidental to the activity. On the other hand, students are likely to remember some of the biographical information about the candidates because the format of the activity requires them to work with that information. However, expecting students to commit the biographical information to memory, such as which college Alexander Hamilton attended, seems very questionable at best. The biographical information serves a legitimate and necessary purpose in the activity, but in the sweep of human events it is on the same level as the name of Robert E. Lee's horse (Traveler): historical trivia.

The biographical information in the "Presidency" activity serves as a vehicle to help students consider factors that influence the election of a president. In that context, an appropriate learner objective for the *content focus* of this activity would be: "Upon completion of this activity, learners will identify at least seven factors that could influence voters in their decisions about a candidate's qualifications for the presidency."

In the activity, students are also asked to identify the best- and least-qualified presidential candidate, and then reach group consensus about their choices. The students' involvement in a group decision-making process, as well as their responses to questions like "What process did the group use in reaching its decision?" and "Did some factors weigh more heavily in that decision than others?" are just as instructionally significant as whichever candidates the group selects. The point is that the group's decision-making process reflects a *process/skills* focus for this activity that deserves as much attention as their final decisions. A sample learner objective for the process/ skills emphasis of the activity would be: "Given the constitutional qualifications for president, students will (a) identify additional qualifications (for the presidency) that they feel are appropriate, (b) determine if these qualifications are acceptable to a group of peers, and (c) defend or modify the selection of potential candidates to reach group consensus." In other words, the "Presidency" activity could serve as a vehicle for (1) identifying and learning about factors that may influence the selection and election of a presidential candidate, which is its content focus, and for (2) analyzing and learning about a group decision-making process, which is its process focus.

• •

Other multidisciplinary subjects

middle-school programs. Most language arts, science, and social studies programs are organized on this basis. A typical elementary science program, for example, will have separate chapters on plants (botany), animals (zoology), the earth's crust (geology), insects (entomology), and weather (meteorology), each of which reflects a separate discipline in its own right. Language arts and social studies follow a similar pattern, although the specific disciplines are different.

——● **Contemporary Implications**

In the course of the debates between the unified studies and separate-discipline advocates, some individuals who favor teaching the disciplines separately referred to social studies as a kind of "social stew," a subject closely akin to "mystery meats" sometimes served in school cafeterias. Individuals who favored the unified approach to social studies would sometimes accuse the separate-discipline advocates of trying to turn young children into miniature historians and geographers, which wasn't necessarily helpful for teaching children to live in modern society. As the debates continued in academic circles, most teachers found they could

STANDARDS

How the standards evolved

close their classroom doors with relative assurance that the debates would have little impact on their daily activities. But then, in the 1990s, came the standards.

Nominations for the organizations that would create the national standards for the subjects taught in American schools came largely from the Department of Education and were submitted to the U.S. Congress for its approval. During this period, some key individuals in the Department of Education happened to be strong advocates for teaching the disciplines separately. When Congress approved the nominations in 1993, there were to be standards for science, mathematics, history, geography, economics, and so forth, but standards for unified social studies programs were nowhere to be found. The NCSS was understandably appalled. How could Congress fail to recognize social studies?

While the nominees began developing their proposed standards, the NCSS began a belated effort to (1) create standards for teaching social studies, and (2) have Congress recognize social studies as a subject area unto itself. That undertaking was undoubtedly assisted by a fortuitous turn of events (depending on your perspective, of course). When the draft version of the proposed history standards were submitted for approval, even some separate discipline supporters objected to them. Apparently the proposed standards devoted (1) too much attention to African-Americans, Native Americans, and other minorities and (2) far too much attention to failures and atrocities committed over the course of U.S. history (Zemelman, Daniels, & Hyde, 1998). For example, most history texts traditionally treat the topic of the westward expansion of the United States under subtitles such as "How the West Was Won." The idea of changing to a perspective more sympathetic to Native Americans—"How the West Was Lost" (or Stolen)—apparently irritated quite a few people, including some members of Congress and some individuals in the Department of Education. Questions involving "Who is right here?" or "Who should be offended?" became moot when the U.S. Senate voted 99 to 1 to reject the draft version of the proposed history standards.

Problems!

Congress ultimately approved both the NCSS standards for social studies and the separate standards for the social science disciplines—history (revised), geography, economics, and so forth. As a result, social studies teachers have an array of standards to inform their teaching.

Because all the standards focus on different aspects of social behavior, it is reasonable to ask whether there is much duplication. The general answer is no. For the most part, the historians, geographers, economists, and so on were very discipline specific. For example, the history standards identify five standards for Historical Thinking (which are included in the Resource Handbook at the end of this book), but these are quite different from the five themes of Geography, (which are included in Chapter 2). So instead of duplication, there is often great specificity—lists of hundreds of facts and topics deemed essential for student competence in the discipline. We sometimes wonder whether many people have read all the standards, because when you include the NCSS materials with the standards from the separate disciplines, the result is an impressive stack of documents approaching the size of an unabridged dictionary.

A wealth of standards

Social studies is unique among the subjects taught in elementary and middle schools because it is the only one that has such a wealth of standards. In addition to the NCSS standards for social studies and the standards for history and the social

science disciplines developed by other organizations, there are also standards (sometimes called "outcomes") that were developed by the states and are often referenced to state-mandated tests. With so many standards to choose from, the pertinent question becomes: Where does a teacher begin?

We concur with the NCSS recommendation that teachers use the social studies standards, which are organized around ten broad themes, to address overall curriculum design and comprehensive student performance expectations. Teachers can then use standards for individual disciplines (for civics and government, economics, geography, and history) to provide focused content for grade-level strands and specific courses. Sometimes a discipline such as history will take the lead, while other disciplines, such as geography and economics will play supporting roles. At other times, separate disciplines such as history, geography, and economics will be equally involved, thus reflecting the multidisciplinary nature of social studies.

The NCSS Themes

The ten themes from the NCSS standards (as detailed in the Resource Handbook) are as follows:

1. Culture
2. Time, Continuity, and Change
3. People, Places, and Environment
4. Individual Development and Identity
5. Individuals, Groups, and Institutions
6. Power, Authority, and Governance
7. Production, Distribution, and Consumption
8. Science, Technology, and Society
9. Global Connections
10. Civic Ideals and Practices

STANDARDS

The complete NCSS standards are available on-line at the Internet address listed in both the following Technology Update and in the "Suggested Readings and Resources" section at the end of the chapter.

Performance Expectations

What children are expected to do

Performance expectations for each of the NCSS themes are presented in three clusters: (1) for the early grades, (2) for the middle grades, and (3) for high school. The following example for the early grades reflects the performance expectations for the theme Culture.

Social studies programs should include experiences that provide for the study of culture and cultural diversity, so that the learner can

a. explore and describe similarities and differences in the ways groups, societies, and cultures address similar human needs and concerns.
b. give examples of how experiences may be interpreted differently by people from diverse cultural perspectives and frames of reference.

Standards for Social Studies, History, and Social Sciences

This is the first Technology Update, each of which is keyed to the content of the chapters in this book. Most Updates require access to the Internet and will direct you to additional resources and materials related to teaching elementary and middle school social studies. In this instance, we provide more detailed sources for standards that apply to teaching social studies.

Note that Internet addresses sometimes change or cease operation. In the event that a listed address fails to work correctly, you can use a standard search engine to locate a new address.

The three best sources for standards-related materials are:

1. The Home Page maintained by The National Council for Social Studies (NCSS), at:

    http://www.ncss.org

    This site has the complete NCSS standards on-line along with many other social studies–related sites and materials.

2. Resources for Social Studies Teachers at:

    http://www.csun.edu/~hcedu013/

This site, maintained by Dr. Marty Levin, at California State University, Northridge, includes standards among a wealth of other social studies–related materials.

3. Putwest BOCES at:

    http://putwest.boces.org/StSu/Social.html

In addition to the various national standards, this site also links to states that have adopted standards or standards-related materials.

Most of these sites have links that enable you to reach the other sites without having to enter the full address. They also provide links to standards-related materials from other organizations including:

The American Historical Association at:

    http://web.gmu.edu/chnm/aha

The Center for Civic Education at:

    http://www.informall.org:80/showcase/civnet/
    partners/center/center.html

The National Center for History in the School at:

    http://www.sscnet.ucla.edu/nchs

---

   c. describe ways in which language, stories, folktales, music, and artistic creations serve as expressions of culture and influence the behavior of people living in a particular culture.

   d. compare ways in which people from different cultures think about and deal with their physical environment and social conditions.

   e. give examples and describe the importance of cultural unity and diversity within and across groups.

⬤ Classroom Example

Most standards documents include examples of classroom activities illustrating how learning experiences can be designed to help students meet performance expectations. For example, an exemplary classroom activity for the NCSS theme of culture describes the experiences of Carlene Jackson, a teacher who uses a new program to develop geographic understanding among students in her first-grade class. Upon examining her class list (before the first day of school), Ms. Jackson determines that she might have students of Mexican, Vietnamese, and Korean ancestry, as well as of African-American and European-American backgrounds. Jackson and her students decide to study how families meet their basic needs of food, clothing, and shelter in five places: their own community; Juarez, Mexico; Hanoi, Vietnam; Lagos, Nigeria; and Frankfurt, Germany. The students read books and stories, look at photos and slides, watch videos, and talk to speakers from their cities. Students sharpen their reading, writing, and speaking skills and learn new geography skills such as map reading. For each city, they read and discuss something about its location, climate, region, and people. This activity addresses performance expectations a, b, and d.[1]

An example, continued

Regardless of whether you favor a unified approach to social studies or teaching the social science disciplines, an even more basic question needs to be addressed. It is: "Why teach either unified social studies or courses in the separate disciplines in elementary and middle schools, when courses in high schools and college often repeat essentially the same material? This question is the focus of the next section.

Social Studies and Citizenship Education

Our democracy was still in its infancy when the French observer, Alexis de Tocqueville (1947), wrote, "The Americans are hardly more virtuous than others, but they are infinitely better educated (I speak for the masses) than any other people of my acquaintance." De Tocqueville went on to say that an educated citizenry "the mass of those possessing an understanding of public affairs, a knowledge of laws and precedents, a feeling for the best interest of the nation, and a faculty of understanding them, is greater in America than any other place in the world." De Tocqueville wrote these words almost two centuries ago, when it was rare for students to attend school through the eighth Grade, and even rarer for students to attend a college or university. It was also a time when democracies were rare and most of the world was ruled by kings and emperors.

Democracy demands an educated citizen

When governing power is vested in a single individual, such as an absolute monarch, there is little need to educate the masses; the monarchs make all the decisions and the people simply follow. But when governing power is vested in the people, as in a democracy, and when people participate in determining whether something is or is not for the common good, new expectations arise. The citizens in a democracy have a right—even a duty—to expect our citizen colleagues to be knowledgeable, to deal morally and ethically with others, to challenge and critically question ideas and proposals, to make good and defensible decisions, and to be concerned about the welfare of others and the common good (see Gross & Dynneson, 1991). The first point here is that a democratic form of government imposes responsibilities on everyday citizens that were virtually unknown when De Tocqueville wrote his immortal words. A second but closely related point is

---

[1]Abridged from the Executive Summary, *Expect Excellence: Curriculum Standards for Social Studies.* Copyright 1994 by the National Council for the Social Studies. Reprinted by permission.

that schools—along with the family and the church—were charged with making students knowledgeable and responsible enough that they could handle the duties of citizenship just described.

Educating students before they leave school

For most of the nineteenth century and at least the first two decades of the twentieth century, it was common for students to leave school at the end of elementary (or grammar) school, usually Grade 8. This was a time when students moved directly from elementary schools to high schools, assuming they planned to attend a secondary school. (The first junior high school was not created until 1909–1910.)

During much of the nineteenth and early twentieth centuries, many students were the children of recent immigrants—children who typically had little knowledge of America's history, geography, or its democratic heritage. Thus it made sense to try to provide these students with an awareness of these subjects before they left school (at Grade 8), which necessarily meant during the elementary grades. But even if students did not leave school by Grade 8, which a growing number did not, the elementary courses were seen as preparation for similar courses offered in high schools—a situation that still remains today.

When junior high schools became popular in the 1920s and 1930s and thereafter, they typically housed Grades 7, 8, and 9. And as school districts began establishing junior high schools, two things often happened. First, Grade 6 marked the end of elementary school, and, second, many students elected to leave school at the end of junior high, or Grade 9. During this era, high schools typically regarded their primary mission as preparing students for colleges and universities, even to the extent of offering required courses in Latin and Greek.

The "reasons" for the repetition in social studies

The reason for this brief and considerably oversimplified journey through the history of education is to indicate why there is so much apparent repetition of social studies courses through the grades. When many students dropped out of school at the end of Grade 8, the social studies courses intended to prepare them to be knowledgeable citizens were taught at the elementary school level. A similar rationale was often applied when junior high schools were created; it was necessary to train students in the responsibilities of citizenship before they left school at Grade 9. The rationale for teaching similar courses at the high school level was similar but usually had elements of preparing students for higher education as noted earlier.

It's common knowledge that most students no longer leave school at the end of Grades 6 or 8; if nothing else, doing so is against the law in some states. Thus it is reasonable to ask why elementary schools today offer a social studies curriculum that is often similar to what they offered fifty to a hundred years ago, when students left school at the end of their elementary years? Or why most junior high schools offer a social studies curriculum similar to what they offered when many students left at the end of Grade 9?

The power of tradition, again

There are probably several answers to these questions. First, the situation is undoubtedly another example of the power of *tradition* that we noted in the prologue. As new layers of schooling evolved, there apparently was a reluctance to reexamine what was being done at the lower layers. Therefore, many schools at the lower levels continued doing what they had always done, regardless of whether it was repetitious. Second, tradition itself may be used as a reason for maintaining the status quo. "We've taught American history at fifth grade for over fifty years, and we see no reason to change. Period!" Recognize that this "reason," when stated authoritatively, can evoke considerable intimidation. Finally, and because the repetition of social studies courses is difficult to ignore, we suspect that another rationale was added to the existing notion of preparing future citizens. This line of reasoning is based on the idea that schools exist to "get children ready for" something, usually another level of schooling. You have surely heard the claim that the purpose of day care is to get kids ready for elementary school, the purpose of elementary school is to get kids ready for junior high, and so on up the line. When two or more of the claims are combined, as in "We've always taught 'this' in fifth grade, and besides, we are getting your child ready for junior high school (or some other level of schooling)," whoever is questioning or complaining faces an uphill struggle.

The purpose of social studies: citizenship education

The main point here is that schools in general and social studies in particular share the common goal of training the young to be responsible citizens, which, in a more condensed form, is referred to as *citizenship education.* The schools' mission of citizenship education is broad and encompassing, whereas social studies shares a somewhat smaller piece of the action. The relationship between social studies and citizenship is reflected in the NCSS's (1994) definition of social studies, which states that a major purpose of social studies is "to help young people develop the ability to make informed and reasoned choices as citizens of a culturally diverse, democratic society in an interdependent world" (p. 2).

Almost everything students learn in schools can help to make them more knowledgeable, and, thus, good (or perhaps better) decision makers and citizens. But there is more to citizenship that simply subject-matter knowledge. Citizens in a democracy must also be conversant with the attitudes and predispositions that are essential parts of the literacies of citizenship.

The Literacies of Citizenship

At one time, *literacy* referred almost exclusively to the ability to read, write, speak, and use language effectively. Today it can refer to a variety of aptitudes, including cultural literacy, historical literacy, scientific literacy, mathematical literacy, and so forth. This section focuses on three literacies, multicultural, civic, and community, that seem both essential and unique to citizens who live in a democracy.

Multicultural Literacy. This form of literacy reflects the unique nature of American society. As MacIntyre (1990) suggested in "How to Be a North American," we who live in a nation of immigrants must be able to deal effectively with two cultures simultaneously: one based on our common "American" heritage, and the other based on the particular ethnicities from which we derive. All of us contribute to the common American culture, and, as MacIntyre points out, if we were to lose the contributions that our ethnicities afford us, we would have nothing to bring and nothing to give. However, MacIntyre also warns that "if each of us dwells too much, or even exclusively, upon his or her own ethnic particularity, then we are in danger of fragmenting or even destroying the common life" (p. 5). More recently, Salinas (1997) warned that if we as a nation are unable to

We live in several cultures simultaneously

maintain a reasonable balance between our competing loyalties, first to our individual ethnicities, and second to the larger American culture, we will join the ranks of the world's other multiethnic nations—the Bosnias and Serbias of the world—as a battleground of perpetual ethnic discord.

DIVERSITY

The goal of multicultural literacy is to develop citizens who have the knowledge and ability to understand events and experiences from different perspectives. This "understanding" derives from the ancient Greeks, who, according to Arendt (1961), "sought not to understand one another as individual persons, but to look upon the same world from another's standpoint, to see the same in very different and frequently opposing aspects" (p. 51). In this context, for example, it is as important for white, Anglo students to understand how slavery was viewed from the perspective of an enslaved person, as it is for African-American students to understand how slavery was viewed from the perspective of white persons living in the seventeenth and eighteenth centuries, and much of the nineteenth century. Those two views will obviously be quite different. A second but vitally important element of multicultural literacy—the willingness to suspend judgment—may be even more difficult to achieve. In the context of slavery, for example, it is one thing to say that "1 understand where they (either slaves or slave owners) were coming from." However, it is quite another to accuse contemporary Americans of being "wrong" because they reflect the ethnicity of either slave or slave owner. It is also one thing to judge the rightness or wrongness of activities in their historical perspective, but another to transfer those judgments to modern-day activities.

Willingness to suspend judgement

Multicultural literacy should be the end product of a *multicultural education*. Both concepts share a common goal: enabling students to view concepts and issues from multiple ethnic perspectives, and from the points of view of the cultural, ethnic, and racial groups that were most intimately involved in the event or issue (see Banks, 1989, 1997). It is not essential that students understand every possible point of view on every possible issue, nor is it essential that they accept or adopt a divergent view. But everyone needs to understand that any question or issue has at least two sides.

Multicultural education

The concept of multicultural education has been around for at least two decades, but it—like most topics in this chapter—is still a matter of continuing debate. For example, some people argue that there is no common American culture, and hence no beliefs that unite us; rather, there is just a common American society in which all of us live (see Asante & Ravitch, 1991). Others argue that the current curriculum is too biased toward the European origins of American culture—or what is sometimes called a "Eurocentric" curriculum. Some individuals believe that the Eurocentric curriculum should be replaced by infusing African-American studies into every course. Those who make such claims are referred to as Afrocentrists, and the resulting curriculum is referred to as Afrocentric.

Bias in the curriculum

There is a Eurocentric bias in the existing curriculum. As just one example, too many Americans are unaware that Sante Fe (New Mexico) was a thriving community before the Pilgrims ever stepped onto Plymouth Rock (and despite the fact that the Spanish who controlled Mexico at the time were of European origin). The question here is: Should a curriculum that is biased in one direction be replaced by curriculum biased in another direction? In her response to a controversial proposal for a new social studies program for New York State, Ravitch (1990) noted that "you can't have a curriculum opposed to bias that is itself biased" (p. B4). We deal with other potentials associated with multicultural education in more detail in Chapter 4, but from this limited treatment it should be clear that most schools do not yet have a multicultural curriculum that effectively addresses the goals of multicultural literacy.

Civic Literacy.   Civic literacy refers to a form of political socialization that ensures that future citizens develop the knowledge, attitudes, and values that are consistent with the society's political system. This is obviously a much smaller body of information than multicultural literacy. Developing civic literacy is something that many schools already do, at least up to a point. It involves understanding the following:

The political principles on which our government is founded
Our political system and how it *really* works
The functions of government, both real and perceived
That a democracy places more responsibilities on citizens than do most other
    forms of government
That political liberty hinges on the level and quality of civic and civil discourse,
    which also depends largely on the extent to which citizens participate and are
    willing to reason together

The students you encounter, including even kindergartners, will have already begun to acquire some of the attitudes and values associated with civic literacy. For example, most young children usually have a highly developed sense of "fair play." At the same time, other attitudes, like "the government is responsible for taking care of everyone," will be simplistic and perhaps even inconsistent with democratic citizenship. It can be difficult to determine where the citizen's responsibilities end and the government's take over, as in matters related to welfare or health care. Developing civic literacy means that citizens are aware of the different points of view on issues, not that they adopt a liberal or conservative stance. Many younger children will neither care about nor be able to understand some of the elements just listed, especially theoretical or complex explanations of the role and functions of government. As a consequence, the development of civic literacy clearly extends throughout the entire school (K–12) experience and beyond.

Civic literacy extends beyond the narrower notion of "government" that most of us were exposed to in schools—such as the idea that there are 435 members of the House of Representatives—and focuses on helping children understand and develop the abilities that will be expected of them as citizens. This can mean helping children understand the need for rules and laws, and how the two are different. It also extends to helping children understand those things for which they as individuals are responsible, which includes the respect of self and others, as well as things for which the government is responsible, such as defense from foreign invasion. It also extends to elements for which the individual and the government share mutual responsibility, such as the safety of the neighborhood.

Elements of civic literacy

A long-term enterprise

Community Literacy.   In some areas of the country, people are virtual prisoners in their own homes. Some of them keep their window shades down at all times and dare not sit on their porches for fear of being injured in a drive-by shooting or drug-related gun battle. In this kind of environment, it is heartening to read about neighbors who band together in a spirit of community to rid their neighborhoods of criminal elements. Those neighbors' efforts do not reflect a return to the days of vigilante justice, because they almost always work in cooperation with the police. Important as it is to rid neighborhoods of criminal elements, the key here is to ensure living situations for all people that do not compromise the quality of daily life. All of us depend on each other to provide positive and supportive living environments, and by working together in a spirit of community, citizens in a democracy can influence the moral, social, and physical environments in which they live.

You may have read newspaper stories about the juveniles who randomly shot seven children at a roller skating rink. According to Barnicle (cited in Martin, 1995), the mother of one accused juvenile claimed that "the police should have been there to take the gun away from my son before he went inside" (p. 356). It is common for parents to defend their children, but for the mother to argue that the police, not she or her son, were responsible for the shootings illustrates one aspect of the problem. In this instance and others like it, it is the social environment—or more precisely a failure in the social environment in the "community" of morally responsible citizens—that permits the wanton taking of human life, often without remorse. The dilemma results when an unwritten rule of modern life, "Keep your nose out of other people's business," conflicts with the community's responsibility to control its members. It's a matter of determining where an individual's rights end so that the group's continuing survival is not threatened. As Bell (1990) suggested, the corruption of society occurs when self-centered individualism runs rampant and without regard for social costs or moral consequences, a situation that can ultimately lead to self-destruction of the environment itself.

The community in a democracy (and in community literacy) exists to provide the broadest and most effective environment for people to develop as citizens and as individuals. Our relationship with that community is reciprocal: The social environment affects the kinds of things that we as citizens can do, just as we, as individuals, influence the environment itself. The responsibility for a safe and effective social environment does not rest solely with Congress, which has passed crime bill after crime bill, nor with the city council, the police, or the schools. It is a societal responsibility that rests with all of us, as citizen members of a democratic community. The point is that citizens in a democratic society, working together in a spirit of community and for the common good, can reflect Abraham Lincoln's famous words—"government of the people, by the people, and for the people." And this, after a somewhat convoluted journey, is the goal of community literacy.

These literacies of citizenship—multicultural, civic, and community—suggest multiple goals for social studies education.

The "spirit of community": acting together

Individual rights and the common good

Reciprocal relationships

●Why Teach Social Studies—Revisited

Everything schools do is, in theory at least, geared toward citizenship education. This means that social studies and all the other subject areas contribute to making an individual a responsible citizen—even algebra, literature, and physical education! Unfortunately, this line of reasoning, although accurate, is so global that it seldom provides the specific guidance some people seek. With that in mind, this section addresses more specific goals for teaching social studies. The question here is: What does social studies contribute to citizenship education?

The four basic purposes for teaching social studies are as follows:

Goals for teaching social studies

* Teaching young citizens about our collective cultural heritage—about where we as world cultures have come from, where we are, and where we may be going
* Teaching young citizens to think and process information skillfully and intelligently
* Teaching young citizens about human behavior
* Teaching young citizens to act morally and ethically in accordance with what they know

Transmitting the human story

If you think that "teaching about our cultural heritage" is simply a longer way of saying "learning history," you are partially correct. The problem is that history tends not to include the other social science disciplines—archaeology, anthropology, geography, and so forth—all of which can contribute to understanding how we got to be the way we are. Our cultural heritage extends to the origins of human civilization, the development of cultures throughout the world, literary and technological achievements, and the different ways we humans have devised for explaining our place in the universe. One of the main purposes for teaching social studies is to transmit that "story"—that knowledge and its associated attitudes and values—to students.

Teaching thinking

"Teaching children to think skillfully" is a phrase that educators are often fond of, even though it seldom communicates especially well. Nevertheless, if you examine most state-mandated tests, you will find that one aspect they almost always focus on may be referred to by a variety of names, including *critical thinking, reflective thinking, problem solving,* or, simply, *inquiry.* There are subtle differences between these terms, but they are more similar than they are different; all of them involve doing something with information. At the risk of burdening you with even more vocabulary, we think the expression "information-processing skills" is more descriptive of what people actually do when they think and thus have adopted it throughout this book.

Information-processing skills refer to what people do with information—how they mentally manipulate and process various pieces of data. These include skills such as hypothesizing, identifying relevant and irrelevant information, hypothesis testing, and generalizing. Consider, for example, that when the children's tale of *Hansel and Gretel* is told in Africa, the wicked witch's house is made of salt, not candy (as in Europeanized versions.) Upon learning this, you may find yourself saying "something is wrong here." You may also find yourself trying to explain why the two tales are so different. Could it be that in parts of Africa, salt is more highly prized than candy? Or that candy is so foreign to some cultures that the children would be unable to understand why Hansel and Gretel found it so attractive? The underlying phenomenon here is that some African cultures value salt more highly than gold (or candy).

You may have found yourself comparing one or more pieces of information from the preceding example to determine whether they "fit." That is one aspect of teaching information-processing skills: determining whether the various pieces of information agree and are logically related to one another. Another aspect of processing information includes creating possible explanations or hypotheses that might explain a situation. Helping children to process information—otherwise known as thinking—is one of the purposes for teaching social studies. Incidentally, an excellent technique for teaching thinking skills is through *modeling*, that is, by walking (and talking) students step-by-step through the process that you used. We'll elaborate on using social studies as a means for teaching thinking skills throughout this book.

The goal of "teaching children about human behavior" may sound like it's shorthand for "teaching psychology," but it is actually broader than that. Earlier in this chapter you may recall that we suggested that each of the social science disciplines focuses on a different aspect of human behavior. However, history, and to a lesser extent geography, so dominate most social studies programs that some students never study anthropology, sociology, psychology, or the other lesser known social sciences. And even when students take courses in these disciplines, their emphasis sometimes focuses on findings in the field—such as when certain products are scarce, the price tends to increase—as opposed to the techniques the disciplines use to identify patterns in human behavior. It may sound as if we are being critical here, but our concern is that too often courses in the social science disciplines focus almost exclusively on the findings of previous social scientists, and with relatively little emphasis on the processes they used to discover the tendencies in human behavior.

Studying findings and processes

The last goal, "teaching young citizens to act morally and ethically in accordance with what they know," was an oft-cited purpose of schools (and social studies) at the turn of the last century. At the time, it was called character education. The character education movement fell out of favor in the middle of the twentieth century, for reasons detailed in Chapter 6. By the mid-1990s, however, schools at all socioeconomic levels were increasingly besieged by irresponsible and sometimes immoral behaviors. Long-cherished values such as honesty, responsibility, and treating others with mutual respect were being replaced by new codes of conduct. These included behaviors such as lying whenever it serves your purpose (especially if you don't get caught), and treating other individuals any way you want to. The corollary here is that if someone doesn't like how they are being treated, as in "He's lookin' at me," a fight could result. Even more extreme situations have been widely reported in the press and occur when students bring weapons to school and open fire on their fellow students or teachers. Since the mid-1990s character education has enjoyed a rapid rebirth as more and more schools adopt character education programs, such as "Character Counts." This complex issue is the focus in Chapter 6.

The return of character education

● Promoting Democracy in the Classroom

Someone once said that democracy is something you live, not something you teach. The parallel here is that if the purpose of schools and social studies is to prepare youth of the society for democratic citizenship, we need to give them some experience with democratic process and ideals prior to sending them out to face the world at graduation. In this section, we explore how teachers can begin to "do" democracy in their classrooms.

Students cannot learn the responsibilities of democratic citizenship while sitting in classrooms run by dictators. The two formats are incompatible. At the same time, however, everyone knows that teachers must deal with a host of constraints that operate against the creation of a pure classroom democracy. First, teachers have legal and ethical responsibilities for the safety, welfare, and learning of their students, and thus they cannot relinquish their overall authority as teachers. In addition, and because teachers seldom have had much experience with democratic classrooms as students, we suspect that "doing democracy" in the classroom is something that evolves over time, as opposed to something that teachers jump into immediately.

"Doing" democracy in the classroom

A key element in moving toward a democratic classroom is your students' prior classroom experience. Most of them will not have experienced many of the responsibilities that the role of classroom citizen demands. Some students may find that it is easier to be a spectator or a follower, which requires only simple obedience, than to participate in self-governance. Be advised also that helping students become accustomed to the more demanding role of participant can be fraught with problems.

Children play a real role in classroom governance

A growing body of research suggests that it is impossible to teach children the moral and ethical behaviors associated with democratic citizenship—things like respecting the right of others to voice their opinions even if they differ from yours—in twenty-minute lessons taught on every other Thursday. Likewise, teaching ethics, morals, and values should be part of a whole-school enterprise, not something that individual teachers do in isolation. Recognize also that even in the most democratic, student-focused classrooms, the students are not and cannot be the primary source of curriculum. Even though asking students a question like "What would you like to study today (or this week, or month)?" would seem to reflect the epitome of a child-centered classroom, it fails to recognize that children do not know what they do not know. In other words, students cannot indicate the desire to study something they have never heard of. The point is that even in democratic classrooms, some elements always remain the teacher's prerogative.

The common good

A final element critical to operating a democratic classroom is the need to maintain an unswerving focus on the common good. No matter how much individual students may wish to follow their whims and impulses, the criterion for determining whether or not behavior is acceptable is the extent to which it reflects a shared conception of justice based on the common good. It is not your responsibility as teacher to be the sole determiner of the common good, even though that may be the case from time to time; all students should participate in that determination. In group situations, our right to do our own thing must be tempered by a concern for others, by the common good. It is one of the primary rights and responsibilities of democratic citizenship.

SUMMARY

Social studies is a composite subject created for teaching purposes that draws its content from history and the social science disciplines—geography, sociology, political science, economics, anthropology, and psychology—and to a lesser extent from philosophy, religion, and the fine arts. The main purposes for teaching social studies include (1) teaching children about our cultural heritage, (2) teaching children to think skillfully, (3) teaching about human (social) behavior, and (4) teaching children to act morally and ethically according to what they know. Because these purposes are not mutually exclusive, teachers will often deal with two or more of them simultaneously.

The overarching goal of social studies is citizenship education: that is, training students to be effective participants in a democratic society. Because educating responsible citizens is the major responsibility of schools everywhere, so citizenship education is an all-school enterprise, not the responsibility of social studies alone. Citizens in democratic societies have special responsibilities that are often denied their counterparts in totalitarian societies, where leaders make the decisions and citizens merely follow. For example, citizens in democratic societies must be able to strike a balance between the common heritage that all of us enjoy and the contributions that individual ethnicities make to our cultural mosaic—what we have referred to as multiethnic literacy. At the same time, citizens in a democratic society must recognize their responsibilities for maintaining a civic environment that welcomes their voice in determining how government will function—what we have referred to as civic literacy. And finally, citizens in a democratic society must recognize their responsibilities for maintaining secure living environments that ensure the continuing safety of one's family and community, yet still enable individuals to achieve their aspirations—or what we have referred to as community literacy. We suggest that these literacies of citizenship are essential to nurturing and maintaining a representative democracy, and as such, reflect an ongoing challenge that all of us share.

SUGGESTED ACTIVITIES

1. In the example in the chapter introduction, the Ramirez teachers usually wait until after students have asked about time zones prior to explaining how they work. Because the teachers know the children are likely to have a problem with time zones, wouldn't it be better if they simply explained time zones prior to the students' request? Is anything gained by waiting?

2. In the cooperative biographies example, Ms. Lindquist predetermined several elements of the activity, notably that each group would have five members, and each biography would have five chapters. Do you think Ms. Lindquist was justified in imposing these requirements, or would it have been better if each group had determined how many members it would have and the number of chapters in their biography?

3. In his article "The Futility of Trying to Teach Everything of Importance," Grant Wiggins (1989) argues that when teachers repeatedly claim that *everything* they teach is important, then nothing will seem important to students. The ultimate test, Wiggins suggests, occurs when students say "*This* is important," and when the teacher is silent on the matter. How to you respond to Wiggins's claim?

4. Some people suggest that most teachers don't know enough about different ethnic perspectives to teach multicultural education with any assurance. Others suggest that some individuals resist a multicultural approach because it threatens the Anglo mainstream power structure that dictates what is or is not taught in American schools. Decide the extent to which either of these contentions reflects your personal position.

SUGGESTED READINGS AND RESOURCES

Introductory Note: This section contains both print and electronic resources and is organized by categories that correlate with major topics in the chapter. The resources located under the heading "General," for example, expand on the overall focus of the chapter, and additional resources are included under their respective headings.

Print Resources

GENERAL RESOURCES

Robert D. Barr, James L. Barth, & S. Samuel Shermis. (1977). *Defining the social studies*. Bulletin 51. Washington, DC: National Council for the Social Studies. This classic book is one of the standard works for clarifying the competing philosophies of social studies.

Jere Brophy & Bruce VanSledright. (1997). *Teaching and learning history in the elementary schools.* New York: Teachers College Press. Most of this book focuses on the very different techniques that three fifth-grade teachers use to teach fifth-grade American history. However, the first two chapters also present an excellent overview of recent research.

David W. Saxe. (1991). *Social studies in schools: A history of the early years.* Albany, NY: State University of New York Press. This book is a detailed, well-written, blow-by-blow account of how social studies was created.

SOCIAL STUDIES STANDARDS

Mary E. Haas & Margaret A. Laughlin. (1997). *Meeting the standards: Social studies readings for K-6 educators.* Washington, DC: National Council for the Social Studies. This is a useful collection of readings.

DeAn M. Krey. (1998). *Children's literature in social studies: Teaching to the standards.* Bulletin 95. Washington, D.C.: National Council for the Social Studies. This book is filled with annotated lists of children's books published during the 1990s that are key to the ten NCSS thematic strands. Very useful.

Margaret A. Laughlin & H. Michael Hartoonian. (1997). *Succeed with the standards in your social studies classroom.* Portland, ME: J. Weston Walch. This book contains ready-to-use reproducible activities for the ten NCSS themes.

Tarry Lindquist. (1997). *Ways that work: Putting social studies standards into practice.* Portsmouth, NH: Heinemann.

T. Lindquist & D. Selwyn. (2000). *Social studies at the center.* Portsmouth, NH: Heinemann. Lindquist and Selwyn provide lots of examples of good social studies teaching and then show how these reflect the standards. Highly recommended.

National Council for the Social Studies. (1994). *Expectations of excellence: Curriculum standards for social studies.* Washington, DC: National Council for the Social Studies. This is a well-written compendium.

MULTIETHNIC LITERACY

Peter D. Salinas. (1997). *Assimilation, American style.* New York: Basic Books. In this short but brilliant work, Salinas argues that in the past thirty years we have moved toward a policy of enhancing ethnic consciousness, but at the expense of America's historic commitment to assimilation. If you read Salinas, you should also read Nathan Glazer's (1997) *We Are All Multiculturalists Now* (Cambridge, MA: Harvard University Press), to get the other side of the coin.

COOPERATIVE BIOGRAPHIES

M. Zarnowski. (1990). *Learning about biographies: A reading-and-writing approach for children.* Urbana, IL: National Council for Teachers of English and the National Council for the Social Studies. We agree with Tarry Lindquist that this little book is an invaluable resource for teachers thinking about doing a biography project with their students.

Internet Resources

Introductory Note: Web sites sometimes change Internet addresses or cease operating entirely. All the addresses supplied here were operating when this book was printed, but should any of them fail to work properly we suggest you enter the topic or target organization in any standard search engine.

The National Council for the Social Studies

http://www.ncss.org/online/home.html

This site, maintained by the largest professional association for social studies, is an excellent place to begin. Contains a wide variety of materials, including information about social studies, teaching techniques, lesson plans, networks, and information about professional development and travel opportunities.

ERIC Clearinghouse for Social Studies/Social Science Education ERIC/Chess

http://www.indiana.edu/-ssdc/eric-chess.html

This site is maintained by the national clearinghouse for social studies materials, including curriculum guides, teaching units, journal articles, and bibliographies.

Social Studies Sources

http://education.indiana.edu/-socialst/

This site is maintained by Indiana University and links to a variety of topics including American and world history, government, geography, news groups, and other sources.

CSS Journal

http://www.cssjournal.com/journal/sites.html

This site offers links to hundreds of social studies sites on the web.

Social Studies Around the Web

http://www.li.net/~ndonohue/ssus.html

Created by a teacher, Nancy Donohue, this site links to hundreds of topics. Well organized and easy to navigate.

Resources for Social Studies Teachers

http://www.csun.edu/~hced013/

This site, which is maintained by Dr. Marty Levine, California State University, Northridge, was one of the first and remains one of the most useful resources for anyone planning to teach social studies.

ePALS Classroom Exchange

http://www.epals.com/index.html

The ePALS Web site encourages teachers and students to share educational experiences through the classroom exchange. This site boasts an E-mail membership of over fifteen thousand classrooms in more than one hundred countries. Each participating teacher provides a brief introduction as well as information on grade level and class size.

Partner Schools

Intercultural E-Mail Classroom Connections

http://www.stolaf.edu/network/iecc/

This free service is offered by St. Olaf College in Minnesota.

Developing Educational Standards

http://putnamvalleyschools.org/Standards.html

If you are looking for information on standards, this site has it. This Putnam Valley (NY) schools site provides access to the educational standards for fifteen subjects, all fifty states, the U.S. government, and a few other nations.

2

History and the Social Sciences: The Knowledge Base for Social Studies

Key Questions

- What is the academic knowledge base for social studies?
- How has the human experience influenced what we think, do, and value?
- What is science, and what is its relationship to social studies programs?
- How do the social sciences differ from history?
- On what areas of the human experience do the social science disciplines focus?
- How does one teach history and the social sciences to young children?

Key Ideas

- Individually and collectively, all of us learn from past experience.
- History and the various social sciences study different aspects of the human experience. Collectively they are sources of content for social studies programs.
- History has a history, as do each of the social science disciplines. The parts of the human experience that these disciplines study, as well as how they study it, have changed over time.
- Science, as in social *science* discipline, refers to a rigorous process for producing and validating knowledge.
- Findings from the social sciences are usually stated as tendencies or probabilities, not absolutes.

Introduction: On Waiting in Line

Have you ever found yourself waiting in line at a bank, post office, or supermarket, only to discover that all the other lines are moving faster than yours? Which of the following describes your reaction when this happens?

a. Do you think about changing lines?

b. Do you scowl at the person causing the delay?

c. Do you continue waiting impatiently until it is your turn?

d. Do you do all of the above?

Snake lines

In these situations, my response would be "All of the above." To avoid these kinds of responses, many businesses—airports, banks, and fast-food restaurants especially—have shifted to "snake lines." This is where all the windows or stations are served from a single-file line. Snake lines are no more efficient than separate lines, but they are much fairer, because you cannot get stuck in a line that's moving slower than all the others.

Lining up is culturally related

In some nations, waiting in line is referred to as "queuing up." New Yorkers call it "waiting on line." Yet regardless of what it is called, social scientists have found that "queuing up" is part of a complex social system that involves culturally specific principles of fairness and justice. This means that for those of us who live in the Western world, the people from some cultures seem to know how to line up "properly" and others don't. For example, when the Walt Disney Corporation opened Euro-Disney in France, they had expected ticket buyers to line up in the same orderly way they do at Disney locations in California and Florida. But to Disney's dismay, the lines for both rides and tickets at Euro-Disney were chaotic. Disney's experience was consistent with what social scientists had noted previously: the more a society values equality, the more fairly its members will queue up.

How perceptions influence reality

Social scientists have found that it's not how long people actually wait in line that matters, but their *perception* of how long they *think* they had to wait. People often felt that they had waited 30 percent longer than they actually had. A similar phenomenon occurred when high-rise office buildings and hotels were first constructed and workers began complaining about long waits for the elevators. The researchers suspected that instead of installing more new elevators or speeding up the existing ones, there might be a less costly solution: provide something for the people to do that would influence their perception of the time they spent waiting. The researcher's recommendation was to install mirrors in the elevator lobbies. The complaints declined markedly. The next time you're in a major hotel or high-rise office building, take notice of the decor in the elevator lobbies.

Significance?

Researching how we humans respond to waiting in line may seem like pretty banal stuff. You might even want to ask, "Shouldn't those researchers be studying something more significant?" But imagine that you are the architect of a high-rise building and you are confronted by an angry chief executive officer (CEO) who says, "Look at all these complaints! You didn't install enough elevators." Do you install more elevators, which is an expensive proposition? Or tell the CEO to ignore the complaints? If you are aware of the social science findings, you could propose a far less expensive alternative that CEOs and many other people would probably never think of: mirrors.

Most of us are not architects (or CEOs) who might reap direct benefits from this research. So the next question is: Should students be expected to study these findings as a part of social studies? In addition to offering some insights into human behavior, the findings about waiting in line could reflect persistent behavior patterns that may emerge in other settings. Students could investigate questions such as: In what ways (besides waiting in line) does perception influence our view of reality? Or, in what other ways besides waiting in line do cultures that place less value on equality differ from ours? The waiting-in-line findings are insignificant and almost trivial by themselves, yet they could serve as a vehicle for reaching other more significant ideas about human behavior. How information can serve as a vehicle for developing ideas in other contexts is explained throughout the balance of this book.

Chapter organization

This chapter focuses on history and the social sciences, both of which reflect the largest portion of the knowledge base from which social studies is drawn. First we consider history as a field of study and look at some of the problems associated with teaching history to young children. We then examine the individual social science disciplines and what it means to be historically, geographically, and politically literate. Finally, we turn to what all of this means in terms of those portions of the human experience that we as teachers pass on to the young in the form of social studies.

History and the Human Experience

A historical clock

Many of the things that affect our lives today are of comparatively recent origin, historically speaking. Laptop computers, pagers, and cellular phones are just a few that come to mind, but consider that, in the perspective of historical time, even things like the printing press are relatively recent innovations. This becomes especially evident when historical time is depicted through the metaphor of a clock. Imagine the face of a clock on which every minute represents fifty years—a substantial part of anyone's lifetime. On that basis, the entire clock face represents three thousand years—or from about 1000 B.C.E. (before the Christian Era) to A.D. 2000 (see Figure 2.1). (Portions of this material are based on Postman and

FIGURE 2.1 The Sequence of Inventions

Today

One minute = 50 years

Weingartner [1969].) On this scale, the printing press would have been invented only nine minutes ago, television about a minute ago, and fax machines and cellular phones in the last second or two. In the field of medicine, it would have only been about three minutes ago that doctors began curing more people than they harmed. Likewise, it has also been only seconds since medicine achieved some of its most significant developments—organ transplants, laser surgery, synthetic drugs, and many other things we take for granted today.

TECHNOLOGY

The clock metaphor illustrates that life today is much faster paced than it was in years past. An hour is still sixty minutes long, of course, but changes and innovations—particularly technological innovations—have become an accepted and even expected part of modern life. Yet as quickly as changes are occurring today, history shows that change was also a facet of life in the past, although the pace was much slower.

Two areas that have changed significantly over time are not in technology or medicine, but in how we look at ourselves as human beings, and how we regard

How we view ourselves

the world in which we live. It's been only recently that we have understood our historical past well enough to realize that how we think of ourselves as human beings can differ from how members of other cultures view and think of themselves. And only recently have we come to understand that our definition of what it means to be human has changed over time. The information in Table 2.1 is oversimplified, but it reveals some of those changes.

History and the World Children Know

One of the values in teaching and studying history is the extent to which it can help young citizens view the human experience in its broader context and understand events from different perspectives (Arendt, 1961). We will use the phe-

History as understanding

nomenon of slavery to illustrate how this occurs.

It is widely known that during the seventeenth and eighteenth centuries and portions of the nineteenth century, thousands of African-Americans were enslaved and brought to this country against their will. It is less widely known that during the same period slavery was also practiced elsewhere in the world, especially in parts of Asia and North Africa. Most women in harems, for example, were not there of their own free will. Even today, parents in some parts of Southeast Asia sell their daughters into virtual slavery working in the brothels of larger cities like Bangkok.

Shift now to your twentieth-century classroom. You have reached the section of every American history textbook that deals with the three-corner (or triangular) trade. This was where American ships would haul cargoes of naval stores (lumber, pitch, etc.) or other products from New England to southern Europe—

Three-corner trade

the first leg of the triangle. The ships then sailed to North Africa, where the captains would purchase cargoes of slaves. The enslaved people would then be transported to ports in the southern United States or the Caribbean, where they were sold. To complete the triangle, the ships would pick up cargoes of agricultural products—often rum, cotton, and sugar—and transport them back to New England, where their voyage had begun originally. It was a lucrative trade that made many shipowners wealthy.

TABLE 2.1 What It Means to Be Human: A Western Historical Perspective

When	Conceptual Framework	Implications
Ancient Times	Without necessarily making any reference to the real world about them, human beings were believed to be able to use their unique mind to reason about their condition.	The world was what human beings said it was. Humans were unique and set apart from the rest of the world. The concept of science at this time was the application of reason to morality and virtue.
Early Christian Era	Religious frameworks found men and women to be part of a larger scheme and to serve purposes for existence that transcended their earthly experience. The application of the human mind and reasoning ability found rational reasons for following reasoned authority and authorities.	Mind was pure and good and physical needs and desires were viewed as evil. Humans were seen as having two dimensions—the soul and the body. Men and women were born in sin, and human effort was directed toward redemption and the "other world."
Renaissance	The political framework found men and women recognizing social realities found in existing social conditions. Power, control, leadership, and forms of social organization were based on political realities. Machiavelli's precepts emerge. Note: some argue that Machiavelli was the first political *scientist*—a scientist because he built his framework by observing and generalizing from the real world.	Beginning of the nation-state and nourishment of loyalty to earthly concerns now ran parallel to religious ideals. Beginning to use observed and observable information upon which to build ideas, people started to become increasingly aware of the complexity of their world. This movement modified their "way of knowing."
18th and 19th Centuries	The economic framework emerged. The human condition began to focus on industrializing, on ideological justifications for property, and the accumulation and distribution of wealth. The industrial revolution was under way. Adam Smith, Karl Marx, and others observed and interpreted the human experience as basically economic. Economic activity was part of the "natural" world. Human behavior was subject to "laws" just as the natural world was.	There was a definite relationship between people's "daily bread" and their larger conceptual frameworks of politics and religion. Class distinctions emerged, and economic mobility was related to social mobility. The organization and rules for economic activity fed nation-state rivalry, the need for justifying imperialism, and the need for explaining differing economic "levels." Natural laws pertaining to government, economics, and social class emerged as "right" when viewed as a larger, observed pattern of human experience. This led to a view of natural progress that human beings couldn't control.

(continued on next page)

When	Conceptual Framework	Implications
Early 20th Century	The psychoanalytic conceptual framework found men and women at the mercy of their subconscious and deterministically influenced by experiences. The framework reintroduced the individual and raised concern with the ego, superego, and id. Each individual was a product of his or her environment—especially the early environment that acted in screening subsequent experiences. Freud's interpretation helped sharpen this framework.	The primary focus appeared to be on the individual, and this seemed compatible with political and economic world-views that seemed to carry weight. Emphasis was *not* on the individual deliberately interacting with experience but on the impact of early experiences that "conditioned" the psychological sets that an individual carried through life. Stress was on the inner person and the psychological impact one's life history carried.
Middle 20th Century	The physical sciences had struggled into maturity. The social sciences commenced to scientifically (empirically) study human behavior. Instead of emerging with set and unchanging "laws" of human behavior, the social sciences, through systematic research, came up with findings stated in "if-then" terms—findings stated in probability rather than certainty. Aspects of human behavior became the provinces of specific disciplines, as potential sources for understanding and explaining the human condition. The proper study of humans was humans. Previous conceptual frameworks that focused on external absolutes became challenged through the application of a maturing science to the area of human behavior.	The social science concept of human beings freed people from any sort of absolute determinism. It portrayed human beings as organisms interacting with artificial and natural environments. Rational applications of social science findings again brought focus to *Homo sapiens* as a learning/teaching and valuing species. Social concern moved from "other-worldliness" to the human condition on this planet. Ways of "knowing" shifted from logic and reason to observable human phenomena. In a continuing struggle, men and women assumed responsibility for their life choices. As John Dewey maintained, the purpose of life is life. Social science provided different information with which to help adapt and control. The choices, difficult as they are, are ours to make.
Turn of the 21st Century	Traditional ways of knowing, including the natural epistemology provided by science, as well as the notions of objectivity and rational rules for evidence, are being challenged in the academic community. The turn of the century is a time of ferment as the conceptual framework seems to be moving from a form of rationalism—rooted partly in the Enlightenment and based on the canons of science—to a form of intellectual relativism that accommodates multiple methods and procedures for knowing.	The implications of competing ways of knowing are not entirely clear. However, it appears there will no longer be a single standard for measuring and judging what one knows and how one knows. What this will mean for the structure and nature of the school curriculum and the academic disciplines is not clear. Also unclear is the mechanism—other than sheer numbers and power—that societies will use to resolve social conflicts, or whether the courts will need to establish new rules for handling evidence. The implications are substantial.

Against this background, consider one of your fifth graders who asks: "How could those people buy and sell human beings? Don't they know it's wrong? Don't they have a conscience?" The student's questions are reasonable, and common. How will you respond?

Different ways of viewing the world

In developing your response, consider that your students are products of twentieth-century thinking, and, as suggested in Table 2.1, are likely to believe in self-determination. They are also likely to believe (as your student has already indicated) that buying and selling human beings or keeping them in bondage is immoral and illegal. It has probably never occurred to most children that people in other times and places, including the seventeenth and eighteenth centuries, looked at their world quite differently than today's children do.

The problem of helping children understand different views of the world is compounded because elementary textbooks almost never deal with different views. This means that you are essentially on your own. In this context, the first time you say "natural laws," you are apt to get some bewildered looks from students. Nevertheless, people in the seventeenth and eighteenth centuries who considered themselves moral individuals were able to rationalize the practice of slavery on the basis of one or more so-called laws of nature, or "natural laws." The natural law that applied to slavery was based on the notion that some human groups were ranked as "higher" or "lower" than others, usually along racial lines. By virtue of their ranking, members of lower groups were considered eligible for domination, subservience, and even enslavement.

"natural laws"

Unless you are willing to explain how people in the seventeenth and eighteenth centuries viewed the world, including the concept of natural law, providing intelligible responses to your student's question will be difficult. An adequate though not very comforting compromise is to say something like "What those people did was wrong by our standards today. I'm not trying to excuse what they did, but people at that time didn't look at their world in the same way we do." If you think that the last line is too much, you could ignore it. However, unless you've laid some preliminary groundwork with your students, they won't understand the notion of world-view any more than the notion of natural laws.

Helping Young Children Connect with the Past

Part of the dilemma arises because of the way history is often presented in schools. From your experience, you know that most history courses are organized as chronological surveys in which you begin somewhere in the past and then work slowly toward modern times. But, as Levstik and Barton (1997) noted, "Too often, history instruction is simply a march through time that never quite connects to the present" (p. 1). When history survey courses finally get to the present day—if they do—it is typically in a hurried treatment that occurs during the last week of May, when most students are looking forward to the end of school.

Chronological surveys

You may also recall that when history is taught chronologically, one event usually leads up to, or is said to "cause," a later event. The Boston Tea Party, for example, is often presented as a cause that led to the Revolutionary War, just as slavery and states' rights are usually identified as causes of the Civil War. In this context, ask yourself whether the colonists who participated in the Boston Tea Party were saying to themselves, "We are causing the Revolutionary War!" Even if most colonists wanted a war with England, which some of them did, they could not say they were causing the Revolutionary War—at least not until the war itself actually occurred. Likewise, the first enslaved person arrived in this country in 1619, but the Civil War did not occur until 1861, almost 250 years later. Is it possible that a cause existed for five generations? What actually happened, of course, is that beliefs changed over those 250 years, and the natural laws that had once made enslavement a tolerable practice were gradually replaced by even stronger beliefs in self-determination for all people. The first point here is that slavery became a cause of the Civil War, even though it didn't start out that way. The second point is that historians can look at past events, such as the Revolutionary or Civil wars, and then, with the hindsight that history permits, go back to identify what caused those events. Despite the image that many textbooks convey, children need to understand that the cause-effect nature of history always occurs after the fact. Our third point is that although historians can rightfully focus on explaining the past, they cannot predict the future. Even after analyzing events that are occurring today, no reasonable historian would say: "These events *will* cause the Caribbean War of 2008." Forecasting is the business of meteorologists, not historians.

"causes" and "effects"

Yet another factor that influences how young children understand history is the way they perceive the passage of time. Very young children often think of time in terms of tonight, tomorrow, and perhaps next week. If you have any doubt about this, recall those holiday eves from your childhood when you wondered if it would *ever* get dark? Perhaps you've also noticed that your birthdays (and possibly the holiday seasons) come around more quickly than they used to. As adults, we know that time has not speeded up; rather it's our perception that changes. The time that once crept along so slowly when we were children somehow speeds up as we get older. The point here is that for young children who measure time past by the number of "longs" they attach to "ago"—as in "It happened a long, long time ago"—trying to instill precise historical dating is probably an exercise in futility. All of us eventually develop the ability to deal with the past, including the distant past, but expecting young children who have lived a decade or less to understand historical time is probably a case of imposing adult views onto children who look at their world quite differently.

History looks back, not forward

How children perceive time

Two additional factors, one peculiar to history and the other pertaining to how we as adults expect children to deal with history and the other subjects they study, also have a bearing here. The distinguished historian Arnaldo Momigliano (1982) noted that although history has existed as a research and literary activity for at least twenty-five centuries, it has been a subject taught in schools and universities for only two or three centuries. Momigliano went on to note that in the two thousand years before it became a school subject, "history was written for *adult* minds" (p. 245). Although young children can deal with history, teachers need to be sensitive to (1) how they approach it as a subject, and (2) the kinds of expectations that they impose on children who are expected to learn it.

History was originally for adults

● History for Young Children

A growing body of research (see Brophy & VanSledright, 1997; and Levstik & Barton, 1997) indicates that young children can deal with history quite readily. However, teachers must approach history in ways that accommodate young children's abilities and prior experiences. Sometimes this can mean avoiding certain practices. For example, when history was first introduced as a school subject, the prevailing educational view was that children were "miniature adults"—individuals who needed only proper guidance and training to function effectively as adults. At that time, the dominant educational technique for providing that training was called "mental discipline" or "mind training." From this perspective, the mind was regarded as a muscle that would "strengthen" and respond to exercise, just as skeletal muscles do. The usual procedure for training children's minds, and thus building mental discipline, was by providing children with long and often onerous mental exercises—things like memorizing the presidents *and* vice presidents of the United States, in order. History and geography provided ideal subject matter for the advocates of mental discipline—just look at all the facts children could be expected to memorize.

Providing miniature adults with mental discipline

The "mental discipline" notion has died a lingering death, as did the conception of children as "miniature adults." Despite the huge body of research (e.g., Piaget, 1950; Egan, 1979; Elkind, 1982) that shows that young children do not think and reason as adults do, at least not initially, some parents today still dress their children in designer clothing and otherwise put the trappings of adulthood onto their children.

How then should you approach history with young children? Here is a brief summary of practices that are based on a growing body of research (see Brophy & VanSledright, 1997; Bruer, 1993; Bruner, 1986; Caine & Caine, 1994; Gardner, 1991; Good & Brophy, 1994; Levstik & Barton, 1997; Levstik & Pappas, 1987; Thornton & Vukelich, 1988).

Recommended practices

★ Avoid trying to cover long periods of time very quickly. Try focusing instead on one historical era, and then providing in-depth narrative accounts for that period. Better yet, let your students become involved in those detailed accounts. With a teacher's help, young children can often make sense of the original source materials found in journals, diaries, biographies, pictures, and historical documents.

★ Avoid broad and sweeping statements such as "Reconstruction was a time of turmoil," at least until students have had the experiences that will permit them to know what such statements mean. Instead of painting history with a "broad brush," try focusing instead on *particular* history, that is, on narrative accounts where *a* person (or small group of persons) deals with *a* particular problem in *a* particular place at *a* particular time, and under *a* particular set of circumstances. Especially useful in this respect are fictionalized diaries based on original sources but that avoid the archaic language that can sometimes cause problems for young children. Two of our favorites in this genre are Kristiana Gregory's *The Winter of the Red Snow: The Revolutionary War Diary of Abigail Jane Stewart* (1996) and *Across the Wide and Lonesome Prairie: The Oregon Trail Diary of Hattie Campbell* (1997). The red snow in the title of the Revolutionary War diary refers to the bloody footprints left by George Washington's troops as they marched bootless in the ice and snow en route to their camp at Valley Forge over the winter of 1777–78. Consider that even if children already know about Valley Forge, details like the bloody footprints can motivate reluctant readers. Likewise, the Oregon Trail diary does a wonderful job conveying the hardships and the occasional joys that occurred

"Particular" history

Living history museums can offer wonderful opportunities for stepping back into the past. *(© Joel Gordon)*

Fictionalized diaries

during that arduous eight-month journey from Missouri to Oregon. Note also that although the Gregory diaries are written from the perspective of girls between eleven and thirteen years old, most boys find them as engrossing as girls. The point here is that in teaching history to young children, try to use materials that will personalize events and make them real.

★ Avoid using outlines as an introductory activity. If you remember making an outline after you wrote your report (on whatever the topic), as noted in the prologue, don't expect your students to approach outlines any differently. Outlines of historical events that children have not yet studied are simply lists—often disjointed lists. Outlines (and timelines) are excellent devices for organizing preexisting information and are especially useful as concluding or synthesizing activities. On the other hand, neither you nor your students can organize information that you do not have (which may explain why you wrote your outline after you had written your report!)

Time and specificity

The research (see Levstik & Barton, 1997) suggests that two keys to teaching history to young children successfully are *time* and *specificity*. For example, let's assume that you want your students to understand the role that the Underground Railroad played before the Civil War. You could probably convey this information in a ten- to fifteen-minute minilecture, or you could have students spend several days reading a biography of someone who lived through that period, possibly Harriet Tubman. Which would you do? Despite the time it takes, we would opt for the biography. It would personalize events surrounding the Underground Railroad in ways that children can relate to, and it would also permit you to *scaffold,* that is, to build on students' prior knowledge and experiences. In the absence of scaffolding, children may be forced to treat new knowledge as isolated and highly perishable pieces of information. A final but not insignificant reason to use the Harriet Tubman biography specifically is that most students love it.

Coverage vs. specificity

The issue here is not whether you could "cover the material" in less time via other means, but whether you could do it with the specificity, immediacy, and poignancy that most biographies, diaries, and primary source materials do. This is essentially the same "less is more" issue that we considered in Chapter 1. In addition, and although these guidelines are applicable to teaching history to very young children, they are also applicable to older children, even adults.

Where do social studies textbooks fit in here? Many teachers, expecially beginning teachers, use textbooks as their main organizer and then supplement the text with primary source materials. It is not unusual for some primary source materials to be included as part of a total textbook package. In other instances, teachers (such as Tarry Lindquist from Chapter 1) organize most of their teaching around primary source documents and then use textbooks to help their students pull everything together.

History and the Social Sciences

This section explains why most social studies educators use the expression "history and the social sciences," instead of lumping the two together. It then examines the social science disciplines, how they are organized, and areas of the human experience they usually focus on.

● History

History is not a social science discipline, which is why we use the expression "history and the social sciences" throughout this book. History actually falls into a grey area that lies between the social sciences and the humanities. This is not a defect or deficiency; it simply reflects the nature of that vast and wonderful discipline.

Why history is not a social science

History differs from the social sciences in at least two significant ways. First, historians focus on the past—which is not exactly a revelation, we're sure. However, because the events of history are in the past, it is physically impossible for historians to move backward in time to control and reproduce historical events experimentally in the same way scientists can control events in a laboratory. This is why historians cannot predict future events with a reasonable degree of accuracy. Historians often reconstruct events from historical documents, but this too can pose other problems: Historians cannot be certain they have all the pertinent documentation. Neither can they be certain that whatever documentation they have reflects an unbiased account of the events in question. In times of war, for example, the losing side's records are often destroyed or lost, sometimes intentionally. This situation is what possibly led the noted historian Henry Steele Commager (1980) to comment that, over the centuries, history is typically written by the victors, not the vanquished.

In most social studies programs, history is treated as a social science discipline, even though it does not meet all the procedural requirements of a science. At the factual level—the names, places, and dates that we typically associate with history—there is probably no problem in treating it that way. But if, as Momigliano (1982) noted, "we take it for granted that history can answer questions about the purpose of life or about the shape of the future—which history cannot answer—we are placing ourselves and history in a false position" (p. 495).

Historical viewpoints and objectivity

Elementary and middle-school students typically believe that everything in their history textbook is fact, an agreed-upon and unquestioningly true record of the past. It wasn't until we majored in history in college that we discovered there were different schools of history, and that historians may interpret the same events very differently. The point is that no historical account is entirely objective. Events of history are always interpreted through human eyes, and everyone knows that if six different people observe the same event, you can get six different accounts of what occurred. Historians must decide which (of those six or more) accounts are the most plausible, and even then there is always a lingering doubt. Did the historians miss something, or overemphasize one account at the expense of others? Such questions simply reflect the often incomplete and interpretive nature of history. This also suggests why history's niche among the branches of knowledge is often more closely associated with the humanities than the sciences.

Selected Focal Areas of History

Civilization	Change	Continuity	Progress
Chronology	Bias	Invention	Leadership
Colonization	Perfectability	Historical records	Exploration

Geography

Geography is the science of place and space. Geography's two major areas of study are (1) places on the earth, and (2) the interaction between places and the people who live in them. These areas are the focus of geography's two major subdisciplines: *physical geography* and *cultural geography.*

The components of geography

Physical geography, which is one of the oldest of the social sciences, focuses on the physical characteristics of place. Physical geographers study place location, landforms, climate, resources, and the other facets of our habitats on earth. When you learned about the capital of Belgium (Brussels), the mountains that separate France and Spain (the Pyrenees), or the major American river that flows into the Gulf of Mexico (the Mississippi), you were studying physical geography.

Cultural geography focuses on the interaction between peoples and their environments, or, in other words, how people use the spaces in which they live. Cultural geographers look mainly at the effects of human intervention on the environment. These include how people are distributed on the earth's surface, how they use resources, how they develop transportation and communication systems, and so forth. If you remember studying how the scarcity of usable land forced farmers in the Orient to build terraces on the steep hillsides, you were dealing with cultural geography.

A third subdivision of geography is *cartography*—mapmaking. Maps and aerial or satellite photographs (from which most maps are made) are among geographers' most important tools for displaying and analyzing the phenomena they study.

Geographic Literacy.   Although geography is second only to history as a mainstay of the social studies curriculum, most of the geography that students study occurs in elementary and middle schools, primarily in Grades 3 through 7. Rather than having students take additional courses in "pure" geography, the emerging view is that geography and history are complementary subjects that are best taught together in the social studies curriculum (see Bednarz, 1997). When you think about it, every event in history occurred somewhere on earth, and sometimes where the event occurred influenced its outcome. As Bednarz noted, there are good geographic reasons why the Revolutionary War "Battle of Bunker Hill" was actually fought on nearby Breed's Hill (p. 140).

Complementary subjects

In the past, most efforts to assess geographic literacy were based almost solely on the student's knowledge of physical geography. This means that students were expected to answer questions such as "What is the capital of the Philippines?" and "What are the five major rivers of Africa?" Information of this kind is sometimes derisively referred to as "place-name geography," but it still plays a role in many social studies programs and as a component of geographic literacy. Contemporary measures of geographic literacy often include aspects of place-name geography but in many instances have been broadened to include elements of critical and creative thinking and the use of geographic resources. These dimensions are reflected in the following exemplary geographic literacy tasks designed for fourth-grade students:

Place-name geography

* Locate the seven continents and four oceans on a world map.
* Locate specific geographic features, such as the Ozark Plateau or the Susquehanna River, on a map of North America.
* Tell a story about what it is like to travel to or live in another region of the country or world.
* Find answers to questions, such as "What are the five largest cities in your state?" by using an encyclopedia, atlas, gazetteer, computer database, or other resources.
* Measure the distance between two places on an interstate highway map.
* Describe the relative location of your local community in terms of its situation in your state and region, such as "My town is halfway between the state capital and the largest city in the state" (Henry, 1994, p. 4D).

Performance standards

Selected Focal Areas of Geography

Landforms	Location	Areal specialization	Demographics
Region	Migration	Habitat	Population density
Resources	Ecosystem	Climate	Spatial interaction

TECHNOLOGY UPDATE

G.I.S.: Geographical Information Systems

G.I.S., or Geographical Information Systems, refers to powerful computer software that can store and display a variety of geographical information. G.I.S. programs such as the *Mapmaker's Toolkit* (Tom Snyder Productions) and *Mapping the USA* (ERIM International) are suites of databases, including maps and photographs—both current and historical—that are integrated or georeferenced. This means the materials are designed so that two or more pieces of information will fit together and can be displayed simultaneously. If you have ever tried to compare two maps of the same area, both in different scales, you know what a problem that can be. And if you have never tried doing this, what may sound like a simple matter can easily prove otherwise.

A brief example based on an older technology may help to clarify how a teacher could use G.I.S. software effectively. Imagine if you will that you have made overhead transparencies of three different maps, all in the same scale, of southern California from San Diego to the Los Angeles area. The first transparency shows population density, which in the Los Angeles and San Diego metropolitan areas is dense indeed but is significantly sparser in desert regions. On top of this map you overlay a second transparency (map) that shows the yearly rainfall. By projecting the two maps simultaneously, your students should be able to see that people tend *not* to live in areas that get less than ten inches of rainfall—the geographical definition of a desert—each year. But again, trying to locate maps in the same scale and that contain just this information—population density and rainfall—*and* that are not cluttered with additional details, such as city names and roadways, is an almost impossible task. If you don't have access to G.I.S. software, you may want to visit Atlapedia Online at **http://www.atlapedia.com/index.html,** where you can download maps and up-to-date statistical information about every country in the world.

Once children have determined where people tend to live (and where they don't), you might then remove the rainfall map and place your third transparency—a map of the roadways in the area—on the overhead projector. It should quickly become apparent that highway systems in the San Diego–Los Angeles areas are far more complex than in a desert community like Needles, California, where roads are few and far between.

Teachers in technologically advanced schools need not endure the time-consuming hassle of locating and making the necessary maps and overhead transparencies; rather, they need only punch a few keys on their G.I.S-equipped computer. Whether you use the older technology (overhead transparencies) or the G.I.S. programs, the activity can lead to at least two powerful geographic ideas: that people tend *not* to live in areas that receive less than ten inches of rain a year, and that as the population density increases, highway systems tend to become more complex. The G.I.S. software greatly simplifies the process of selecting and layering maps that show only the geographic features a teacher wants to display. To paraphrase the housekeeping guru, Martha Stewart, G.I.S. is a good thing.

●— Anthropology

A focus on culture

Anthropology is the study of culture—the different ways of being human. Using artifacts, written and oral accounts, and on-site observations, anthropologists strive to develop profiles of cultures around the world. Anthropologists often use maps in their studies, but among their most important tools are cameras or camcorders, tape recorders, field notebooks, and laptop computers.

The discipline of anthropology is organized much like geography: its two major subdisciplines are *physical anthropology* and *cultural anthropology*. Physical anthropology focuses on the physical characteristics of humans and, in some

Five Fundamental Themes of Geography

The Joint Committee on Geographic Education (1984, pp. 3–7) identified five fundamental themes that are intended to capture the essence of geography and serve as guidelines for geographic education in the schools.

Location

THEME ONE: *Location: Position on the Earth's Surface*

Absolute and relative location are two ways of describing the positions of people and places on the earth's surface.

Place

THEME TWO: *Place: Physical and Human Characteristics*

All places on earth have distinctive tangible and intangible characteristics that give them meaning and character and distinguish them from other places. Geographers generally describe places by their physical or human characteristics.

Relationships

THEME THREE: *Relationships Within Places: Humans and Environments*

All places on the earth have advantages and disadvantages for human settlement. High population densities have developed on flood plains, for example, where people could take advantage of fertile soils, water resources, and opportunities for river transportation. However, flood plains are periodically subjected to severe damage. By comparison, population densities are usually low in deserts, yet some desert areas, such as Israel, have been modified to support large populations.

Movement

THEME FOUR: *Movement: Humans Interacting on the Earth*

Human beings occupy places unevenly across the face of the earth. Yet these people interact with each other; that is, they travel from one place to another, they communicate with each other, or they rely upon products, information, and ideas that come from beyond their immediate environment.

Regions

THEME FIVE: *Regions: How They Form and Change*

The basic unit of geographic study is the region, an area that displays unity in terms of selected criteria. We are all familiar with regions showing the extent of political power, such as nations, provinces, countries, or cities, yet there are almost countless ways to define meaningful regions, depending on the problems being considered. For example, Indiana as a state is a governmental region, Latin America as an area where Spanish and Portuguese are major languages can be a linguistic region, and the Rocky Mountains as a mountain range is a landform region.

Historical and archaeological artifacts can bring the real world into the classroom. (© Susie Fitzhugh)

The components of anthropology

cases, animals. The fact that one branch of physical anthropology, *primatology,* focuses on the behavior of nonhuman primates—apes, baboons, and gorillas—harkens back to a time when anthropology was considered a subdiscipline of biology. Anthropologists who focus on studying fossils (instead of living beings) reflect a subspeciality known as *paleoanthropology* or *paleontology.*

Cultural anthropology (or social anthropology) is the broad descriptor for the study of culture. Some cultural anthropologists employ a "cross-cultural perspective" to study the behaviors of past or present cultures. Others narrow their study to a single culture or ethnic group, such as the Hopi, the Maori of New Zealand, or former Puerto Ricans who now live in the Spanish Harlem neighborhood of New York City. Anthropologists who study single ethnic groups are called *ethnographers,* or literally, "individuals who map an ethnic (or culture)."

The power of language

Anthropological linguistics or *linguistic anthropology*—the two terms are interchangeable—focuses on the study of language and its use in social contexts. Most anthropologists agree that the creation and use of language is one of the key elements of human adaptation. As a result, linguistic anthropologists study the structure of a group's language, how they acquire it, and what it shows about their relationship to other groups.

Archaeology reflects a subspeciality of anthropology that focuses on the remains from lost or past civilizations. The materials could be a single piece of

Selected Focal Areas of Anthropology

Culture	Acculturation	Diffusion	Customs
Ethnology	Tradition	Language	Kinship patterns
Rituals	Enculturation	Innovation	Tools

broken pottery or the contents of an entire city, as in Pompeii, Italy; but they usually fall somewhere in between. By studying these remains, the archaeologist's goal is to discern the way of life of the peoples who used them.

● Political Science

Government and political behavior

Political science is the study of how human beings think, organize, and act politically (Brody, 1989). However, some totalitarian societies, such as China, do not recognize political science as a legitimate area of study (Theroux, 1997). Specializations in political science include public administration, international relations, political theory, and the study of policymaking and political behavior.

All societies develop ways to maintain social order, which are usually called governments, and most societies endow their governments with power and authority over members of the society. The form of government may be very simple—a chief and a council of elders or sometimes just a chief who acts unilaterally—or it can be more complex, as in the executive, legislative, and judicial branches of the U.S. government. The authority of government may be reflected by rules, which when written are called *laws* or when unwritten are called *mores* or, more simply, *tradition*.

In our society, decisions about whether someone has violated the law are vested in the judicial branch of government. In other societies, those decisions may be vested in the same bodies or persons who make the laws—a chief, a council, or some similar individual or group. In our society, the legislative, executive, and judicial branches of government are separate, at least theoretically. Ongoing issues like the abortion question have refocused attention on the way in which the Supreme Court interprets the law, thus determining what is or is not lawful behavior.

Civics emphasis

Political science appears in most elementary and middle-school social studies as *government* (or *civics*). The major emphasis is on the law-making process and the form and structure of government at the local, state, and national levels. A second emphasis emerges at the upper elementary and middle-school grades when students study the historical evolution of the American government—from colony to confederacy to republic.

Selected Focal Areas of Political Science

Government	Authority	Power	Monarchy
Citizenship	Democracy	Fascism	Judiciary
Socialism	Federalism	Communism	Due process

Sociology

Many of us voluntarily join a variety of groups—school groups, the PTA perhaps, religious groups, or social or service groups such as the Lions Club or the Rotary. At the same time, all of us are members of other groups—cultural, ethnic, or age groups, such as teenagers, "yuppies," or seasoned citizens—simply because of who we are. Whether one is a teenager, a young adult, or a Golden Ager is not a matter of choice. But sociologically speaking, all of the groups to which you belong influence your behavior, just as you influence the behavior of the group itself.

Sociology is the study of human groups, how they form, and how they function. During the 1800s, sociology was very broadly defined as the study of all aspects of human life and social activity (Dawson, 1929). Almost everything "social" was subsumed under either sociology or history. However, as the other social science disciplines began to carve their niches from the human experience, people tended to drop the generic "sociology" and refer to the more specialized disciplines, such as political science. *Sociology* was retained as a term, but its focus was narrowed to the discipline concerned with the study of group behavior.

The study of group behavior

Sociology has an array of subdisciplines. Some of these include economic, organizational, political, rural, and urban sociology; the sociologies of knowledge, law, religion, and medicine; human ecology; the history of social thought; sociometry and other small-group research; survey research; and special fields such as criminology and demography.

Sociology's focus on groups sometimes overlaps with other social science disciplines, mainly anthropology and political science, which also deal with human behavior in group settings. At times, the question becomes one of who is overlapping whom. Sociology and political science typically focus on modern, industrialized societies, whereas anthropology usually focuses on preliterate societies. Yet when sociologists, anthropologists, and political scientists all focus on a contemporary society, some overlap is probably unavoidable. However, each discipline typically examines phenomena from a different perspective and, in so doing, adds richness and depth to what we know about the human condition.

How disciplines may overlap

Selected Focal Areas of Sociology

Groups	Socialization	Discrimination	Stratification
Social class	Social status	Society	Norms
Role expectations	Segregation	Social mobility	Power

Economics

Economics is the study of systems for producing, distributing, exchanging, and consuming goods and services. The economy of a society may be based on trading grain or beads or tobacco or money, but regardless of its medium of exchange, an economy underlies every society. Subdisciplines in economics include economic history, agricultural economics, industrial economics, international economics, public finance, and certain aspects of business management.

The "science" of scarcity

Scarcity is the engine that drives economies everywhere. If we lived in a utopian world where everyone had everything that they could ever want or need, scarcity would not exist and an economy would be unnecessary. In the real world, there are more things we want and need (or think we need) than there are resources available to satisfy them. Thus we must allocate resources to balance our wants and needs with the resources available to us. In the process, we may be forced to settle for a compact Ford or Chevrolet instead of the Corvette we always dreamed of. Economics is sometimes called the science of scarcity because of the central role it plays in every economy.

One of the two major areas of study within economics is *microeconomics,* which focuses on specific segments of the larger economy. These segments may include individual consumers or households, or businesses that serve a particular segment of the market, such as retail sales or medical services. The other major area of economics, *macroeconomics,* studies the economy as a whole. Macroeconomists typically study the complex web of relationships among such things as the money supply, the inflation rate, business and industrial inventories, and the unemployment rate.

The findings of macroeconomists often provide the basis for governmental intervention in the economy, whether it be to maintain lower interest rates or low inflation, or to reduce unemployment. Strictly speaking, actions designed to maintain low interest rates, low inflation, and full employment are matters of social policy, *not* economics per se. Economists do not intervene in the economy; rather, they provide the data that enable social planners—who are usually employed by government—to do the actual intervention.

Macroeconomics focuses on economic elements, like inflation and the gross national product, that can have a profound influence on consumers. At the same time, macroeconomics can seem abstract and far removed from day-to-day living. Few of us, for example, may pay much attention to changes in the interest rate until it becomes so high that we can't afford taking out a loan to purchase something. Likewise, trying to understand abstract concepts such as inflation, much less what causes it, can be frustrating for young children and adults alike. Inflation is an abstraction that no one has ever seen, although we do see its effects in higher prices. In place of abstract concepts like inflation, the economic components of elementary and middle-school social studies programs usually focus on *consumer economics,* which aims at helping children become informed consumers. Most social studies programs also deal with basic concepts of microeconomics, such as resources, wants and needs, production, consumption, and exchange.

Allocating resources

Intervening in the economy

Consumer economics emphasis

Selected Focal Areas of Economics

Goods	Services	Production	Exchange
Resources	Profit	Scarcity	Supply and demand
Consumer	Labor	Needs and wants	Price

● Psychology

Psychology is the study of behavior—animal or human, instinctive and learned. The psychologists who study rats in a maze or chickens pecking at buttons to obtain food may be interested solely in the animals' behavior or may be searching for clues to human behavior, or both. Humans are infinitely more complex than rats or chickens, of course, which is why findings based on animal behavior don't always transfer to human beings. The point is that psychology is the study of behavior, broadly speaking, not human behavior alone.

Behavior is a tremendously complex and varied subject, and so is the discipline that studies it. Some subdisciplines of psychology use procedures more common to medicine and the natural sciences, such as treating disturbing or abnormal conditions, including mental illnesses. Still others focus almost exclusively on human behavior and are clearly social sciences.

The study of behavior

The fields of psychology most pertinent to the social studies include social psychology, which focuses on the behavior of humans in groups and group settings; cognitive psychology, which focuses on intellectual functions such as memory, perception, learning, and reasoning; and developmental psychology, which deals with the development of human behavior over the lifetime. Other related subdisciplines include personality psychology, which deals with the nature and development of personality, and psycholinguistics, which examines the development of language and language skills.

More common in health programs

Content drawn from psychology is common in elementary and middle schools, but it is more often part of the health curriculum, not social studies. Most health programs consider topics such as the nature of thinking and learning, the stages of human development, and the influences of heredity and the environment on human behavior, all of which derive from psychology. Also common to schools is what could be called "applied psychology." This is reflected by teachers' efforts to help students (1) build their self-concept and self-esteem, (2) deal with possible feelings of inadequacy, (3) cope with physical or verbal abuse, and (4) maintain good relationships with adults and peers. Although the elements of "applied psychology" are an inescapable part of teaching, they seldom occur as a formal subject. Whether psychology is treated as health or social studies, it remains a fertile source of social content.

Selected Focal Areas of Psychology

Learning	Personality	Motives	Self-concept
Perception	Aggression	Attitudes	Traits
Instinct	Conditioning	Punishment	Reinforcement

●── Related Disciplines

Other fields of study besides the social science disciplines apply the processes of science to social phenomena. For example, the field of psychiatry, which we normally think of as part of medicine, could be considered a social science (see below). The following are related disciplines that may be incorporated into social studies programs:

Related fields of study

Law—including jurisprudence, the major legal systems, legal theory, and the relation of law to the other social sciences.

Psychiatry—including theories and descriptions of the principal mental disorders and methods of diagnosis and treatment.

Statistics—including theoretical statistics, the design of experiments, sampling errors, sample surveys, governmental statistics, and the use of statistical methods in social science research. Note that statistics are mathematical tools that scientists use to determine the probability that the phenomenon they observed in a sample of the population is an accurate reflection of the entire population. In other words, scientists use statistics to test the probability that their findings are valid and not simply random or chance occurrences.

Natural Sciences—including biology, geology, and environmental sciences.

Major Findings from the Social Sciences

Findings from the social science disciplines can take many different forms. Sometimes they are presented as generalizable statements that apply at all times and in all places. For example, all cultures develop a means for social control—that is, for governing the conduct of their members. This means that all cultures hold certain expectations of how their members should behave. Other social science

Generalizations

findings are presented in the "if-then" format that we described earlier, and describe how people will tend to behave. Thus, for example, the members of a group will tend to perceive the group's collective opinion as closer to their own than it really is. Such findings provide a basis for anticipating and interpreting the behavior of others, but because they are based on tendencies, not absolutes, the behaviors they predict will not always occur.

In many (some will say too many) cases, data from the social sciences consist of factual, uninterpreted, documentary information. You could, for example, find out how many acres of farmland were harvested in 1957 or how many bushels

Raw (uninterpreted) data

of wheat were produced in Kansas in 1994—assuming that you needed that kind of information. In still other instances, social science findings can reflect reinterpretations of previously existing information. This might include a reconsideration of the role that slavery played as a cause of the Civil War, or a new explanation for why the food problem in India might be further complicated if the Hindus were to eat their sacred cows.

Regardless of the form the data take, social scientists are continually adding to the fund of knowledge. That's why social studies books get thicker, not thinner. The efforts of individual social scientists are usually systematic and well organized, but because there is no systematic way of managing all the information they produce, their findings are scattered throughout hundreds of sources—journals, magazines, even the Internet. Some of them, like the findings about waiting in line, eventually appear in textbooks.

An ever-growing body of knowledge

The following sample generalizations, which are stated in nonacademic language, are based on history and the social sciences. They apply to human activities regardless of social situation, cultural background, or geographic location and could serve as a foundation (or part of one) for social studies programs.

* People all over the world are the same in some ways and different in other ways.
* Human beings learn to behave the way they do.
* Most human beings learn social habits, many of which they perform automatically and without thought. These patterns of behavior can help others predict how people will behave.
* Most people think that their ways of thinking and doing things are natural and right.
* All people can learn from past experience and can accept or change their ways of living.
* A change in one part of a person's life often requires changes in other parts of their life.
* Most people live in several different group settings simultaneously. This may cause conflict for the person if the groups expect different kinds of behavior.
* Most people carry a "map" of their social worlds in their mind.
* Most groups in which people live are dependent upon other groups (in which they don't live). This can lead to cooperation or conflict.
* People learn to play certain roles that may change over time and with new situations.
* Most human behavior is aimed toward satisfying some purpose or achieving certain goals.
* All human beings are born with the same physical needs, but how these needs are satisfied differ from one person to another.
* People living in the same group tend to share values and behaviors that are similar.
* Every human group has ways of handling how people work, how resources are used and distributed, and how the group's "wealth" is to be managed.
* In most groups, individual members depend upon one another for satisfying needs and wants.
* How people use their physical environment depends on what is available, what is wanted, and how the group manages itself.
* All human groups develop ways for handling disagreements.
* Most groups of people believe in myths and legends that help them interpret and make sense of their world.

Most behavior is learned

Most human behavior is purposeful

All societies have rules they live by

These findings could become the major ideas—the content—around which social studies instruction is organized. In this instance, content refers to two different but mutually supporting ideas: (1) the information and ideas contained in a particular subject area, such as social studies, and (2) the subjects or topics that matter in a specific field of study. If you consider the two different meanings, a significant aspect of social studies teaching may emerge: being a teacher is different from being a scholar. Teachers must identify and use specific information and ideas to ensure that their students learn to identify and use information and ideas. Scholars, on the other hand, usually identify information and ideas to be used in developing more content and more effective modes of inquiry. This is not to suggest that scholars can't teach, or that teachers cannot also be scholars. The point is that although teachers have some dependency upon the scholars' work, teachers and scholars may view content from different perspectives.

The knowledge base for social studies

The social science disciplines were originally created to aid in the scholarly pursuit of knowledge. Yet the content and findings from history and the social sciences furnish the raw materials—the knowledge base—upon which social studies programs are built. How one chooses to select, organize, and use these raw materials will determine the nature of the program, which is our focus in Chapter 3.

●——— COMMENTARY   **Social Studies or Social Science Education**

When most of us were in elementary and middle schools, we studied social studies, not social science. We learned the names, dates, and places of history and geography, and we occasionally sampled some of the other social science disciplines. What we did not study much about was how scientists work with information and how they validate their findings. Occasionally we put information into chart and graph form, but it was usually decontextualized data—stuff like graphing the amount of wheat grown in Kansas from 1970 to the present. Some of us may have experienced the problems associated with polling or conducting a survey to determine the most popular soft drink or peanut butter, and whether students' taste for such products change from kindergarten to sixth grade, but such activities may have been the exception, not the rule.

When the knowledge base of history and the social sciences is drawn on to produce a social studies program, what often gets omitted are the processes of science. In other words, most social studies programs leave out the "science" part of social science. We are not suggesting that we need to put science back into social studies, because for the most part it was never there to begin with. We do suggest, however, that the information processes of science should be part of every social studies program. Helping students to gather, process, and evaluate information would be useful in its own right and would also help move from traditional social studies toward social science education.

● ●

SUMMARY

The human experience is that colossus from which all social studies stem. Our collective knowledge of the human experience is so all-encompassing that scholars created smaller, more manageable bodies of knowledge to organize what we know. Yet even these smaller bodies of knowledge, like geography and biology and medicine, have grown to massive proportions.

Somewhere in the human experience, scholars began referring to the smaller branches of knowledge as *disciplines*. At another point in the human experience, scholars who specialized in certain disciplines adopted rigorous (disciplined) processes and procedures, called *science*, for adding new knowledge to their fields of study. Consequently, the social science disciplines today represent organized bodies of knowledge in which scholars employ the processes of science to study selected aspects of the human experience.

The fields of study most pertinent to social studies are history and the social science disciplines of geography, political science, economics, anthropology, sociology, and psychology. Because some aspects of psychology are affiliated with the natural sciences, and others are closer to the social sciences, psychology—like history—can fall into a grey area. Psychology can provide a kind of bridge between the natural and social sciences, whereas history provides a bridge between the social sciences and the humanities. The point is that how curriculum developers and others classify the various disciplines that focus on the human experience can influence the topics that are included in a social studies program.

Recent research suggests that even young children are often able to study history and historical events, but they must do so in ways that accommodate their limited range of experiences. The key element in presenting historical events to young children is to make them as personalized and specific as possible. This means that sweeping statements, such as "The Reconstruction period (after the Civil War) was a difficult time for many people," will probably be meaningless to young children unless they have had prior experiences with the problems that people actually faced during that era. Historical narratives, including historical fiction in which someone does something to someone, can often provide the immediacy and involvement that young children require. Young children must be able to see how history relates to their lives, but the same principle is also appropriate for older students—even adults.

SUGGESTED ACTIVITY

1. When historians write history, they look to an event and then seek out the causes for it. In other words, the Stamp Act was not a cause of the American Revolution until the revolution actually began. Prior to the Revolution, it was simply a troublesome law that the colonists had to deal with. Consider how things would be different if history were taught in reverse chronological order, beginning with the present and moving back to the past.

SUGGESTED READINGS AND RESOURCES

Print Resources

GENERAL RESOURCES

Linda S. Levstik & Keith C. Barton. (1997). *Doing history: Investigating with children in elementary and middle schools.* Mahwah, NJ: Lawrence Erlbaum Associates. This engaging book is packed with countless examples of appropriate classroom practice on teaching history to young children. It belongs on your "must read" list.

Raymond H. Muessig (Ed). (1980). *Study and teaching of social science series.* Columbus: Charles Merrill. Each of the 100-page volumes of this aging but still useful series focuses on a social science discipline. The authors and volume titles are as follows: Henry Steele Commager & Raymond H. Muessig. *The study and teaching of history.* Jan O. M. Broek, Henry Hunker, Raymond H. Muessig, and Joseph M. Cirrincione. *The study and teaching of geography.* Pertti J. Pelto & Raymond H. Muessig. *The study and teaching of anthropology.* Roman F. Warnke, Raymond H. Muessig, & Stephen L. Miller. *The study and teaching of economics.* John A. Straayer & Raymond H. Muessig. *The study and teaching of political science.* James A. Kitchens & Raymond H. Muessig. *The study and teaching of sociology.*

Patricia L. Roberts. (1997). *Literature-based history: Activities for children, grades 1–3,* and (1996). *Literature-based history: Activities for children, grades 4–8.* Boston: Allyn & Bacon.

Both of these books offer abundant teaching ideas and activities as well as supplementary children's books that can make history come alive for young children. An excellent teaching resource.

OTHER

Kristiana Gregory. (1996). *The Winter of the Red Snow: The Revolutionary War Diary of Abigail Jane Stewart,* and (1997). *Across the Wide and Lonesome Prarie: The Oregon Trail Diary of Hattie Campbell.* New York: Scholastic. These slender volumes capture the joys and tribulations of the winter of 1777–78 at Valley Forge and the eight-month journey from Missouri to Oregon. Excellent for reading aloud. Highly recommended.

Internet Resources

Introductory Note: Internet sites related to teaching history and the social science disciplines are so extensive that to keep this section manageable we have presented only a partial listing here. The focus here are sites maintained by social studies–related professional organizations. Finally, Web sites sometimes change their Internet addresses or cease operating entirely. All the addresses supplied here were operating when this book was printed, but if any of them fails to work properly, we suggest that you enter the topic or target organization in any standard search engine.

HISTORY

National Council for History Education

http://www.history.org/nche/main.html

The organization promotes the study of history in the schools and offers links to other Web sites pertaining to teaching history.

The National Center for History in the Schools

http://www.sscnet.ucla.edu/nchs

This site is the home of the history standards.

Library of Congress—American Memory

http://rs6.loc.gov/amhome.html

This outstanding site contains a wide range of downloadable history-related resources including photographs, and audio and video materials. Highly recommended.

GEOGRAPHY

National Council on Geographic Education

http://multimedia2.freac.fsu.edu/ncge/

The National Council on Geographic Education provides excellent resources related to teaching geography.

National Standards for Geography

http://www.nationalgeographic.com/xpeditions/main.html

This site, which is maintained by the National Geographic Society, contains the eighteen national standards for geography (titled "Geography for Life") and a wealth of other teaching resources—lesson plans, maps, and so on.

GEOGRAPHY LESSON PLANS

http://www.eduplace.com/ss/autoact/ss-l.html

This site, maintained by Houghton Mifflin, offers a collection of geography lesson plans for Grades K–6.

POLITICAL SCIENCE/GOVERNMENT

Center for Civic Education

http://www.civiced.org/stds.html

This site is maintained by the Center for Civic Education and contains the complete *National Standards for Civics and Government* document. In addition to other links, this site also provides an executive summary of *Civitas: A Framework for Civic Education,* a program for improving teaching about democratic government practices (at: http://www.civiced.org/civitasexec.html).

ECONOMICS

National Council on Economic Education

http://www.nationalcouncil.org/

This site is maintained by the largest professional organization for promoting economic education in the schools and offers a variety of information and curriculum materials for K–12 economics programs.

EcEdWeb

http://ecedweb.unomaha.edu/ec-cncps.htm

This site, maintained by the economics education center at the University of Nebraska at Omaha, offers curriculum guidelines, program information, and other economic education materials of interest to elementary and middle-school teachers.

SOCIOLOGY

Teaching and Academic Resources—Sociology

http://www/asanet.org/teaching.htm

At this site the American Sociological Association provides information on sociology-related teaching approaches and curriculum. Primarily aimed at college and university faculties.

ANTHROPOLOGY

American Anthropological Association

http://www.ameranthassn.org/resinet.htm

At this site the American Anthropological Association offers a wide range of information and links to other sites related to teaching anthropology.

PSYCHOLOGY

American Psychological Association

http://www.apa.org/ and **http://www.apa.org/psychnet/**

This site, maintained by the American Psychological Associ- ation, offers wide-ranging information related to the gen- eral subject of psychology. Adding "psychnet" to the original address will take you to links to other psychology-related Web sites.

How Social Studies Programs Are Organized

Key Questions

- What topics are taught in social studies, and when?
- What are common patterns for organizing social studies programs?
- How important is sequence to a social studies program?
- How does the nature of social studies influence the creation of social studies programs?

Key Ideas

- The predominant organizational pattern for elementary social studies programs is the expanding-environments pattern.
- Developmental considerations, including how children develop concepts of time, space, and distance, influence the organization of social studies programs—or should.
- Traditional social studies programs usually examine various facets of a topic.
- Alternative social studies programs usually examine various facets of a concept or idea.
- Because social studies does not have the inherent structure of a subject like mathematics, teachers often have more flexibility in designing a social studies program than they realize.

Introduction: On Framing the Constitution

New York is one of almost twenty states, including California, Texas, and Virginia, where social studies programs are determined primarily at the state level. This sometimes means that what gets included in, or is omitted from, the state's social studies curriculum may depend on how successfully individuals or groups can lobby for their cause at the state level.

This phenomenon became apparent when the New York Board of Regents (the state board of education) was considering the adoption of a new, multicultural social studies program. As one aspect of the proposed program, students would be expected to learn that the framers of the U.S. Constitution were inspired by two factors: the European Enlightenment, and the Iroquois Confederation—the alliance of seven tribes of indigenous people from New York and nearby areas.

Most historians readily acknowledge the Enlightenment's impact on the framers of our constitution. The Enlightenment reflected the belief that common people were capable of deciding the common good. However, no social studies program we know of has included the Iroquois Confederacy as a contributing factor to the Constitution. Some people in New York apparently questioned this also and began asking, "How does anything—not just the Iroquois Confederation—get into the (state-mandated) social studies program?"

New York State experience

Jack Weatherford contends in his book *Indian Givers* (1988; see also Johansen, 1982) that the Iroquois helped the colonists resolve the dilemma of how to join the thirteen colonies into one country without each one giving up its powers. A confederacy, which is a voluntary association of separate states, does that. The United States actually operated as a confederacy under the Articles of Confederation from the Revolutionary War in 1776, and 1789, when the Constitution was ratified. However, in 1988, Congress passed a joint resolution acknowledging the historical debt that the United States owed "to the Iroquois Confederacy and other Indian nations for their demonstration of enlightened democratic principles of Government."

Whether the Iroquois Confederacy did or did not influence the framers of the Constitution was one aspect of an often heated debate in New York between supporters of the new curriculum and others who argued that history was being rewritten to serve political purposes. The controversy grew even more heated when people learned that the Iroquois's contributions to the Constitution were included in the New York social studies program after a delegation of Iroquois had visited Thomas Sobol, the state's commissioner of education (see Starna, 1990). Armed with the congressional resolution, the Iroquois apparently convinced the commissioner that New York's social studies program should be changed—a decision that would affect countless teachers and the 2.5 million school children who live in that state.

The issue here is: Is failing to include the alleged Iroquois contribution to the Constitution a glaring omission that should be changed (in New York and elsewhere), or is this an instance where certain predisposed individuals are attempting to rewrite history to make it come out the way they want it to? World history is replete with examples where dictators had their nation's histories rewritten to make them come out the way they wanted them to. We mean no disrespect to the Iroquois; the point here is that decisions about the social studies that you will be expected to teach are increasingly being made at the state level, and not in local school districts as was once the case. This incident in New York is not an exception, because similar situations (usually involving different content) have occurred elsewhere (see Cornbleth & Waugh, 1995).

Whose history?

A growing trend

This chapter examines the organization of contemporary elementary and middle-school social studies programs and factors that often influence them. Throughout the chapter, the terms *program* and *curriculum* are used interchangeably. Authorities sometimes distinguish between the two, usually using *curriculum* to indicate the broad framework within which teachers may develop their own *programs,* yet in many schools today you will hear expressions such as "our social studies program" or "our map skills program." Because *program* seems to be edging out *curriculum* in common usage, we follow that convention in this chapter.

The next section presents the predominant curriculum pattern for elementary and middle-school social studies programs. Following that is an examination of several alternative curriculum patterns and a sampling of factors that can influence how social studies programs are organized.

The Dominant Curriculum Pattern: Expanding Environments

Figure 3.1 illustrates the organizational approach to social studies that was created in the mid-1920s, became increasingly popular during the 1940s and 1950s, and continues to dominate programs throughout the country today. You may find occasional variations on the *expanding-environments* approach to social studies, some of which are described later in this chapter, but for all practical purposes it is a national curriculum (see Joyce, Little, & Wronski, 1991). This organizational pattern is also known as *expanding horizons, widening horizons,* or the *expanding communities of man.*

The organizing principle   The organizing principle for the expanding-environments approach is a mixture of physical and conceptual distance. The sequence begins with the environments (or communities) that are physically closest to the child, such as the home, school, and neighborhood. It then progresses through environments that are successively more distant: the local community, the state (or region), the nation, and finally the world. Because all of us live in these environments simultaneously, the assignment of certain environments to certain grade levels is done for instructional simplicity and convenience.

● A Composite K-8 Program

When the expanding-environments principle is translated into an actual curriculum, the result is similar to the composite program shown in Table 3.1. The table, which reflects the commonalities among four widely used textbook series, shows

FIGURE 3.1 Expanding-Environments Approach to Social Studies (K–6)

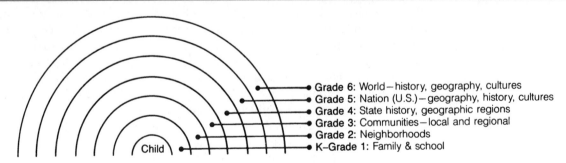

Grade 6: World—history, geography, cultures
Grade 5: Nation (U.S.)—geography, history, cultures
Grade 4: State history, geographic regions
Grade 3: Communities—local and regional
Grade 2: Neighborhoods
K–Grade 1: Family & school

Child

TABLE 3.1 Composite Social Studies Curriculum (K–8)

Grade	Focus/Title	Typical Sequence/ Unit Topics	Dominant Discipline
K	*Getting Started*	Learning About My World	The social science disciplines are integrated throughout all units.
		Families/Community Helpers	
		Transportation and Communication	
		Special Days	None
1	*Families, Homes, and Neighborhoods*	Our Earth	Geography/Map Skills
		Families Meet Their Needs: Food, Clothing, Shelter	The social science disciplines are integrated throughout all units.
		Families at Work	
		The Neighborhood	
		Holidays Around the World	
2	*Neighborhoods and Communities*	Exploring Our Earth	Geography/Map Skills
		Urban, Suburban, and Farm Communities	The social science disciplines are integrated throughout all units.
		Communities—Today and Yesterday	
		Transportation and Communication	
		Communities Celebrate Holidays	
3	*Communities and Resources, Here and There*	Map and Globe Skills	Geography/Map Skills
		Living in Different Communities	Integrated
		Governing Communities	Political Science
		How Communities Change	Integrated
		Farm and Ranch Communities	Integrated
		Communities Around the World	Geography/History
4	*Regions Near and Far*	Our Earth	Geography/Map Skills
		Regional Studies Emphasis: Units on Forest, Plains, Mountain, and Desert Regions, e.g., The Pacific Northwest, etc.	Geography
		Working Together Around the World	Economics
		State History Emphasis: Major Resources and Land Forms	Geography
		Early Settlements	History
		Governing Our State	Political Science
		Our State Today	None/Integrated

(continued)

TABLE 3.1 Composite Social Studies Curriculum (K–8) *(continued)*

Grade	Focus/Title	Typical Sequence/ Unit Topics	Dominant Discipline
5	*Our United States*	Map and Globe Skills	Geography/Map Skills
		Founding the New World	History
		Building a Nation	History
		Establishing a Government	History/Political Science
		A Divided Nation (Civil War)	History
		Our Nation Expands Westward	History
		Our Nation Today	History
		Regional Geography of the United States: Units on New England, the Mountain States, the Pacific States, etc.	Geography Geography/History
		Map, Globe, and Graph Skills	Geography
6	*Our World Today*	**World History Emphasis:** Classical Civilizations: Egypt, Greece, Rome	History
		The Industrial Revolution through the Twentieth Century	History
		Eastern Hemisphere Emphasis: Our World Today: Units on Europe, Africa and the Middle East, Asia, and Australia	Geography and history are integrated in all units.
		Western Hemisphere Emphasis: Our Neighbors to the South: Units on Mexico, South and Central American nations	History and geography are integrated in all units.
		Our Neighbors to the North: Units on the Canadian Provinces, etc.	History and geography are integrated in all units.
7	*State History, World History, or World Geography*	Early Times to the Present	History
		Selected Civilizations	History
		Regions of the World	Geography
8	*U.S. History*	See Grade 5 except for the geography	History

the common topics, the typical sequence of units, and the social studies disciplines emphasized within the units.

● Scope and Sequence Summarized

Kindergarten. Most social studies programs for kindergarten are designed to familiarize children with their developing selves and their new environment—the school. No social science discipline predominates in kindergarten programs, and the sequence of topics has no particular logic. And although the "Special Days" or holidays unit is listed last in kindergarten and in Grades 1 and 2, teachers often draw on it extensively throughout the year, in what is sometimes referred to as the "holiday curriculum."

Focus: Self and School

Grade 1. First-grade programs typically focus on the family, the school, and the neighborhood. The social science disciplines are usually integrated throughout, although consumer economics often gets more attention than the others. The emphasis on holidays also continues.

Focus: School and family

Grade 2. Second-grade programs traditionally focus on neighborhoods, but this focus is often broadened to include communities and "community helpers." This broadening has occurred, in part, because of how neighborhoods have changed. Fifty years ago, the residents of a neighborhood were often ethnically similar (Polish, Italian, Chinese, etc.), and many neighborhoods had stable populations and well-established social systems; often a person was born, got married, and eventually died in the same neighborhood. As the U.S. population has become increasingly mobile, the stability of many neighborhoods—along with the social control and cohesiveness that they once enjoyed—has largely disappeared. Thus in many areas today, neighborhoods are no longer cultural enclaves but simply places where one resides.

Focus: Neighborhoods

Second-grade programs usually deal with different types of neighborhoods and communities—rural, urban, and suburban. Identifying connections between the students' local community and communities elsewhere in the nation or world is often the focus of the last unit.

Grade 3. After an obligatory first unit on maps and globes, the emphasis in third-grade programs turns to communities in the generic sense of the term. The initial focus is usually on communities in different geographic environments, and then shifts to an emphasis on political, economic, and social aspects of community life. Selected cities, both contemporary and historic (e.g., Washington, D.C., Williamsburg, Virginia), are often presented as case studies.

Focus: Communities

Grade 4. Most fourth-grade social studies programs focus on the geographic regions of the United States, which are often compared with similar regions elsewhere in the world. Geography—physical, social, and economic geography—is the

Focus: Regions/the state

Map and globe skills are part of most social studies programs from Grade Two onward. (© *Jean-Claude Lejeune/Stock Boston*)

dominant social science discipline. However, many states, including California and Texas, have either supplemented or replaced the regional geography emphasis with a first course in state history and geography.

Grade 5. The historical emphasis of fifth-grade programs is clearly evident in Table 3.1. The emphasis on geography in Grade 5 depends in part on the program for Grade 4. In areas where state history is emphasized in Grade 4, a regional geography emphasis is usually incorporated into Grade 5. However, when regional geography is treated in Grade 4, American history is the main focus in Grade 5.

Focus: U.S. history and geography

The trend toward limiting the scope of fifth- and sixth-grade programs seems to reflect a growing acceptance of the "less is more" approach that we noted earlier. Instead of trying to teach all of American history in the fifth-grade year, schools are increasingly dividing the content into two parts. For example, in the California program (illustrated in more detail shortly), fifth-grade history ends at 1850. Recent American history is not picked up again until Grade 8.

Grade 6. The scope of many sixth-grade programs is often even broader than for fifth grade. A common pattern is to devote the first semester to a survey of world history and the second semester to a study of the geography of nations in the Eastern Hemisphere.

Focus: World history and geography

If there is one grade where there is too much content to teach effectively, this is it. It is almost impossible to do justice to world history in a typical ninety-day semester, much less the geography of nations of the Eastern Hemisphere in a second ninety-day semester. This is why some states have split the course into two or more segments. In the California program referred to earlier, the sixth-grade program is limited to ancient civilizations prior to A.D. 500.

Grade 7.   The guiding principle of the expanding-environments approach exhausts itself at Grade 6; it is strictly an elementary (K–6) program. The grade-to-grade sequence in secondary (7–12) social studies programs is topical, but there is no apparent guiding principle for organizing or sequencing courses or topics.

Focus: Varies considerably

Social studies programs for Grade 7 seem to have more variability than at any other grade level. Some seventh graders will study either world geography or world history, which are extensions of what they studied in Grade 6. Others will study state history, which is theoretically an extension of what they studied in Grade 4 but often has significant repetition. In still other areas, seventh-grade programs will combine both elements: one semester of world geography and one semester of state history.

Focus: U.S. history

Grade 8.   In Grade 8, the study of American history is almost universal, but without the emphasis on geography that occurred in Grade 5. Significant deviations occur in schools where American history is treated over a two-year period. In those cases, the eighth-grade program may focus on American history through 1850, 1860, 1877, or another convenient date, and the "second half" is treated at another grade level (usually Grade 9 or 11).

● Selected Program Features

This section presents selected features from all levels of the composite program illustrated in Table 3.1.

Scope

1. *Large increases in the scope of the program from grade to grade*—Primary-level social studies programs are sometimes faulted for dealing with a very limited range of material. At the same time, the scope of intermediate-grade (4–6) programs is often extremely broad.

Map and globe skills

2. *Separate units on map and globe skills at most grade levels*—Map and globe skills are vital components of social studies programs, but when they are presented in isolation, they are often decontextualized and seemingly without purpose. Instead of teaching map and globe skills as a separate unit, we recommend integrating these skills into lessons throughout the year in contexts where those skills provide information that your students can actually use.

A global emphasis

3. *An emphasis on developing a global view*—This emphasis is reflected by units or chapters that have an "our world" perspective in their titles. The intent is to help students understand that many problems, such as providing food and shelter and maintaining world peace, are common to people around the globe.

Holidays

4. *The continuing presence of the "holiday" curriculum*—Much of the primary (K–3) curriculum is devoted to observing and celebrating holidays and festivals throughout the year. This long-standing practice has added life and color to classrooms for many years and has been the reason for holding countless parties. We urge caution here because in some classrooms the "holiday" curriculum gets so much emphasis that it overwhelms everything else.

In a scathing review of four primary-level social studies textbook series, Larkins, Hawkins, and Gilmore (1987) argue that "adherence to the sequence of family, neighborhood, community is in part responsible for the trivialization of social studies in the first three grades" (p. 301). The authors cite many examples that support their contention, but one involving the study of birthday parties is especially illustrative:

> [The textbook publisher] is also convinced that children must be taught about birthday parties. A Chinese-American family is shown with a birthday cake. An American-Indian family is shown with a birthday cake. And a nonminority American family is shown with a birthday cake. A superficial dribble of noninformation about the differing cultural backgrounds of the three families is thrown in to help fill out the ten pages devoted to birthday parties. Danny's Chinese-American grand-

mother tells him how birthdays are celebrated in China. Unfortunately, neither she nor Danny share that information with the reader. Maria's father tells her about birthdays on the Chippewa reservation, but neglects to tell us. And Jane's mother tells her, but not us, about what it was like to grow up in West Virginia. (p. 304)

Had these texts told us how birthdays are celebrated in China, on the Chippewa reservation, or even in West Virginia, that ten-page section might have been salvaged. In the absence of such information, we find ourselves wondering (1) what it is about birthday parties that children need to learn in school, and (2) is this not the kind of knowledge children will learn without instruction? We share Larkins, Hawkins, and Gilmore's concern about the damage such treatments can do to children's, teachers', and the public's perception of the importance of social studies as a curriculum offering in the schools.

5. *Multidisciplinary social studies tends to diminish at the higher grades.* The multidisciplinary nature of primary social studies programs is clearly evident on Table 3.1. Also evident, however, is the emphasis on single disciplines that begins in Grade 4 and continues through the middle (and high) school years.

———● Expanding Environments Reconsidered

The organizing principle for the expanding-environments approach—studying nearby environments before more distant environments—seems to make eminent sense. Each environment seems to build on the previously studied environment, and in a logical sequence that's readily evident to most adults.

The expanding-environments pattern also seemingly reflects the educational principle of "beginning with the concrete and moving to the abstract." Families (Grade 1) and neighborhoods (Grade 2) are certainly more concrete and real for most children than are states (Grade 4) or the nation (Grade 5). When third graders are studying their community, they are learning about something fairly concrete, something most of them have experienced simply by having lived in a community. However, when children study "the state" in fourth grade, they move to something that is often beyond their immediate view of the world. States have physical dimensions—boundaries, a capital, and so on—of course, but the state is a phenomenon of political organization; it is lines on a map that can't be seen anywhere else.

Although states are smaller and less-distant environments than the nation (which children study in fifth grade), and although children do indeed live in a

Conceptual versus physical distance

state, these factors do not make the state any less an abstraction. Likewise, fifth-grade children cannot "see" the United States, except by looking at a map that is itself an abstract representation of the country. Eventually most children gain the experience that enables them to deal with the different worlds in which they live. Our point here is that abstraction is determined by conceptual distance—the extent to which a phenomenon is within or beyond a child's realm of experience—*not by physical distance.* From this perspective, the expanding-environments approach is not so much a logical progression from concrete to abstract as a quantum leap that occurs after third grade.

Role of sequence

The sequence in which children study different environments is neither as rigid nor as important as it might seem. In more practical terms, this means that it is not necessary for primary-level children to study their families (or *the* family) before they study the (their) neighborhood, for example. Neither is it necessary for children to study the American family prior to studying Russian families or any other family around the globe. Rather, if the family is the focus of study, we think an appropriate way to study it is by examining various families in the neighborhood and in other nations.

Despite its continuing popularity, the expanding-environments approach is not without some other problems. For example, most kindergarten and first-grade children are not aware of, nor do they necessarily understand or care about, the sequence of environments they will study over the next six years. They almost never concern themselves with the "whole," with how one topic relates to other topics they will study; rather, their concern is with what they are studying today. For most young children, the future—next week perhaps—is so distant that they hardly even think about it. At the other end of the program, it is not clear whether sixth, seventh, or eighth graders necessarily understand the organizational pattern of social studies that they've been exposed to. But then, perhaps children don't need to understand the overall pattern of what they study; that's a question researchers have yet to investigate.

Do children see a forest or just the trees?

An important consideration in organizing any instructional program rests on the nature of the underlying subject areas. Although the expanding-environments pattern makes it seem otherwise, social studies does not have the same kind of inherent structure or prerequisites as does a discipline like mathematics. In teaching arithmetic, for example, you must begin with counting, addition, and subtraction, for these are legitimate prerequisites for other arithmetic processes. In social studies, on the other hand, it is not necessary for children to know anything about families in order to study communities, nor is it necessary for them to have studied American history before they study the history of ancient civilizations. The point is that the mathlike sequence of the expanding-environments pattern makes social studies appear to be an inherently structured subject based on prerequisite learnings when, in fact, a social studies program can be assembled in many different ways.

Variations on the source of "structure"?

You could, for example, teach first graders a unit on the Stone Age, instead of waiting until Grade 6 as called for by the expanding-environments approach. You would need to make adjustments for the children's limited reading ability, but there is nothing so inherently complex about the Stone Age as to be beyond a first grader's comprehension. Or you could use chronology as your organizer and begin teaching

It may seem to be common sense to begin studying nearby environments—like the family, home, and school—before tackling more distant environments. This is also one of the basic premises of the traditional expanding-environments approach to social studies. But this is one time when common sense may fail us. Studying things that we are extremely familiar with and close to, such as our families, our language, and ourselves, is often very difficult, simply because we are too familiar with them. Our families, for example, are so much a part of our everyday lives that we often take them for granted. Likewise, each of us has a vast body of feelings and information about families in general and about our own family in particular, but because of our upbringing and prior cultural experiences, most of us (including children) have developed perceptual blinders that

keep us from thinking about families objectively. Common sense notwithstanding, things that are more physically distant from us are often easier to study objectively.

When first graders study "the family," you sometimes find them studying Japanese families. They are not doing this because there are things about Japanese families that everyone should know, but because information about (or from) other cultures can provide a basis for *contrast,* that is, a way to relate the unfamiliar with phenomena that we know well. In other words, first graders can study Japanese families as a vehicle for studying American families, for learning how they are alike and how they are different. When first graders discover that Japanese children do not celebrate their birthdays every year, they simultaneously discover something about themselves and about their own culture.

first graders about ancient civilizations (Egypt, Greece, etc.) as many European nations do. The single exception to everything said here is the area of map skills. This is because most map skills, especially latitude and longitude, are based in mathematics, as illustrated in Chapter 13. We examine some alternatives to the expanding-environments pattern later in this chapter.

Alternative Organizational Patterns

From time to time, various groups and individuals have proposed alternative elementary programs. Most of them are variations on the expanding-environments approach, but in other instances, they ignore the expanding-environments pattern entirely. This difference is the basis for this section's organization.

──● Variations on the Expanding-Environments Pattern

NCSS alternatives

The National Council for the Social Studies (NCSS) (1989) has endorsed three alternative curriculum models for social studies, one of which is shown in Table 3.2. Although this proposal is not a radical departure from the expanding-environments approach, it claims different motives. Those motives, along with the other two recommended models, are included in the Resource Handbook.

Most state social studies programs are similar to the composite program presented earlier (see Table 3.1). However, the California History–Social Science Framework represents an exception to the rule. It attempts to (1) incorporate appropriate children's literature at each grade, (2) incorporate more multicultural

TABLE 3.2 NCSS Proposed Social Studies Program

Grade Level	Content
Kindergarten	Awareness of Self in a Social Setting Socialization experiences to bridge home life with life in schools
Grade 1	The Individual in Primary Social Groups: Understanding School and Family Life Specialized roles, family structure, interdependence, the need for rules and laws
Grade 2	Meeting Basic Needs in Nearby Social Groups: The Neighborhood Social functions including education, production, consumption, communication, and transportation within a neighborhood context
Grade 3	Sharing Earth Space with Others: The Community Same social functions of Grade 2 except in the context of the community in a global setting
Grade 4	Human Life in Varied Environments: The Region Geographic and cultural regions; the state as a political region, as may be required
Grade 5	People of the Americas: The United States and Its Close Neighbors Emphasis on the development of the United States, core values, significant individuals, history and geography of Canada and Mexico
Grade 6	People and Cultures: The Eastern Hemisphere Major geographical regions, historic and economic development, political and value systems

Source: NCSS Task Force on Scope and Sequence, "In Search of Scope and Sequence for Social Studies." Reprinted by permission from National Council for the Social Studies *Social Education.*

● ——— **COMMENTARY How States Affect Textbooks, and Vice Versa**

Whenever states opt to change their social studies programs, they could create something that doesn't "fit" any of the current textbook series. This was potentially the case when California decided to limit its sixth-grade program to ancient civilizations prior to A.D. 500. This was not a problem in a state as large as California—which has 11 percent of the nation's schoolchildren—nor would it have been a concern in other large states like New York and Texas. In large states, the textbook market is so huge that most publishers will design materials to fit the state's program. For years, most publishers have offered specialized state history books (at Grade 4) for larger states. However, in smaller states, publishers typically offer a regional geography book that they also market nationwide. Thus if you live in states such as North Dakota or New Hampshire, and if one of the smaller publishers has not produced a book to meet your needs, you may need to settle for a generic textbook that is marketed nationwide. It is a matter of economics. Should you encounter a new, fifth-grade text that goes only to 1850, it is fairly safe to assume the book was designed for another state's program, in this case, California.

TABLE 3.3 Selected Children's Literature Used in the California Social Studies Program (Abridged)

Grade	Topic	Children's Literature
K	Learning and Working, Now and Long Ago	*Jack and the Beanstalk, Goldilocks, Aesop's Fables*
1	A Child's Place in Time and Space	*Little Toot, Little Red Lighthouse, Mike Mulligan and His Steam Shovel*
2	People Who Make a Difference	*Johnny Appleseed* Other myths, folktales, and legends
3	Understanding Continuity and Change	*White Stallion, Wagon Wheels, The Drinking Gourd*
4	California: A Changing State	
5	The Making of a New Nation, to 1850	*Immigrant Kids* *Waiting for Mama*
6	Ancient Civilizations, to A.D. 500	Selections from Greek and Roman literature and the Bible
7	The Medieval World, A.D. 500 to 1789	*Pillow Book, Song of Roland* *Tale of Genji*
8	U. S. History, 1783–1914	*Huckleberry Finn, My Ántonia*

and historical content than do most traditional programs, at the primary grades especially, and (3) at the same time reduce the scope of the history covered at the intermediate level. Table 3.3 shows the major topics and selected children's literature for each grade in the California program.

● A Distinctive Variation: The CORE Curriculum

The CORE Knowledge Program

Until the early 1990s, most variations to the traditional expanding-environments approach to social studies were produced by states, like the California program just considered. However, in 1991, a group of educators were inspired by E. D. Hirsch's book *Cultural Literacy* (1988) and decided to use it as the basis for an elementary curriculum that would have national circulation. The last section of *Cultural Literacy* contained an alphabetical listing of five thousand names, dates, phrases, and concepts ranging from names such as Aaron (Hank), through colloquial sayings such as "A stitch in time saves nine" to places around the globe, such as Zurich (Switzerland), that Hirsch believed reflected the "core" knowledge that everyone should know to be considered "culturally literate." However, Hirsch did not identify his criteria for selecting the five thousand items, and this reluctance has remained a bone of contention among his critics. Nevertheless, the educators organized those random elements into an instructional program.

The product of the group's effort is called the CORE Curriculum. In this instance, CORE is not an acronym; rather, it refers to the "core" of fundamental knowledge that was referred to above. The CORE Curriculum is a comprehensive program that is designed to comprise 50 to 60 percent of an elementary curriculum. It also covers all subject areas except reading. A second distinguishing feature of the CORE Curriculum is its content specificity; it lays out exactly what teachers are expected to teach in each subject and at each grade level. The Core Knowledge Foundation makes teacher-developed sample units available at its Web site (**http://www.coreknowledge.org**), but it does not otherwise specify how teachers should teach the material.

CORE is not an acronym

E. D. Hirsch, Jr., is among the individuals we identified in Chapter 1 as critics of multidisciplinary social studies. He argues that multidisciplinary social studies does not allow children to study history and geography in enough depth to enable them to become historically and geographically literate. Because of Hirsch's position, it should be no surprise that the words *social studies* do not appear in the CORE materials. Instead, the CORE Curriculum's "social studies" component is organized around three strands: World Civilizations, which focuses primarily on world history; American Civilizations, which includes American history and studies of other Western cultures—the Incas, Aztecs, and so on; and Geography. Table 3.4 shows how the "social studies" component of the CORE Curriculum differs from a traditional social studies program.

History and geography are treated separately

In place of the expanding-environments pattern, the CORE program reflects an organizing principle that has been used for many years throughout much of Europe: historical chronology. In practice, this means that students study older civilizations before they study modern civilizations. This seemingly modest change has some far-reaching consequences because it means, for example, that first graders will study ancient Egypt, and second graders will study ancient Rome, both topics that are far removed from the family, school, and neighborhood focus of traditional social studies programs at those grade levels. At the same time, spreading the study of world and American civilizations across the grades (from K through 6) means that instead of having to consider almost all of American history at Grade 5 and almost all of world history at Grade 6, as is the case in traditional social studies programs, both teachers and children have opportunities to examine these areas in greater depth than would otherwise be the case.

The organizing principle: chronology

Since the CORE Curriculum was created in 1991 it has been adopted by more than a thousand schools across the country (Whitmire, 2000). This acceptance has been fairly rapid, especially considering that none of the currently available textbook series are geared to it. Teachers sometimes use one of seven books that accompany the program, variously titled *What Your Kindergartner* (First Grader, Second Grader, etc.) *Needs to Know* (Hirsch, 1991–1993), which highlight the topics taught at each grade level. In place of regular textbooks, CORE teachers usually make extensive use of informational books and whatever other resources they can lay their hands on. It almost goes without saying that the CORE Curriculum places a heavy burden on teachers, especially during their first year using the program.

No textbook, per se

Does the CORE Knowledge Program work? It seems to, but until recently, the data on student performance has been limited. Information provided by the Core Knowledge Foundation (Marshall, 1996) indicated that administrators in CORE

TABLE 3.4 Comparison of Traditional Social Studies and CORE Curriculum

Grade	Traditional Programs	CORE Curriculum Strands		
		World Civilization	American Civilization	Geography
K	Family and School	Seven Continents	American Geography Native Americans Columbus/Mayflower	Maps and globes
1	Family and Community	Early Civilizations: Egypt, etc. World Religions Mexico	Early Civilizations: Mayas, Incas, Aztecs Early Colonies to Independence	Place location for topics at left
2	Neighborhood	Ancient Civilizations: India, China, Greece Modern Civilizations: Japan	The Constitution Westward Expansion Civil War	Geography of the Americas and World Civilizations
3	Community	Ancient Rome Byzantine Civilizations	Earliest Americans The 13 Colonies	Geography of the Mediterranean
4	The State	The Middle Ages Islam and Holy Wars Medieval Africa and China	American Revolution The Constitution Presidents and Heroes	Mountains Geography of Africa
5	The Nation (U.S. History)	Meso-Americans: Mayas, Aztecs European Exploration Renaissance English Revolution Russia	Westward Expansion The Civil War Reconstruction	The Political Geography of Europe Geography of topics at left
6	The World (World History)	Lasting Ideas from Ancient Civilizations: Judaism and Christianity, Greece and Rome, Capitalism and Socialism Latin America	Immigration, Industrialization, Urbanization America as a World Power	Geography of topics at left

schools credit the program with improving students' performance on standardized tests. More recently, in a rigorous study conducted in Oklahoma City (Whitmire, 2000), three hundred students from CORE Knowledge schools were matched on five criteria with a comparison group of three hundred students from traditional (non-CORE Knowledge) schools. The matching criteria included: age, grade level, race, sex, income level, and students' scores on the (standardized) Iowa Test of Basic Skills. To be included in the study, each student had to match on all five criteria. The results? After one year, almost all the CORE Knowledge students scored higher than the non-CORE Knowledge students—not on average, but individually! Researchers are currently following up on this study to determine whether other factors may have played a role, such as more motivated teachers among the CORE Knowledge group.

What the Critics Say About CORE Knowledge. Criticisms of the CORE Knowledge Program typically focus on three elements: (1) concerns that the program is developmentally inappropriate, (2) concerns that the program is essentially a nineteenth-century course of study repackaged for the twenty-first century, and (3) concerns about how its elements were identified for inclusion. It is oversimplified but essentially correct to say that concerns about the developmental appropriateness (or inappropriateness) of the CORE stem from individuals' beliefs about what kinds of experiences are within (or beyond) a child's realm of experiences, and thus, what he or she is "ready for." Some critics cite the expectation that first graders will study ancient Egypt as an example of developmentally inappropriate subject matter. And when you think about it, few things might seem further removed from a seven-year-old's life than ancient Egypt. On the other hand, if you talk to first-grade CORE Knowledge teachers, they are likely to tell you that although they initially had concerns about the developmental appropriateness of topics like ancient Egypt, those concerns vanished when they saw how enthusiastically their students responded.

A second and perhaps more fundamental criticism involves the question of whether traditional knowledge—what some critics refer to as nineteenth-century knowledge—is what students need to live in the twenty-first century. One of our colleagues, for example, refers to CORE Knowledge as "the curriculum based on dead white males." CORE supporters usually respond that most of the core of common knowledge on which cultural literacy is based is indeed rooted in the past. A related criticism has focused on the strong Euro-American bias in the literary selections. For example, Peterson (1995) noted that over 80 percent of the poetry and literature selections are Euro-American, and over one-third of the non-European selections have animals as the main characters. This, Peterson argues, sends a not-so-subtle message that stories about non-European cultures are not as serious. Then, too, the inclusion of classic tales, such as Snow White and Cinderella, where passive females are rescued by handsome princes, have raised questions about gender equity. Still other critics have chastized E. D. Hirsch for his reluctance to identify the criteria he used for selecting the five thousand elements of "cultural literacy" (see Apple, 1993).

The Core Knowledge Program is a distinctive variation from traditional social studies programs that requires much more teacher planning than do most traditional programs. Other approaches that teachers can take to create distinctive variations include using a thematic-unit approach or attempting to build a spiral curriculum or a concept-based social studies program. We consider these variations in the next section.

Developing Social Studies Programs

You probably don't plan to design an entire social studies program in the next week or so, but this section provides an overview of program development elements that every teacher and program developer must consider.

● Basic Program Design Elements

The essential aspects of creating any instructional program are captured in four little words: *what, why, when,* and *how. What* am I expected to teach? *Why* am I expected to teach "this" instead of "that"? *When* in the year am I expected to teach something? And *how* am I supposed to do that? These are the basic questions of curriculum planning that teachers usually refer to as their "scope and sequence."

What to study

Scope.   The first decision in determining a social studies program involves scope. In other words, what segments of the universe of social studies knowledge will be taught? In more practical terms, the question is one of whether a unit on "the farm" or "desert communities," for example, will or will not be included in a social studies program.

Concerns related to scope, or the *what* you plan to teach, must always be considered in relation to the question of *why* (or *why not*). Answering a question like Why should we include a unit on the farm?, for example, gets into matters of the program's rationale.

Why study it?

Rationale.   The question *why* ("this" topic instead of "that" topic) is a request for a rationale—a reasoned statement of justification about why children should be taught and expected to learn certain subject matter.

The curriculum guides that most new teachers receive seldom provide a justification for why the selected topics are worth being studied. Somewhere along the line, whoever created the program had to address that question, but the reasons why certain content was selected and other content ignored are seldom conveyed to teachers. As a result, you may find yourself wondering why you are expected to be teaching something. And if you aren't sure why you are supposed to be teaching something, it probably won't be long before your students are asking the same question.

In what order and at what grade?

Sequence.   After determining what topics should be taught, and why, it then becomes necessary to decide *when*—at what time and in what order, or sequence—to teach them.

Sequencing subject matter has two dimensions: a "between-grades" dimension and a "within-grade" dimension. First, it's necessary to determine at which grade level something will be taught. For example, having decided that a unit on "the farm" should be included in a program, the between-grade question is, At which grade level should "the farm" be taught? Once that question has been answered, the second element involves determining when (at what time during the year) it should be taught within that grade level.

The within-grade-level question concerns the sequencing of units within a grade level. For example, having determined that Greece, Rome, and ancient Egypt should be taught at a certain grade level (probably Grade 6), the next decision is to determine the order in which those topics will be taught. Sometimes that sequence may be based on a logical progression, such as from simple to complex; in other cases it may be arbitrary. When history is involved, as in this example, the sequence is invariably based on chronology. On that basis, you will teach ancient Egypt first. But which will come next—Greece or Rome?

Making it meaningful **Synthesis.** How will everything be pulled together into a whole that is meaningful to students? There probably isn't any one best basis for sequencing a social studies program, but the program needs to be organized around something. To illustrate the importance of the synthesis, consider a third-grade social studies program that asks you to teach the following sequence of topics:

1. explorers
2. the geography of Australia
3. community helpers
4. transportation
5. the Civil War

If there is something—a theme, an approach, anything—that can pull these topics together so that they make sense, it isn't apparent. However, young children may not care about the sequence of topics they study as long as they are interesting. In some respects, sequencing may be more of a problem for adults than for children.

● Subject-Matter Considerations

Social studies seldom imposes the kind of prerequisite prior learnings that you might associate with a subject such as mathematics. Children's vocabulary and reading ability may limit what you can teach, but this holds true for almost every subject area. The absence of a hierarchy or predetermined sequence in which history or social studies must be taught means that teachers have more latitude to use other factors, such as students' interests and abilities, as a basis for selecting content.

No hierarchy = more flexibility

There are many possible entry points to studying about the human experience, and some of these possibilities are illustrated in Table 3.5. By mixing and matching items from the various columns of Table 3.5, it is possible to create hundreds of alternative configurations for social studies. Each of these will reflect a different orientation and a different blending of content and instructional purpose.

Alternative entry points

TABLE 3.5 **Alternative Ways of Looking at Social Studies**

Objects of Study	Disciplines	Major Findings and Ways of Knowing	Instructional Purposes
The community	Anthropology	Value statements	Miniature scholars
Native Americans	Economics	Descriptions	Cognitive skill development
Area studies	Geography	Nonempirically based feelings	Accumulation of knowledge
The United States	History	Principles (analytic or empirical)	Concept development and testing
Non-Western civilization	Philosophy		Creative use of individual and collective experience
The environment	Political science	Generalizations based on observations and probability	
Change processes	Psychology		Indoctrination
Minorities	Sociology		Social control
Local, state, and national government			
Citizenship			
Consumer economics			

When we suggested that social studies could be approached in many different ways, we doubt that you anticipated quite this many possibilities!

● Developmental Considerations

Creating a viable social studies program must also consider young children's abilities to deal with elements like time, space, and distance.

Children's concepts of time

Time.   It isn't entirely clear how children develop a sense of time, especially historical time. Apparently children's conceptions of time—including personal time, social time, and historical time—develop at different rates and so gradually that children are unaware of what is taking place.

When young children enter elementary school, they have a fairly secure conception of "yesterday." But events that happened to them prior to yesterday—two weeks, two months, or two years ago—are usually thought of as happening "a long time ago," somewhere in a vast and undifferentiated past. However, because young children sometimes have difficulty differentiating the time span of past events does *not* mean that they have forgotten what happened. Children can often describe past events—vacations, birthday parties, or other experiences—in excruciating detail. They can tell *what* happened, but they may be unable to provide an accurate time frame for *when* the events took place.

So All Can See

Asking your class to crowd around one 14-inch computer screen is probably inviting problems. Someone is almost sure to step on someone else's foot, whether intentionally or not. How then do you use computer-based technology so that everyone can see, but without having to crowd around a single monitor?

There are at least four possible solutions to this problem. One is to use a liquid crystal display (LCD) device that fits on an overhead projector and that projects the computer-driven image on a screen. The image is not always as bright as you might hope for, and special overhead projectors that don't produce too much heat are required.

A second option is to get a device that projects the computer-driven image on a screen. Computer projectors are becoming less expensive than they once were ($250 and up), and they permit large groups to view the image simultaneously. A third option is to get one of the "black boxes" that will project computer images through a TV set. This is a less costly option ($100 or so) than the others because most schools already have the TVs available. A fourth option is to download the files onto a disk and then allow children to view them when it is their turn to use the computer. The disk option is the least costly, but it does not permit the entire class to view the images simultaneously. Nevertheless, it is a plausible alternative as schools acquire the resources to use computer-based technology effectively.

At about age ten or eleven, children's conceptions of time apparently permit them to feel an awareness (but not a complete understanding) of the historical past. All of this does *not* mean that history is out of the question for younger children, however. Even very young children can often relate vicariously to the individuals and events of history, particularly if those events are presented in narrative (story) form.

Space and Distance.   Children's conceptions of space—how they fit into their environment—and distance (physical remoteness) seem to develop in ways similar to their conception of time. Initially, distance is measured by the number of *fars* they attach to *away*. As any young child can tell you, "far, far away" is much farther than "far away."

Children's views of space and distance

Eventually everyone develops conceptions of time and space. It's something all of us do, simply through the process of living. Thus we question whether trying to speed up processes that will occur normally is a good investment of your time. Instead of trying to accelerate the way your students perceive time, space, or distance, you can teach educationally valuable things that do not require them to alter the way they view their world.

──● Organizational Considerations

This section presents three distinctive ways to organize subject matter for a social studies program. These include: (1) thematic units, which integrate elements from several subject areas, (2) spiral curricula, where early learnings provide the basis for later learning, and (3) a concept-based approach, which provides a way for children to organize what might otherwise be isolated facts.

Thematic and Topical Units.   The whole-language approach to reading and language arts has come under fire in some parts of the country. Nevertheless, the underlying belief that the components of language—reading, writing, spelling, handwriting, and so on—are best learned and taught in contextualized settings instead of as separate subjects makes intuitive sense. Teachers in whole-language classrooms often provide those settings by organizing units around a theme or topic, such as "desert environments," "time," or even "bears" or "dinosaurs."

Fusion

More and more teachers are recognizing that it is possible to integrate elements from several subject areas into what are sometimes called *transdisciplinary units*. It is needlessly redundant, for example, to study a unit on desert environments in science at one point in the year, and then study a unit on desert communities in social studies later in the year. By carefully selecting themes and topics, and by identifying learning experiences that seem to cluster together, it is possible and often desirable to integrate across subject areas.

Is it a worthwhile topic?

The potential themes for integrated units are almost endless, and we provide a detailed example of a technique for identifying potential activities for thematic units in Chapter 8. However, a word of caution is in order here: Be certain that the theme you select is worth studying. Children might very well enjoy a three-week unit on bears, for example, but you need to ask yourself just how much about bears children need to know. Does a unit on "bears" have enough substance and learning potential to warrant spending three weeks on it?

Figure 3.2 shows an abridgement of a web for a thematic approach to time that was developed by Pappas, Kiefer, and Levstik (1995). The original of this figure fills two 8½-by-11-inch printed pages.

Figure 3.2 shows that the overall theme of time was divided into several subthemes, including "Changes over Time," "Personal Time," and "Measuring Time." Instructional activities and relevant works of children's literature were then identified for each subtheme. Titles of the children's books for each subtheme are shown in italics, and complete citations are provided in the references for this chapter.

Spiral Curricula.   The basic premise that underlies a spiral curriculum is that once students learn an idea, teachers can help them build on what they know by extending those ideas to new situations. It is the scaffolding process that was referred to earlier.

Scaffolding

Helping students apply ideas to new situations may seem like common sense. Yet too often ideas that students are expected to learn are treated in isolation, and students have nothing to connect them to. In a spiral approach to content, concepts and generalizations are introduced in the primary grades and then expanded upon as the children progress from grade to grade. The key in the expansion process is not simply to present new applications of the idea, lest the students treat them as totally new ideas. It's often necessary to help students understand how a new application of an idea is connected to an earlier application.

FIGURE 3.2 Partial Web for Thematic Unit: Time

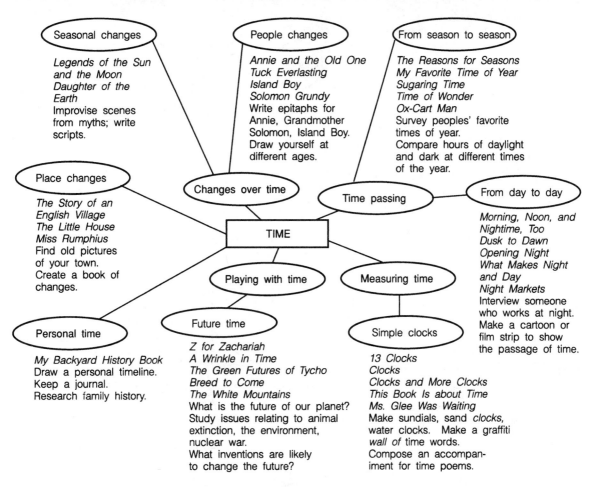

Seasonal changes

*Legends of the Sun and the Moon
Daughter of the Earth*
Improvise scenes from myths; write scripts.

People changes

*Annie and the Old One
Tuck Everlasting
Island Boy
Solomon Grundy*
Write epitaphs for Annie, Grandmother Solomon, Island Boy.
Draw yourself at different ages.

From season to season

*The Reasons for Seasons
My Favorite Time of Year
Sugaring Time
Time of Wonder
Ox-Cart Man*
Survey peoples' favorite times of year.
Compare hours of daylight and dark at different times of the year.

Place changes

*The Story of an English Village
The Little House
Miss Rumphius*
Find old pictures of your town.
Create a book of changes.

Changes over time

Time passing

From day to day

*Morning, Noon, and Nightime, Too
Dusk to Dawn
Opening Night
What Makes Night and Day
Night Markets*
Interview someone who works at night.
Make a cartoon or film strip to show the passage of time.

TIME

Personal time

My Backyard History Book
Draw a personal timeline.
Keep a journal.
Research family history.

Playing with time

Measuring time

Future time

*Z for Zachariah
A Wrinkle in Time
The Green Futures of Tycho
Breed to Come
The White Mountains*
What is the future of our planet?
Study issues relating to animal extinction, the environment, nuclear war.
What inventions are likely to change the future?

Simple clocks

*13 Clocks
Clocks
Clocks and More Clocks
This Book Is about Time
Ms. Glee Was Waiting*
Make sundials, sand *clocks,* water clocks. Make a graffiti *wall of* time words.
Compose an accompaniment for time poems.

Source: From *An Integrated Language Perspective in the Elementary School: Theory into Action* by Christine C. Pappas, Barbara Z. Kiefer, and Linda S. Levstik. Copyright © 1995, 1990 by Longman Publishing Group. Reprinted with permission.

● ●

Expanding on an idea

Figure 3.3 shows an example of the spiral development of a generalization as described by Hilda Taba (1967). This spiral focuses on the development of generalizations (as opposed to a sequence of expanding environments). For example, the notion that geography and natural resources influence how people live is first introduced in the primary grades and then expanded upon in different contexts at higher grade levels.

Concept-Based Approaches. In most traditional social studies programs, the emphasis is on learning the information associated with whatever topic is the focus.

FIGURE 3.3   The Spiral Development of a Generalization

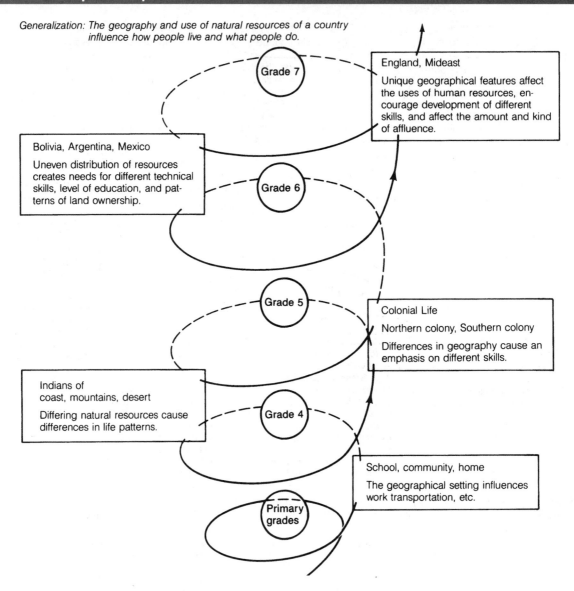

Generalization: The geography and use of natural resources of a country influence how people live and what people do.

Grade 7

England, Mideast

Unique geographical features affect the uses of human resources, encourage development of different skills, and affect the amount and kind of affluence.

Bolivia, Argentina, Mexico

Uneven distribution of resources creates needs for different technical skills, level of education, and patterns of land ownership.

Grade 6

Grade 5

Colonial Life

Northern colony, Southern colony

Differences in geography cause an emphasis on different skills.

Indians of coast, mountains, desert

Differing natural resources cause differences in life patterns.

Grade 4

School, community, home

The geographical setting influences work transportation, etc.

Primary grades

Source: *Teacher's Handbook for Elementary Social Studies* by Hilda Taba, Mary C. Durkin, Anthony H. McNaughton, and Jack R. Fraenkel. © 1967 by Addison-Wesley Publishing Company. Used by permission of Pearson Education, Inc.

If the topic was Holland, for example, you probably learned about tulips, and chocolate, and cheese. If the topic was China, you probably studied things associated with the geography and climate of China, China's government, China's resources, and other aspects of life in that nation. If the next unit was Japan, you went

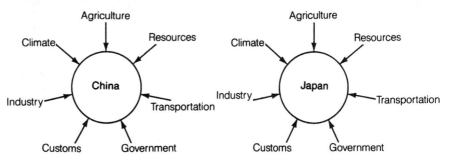

FIGURE 3.4   A Traditional Topic-to-Topic Approach

Source: *Teacher's Handbook for Elementary Social Studies* by Hilda Taba, Mary C. Durkin, Anthony H. McNaughton, and Jack R. Fraenkel. © 1967 by Addison-Wesley Publishing Company. Used by permission of Pearson Education, Inc.

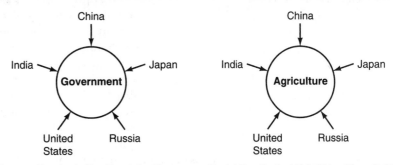

FIGURE 3.5   A Concept-Based (Selected-Dimensions) Approach

Source: *Teacher's Handbook for Elementary Social Studies* by Hilda Taba, Mary C. Durkin, Anthony H. McNaughton, and Jack R. Fraenkel. © 1967 by Addison-Wesley Publishing Company. Used by permission of Pearson Education, Inc.

through the same process again, this time studying Japanese agriculture, the climate of Japan, and so forth. This topic-by-topic approach is illustrated in Figure 3.4.

Topical vs. concept-based approaches

A quite different approach is based on following a single concept or idea through several different applications. In other words, the concept-based approach is based on the idea that it is not necessary to study every country in the world to be able to say something about how nations organize their governments, practice agriculture, or use their resources, and so on. By studying only selected nations (instead of the entire universe of nations) it is possible to identify patterns among nations. Figure 3.5 illustrates that it is possible to identify *patterns* in agricultural practices by studying agriculture in China, India, Japan, Russia, and the United States.

In traditional programs, students often become so concerned with the "parts"—the climate, the government, the customs, and so on—that they may not see the "whole." By focusing on agricultural practices in Thailand, in Laos, in

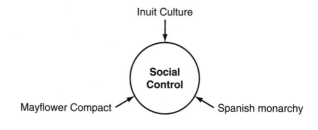

FIGURE 3.6   An Approach to the Concept *Social Control*

Inuit Culture

Social Control

Mayflower Compact   Spanish monarchy

● ●

China, and in Japan, children tend to treat each nation separately, and in that process may miss the point of agricultural practices that are common to heavily populated areas in the Pacific Rim or elsewhere.

An emphasis on the whole In a concept-based approach, the focus shifts from the parts to the "whole." This parts/whole emphasis is illustrated by the questions associated with each approach. In a topic-by-topic approach, at least seven questions are generated, all of which follow this general form: "What is Chinese (agriculture, transportation, etc.) like?" The same questions are then asked about Japan. The result may be fourteen or so pieces of discrete data. In a concept-based approach, however, such an examination has fewer questions, and each is studied in greater depth.

When to use which approach A concept-based approach can help students become aware of patterns that exist among cultures, but it is not appropriate for some elements, especially truly unique elements such as a culture's customs and rituals. For example, if your interest is in Japanese customs, it will be necessary to study Japan. On the other hand, if you are interested in determining whether some customs are common to nations in the Far East, you would need to study several Far Eastern nations to decide.

Perhaps one reason that concept-based instruction has not been more widely accepted is that most teachers lack familiarity with it. Not having experienced concept-based instruction as students, they will tend to use the topic-to-topic approach with which they are more familiar. In a concept-based program, for example, the children might study the sixteenth- and seventeenth-century Spanish monarchs, the Mayflower Compact, and the Inuit (Eskimos). From a traditional perspective, these would be seen as three separate and unrelated topics, but as Figure 3.6 illustrates, the focus for all three is the concept "social control."

A concept-based approach to social control You may recall that the Mayflower Compact was produced by the travelers on the good ship *Mayflower*, who agreed in writing to govern (control) themselves for the common good. The Inuit on the other hand govern themselves by elaborate but unwritten laws and traditions. The Spanish monarchy serves as an exemplar of absolute control based on the divine right of kings. The differences among these forms of social control provide the basis for contrast.

Concept-based programs may sometimes seem a little piecemeal, especially to individuals who are familiar with traditional topic-based approaches. As a result, some teachers occasionally provide in-depth case studies of a single culture, subculture, or nation. However, a concept-based approach to social studies allows children to learn about human behavior in general, as opposed to learning unrelated ideas about many different subjects.

SUMMARY

Traditional K-6 social studies programs are based on the expanding-environments (or expanding-horizons) approach, where children progress from environments they are close to—such as the home, family, school, and neighborhood—in the primary grades, to more distant environments—the state, the nation, and the world—at the intermediate grades. The organizing principle for expanding environments exhausts itself at the end of Grade 6 (what do you study after you have examined the world?), so middle-school programs at Grades 7 and 8 typically repeat elements that students studied at the elementary grades. Grade 7 programs often focus on state history, or world geography, while Grade 8 programs usually deal with American history, but without the geography elements common in most elementary programs.

The CORE Knowledge Program is a recent and distinctive variation to traditional K-8 programs, especially in the area of social studies. Because of E. D. Hirsch's philosophical belief that multidisciplinary social studies does not permit students to study subjects in depth, the CORE Knowledge Program focuses on three strands that students study at each grade level: World Civilizations (world history and geography), American civilizations (history and geography), and geography. The organizing principle for the "social studies" portion of the CORE Knowledge Program is historical chronology. This means that children in the early grades study ancient civilizations, such as Egypt, Greece, and Rome, instead of waiting until Grade 6, as is more common in traditional programs.

Other variations to traditional social studies programs include: (1) the thematic unit approach, in which content from several subject areas is integrated around a topic such as "the desert," or "time"; (2) a spiral approach to curriculum, in which new ideas and applications build on the ideas that students have learned previously, and (3) a concept-based approach, in which children examine patterns among cultures, such as how they organize their governments, practice agriculture, or exercise control over their citizens.

SUGGESTED ACTIVITIES

1. Do you think it is important for children to understand the logic (the *why*) of what they are studying? In math? In social studies? In anything?

2. Determine how the old saying "familiarity breeds contempt" might apply to the expanding-environments approach to social studies.

3. Go to your curriculum library or resource center and get three or four texts, each for the same grade level but from different textbook series. Do a content analysis, comparing the topics they cover, the approach they take, and the things they do and do not emphasize. If you work in a small group of six to eight members and each member takes a different grade level to study, you will have a composite of the similarities and variations among textbook series, any one of which you might find yourself teaching from.

4. Review the assumptions on which the expanding-environments approach to social studies is based—for example, that children should be exposed to the world by Grade 6. Then, in small groups, outline the characteristics of a K–8 social studies program that follows alternative assumptions of your choosing.

SUGGESTED READINGS AND RESOURCES

Print Resources

E. D. Hirsh, Jr. (Ed). (1992). *What your third grader needs to know.* New York: Doubleday. This is one book from the Core Knowledge series edited by the author of *Cultural Literacy;* other books have similar titles for different grade levels, for example, *What your first grader needs to know.* Various sections cover language arts, American and world civilization, fine arts, mathematics, and the natural sciences.

Catherine Cornbleth & Dexter Waugh. (1995). *The great speckled bird: Multicultural politics and educational policy-making.* New York: St. Martin's Press. If you are interested in exploring how political pressures can influence the curriculum, this book is where you should begin.

Stephanie Steffy & Wendy J. Hood (Eds.). (1994). *If this is social studies, why isn't it boring?* York, ME: Stenhouse. This book is just as delightful as its title. It contains fifteen first-person essays by teachers and others describing how they brought new life to social studies classes by integrating different kinds of literature.

William W. Joyce, Timothy H. Little, & Stan P. Wronski. (1991). "Scope and sequence, goals, and objectives: Effects on social studies." In J. P. Shaver (Ed.), *Handbook of social studies teaching and learning* (pp. 321–331). New York: Macmillan. This section of the *Handbook* provides a good summary of recent research on social studies curriculum patterns.

Internet Resources

Introductory Note: Web sites sometimes change their Internet addresses or cease operating entirely. All the addresses supplied here were operating when this book was printed, but if any of them fails to work properly, enter the name of the target organization in any standard search engine.

CORE Knowledge Program

http://www.coreknowledge.org

Information on this program is available at this Web site or from the CORE Knowledge Foundation, 801 East High Street, Charlottesville, VA 22902; 804-977-7550. A periodic newsletter, *Common Knowledge,* is also available.

H-Net, Humanities and Social Studies Online

http://www.h-net.msu.edu/

This site contains the Michigan State University collection of discussion networks and information on a wide range of subjects. A useful site for making contact with others interested in teaching social studies.

The Resource Center of the Americas

www.americas.org

This Web site offers innovative and challenging curricula designed to build bridges between people throughout the Americas. The Center also offers a huge lending library of books, periodicals, and videos on the Americas.

The Social Studies Curriculum: Conceptual Teaching

http://www.sasked.gov.sk.ca/docs/midlsoc/g6currss.html

This highly recommended Web site is maintained by the provincial Department of Education in Saskatchewan and offers useful information about the grade-level placement of concepts and associated social studies skills.

Social Studies Concepts for Early Childhood

http://www.osr.state.ga.us/bestprac/social/ss_toc.html

This site is maintained by the State of Georgia Office of School Readiness and offers an excellent list of social studies–related concepts designed for use with prekindergarten students.

Contexts for Teaching

Social Studies

Part 2 examines the factors that furnish a context for teaching social studies— or any subject—in schools today.

The first two chapters are devoted to the increasingly culturally and educationally diverse student audiences in schools everywhere. A significant portion of Chapter 4, The Dimensions of Cultural Diversity, focuses on multicultural education as a means for addressing cultural diversity. Other sections of Chapter 4 address the diversity that students from specific cultural and ethnic groups may reflect. Chapter 5, The Dimensions of Instructional Diversity, focuses on meeting the needs of students who may be physically or emotionally challenged, display learning disabilities, or have preferred learning styles.

In turn-of-the-century schools, *character education* was used to describe efforts to mold children into responsible citizens. Over the years the term "character" fell into disfavor, for reasons described in Chapter 6, Developing Character and Values. Devoting a major section of this chapter to building character, as well as the inclusion of the term *Character* in the title, reflect changes in the broader society that are imposing new demands on what schools and teachers do.

Chapter 7, Social Studies: Gateway to Literacy, focuses on language literacy and children's ability to encounter social studies. This does not mean that social studies should be taught as reading, especially the type where children open their textbooks and begin reading aloud. Rather, the emphasis is on using social studies to enhance children's literacy skills without doing a disservice to either social studies or literacy.

4

The Dimensions of Cultural Diversity

Key Questions

* What kinds of diversity should you anticipate in your classroom?
* How do you accommodate diverse students' interests and abilities?
* How can teachers avoid cultural and gender bias?
* How can teachers approach multicultural education?

Key Ideas

* Diversity is a normal part of life in classrooms today.
* The range of diversity in any classroom can be astounding—religious, ethnic, cultural, physical, intellectual, and social.
* Racism and sexism can be either personal or institutional, and conscious or unconscious.
* Multicultural activities must be authentic; otherwise they can lead to inaccurate stereotyping.

Introduction: On Mottoes and Metaphors

DIVERSITY

The eagle on the Great Seal of the United States, which is on the back of a dollar bill, is holding a ribbon or scroll in its beak. Inscribed there is our national motto: *e pluribus unum*—"Out of many, one." The notion of *E pluribus unum* is such a dominant theme in the multicultural education literature that it seemed to provide an appropriate introduction to this chapter on diversity.

Are we one? or many? or both?

The current interest in *E pluribus unum* focuses not on "the many," for we are indeed a nation of immigrants, but on *unum*—the "one." As noted in Chapter 1, the question today is, Is the United States *one*—a nation with a common culture that binds us together? Or would our national character be better described by *E pluribus pluribus*—out of many, many? As Barber (1992) suggested, the diversity of America is at once a virtue, a source of pride, a brave boast, a troubling reality, and an unsettling problem that muddles what it means to be an American.

When people try to describe the American character, they sometimes turn to metaphors. For example, our society, and schools especially, were once described as a "melting pot" from which recently arrived immigrants were expected to

96

emerge as "Americans." Regardless of an individual's prior ethnicities—whether they were Italian-Americans, African-Americans, or Chinese-Americans—the idea was to get rid of that hyphen and make everyone fully qualified members of the mainstream American culture.

Changing metaphors

The problem with most metaphors is that they seldom "fit" perfectly. Many people's problem with the melting pot image stemmed from the belief that America is not a single culture but a multitude of cultures, each with traits and characteristics that contribute to the larger society. When the melting pot notion fell into disfavor about thirty to forty years ago, some people turned to a "salad bowl" metaphor, in which each ethnicity retains its separate identity but still contributes to the whole. Describing America as a salad bowl was an improvement over the melting pot, but this metaphor too has problems. Among other things, it's too easy to overemphasize the ingredients in the salad and neglect the importance of the bowl—which represents the beliefs and values that all Americans have in common.

The American mosaic

Instead of a food-related metaphor, consider describing American society as a mosaic—a work of art when it is assembled, but simply a collection of individual pieces before it is put together. The parts-whole relationship of a mosaic also captures the duality of *cultural pluralism* that we noted in Chapter 1. This is because all of us must deal with at least two cultures, sometimes simultaneously: the common American culture that everyone shares, and our individual ethnicities that set each of us apart from other people. If you question whether there are beliefs and values that all of us share, consider what would likely happen if the people who argue that we have no common values were denied their right to state that position. We suspect that phrases like "freedom of speech" and "the Bill of Rights" would appear as if out of nowhere.

● Why Diversity Has Become a Concern

The diversity that you and every teacher must deal with has grown tremendously in the last twenty or so years. One reason for this is *desegregation,* in the broadest sense of that term. *Brown v. Topeka Board of Education* (1954) marked the beginning of the end of racially segregated schools, although the effects of the Supreme Court's ruling were by no means immediate.

Why classrooms are more diverse today

The end of overt racial segregation has accounted for some of the increased diversity in classrooms today, but the end of another more subtle form of segregation also had a discernible impact. The Individuals with Disabilities Education Act of 1990, which extended Public Law 94-142, continued to reduce the number of physically and educationally disabled students who were formerly segregated into separate, often special education, classrooms. The legislation did not abolish separate classes entirely, but it did require that students be placed in the *least restrictive environment:* that is, environments that best met the student's needs. That environment might be a regular classroom, a regular classroom plus special services in separate classrooms (which are known as pull-out programs), placement in a totally separate classroom, or, in the most extreme cases, institutionalization. The key point is that one effect of PL 94-142 and subsequent legislation was to increase substantially the diversity in regular classrooms.

Three other factors also account for the increased diversity in classrooms today: (1) demographic changes resulting from new immigration, (2) increasing minority populations, and (3) an increased recognition of the ethnicities of all students, many of whom had been in classrooms all along. For example, there is an elementary school in San Francisco where students may speak one or more of twenty-seven different languages in their homes. This situation, both in California and elsewhere, has resulted largely from increased immigration—primarily from Mexico, Central America, and the Pacific Rim. As a consequence, in many of the large school districts in America, the majority of students are currently non-white or soon will be.

When the melting pot was the prevailing metaphor, the dominant belief was that the faster newly arrived students dropped the hyphen and began thinking of themselves as "Americans," the better. But if you think about it, expecting people to submerge their ethnicities was tantamount to asking them to deny their heritage. It was a nearly impossible expectation to begin with, as many third- or fourth-generation, American-born offspring of immigrants and enslaved peoples will readily attest. It is also an expectation that diminishes one of the qualities on which our nation of immigrants was built. Instead of denigrating or trying to erase individual ethnicities, many people today prize them for the contributions they make to the mosaic of life in America. Some people are reinserting that infamous hyphen to describe themselves as African-Americans or European-Americans, even though it has been centuries since their ancestors came from either Africa or

Europe. It's the heritage that matters, not the time span. This chapter examines the educational impact that the increasingly diverse American culture has and will have on those of us who teach its future citizens. To provide a context, a profile of a classroom that reflects some of the different kinds of diversity you are likely to encounter in your own classroom is presented. The focus then turns to ways in which you can address some forms of diversity, including cultural, racial, gender, and religious differences. Chapter 5 follows up with the various physical, emotional, and learning disorders that may exist regardless of race and ethnicity. For lack of a better term, the latter group is referred to as reflecting educational or "instructional" diversity.

A Classroom Profile

The following vignette illustrates the diversity you are apt to encounter, regardless of where you teach. This vignette describes a fourth-grade classroom at Roscoe Hunt Elementary School, a racially and ethnically mixed magnet school located in a lower-middle-class neighborhood. Hunt Elementary serves neighborhood children as well as students from other parts of the city who want to take advantage of its enhanced programs in math and science.

Mary Jane Blanchard is in her third year of teaching fourth graders. She has between twenty-two and twenty-six students in her class—the number changes almost weekly. Every so often a student will leave and a new student will arrive or a former student will return. For example, one former student, Tyrone, has recently returned after spending three months living with his aunt in Chicago. Only seventeen of the twenty-four currently enrolled students began the year with Ms. Blanchard.

Students may reflect multiple forms of diversity

The mobility of students in Mary Jane's classroom is high, but not as high as at Ramirez Elementary, the school featured in Chapter 1. Likewise, the diversity in Mary Jane's students is not all that uncommon, although she, like any teacher, has a couple of students who are exceptions to the rule. Note also that although the following list looks long, this is because some students reflect multiple forms of diversity or exceptionality. Some of Ms. Blanchard's students include the following:

Academic considerations

* Five students—Tyrone, Trisha, Jesus, Miguel, and Maria—whose reading skills are *at least* one-half year below grade level; all of them spend a part of each day in the Resource Room, where they receive special tutoring in academic skills. Two of these students, Trisha and Miguel, have difficulty remembering what they read.
* Six students—Juan, LaShawna, Melissa, Gina, Richard, and Chen Lee—who, although they are fourth graders, have reading, math, and language skills that are at the sixth-grade level or above.
* Three students—Tyrone, Richard, and Christi—who have illegible handwriting, despite all Ms. Blanchard's efforts otherwise.
* Three other students—Jesus, Miguel, and Maria—who come from homes where Spanish is the dominant language.
* One student, Trang, who spoke no English at the beginning of the year (and no one in the school spoke Vietnamese).

Emotional considerations

* One student, Heather—a girl with apparently normal intelligence who spends her day huddled in her seat with her coat pulled over her head, almost as if she were withdrawing from the world.
* One gifted student, Chen Lee, who is a very hard worker and who places extraordinary emphasis on memorization. In math, for example, she memorizes the answers *and* the problems.
* One student, James, who has muscular dystrophy and is confined to a wheelchair.
* Another student, Jason, who takes the drug Ritalin to calm his hyperactivity.

Religious diversity

* Two students, Amy and Melissa, whose parents have requested that their children be excused from any lessons involving witches, ghosts, goblins, or other supernatural beings, all of which are offensive to their religious beliefs. In addition, Melissa's parents have requested that she be excused from saying the Pledge of Allegiance during the opening exercises, again because of the family's religious convictions.
* Six students—Tyrone, LaShawna, Patrick, James, DeLeon, and Charles—who come from single-parent homes. Four students live with their mother, one lives with his grandmother, and Charles lives with his father.
* Finally, one student—Tyrone—who apparently doesn't like Ms. Blanchard or Roscoe Hunt school and has decided that he will not learn in this setting.

Lest you think otherwise, Mary Jane Blanchard's class is *not* an uncommon example. If you have doubts about this, consider the kinds of diversity she does not have in her classroom—at least not this year. She does *not* have students who

* have limited vision or hearing,
* are cognitively disadvantaged,

* are absent from school more than three days every week,
* have infant alcohol or "crack baby" syndrome,
* have known tobacco, drug, or alcohol addictions, or
* are abused.

All classrooms are diverse, some more so and some less so than Mary Jane Blanchard's. This means that all teachers must adapt their teaching in ways that accommodate their students' needs. Some forms of diversity may require major instructional changes, like accommodating Trang's limited ability with English or Trisha's lack of reading skills. Other forms of exceptionality, such as making sure that Jason gets his medication on schedule, don't require instructional modifications, but they are things that a teacher must keep in mind. The forms of diversity and exceptionality reflected in Mary Jane Blanchard's classroom, and that are considered in this chapter, include

Cultural diversity summarized

* cultural and ethnic diversity. Mary Jane's class currently has mainstream Anglo, Latino, African-American, Cuban-American, Mexican-American, mixed Anglo-Mexican American, and Haitian-American students. In addition, she teaches a variety of Asian-Americans, including students whose ancestry includes China, Taiwan, Vietnam, Laos, and Japan.
* religious diversity, especially as reflected by Amy and Melissa.

In the following sections, we look at how teachers can accommodate cultural, ethnic, and religious diversity.

Responding to Cultural and Ethnic Diversity

● The Three Little Pigs Revisited

Few of us can forget "The Three Little Pigs," that tale filled with delightful opportunities for huffing, puffing and "blo-o-wing" the house down." As is the case for many children's stories, it is useful to look beneath the surface for hidden messages. For example, doesn't the "Three Little Pigs" extol the virtues of brick homes and, by implication, the people who build them? And isn't one of its underlying messages that hardworking people should build brick houses—homes that can withstand adversity? In addition to "brick is best," the story also seems to belittle homes made of straw and wood (sticks), as well as the "lazy types" who build them. It seems to say that "If those people would take some initiative and were willing to work a little harder, they could build themselves a good (brick) house too!" Then consider the countless thousands of people in the world who don't have a brick kiln nearby and who probably couldn't afford to buy bricks even if they did. They are likely to build their homes from inexpensive and readily accessible materials, like adobe, or stone, or logs. In very warm climates, some people's homes may consist of raised bamboo platforms that are open to the cooling breezes. Certainly such homes would not meet the standard set in "The Three Little Pigs." The question here is whether a home—any home—that is not built from bricks is necessarily inferior.

Hidden messages

It would be easy to overstate the effects of inaccurate and possibly hurtful stereotyping in children's tales like "The Three Little Pigs." But should teachers simply ignore it entirely? Or should they stop using such stories because of the questionable stereotyping they contain? On one hand, most children seem readily able to handle fantasy, including pigs that talk and wolves that huff and puff. But in this case, a follow-up explanation of housing in different parts of the world, perhaps accompanied by pictures downloaded from the Internet, could mitigate some of the inaccurate stereotyping.

"The Three Little Pigs" is not alone among materials that can foster a particular world-view in the young (see Christiansen, 1994). The contemporary media is filled with programming that often generates stereotypes that are only slightly more open and varied than media of thirty-five to forty years ago. For example, and assuming that you have seen reruns of "The Lone Ranger," imagine how different that program might be if it were retitled, "The Story of Tonto (and his trusty companion, the Lone Ranger)." The notion that heroes are virile white males is so deeply embedded in our popular culture that in the movies, short and heavy-set males (like Danny DeVito, perhaps) must be satisfied with Oscar nominations for best supporting actor. It would be more politically correct to refer to Mr. DeVito as height-challenged (short), and weight-challenged (heavy-set)—but you probably get the message. A similar situation probably exists for DeVito's female counterparts, such as the highly regarded actress, Kathy Bates. Thirty years ago, DeVito and Bates would have been referred to as "character" actors, so apparently even the Oscar terminology has changed to reflect a more encompassing (or less exclusionary) view of people in show business.

Individuals have only limited power to alter the stereotyping presented in the media. But as teachers we can select the media we use with students and thereby control at least to some extent the intentional and unintentional racial and gender bias that might otherwise occur. Some of these options are explored in the next section.

Cultural Diversity

Children of color

Lisa Delpit (1995), in *Other People's Children,* writes about teachers who, when facing a multiracial class, sometimes say things like "I don't see color, I only see children" (p. 177). Would you consider this a situation where to acknowledge children's color is to insult them? Or is it a matter of fairness, of treating all children alike, regardless of race, color, or creed? Or is it a matter of taking a standard for fairness too far? Delpit questions the real message that this otherwise well-intentioned statement sends. For example, is it suggesting that there's something wrong with being black or brown, and that it should *not* be noticed? Delpit suggests, on the other hand, that if one does not see color, then one does not really see children.

There is certainly nothing wrong when teachers try to maintain standards of fairness and respect that apply to all students—and hopefully between students. To do so might be a welcome departure from the name-calling and put-downs that characterize too many classrooms today. But Delpit suggests that carrying the fairness standard too far could have unintended consequences. For example, when some Native American students are called on to answer questions, they will remain silent—even when they know the answer. Such behavior may have led to the stereotype of the "nonverbal Native American." It may also cause some teachers to avoid calling on Native American students in large-group activities so as not to embarrass them publicly. Unlike white, middle-class society, where everyone's contribution is valued, many Native American parents (as well as parents from Oriental cultures) expect their children to sit quietly and observe—to be seen but not heard. The matter is further complicated by the fact that quick responses from Native American children are likely to be considered rude or disrespectful (Stokes, 1997). The first point here is that Native American children, who are usually as verbal as children anywhere *in small-group settings,* may find themselves caught between the differing expectations of two cultures. The second point is that although teachers are sometimes aware of some aspects of Native American cultures—such as their close relationship with the land and nature—teachers may not be aware of the differences in child-rearing practices, differences that can lead to erroneous conclusions and unintentional stereotyping. A third point concerns teachers who claim that to succeed in our culture, Native American children must (among other things) overcome their reluctance to talk in front of large groups. Part of that argument is surely valid, although it is not a foregone conclusion that Native American children will necessarily opt for success in the larger society. The other side of the coin is that members of most minority groups will face intangible penalties if they seek to leave the warmth and support of their familiar culture so as to affiliate with and achieve "success" in a less familiar culture. In other words, not everyone wants to look like Vanna White and sound like Dan Rather, no matter how highly those personae may be valued in the dominant culture.

Even if you anticipate teaching in an area where there are few Native American students, children from other cultures may have equally unique ways of responding to the events around them. At the risk of overgeneralizing, some of these cultural differences are summarized here:

* Children from cultures that have strong, group storytelling traditions—which includes some Native American, Inuit, and Native Hawaiian groups—often prefer activities that demand lots of talking and small-group activities. As you might expect students from these cultures often become frustrated with worksheet activities that they must complete individually and silently.
* Many students of Asian origins are reluctant to ask questions and express personal opinions because doing so may be considered rude and disrespectful to adults. In Korean and Japanese cultures especially, the idea that students must ask questions implies that the teacher did such a poor job in the initial teaching that additional questions were necessary. In other words, asking questions is not necessarily a way for students to clarify things they do not understand, but rather becomes a subtle way to attack the teacher.
* Many Latino and Hispanic *male* students will often look you boldly in the eye when you talk with them, regardless of whether you are male or female. However, many Latino and Hispanic *female* students (and some males) are trained to avoid looking directly at adults, especially males. They will sometimes

Cultural patterns (margin)

Intangible penalties (margin)

Cultural traditions (margin)

look at the ceiling, or more often the floor, but they will avoid looking at some adults even if the adult says, "Look at me when I am talking to you." What we may interpret as disrespectful behavior may in fact be the ultimate sign of respect in cultures where one does not look into the eyes of someone older, someone you respect.

Students from other cultures will sometimes display culturally defined behaviors that are polar opposites from what we consider appropriate. For example, individuals from some Oriental cultures indicate sympathy by laughing (usually while covering their mouth with their hands). This can be disconcerting for an uninformed teacher who, for example, announces to the class that he or she was absent to attend a relative's funeral, and then finds that some of their Oriental-American students cover their mouths and laugh. Instead of taking offense and saying, "This is not a laughing matter," a more culturally appropriate response would be a simple "Thank you."

★ African-American students sometimes respond to teachers' questions in ways similar to the Native American students noted earlier. They may give short answers, flippant responses, or none at all. In traditional African-American communities, children are (1) seldom expected to contribute to adult discussions or (2) to ask direct questions (Shade & New, 1993). In addition, African-American students are likely to follow the "rules" that govern conversation in their native cultures or homes, rules that often differ considerably from the more restrained and laid-back conventions that govern conversations among Anglos. These differences are often reflected in the (1) passion, (2) animation (gestures), (3) pacing (fast) and (4) volume (often loud) of conversations among African-American speakers.

──● Teaching Implications

Children from most non-Western cultures will seldom voluntarily tell you, for example, that "I don't ask questions because you'll think I'm rude." This means that identifying the cause for apparently troubling behaviors can become a form of "discovery" learning for teachers. Perhaps the easiest way to deal with this is to ask the child directly about your concerns—in private and in the least threatening way possible. If the child says, "Yes, talking in front of the group really bothers me (for whatever reason)," the next question concerns whether this is something children will need to live with, or whether you are willing to use an alternative strategy that does not place students in an embarrassing position or leave them open to ridicule. Teachers may also need to clarify their motives by asking them-

selves why they are conducting question-and-answer sessions in a large-group format. Because it's convenient? Because they haven't really thought about it? Or do they believe that children will learn from and remember the other students' responses? Unless you can satisfy yourself that there are good reasons for using a whole-group, question-and-answer activity—sometimes erroneously referred to as a "discussion"—consider using a strategy where students respond to your questions in small groups. You then appoint one group member to report the group's findings to the larger group. This minor procedural change will (1) permit more students to participate simultaneously and (2) change the student's role from being "an answerer" to that of "a reporter." Such a subtle shift can eliminate many of the pressures that can cause problems for nonwhite students, especially students from Oriental and Native American cultures.

Alternate strategies

Many of the considerations that apply to nonwhite students also apply equally to African-American students, who are also obviously nonwhite. The research suggests that African-American students do better in school when teachers provide opportunities for them to think out loud and talk with their classmates in informal, conversational settings, all of which are usually most feasible in small-group settings. The research also suggests that African-American students benefit from highly participatory activities, including role playing and dramatic play, and by having teachers present materials auditorily, through music, chants, and rhyme (Gay, 1991, 1997; Delpit, 1995; Ladson-Billings, 1995; Share & New, 1993).

Role playing and dramatic play are treated in Chapter 11, but consider a brief example of how you might incorporate an auditory approach to fifth-grade American history. Assume that the class has been studying the origins of the Revolutionary War, and you want students to understand that the British Parliament already knew the American colonists were in ferment. After creating small groups, you randomly assign each group the task of summarizing and then presenting either the American or the British prewar position to the entire class. In addition, each group's report must be presented as a "rap." Because the grammar in many raps is purposefully atrocious, you might offer extra credit for raps that use good grammar (as would certainly be the case for Parliament's message to the colonists).

● Does Everybody Really Know?

Exploring a different perspective

The first point here is that children from other cultures often react to everyday situations in ways that are traditional and wholly acceptable in their respective cultures. The second and perhaps more important point is that children from other cultures often assume that you understand and accept their responses to situations. Their notions for how they should demonstrate respect and express sympathy, for example, much less for what are the "correct and appropriate" ways to respond to situations, are behavior patterns they have grown up with. Such children are often inclined to believe that "everybody knows" about them. This means that your students may be quite unaware of why you reacted so strongly when they refused to look you directly in the eye or used laughter to express their sympathy. They are likely to assume that everybody understands that laughter can be a normal and perfectly appropriate expression of sympathy–as it is in their culture–or that one should not look directly at a person he or she respects. The students may be equally unaware that their behavior is culturally determined, just as you may be unaware of the basis for their seemingly aberrant behavior. Because most children are not inherently mean-spirited, when encountering behaviors that you cannot explain, consider stopping for a moment, taking a deep breath, and then saying something like "O.K." in as accepting a way as you can. Because it would be unfair to the children to drop matters at this point, you should probably talk with the child privately. You may also want to make inquiries about the children's behaviors among people you know and trust, preferably people with immediate knowledge of the cultures in question.

━━━━● **"Being Bad Is the Way We Are"**

Marc Elrich (1994) teaches in a school on the outskirts of Washington, D.C. All but two of the twenty-nine students in his sixth-grade class are African-American or Hispanic, and most of them are of low socioeconomic status—in other words, they are poor. In some respects, Marc doesn't face the range of diversity that Mary Jane Blanchard must deal with, but he faces some difficult problems nonetheless.

Marc teaches in a school that offers a range of programs that are meant to teach children to celebrate and prize their diversity. Yet despite the school's programs, many of Marc's students have such low self-esteem and low expectations for themselves that by the age of ten or eleven, many of them have opted out of the educational system.

Another classroom example

On one occasion Marc showed a film that he hoped would provoke a discussion of self-esteem. The film was based on a Langston Hughes story about an African-American youth who attempts to steal the purse of an elderly African-American lady. The youth fails, and the woman takes him into her home, where she applies a generous amount of love and understanding. The messages: love is a powerful medicine, and, with love, all of us can become better people.

In the postfilm discussion, it quickly became apparent that Marc's students hadn't bought the message. For example, one student said, "As soon as you see a black boy, you know he's gonna do something bad!" Marc's question: "Just because he's black, he's bad?" Student: "Everybody knows that black people are bad. That's the way we are." Marc: "Do you mean 'bad' like 'cool' or 'tough' or 'hot,' or do you mean 'bad' as in 'not good' or 'evil'?"(p. 12). The student meant the latter.

As the discussion continued, a disturbing picture began to emerge. Marc's students were nearly unanimous about the following comments:

Students' self-images and prejudices

* "Black people don't like to work hard."
* "Black boys expect to die young and unnaturally."
* "White people are smart and have money."
* "Asians are smart and have money."
* "Asians don't like blacks or Hispanics."
* "Hispanics are more like blacks than whites. They can't be white so they try to be black."
* "Hispanics are poor and don't try hard because, like blacks, they know it doesn't matter" (pp. 12–13).

Good at being bad

In subsequent discussions, Marc's students indicated that people who can afford the material goods associated with the "good life" get their money through guns and dealing in drugs. They also believed that wimps die young and live in fear, whereas tough guys die young but are proud. Likewise, bosses are white and workers are black, and black people don't do important things, except in school books. "But," Marc also indicated, "my students don't lack for pride. They are, in fact, quite proud of what they are. They were good at being bad, some were excellent at it, and the badder they were, the greater their social status" (p. 14).

Another Marc, in this case Mark Twain, once said, "I never let my schooling interfere with my education." Marc Elrich's students had obviously learned some powerful lessons, perhaps not what we might have wanted and hopefully not in school, but powerful nonetheless. In reflecting on his experience, Marc indicated:

Students' responses to special programs

> I gave a lot of thought to how we teach students to value diversity. The thoughts and words of my students make a mockery of our [school's] celebrations. Setting aside a month for black history or women's history seems strange and artificial to most students regardless of color. These children aren't naive. What are the seven other months: White Male History Months? History needs to be inclusionary, but it also needs to be natural so children come to see that there's nothing strange or odd about black people or women achieving success. I have begun to fear that singling out groups for special attention does more to foster suspicion, jealousy, and cynicism, than it does to promote understanding, empathy, and community (p. 14).

Children are perceptive observers of their world, and for one to believe that teachers can change those views by teaching occasional lessons on successful African-Americans, Asian-Americans, or whatever, may be naive. As Elrich noted, ". . . children form their own impressions early on, and they sense the dissonance between the reality of life and the pretty pictures offered in school. If we are concerned with our children genuinely valuing diversity and with all children developing high self-esteem, then we have to offer our children genuine knowledge and insight into the world in which they live. I don't think we do" (p. 15).

Powerful lessons

Whether schools can single-handedly eliminate the kinds of stereotyping that Marc Elrich's students reflect is debatable. The fact that streetwise children may consider the examples of successful minorities that appear in textbooks—the Jackie Robinsons and the Martin Luther King Jrs.—as exceptions, as people far removed from the life they know, suggests that some of the underlying problems associated with racism extend beyond what schools can influence on their own.

Multicultural education programs (considered later in this chapter) may be able to address some of these problems, but for this to occur, students, teachers, and communities that the schools serve must regard multicultural education as an integral part of the school program, not simply an add-on designed to placate (or mislead) minority children.

Sexism and Gender Equity Education

Sexist stereotyping

The first illustration in a first-grade social studies book from the 1960s shows a neatly dressed woman (possibly Beaver Cleaver's mother) standing on the front steps waving good-bye to her children as they board the school bus. Several pages later, a briefcase-carrying male arrives home from work (according to the text) and is shown, his feet on the ottoman, reading the newspaper while the woman (who we know by then is the wife and mother) is shown preparing dinner in the kitchen. When the family goes on trips—which families do often in first-grade books—guess who drives?

After over a decade of enhanced awareness of the need for more gender-equitable treatments, the messages that such illustrations can convey to children should hardly be lost on any of us. They begin with "A woman's place is in the home" and go on from there. Such messages are simplistic and sexist, and they inaccurately depict the

Diversity and Multicultural Resources on the World Wide Web

The Internet offers an almost mind-boggling array of resources for diversity-related topics. Listings in addition to those highlighted here are contained in the Suggested Readings and Resources section at the end of the chapter.

An excellent source for multicultural/ethnic studies materials is the **Balch Institute for Ethnic Studies** at:

> **http://www.avalon.net/-librarian/Balch Web/ balch.html**

This site has extensive listings of materials related to multicultural issues, many of which are downloadable. It also contains samples of historical materials that reflect stereotyped images of various ethnic and cultural groups.

The Montgomery County Maryland Public Schools maintains an outstanding program titled **"Making Multicultural Connections Through Trade Books"** at:

> **http://www.mcps.k12.md.us/curriculum/ socialstd/MBD/Books_Begin.html**

In addition to providing an extensive database of children's trade books for specific cultures, this site also identifies (a) relevant technology and (b) how that technology can be used with specific books. For example, Patricia Polacco's delightful stories, *Chicken Sunday* (New York: Scholastic, 1992) and *Rechenka's Eggs* (New York, Putnam and Gosset, 1998), both involve intricately designed, Ukranian (Easter) eggs—which are also known as "Pysanky" eggs. The program identifies relevant children's books and then links to software, in this instance *Kid Pix Studio* (Broderbund), and the *Kid Pix Around the World Activity Book* by Barbara Chan (Addison Wesley, 1994), which children can use to make their own Pysanky eggs.

An excellent source for gender-equity related materials is maintained by the **American Association of University Women** at:

> **http://www.aauw.org/4000/resources.html**

Of particular interest at this site are links to "Gender Equity Resources for K-12 Teachers."

roles and responsibilities of both women and men in modern society. Current social studies textbooks are far less guilty of such treatments, and typically show single-parent families, women in roles traditionally viewed as male, and men in roles traditionally viewed as female. However, recent studies suggest that instructional materials sometimes insert pictures of females, but say nothing about their substantive contributions (Kames, 2000). An annotated bibliography of women's contributions throughout history is included in the Resource Handbook.

Failing at Fairness

In a now-classic report that was published as *Failing at Fairness: How American Schools Cheat Girls* (1994), Myra and David Sadker analyzed a large group of social studies text materials and found that females were seriously underrepresented. In one sixth-grade, world history text, for example, only eleven female names were mentioned, and none of them were adult American women. As further evidence of the male-dominated curriculum, the Sadkers asked students at all levels of schooling to identify twenty famous American women from history who were not athletes or entertainers. The majority of students flunked miserably—most had difficulty identifying ten women, even though some of them had included names like Aunt Jemima and Betty Crocker to beef up their lists.

Thanks in part to efforts by the Sadkers and others, current texts are less guilty of slighting women than was true just ten years ago. African-American women, for example, such as Sojourner Truth (a former slave) and Harriet Tubman are presented

A female pilot in the classroom can speak volumes about the increasing equity among individuals of either gender.
(© Michael Zide)

more prominently than in the past. Yet other contemporary materials may still be guilty of promoting gender bias. For example, Bigelow (1996) suggests that the popular computer simulation, *Oregon Trail* (MECC) can contribute to gender bias because even if students elect to play a female character, which is a selection they make at the beginning of the simulation, most subsequent decisions they are asked to make were usually made by males, not females. This does not mean *Oregon Trail* is unsuitable for children, but it does mean that some of the cautions that apply to classic fairy tales also apply to contemporary materials.

Guidelines for identifying sexism and racism in children's books are presented in Figure 4.1 on pages 109 to 110.

The immediate goal of gender equity education involves the equal treatment of people regardless of gender, but it is part of a broader goal that encompasses the inclusion of individuals regardless of gender, race, age, religion, or economic position. Gender equity education focuses primarily on helping children develop a perspective—a way of looking at the world and how individuals are treated within that world—not on learning a body of information. You can play a key role in that process, especially by selecting teaching materials in which the gender role treatment is balanced and equitable (Flynn & Chambers, 1994). You can also call attention to the inequitable treatment of individuals of either gender in whatever situations or materials the children encounter.

Current materials may reflect subtle gender bias

The goal: inclusion

Racism and Sexism: Institutional or Personal?

In situations involving perceived racism or sexism, two questions usually apply. One, is the apparent racism or sexism personal or institutional? And, two, is it conscious

Racism and sexism in children's books range on a continuum from blatant and intentional to subtle and inconsequential. The following are elements to consider.

1. The Illustrations

_____ **Look for Stereotyping.** Stereotypes are oversimplified generalizations about a particular group, race, or sex, and usually carry derogatory implications. Look for instances where characters are ridiculed or demeaned because of their race or sex.

_____ **Look for Tokenism.** Do the nonwhite characters look just like whites except for being tinted or colored in? Are minority faces depicted with distinctive features?

_____ **Look at Who's Doing What?** Are minorities depicted in subservient and passive roles or in leadership and action roles? Are males shown as the "doers" and females as the observers?

2. Check the Story Line

The following checklist suggests some subtle forms of bias to watch for.

_____ **Standard for Success.** Must people of color adopt "white" behavior standards to get ahead? Is "making it" in the dominant white society projected as the only ideal? Must people of color exhibit extraordinary qualities—excel in sports, get A's, and so on—to gain acceptance and approval? In friendships between white children and children of color, is it the child of color who does most of the understanding and forgiving?

_____ **Resolution of Problems.** How are problems presented, conceived, and resolved in the story? Are people of color considered to be "the problem"? Are oppressions faced by women and people of color represented as causally related to an unjust society? Are the reasons for poverty and oppression explained or presented as inevitable? Does the story line encourage passive acceptance or active resistance? Are the problems faced by a person of color resolved through the benevolent intervention of a white person?

_____ **Role of Women.** Are the achievements of girls and women based on their initiative and intelligence, or are they due to their good looks or their relationship with boys? Are sex roles incidental or critical to characterization and plot? Could the same story be told if the sex roles were reversed?

_____ **Use of Loaded Words.** Loaded words have insulting overtones and include examples such as *savage, primitive, conniving, lazy, superstitious, treacherous, wily, crafty, inscrutable, docile,* and *backward.* Look for sexist language and adjectives that exclude or ridicule women, or use the male pronoun to refer to both males and females.

3. Look at the Lifestyles

Are people of color and their settings depicted in ways that contrast unfavorably with the unstated norm of white middle-class suburbia? If the nonwhite group is depicted as "different," are negative value judgments also implied? Are people of color depicted exclusively in ghettos, barrios, or migrant camps? In depicting another culture, do the illustrations and text offer genuine insights into another lifestyle? Look for inaccuracy and inappropriateness in the depiction of other cultures. Be wary of the "quaint-natives-in-costume" syndrome, which is usually most noticeable in areas like clothing and customs, but can extend to behavior and personality traits as well.

4. Weigh the Relationships Between People

—— **Power.** Do the whites in the story possess the power, take the leadership, and make all the important decisions? Do people of color and females function in essentially supporting roles?

—— **Family Relationships.** In African-American families, is the mother always dominant? In Latino families, are there always lots of children? If the family is separated, are societal conditions—unemployment, poverty—cited among the reasons for the separation?

5. Note the Heroes

The key question to ask here is: "Whose interest is a particular character serving?" Are minority heroes (when they appear) admired for the same qualities that have made white heroes famous, or because what they have done has benefited white people?"

6. Consider the Effects on a Child's Self-Image

Are norms established that limit a child's aspirations and self-concepts? Are African-American children continuously bombarded with images of the color white as the ultimate in beauty, cleanliness, virtue, and so on, and the color black as evil, dirty, menacing, and so on? Does the book counteract or reinforce exclusively positive associations with the color white and negative associations with black?

Do individuals of one sex perform all of the brave and important deeds? Are individuals of either sex denigrated because they are not fair-skinned or slim of body? Are there one or more characters with whom children of color can readily identify to positive and constructive ends?

7. Author's (or Illustrator's) Background, Qualifications, and Perspective

Analyze the biographical material (on the jacket flap or the back of the book) to determine whether the author(s) or illustrator(s) seem qualified to deal with the subject. If the author and illustrator are not members of the group being written about, is there anything in their background that would recommend them as the creators of this book? The same criteria apply to books that deal with the feelings and insights of females. Look carefully to determine whether the author's perspective substantially weakens or strengthens the value of his/her written work. Are omissions and distortions central to the overall character or "message" of the book?

8. Look at the Copyright Date

Only recently has the children's book world begun to reflect the realities of a multiracial society and the concerns of feminists. Copyright dates can be a clue as to how likely the book is to be overtly racist or sexist, even though recent dates are no guarantee of a book's relevance or sensitivity.

Abridged and adapted from the Council on Interracial Books for Children, "10 Quick Ways to Analyze Children's Books for Racism and Sexism."

Unconscious bias

or unconscious? The majority of teachers we meet are fair and caring people who go out of their way to avoid intentionally racist or sexist behavior. Most of them, for example, would not refer to a black male student as "boy," for doing so could be perceived as personally and consciously racist. But the same teachers may unconsciously engage in what are perceived as racist or sexists acts by, for example, assigning only

MODEL STUDENT ACTIVITY

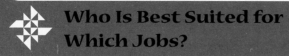

Who Is Best Suited for Which Jobs?

Introductory Note: Lessons like the one that follows can sometimes be problematic if parents perceive that you are trying to instill a particular point of view in their children. Therefore, make certain that this lesson corresponds closely with the curriculum for your grade level.

Grades:

3 through 8

Overview

This lesson is based on a survey of your students regarding which gender—male, female, or both—is best suited to certain jobs or tasks.

Objectives

1. The teacher will determine the extent to which students have stereotyped expectations about who should hold various jobs.
2. Students will show that they understand the word *stereotype* by correctly identifying certain expectations about jobs as stereotypical.

Procedure

1. Discuss the vocabulary important to this lesson: *stereotype, bias, opinion.*
2. Before you give the questionnaire to students, make sure they understand that you want honest opinions. Stress that there are no right or wrong answers and that you are not testing them on facts. Make it clear that they don't need to put their names on the questionnaires.
3. Divide the class into small groups (to facilitate tallying the results later). Hand out the questionnaires and allow students up to thirty minutes to complete them (individually).
4. Collect the questionnaires from each group and then give each group's responses to another group for tallying. Provide groups with blank questionnaires that they can use for summarizing the responses.
5. Use an overhead transparency of the questionnaire to summarize the small-group's tallies.
6. Lead a group discussion. Possible topics include:

   * What are the occupations that mostly men go into? Why do you think so?
   * What are the occupations that mostly women go into? Why do you think so?
   * Can both men and women hold those jobs? Why do you think so?
   * What job would you like to have? Give several reasons.

7. Be ready to counter stereotypical ideas with information about women astronauts, women scientists, male librarians, male secretaries, and male nurses. Ask students for examples from their own experience or from TV, magazines, or the Internet.

(continued)

Who Should?

Part I. For each of the jobs listed below, decide whether you think it should be done by a man, a woman, or could be done equally well by both. Circle 1 under MAN if you think only a man should do the job; circle 2 under WOMAN if you think only a woman should do the job; or circle 3 under BOTH if you think both a man and woman should do the job. Circle only one answer for each job.

	MAN	WOMAN	BOTH
1. airplane pilot	1	2	3
2. astronaut	1	2	3
3. carpenter	1	2	3
4. chef	1	2	3
5. doctor	1	2	3
6. lawyer	1	2	3
7. librarian	1	2	3
8. lifeguard	1	2	3
9. nurse	1	2	3
10. president of USA	1	2	3
11. race-car driver	1	2	3
12. secretary	1	2	3
13. telephone operator	1	2	3
14. truck driver	1	2	3
15. nursery school teacher	1	2	3

Part II. When there are class jobs to be done, who do you think *should* do them? Circle a number to show your answer.

	BOY	GIRL	BOTH
16. messenger	1	2	3
17. class president	1	2	3
18. eraser cleaner	1	2	3
19. class secretary	1	2	3
20. class treasurer	1	2	3

Part III. Now what about things at home? Circle a number to show your answer.

	MAN	WOMAN	BOTH
21. When children misbehave, who should correct them?	1	2	3
22. Who should teach good manners?	1	2	3
23. Who should take care of a sick child?	1	2	3
24. Who should teach children right from wrong?	1	2	3

Part IV. Here is a list of jobs that people do at home. Circle who you think *should* do the job.

	MAN	WOMAN	BOTH
25. washing dishes	1	2	3
26. taking out the trash	1	2	3
27. grocery shopping	1	2	3
28. paying bills	1	2	3
29. cooking	1	2	3
30. fixing things	1	2	3
31. dusting furniture	1	2	3
32. scrubbing floors	1	2	3
33. sewing	1	2	3
34. working in the yard	1	2	3
35. moving furniture	1	2	3
36. doing the laundry	1	2	3

Part V. Here is a list of spare-time activities. Circle who *should* do them: a man, woman, or both.

	MAN	WOMAN	BOTH
37. playing football	1	2	3
38. swimming	1	2	3
39. playing the piano	1	2	3
40. going to sports events (like baseball games)	1	2	3
41. working out in a gym	1	2	3
42. helping in a hospital every week	1	2	3

The "Who Should?" survey was abridged and adapted from material originally developed by the Highline School District, Project Equality, Seattle, WA 98166.

This activity was abridged and adapted from "Awareness of Sex Bias and Equity" originally developed by Carol Hankinson, Waiahole Elementary School, Hawaii, and Amy Okumura, Beverly J. Pu, and Yuriko Wellington, Hana High and Elementary, Hawaii, and appearing in *Oceans of Options: Sex Equity Lessons for the Classroom,* which was published by the Far West Laboratory for Educational Research and Development, 730 Harrison Street, San Francisco, CA 94107.

boys when heavy things need to be carried to the office or library, or by apparently using a double standard to judge the behaviors of boys and girls—"Boys will be boys, you know." On the other hand, a teacher who, after becoming aware of a textbook that distorts the images or contributions of people of color, decides to use it anyway—without saying anything or providing opportunities for students to investigate the bias—could be considered to have committed a consciously racist act.

Institutional bias   Institutional racism and sexism are usually more difficult to see and, thus, avoid. For example, many people may not be aware that there are more males than females in administrative positions in public schools, especially at the superintendent level—where the proportion of women is tiny. In still other instances, school practices that are designed to serve one purpose can sometimes have the effect of being racist or sexist. Homogenous grouping (or tracking) is one example. Some people argue that when schools group their students by ability, teachers are (a) better able to target individual needs and (b) students will learn more. Others argue that although homogeneous grouping "works" for high-ability students, it can have discriminatory consequences for students in the lower tracks, especially for the poor and minority students who tend to inhabit these tracks. Not only are students in the lower tracks often seen as less able, but some students come to see themselves as less able—"well, we are the lower group, you know, we're not supposed to 'get' this stuff."

Raising one's awareness   Conscious institutional racism and sexism is very difficult to combat on an individual basis. The same is true of conscious personal racism and sexism. In either case, individuals or groups are knowingly supporting a particular agenda. Unconscious racism and sexism is a different matter, because it lacks conscious motivation—it may simply be the effect of actions that someone hasn't thought about. Combating unconscious racism and sexism is largely a matter of bringing the effects of the actions to a conscious level. As opposed to comments such as "You're being a racist (or sexist)," which can be construed as a personal attack that raises one's defense mechanisms, consider focusing on the actions, not the individuals. A question such as "I wonder if some people think that (the action) is racist (or sexist)?" may be sufficient to bring an unconscious action to the conscious level where it can be dealt with.

Multicultural Education

There is no single, agreed-upon definition for *multicultural education*. Some individuals prefer a stronger descriptor. For example, Enid Lee (1994) prefers "antiracist education." Whatever descriptor you elect to use, multicultural education and cultural pluralism reflect the notion that the richness of our society is rooted in every nook and cranny on the globe. This means that all peoples must be treated in ways that recognize and respect their inherent dignity and their contributions to society. The basic goal of multicultural education is to help all children—regardless of ethnicity, gender, disabilities, or social class—understand and appreciate events and people from various points of view. Those points of view may reflect cultural and ethnic similarities and differences, as well as identify alternative choices for people regardless of their situation.

Goal

The literature on multicultural education is vast, and some of it reflects attempts by individuals to push a particular agenda. For example, consider the following survey of cultural awareness (Grant & Sleeter, 1989) in which you are asked to match the following individuals with their occupations. The answers are at the end of the chapter.*

Multicultural awareness?

_____ 1. Richard Wright	a.	African-American historian
_____ 2. Mary McLeod Bethune	b.	African-American psychiatrist on Harvard faculty
_____ 3. Rudolfo Acuña	c.	African-American opera singer
_____ 4. Patsy Takemoto Mink	d.	Founder and former president of a college
_____ 5. Marion [sic] Anderson	e.	Mexican-American historian
_____ 6. Larry Itliong	f.	African-American male novelist
_____ 7. Reies Lopez Tijerina	g.	Mexican-American political leader
_____ 8. Lerone Bennet	h.	Author of children's books
_____ 9. Alvin Poussaint	i.	Philippino-American labor leader
_____ 10. Yoshiko Uchida	j.	Former member of Congress

Some people breathe a sigh of relief when they get to Marian Anderson, the acclaimed African-American opera singer. Often this is the first entry they recognize. In desperation, they sometimes turn to a process of elimination based on the perceived ethnicity of the individual's last name. They might also ask where was Ella Fitzgerald, Ernie Banks, Kathleen Battle, Joycelyn Elders, Henry B. Gonzales, and Cesar Chavez—people they had heard of.

Building mutual respect

With due respect to Grant and Sleeter, one might question whether this is a legitimate survey of cultural awareness. Or perhaps it was designed to heighten one's awareness of what one does not know. The point is that the goal of multicultural education is *not* to replace Eurocentric trivia with a different kind of more politically correct trivia. Rather, multicultural education is intended to develop the knowledge, perspectives, and frames of reference that build *mutual respect* between and among all peoples.

——● Approaches to Multicultural Education

Multicultural education can be embraced in different ways, some more and some less effective than others. One of the ways to look at this is to think of multicultural education as a continuum that ranges from discrete activities that teachers occasionally employ to a broadly comprehensive program where multicultural elements are integrated into the program on an ongoing basis. (Note that portions of this treatment are based on Banks, 1989). Various phases of such a continuum, each more comprehensive than the one that precedes it, include:

1. **Contributions Approach.** Examples include the addition of discrete activities and units that focus on heroes, holidays, and unique cultural phenomena.

2. **Additive Approach.** Examples include the addition of content and themes, such as incorporating works of African-American literature into an existing Amer-

---

*Source: From *Turning on Learning: Five Approaches for Multicultural Teaching* by Grant/Sleeter. Copyright 1989. Reprinted by permission of Prentice-Hall.

ican history course. At this stage, the curriculum is added to but remains otherwise unchanged.

3. **Transformational Approach.** At this level, the structure of the curriculum is changed to focus on issues and events from the perspective of different cultural and ethnic groups.

4. **Social Action Approach.** At this most comprehensive level, the curriculum is restructured to focus on important social issues, with the clear expectation that students will engage in actions to help resolve them.

Each of these approaches is examined in more detail below.

Contributions Approach. This approach to multicultural education is one of the more common, especially in schools where teachers elect to approach multicultural curriculum on their own. Special culturally oriented events such as "Black History Month" or "African- or Native-American Heritage Day" characterize this approach, as do insertions of special lessons on ethnic heroes such as Crispus Attucks (the first African-American to die in the Battle of Concord), Cesar Chavez (the organizer of Mexican-American farm workers), or even Rosa Parks (who initiated the Montgomery bus boycott).

Stage one: Contributions

CAUTIONS AND LIMITATIONS

The contributions approach to multicultural education has some limitations, not the least of which is that children will see it as a curriculum add-on designed to appeal to a certain population. If there is a question about this, consider the responses of Marc Elrich's students to the inclusion of certain African-American heroes in their textbooks.

Limitations and liabilities

A second and perhaps more serious limitation of the contributions approach is that well-intentioned activities can sometimes do as much harm as good. The special days set aside to honor certain cultural or ethnic groups, or the eating of ethnic foods that Elrich (Banks and many others) referred to, can unintentionally convey inaccurate information and create negative stereotypes.

For example, I thought that, when our son went to camp, where a sizeable contingent of his fellow campers would be from countries in Eastern Europe and Russia, the experience would be useful to him. What better way to get to know people from other cultures than to live with them for a week? He returned from camp asserting that Russians stank! They didn't wash or take showers, he said.

While I knew that people from some cultures in Eastern Europe did not bathe as often as many Americans, and that some of them regard deodorants as feminine, I was not prepared for the vehemence of my son's reaction, nor could I temper his conclusion. To this day, and with no experience to the contrary, my son still believes that Russians stink.

CRAFT ACTIVITIES

Arts and crafts activities must also be treated carefully, or they too can sometimes be misleading. On one occasion, for example, we visited a kindergarten class in which the children were studying Native Americans. They had dyed elbow macaroni with red, orange, yellow, green, and blue food coloring. After the macaroni had dried and was strung on strings, the children proudly displayed their "Indian necklaces." The teacher's motives were well intended; she wanted a hands-on activity that related to the unit, preferably one the students could complete quickly. The problem here was with what the children learned from the activity: that Native Americans wear necklaces made from colored macaroni—which no self-respecting Native Americans do.

The context is important

Having students create a macaroni necklace can be an engaging craft activity that may be worth doing on that basis alone. However, problems can arise if the teacher introduces it with "Today, boys and girls, we are going to make necklaces like the Native Americans used to wear." Justifying activities on a multicultural basis can easily become misleading, and can provide learnings that go beyond what the teacher intended. Multicultural education is an area where otherwise well-intended activities, like the African-American History Month that Marc El-rich referred to, could be regarded as an insult.

Adding new elements to the existing curriculum.

Additive Approach.   The additive approach to multicultural education involves the inclusion of books, units, or courses that add to the existing curriculum but do not change it substantially. It would also be reflected by a teacher who, for example, decides to teach a unit on the internment of Japanese-Americans in special camps during World War II—a topic often omitted from textbooks. The teacher might base the unit on Yoshiko Uchida's *Journey to Topaz: A Story of the Japanese-American Evacuation* (1971) and Ken Mochizuki's (1993) *Baseball Saved Us,* an easy book that traces how Japanese-Americans imprisoned in a desert internment camp built a baseball field to relieve the monotony.

Limitations of the add-on approach

The add-on approach is a legitimate stage in the development of a truly multicultural curriculum, particularly for teachers working on their own. However, it has some limitations. For example, Banks (1989) noted that students may see the units as appendages rather than as an integral part of the overall course of study. Occasional add-on units can provide different cultural perspectives, but they are unlikely to show how the histories and cultures of various groups are interwoven over time.

Transformational Approach.   This approach focuses on transforming the existing curriculum within and across subject areas by "the infusion of various perspectives, frames of reference, and content from various groups that will extend students' understanding of the nature, development and complexity of U.S. society" (Banks, 1989, p. 203). In other words, the transformational approach involves restructuring the existing curriculum so that it routinely provides a variety of cultural perspectives.

Multicultural activities should be an ongoing part of social studies. *(© Marc W. Bernsau/The Image Works)*

Transforming the existing curriculum

A transformed curriculum should, in Bank's (1989) view, reflect the process of *multiple acculturation*. Instead of focusing simply on contributions per se, the "emphasis should be on how the common U.S. culture and society emerged from a complex synthesis and interaction of the diverse cultural elements that originated within the various cultural, racial, ethnic, and religious groups that make up U.S. society" (p. 161).

Social Action Approach.   This approach builds on the transformational approach by adding dimensions that ask students to make decisions and take appropriate actions in light of their decisions. Banks (1989) contends that traditional schooling often fosters political passivity and socializes students to accept existing ideologies and practices rather than helping them to become skilled participants in social change. As Banks states, "to participate effectively in democratic social change, students must be taught social criticism and must be helped to understand the inconsistency between our ideals and social realities, the work that must be done to close this gap, and how students can, as individuals and groups, influence the social and political systems in U.S. society" (p. 205).

Moving from knowledge to social action

Assessing Multicultural Activities

The four approaches to multicultural curriculum that Banks described reflect one way of looking at multicultural literacy. The key element in all of them involves the nature of culture itself.

The Cultural Pyramid.   Artifacts, relics, and foodstuffs are among the most visible and readily available aspects of a culture. At the same time, they are among

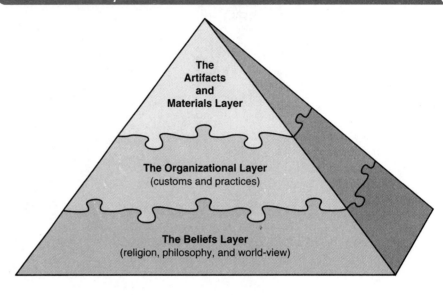

FIGURE 4.2 The Pyramid of Culture

The
Artifacts
and
Materials Layer

The Organizational Layer
(customs and practices)

The Beliefs Layer
(religion, philosophy, and world-view)

● ●

The layers of culture

the *least* significant aspects of the total cultural mosaic. Figure 4.2 shows that the basis of every culture rests in its fundamental beliefs and attitudes—in its cosmology or world-view. A second component is reflected by the way the culture has organized itself—the organizational layer—and by the customs and practices the culture follows. Those customs and practices usually reflect the group's underlying beliefs. At the top of the cultural pyramid are the materials and artifacts the culture uses, including the foods it considers suitable for consumption.

Consider, for example, that Jews who follow the kosher tradition do not serve meat and dairy products on the same dish. This practice reflects the organizational layer—the middle layer—of the cultural pyramid. The reason for serving meat and dairy products separately is rooted in the Jewish faith, in the belief layer of culture. Because of their beliefs, kosher Jewish families have two sets of china and kitchen utensils, one used exclusively for dairy products and another for meat and other foods. The dishes themselves reflect the artifacts and materials layer of culture.

Establishing a cultural context

Considered in isolation, the two sets of china in kosher Jewish families or the practice of serving meat and dairy products separately may seem nothing more than quaint customs or cultural oddities. The same would be true of the Amish's refusal to use electrically powered appliances or to drive automobiles. In any multicultural activity, it is essential that students understand how a culture's artifacts, customs, and practices are related to the underlying basis in belief. If those relationships and connections are *not* made, children could easily regard unfamiliar groups as cultural eccentrics.

Multicultural Activities with Substance

Despite some questionable activities that are passed off as multicultural education, there are legitimate and educationally defensible ways to deal with some of them. For example, teachers who have their students build a tepee or models of other cultural artifacts must make certain that students clearly understand that they are re-creating historical or cultural events, and imperfectly at that. For food-related activities, recognize that in many cultures the preparation and presentation of food is often more important than eating. For tortillas or Indian corn bread, for example, let students experience what it is like to grind the corn into flour—as some people in Mexico and some Native Americans still do today. Be advised, however, that grinding corn by hand is boring and tedious; and it takes a long time to grind enough corn to make a single tortilla. Students may become frustrated at their lack of progress, but with that frustration may come a new appreciation of what some people must do to obtain food.

More than meets the eye

Likewise, instead of serving canned spaghetti, consider having your students make spaghetti from scratch, as many Italian-Americans do. All it requires is some flour, an egg, and a little water kneaded together on a clean surface, like a clean desktop. No bowls or utensils are needed except for a rolling pin, a knife to cut the dough into thin strips, and a large pot of water in which to cook it. (Note that homemade spaghetti is flat, not round like the commercially prepared product.) While their pasta is drying, one group of students can research the recipe and then prepare a tomato-based sauce characteristic of southern Italy. Another group can research and make a clear or cream-based sauce like those served in northern Italy. In this activity, cookbooks—the Time-Life series is wonderful for this—can become reference books. There is a world of difference between what children can learn from the spaghetti activity described here, and what they can learn from heating and eating canned spaghetti.

Include resesarch

Food-related activities is an area that has a high potential for abuse. The rule of thumb should be: if you wish to use food-related multicultural activities, do them in educationally defensible ways. If that takes too much time—and such activities can require lots of classroom time—then don't do them at all. Multicultural education clearly demands unusual sensitivity to and respect for the peoples of all cultures.

Respecting Religious Diversity

Some public school teachers mistakenly believe that they cannot mention religion in their classrooms. If that were the case, it would be impossible to teach about any of the world 's religions—Islam, Hinduism, Buddhism, and so forth. Not only have the courts sustained teachers' (and schools') rights to teach *about* religion, but they have also indicated that information about religion is necessary to a good education. This means that you could do an in-depth analysis of Christian and non-Christian religions if you wished to, as long as it is relevant to the course of study. It also means that teaching about religion should be handled as objectively as possible, and without any suggestion that teachers are attempting to sway their students' beliefs.

Teaching religion vs. teaching <u>about</u> *religion*

You may recall that because of their religious beliefs, the parents of two students in Mary Jane Blanchard's class had requested that their children be excused from Halloween activities involving witches and goblins. In addition, Melissa's parents had requested that she be excused from saying the Pledge of Allegiance during morning exercises. In both instances, the underlying issue involves the parents' and children's rights to the free exercise of their religious beliefs under the First Amendment.

Respecting First
Amendment Rights

How did Mary Jane Blanchard handle the parental requests? In the case of Halloween observations, the school board had previously passed a policy banning black cats, witches, and symbols of the occult from all school-based activities, in-

---

COMMENTARY **The Scope of Diversity**

Among the myths in education is the notion that diversity occurs only in classrooms inhabited mainly by African-Americans. However, plenty of diversity exists in suburbia too.

When I first accepted the offer to teach sixth grade in the Quaker Ridge School in Scarsdale, New York—one of the wealthiest school districts in the country—I could not help but think what a delight it would be to teach those "smart little rich kids." I had from twenty-seven to thirty-six students in the classes I had taught previously in rural Ohio, but in Scarsdale, my largest class had nineteen students and the smallest, nine. This, I thought, was going to be a teacher's dream.

You can probably see where this is leading. It wasn't long into the school year before I found that some of my preconceived notions were incorrect. The idea that these students were "smart little rich kids" was one of the first to fall by the wayside. None of my children's parents were on welfare, and the free lunch program was nonexistent. However, I soon discovered that in wealthy communities like Scarsdale, many parents send their children to private schools. Although most of my students lived in comfortable homes, almost half of them were the children of housekeepers, chauffeurs, maids, and cooks and were often restricted to cramped "help's quarters" within the larger homes. Even though many of my students came from the higher end of the economic spectrum, an almost equal number came from the lower end; there were few middle-class students, economically speaking. In addition, and even though most of my students didn't need to worry where their next meal was coming from, they were neither smarter nor any less intelligent than the students I had taught previously.

In three years of teaching in rural Ohio, I had not encountered an African-American or an Asian-American student. This was not the case in Scarsdale. Three African-American students and four Asian-American students were among that sea of fifty or so shining faces I saw each day. One African-American student whom I especially remember was Clarence, whose parents were both prominent physicians. Clarence was among the brightest students I have ever encountered, but homework was a lost cause with him; he didn't think he needed it, and based on his performance without it, I eventually agreed.

My four Asian-American students performed as the stereotype says they will: they worked harder and more conscientiously than most of the other students that I dealt with that year. At one point I asked one of them if she ever relaxed, but her blank look suggested that I didn't understand her cultural mores.

Yet another incident indicated how provincial my perspective on diversity had been. While teaching in Ohio, I had the unenviable task of organizing the school's assemblies. We sang patriotic songs at Thanksgiving, Christmas carols at Christmas, and so forth. Upon moving to Scarsdale, I made the mistake of mentioning my prior experience handling assemblies, and they once again became my responsibility. The Thanksgiving program went as well as such programs usually do, but when I sat down with the music teacher (and pianist) to select the carols for the Christmas program, I was informed that (1) we were planning a "Winter Holiday Program," and (2) my old list of carols—which included "Oh Come All Ye Faithful" and the like—would be inappropriate in a largely Jewish community. We quickly discarded the religious carols and sang "Winter Wonderland" and "Santa Claus Is Coming to Town" instead. However, this incident caused me to reflect on how many non-Christian families in Ohio I may have unintentionally offended.

Every classroom and school reflects diversity, even when you may not expect it (or should know better).

cluding Halloween. Such policies are often extensions of actions originally intended to curb gang-related activities. In any event, the Board policy effectively eliminated both the activities in question and the need to excuse Amy and Melissa; Ms. Blanchard adjusted activities for her entire class accordingly. More and more schools are adopting similar policies, but in schools that do not have them, honoring the parent's request is recommended. For other matters, especially attempts to censor certain books, most schools have established procedures for determining whether the protested content or activities serve an overriding and compelling educational purpose.

Investigate existing procedures

At one level, the request to excuse Melissa from saying the Pledge of Allegiance became a kind of nonissue. Over fifty years ago the Supreme Court ruled that students cannot be compelled to say the Pledge of Allegiance. But for questions about whether teachers can ask students to stand during the Pledge (even if they do not say it)—where standing can be regarded as a means for honoring something—or whether teachers can permit the student to leave the classroom during the Pledge, the answer is: it depends. The Supreme Court has not ruled on either question, but many federal circuit and state courts have. The problem, according to our school law specialists, is that the various courts have not ruled consistently one way or the other. This effectively means that what is or is not legal depends on the rulings (or absence of rulings or local policies) in the legal jurisdiction where you teach.

Court rulings

Excusing Melissa from saying the Pledge was problematic for Ms. Blanchard in the sense that she pondered long about how she would present Melissa's nonparticipation to the rest of the class. She finally decided to tell them "The Pledge of Allegiance is a way of showing our respect for the flag and what it stands for, but some people's religious beliefs—like Melissa's—do not permit them to say the Pledge. We are going to respect Melissa's beliefs too." It turned out that what Mary Jane had worried about was a bigger problem for her than for her students. Melissa stood for the Pledge without being asked to, but she did not speak the words. For Melissa's classmates, this procedure had been going on since they were in kindergarten and was nothing out of the ordinary.

Respecting cultural diversity

The basic requirement for dealing with the ethnic, religious, and cultural diversity in classrooms today is a healthy respect for each individual's heritage, including the teacher's, and for the deeply held beliefs associated with that heritage. For those of us who teach, diversity in all of its forms demands that we demonstrate an honest and supportive sensitivity to what individuals bring with them to the classroom.

SUMMARY

Four factors have contributed to the phenomenal diversity in classrooms today: (1) desegregation, (2) increased immigration, (3) rapidly growing minority populations, and (4) growing recognition of the ethnicity of students who were in classrooms all along. Of these factors, the end of segregation has two dimensions; the first dimension involves ending the practice of segregating schools along racial lines, and the other involves removing students with handicapping conditions from separate classrooms and returning them to the mainstream of public education—regular classrooms.

This chapter has focused primarily on cultural and ethnic diversity. Children from the various cultures that make up the American mosaic often bring with them different and sometimes unique ways for addressing common situations. As a consequence, some children avoid looking adults in the eye when they are talking to them; to do otherwise would be considered disrespectful. Likewise, children from some cultures avoid asking (and sometimes answering) a teacher's questions so as not to be what, in their culture, would be considered rude. The idea that schools should act as melting pots that will eradicate cultural practices so as to "Americanize" children has fallen into disfavor, but traces of it still exist. For example, suggesting to a child that "we do it differently here" can be interpreted in different ways. The key is the teacher's implicit message, which, admittedly, is not easy to determine out of context. Is the teacher's real message, "Don't do that anymore," or is it "I'm just telling you this so you know there's another way you could do that"? One statement is obviously a put-down, and the other is intended for the child's information, and most children are skilled enough observers of human behavior to recognize the difference between the two.

This chapter also focused on forms of racism and sexism that are perpetuated in the media and educational materials. The popular media has broadened its once narrowly defined definition of "hero" to (occasionally) include individuals other than handsome, white males, but the classic tales that parents and teachers read to children often con-tain a healthy dose of racial and/or sex-role stereotyping. Parents who read stories to their children at bedtime are at a disadvantage, because they cannot engage in a discussion with their sleeping child about whether people who, for example, build their houses of sticks or straw are less worthy than people who build their homes from bricks. Most teachers don't face those limitations and are probably remiss if they permit such blatant stereotyping to go without comment. People should not "ruin a classic story with excessive analysis," of course, but neither should a teacher perpetuate cultural, racial, or sexist myths by saying nothing about them. This is not an "all or nothing" matter, but rather one of assessing whether the perspectives depicted in classic tales correspond with the prevailing views in contemporary society.

Multicultural education has become the major means for recognizing the multiple cultures and ethnicities that exist in almost every classroom. Multicultural education is a multifaceted effort aimed primarily at helping all children, regardless of ethnicity, gender, disabilities, or social class, to understand and appreciate events and people from various points of view.

SUGGESTED ACTIVITIES

1. Design a poster or bulletin board that uses a metaphor to describe our multicultural society. Consider pizza as a possibility, but do not restrict yourself to food-related products. Then determine in what respects your description might be distorted.

2. Determine which of the following statements best describes the U.S. culture: (1) The whole is greater than the sum of its parts. (2) The whole is equal to the sum of its parts. (3) There is no whole, just parts. Support your evidence with reasons and examples.

3. The need for teachers to respond to diversity in their classrooms has received much attention, but there is growing concern that this emphasis may be too one-sided. Don't teachers have personal rights that should be acknowledged and respected just as much as the rights of their students? Should teachers who do not wish to celebrate holidays be forced to do so anyhow? And what about teachers who do not wish to say the Pledge? What kind of role model are they presenting to students? Either individually or in small groups, establish a clear position on these questions, giving reasons and examples for support.

4. Obtain a fifth-grade social studies text. Using the index entries for "Native Americans" and one other identifiable ethnic group as a guide, assess the overall balance of the way the two groups are treated. Support your claim with evidence from the text.

5. Lisa Delpit, in *Other People's Children,* describes an activity designed to show how difficult it is to change one's existing speech patterns. Try teaching someone a new dialect in which the consonant cluster "di" is added in front of every English word. Be advised that this is "Dimuch diharder dithan diit dilooks."

SUGGESTED READINGS AND RESOURCES

Print Resources

GENERAL RESOURCES

Bill Bigelow, L. Christensen, L, S. Karp, B. Miner, & B. Petersen. (1994). *Rethinking our classrooms: Teaching for equity and justice.* Milwaukee: Rethinking Schools. The title of this thought-provoking collection of articles and teaching activities says it all. Developed by a group of teachers from Milwaukee (WI), this volume also includes contributions from noted authorities in the field. Excellent.

MULTICULTURAL EDUCATION

James A. Banks. (1997). *Educating citizens in a multicultural society.* New York: Teachers College Press. This paperback reflects Banks's latest contribution to the multicultural education literature and directs special attention to the relationship between multicultural education and citizenship education.

Eugene Garcia. (1994). *Understanding and meeting the challenge of student cultural diversity.* Boston: Houghton Mifflin. This book provides excellent treatments of the different types of diversity in classrooms today and ways in which teachers can respond appropriately to them.

Enid Lee, Deborah Menkart, & Margo Okazawa-Rey (Eds.). (1998). *Beyond heroes and holidays: A practical guide to K–12 anti-racist, multicultural education, and staff development.* Washington, DC: Network Educators on the Americas. This is an excellent collection of articles by a remarkable range of authors.

Nancy Schniedewind & Ellen Davidson. (1998). *Open minds to equality: A sourcebook of learning activities to affirm diversity and promote equity* (2nd ed). Boston: Allyn & Bacon. This excellent and wide-ranging collection includes brief background materials and a variety of learning activities, many of which are ready for duplication.

WOMEN'S HISTORY/GENDER-EQUITY

Not all of the books listed here are intended for young children, but all of them provide an inclusive history. They include:

Joy Hakim. (1999). A *history of US.* New York: Oxford University Press Children's Books, ten volumes.

Christine Lunardini. (1994). *What every American should know about women's history.* Holbrook, MA: Bob Adams.

Wilma Mankiller, Gwendolyn Mink, Marysa Navarro, Barbara Smith, & Gloria Steinem (Eds.). (1998). *The reader's companion to U.S. women's history.* Boston, MA: Houghton Mifflin.

Howard Zinn. (1995). *A people's history of the United States: 1492 to the present.* New York: Harper Perennial Library.

_____. (1998). *The twentieth century: A people's history.* New York: Harper Perennial Library.

GENDER EQUITY LESSON MATERIALS

Oceans of options: Sex equity lessons for the classroom. Far West Laboratory for Educational Research and Development, 1855 Folsom St., San Francisco, CA 94103. This is an interesting collection of sample lessons.

Internet Resources

Introductory Note: Web sites sometimes change their Internet addresses or cease operating entirely. All the addresses supplied here were operating when this book was printed, but if any of them fails to work properly, enter the name of the target organization in any standard search engine.

MULTICULTURAL/ETHNIC INTERNET RESOURCES

National Association for Multicultural Education

http://www.inform.umd.edu/NAME/index/natoffice.html

This site is maintained by the National Association for Multicultural Education and includes references to multicultural reference materials, promising classroom practices, and sources of teaching materials.

Multicultural Education Resources

http://gilligan.esu7.k12.ne.us/~esu7web/resources/multi.html

This highly recommended site is maintained by Nebraska's Educational Service 7 and includes links and information on almost every topic related to multicultural education—diversity, ethnicities, immigration, and so on. This site also has listings for individual ethic groups, such as Russians, French, Hawaiians, and so on.

The Resource Center of the Americas

http: www.americas.org

This organization focuses on creating innovative curricula that build bridges between people throughout the Americas. It also offers a lending library of thousands of books, periodicals, and videos. Periodic E-mail updates of new resources can be found at **bookstore@americas.org.**

Resources for Afro-American History

http://www.libraries.rutgers.edu/rulib/socsci/hist/afrores.html

This site provides extensive listings of resources related to African-Americans.

GENDER EQUITY–RELATED INTERNET RESOURCES

Upper Midwest Women's History Center

http://www.hamline.edu/~umwhc/

This site focuses primarily on ways to incorporate women's history into school programs.

Women's Studies

http://www.library.upenn.edu/resources/interdiscipline/gender/women/women.html

This site provides links to women's issues in history, music, religion, African-American studies, and numerous others.

http://www.hist.unt.edu/09w-amm6.htm

This site offers an extensive collection of links related to women's studies, including resources, guides and programs, history, great women, and women in the professions.

Answers to Cultural Awareness Activity

1. f His most well-known novel is *Native Son*.
2. d The college was called the Daytona Educational and Industrial School; it was for African-American girls.
3. e Best-known book is *Occupied America*.
4. j She was a representative from Hawaii; the only Asian-American woman to serve in Congress.
5. c (No answer provided in original.)
6. i Helped organize the grape boycott with Cesar Chavez.
7. g Fought state and federal authorities for land grants to Hispanics, which were legally protected by the Treaty of Guadalupe.
8. a Best known for his book, *Before the Mayflower*.
9. b Publishes widely in both scholarly and popular literature, such as *Ebony*.
10. h Former Japanese-American internment camp prisoner who has published numerous stories.

5

The Dimensions of Instructional Diversity

Key Questions

* What is instructional diversity?
* How do physical and emotional disabilities influence instruction?
* How do teachers adapt instruction to meet individual needs and still keep their sanity?
* What is learning style, and how does it affect the ways in which students learn?

Key Ideas

* Instructional diversity includes academic and linguistic diversity, and students with physical and emotional disabilities.
* Academic diversity includes students working below grade level in one or more subject areas, and gifted students.
* Linguistic diversity is often reflected in students for whom English is a second language.
* Various strategies can be used to tailor instruction to meet students' needs.

Introduction: On "Falling through the Cracks"

DIVERSITY

In the not too distant past, when schooling was a "one-size-fits-all" enterprise, some students invariably "fell through the cracks." Sometimes they failed in certain subjects, sometimes they got poor grades or had work habits that left a lot to be desired, and sometimes they just had problems learning. Some of those kids dropped out of school as soon as they could; some still do. You can almost bet that many students who "fell through the cracks" were at least a half-grade level or more behind in reading. And some of them may have been auditory learners who rely heavily on listening, as opposed to more visually oriented learners—which includes most teachers—who rely on how things look.

125

For a quick test of your learning preference, think about how you deal with situations when you are writing something and encounter a word that you are not sure how to spell. Using the dictionary is always an option, of course, but after ten minutes looking up *pneumonia* under the letter "N," you may turn to another strategy. Do you (1) sound out the word and go with the result, (2) change to a different word that you know how to spell, or (3) write the word three different ways and then pick the one that "looks right"? Auditory (hearing-oriented) learners are more likely to use techniques 1 and 2, whereas visual learners often rely on technique 3. Because auditory learners may lack an accurate visual image of words, they often encounter problems with words containing silent letters (like *pneumonia*) and words like *nickel* and *pickle,* where there are no sound cues as to whether the word ends with "el" or "le." But then, even ardent visual learners are not above using technique 2—changing to a different word—especially if the teacher or reader has a "thing" about spelling.

It is also likely that some students who "fell through the cracks" were nonnative speakers of English, usually known as English as a Second Language (ESL) students. It is not the students' fault that they were born into families where the native language is Spanish, Vietnamese, Laotian, or any of hundreds of others. Likewise, there's no question that ESL students must become proficient in English. The problem for most ESL students is making the transition to English, and the insensitivity they occasionally encounter along the way.

State-mandated competency testing has put students who might otherwise have fallen through the cracks into a different light. In almost every state the focus is on how *all* students perform, not just those who have traditionally done well. Under clearly defined circumstances, some students can be exempted from state-mandated tests, but the process typically involves more paperwork than you would believe—paperwork designed to prevent students from slipping through the system untested. This means that making provisions for ESL students or other students who are experiencing problems has become significantly more important than was true in the past. Even small groups of low-performing students can affect a school's overall performance rating, which can bring with it unwanted and unfavorable publicity. The point is that state-mandated tests seldom permit the kind of selective testing that schools might use to conceal the performance of students who, in the past, might have slipped by unnoticed.

A second related point is that the practice of shipping students with disabilities to special education classrooms was limited even before competency testing became as popular as it is today. As noted in Chapter 4, the Individuals with Disabilities Education Act of 1990 reduced the number of physically and educationally disabled students who were formerly segregated into separate, often special education, classrooms (Turnbull, Turnbull, Shank, & Leal, 1999). The *least restrictive environment* provision of that legislation permits students to be placed in special education classrooms full time only if their needs cannot be met in either (1) a regular classroom or (2) a regular classroom combined with a program of special services (what are known as pull-out programs).

The overarching point is that two elements—mandated competency testing, combined with the disabilities legislation—have had profound effects on what it means to be a "regular" classroom teacher. Every teacher must be able to adjust his or her instruction to accommodate the needs of educationally diverse students.

How do you learn best?

Non-English speakers

State-mandated testing closes some of the "cracks"

Emphasis on inclusion

Classroom Profile, Part Two

DIVERSITY

The previous chapter provided a preliminary profile of the students in Mary Jane Blanchard's fourth-grade class at Roscoe Hunt Elementary. We revisit the same classroom in this chapter but focus primarily on educationally diverse students. The students whose diversity falls within the scope of this chapter include:

Instructional diversity

★ Five students—Tyrone, Trisha, Jesus, Miguel, and Maria—whose reading skills are *at least* one-half year below grade level; all of them spend a part of each day in the Resource Room, where they receive special tutoring in academic skills. Two of these students, Trisha and Miguel, have difficulty remembering what they read but can remember—almost verbatim—things that they hear.

Gifted and talented

★ Six students—Juan, LaShawna, Melissa, Gina, Richard, and Chen Lee—who have reading, math, and language skills that are at the sixth-grade level or above. LaShawna, Chen Lee, and Richard are considered gifted.

★ Three students—Tyrone, Richard, and Christi—who have illegible handwriting, despite all of Ms. Blanchard's efforts otherwise.

★ Three students—Jesus, Miguel, and Maria—who come from homes where Spanish is the dominant language.

★ One student, Trang, who spoke no English at the beginning of the year (and no one in the school spoke Vietnamese). With voluntary assistance from several classmates, Trang now speaks passable English and in just four months has made remarkable progress.

Emotional considerations

★ One student, Heather, is a girl with apparently normal intelligence and physical development. Heather can do fourth-grade work but apparently prefers not to. Instead, she spends her day huddled in her seat with her coat pulled over her head, almost as if she is withdrawing from the world. Heather will answer direct questions from Ms. Blanchard, but her responses are monosyllabic and barely audible; she will not look at the teacher, even when asked to do so. Heather has not uttered a complete sentence all year and avoids interacting with other students as much as possible. Heather has no real friends in the class, but neither does she have any enemies. The other students are patiently tolerant of Heather, and some are almost protective of her.

Need for structure

★ One gifted student, Chen Lee, is an extremely hard worker who places extraordinary emphasis on memorization. In math, for example, she memorizes the answers *and* the problems. Chen Lee also has "high structure needs"; that is, she has difficulty dealing with independent problem solving and unstructured or open-ended activities. Chen Lee often became frustrated when Ms. Blanchard gave topical assignments, such as "read the next section in the text." This is no longer the problem it was, because to accommodate Chen Lee's need for structure, Mary Jane now provides page numbers for all assignments.

★ One student, James, who has muscular dystrophy and is confined to a wheelchair. The school district provides a full-time aide who assists James and helps him get from place to place. Because James is unable to write, he dictates all written assignments to his aide.

★ Another student, Jason, who takes the drug Ritalin to calm his hyperactivity. The difference between Jason's pre-Ritalin behavior and his behavior today is like night and day. Jason's parents have given Mary Jane permission to administer Jason's midday dose of Ritalin; in fact, they have asked that he take it at 11:30 sharp, so that he will be ready for his evening dose when he gets home from school. Both Jason and Ms. Blanchard sometimes get involved in activities and forget about Jason's medication schedule, but Richard has volunteered to remind them.

★ Another student, Gina, a Type 1 (early onset) diabetic. Gina wears an insulin pump and usually manages her condition without assistance. However, about once every six weeks, her blood glucose level gets too low and she slips into a diabetic coma. If this occurs on one of the three days a week when the school nurse is at Roscoe Hunt, she will administer a potentially life-saving glucose injection. If coma occurs when the nurse is not present, Ms. Blanchard administers the injection.

★ Finally there is Tyrone, a student whose disabling condition is apparently of his own choosing. When Tyrone returned from a two-month visit to his aunt, Ms. Blanchard greeted his return with mixed feelings. So did Tyrone. He begged his mother to let him attend another school, and Ms. Blanchard suggested the possibility in a parent-teacher conference. But Tyrone's mother was adamant. She told him, "You started the year at Roscoe Hunt and you're gonna to finish here, so quit complainin'." Tyrone has problems with reading and handwriting, but something about his relationship with Ms. Blanchard has apparently "turned him off." Ms. Blanchard is at a loss to explain it. It's not that Tyrone cannot learn, because he can be very articulate when he wants to be, but he has apparently decided that he won't learn from Ms. Blanchard. Sometimes he just sits there, staring at Ms. Blanchard defiantly, almost daring her to teach him. As Ms. Blanchard says, "I've had lots of students who had learning problems—who couldn't learn—but I've never dealt with students who've decided they won't learn. We are at odds, and I'm not sure I know what to do."

We'll examine each of these students in the balance of this chapter.

Responding to Physical and Emotional Diversity

Mary Jane Blanchard does not have sight- or hearing-impaired students in her class this year, but if she did, there are some no-cost, commonsense things that she could do to make life easier for them. These include things like seating sight- and hearing-impaired students toward the front of the classroom. Ms. Blanchard also offered James, the wheelchair-bound student, a seat near the door; that way he wouldn't have to thread his way through a roundabout route to reach his desk. However, James felt that his aide would be distracting to the rest of the class if they were in the front of the room, so he opted for a seat near the rear. Based on James's decision, Ms. Blanchard now keeps an extra-wide aisle on one side of the room. Such seemingly minor accommodations can have important consequences for children with physical impairments.

Diversity is the norm in most classrooms today.
(© Evan Johnson)

Once you move beyond simple, no-cost accommodations, making provisions for students with physical impairments typically requires additional funding, which necessarily means some form of administrative involvement. A key element for children with physical disabilities—although not those with emotional disabilities—lies **Removing barriers** in removing the barriers that hinder their physical access to buildings, classrooms, and other ancillary services. Stairways, drinking fountains, and rest room facilities can still pose problems for children with physically disabling conditions, but most schools have already modified their facilities to accommodate them.

● Emotional Impairments

When we talked with Ms. Blanchard about Heather, the student with the (apparent) emotionally disabling condition who we described earlier, Mary Jane said, "I just didn't know what to do about Heather. At first I tried creating some special assignments for her—really interesting activities, you know—but she still just sat there with her coat pulled over her head. I got so frustrated that I finally called **Seeking help** the school district's Diagnostic and Counseling Center. They came out and observed her and agreed they would work with her for an hour every week. After three weeks, nothing had changed, so I complained again. Then the counselors began working with her for an hour every day, but there was still no change in her behavior. We were finally able to obtain some medical testing, which indicated that Heather had a chemical imbalance that had caused a form of depression. It took a while for them to get her medications adjusted correctly, but today she acts like a perfectly normal fourth grader."

Helping students with emotionally disabling conditions (including, in Heather's case, an underlying medical problem) is often difficult, in part because

Not long ago, over five hundred staff members—including the teachers, administrators, clerical and custodial personnel, and school bus drivers—in a 28,000-student school district in Virginia were trained to administer glucose injections to students like Gina, the diabetic student from Ms. Blanchard's class. In other instances, teachers may find themselves responsible for performing urinary catheterizations, suctioning a child's trachea, or feeding a student through a stomach tube (Temple, 2000). Not all these situations occur in every class, of course, and in reality they represent only a tiny fraction of the students that teachers encounter during a year. Nevertheless, being responsible for performing such medical procedures can seem a little daunting. Nowhere in our training did anyone suggest that we would be responsible for suctioning a child's tracheotomy tube, for example, nor were we trained how to do it.

Both the National Education Association and the American Federation of Teachers strongly oppose holding teachers responsible for tending to students' health needs. On the other hand, parents of children with physical infirmities typically claim that their child's disability is a 24-hour-a-day condition, not something that ends when they enter a classroom. To make their point, a growing number of parents (and the courts) are invoking the provisions of some fairly old, federal legislation—the 1977 Individuals with Disabilities Education Act (IDEA), and the Vocational Rehabilitation Act of 1973, which prohibit discrimination against the disabled in any federally funded programs. In most instances, the courts seem to have supported the parents' position.

Determining who should perform medically related procedures is a matter of dispute in some areas. Asking teachers to assume responsibility for such tasks is, for the school district at least, a no-cost option. Whether there is an emotional cost to the teachers who assume those responsibilities is another matter, of course. Some school districts have banned teachers from such health-related tasks and have hired nurses and aides to tend to children with health-related disabilities. Unfortunately, this seemingly obvious solution is complicated by several factors, not the least of which is the serious shortage of nurses in most parts of the country (Temple, 2000). When you combine this with the fact that the salaries for nurses working in hospitals or private practice can equal or exceed a principal's salary, whereas school district salaries are typically one-third to one-half of what nurses could earn elsewhere, you see other dimensions of the problem.

It is politically expedient for most school districts to keep their tax rates as low as possible. Yet despite this I believe they should (1) offer and pay for appropriate training for whatever medical procedures teachers may be required to perform, *and* (2) provide liability insurance for teachers who are asked to accept such responsibilities. Dealing with serious medical conditions is not something most teachers were trained to do. Consider also that some school boards pay for a superintendent's professional liability insurance (or increase their salary accordingly), for what are seldom life-and-death matters. Thus it seems reasonable and just for school boards to indemnify teachers for what could really become life-or-death matters.

few teachers have the training needed to cope with severe emotional disabilities. Once Heather was properly diagnosed, her disability responded quickly to treatment. But the outlook is not so optimistic (or quick) for students with purely emotional disorders. These situations can become more complicated if the children's

Troubling problems problems are caused by child abuse or, more commonly and seemingly less offensive, a divorce in the family. Not all learning disabilities result from abuse, emotional problems, or divorce, of course, but sudden changes in academic performance are often symptoms of underlying emotional (or sometimes physical) problems. Because there are so few instructional options that a teacher can use, the key lies in identifying and orchestrating school and community support services that can deal with emotional disabilities, as Ms. Blanchard did for Heather.

Also, when you encounter children with emotional disabilities, you will undoubtedly be reminded of how complex and fragile our emotions really are.

Accommodating Educational Diversity

Diversity that can be expected

You are almost certain to encounter students, like those in Mary Jane Blanchard's class, who are *at least* one-half year below grade level, or who have difficulty remembering what they read but can remember almost everything they hear. You may also have students who excel academically and are considered gifted, but who quickly become bored with routine schoolwork. You are just as likely to have one or more students who have "high structure needs," and thus have difficulty dealing with independent problem solving and unstructured or open-ended activities. You are also likely to have students who abhor small-group work, and still others who thrive on it.

Educational diversity includes students, such as those just described, who have nonethnic and nonculturally related conditions or preferences that influence what and how they learn. These conditions can influence the kind of instruction a teacher offers, the form in which he or she offers that instruction, and the way in which students respond to it.

The Learning Disabled (LD)

Responding to students with learning disabilities

Learning Outside the Lines (2000) is a remarkable book by two remarkable authors, Jonathon Mooney and David Cole. Mooney was diagnosed as learning disabled in elementary school, didn't learn to read until he was twelve, still can't spell, and dropped out of school for a while when he was in the sixth grade. Mooney recently graduated magna cum laude from Brown University with a degree in English literature. David Cole, also a recent honors graduate from Brown, was diagnosed with attention deficit hyperactivity disorder (ADHD) in first grade and was taking the drug Ritalin before he entered second grade. Cole took himself off Ritalin when he was an adolescent, because he didn't like the way it made him feel, but he resumed the drug regimen when he entered Brown and continues it still.

Students who don't "fit" the system

Much of *Learning Outside the Lines* focuses on the anguish that Mooney and Cole experienced in school. Their problems, and those of learning disabled students elsewhere, may result at least in part from the fact that they don't "fit" the system. It is not a matter of conscious rebelliousness or desire to "do their own thing;" they just could not accommodate the system. Jonathon Mooney, for example, spent most of second grade sitting in the hallway for disrupting class. By third grade, Mooney's inability to read had become almost unbearable, and he spent countless hours wondering "what's wrong with me." Mooney claims that he was so angry and ashamed, he could taste the stomach acid come up into his throat. He even imagined killing the teacher, and also learned to hide in the bathroom to escape reading out loud.

According to Mooney, a psychological turning point occurred when his mother read him *Leo the Late Bloomer* (Kraus, 1998), a story about a lion who couldn't read. After hearing about Leo, Jonathon was more willing to accept the fact that he was not a "weird klutz." Nevertheless, his writing and spelling were atrocious, and even in Grade 3, he did not have the ability to look at words to determine what they meant. His teachers tried to be helpful, but they couldn't seem to find the right words or examples. For example, Mooney's teachers would often urge him to "focus on the words," but he had no idea what "focus" meant or how to do it. It's the kind of situation that students face when teachers talk in generalities, such as "you need to improve your work," but the student has no idea where to begin to do that. In addition, and because Mooney was unable to read, he had no idea what the symbols represented nor could he decipher which words were spelled correctly. Jonathon sometimes erupted in fits of temper, and his teachers occasionally (and understandably) responded in a similar fashion—"Here I am trying to help you, and you 'blow your top' at me." Jonathon was frustrated and so were his teachers. So, where would you as a teacher go from here?

Frustration all around

Learning disabled students are often bright and otherwise capable individuals. For example, David Cole's IQ was so high that despite his disability he was permitted to skip grades. In some instances, LD students can excel athletically, and most of them get along well socially, as long as they, like Jonathan Mooney, can cope with their feelings of inadequacy. In most instances, LD students would love to read and spell well, but no matter how hard they try they just can't. Such ongoing academic problems can lead to what Thomas (2000) calls "chronic success deprivation." Thomas suggests that most of us need to be successful at something—no matter how small or insignificant—and that ongoing failures can lead to the feelings of despondency and desperation that Mooney described earlier. Data from the U.S. Department of Education (1996–97) indicate that almost 50 percent of the adolescents in detention facilities have been diagnosed with moderate to severe learning disabilities. Both Mooney and Cole followed this pattern. Mooney was sent to a detox center after several drug-related arrests, and Cole spent most of his high school years in detention.

Coping with feelings of inadequacy

Students with learning disabilities can often cope successfully after they leave school, despite their inadequacies in certain academic areas. The literature is filled with examples of people—like Charles Schwab, the stock broker, and John Chambers, the CEO of high-tech Cisco Systems—both of whom have severe learning disabilities, and both of whom are multimillionaires today. As a footnote here, the mission statement for Cisco Systems, a multibillion-dollar corporation, is a hand-drawn sketch. This undoubtedly reflects the fact that writing is not one of John Chambers's strong suits, and that learning disabilities are not something you necessarily outgrow. Perhaps the ultimate irony is that the place where most LD students cannot succeed is in school.

Success despite the odds

Two issues that are almost always associated with LD students involve performance standards and the related issue of fairness. Here's how Jonathon Mooney describes one aspect of the problem. "I'd think 'I've got to write, but I can't spell, so they won't know what I'm trying to say.' So I dumb down my writing to not get busted on spelling. How stupid is that?" He remembers not the teachers in the resource room who tirelessly and unsuccessfully tried to teach him to spell, but the teachers who "bent" the rules to accommodate his disabilities—like the (few) teachers who said they wouldn't "count his spelling." Computer-based spelling checkers can sometimes help here, but even with such aids, the words in question need to be reasonably close.

Performance issues

The standards issue for LD students include questions such as: How important is it that every word be spelled correctly? And, how important is it that the paper be written? Would a report on tape be equally acceptable? The fairness issue arises if the answers to these questions are different for students who are not learning disabled—and if the LD students feel that things are being "dumbed down" just for them.

Accommodating LD students *can* be among the most heart-wrenching problems in teaching. Being stern and hard-nosed usually doesn't work, because most LD students really do try. Encouraging them to "try harder" seldom works, because they are often trying as hard as they can. Giving LD students poor grades usually doesn't work, because they've been that route before. What LD students really seem to need is success—just a tiny bit of success—to offset all the failures with which they are all too familiar. Working with LD students is clearly an area where there are no quick fixes.

● Willful Nonlearning: A Special Situation

Accommodating students who can learn but have chosen not to is among the more perplexing problems a teacher can face. Situations like the one described here, which are probably more common than you might imagine, often involve a clash of wills—the teacher's and the student's. It should also become evident that willful nonlearning can involve a potpourri of elements, including elements of cultural diversity, perceived racism, language skills, emotional diversity, instructional decision making, and in the final analysis, a heavy dose of stubbornness.

Tyrone—Mary Jane Blanchard's student (who we met earlier in this chapter) has decided that he will not learn from Mrs. Blanchard. However, asking his mother if he could transfer to another school suggests that he has not opted out of schooling altogether. The relevant question here is, What has turned Tyrone off?

Some background on Ms. Blanchard may be useful. Like most teachers, Ms. Blanchard is a kind, decent, and caring individual. She attended a largely white suburban school, where, because the school used homogenous grouping (where children with similar abilities were grouped together), the children from the few African-American and Hispanic families in the district tended to be assigned to the lower tracks. Assigning the preponderance of minority children to lower tracks continues to be a common situation in schools around the country. That practice also has been the object of criticisms that go well beyond the classroom (see Bigelow, 1994; Schwabe, 1994).

Throughout her public school experience, Mary Jane Blanchard was assigned to the "accelerated" or "college prep" tracks. As a result she had little meaningful interaction with minority students until she began teaching at Roscoe Hunt Elementary. Mary Jane was also raised in a home where standard English was the norm, and seldom makes errors in grammar, spelling, or pronunciation. Tyrone, on the other hand, has no standard for judging the correctness of Ms. Blanchard's English, because it is different from the language spoken in his home. According to Tyrone, "Ms. Blanchard talks like my mamma do when she talkin' to someone important on the phone." Tyrone continues: "Ms. Blanchard says we all gotta learn to speak an' write good English, but when I say somethin' she puts me down. I can't say three words but she's gonna correct two of 'em. So then I says,

Fairness

When strong wills clash

An aspect of tracking

Standards?

'Two can play dat game', an' I quit talkin'. But Ms. Blanchard she don't let me. She says I gotta talk. And when I talk, she put me down again. An' she looks at me kinda funny like."

Ms. Blanchard has a different perspective. She indicates that "What Tyrone says is basically true; I do insist that everyone write and speak good English in my class—it's the kids' key to success. My problem with Tyrone is his atrocious oral language. His written language isn't too bad—even though he has lots of spelling problems and his handwriting is so awful I can hardly read it—but how he talks really bugs me. When I correct him, he gives me hateful looks."

Another dilemma

With this information as background, how would you assess the situation? Is this an instance where Tyrone is being too sensitive? Or are Ms. Blanchard's expectations unreasonable? Ms. Blanchard obviously wants everyone to use standard English in her classroom, even though this seems to pose a problem for Tyrone. Would it be fair if Ms. Blanchard allowed Tyrone to use the oral language that he is familiar with but insisted that everyone else used "correct" English?

Standard English may be a "foreign language"

Consider that Tyrone's rejection of Ms. Blanchard results not from deep-seated feelings of animosity or racism on her part, but from a common assumption among people for whom standard English is essentially a native language. That assumption is based, in part, on the notion that "I learned to speak English correctly, you can too." Unfortunately, native speakers of standard English seldom realize how difficult it is for individuals to change their speech patterns to conform to standard English, a language form with which they have little or no experience. In other words, for American children who grew up speaking regional or ethnic dialects (sometimes both), standard English can be a "foreign" language.

Teachers' efforts to change a child's oral language can often carry with them the implicit notion that "how you speak at home (or wherever you learned to talk this way) is wrong." Regardless of how effectively and successfully the child has communicated in the past, the underlying message—that they need to change the way they speak—can be very disconcerting. This could be an instance where Ms. Blanchard's implicit message about "wrongness" may be more powerful than anything she says to the contrary.

Unintended consequences

If Tyrone had a model of standard English that he carried around in his head with him, it's doubtful that he (or Ms. Blanchard) would have a problem. But he does not. As a result, when Ms. Blanchard corrects Tyrone's speech, he doesn't necessarily understand why his speech pattern is "bad" and another one that he isn't familiar with is better. In other words, Ms. Blanchard's efforts seem to have created a situation where she is denigrating a language form that Tyrone has (a) used for years and (b) grown comfortable and been successful with (except in Ms. Blanchard's class). In other words, Ms. Blanchard may be threatening something that Tyrone holds near and dear. Herbert Kohl (1994) suggests that willful nonlearning tends to occur "when someone has to deal with unavoidable challenges to her or his personal and family loyalties, integrity, and identity" (p. 134).

There are no quick remedies for dealing with students like Tyrone, who are able to learn but have chosen not to. This situation is complicated by the fact that Ms. Blanchard thinks that she is (a) is not being unreasonable and (b) is acting in Tyrone's best interests. Ms. Blanchard could try pressuring Tyrone to change his attitude, but because a teacher cannot force someone to learn who chooses not to, Tyrone holds the power here. One option for Ms. Blanchard involves begging or pleading with Tyrone, but this (a) would tend to reinforce the power position that Tyrone already has and (b) is unlikely to address the root of the problem.

Ms. Blanchard must talk with Tyrone one-on-one, to be sure, but before she does that, she would be wise to rethink the situation and some of her expectations. The basic problem here seems to be Ms. Blanchard's insistence on standard English usage in both written and oral language. It is one thing to insist on standard English in written work, where because the writing process is slower than speaking, writers have the opportunity to consider different ways in which they could be saying something. But oral language is much more a spur-of-the-moment activity. As Hennings (1994) notes, continually correcting a student's oral language may eventually cause that student to stop talking entirely. In oral language situations, the speaker's main concern is getting her or his message across. Trying to force speakers to attend also to the *form* or correctness of their message immeasurably complicates the seemingly simple process of speaking.

Analysis. Ms. Blanchard probably needs to reflect on her standards, but under no circumstances should she accept everything that students wish to say in written or oral form. The classroom's ground rules for treating everyone with respect rule out both cursing and intentionally hurtful statements, either written or oral. But Ms. Blanchard's dilemma seems to stem not from the high standards for written communication in her classroom, but from her intolerance for nonstandard *oral* language forms. If Ms. Blanchard were willing to accept more variance in her student's oral language, she might have avoided the situation where she was seen as putting down the language spoken in her students' homes—even if that was not her intent. This situation reflects one of the realities of teaching: no matter how noble and pure their motives, most teachers cannot control how they are perceived by others, including their students.

──● Learning Style

Some people can't wait until someone quits talking so that they can read the instructions—whether they are making a cake or whatever. Others will say, "Don't bother me with that, just tell me how to do it." Another group of people will say, "Just let me do it." These examples reflect three preferred approaches to learning, or what is sometimes referred to by the generic term *learning style* (see Dunn & Dunn, 1992).

Learning style, in abbreviated form, refers to how people would prefer to learn about things. Some people, for example, prefer to learn through reading; others prefer to learn through listening; and still others prefer to learn by manipulating objects or materials. If you are a person who prefers to learn about something through reading—or what is sometimes called a "*visual* approach to learning"—you may be able to remember where words or pictures are located on a page. Given your preference, you may find yourself becoming impatient with people who repeatedly ask for expanded verbal explanations. On the other hand, people like Mary Jane Blanchard's students, Trisha and Miguel, very much prefer *auditory* explanation and instructions. Auditory learners often have difficulty remembering what they read, but they can sometimes recall verbal explanations with the same precision that visual learners remember where words are located on a page.

Do both parties need to give a little?

Accepting nonstandard language

Preferred approaches to learning

Lest it seem otherwise, education is not an ongoing battle between visual and auditory learners. The point here is to suggest that problems can arise when visually oriented teachers fail to provide the verbal explanations that sound-oriented learners rely on. As Ms. Blanchard says, "I sometimes explain stuff that seems obvious, but I know that at least some of my kids need that explanation." The fine line that teachers must determine, of course, is when they have explained something in enough depth to satisfy their auditory learners, but without boring their visual learners in the process.

Appealing to different styles

Manipulative learners include students who cannot wait until everyone quits talking or reading so they can get their hands on whatever they are expected to do. The use of manipulatives is an important component in some areas of teaching, especially mathematics education, but it is not simply because hands-on techniques appeal to manipulative learners. Manipulative materials often permit students—whether visual, auditory, or manipulative learners—to see what might otherwise be abstract concepts in more concrete terms. This means that instead of having to memorize that $2 + 2 = 4$, students can actually see that when you combine one set of 2 beans with another set of 2 beans, you will have a total of 4 beans.

Using nonverbal feedback from students

You will undoubtedly have a mixture of visual, auditory, and manipulative learners in your classroom. Thus, the fine line referred to earlier will most likely lie in appealing to different learning styles, but without going overboard on any one style so that it "turns off" the others. One key here lies in closely observing your students' nonverbal communication, especially their expressions. For example, after giving a long verbal explanation, your visual learners' eyes may have begun to glaze over. This is O.K. so long as it doesn't go on too long. However, if your manipulative learners' eyes also begin to glaze over, you face the prospect of losing the attention of two groups—the visual and manipulative learners. When this happens, you may wish to move quickly into the activity and provide extra assistance individually.

Observing patterns of responses

How do you know which of your students are visual, auditory, or manipulative learners? The key here is by observing their responses to different classroom situations. Students who open a textbook (not a novel) without being told to do so are likely to be visual learners. Students who ask you a million questions, and can't seem to begin an activity without precise instructions, are probably either auditory learners or students who need lots of personal attention (perhaps both). Then you will have students who don't seem to have a clear preference one way or another. That's because learning style is a preference, not a trait etched in granite. Actually, learning style is like people's feelings about broccoli; some people love it, some hate it, and others are indifferent to it. And like most preferences, learning style can vary by degrees. Some students have strong preferences for visual, auditory, or manipulative learning, whereas other students have no real preference and can take whatever comes. Note that a sample learning style inventory is presented in Part I of the Resource Handbook.

Accommodating students' preferred learning styles may make students feel more comfortable and satisfied, but this does not mean that learning style necessarily reflects the only way a child can learn. For example, auditory learners can learn using visual and manipulative approaches, even if that is not their preferred style. Good and Brophy (1999) also note that, "accommodating students' preferences is not the same as meeting their needs" (p. 349). Good and Brophy cite several studies that suggest that although tailoring instruction to students' preferences may improve their attitudes toward learning, it can also produce *less* achievement than teaching them in other ways. The implication here is that teachers should strive for teaching activities that appeal to a variety of learning style preferences as opposed to relying extensively on activities that appeal to only one learning style. In addition to their preferred learning styles, other factors can influence how a learner learns. These include:

Attitudes vs. performance

Factors that influence learning style

* Environmental factors, including studying with music playing, in complete silence, or somewhere in between
* Sociological factors, including working alone or in groups
* Emotional factors, such as working in open-ended or highly defined assignments
* Physiological factors, such as studying while standing, sitting, or lying on the floor
* Psychological factors, such as one's preference for visual, auditory, or manipulative sources

Need for Structure. A related aspect of learning style involves the extent to which students prefer open-ended activities, where they define most of the elements themselves, or—at the other end of the continuum—where they insist on having *everything* spelled out for them in advance. In this context, structure refers to how highly the teacher specifies or organizes a task in advance. Consider how you approached writing papers in the courses you have taken. Did you insist on precise instructions, perhaps including such things as the absolute minimum length of the paper, the number of footnotes, acceptable type fonts, the width of margins, and so on, or were you more willing "to go for it" until you met the assignment? You have too much experience to know that most students do not ignore factors that can play a role in grading, such as the number of references or proper font sizes, but you may also ask yourself, what is most important—the substance of the paper or its format? Such a question is unlikely to occur to students with high structure needs, because their main concern is with meeting the established expectations. They want to be certain that *everything* about their paper is within the guidelines. It may not matter that their paper says nothing, because they often hope to get a good grade simply because they met all the structural requirements. It is part of the "grading game" familiar to everyone in schools today.

Varying tolerances for ambiguity

An example of intolerance for ambiguity

An example of one student who faces the "structure" dilemma is Chen Lee, one of Mary Jane Blanchard's gifted students, who has "high structure needs." She is very uncomfortable in unstructured situations; she wants to know what task is to be done, exactly how that task should be done, when it must be done by, and in some instances, how to know when she is finished. Students like Chen Lee stand in contrast to students who have low structure needs, who can tolerate ambiguity in the tasks they are expected to do, and who often prefer to decide things for themselves.

Because you are likely to have both kinds of students in your classroom, two aspects about the need for structure are worth noting here. First, there appears to be no link between a child's need for structure and their intelligence (as need for structure is traditionally defined). This means that although Chen Lee is a gifted student, the same needs may appear among normal and low-ability students. A second aspect about the apparent need for "structure" is that it is a one-way relationship. Children with low structure needs may prefer open-ended and unstructured tasks, but they can also tolerate highly organized assignments, whereas students like Chen Lee are often frustrated with open-ended tasks. Therefore, if you are going to err, do so in favor of providing more structure, not less, to the tasks you assign.

You may also want to use your students' structure needs as a basis for creating groups. By putting students with high structure needs in one or two groups—which will be heterogeneous in terms of sex, ethnicity, and so on—you can provide them with the very specific guidance they feel they need, but without stifling the creativity of your other groups who are more comfortable making decisions among themselves.

Cooperative Learning

Cooperative learning is an approach to instruction in which students deal with learning tasks cooperatively, usually in small groups. The extended example in Chapter 1 of how Tarry Lindquist's class writes cooperative biographies reflects one teacher's approach to cooperative learning. In general, the teacher acts as a guide and consultant and other students serve as resources. Each individual is accountable for the group's effort, and all group members must learn the material in question. Typically, everyone in the group receives a common grade. In theory, students who goof off or don't contribute to the group's effort will be subjected to intense peer pressure, but in reality, some students willingly fade into the background and let others do all the work. The cumulative research findings (Johnson & Johnson, 1987) suggest that cooperative learning can lead to higher achievement, enhanced self-esteem, and improved attitudes toward teachers, other students, and school itself.

Cooperative learning provides an environment in which all students can contribute according to their abilities. However, cooperative learning necessitates some modifications in the competitive work ethic that has prevailed in classrooms for years. In its simplest form, the work ethic is based on the notion that each student must do his or her own work, and that working with someone is tantamount to cheating. The individual work ethic effectively negates almost any kind of cooperative group enterprise. This necessarily means that the cooperative model should be applied to tasks where students are expected to work cooperatively, and the competitive, individualistic model should be applied to tasks that students are expected to deal with on their own. Trying to mix the two approaches can give rise to problems and probably explains why legitimate small-group work has often played second fiddle in many schools. In the final analysis, few things are more basic than working successfully with others.

The Jigsaw Method. The *jigsaw* name for this variant form of cooperative learning derives from an analogy to a jigsaw puzzle, which is not complete until the separate pieces are reassembled back in place. It is the technique that Ms. Lindquist used in the cooperative biography project described in Chapter 1. You may recall that Ms. Lindquist created five working groups, each with the task of producing a biography of Abe Lincoln. The individual members of each group were responsible for producing one chapter—one student would create the chapter on Lincoln's early life, another the chapter on Lincoln as president, and so on. The jigsaw comes into play when members leave their original (working) group and meet together in a new, task-alike group—the students responsible for the chapter on Lincoln's early life meet together as a group, the students responsible for Lincoln's presidency meet together, and so on. You may wish to reexamine Figure 1.1 in Chapter 1 to see a visual depiction of how jigsaw groups are organized.

Using working groups and task-alike groups

Mary Jane Blanchard also uses the jigsaw method on occasion. In one instance, she organized her twenty-five-member class into five heterogeneous working groups of five students each. Each working group gets the same assignment: to produce a pictorial collage that shows examples of, and clearly distinguishes among, goods and services in five different areas—health, food, transportation, housing, and education. Each working group member is responsible for one area (or puzzle piece). For example, Student A on each team has health, Student B has food, and so forth. The working groups meet initially to clarify their assignment and assign topics. Then the working group disband temporarily and reconvene in task-alike groups. In this case, all the students working with health-related goods and services meet together, all food-related members meet as a group, and so forth. The task-alike groups work together to consider such things as the kinds of pictures that would show their respective areas, and whether a picture of a nurse, for example, would show a good or a service. Once the task-alike group members are certain what they are after, they can reassemble as their original working groups. In this instance, they work individually to collect pictures from the magazines supplied by Ms. Blanchard. Mary Jane also provides guidance and support throughout the activity, because cooperative learning is not intended as a technique in which students must work totally on their own. After the team members have completed their tasks, the original working team members reassemble to develop their collages. The problem the working teams must deal with now, if they have not done so already, is to figure out how they can present their information so that the goods and services for each area are displayed clearly and separately from the other areas. The complete collages are hung around the room and shared during the debriefing. Also considered during the debriefing are the problems that the teams encountered in completing their tasks and how they dealt with them.

The jigsaw in practice

A less-structured alternative to the jigsaw technique involves assigning projects to small teams of students and then allowing the teams to work out their own procedures, thus eliminating the task-alike groups. Regardless of which approach a teacher takes, the problems that students encounter as they work together must be considered together with whatever content they learn.

An alternative

● Multiple Intelligences

Just as some of us have preferred learning styles, so some of us are also artistically, musically, or athletically inclined and others of us are not. Ask yourself why some people can play a musical instrument without lessons, whereas for others of us it is a lifelong struggle. These abilities or inclinations have become the focus of a growing body of theory and research related to multiple intelligences.

An expanded view of intelligence

Intelligence has traditionally been thought of as a single, inherited entity that enabled people to learn almost anything, provided it was presented in an appropriate way (see Gardner, 1993). Anyone who has taken traditional intelligence (IQ) tests know that those instruments place a premium on one's ability to manipulate words—what Gardner (1993) calls "linguistic intelligence"—and on one's ability to solve logical or mathematical problems—what Gardner calls "logical-mathematical" intelligence. All of us know that schools recognize other talents, especially athletic skills, and in high schools at least, offer classes like band, choir, art, and shop where students can apply those talents. But most people will agree that this is an area where not all things are valued equally. Telling your mother that you flunked shop, for example, is usually a less serious crime than flunking something like English. The point is that most schools focus on linguistic and logical-mathematical intelligence.

The eight intelligences

A growing number of authorities believe that multiple intelligences are each quite independent of each other and that each has its own strengths and constraints. In addition to linguistic and logical-mathematical intelligence, which he originally suggested, Gardner has identified six other intelligences: musical, spatial, bodily-kinetic, interpersonal, intrapersonal, and naturalistic. Gardner's most recent addition, *naturalist intelligence* (see Gardner & Checkley, 1997) refers to an individual's ability to identify patterns in nature and discriminate among living things. Some individuals, for example, can discriminate between animals that are O.K. to hunt, and those that are better to run away from lest they kill you before you can kill them. Likewise some individuals can readily distinguish between varieties of wild mushrooms that are safe to eat, and others that cause dire consequences if you eat them.

Reviving an old idea

Some people think that Howard Gardner created the notion of multiple intelligences, but he actually popularized and expanded on an ancient idea. Over two millennia ago, the ancient Greeks viewed intelligence as a multifaceted phenomenon that included shrewd intelligence, analytic intelligence, aesthetic intelligence, spiritual intelligence, and others (Rosenthal, 1971). The first point here is that although the concept of multiple intelligences has been around for over a thousand years, it was largely ignored or minimized until recently. The second point is that differences in individuals' learning style could reflect differences in their underlying intelligences. The third point is that the diversity reflected in multiple intelligences could mean that there are multiple ways to teach something.

As researchers continue to explore multiple intelligences and learning styles, it is becoming ever more apparent that the two concepts are related. This is reflected in Table 5.1, which correlates the two notions. Table 5.1 also indicates potential activities that appeal to different intelligences. However, if you examine those activities closely, many of them seem very appealing, the kinds of things that most children would enjoy. Clearly, multiple intelligences and learning styles are areas where there is still much to be learned.

TABLE 5.1 Multiple Intelligences and Learning Styles

Children Who Are Strongly	Think	Love	Need
Linguistic	in words	reading, writing, telling stories, playing word games, etc.	books, tapes, writing tools, paper diaries, dialogue, discussions, debates, stories, etc.
Logical-Mathematical	by reasoning	experimenting, questioning, figuring out logical puzzles, calculating, etc.	things to explore and think about, science materials, manipulatives, trips to the planetarium and science museum, etc.
Spatial	in images and pictures, doodling, etc.	designing, drawing, visualizing imagination games, mazes, etc.	art, LEGOs, videos, movies, slides, puzzles, illustrated books, trips to art museums, etc.
Bodily-Kinesthetic	through sonintic sensations	dancing, running, jumping, building, touching, gesturing, etc.	role play, drama, movement, things to build, sports and physical games, tactile experiences, hands-on learning, etc.
Musical	via rhythms and melodies	singing, whistling, humming, tapping feet and hands, listening, etc.	sing-along time, trips to concerts, music playing at home and school, musical instruments, etc.
Interpersonal	by bouncing ideas off other people	leading, organizing, relating, manipulating, mediating, partying, etc.	friends, group games, social gatherings, community events, clubs, mentors/apprenticeships, etc.
Intrapersonal	deeply inside of themselves	setting goals, meditating, dreaming, being quiet, planning, etc.	secret places, time alone, self-paced projects, choices, etc.

Source: Based on Harold Gardner. (1993). *Multiple intelligences: The theory in practice.* New York: Basic Books.

SUMMARY

In this chapter, several issues related to the instructional diversity you will face in your classroom were examined, not the least of which is the difficulty that schools face in moving away from a one-size-fits-all educational model. Just the thought of providing instruction geared to divergent learning styles or a particular intelligence, for example, may panic some people. History suggests that in movements of this kind, there will be a series of refinements, each of which offers more specific guidance to classroom teachers. However, history also suggests that there will be some gross errors, some backtracking, and some people who go overboard or use the movement to serve their own ends. As a teacher, you will be pushed and pulled in various directions and will be told that you should do this instead of that. Surviving in this environment probably requires two things above all others: healthy doses of (1) thoughtfulness and (2) common sense.

SUGGESTED ACTIVITIES

1. There is a widespread belief that schooling should be the same everywhere, and that providing special programs for exceptional students is somehow undemocratic. To what extent, if any, does this feeling conflict with the principle that every child has the right to an education appropriate to his or her needs and abilities?

2. If a student like Jonathon Mooney, coauthor of *Learning Outside the Lines,* were in your class, it wouldn't be long before you realized what Jonathon already knows: that he cannot read or spell. Would you continue giving him poor grades in reading or spelling? Would you ask him to look up the words in a dictionary (which he can't read)? Or would you not grade spelling, as some of his teachers did? What would you do?

3. Teachers who use cooperative learning groups extensively often find that in classes where everyone receives the same instructions, some groups work well while others flounder helplessly. What factors may account for this, and what steps would you take to correct the problem?

SUGGESTED READINGS AND RESOURCES

Print Resources

Howard Gardner. (1983). *Frames of mind.* New York: HarperCollins Basic Books. This is the book that sparked the interest in multiple intelligences.

Daniel Hallahan & James Kauffman. (1997). *Exceptional learners.* Boston: Allyn & Bacon. This special education text takes the position that in dealing with exceptional children, the emphasis should be on their abilities, not their handicapping conditions.

Educational Leadership. (September 1997). This highly useful theme issue focuses on teaching for multiple intelligences.

Jonathon Mooney and David Cole. (2000). *Learning outside the lines.* New York: Simon & Schuster. This book offers remarkable insights into what it is like to be learning disabled.

Internet Resources

Introductory Note: Web sites sometimes change Internet addresses or cease operating entirely. All the addresses supplied here were operating when this book was printed, but should any of them fail to work properly, enter the topic or target organization in any standard search engine.

New Horizons for Learning

http://www.newhorizons.org/

This organization focuses on how people learn. It has links to issues ranging from brain research to learning styles to lesson plans. Recommended.

ESL/BILINGUAL EDUCATION

TESOL

http://www.tesol.edu/index.html

This is site is maintained by TESOL, Teachers of English to Speakers of Other Languages, which focuses on helping to improve the English-language proficiency of people who are nonnative speakers of English. It has numerous links to other Web sites on ESL.

National Clearinghouse for Bilingual Education

http://www.ncbe.gwu.edu/

This recommended site contains information of interest to teachers who work with nonnative speakers of English.

Language Development Strategies

http://www.lalc.k12.ca.us/laeplsmartlSunrise/lang.html

This site focuses on materials, strategies, and sample lesson plans for assisting limited-English-proficiency students. Information pertains to English language development, second-language acquisition, and self-image and multicultural learning.

SMALL-GROUP STRATEGIES

WWW Constructivist Project Design Guide

http://www.ilt.columbia.edu/kl2/1ivetext-nf/ webcurr.html

This site, which is maintained by Columbia University, offers resources for developing cooperative learning units.

Teachers Helping Teachers

http://www.pacificnet.net/~mandel/

This site is a resource for getting teaching ideas and information about a variety of topics of interest to teachers. Teachers share their insights with each other.

A Guide to Maximizing Learning in Small Groups

http://www.cs.ukc.ac.uk/national/CSDN/html/EDUres/ small-group-learning.html

This site offers guidelines for working with students in small groups.

Developing Character and Values

Key Questions

● What gives schools and teachers the right to intervene in children's values and morals?

● How sensitive must teachers be to parental and community expectations?

● What are the moral implications associated with teaching or *not* teaching values and character?

Key Ideas

● The school's role in teaching values and character continues to be controversial.

● Every teacher teaches values and morals, whether explicitly or implicitly; it's an unavoidable fact of teaching . . . and living.

● Community expectations concerning values education are seldom consistent, nor are they necessarily known in advance.

● The key components of character education are (1) values themselves and (2) a process of valuing. General agreement on these components does not exist.

● Alternative approaches to values education include (1) inculcation, (2) literature-based techniques, (3) values clarification, (4) moral reasoning, and (5) values analysis.

● The "hidden curriculum" is a powerful instrument of instruction.

Introduction: The Reemergence of Character Education

Teachers cannot avoid teaching morals and values even if they want to. Everything they say and do, everything they study and discuss in class, even how they operate their classrooms, will reflect the values and standards that guide their conduct. Simply by observing your actions and deeds, your students will learn what you

144

think is important, valuable, and worth cherishing—and what is not. Without your saying a word about respecting others, for example, your students will know whether you respect them as individuals.

Children will not necessarily adopt your values or any teacher's values. In fact, some children's value systems may prompt them to reject what you hold dear. When that happens, it's difficult not to take the child's rejection of what you value as a rejection of you personally. It takes a strong person who, in the face of defiance and rejection, can still say to a child, "I care about you regardless of how you feel about me." At the same time, the child's out-of-school environments may also reflect a self-centered, "do your own thing" mentality that directly contradicts many of the behaviors you are trying to model. Nevertheless, for those of us who intervene in children's lives, teaching morals and values is an inescapable fact of life.

When the first edition of this book was written over twenty years ago, serious questions were being asked about the school's role in teaching morals and values. At the time, the nation was extracting itself from the war in Vietnam, and teaching even long-cherished values like patriotism had become controversial. As new faculty members, we witnessed antiwar riots and protests on our campus and elsewhere among individuals who believed that the Vietnamese conflict was an unjust war that the United States should get out of as quickly as possible. Many of those protestors also believed that the notion of patriotism as "Our country, right or wrong," was itself wrong, and that expecting them to support an unjust war was immoral. Such antiwar views often clashed with the views of other Americans who believed that the nation was obliged to support its armed forces, regardless of whether they personally supported or opposed the war. Those were troubling times indeed.

When the United States was involved in the Korean conflict in the early 1950s, similar protests did not occur. In the time between the two wars, the moral climate had changed dramatically. Beginning after World War II and continuing into the 1960s, more and more people in America (and around the world) began to embrace a rampant form of individualism that was divorced from notions of social responsibility. Also emerging at that time was a movement toward *logical positivism:* that is, the tendency to distinguish between facts, which were scientifically verifiable, and matters involving morals and values, which were regarded as expressions of personal feelings or preferences. Thus, when someone advocated a particular course of action as "the right thing to do," the usual responses were "Says who?" and "Nobody can force me to do anything I don't want to." Values and morals were becoming personalized and privatized, and moral and value issues were increasingly seen not as matters of doing the right thing, but as matters of personal judgment. For many Americans, morality was becoming a matter of "doing one's own thing. "

Lickona (1993) suggests that the era between the Korean and Vietnam wars and into the 1970s and 1980s was marked by a worldwide rise in *personalism*. This was and is a social movement that celebrates the autonomy of individuals, and their individual rights and freedoms. As Lickona stated, "Personalism rightly protested societal oppression and injustice, but it also delegitimized moral authority, . . . turned people inward toward self-fulfillment, weakened social commitments (for example, to marriage and parenting), and fueled the socially destabilizing sexual revolution" (p. 6).

Values permeate everything teachers do

Troubling times

Individualism and the personalization of morals

President Theodore Roosevelt once said, "To educate a person in mind and not in morals is to educate a menace to society." Nevertheless, the legitimacy of teaching morals and values in the schools began to be questioned during the 1970s and 1980s. In the process, many schools and teachers began consciously avoiding explicit instruction in moral and ethical principles, at least to the extent they could (see Sizer, 1985). In place of the school's traditional role in character education, they began focusing almost exclusively on the knowledge component of education—on transmitting "smartness."

Questioning the school's role in teaching values

The concerns for self-fulfillment and individual rights continued through the 1980s and into the 1990s, but disheartening signs arose on the horizon. Many families were no longer the stabilizing force in society they once were; crime and corruption were increasing; everyday life was becoming increasingly uncivil; and sex, nudity, and violence were becoming commonplace on TV and in the movies.

By the mid-1980s, some authorities had begun to call for a return to the school's former role of providing explicit instruction in morals and values. For example, Ryan (1986) contended that by *not* treating values explicitly, the schools were doing only half their job.

Calls for returning to teaching morals and values

By the mid-1990s, the occasional voices suggesting that our society was facing a growing number of problems had become a chorus. Some individuals, like William Kilpatrick (1992), suggested that in addition to persistent educational problems—like Johnny's inability to read well—an even more serious problem is that Johnny doesn't seem to know the difference between right and wrong. The contention among many observers was that schools could not remain morally and ethically neutral, but must return to their traditional role of teaching character education. In the late 1990's, character education was returning to many schools, in some cases with a vengeance.

Character education

The schools had some valid reasons for backing off from traditional character education in the 1960s and 1970s. How, for example, could teachers continue to teach about "doing the right thing" when the larger society said, in effect, "It's O.K. to do your own thing"? Schools always tend to mirror the larger society, so to whatever extent the society says "we are going in this direction," the schools inevitably follow (see Rogers & Frieberg, 1994). When society effectively said "Back off on teaching values as moral absolutes, " schools did. Today, however, more and more people are turning to schools to do something about the problems facing our society. Yet there is no clear consensus on (1) how schools should accomplish the task, or (2) whether schools have the tools and skills necessary to remedy moral problems.

Schools mirror the society

Can schools do the job?

The first part of this chapter examines some current attempts to reestablish character education in the schools. The following sections explore alternative approaches for dealing with value issues.

Terminology Clarified

The area of morals and values can easily become a morass of vague terms, so the following definitions are included:

Ethics defined, from the Greek

Ethics comes from the Greek *ethikos* and refers to norms and standards for judging behaviors as right and good or wrong and bad. In popular usage, ethics is typically used in connection with how we conduct our relationships with others; for example, persons who act unethically always do so in relationship to someone else.

Morals defined, from Latin

Morals is the Latin version of the Greek *ethikos* and carries the same meaning. In popular usage, *morals* often refers to the norms and standards that guide behavior.

Values defined

Values are ideas that serve as standards of conduct, beauty, efficiency, or worth. No one has ever seen an individual's values because they, like all ideas, are mental constructs. But we can observe how people behave, which indicates what they value.

Ethics and aesthetics

The standards we use for determining beauty are usually treated separately from standards of conduct, efficiency, and worth. For example, what we enjoy and find beautiful, such as a spectacular sunset, is said to reflect *aesthetics*. Aesthetic matters, such as whether you like or dislike modern art or classical music, seldom involve moral or ethical considerations. One way to think of this is that morality and ethics deal with "right" and "wrong," whereas aesthetics deals with what we think of as good or bad, beautiful or ugly.

Virtue defined

Virtue, a term popular in the Victorian era, is enjoying a rebirth (see Bennett, 1994; Doyle, 1997; Himmelfarb, 1995). It refers to qualities that all individuals should strive for, such as honesty, truthfulness, self-respect, and self-reliance. Himmelfarb suggests that the need to distinguish between virtues and values has come about because values in popular usage can refer to "beliefs, opinions, attitudes, feelings, habits, conventions, preferences, even idiosyncrasies—whatever any individual, group or society happens to value, at any time and for any reason" (p. 3). Some authorities use the term *core values* to describe virtues such as those noted above and to set them apart from other values.

Character

Character refers to virtuous behavior—behavior that conforms to valued norms and customs.

Building Character

When one of the school's missions was to "melt" newly arrived immigrants into the mainstream society, the teaching of values and morals was usually called *character education*. That term is enjoying a rebirth today, but you will sometimes hear it called *values education* or *moral education*. All three terms refer to what schools do to help children become ethically mature adults who are capable of practicing moral thought and action in democratic ways.

Traditional techniques

As part of their character education mission, many schools in the 1920s and 1930s devised pledges and codes of conduct. The "Children's Morality Code," for example, stressed duty, good health, good workmanship, and teamwork in addition to the core values previously noted (Leming, 1993). Teachers also used techniques that included preaching, modeling desired behaviors, and, occasionally, mocking children who deviated from what was expected. Whatever success the schools enjoyed in these efforts was judged by the extent to which the core values (or virtues) were incorporated into students' belief systems and, ultimately, their behavior.

Teaching character is clearly a more complex enterprise than teaching content oriented lessons. For example, what exactly would you teach if you wanted your students to demonstrate respect for others? There is some excellent children's literature that you could use, but unlike conventional subjects, character traits do not have any easily defined content. You might resort to preaching platitudes like "Be nice to others," but the research indicates that such exhortations, as well as various codes and pledges, are unlikely to have any lasting effects on students' character (see Leming, 1993).

What to teach, exactly?

What Is Good Character?

The purpose of character education is to develop good character in the young. One authority, Thomas Lickona, suggests that "good character consists of knowing the good, desiring the good, and doing the good" (1993, p. 9). Lickona's definition, broad as it is, highlights a major difference between character and conventional knowledge-based subjects. In addition to a cognitive (or knowledge) dimension that character traits share with conventional subjects, character also has an attitudinal (or feeling) dimension and a psychomotor (or behavioral) dimension that conventional subjects usually lack. Many children already know about values like honesty and truthfulness, for example, but nobody needs to tell you that some children (and adults) will still be dishonest or lie whenever it suits their purpose. What they may lack is an attitude, a disposition, a conscience if you will, that disposes them to do the right thing regardless of its ultimate effect on

The multidimensional nature of character

Simply knowing about character is inadequate

Is this the future of teaching in the age of technology? © *1997. Reprinted courtesy of Bunny Hoest and PARADE Magazine.*

"Keep your eyes on your own monitor, and don't e-mail anyone."

them. The affective, or dispositional, component of character provides an essential bridge between character's cognitive (or knowing) dimensions and a person's actions. The cognitive, affective, and behavioral dimensions of character, as identified by Lickona (1993), are summarized in Table 6.1.

A bridge between what people know and do

● Which Values Should Be Taught?

Parents who oppose character education usually do so out of fear that schools will try to indoctrinate their children about gay rights, abortion, premarital sex, and similar matters. The issue is compounded because of individuals who want schools to deal explicitly with such issues. The issue is even further compounded by one segment of the character education movement that defines character very narrowly—as helping adolescents avoid premarital pregnancy. Most character education programs, however, focus not on a political agenda or avoiding pregnancy, but on developing core values, or virtues, that are (1) basic to morality and (2) that almost no one opposes. These virtues (or core values) include respect, the dignity of the individual, personal and civic responsibility, honesty, trustworthiness, fairness, caring, and courage. (All these values are elements of the community literacy referred to in Chapter 1.)

A focus on virtues (core values)

TABLE 6.1 The Moral Components of Character

Dimension	Trait
Cognitive	1. Awareness of the moral dimensions of a situation
	2. Knowing moral values, like truthfulness, and what they require in concrete cases
	3. Perspective taking, the ability to look at situations from various perspectives
	4. Moral reasoning, the ability to differentiate among different rationales and motives for behaving in certain ways
	5. Thoughtful decision making, the ability to assess alternative courses of action
	6. Moral self-knowledge
Affective	1. Conscience, the felt obligation to do what one judges is right
	2. Self-respect
	3. Empathy
	4. Love of the good
	5. Self-control
	6. Humility, a willingness to recognize and correct our moral failings
Behavioral	1. Competence, skills such as listening, communication, and cooperating
	2. Will, which mobilizes judgment and energy
	3. Moral habit, a reliable disposition to respond to situations in morally good ways

Source: Abridged from Thomas Lickona, "The Return of Character Education," *Educational Leadership,* 51 (1993), 10.

Some schools integrate elements of character education into their programs without using an explicit label, like *character education,* whereas other schools may use terms such as *positive conflict resolution.* One expression you commonly hear in schools today is "character counts," a sentiment we agree with entirely. However, it is also the name of a popular, commercially available character education program. Regardless of how they refer to character education, most schools involve parents in meetings that focus on the values they intend to promote. Almost never do those schools encounter anyone who argues, for example, that lying is better than telling the truth.

Different labels

● Dealing with the Hidden Curriculum

The notion of the *hidden curriculum* has been around for years, but references to it occur increasingly throughout the character education literature (see Berreth & Scherer, 1993; Leming, 1993; Lickona, 1993; Lockwood, 1997; Ryan, 1993). This seems to reflect growing recognition that profound teachings are often conveyed by the hidden curriculum, that is, in the day-to-day schooling practices that all students experience but that are not part of the formal school curriculum. Consider, for example, teachers who talk about the importance of cooperation but then set up instructional programs in which students must compete for every reward. Other students will remember teachers for whom putting an incorrect heading on an otherwise perfect paper could produce devastating results.

Classroom Management Practices. Many classroom management programs, including Lee Canter's popular Assertive Discipline (1989) and others like it, feature a series of systematic consequences for students who misbehave. For a first offense, the student's name goes on the board; for a second offense, the student must stay after school, and so forth. Although negative consequences can tend to reinforce the teacher role of "prison guard," they are usually only one part of such plans. As Canter notes, "The key to Assertive Discipline is catching students being good: recognizing them and supporting them when they behave appropriately" (p. 57). Rewarding students for good behavior might seem an appropriate balance for negative consequences, but as Kohn (1997) points out, this aspect of most management plans can sometimes undermine a character education program.

Rewarding good behavior can have unintended consequences

Regardless of the specific management plan teachers use, the key concern is how they reward good behavior. Providing students with tangible rewards can be an effective technique in the short run but could have negligible or negative long-run effects. According to Kohn, questionable reward systems include (1) providing "bonus bucks" (or punching tickets or putting marbles into a jar) that can be redeemed for an ice cream or pizza party, and (2) rewarding children with a leaf to hang in their "Forest of Virtue." Equally questionable, according to Kohn, are activities such as targeting a certain value on a particular day of the week—"If it's Thursday, this must be Respect Day"—and then rewarding children for demonstrating that day's value. One could ask, "What's wrong with respecting others on Mondays, or any other day of the week?" Even worse than tangible rewards, in Kohn's view, are awards that are so limited that

The downside of tangible rewards

only a few children can get them: "This week's winner of the Hard Worker Award is. . . . " Such awards—assuming children really value them—force children to compete with their peers and thus to regard their classmates as potential obstacles to success.

Extrinsic vs. intrinsic motivation

Using tangible rewards for virtuous conduct is a form of extrinsic motivation that can undermine intrinsic motivation. What children can learn from such practices is not that virtuous behavior is good, desirable, and something worth doing on its own merits, but that the purpose of "being good" is to earn rewards. Frequent rewards for children who demonstrate virtuous behavior can make them *less* likely than other children to continue demonstrating those behaviors (Fabes et al., 1989; Grusec, 1991, cited in Kohn, 1997).

An alternative to tangible rewards

Should you find yourself teaching in a school that has adopted Assertive Discipline, or a similar management plan, your options are necessarily limited. Because ignoring the school's plan would probably be unwise, you should consider modifying the plan, especially to the extent to which you provide tangible rewards for desired behaviors. In place of tangible rewards, consider offering free time or using classroom meetings as they are described in William Glasser's *The Quality School* (1990) and his earlier works. From time to time, you might want to conduct classroom meetings that focus on whether it is "right" to reward people for doing what they ought to do anyhow.

The basic point here is that the hidden curriculum and classroom management practices must complement, or at least not contradict, everything else that schools and teachers do. In one study, Williams (1992) went so far as to suggest that "respect is best taught through a hidden curriculum of modeling and quality teaching" (p. 22). The hidden curriculum and questionable classroom management practices are such powerful forces that to ignore them could negate the purpose of a character education program.

● Guidelines for Character Education

Successful character education programs are comprehensive and schoolwide. For example, you may establish your classroom as a caring moral community, a place where students respect and care about one another and feel membership in and responsibility to and for the group (Lickona, 1993). However, what you do in your classroom is more likely to have long-term results if the entire school functions as a caring moral community, where your classroom reflects the norm, not an exception, for classrooms throughout the school. Should you eventually teach in a school that does not have a schoolwide program, you can still operate your classroom as a caring, moral community, but don't be surprised if you feel like a lone voice in the wilderness.

Schoolwide efforts

Lickona (1993, pp. 10–11) recommends the following schoolwide actions to support character education:

Schoolwide actions

* *Fostering care beyond the classroom.* Using positive role models to inspire altruistic behavior and providing opportunities at every grade level to perform school and community service

* *Creating a positive moral culture in the school.* Developing a schoolwide ethos . . . that supports and amplifies the values taught in the classroom

Many schools are including a community service component in their character education programs. *(© Jonathan A. Meyers)*

★ *Recruiting parents and the community as partners in character education.* Letting parents know that the school considers them their child's first and most important moral teacher, giving parents specific ways they can reinforce the values the school is trying to teach, and seeking the help of the community, churches, businesses, local government, and the media in promoting the core ethical values

Lickona also recommends the following as activities that individual teachers can use in their classrooms:

Things teachers can do

★ *Acting as caregiver, model, and mentor.* Treating students with love and respect, setting a good example, supporting positive social behavior, and correcting hurtful actions through one-on-one guidance and whole-class discussions
★ *Practicing moral discipline.* Using the creation and enforcement of rules as opportunities to foster moral reasoning, voluntary compliance with rules, and a respect for others
★ *Creating a democratic classroom environment.* Involving students in decision making and sharing the responsibility for making the classroom a good place to be and learn

* *Teaching values through the curriculum.* Using ethically rich content of academic subjects (such as literature, history, and science) as well as outstanding programs, such as the Heartwood Ethics Curriculum for Children (which is described shortly)
* *Using cooperative learning.* To develop students' appreciation of others, perspective taking, and ability to work with others toward common goals
* *Developing the "conscience of craft."* By fostering students' appreciation of learning, capacity for hard work, commitment to excellence, and sense of work as affecting the lives of others
* *Encouraging moral reflection.* Through reading, research, essay writing, journal keeping, discussion and debate
* *Teaching conflict resolution.* To help students acquire the essential moral skills of solving conflicts fairly and without force

A moral imperative

The movement toward reestablishing character education will undoubtedly be challenging. If nothing else, many teachers today grew up in a cultural milieu that encouraged the personalization and privatization of moral values. Also, many questions exist for which there are no clear answers. Why, for example, do some people consistently act in morally responsible ways and others don't? And, can schools provide the same kind of moral anchors that families have provided in the past? Despite the unanswered questions, the consensus in the literature is that character education has become a moral imperative.

Other Approaches to Values Education

Amenable to moral and ethical issues

Most of the approaches to values education dealt with in this section are amenable to ethical questions or to issues involving the moral and ethical standards that influence one's behavior.

● Inculcation

Throughout human history, *inculcation* (or exhortation) has been a common technique for molding human behavior. It refers to the process of making an impression on the mind through frequent repetition, insistent urging, or modeling. Inculcation, like brainwashing, is based on the premise that if you show or tell people something often enough, eventually they will behave accordingly.

Repeated telling

Whenever you hear parents (or teachers) saying things like "Good girls (or boys) don't do *that* kind of thing, " they are using inculcation. Somewhere along the line, the parents identify the desired behavior, such as "Children should respect their elders. " Then, over the years, they provide appropriate reinforcement—a nod or smile of approval when children demonstrate the desired behavior and a gentle reminder when they don't.

For centuries parents have successfully inculcated desired values and behaviors in their children. And the children will usually behave as they are expected, at least when their parents are present. Even though many parents have used inculcation successfully, research suggests that it does not work equally well for teachers. The research doesn't indicate why this is so, but it most likely has to do with contact time. Parents can consistently reinforce desired behaviors in their children from their birth onward. Teachers, on the other hand, have only a 180-day school year in which to accomplish the same thing. And children know that, come each September, they will have a different teacher who will probably hold different expectations.

● Literature-Based Techniques

Literacy springboard to teaching values

Most children have heard the famous lines "1 think I can, I think I can, I think I can," and "1 thought I could, I thought I could, I thought I could." They are from Watty Piper's (1930/1954) children's classic, *The Little Engine That Could*. Through diligence, perseverance, and a lot of effort, a little switch engine is able to pull a trainload of Christmas food and toys to the children who live on the other side of the mountain. If some of your students have heard the story, you can still read it again—even students familiar with the story will enjoy it another time. Children's stories like *The Little Engine That Could* can provide the basis for a follow-up discussion of how diligence, perseverance, and patience, combined with a positive attitude, can often overcome overwhelming obstacles. The children can also talk about times when positive attitudes have helped them complete challenging tasks or do things that they were afraid to do.

Examples

If you want to focus on behaving responsibly, you might consider reading Chris Van Allsburg's (1988) delightful tale, *Two Bad Ants*. This story focuses on an ant colony that sets out to retrieve a huge mound of delicious crystals (sugar) their scouts have located. But instead of returning to the colony with all the other ants, the two bad ants decide to remain and feast for a while. The crystal pile soon becomes a dangerous place, and the two ants eventually end up in a coffee cup, are put down into the garbage disposal, and even get blown out of an electrical outlet where they are trying to hide. Needless to say, the ants suffer severe consequences for their actions.

Still in the context of responsible behavior, older students will enjoy Kate McMullan's (1991) *The Great Eggspectations of Lila Fenwick*. In this story, a librarian tries to teach sixth graders about responsibility by having them care for a hard-boiled egg as if it were a newborn baby. Lila discovers that many of her usually great ideas backfire on her as she tries to care for her egg.

So many literary works can serve as springboards for values-oriented discussions and activities that an extended listing of children's stories is included in the Resource Handbook. These stories are organized by the main values they focus on—sharing, responsibility, and so on.

A literature-based approach to values education can be as organized (or unorganized) as you wish to make it. The basic procedure is to read the story to your students and then conduct a follow-up discussion or share-and-tell session. The discussion period should be regarded as a time to talk with children about the values in question, and not an opportunity to moralize.

Other literature-based programs

Two character education programs that make use of children's literature warrant special mention here. They are the Heartwood Ethics Curriculum and the Exploring Ethics through Children's Literature Program. The Heartwood program was developed by an attorney from Pittsburgh who was appalled by the lack of remorse among the young defendants she represented in court, as well as by some retired teachers from the Pittsburgh area. The Heartwood materials are based on Newbery award–winning, multicultural books (stories) that address core values such as courage, loyalty, justice, respect, hope, honest, and love. The Exploring Ethics through Children's Literature Program follows a similar format.

Resources. Character education is such a "hot topic" that there many resources at your disposal. Some organizations offer character education programs, and others offer support services such as workshops; some offer both. A listing of character education resources is included in the Resource Handbook.

Values Clarification

Clarifying what our values are

Values clarification is one of the rare techniques whose title describes exactly what it tries to do: Help individuals *clarify* what their values really are. The underlying premise is that most individuals are not clear about what their values are until they are confronted by situations that cause them to examine their values.

Values clarification is a value-neutral approach that was created in the mid-1970s when the explicit teaching of values was declining. Rather than trying to instill or impose certain values, values clarification is based on a seven-phase valuing process, as follows:

Choosing

The valuing process

1. Encourage children to make choices, and to make them freely.
2. Help them *discover alternatives* when faced with choices.
3. Help children weigh alternatives thoughtfully, reflecting on the *consequences* of each.

Prizing

4. Encourage children to consider what it is that they prize and *cherish*.
5. Give them opportunities to *affirm their* choices to others.

Acting

6. Encourage children to act, *behave,* and live *in accordance with their choices.*
7. Help them be aware of repeated behaviors or patterns in their life *[emphasis added] (Raths, Harmin, & Simon, 1978, pp. 28, 38).*

The Clarifying Response. A key element of values clarification is the clarifying response. This refers to how teachers respond to students, either individually or as a class, to help them identify what is important and desirable. In many instances, the exact form of the clarifying response will be situational and may take the form of a question, as illustrated in the following exchange:

TEACHER: Bruce, don't you want to go outside and play on the playground?

STUDENT: I dunno. I suppose so.

The clarifying response

TEACHER: Is there something that you would rather do?

STUDENT: I dunno. Nothing much.

TEACHER: You don't seem much to care, Bruce. Is that right?

STUDENT: I suppose so.

TEACHER: And mostly anything we do will be all right with you?

STUDENT: I suppose so. Well, not anything, I guess.

TEACHER: Well, Bruce, we'd better go out with the others now. You let me know sometime if you think of something you would like to do. (Dialogue adapted from Raths et al., 1978, p. 55.)

The intent here is not to get the student to adopt the values clarification process in a fifteen-second exchange. Clarifying responses should encourage students to examine their ideas, but without the teacher moralizing, criticizing, evaluating, or otherwise suggesting that they have a "right answer" in mind (Raths et al., 1978). The exchange must be genuine or it will fall flat on its face.

Productive clarifying response questions include the following:

Suggested clarifying responses

Is this important to you?

Are you happy about that?

Did you think of other (alternative) things you could do?

Would you really do that or are you just talking?

What other possibilities are there?

Would you do the same thing over again?

Is it important enough that you would be willing to share your idea (project, experiences, etc.) with the others? (Raths et al., 1978, pp. 59–63)

What Critics Say About Values Clarification.   Most criticisms of the values clarification approach have focused on techniques that (1) could jeopardize the student's right to privacy, (2) could place teachers in the role of a trained counselor (or psychiatrist), (3) fail to distinguish between moral and nonmoral issues, and (4) suggest that all value beliefs are equally valid (ethical relativism) (Lockwood, 1977). It is difficult for students to state their beliefs publicly without disclosing personal information about themselves and their relationships with others, including their families. Thus any of the clarifying questions could lead to a potential invasion of the student's right to privacy. Invasion is even more likely if explicit questioning techniques are used, for example, if students are asked to identify who in their family brings them the greatest sadness. Then, too, the clarifying questions as shown on page 155 are much like those that trained counselors and psychologists use in group therapy sessions. For example, it is easy enough to ask a child, "Is that important to you?," but the child's responses could go beyond those you are trained to handle.

Values clarification activities have also been criticized for failing to distinguish between moral (ethical) and nonmoral (aesthetic) value issues. There is obviously nothing immoral about asking students to identify their favorite foods, or how they would spend their allowance, both of which are a matter of personal priorities. However, in a popular values clarification activity called "The Bomb Shelter," students are asked to select which six of ten candidates—which include a doctor, a violinist, a police officer, and a law student and his wife—should be per-

Potential to invade one's privacy

Simple questions can have hard-to-handle responses

Treating aesthetic and moral issues alike

When students help each other, both may gain from the experience. (© *Jean-Claude Lejeune*)

mitted to enter the shelter. Candidates who are not admitted will presumably die. Asking children to determine which individuals should be permitted to live and which should die, or whether doctors make greater contributions to society than do violinists, are far different matters from asking about a student's favorite flavor of ice cream. This is purely a judgment call, so ask yourself if it is appropriate to place children in situations where they must make (1) life-or-death decisions, or (2) judge the relative merits of different occupations.

Ethical relativism

A final criticism of the values clarification approach is that it tends to promote *ethical relativism.* This means that instead of using overarching moral principles, such as the dignity of the individual and the sanctity of human life—principles that should apply in all situations—the values clarification approach seems to suggest that individuals' actions should be governed by the situations in which they find themselves, and by what is practical or expedient. This criticism arises, in part, because there is no justification phase in the seven-step valuing process (page 155). Because students are not asked to justify or defend their decisions, they could come away with the impression that one person's views are as good as anyone else's, regardless of the situation.

After reviewing over seventy-five studies involving values clarification approaches, Lemming (1985) found that they seldom produced the kinds of attitudinal or behavioral changes the researchers had anticipated. Lemming therefore suggested that the popularity of values clarification activities may result, in part, from their widespread availability for classroom use.

───● Moral Reasoning

The *moral-reasoning* approach to values education is closely associated with the work of the late Harvard psychologist Lawrence Kohlberg and his associates. Kohlberg first developed a theory that dealt with how children learn to reason morally and then developed a teaching strategy to help children improve the quality of their moral reasoning. To determine what makes one kind of moral reasoning "better" than another, it's necessary to understand the moral development theory on which Kohlberg's teaching strategy is based.

Moral Development.   Kohlberg's research focused on the question "How do individuals develop the ability to reason morally (to justify their actions)?" After investigating moral reasoning among individuals of various ages and from various cultures, Kohlberg identified a developmental sequence, which is shown in Table 6.2. (At one time the developmental sequence had six stages, but Kohlberg redefined his model so that Stage 5 now incorporates what was formerly in Stage 6.)

Implications

In Jean Piaget's scheme for cognitive development, sooner or later almost everyone reaches the last stage, formal operations: the ability to think and reason abstractly. However, Kohlberg found that fewer than 25 percent of American adults ever reach Stage 5 (Principled level) in the development of their moral reasoning. If you consider that the moral basis of the Bill of Rights reflects Stage 5 reasoning, Kohlberg's findings suggest that many citizens may neither understand nor appreciate the fundamental moral principles upon which the nation was founded. This also helps to explain why many fifth- and eighth-grade teachers get frustrated teaching a required unit on "the Constitution"; the majority of their students may be operating at Stage 3, the level at which their primary interest is in gaining the social approval of others, as opposed to the Stage 5 reasoning on which the Constitution is based.

75 percent don't reach Stage 5

In Kohlberg's developmental scheme, each stage serves as a basis for the next. But unlike developmental schemes that link children of certain ages with particular stages, Kohlberg found that the age-stage relationship is less evident in moral reasoning. As Lickona has noted, "In general . . . Stages 1 and 2 dominate in the primary school years and persist in some individuals long beyond that. Stage 3 gains ground during the upper elementary grades and often remains the major orientation through the end of high school. Stage 4 begins to emerge in adolescence. Only one in four persons moves on in later adolescence or adulthood to Stage 5" (1977, p. 39). Note also that individuals who can reason at higher levels may sometimes use lower-level reasoning to justify their actions.

Using Moral Dilemmas.   Kohlberg's research suggests that students will be stimulated to move to the next stage of moral development upon repeated exposure to higher levels of moral reasoning. Such exposure can be gained by helping students work with moral dilemmas. These are stories or situations that involve conflicting moral principles and in which students must identify and evaluate alternative courses of action. Dilemmas necessarily involve situations in which the alternative courses of action are either desirable or undesirable, but

TABLE 6.2 Kohlberg's Stages of Moral Development

Level	Stage	Characteristics
Principled: Concern for fidelity to self-chosen moral principles	5	*Motivator:* Internal commitment to principles of "conscience"; respect for the rights, life, and dignity of all persons. *Awareness:* Particular moral/social rules are social contracts, arrived at through democratic reconciliation of differing viewpoints and open to change. *Assumption:* Moral principles have universal validity; law derives from morality, not vice versa.
Conventional: Concern for meeting external social expectations	4	*Motivator:* Sense of duty or obligation to live up to socially defined role and maintain existing social order for good of all. *Awareness:* There is a larger social "system" that regulates the behavior of individuals within it. *Assumption:* Authority or the social order is the source of morality.
	3	*Motivator:* Desire for social approval by living up to good boy/good girl stereotype; meeting expectations of others. *Awareness:* Need to consider intentions and feelings of others; cooperation means ideal reciprocity (golden rule). *Assumption:* Good behavior equals social conformity.
Preconventional: Concern for external, concrete consequences to self	2	*Motivator:* Self-interest: What's in it for me? *Awareness:* Human relations are governed by concrete reciprocity; let's make a deal; You scratch my back, I'll scratch yours. *Assumption:* Have to look out for self; obligated only to those who help you; each person has own needs and viewpoints.
	1	*Motivator:* Fear of getting caught; desire to avoid punishment by authority. *Awareness:* There are rules and consequences of breaking them. *Assumption:* Might makes right; what's regarded by those in power is "good"; what's punished is "bad."

Source: Based on material in Thomas Lickona, "How to Encourage Moral Development," *Learning,* 5 (March 1977), 37–42.

Dilemmas involve conflicting moral principles

not both. When the two elements are mixed, there is no dilemma; the individual merely follows the most desirable course of action.

A simple moral dilemma suitable for younger children might involve a seven-year-old girl named Holly who comes upon a small boy whose kitten is stranded in a tree. Tears stream down the boy's cheeks as he pleads with Holly to rescue his kitten. Although Holly is sympathetic, the last time she climbed a tree she fell and

Holly and the Cat in the Tree—Procedure for Young Children

Introduce the Situation

TEACHER: One day, a little girl named Holly was walking down the street.

Role-Playing

TEACHER: We need someone to play Holly and the little boy. James? Do you want to play Holly?

JAMES: I'm not playin' no girl.

TEACHER: Sure you can, James. We're just role-playing.

JAMES: (Shakes his head no.)

TEACHER: Okay, Rosemary . . .

(Two students role-play a possible solution for the incident.)

1. Minidiscussion
   TEACHER: Did they manage to solve the problem? (Brief discussion follows. If a child wants to suggest a different solution, move to part 2 immediately. If not, the teacher suggests another solution, secures new role players, and the incident is reenacted again.)

2. Role-play another alternative.

   Continue (1) and (2) until children are satisfied they have identified the possible alternatives.

Debriefing

1. Review briefly.

TEACHER: Let's see. In the first incident, Holly disobeyed her daddy and climbed the tree. In the second, she went to get somebody else to help. What happened in the third incident?

LOUISE: Holly made the boy get someone else to help.

TEACHER: Thanks, Louise. Then in the fourth incident. . .

2. Evaluate alternatives.

TEACHER: Were some solutions better than others? And do you think Holly's father should punish her for disobeying?

(Students' responses will vary.)

TEACHER: (Summarizing) It's good to help a person in need, but we should obey our parents too. Sometimes we need to look for a way to do both things. It's hard, sometimes, isn't it? (More discussion may follow.)

The debriefing is not an opportunity for the teacher to moralize or present "right" answers, Rather, the pluses and minuses of each alternative should be summarized.

sprained her wrist. After that incident Holly promised her father she wouldn't climb any more trees. What should Holly do? (Lickona, 1977, p. 37.)

Holly could do many things, including trying to get help from an adult or breaking her promise to her father. By exploring such alternatives in group settings, moral dilemmas are intended to expose students to different and, it is hoped, higher stages of moral reasoning. For younger children, the dilemmas should involve relatively few characters and moral principles (obedience to authority versus helping a friend in need, for instance). Note also that changing just one element in the kitten moral dilemma, such as changing the kitten in a tree to a kitten trapped on a telephone pole, can alter the situation dramatically.

Exposure to higher levels of reasoning

Heinz and the Druggist

In Europe, a woman was near death from a special kind of cancer. There was one drug that the doctors thought might save her. It was a form of radium that a druggist in the same town had recently discovered. The drug was expensive to make, but the druggist was charging ten times what the drug cost him to make. He paid $200 for the radium and charged $2,000 for a small dose of the drug.

The sick woman's husband, Heinz, went to everyone he knew to borrow the money, but he could only get together about $1,000, which is half what it cost. He told the druggist that his wife was dying and asked him to sell the drug cheaper or let him pay for it later. But the druggist said, "No, I discovered the drug and I'm going to make money from it." So Heinz gets desperate and considers breaking into the man's store to steal the drug for his wife.

Question: Should Heinz steal the drug?

Procedure

1. Ask students to identify what should be done and why. "What should Heinz do?"

2. Divide the class into small groups, either in terms of those who support a particular course of action or at random. Ask them to discuss their reasons and justify the course of action they have chosen. "Why should Heinz do what you think he should do?"

3. Permit groups to summarize and clarify their positions.

4. Ask additional probing questions:

   * Is the welfare of one's relatives more important than the welfare of others?

   * Should Heinz steal the drug for a stranger? For a pet that he loves?

   * It is against the law for Heinz to steal. Does that make it morally wrong? Why or why not?

Students should be encouraged to express reasonable value positions, though it is not necessary that they arrive at consensus.

Source: From *Models of Moral Education: An Appraisal* by R. H. Hersh, J. P. Miller, and G. D. Fielding. Copyright 1980 by Longman Publishers. Reprinted with permission.

The Model Student Activity above is designed for older students. It is based on a classic moral dilemma involving a husband's attempt to secure a drug for his sick wife. How students justify what Heinz should or should not do will identify their level of moral reasoning, as illustrated below:

Stage level reasoning

* *Stage 1:* Heinz should not steal the drug because he will be severely punished if he does.
* *Stage 2:* Heinz has the right to steal for his wife *if he wants to;* besides, a judge would understand and wouldn't punish him.
* *Stage 3:* Heinz has an obligation to help his wife, even if it means stealing for her. Besides, the druggist is being cruel and selfish; doesn't he have a heart?
* *Stage 4:* Heinz has an obligation to obey the law; by stealing the drug and thus breaking the law, he will be harming the society.
* *Stage 5:* Stealing and the law are not issues. Heinz should work to see that scarce drugs are distributed fairly, but even if that fails, the sanctity of human life exceeds everything else.

The small-group decision making and the extended discussion of complex issues associated with moral dilemmas can demand a level of experience and so-
phistication that some younger children cannot handle. "Heinz and the Drug-

Designing simple dilemmas

gist," for example, involves too many elements for young children to deal with
simultaneously.

What Critics Say About Moral Reasoning.   Much of the criticism directed to-

Adequacy

ward the moral-reasoning approach has questioned either the adequacy of
Kohlberg's theory or the contention that higher-stage reasoning is necessarily better than lower-stage reasoning. Harvard psychologist Carol Gilligan (1977, 1982),
for example, contends that women tend to score lower than men on Kohlberg's

Gender differences

scale, not because of deficiencies in women's moral reasoning, but because
women often use a different basis—an ethic based on interpersonal caring—for
determining morality.

Earlier questions about whether discussing moral dilemmas results in movement from one stage to the next have largely been resolved. Leming (1985) states
that "unlike the values-clarification approach, the weight of the evidence supports the claim . . . that the discussion of moral dilemmas can stimulate development through the stages of moral reasoning" (p. 131). For this to occur, however,
moral-dilemma discussions must take place regularly, not just once or twice during a semester.

Caring: An Alternative Ethic for Moral Reasoning.   The moral-reasoning
approach is based on the ethical ideal of justice. In that context, the most prized
values are the equality of human rights and the dignity of human beings
(Woolever & Scott, 1988). On the other hand, some authorities (Gilligan, 1977,

Justice is one aspect of morality

1982; Kohn 1997; Scott, 1987) argue that although nothing is wrong with justice
as an ethic, using it as the sole defining standard for morality is too limiting.
Those authorities (and others) argue that justice does not adequately reflect the
caring and supportive behaviors on which human relationships should be based.

As an example of this, Brogmann (1992) suggests that the "Heinz and the
Druggist" episode reflects the main point of contention between the masculine
and feminine moral voice. Brogmann argues that the masculine way is to rest
one's case on the universal principle that life comes before property, which
means that Heinz should steal the drug. The feminine approach, Brogmann contents, is to consider the consequences that stealing would have on Heinz and his
wife, and to explore alternatives to stealing; such as borrowing the money or seeing an understanding between Heinz and the druggist (see also Gilligan, 1982).
The point here is that justice is only one of the bases that can be used to resolve
this dilemma.

The following dilemma reflects elements inherent in an ethic of caring.

An example of caring

Bob, a top high school swimmer, was asked to teach young children with physical
disabilities to swim. This would help strengthen their legs, possibly enabling them
to walk. Bob was the only one in town who had the life-saving and teaching experience to do this job well. But helping these children would take most of Bob's free
time after work and school, time that Bob would otherwise use to practice for some

important, upcoming swimming contests. If Bob did not use his free time to practice, his chances of winning the contests, and possibly receiving a college scholarship, would be greatly lessened.

Should Bob agree to teach the disabled children? Why or why not? (Adapted from Mussen & Eisenberg-Berg, 1977, p. 121)

Prosocial behaviors

Integral to an ethic of caring are *prosocial behaviors:* that is, actions that aid other people without the expectation of direct rewards. Prosocial behaviors, such as that illustrated in the preceding dilemma, can sometimes involve personal costs or sacrifices. Prosocial behaviors, such as sharing, helping, sacrificing, and giving, are motivated by empathy, altruism, respect, sensitivity, nurturing, and a sense of caring.

● Values Analysis

"Should students be permitted to go outside on the playground for recess, weather permitting?" This may seem like an innocuous question, but as more and more schools remove their playground equipment and do not permit students to leave the building during recess, it's being debated in many communities. When children ask it, it's the kind of question that also lends itself to values analysis.

Analyzing the values in an issue or question

The values-analysis approach to values education emphasizes careful, deliberate, discriminating analysis. The idea is to examine value questions as rationally and unemotionally as possible and then arrive at a decision. In contrast to moral reasoning, where students take a position and then justify it, values analysis would have students refrain from taking a position until they have analyzed the issues involved.

The phases of values analysis

The following tasks are essential to the analysis of the recess question or any value question or issue:

1. *Identifying the issue.* The underlying issues in allowing children to go out onto the playground for recess usually involve one or more of the following: (a) the children's safety, (b) the legal liability and costs that the school may face in the event of injury, and (c) teachers' distaste for playground supervision responsibilities. The issue also may involve whether the recess policy is districtwide or whether each school can establish its own.

What are the value issues?

2. *Clarifying the value question.* Dealing with this element is not as easy as it appears. Ostensibly the value question is whether children's safety is more important than their need for physical exercise. However, whether safety, the avoidance of legal liability, or some other factor or combination of factors is the main motivation must be determined.

Do we have the data we need?

3. *Gathering and organizing evidence.* See Step 4 below.

Are our data accurate and relevant?

4. *Assessing the accuracy and relevance of the evidence.* For the recess question, Steps 3 and 4 of values analysis can occur simultaneously. To facilitate this, the teacher could place the following on the board or in a more permanent location in the classroom:

Reasons for Children to Go Outside for Recess

1. Need for physical activity
2. Need for a change of scene

Reasons for Children to Stay Inside for Recess

1. Safety
2. Lawsuits
3. Other??

The visual display helps children keep track of what portion of the issue they are dealing with. Various individuals can be invited to give their views: an attorney knowledgeable about school litigation, a school board member, the principal, a telephone interview with a principal whose students go outside for recess, and so on. Students could also survey teachers in the school for their opinions.

What are the alternatives?

5. *Identifying potential solutions.* The key question here is, What are the options? Are there other means for providing a break and physical activity for children?

Do our "solutions" create other problems?

6. *Identifying and assessing the possible consequences for each solution.* The children need to consider questions such as: Would running around in a crowded gym be any safer than going outside? What if the gym is already scheduled? If legal liability is the problem, can insurance cover this? And if so, is there money to pay for such insurance? And, if insurance were possible, would the administration permit going outside?

7. *Choosing among the alternatives.* Determining viable alternatives will hinge on the assessment done in Step 6 above.

What is the best course of action?

8. *Deciding and taking appropriate action.* The latter phases of value analysis depend on what happens in the earlier steps. In the recess question, students may decide to petition the principal to review the current policy. This kind of action is only appropriate if the students have determined it is the kind of issue on which the principal or another administrator can act. Students may find that, in today's world, their health and safety cannot be compromised.

As the preceding example illustrates, values analysis is not a "quickie" process. It need not be as elaborate as described here, yet some steps in values analysis, including gathering and assessing evidence, can require considerable time to do well. The overall intent is to wean students from the teacher's influence so that they can follow the processes on their own.

What Critics Say About Values Analysis. Values analysis has many supporters and few critics. Nevertheless, because some elements of values analysis are similar to the other approaches to values education, some of the same cautions may be in order. For example, elements of values analysis rely heavily on teachers asking a series of questions. Sometimes a single student may respond to a sequence of three or four questions (or more if elaboration is required). In a class of twenty-five students, a teacher could find herself engaged in a dialogue with one student. Hopefully the other twenty-four children will be interested enough to pay attention, but the longer the minidialogues go on, the more likely young children are to become disinterested. In light of this, several cautions seem prudent:

1. Teachers should be especially sensitive to the interest level of students who are not participating actively.

2. When possible, the approaches should be used in a small-group format.
3. When student interest begins to sag, summarize and move on to something else.
4. For values analysis especially, do not begin unless the issue is sufficiently involving *and* time is available to see the matter through to resolution.

SUMMARY

Values underlie *everything* a teacher does. It is simply impossible to sterilize lessons to make them value-free. In the 1970s and 1980s, when schools were retreating from their traditional role in building good character, moral education tended to be a hit-or-miss proposition. Teachers might occasionally employ one or more of the approaches presented in this chapter, but there was seldom a coherent program. To varying degrees, the approaches tend to be value-neutral; that is, they help individuals to explore what they *might* do, but they usually refrain from saying what the individual *ought* to do. This value-neutral stance was and is consistent with the privatization and personalization of values and morals that has occurred in the last half of the last century.

In view of the myriad social problems the United States is facing today, and especially the inability of some children to act in morally responsible and acceptable ways, a growing number of schools are moving to reestablish character education programs. Their common goal is to produce students with good character: that is, students who know the good and feel disposed to act accordingly. Character education is a comprehensive, schoolwide effort that focuses on teaching core ethical values such as honesty, respect, responsibility, and truthfulness—values that are essential to the society's continuing survival and that almost no one opposes. Character education also extends to the hidden curriculum, the day-to-day schooling practices that can sometimes contradict, even neutralize, the values that schools and teachers espouse.

Character education is an overarching movement that sometimes incorporates one or more of the alternative strategies we identified in this chapter. Those strategies can provide excellent vehicles for raising moral and ethical questions. However, some of the alternative moral education strategies, especially values clarification, must be approached cautiously.

Character education is the focus of intense interest across the country, in part because of the growing recognition that transmitting knowledge—making students smart—does not ensure that children will act in morally acceptable ways. But whether schools can become caring moral communities remains to be seen. Equally unknown at this point is whether schools can provide moral anchors for children from families that are unable to do so. Until we get answers to such questions, the final chapter on character education cannot be written.

SUGGESTED ACTIVITIES

1. Select and examine at least one chapter in a social studies textbook for any grade level. Determine the extent to which statements within the chapter reflect a value-based agenda.

2. Select an elementary social studies text for the grade level you'd like to teach. For any section of the book you choose, show how you might incorporate values education into your approach to teaching that segment.

3. The Scout Law expected everyone to be trustworthy, loyal, helpful, friendly, courteous, kind, obedient, cheerful, thrifty, brave, clean, and reverent. Determine to what extent these expectations are consistent with the character education movement today.

4. The practice of providing tangible rewards to students for demonstrating good behavior may be successful in the short run, but over time it can undermine a child's intrinsic motivation. Determine how you might resolve this apparent dilemma.

5. Not long ago, a student teacher asked us for "the three best lessons we knew of" that would "make" her students respect each other. Why just three lessons? "Because that's all I have time for." Develop a response for this teacher.

SUGGESTED READINGS AND RESOURCES

Print Resources

GENERAL RESOURCES

William J. Bennett. (1993). *The book of virtues: A treasury of great moral stories.* New York: Simon & Schuster. This book, which was a popular Christmas gift a few years ago, contains classic literary pieces—poems and stories—arranged around ten virtues and sequenced from simple to more complex. For example, the section on Responsibility begins with simple poems for young children, then includes such classics as Tennyson's "The Charge of the Light Brigade," and concludes with a section by Plato, and public documents by Jefferson, Madison, Frederick Douglas, Abraham Lincoln, and Martin Luther King, Jr. The other virtues documented include self-discipline, compassion, friendship, work, courage, perseverance, honesty, loyalty, and faith.

Edward F. DeRoche & Mary M. Williams. (1998). *Educating hearts and minds: A comprehensive character education framework.* Thousand Oaks, CA: Corwin Press. This book offers a nine-component model for a comprehensive character education program. The components include vision, standards, expectations, criteria to guide program development, the role of leadership, necessary resources, training, partnerships, and assessment.

Gertrude Himmelfarb. (1995). *The demoralization of society: From Victorian virtues to modern values.* New York: Alfred A. Knopf. This insightful and sometimes acerbic book by a distinguished historian is not yet another diatribe on what has gone wrong with America. Rather, it is a well-researched history of the Victorian period and focuses on Victorian virtues including hard work, thrift, cleanliness, self-reliance, self-respect, neighborliness, and patriotism.

Alfie Kohn. (1997). How not to teach values. *Phi Delta Kappan,* 78, 429–439. This article provides an in-depth analysis of techniques that are purported to teach values, but probably don't.

Thomas Lickona. (1991). *Educating for character: How our schools can teach respect and responsibility.* New York: Bantam Books. Lickona argues that if we care about the future of our society and our children, educating for character is a moral imperative.

Alex Molnar. (Ed.). (1997). *The construction of children's character: The ninety-sixth yearbook of the National Society for the Study of Education.* Chicago: University of Chicago Press. This book presents a current overview and critical assessment of the theory and practice of contemporary approaches to character education in the schools. Individual chapters by noted authorities provide an excellent cross section of opinion in the field.

Madonna M. Murphy. (1998). *Character education in America's blue ribbon schools: Best practices for meeting the challenge.* Lancaster, PA: Technomic Publishing. This book is full of useful information and succinct evaluations of commonly implemented character education programs, including Here's Looking at You, Quest, and Second Step. It also reviews materials from major character education curriculum development institutes, including the Character Education Institute, The Heartwood Curriculum, and CIVITAS.

Nel Noddings. (1986). *Caring: A feminine approach to ethics and moral education.* Berkeley: University of California Press. Noddings makes the case for human caring as the foundation of ethical responsiveness. She argues that although men often base their ethical decisions on universal principles (à la Kohlberg), women are more likely to base their decisions on feelings, needs, and impressions. Noddings claims that morality should be based on a reciprocity between the person doing the caring (e.g., mother, teacher) and the one being cared for.

Edward Wynne & Kevin Ryan. (1997). *Reclaiming our schools: A handbook on teaching character, academics and discipline.* New York: Merrill. This widely acclaimed book is by perhaps the best known character education proponents in the country. Individual chapters focus on teaching character and discipline, teachers as moral educators, the curriculum as a moral educator, and leadership in moral schools.

OTHER RESOURCES

Information on the Heartwood Ethics Curriculum is available from The Heartwood Institute, 12300 Perry Highway, Wexford, PA 15090 (412-934-1777).

Information on the Exploring Ethics through Children's Literature Program is available from the Critical Thinking Press & Software, PO Box 448, Pacific Grove, CA 93950-0448 (1-800-458-4849).

Internet Resources

Introductory Note: Web sites sometimes change their Internet addresses or cease operating entirely. All the addresses supplied here were operating when this book was printed, but if any of them fail to work properly, try entering the topic or target organization in any standard search engine. Note also that if you enter "character education" into most search engines, you will get hundreds of listings, many of which are for organizations that are trying to market various books and materials. The following are noncommercial sources.

ERIC Clearinghouse

http://www.indiana.ERIc/~eric_rec/ico/bibs/character.html

The ERIC Clearinghouses were created long before the Internet existed, but they still offer excellent sources of information. This one could be subtitled, "more than you want to know about character education."

Two states, California and Utah, offer useful Web sites for character education. They are:

California Character Education Clearinghouse

http://www.cde.ca.gov/character/aboutpg.html

This site, maintained by the California Department of Education's Character Education Project, offers a variety of resources including reviews of character education materials, information about model programs and professional development, an excellent annotated bibliography, and links to other character education Web sites.

Utah Character Education Project

http://www/usoe.k12.ut.ut/curr/char_ed/

This useful site offers many links and resources, very few of which are specific to the state of Utah.

Virtuous Stories

http://www.pbs.org/adventures/Storytime/menu.html

This site features on-line versions of some stories that appear in William Bennett's *Book of Virtues.* The idea is worthwhile, but some of the stories are so abbreviated that PBS's execution leaves something to be desired.

7

Social Studies: Gateway to Literacy

Key Questions

- What are the different forms of literacy?
- How can social studies serve as a gateway to literacy, and vice versa?
- What role does oral language play in building literacy?
- How do children (and adults) construct meaning?

Key Ideas

- Language literacy is the ability to use a standard form of language fluently and effectively.
- Oral language and listening provide the basis for subsequent reading and writing.
- Children (and everyone else) construct meaning by incorporating new ideas into their existing frames of reference.
- Social studies can facilitate language development.

Introduction: People, People, People

For the last fourteen years, Ms. Lynda Esparza has taught second graders at Mesa Verde Elementary School in southern Arizona. Over 80 percent of her students are Hispanic. A few recently arrived from Mexico, some arrived three or four years ago, and others are native-born citizens of the United States. Another 10 percent of Lynda's students are Native American, and the balance are Anglo- and African-American.

We visited Ms. Esparza on a warm November afternoon as she and her class were beginning a social studies unit on community helpers. To find out what her children already knew about communities and community services, Ms. Esparza gathered everyone in the carpeted area. Seated on a low chair and using an overhead projector on a low cart, Lynda told her second graders, "Today, we're going to share ideas about people who work in communities. Remember our rules for brainstorming—everybody gets a chance to speak. After I put down everyone's

Setting the focus

DIVERSITY

ideas, we'll go back and work on them." The children nodded; they had apparently done brainstorming activities before. "O.K., what different jobs do people in communities do?"

Hands shot up. Carlos suggested, "police." Lynda recorded it on the transparency. Maria suggested, "store people," and Lynda asked, "What do you mean, Maria?"

"People who work in stores."

Brainstorming

"What about "mall people?" asked Armondo. "Lots of people work at the mall."

Lynda turned to the class and said, "Let's decide whether we should describe some people by where they work, or whether we should list specific jobs, like clerks or cashiers." The class decided that either way was O.K.

Gracie then suggested "mail people." Because the homophone for *mail* could be confusing for some students, Lynda asked, "Do you mean people like letter carriers, people who work for the post office?"

"Yeah, people like that," Gracie replied.

"Let's put that down as 'postal people,' and then put *mail* in parentheses just so we're sure," Lynda said, demonstrating what parentheses were as she did so. Soon the transparency was filled with a listing of various occupations, some public and some private employees, and some people listed in terms of where they worked. Lynda said, "All these people work in communities, and some of them work for communities. Right now, let's make a 'Beans' poem from our brainstorming."

From the children's expressions, it was clear that they knew what a "Beans" poem was, and that they enjoyed doing it. A "Beans" poem is a form of structured poetry based on "Beans," by Lucia and James Hymes (1960) (shown in Figure 7.1).

FIGURE 7.1 Beans

Beans,
Beans,
Beans.
Butter beans,
Baked beans,
Big fat lima beans,
Long thin string beans—
Those are just a few.
Green beans,
Black beans,
Big fat kidney beans,
Red hot chili beans,
Jumping beans too.
Pea beans,
Pinto beans,
Don't forget shelly beans.
Last of all, best of all,
I like jelly beans!

Source: HOORAY FOR CHOCOLATE (pp. 34–35), © 1960 by Lucia and James L. Hymes, Jr. Reprinted by permission of Addison-Wesley Publishing Company, Inc.

● ●

FIGURE 7.2   A Writing Pattern Based on "Beans"

People,
People,
People,

_____   *people*,
_____   *people*,

_____   _____   _____   *people*,
_____   _____   _____   *people*,

Those are just a few.

_____   *people*,
_____   *people*,

_____   _____   _____   *people*,
_____   _____   _____   *people*,

_____   *people* too.
_____   *people*,
_____   *people*,

Don't forget _____   *people*.

Last of all, best of all,

I like _____   *people* !

● ●

Lynda rose from her chair and dragged an easel filled with large chart paper to an area where everyone could see it. She flipped back the cover sheet to reveal the "Beans" poem format that she had drawn previously, but with blanks where the words had been. Taking a marker, she then said, "Because our poem will be about people, I'm going to put the word *people* where *beans* used to be. She quickly wrote "people" in the appropriate spaces, as shown in Figure 7.2.

Deciding on an ending Lynda then said, "Remember that when we make a 'Beans' poem, one of the first things we decide is how we're going to end it. Let's think about what would make a good last line." Lynda and her students talked about different endings, and finally settled on "I like all people." Lynda then handed the marker to Maria, and said, "Why don't you write this for us?" Maria jumped up, took the marker, and filled in "i like all" in the spaces on the last line before "people." Half a dozen hands went up. Lynda nodded to Placido, who said, "I think Maria needs a capital *I*." Turning to Maria, Lynda asked, "What do you think, Maria?" Maria thought for a moment and said, "Yes, I should have made a capital *I*." She then took her marker and neatly transformed the lowercase *i* into a capital letter.

Interactive writing

With the ending decided, Lynda and the class then began filling in the other blanks. Lynda suggested that they put people who work for the government in the top half of the poem, and people who work in the community in the lower half. For example, when Carlos suggested "fire people," Lynda asked, "Should this go in the top half or the bottom?" Carlos responded that "fire people are city workers, so they belong in the top half." Lynda handed Carlos the marker and he wrote "Fire" in one of the empty spaces. When Armondo was writing "electricity," he spelled it "electrisity." To change the *s* to a *c*, Lynda reached for her roll of correction tape, which is similar to Post-it Notes, and handed a small piece to Armondo, who pasted it over his errant *s*, and then wrote the *c* where it belonged. The result was a product with correct spelling and grammar. If there are a lot of spelling errors or other changes, all the correction tape can create a speckled appearance on the final chart.

When all the blanks were filled in, Lynda asked, "What should we do now?"

Choral speaking

"We chorus it!" her students responded in unison. Lynda picked up a pointer with her right hand and began quietly snapping the fingers of her left hand to establish a rhythm. The students quickly joined in. In unison, and as Lynda pointed to each word, they began chorusing, "People, people, people. . . . "

When the first chorusing was completed, Lynda asked, "Let's see if there is anything we want to change?" Several students offered suggestions, including changing the last line to "*We* like all people." The group debated each suggestion, using more correction tape to make the necessary changes, until the final poem was as shown in Figure 7.3.

Adding variations

After chorusing the revised poem another time, Lynda suggested, "Let's orchestrate this poem—any ideas?" Jason's hand waved vigorously, but his actions violated a rule the class had agreed on previously: A raised hand is sufficient to get attention. If you wave your hand too vigorously or call out "Me, me," you won't get called on. Lynda raised an eyebrow as she looked at Jason, and then called on Lucinda, who suggested, "Let's let the girls be 'people' people, and the boys say the other parts; then we can switch."

Lynda responded, "Shall we try it?" The children nodded. Lynda continued, "The boys and I will say the words until we get to the word *people*. Then we'll stop and our 'people' people (the girls) will say their word." With the same finger-snapping rhythm they had used previously, a chorus of girls' voices began, "People, people, people." A chorus of boys' voices then chimed in with "Police," "Fire." . . . Later, the boys chorused "People, people, people . . . " and the girls added the specifics. After a second time through the poem with the boys as "people" people, Lynda said, "Let's give all our choristers a round of applause." It was a fitting ending for an activity the children had clearly enjoyed.

Determining what students already know

Aside from listing public employees separately from those who work in private industry, there were no profound social studies learnings from Lynda's lesson. Neither was there any effort to determine whether these "community helpers" actually

FIGURE 7.3   People, People, People

People,
People,
People,
Police people,
Fire people,
Electricity and water people,
Friendly, helpful postal people,
Those are just a few.
Teacher people,
Principal people,
Library and cafeteria people,
Doctor and nurse people,
TV people too.
Delivery people,
Store people,
Don't forget McDonald's people.
But last of all, best of all,
We like all people!

● ●

help the community. Those learnings would come later. At this point in the lesson, Lynda was satisfied that her students already knew about many of the jobs available in the community. Whether the students could organize and classify the different occupations they had listed would become the focus for another lesson.

Developing fluency

Lynda's students had participated in an activity that enhanced their oral fluency and that could ultimately enhance their ability to deal with language in different contexts. That, in part, is what language literacy is all about—the ability to read, write, and speak the language fluently and effectively in different situations.

Oral Language and Listening: Bases for Literacy

When Lynda Esparza and her second graders created and then chorused the "People" poem, that activity was more than a cute way to end a social studies lesson. A large body of research (see Button, Johnson, & Ferguson, 1996; Cooper, 1993; Dickinson, 1987; Flood & Lapp, 1987; Pinnell & McCarrier, 1994) indicates that both reading and writing depend, at least initially, on children's facility with speaking and listening. Children who have poor oral language and listening skills are also likely to have poor reading and writing skills. This also means that many students, especially those for whom English is their second language, can benefit from experiences in speaking and using language fluently, comfortably, and confidently.

Prior language learnings

By the time most five- and six-year-old children arrive in school, they have already acquired a vast knowledge of language, most of which they learned without formal instruction. In that process, they will have learned to distinguish separate units of sound (*phonemes*) and meaning (*morphemes*), to discover patterns and rules by which units of phonemes and morphemes are combined into sentences

Planning should encompass what you as a teacher will do and what your students will be doing. *(© Michael Zide)*

(*syntax, grammar,* etc.), and can identify context clues (*semantics*) that guide the social aspects of dialogue. Children don't use the kinds of labels we have here, of course, but when most of them enter school, they already have what linguists call a "fully formed grammar and language system." It matters not whether the children speak standard English, a regional dialect, Black English, or a mixture of English and another language; they will have acquired whatever language they speak through listening and observing, and then by experimenting with their language in social situations.

How do children use listening, speaking, and observing as they acquire language? Were you to observe young children over time, you would likely see them do the following:

★ They rely on listening and speaking as the main channels for learning language (which is obviously true for children who are unable to read or write).

Building and testing theories about language

★ They actively reflect on and analyze what they observe and hear.

★ Based on what they hear and observe, children usually form theories about language and then test those theories in real situations. For example, most children learn that by adding the (bound) morpheme *ed* to certain words, they can talk about things that happened in the past. They test their theory about *ed* by using it in different situations, such as "I walked to the store." However, having discovered the marvelous power that *ed* gives them to talk about things that

Overgeneralizing

happened in the past, many children overgeneralize its application by adding *ed* to verbs of any tense, including *go* or *went.* Thus, it's common to hear young children make statements like "We *goed* to Burger King" or "I *runned* around the track." Eventually, most children discover that their new rule doesn't work all the time. They learn these language patterns without asking questions such as, "When do you add *ed* to a word or use a different word—when do you use *ran* instead of *runned?* Instead they typically look for patterns in the language to identify words that are exceptions to that rule.

The role of prior experience

★ When children lack the correct words for describing something, they usually select from the words that they already know. This is why, upon meeting an elderly man with deep wrinkles, a child might ask, "Why does that man have *paths* all over his face?" (Morrow, 1989). It makes sense, at least from a child's point of view.

Clearly, children do not develop their ability to use language passively; they continually construct or reconstruct language as they learn it (Morrow, 1989). How children learn to use language correctly also transfers to the ways in which they learn (as opposed to memorize) anything. Children (and even adults) construct knowledge by overgeneralizing, by identifying and refining ideas, by testing ideas that may or may not fit their prior experiences, and then by going back through the cycle again. We'll return to this process again later.

●━ Helping Children Develop Fluency in Standard English

Children bring their language from home

Most children come to school fluent in the language of the home. That language may be standard English, the language of schools and textbooks, but it will often reflect at least a regional or ethnic dialect, sometimes both. Most of us are so attuned to the language we grew up with that we notice almost immediately if someone speaks in a different regional or ethnic dialect. To hear someone talk with a southern drawl, perhaps, or say "Hush" instead of "Quiet," is sometimes regarded as quaint or even cute, especially at first. But upon hearing someone repeatedly pronounce *especially* with an "x," as *expecially,*" it probably won't be long before speakers of standard English begin to make judgments about the speaker's intelligence—or lack thereof. In still other cases, the primary language of the home may be something other than English. Thus these children will be learning English as a second language. Either situation can pose problems for children who are becoming fluent in standard English.

English as a Second Language (ESL). We suspect that only people who are truly bilingual can appreciate the problems associated with becoming proficient in two languages simultaneously. Children who are learning English as a second language face challenges that native English speakers seldom encounter. For example, all the children in Lynda Esparza's class know their alphabet, but students whose native language is Spanish tend to pronounce the vowels differently than English-speaking children. What English speakers say as /a/, /e/, /i/, /o/, /u/ are pronounced in Spanish as /ah/, /ey/, /ee/, /o/, /oo/. As a result, native Spanish speakers may have difficulty distinguishing between words like *cut, cat,* and *cot* (see Henning, 1994).

Problems of second-language learners

DIVERSITY

There is a subtle and often unspoken bias against people who—regardless of whatever language they speak in their homes—are unwilling or unable to speak or write standard English. Several years ago, some future entrepreneurs noticed that individuals who represented major corporations based in Texas and the Southwest sometimes had difficulty dealing with their colleagues in corporations based in the East. Upon further investigation, these individuals concluded that a big part of the problem involved how people from southwestern (and southern) regions talked. For example, talking "Texan"—with its lazy drawl and the tendency to say "Y'all"—was often essential to doing business in parts of the Southwest. But the same dialect seemed to become a liability in the East. It is difficult to convince someone from the northeastern United States (New York, Boston, etc.) that the pace of his or her speech is fast—in part, because everybody talks "this way." Likewise, it is equally difficult to convince people who talk at a much slower pace and use regional dialects that people elsewhere may perceive of them as intellectually challenged. Perhaps this is why in the South and Southwest, people who talk rapidly are often regarded with suspicion. On the other hand, people in the Northeast may perceive slow talkers as dimwitted and unable to express themselves with speed and precision. The point here is that the entrepreneurs noted earlier eventually established a school in Dallas to which corporations throughout the South and Southwest send people so they can learn to speak standard English in ways that do not subtly offend people in other parts of the country.

Do people resist changing the speech patterns they grew up with? Of course. Our speech patterns, many of which we may not be aware of, are integral to who we are.

A second brief example may illustrate this point. Whenever you have the opportunity, close your eyes as you listen to a pregame show on the ESPN cable network. Focus your attention on the sportscasters, not the ex-athletes or former coaches—some former athletes sound as if they just came in from feeding the animals (as do some coaches). Until you open your eyes, it's unlikely that you will be able to determine the ethnicity of the sportscasters. Some of them are obviously African-American, some are Anglo, and some are Hispanic, but almost all of them speak flawless standard English.

Some individuals may claim that asking someone to replace a regional or ethnic dialect with standard English is tantamount to asking them to deny their heritage. Still others regard it as a matter of chasing after dollars or of selling out to the Anglos. Regardless of which position you accept, consider the Reverend Jesse Jackson's position. (see Christiansen, 1998). Jackson argues that when people are at home, they are free to speak however they want to. But when anyone wants to communicate to and be accepted by a larger audience, they can eliminate several hurdles by speaking standard English—what the Reverend Jackson calls the "cash language."

· ·

Language differences

Even native English speakers sometimes encounter problems when they first see familiar words in written form. Because English has so many silent letters, what children know and say as /rit/, for example, seems to take on extra letters when it is written as *write*. However, because English-speaking children's pronunciation of the word does not change, their problem is primarily one of recognizing the word in its written form. For Spanish-speaking children, however, the problems are compounded because, except for *h*, all the written letters in Spanish are sounded. Thus, upon encountering a word like *write* in its written form, a native Spanish speaker will want to pronounce it as a two-syllable word, /wreetey/, which is something they have never heard before, even if they're familiar with the English word *write* in its spoken form. In such situations, an ESL child's ability to use context clues becomes even more important than it is for native English speakers.

In some parts of the country, Spanish-language textbooks may be available for social studies and other subjects. However, these texts typically reflect Castilian Spanish, which can be quite different from regional Spanish dialects, like Tex-Mex, that the children are accustomed to hearing in the home. This can mean that, in addition to basic structural differences in the languages, ESL students must often overcome dialectical differences. If the ESL child's native language is neither English nor Spanish, finding appropriate text materials will be almost impossible.

Dialectically Different Children.   Anyone who speaks a regional or social-group dialect exclusively can be regarded as dialectically different. For example, children from New England often add an /r/ to words that end in *a*. Thus, *Cuba* (the country) is usually pronounced /cuber/. On the other hand, children from New York City tend to drop the /r/, as in /pak da cah/ (park the car).

Regional and cultural dialects

DIVERSITY

Dialectically related usages are different from standard English, but they are not substandard forms. Children from Appalachia who say /warsh/ for *wash* or "I done it," for example, are simply repeating the speech patterns they hear and use in their homes and neighborhoods. As different as their pronunciations may be, they are not doing anything "wrong." Teachers who insist on "correcting" such usages in children's oral language may very well send the message that there is something "wrong" with a language form that children feel comfortable with. As Henning notes, "Children who are made to believe there is something wrong with their speech may stop speaking in school, which is counterproductive" (1994, p. 59).

The problems that dialectically different children encounter learning standard English are similar to the problems that ESL students face but are less serious. For a child from Appalachia to discover that there is no *r* in *wash*, for example, is hardly as serious as learning that descriptive adjectives in English go before the noun, not afterwards as in Spanish.

Developing Fluency.   The techniques for helping children become fluent and effective users of standard English are similar to the techniques that children use to learn language in the first place (which is why we went into such detail on that earlier). Children need opportunities to "play" with language. They need oral activities that enable them to build on, transform, expand on, and interpret standard English sentence patterns. They also need to experience the rhythms of standard English, which is one of the reasons that Lynda Esparza had her students chorus the "People" poem in different ways. Children also need to hear standard English used in realistic settings. You may have noticed that Lynda Esparza used the word *shall* correctly during her lesson, and she did so naturally and without making a "big deal" about it. Although even some proficient users of standard English cannot distinguish between when to use *shall* or *will*, Lynda effectively modeled a usage that was not likely to be in many of her children's everyday language repertoires.

Additional suggestions for handling oral language and listening activities include the following:

Playing with language

⋆ Model correct, standard English speech and writing to the best of your ability to do so.

* As you model the language, do it in ways that say to children, "I accept you (and the way you speak) as you are."
* Recognize that the goal is to help children use standard English effectively and fluently, *not* to denigrate the child's (and the family's) existing dialect. Literacy is not a crusade to stamp out regional or social dialects.
* Permit children to use whatever dialects they are most comfortable with in class discussions, storytelling, and creative dramatics.
* React to the message the child is trying to convey and not to the form of speech. Cursing and obscene language are obviously unacceptable.
* Resist the impulse to interrupt children to correct their vocabulary or sentence structure. As Henning notes, "Constant interruption and correction can easily turn a pleasurable sharing time into a period of discomfort that children dread" (1994, p. 60).

Listening Activities

Listening is a combination of what you hear, what you expect to hear, what you observe, and what you recall from your previous experiences. Effective listeners are aware of factors that influence listening. These include (1) thinking ahead of the reader or talker and anticipating the direction of the discourse; (2) assessing the kind(s) of evidence the reader or talker is using; (3) periodically reviewing the author's or speaker's main points; (4) "listening between the words"; (5) constructing ideas instead of just picking up facts; and (6) withholding evaluation of the message until after the reader or speaker is through talking.

Like other language-related activities, listening is probably best approached as part of other ongoing activities. One of the best activities for this is reading aloud to children. What you read aloud should not be restricted to children's literature or limited to the primary grades. Sharing *brief* passages of informational content with older students can be equally appropriate.

Whenever you are reading aloud or it is possible to stop someone who is talking to the class, you might interrupt with *one* of the following questions:

1. What do you think will happen next?
2. What has the author/speaker said up to this point?
3. What is the author's/speaker's main idea?
4. What things [kind(s) of evidence] has the author/speaker used to get us to believe what he or she is saying?
5. Which parts of what the author/speaker said were opinion?
6. How would you have said what the author/speaker said?

Because students (or anyone) may resent the intrusion when their train of thought is interrupted, you must use your judgment about when such questions are appropriate. If students are bored, they probably won't mind the interruption, but then they may not have been listening well enough to answer your questions.

Cassette tape recorders have made it possible to develop homemade listening-oriented activities. By taking a tape recorder with you as you travel, for instance, you can gather interesting materials for listening activities. Consider developing a three-minute tape of sounds at a busy intersection, a shopping mall, or a supermarket. The idea, initially, is to have students *describe what they hear,* not guess what they're hearing. If a child says, "I hear a supermarket," for example, he or she is inferring something rather than describing the sounds. Inferring is a logical extension of describing—usually an inevitable extension—but the students' first focus should be on describing the sounds themselves.

Reading, Writing, and Social Studies

This section is based on two simple yet powerful ideas: Children learn to read by reading, and they learn to write by writing. Reading is that marvelous process by which children gain meaning by decoding written symbols. If children do not understand what they are decoding, they are merely *word-calling,* not reading.

The focus is meaning

Writing is the process of encoding thought and speech into written symbols. Because meaning is inherent in our every thought or utterance, we simply don't think meaningless thoughts. As a result, almost all writing is inherently meaningful, at least to the writer. Unfortunately, what some students do in school might look like writing but is likely to be *pseudowriting* (see Welton, 1982). Certainly you remember reports and term papers that you largely copied from encyclopedias or other sources. That's pseudowriting.

A different perspective on rules

Even the most basic conventions of writing can make sense to children if they are approached from the perspective of writers (or authors) who are trying to convey meaning to readers, instead of as decontextualized rules that writers must follow. Consider: How do writers tell their readers that they've come to the end of an idea? They use a period. How do writers tell their readers that they're beginning a new idea? They begin with a capital letter. How do writers tell readers that they are finished with one cluster of ideas and are ready to move on to a new cluster? A new paragraph.

From thinking thoughts to writing sentences

There are surely millions of students across the country learning rules like "Always end a sentence with a period." Those students really need to understand that a sentence is a thought, an idea in written form, and that the period simply marks the end of the idea. Unfortunately, schools sometimes complicate matters by teaching rules that involve multiple abstractions. Remember, for example, the countless hours you spent drawing one line under the subjects and two lines under the predicates of sample sentences? Ask yourself when was the last time you thought about predicates. The subject-predicate business may be useful if you want to talk about sentences, but you might also ask yourself how often you need to talk about sentences. Most people don't think in terms of nouns, verbs, subjects, or predicates—they think whole thoughts.

Clear thinking leads to clear writing

The points here are several. All of us think in terms of thoughts and ideas that have meaning to us. And when we convert an idea into spoken form, it becomes a statement. When we put a thought or idea into written form, we produce a sentence. However, if decontextualized rules and labels are introduced in the context of writing, the effect can be to make writing more difficult than it really is. All writers must deal with many things as they write, including spelling, punctuation, intended audience, tone, and organization. Yet, to the extent that writing is thinking in a written form, we suggest that the key to helping children produce clear writing is clear thinking.

The primacy of meaning

Reading and writing are complementary processes for getting and conveying meaningful ideas. So, regardless of how you feel about the "whole" language approach to literacy, one of the main contributions of that movement may be the renewed focus it has placed on meaning in all language-related activities.

● Reading and Textbooks

Several factors play a role in helping or hindering children from getting meaning from the materials they read, especially social studies textbooks. You could regard the subtitle for this section as: "Why Are Social Studies Textbooks So Difficult?"

Consider the following passage from a fifth-grade social studies book. As you do so, try to (1) identify the number of ideas it presents explicitly—not those that are implied—and then (2) decide which if any of these ideas is important enough that you would ask a test question about it. If an idea is important enough to be included on a test, it is something students should know and remember.

Sample textbook passage

Little by little, Canada won its freedom from Great Britain. By 1949, Canada was fully independent. Canadians control their own country. They also choose their own leaders. (McAuley & Wilson, 1985, p. 41)

The passage, which amounts to a sweeping summary of recent Canadian history, contains only four short sentences—twenty-seven words in all. Yet the number of ideas that are packed into this space is significant. We identified the following:

Few words, but many ideas

* Canada is a country that now controls itself.
* Canada got its freedom gradually.
* Canada gained its independence from Great Britain in 1949. (This idea could be considered two separate ideas: [1] independence from Great Britain and [2] independence in 1949.)
* Canada was partially independent before 1949.
* The people of Canada select their leaders.

Concept loading

This passage has more ideas than sentences. The extent to which this or any other passage contains ideas that are packed densely, sparsely, or somewhere in between is called *concept loading*. Concept loading contributes to the material's *readability*, that is, to the relative ease or difficulty of reading and gaining meaning from the material. Passages in which ideas are densely packed, and thus have a high concept load, are usually more difficult to understand than passages with a lower concept load.

There are no absolute standards for high or low concept loading, which can vary for different types of materials—novels versus textbooks, for example—so concept loading is a relative measure. However, placing ideas in short sentences does not in itself make those ideas easier to understand. Although the sentences in the sample passage are short, its concept load is fairly high.

Textbooks and Readability. According to Chall and Conard (1991) and others, the readability level of most elementary social studies texts ranges from one to two grade levels above the intended grade level. For example, most fourth-grade books have a fifth- or sixth-grade reading level. This difference tends to diminish during the middle-school years, so that by eighth grade textbooks are likely to be closer to their intended grade level.

What the research says

To understand the abstract concepts and terms that social studies texts often contain, most children usually need concrete examples that they can relate to. The more examples, the better. Yet this is where a confounding element, length, enters the picture. Every example in a book requires space, which adds to a book's length. The overall length of the text becomes a concern, primarily because of the way in which textbooks are perceived. If social studies textbooks were regarded more like dictionaries, as resources to be drawn upon as needed, their length would be irrelevant—except, perhaps, with respect to cost. However, because textbooks are often viewed as something students must "cover" by the end of the year, their length can become a significant factor. Dictionary-size textbooks would strike fear in the hearts of students and teachers alike, and their chances of being adopted are unlikely. Thus textbook authors and publishers are almost forced to maintain a reasonable length and, in the process, are denied the opportunity to clarify abstract concepts and ideas with multiple examples. Presenting large numbers of concepts on each page can make books more efficient, but doing so can also make them more difficult to read and understand.

The dilemma: Adding examples without increasing the length

In response to complaints about high concept loading, most publishers have tried to simplify their materials. However, instead of attacking concept loading directly, which would mean eliminating some abstract concepts and adding examples for others, they usually attack the problem by shortening the sentences, as we saw in the textbook passage about Canada. In theory, short sentences are easier to read than longer, more complex sentences, even though that notion has been disputed by some recent research in reading. Nevertheless, the trend in textbooks is to improve readability (and thus reduce the apparent difficulty level) by reducing sentence length. Even some critics acknowledge that the blame for mediocre textbooks does not rest solely with the publishers (see Sewall, 1988), who must deal with voluminous curriculum guidelines and various other expectations that change from district to district and state to state.

Shorter sentences

● Helping Children Understand Specialized Vocabulary

Every subject has its specialized vocabulary. Literature has its *sonnets* and *metaphors,* science has its *atoms* and *antennae,* and social studies has its *wings, steppes,* and a host of others. For most students, such vocabulary poses a twofold problem. Even though a simple word like *wash* is already part of most students' oral vocabulary and even though the student can probably spell the word correctly, he or she may have never heard of a dry streambed referred to as a *wash.* Likewise, *run* is a regional expression for a brook or stream. Words with multiple meanings like these are called *polysemous,* and they make up about one-third of all commonly used words (Irvin et al., 1995). They often have meanings that are specific to particular content areas—such as *antenna* in science and *wash* in geography.

Terms with multiple meanings

In many instances, polysemous words like *wing, class, bill, branch,* and *fork* are not particularly difficult for students if the teacher can build on the child's existing experiences. In the case of *wash* and *run,* the goal is to associate the word with the child's prior experiences with rivers and waterways, thus adding other terms to their repertoire. Other regional expressions that fit this category are *borough, county, parish; tote, carry; pop, soda, tonic.*

Figurative expressions and abstract concepts

Two categories of terms that can pose more perplexing problems are *figurative expressions,* such as *Fertile Crescent, dark horse, cold war, iron curtain, log rolling,* and *corn belt,* and terms associated with *abstract concepts,* such as *ethnocentrism, nationalism, culture, temperate, democracy,* and *inflation.* Even though none of us have ever seen a belt made from corn, many children already have *corn* and *belt* in their reading and oral vocabularies. Their problem usually arises because they have never encountered these familiar words in their *corn belt* configuration. Abstract terms can pose added problems because they are often not part of the child's oral and reading vocabularies and because they, like figurative expressions, refer to phenomena that are beyond the child's realm of experience. Figurative expressions and especially abstract terms often require more comprehensive teaching strategies, which are considered in detail in the last section of this chapter.

Two final categories of specialized terminology that can affect social studies teaching include the following:

* *Proper names for historically or physically remote personages and places.* Many terms in this category do not follow familiar rules for phonic analysis. Examples: pharaoh, tsar (or czar), Hwang Ho, La Jolla, San Jose.
* *Acronyms and abbreviations.* These can present problems because they are often abbreviations for organizations with which students are not familiar. Examples: OPEC, IRS, GOP, FCC.

Some terms are more important to meaning than others!

In helping children understand unfamiliar vocabulary, a key element to keep in mind is that not all terms are equally important (see Irvin et al., 1995). In many cases, students can get the basic thrust of a passage even if they don't understand every word. For example, consider the following sentence: "With the mechanization that accompanied the agrarian revolution, farmers were able to grow more corn, wheat, oats, and barley." Many students today have never heard of barley, a grain crop used extensively in producing beer, but this word is actually incidental to understanding the text. In addition, because *barley* is presented in association with other grains that should be more familiar to students, the context of the sentence suggests that it is one of several crops that a farmer might grow. Thus, the preteaching of *barley* is not essential, although you could make certain that students understand it in postreading follow-up.

Students are very unlikely to understand the sample sentence above unless they also understand the term *mechanization.* In this instance, *mechanization* is so critical to the meaning of this passage that teachers cannot treat it in the same way they do *barley.* The key here is to anticipate potential problems before students become frustrated. The time-honored technique for doing this is to preteach the term before students read the passage. The teacher should introduce new terms that are vital to understanding the passage—not including *barley*—by writing them on the chalkboard and then defining them before students begin reading. Although this technique tends to treat the vocabulary out of context, it is often

Decisions!

preferable to having students look up the new terms in a dictionary, which at this stage in a lesson too often becomes a ritual in word copying. Thus teachers must be familiar enough with what their students will read that they can decide between terms that are critical to understanding the passage or lesson, and thus demand preteaching, and terms that are incidental or for which context clues will be sufficient.

What Do You Do for Children Who Can't Read the Text?

A nonsolution

The commonsense solution for helping students who have reading difficulties is: get an easier textbook. Unfortunately social studies content varies so markedly from one grade level to the next that it's almost impossible to find easier texts that cover the same topics *and* are appropriate to the student's reading-skill level.

Other options

A second alternative is: don't use the book! There is a vast array of children's literature that is far more interesting than most textbooks. You are more likely to find an easier literary book, even a picture book, on almost any topic, than an easier textbook. Some children's books that you could use either in place of or in addition to the text have already been suggested, and additional annotated bibliographies are presented in the Resource Handbook.

If you feel that your students absolutely must have access to information in the text, you could use one of the following courses of action. Perhaps the least difficult and most readily available option is to read the passages to the students who are having difficulty. However, if you use this approach, have students point to each word in their book as you read from your book. The idea is to have students see each word as you read it, not just listen to your spoken presentation (see Clay, 1993).

Still other possible options

The management problem associated with reading to small groups lies in finding something meaningful for the other students to do. This can be avoided if you (1) have an aide or parent volunteer read to individual children, (2) have one student read to another, or (3) have designed a section of the room as a listening center and have recorded portions of the text available on cassette tapes.

Your third and fourth options, both of which can be time-consuming, involve having small groups of children rewrite *small* portions of the text in their own language and with illustrations after they have finished a section, or rewriting the material in simpler language yourself. If you have the children do the rewriting, be sure that you (1) explain to the children why they are doing this activity, (2) have students work cooperatively in groups but on different sections, and (3) do not use this activity too often—despite its utility, it can pose problems for younger students especially.

Rewriting materials

The feasibility of the fourth option, rewriting material yourself, often depends on the kind of material you are working with. It isn't easy to simplify *statistics*, for example. For text material, this option is further complicated because most texts are written at a very simple level to begin with. Rewriting is a more viable (and often necessary) option if you wish to use advanced material, especially from sources such as *Time, Newsweek,* or social science journals.

A longer-range course of action involves identifying the problem that's keeping the child from reading the text in the first place. No one needs to tell you that

Computers as Writing Tools

Each of the twenty-four students in Mrs. Mary Llanas's combined class of fifth and sixth graders uses one of the four computers in her room to produce a "report" on an African nation. Each report is filled with pictures that students have downloaded from the Internet or reproduced from various books or other sources. When students locate a picture they want to include, they place the book on an easel and use a video camcorder to incorporate the image into their report. Sometimes they use pictures of animals indigenous to the nation or other scenes as the background for the text they write, which appears in a contrasting color in front of the picture. In other instances, pictures are presented with accompanying text either above or below them. In either case, the students are involved with the total visual effect their reports create, not just the words they write.

Other teachers may have their students use "presentation software" as a vehicle for writing activities. The picture below is from a book on colonial occupations. It was produced by Mrs. Judy Rogers's third-grade class using the *Time Trip USA* (EdMark) presentation program. Each student wrote the text for his or her occupation and then incorporated it into the animated program. The animation cannot be shown in this format, but everything movable in this scene actually moves—the horse and carriage, the people, and so on. The children even borrowed a technique from Richard Scarry's popular children's books, which include a tiny worm that peers over the activity on each page. Instead of the worm, Mrs. Rogers's children decided to include a child who pops out of a barrel, as shown in the illustration below. Such computer-based presentation programs offer an excellent medium for motivating students to write.

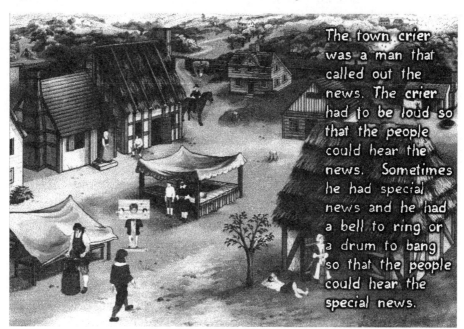

Source: Used by permission of Judy Rogers and Darlinda Rogers.

reading remains a problem for some students, and teachers everywhere are looking for answers to that problem. Until those answers are found, you will undoubtedly be forced to rely on one of the preceding alternative strategies.

● The Reading-Writing Connection

Few educational movements can match the revolution in writing instruction that has occurred over the last decade or so. Whereas writing was once regarded as drudgery, in some classrooms it now rivals recess as a preferred activity.

A growing body of research shows a clear reading-writing connection: improved writing skills can lead to improved reading skills, and vice versa. As young children write, they also come to understand that the words on a printed page were written by somebody—they didn't just magically appear there. As students begin to grasp the concept of author, they begin to realize that authors are responsible for communicating clearly and understandably to others—a responsibility that students assume whenever they write.

Reading and writing are complementary processes

The Writing Process.   One notable aspect of the ongoing revolution in teaching children to write well is the recognition that most traditional writing assignments, where children were given a topic and expected to produce a polished story in one draft, were a far cry from the way in which most authors really write. Moreover, little or no teaching was involved; rather, those assignments were actually tests of the children's existing abilities. It is now recognized that instruction in writing should more closely parallel the processes that most authors follow when they write. Many teachers now follow variations of the writing model shown in Figure 7.4.

Writing: Moving toward what authors really do

Writing Activities.   The potential for realistic writing activities in social studies is almost endless. In most cases, the possible writing activities that are described next require prior class activities or research. However, in many instances, the activities can provide a motive for doing the research.

FIGURE 7.4   A Writing Model

What to write about. Decide on a topic that may be worth pursuing.

Research. Do you need to find out more about the topic?

Initial draft. Write your story.

Two revisions (may be done simultaneously). Focus on (1) content and (2) mechanics.

Extend. Share your writing with others.

★ *"How to's"* are precise, step-by-step descriptions of how to do something. Examples:

1. How to brand a calf
2. How to make soap
3. How to make a peanut butter sandwich

★ *Diaries* or *journals,* or *anecdotes* or *stories* of real or imagined people describing a place, event, or experience. Examples:

1. A visitor to a dairy
2. A pioneer on the Santa Fe Trail
3. A photojournalist in Scotland

★ *Applications* for jobs, describing qualifications for the position and reasons why you would like it. Examples:

1. A sailor on Magellan's first voyage
2. A firefighter
3. The king or queen of England

★ *Letters* written by students themselves or as another person, either real or imagined, containing descriptions, reactions, observations, or attempts to persuade someone to take a certain course of action. Examples:

1. A description of San Francisco (or Fairbanks, Alaska) during the Gold Rush
2. A letter to the mayor asking that the community follow a particular course of action
3. A letter (circa 1860) from a Northerner to a southern relative explaining why the South should not secede from the Union (or vice versa)

★ *Radio scripts* describing events or conditions. Examples:

1. A "You Are There" description of the first Thanksgiving
2. A news broadcast from Paris during the time of Joan of Arc
3. A news bulletin from inside the Alamo (or Nagasaki, Japan, just after the atomic bomb was dropped)

★ *Pamphlets* or *brochures* (with illustrations) that describe places or events. Examples:

1. Washington, D.C.
2. Valley Forge
3. The school

★ *Interviews* (with real or imaginary people) in which students ask and answer questions. Examples:

What was General Lee thinking?

1. An interview with General Lee on the eve of signing the surrender at Appomattox, Virginia, in 1865
2. An interview with Martin Luther King, Jr., circa 1965
3. An interview with a French fur trader, circa 1700

* *Advertisements* for inventions, places, products, and so on. Examples:

    1. The printing press
    2. The water wheel
    3. A medieval castle

* *Biographies* of imaginary children living in other times or places. Examples:

    1. A child living in ancient Sparta
    2. A child living on a plantation in Georgia in 1840
    3. A child living in Sydney, Australia, today

What should a wanted poster for Benedict Arnold say?

* *Wanted posters,* with a picture, description, crime, and so on. Examples:

    1. Benedict Arnold
    2. Jean Lafitte (pirate)
    3. Saddam Hussein

* *Itineraries* for imaginary trips through places past or present. Examples:

    1. A trip on the Underground Railroad
    2. An itinerary for Marco Polo
    3. A sightseeing trip through your community

Before using any of these writing activities, be certain to establish an authentic, purposeful context. Writing a descriptive brochure of Washington, D.C., or a wanted poster for Jesse James, for example, needs to serve a useful purpose. Otherwise, the activities could easily become "writing for the sake of writing."

Helping Children Construct Meaning

Consider the following conversation between a mother and her six-year-old daughter.

MOTHER: What did you learn at school today?

DAUGHTER: Oh, the teacher said we live in a democracy, but I told her that we live in an apartment.

MOTHER: That's nice.

DAUGHTER: What *is* a democracy anyway?

MOTHER: Why it's a form of government, dear.

DAUGHTER: What's a *form?*

Form is yet another of the polysemous (multiple-meaning) words that we noted earlier. Young children often know that *form* refers to the shape of something, and, after experiences like the one above, they may learn that *form* can also refer to a category or type of phenomenon. We used *construct* in the heading for this section because words and ideas (other than our own) are meaningful only to the extent that we can relate them to our prior experiences. For unfamiliar terms, we must rearrange the mental pigeonholes we use to organize and store our past ex-

Relating ideas to prior experiences

DENNIS THE MENACE   By HANK KETCHAM

"THIS IS LINCOLN'S BIRTHDAY, JOEY. YOU KNOW...
THE GUY THEY NAMED THE LOGS AFTER."

*Source: DENNIS THE
MENACE © used by
permission of Hank
Ketcham and © by
North America
Syndicate.*

periences to accommodate the new ideas. That process is often called *accommodation,* although more recently the term *scaffolding,* which more clearly conveys the notion of "constructing" or "building onto," is often used.

Scaffolding

We were reminded of the scaffolding process when we encountered the Dennis the Menace cartoon shown above. We already had many ideas that we associated with Abraham Lincoln—a tall, bearded man in a stovepipe hat, the sixteenth president, teaching himself the law by candlelight, and so forth. Each of these elements reflects an *attribute* that we associated with Lincoln. Also included among those attributes are our attitudes, feelings, and impressions about Lincoln, which, though more difficult to describe, are along the lines of respect for his apparent honesty and an appreciation for the dignity and bearing with which he conducted himself.

Accommodating new ideas

Dennis the Menace suggested a new attribute that we (and perhaps you) had *not* previously associated with Abraham Lincoln. We accommodated this new attribute by adding "toys" to our existing concept. However, we have since learned that Lincoln Logs were invented by Frank Lloyd Wright, the famed architect, who named them after the president who was sometimes called "the log splitter." That piece of trivia could be useful if you ever become a contestant on the TV show

Jeopardy!, but it also suggests that the relationship between Lincoln Logs and our sixteenth president is more tangential than direct.

Testing new conceptualizations

In the earlier example in which the daughter is puzzled by the term *form,* she will probably reconstruct her existing ideas (about *form*) to accommodate the new usage. In addition, at some time in the future she will probably test her newly constructed schema for *form* by using the word in an appropriate situation (or one that she hopes is appropriate). Such testing is a normal part of the language learning process that was referred to earlier, such as when children discover that adding /ed/ to certain words enables them to talk about events that happened in the past.

The problem with definitions

The old rule of thumb—"If you don't know what a word means, you look it up in a dictionary"—is not especially productive for most polysemous terms. For example, a *wing* can refer to the thing that a bird flies with or to a part of a larger building, both of which most children already know. However, *wing* can also refer to a more or less identifiable group of people who belong to an organization, often a political group called a *party,* or it can mean any one of twenty other definitions listed in our dictionary. For children who think of "party" as a kind of celebration, the dictionary definitions for *wing* can create a situation where they must cope with multiple attributes simultaneously, a potentially mind-boggling situation. There are times when using the dictionary to define new terms is appropriate, but this is not one of them.

Helping children understand the various attributes associated with polysemous terms like *wing* is more than simply a matter of definition learning. To approach it in that way would be a classic example of decontextualized instruction—of trying to learn things in isolation and without reference to the phenomena with which they are associated. To provide a context for *wing,* teaching needs to begin with the phenomenon it is associated with, in this case, political parties. If children have only a vague notion of what political parties (or similar organizations) are, which is more than likely, then that becomes the appropriate beginning point for instruction. In other words, trying to teach children about wings when they don't understand the nature and characteristics of political parties is putting the cart before the horse.

Coping with inclusive and narrow ideas

Part of the difficulty that both teachers and students face in understanding abstract ideas like *wing* or *democracy* is their breadth—they are broad concepts with many attributes. In contrast, nonpolysemous words like *barley,* or even a term like *pharaoh,* are often easier for children to handle. Although pharaohs were unique to ancient Egypt, the term reflects a narrower concept with relatively few attributes, as opposed to a broader and more inclusive concept such as *absolute monarch.* Eventually you might wish to help students build the broader concept of *absolute monarch,* but until they are comfortable with narrower concepts—like *pharaohs, kings,* and *emperors*—they may not know what you are talking about.

To summarize briefly, the process of making things meaningful for children or adults involves connecting new ideas with the individual's existing experiences. When children have no previous experiences with the phenomenon in question, like the *wing* of a political party, teachers may need to begin from scratch and provide experiences for them. We've also suggested that broad ideas that have many attributes—like *freedom, democracy,* or *absolute monarch*—tend to be more difficult for children than narrower concepts like *pharaoh,* which, though they may be equally abstract, have fewer attributes that children must accommodate. There

Obviously, students cannot move backward in time and actually participate in the events of history—actually join Christopher Columbus on his voyage, for example. And if your students saw how tiny the *Nina, Pinta,* and *Santa Maria* actually were, they probably wouldn't want to. In lieu of real experiences, teachers can often appeal to children's imagination in ways that support their vicarious participation in events. By using literature to create vivid mental images of historical events, it's sometimes possible to engage children as if they were witnessing the events unfold. These vivid mental images are created by *details.*

Unfortunately, the role of factual details in teaching history is among the most widely misunderstood aspects of social studies instruction. For example, consider the following statements as they might appear in a textbook: "In 218 B.C.E., Hannibal led an army of over 100,000 soldiers across the Alps. He then met and defeated the Roman legions in what is now Italy." The passage is factually accurate but so bland it fails to capture the imagination. It takes details to make the passage come alive, such as the fact that Hannibal was only eighteen years old when he gathered his huge army from various parts of Africa and Europe. Hannibal's army spoke so many different languages that often his troops could not communicate with one another. In addition to the 100,000 soldiers, Hannibal's army also included thirty-seven elephants. Thirty-six of them were African "attack" elephants that had been trained to terrorize enemy soldiers by trampling on them; the elephants practiced on prisoners at the training center in Carthage. The thirty-seventh, an Indian elephant named Syrus, was probably Hannibal's personal pet.

After a harrowing journey across the Alps, Hannibal still had to get his army, its supplies, and the elephants across the Rhone River. The army "borrowed" boats, made rafts, or used anything they could get their hands on to get across the river. But getting the elephants across was another problem; they refused to go onto the rafts that had been built for them. In desperation, Hannibal's soldiers covered the rafts with pieces of sod so that they looked like extensions of the shoreline. Apparently the elephants were deceived, because they willingly walked onto the rafts. However, when boats began towing the rafts toward the opposite shore, the elephants realized something was wrong and panicked. Some reared up, trumpeted loudly, and threw their mahouts (drivers) into the river. Many of the mahouts, who were originally from Africa, had never learned how to swim and were drowned. Some of the elephants also jumped into the river, but they swam to the opposite shore and waited there for the elephants that had remained on the rafts. All the elephants made it safely across the Rhone River.

Individually and in the sweep of human experience, most details appear small and insignificant. It is not important that students come away remembering how many elephants Hannibal had, for example, even though they often do remember such information. The point is that, collectively, details play a vital role in the creation of vicarious experience and subsequent learning. Too often children must deal with test questions such as "How many elephants did Hannibal have?"—questions that ultimately become part of their grade. Because teachers' test questions often define what is or is not important, one must wonder how many students focus their attention on trying to learn what is actually historical trivia. Perhaps some students learn to hate history because the role of factual details continues to be misunderstood.

- -

are so many broad and encompassing concepts in elementary and middle-school social studies that it is often impossible to avoid them. If you find yourself in that situation, one of the strategies in the next section may be appropriate.

———● **Examples of Instruction Designed to Construct Meaning**

The following exemplars illustrate how you might go about managing the idea-building process.

Vocabulary. When you suspect that your students do not understand a narrow concept, such as *isthmus,* you have several options. First, you can *define* it for them: "An isthmus is a narrow strip of land between two bodies of water." However, because few students will have prior experience with an isthmus, your words will mean more if you use a picture or other illustration to provide a visual image of the term. You might also use an *analogy*—for example, "An isthmus is a kind of 'land bridge,' a skinny piece of land that connects two larger land masses." That analogy could be part of a larger explanation in which you use a *simile*—for example, "An isthmus is like a strait, except it's land instead of water." Your explanation for some concepts, such as *peninsula,* might include a description of the origin of the expression: "*Peninsula* comes from the Latin—*pene* for 'almost' plus *insula* for 'island.' In other words, a peninsula is almost an island."

Building on what students know

Having students use a dictionary or glossary is another option for relatively narrow real-world concepts, such as *isthmus* and *peninsula.* But for abstract concepts such as *capitalism* or *imperialism,* dictionary definitions may lead to the situation noted earlier—that is, where one abstraction is defined with other abstractions.

The Taba Model. The following idea-building strategy was developed by the late Hilda Taba and is based on a three-step sequence illustrated in Table 7.1 (Taba et al., 1967). In some respects, this strategy is similar to the way that Lynda Esparza began her lesson in the introduction to this chapter, although she opted not to do the entire process in a single lesson. In this strategy, students are asked first to identify and enumerate items, then to find a basis for grouping or clustering the items together, and finally to identify a label for the items they have clustered. How the three phases might be conducted for a second-grade class is illustrated in the following Model Student Activity.

An old strategy but still useful

TABLE 7.1 Taba's Concept-Formation Strategy

Phase	Overt Activity	Covert Mental Operations	Eliciting Questions
One	Enumeration and listing	Differentiation	What did you see? Hear? Note?
Two	Grouping	Identifying common properties, abstracting	What belongs together? On what criterion?
Three	Labeling and categorizing	Determining the hierarchical super- and subordination	What would you call these groups? What belongs under what?

Source: *Teacher's Handbook for Elementary Social Studies* © 1967 by Taba, Durkin, et al. Copyright Addison-Wesley Publishing Company. Used by permission.

Taba's Concept-Formation Strategy

Phase 1: Enumeration and Listing

TEACHER: Let's start listing on the board the things that you would buy if you went to the store.

DAVID: Apples.

PAUL: I'd buy a steak.

RANDY: Shrimp.

DENNY: I'd buy a puppy.

TEACHER: A puppy is different, isn't it?

MICHAEL: Watermelon.

CARLA: Candy bar.

ANN: Scooter.

TEACHER: Scooter, that's something different again, isn't it?

TEACHER: We've almost filled up our board with things that we would buy. What can we do with these things? Do some of them belong together? Which ones belong together? Which ones could you find in the same place?

DENNY: You can buy a doll and scooter in the same place.

TEACHER: You would buy them in a toy shop, wouldn't you? Let's pick the ones that you might buy in a toy shop. What else would you buy in a toy shop?

RICKY: Squirt gun.

TEACHER: All right, we would buy a squirt gun in the toy shop. What else would we buy in the toy shop? (Taba et al., 1967, pp. 95–99).

Phase 2: Grouping

Students continue to suggest different (and multiple) groupings for some items, such as "steak and watermelon—things at a cookout" or "shrimp and steak, because both are meats." Students may or may not identify a "food" category for items such as apples, watermelon, steak, and shrimp.

Phase 3: Labeling and Categorizing

After the larger clusters have been identified, the teacher then moves to labeling and categorizing by asking, "What would you call these groups?" Responses may include "things you can buy in a store," "things we eat," and "things we use." As Taba and her colleagues (1967, p. 94) noted, it is important for students "to discover that any item has many different characteristics and therefore can be grouped in many different ways. Each of the multiple qualities can be used as a basis for grouping."

Anticipatory Strategies

Anticipatory strategies are teaching techniques that teachers use prior to a learning experience. Some of these strategies, like contextual redefinition and word mapping (explained below) focus on one or two words that are apt to prove troublesome for students. Other strategies, such as KWL charting and SQ3R, are usually designed to set the stage for learning, but also have follow-up components that occur after a learning experience.

Contextual Redefinition. Helping students learn to use the context in which unfamiliar words appear is vital to the process of becoming an independent learner. This was illustrated in an earlier example involving the word *barley,* which we suggested was not important enough to the meaning of the passage that it demanded preteaching. Unlike the *barley* example, students will encounter many passages with unfamiliar words that are critical to understanding and that must be pretaught. In such cases you can use contextual redefinition, a teaching strategy that is based on making and verifying predictions. Phases of the contextual redefinition strategy are as follows:

Selecting problem terms

* *Phase 1:* Select terms that are likely to be unfamiliar to students *and* that are critical to understanding the passage. For purposes of illustration, consider the term *civil service* (after Irvin et al., 1995).

* *Phase 2:* Using an overhead or chalkboard, present each term individually and in isolation.

* *Phase 3:* Ask students to brainstorm possible definitions for each term. Accept all suggestions, including those that are wrong or "off the wall," as in "a civil service is a wedding where everyone is polite" (Irvin et al., 1995).

Deciding on a possible meaning

* *Phase 4:* Help students reach a consensus on the most probable meaning.

* *Phase 5:* Present a sentence or cluster of sentences that illustrates the meaning of the term. For example: "Civil service was created during the T'ang dynasty in China. Using an examination system, government officials were selected based on their qualifications instead of their noble birth."

Modify as needed

* *Phase 6:* Help students modify their earlier definitions if necessary.

* *Phase 7:* Ask one or two students to verify the definition in a dictionary or glossary.

Word Maps. In the example for Phase 5 above, the term *dynasty* might be troublesome for some students. An alternative strategy to contextual redefinition involves creating a word map for the unfamiliar term, in this case *dynasty*. The emphasis in this strategy is on relating unfamiliar terms to students' prior experiences. A sample word map for *dynasty* is shown in Figure 7.5.

The KWL Strategy. Portions of the KWL Strategy occur prior to a learning activity, and other portions take place after the activity. This is reflected in the following vignette, "Why Woodpeckers Don't Hurt Themselves."

VIGNETTE: WHY WOODPECKERS DON'T HURT THEMSELVES

I first met Eric Cederstrom when he was teaching at Harwell Elementary in a mid-sized city. He has since moved into administration, which, as he puts it, "Is where the money is." When I dropped by Eric's third-grade classroom one afternoon, there was a huge sheet of red paper covering one of the chalkboards. Under the heading "Animals," the paper was divided into three columns: (1) Know, (2) Want to Know, and (3) Learned (see Table 7.2). On that first visit, the "Learned" column was still blank.

I said, "Oh, you're using the KWL strategy [developed by Ogle (1989)]." Eric replied, "I don't know whether I'm doing it or it's doing me. We're working on an animal unit, and yesterday we brainstormed what the kids already knew about

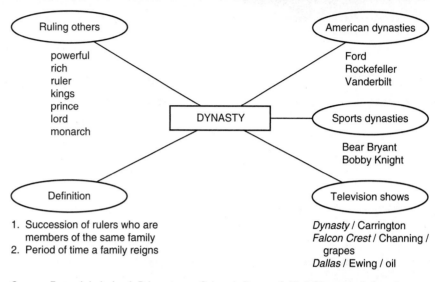

FIGURE 7.5 A Sample Word Map for *Dynasty*

Ruling others

powerful
rich
ruler
kings
prince
lord
monarch

American dynasties

Ford
Rockefeller
Vanderbilt

DYNASTY

Sports dynasties

Bear Bryant
Bobby Knight

Definition

1. Succession of rulers who are members of the same family
2. Period of time a family reigns

Television shows

Dynasty / Carrington
Falcon Crest / Channing / grapes
Dallas / Ewing / oil

Source: From J. L. Irvin, J. P. Lunstrum, C. Lynch-Brown, & M. F. Shepard, *Enhancing Social Studies Through Literacy Strategies* (Washington, DC: National Council for the Social Studies, © 1995). Reprinted by permission of NCSS and J. L. Irvin, J. P. Lunstrum, C. Lynch-Brown, & M. F. Shepard.

• •

animals. Then we talked about what they wanted to know more about. The brainstorming is supposed to activate their prior knowledge, and the 'Want to Know' column identifies what they want to find out. Right now, the kids are at the library getting books on animals."

Unexpected questions

"The 'What They Want to Know' column included a lot of stuff I really didn't expect," Eric continued, "like 'Why don't woodpeckers hurt themselves?' I don't know why woodpeckers don't hurt themselves, and when I wrote that item on the chart, I told the kids that I didn't think we'd be able to answer this one—or why animals have tails or whether they have secrets. But I also didn't get the kinds of things I really wanted to focus on either, like 'What do animals do in the winter?'"

"Maybe not," I answered, "but you got a good indication of what your kids are thinking about."

"That's true; . . . we'll see how it goes," Eric said hopefully.

Unexpected answers

Upon my return to Eric's classroom, all the columns on the KWL chart were filled in. When I asked how it went, Eric responded, "Not bad for the first time using this strategy; as I expected, they couldn't answer some of their questions, but I was also surprised about some of the items, like 'Kangaroos have pockets.' I thought almost everyone knew that."

"So, would you use this activity again?"

TABLE 7.2 KWL Chart for Animals

What We Know	What We Want to Know	What We Learned
1. They can be furry.	1. How do animals communicate?	1. Some lay eggs.
2. Most have four legs.	2. Can sharks jump to the sun?	2. They can have long or short tails.
3. Some animals can fly.	3. How do sharks breathe?	3. Turtles can't get out of their shells.
4. Some animals are playful.	4. Do animals have secrets?	4. Some animals are slow, some are fast.
5. Animals have insides like ours.	5. Do turtles have ears?	5. There are different types of animals.
6. Some animals are mean.	6. How do dogs bark?	6. Some animals swim a lot.
7. Some animals bite.	7. How do animals swim without hands?	7. Some eat a lot.
8. Some animals live in trees.	8. Why do animals have tails?	8. Dogs "talk" with their tails.
9. Some animals live in water or underground.	9. How do people train animals, like Flipper?	9. Some animals have hands.
10. Some animals peck.	10. Why don't woodpeckers hurt themselves?	10. Some animals don't have ears.
11. Some animals have sharp teeth.	11. How do dogs stand?	11. Kangaroos have pockets.
12. Most animals don't talk.	12. How do turtles put their head in their shell?	

Source: Courtesy of Eric J. Cederstrom's Third-Grade Class, Harwell Elementary School, Lubbock, TX.

Making adaptations for the next time

"I think so," Eric said, "but I would do some things differently. I really need to limit the topic more, because 'animals' is way too broad. Maybe we should do reptiles and birds separately. And instead of one master chart, I'll have the kids make their own copies so they can have something to refer to. I'm also thinking about structuring the groups a little more."

Eric Cederstrom's first rendition of the KWL strategy isn't perfect, which he readily admits. However, he had already identified some things he would do differently another time around. The first point here is that the KWL strategy permits students to participate, albeit in a limited way, in clarifying what they are going to learn. A second but equally important point is that planning is an ongoing process that occurs before, during, and after instruction.

PreP (PreReading Plan). The PreReading technique is an anticipatory strategy in which students focus on what they already know about a topic before they begin reading (see Langer, 1981). In many respects, this phase is similar to the "What I already know" phase of the KWL strategy. If the topic is the Revolutionary War, for example, the teacher might ask students what comes to mind when he or she says, "the Revolutionary War." Students' responses may include "Redcoats," "the Stamp Act," or, if students have no notion of the Revolutionary War, silence (or no response). In an attempt to build on students' associations, the teacher may ask a question such as "What made you think of the Stamp Act?" (or whatever the student said). One problem that may arise here occurs when some students recall the Stamp Act, but other students have no idea what everyone is talking about. One purpose of this phase of the strategy is to help the teacher determine whether the students' responses show (1) significant prior knowledge, (2) some prior knowledge, or (3) no prior knowledge. Students whose facial expressions suggest they are "lost" probably belong in Category 3—no prior knowledge. Based on this information, the teacher's decision focuses on determining whether students with no prior knowledge can be successful reading the passage, or whether they need more information before attempting it. But then, if the passage explains the Stamp Act (or whatever the topic) so that readers with no prior knowledge will understand it, using the PreP technique may not be worth pursuing further. In instances where the reading passage is in a textbook, most of which assume no prior knowledge of the topic, the PreP strategy may be only marginally useful.

Assessing students' prior knowledge

SQ3R/SQ4R. The SQ3R and its slightly modified cousin, the SQ4R, are time-honored techniques (Robinson, 1962; Cooper, 1993) for helping students pose their own questions and purposes for reading. The phases of SQ3R, which are done in sequence, include: (1) *survey* the section of the text to get a general idea of what it is about, (2) pose a *question* that is likely to be answered in the text, (3) *read* the section until the reader can answer the question, (4) *recall* the answer to the question without referring to the text, and finally, (5) *review*, where the reader tries to recall the main points learned from the reading. The SQ4R technique follows essentially the same pattern except that it includes a *recite* phase, that is, *survey, question, read, recite, recall*, and *review*. In the *recite* phase, the reader is asked to verbalize the answer to the guiding question.

Survey, question . . .

Follow-up Comprehension Strategies

Follow-up strategies, such as semantic mapping and Somebody-Wanted-But-So summary/review charts, are designed to build upon and to enhance students' initial understandings.

Using Semantic (Concept) Maps. Semantic (or concept) maps are similar to word maps but have a broader focus. Semantic maps are devices that (1) visually depict the attributes associated with an idea or concept, and (2) show the relationships among those elements.

The process of making a semantic map is sometimes called "webbing," probably because the finished product can resemble a spider web. Semantic mapping uses elements that are similar to the Taba strategy, especially since students organize and cluster related elements. To illustrate the mapping process, we use the

Visualizing how elements are related

textbook passage about Canada on page 179. The steps in creating a semantic map are shown below.

The ideas ★ *Step 1: Determining students' existing ideas.* Ask, "When someone says Canada (or whatever your map will focus on), what do you think of?" List the students' responses in key words on the board or an overhead transparency. Their responses, which will be organized in Step 2, may include attributes such as "borders the United States to the north," "is larger than the United States," "national capital is Ottawa," and "bilingual, especially in the eastern provinces, where French is commonly spoken."

★ *Step 2: Clustering related responses.* Help students identify related elements by using symbols to show each relationship—circles around items related to language, boxes around elements related to the economy, and so forth. The purpose of this step is to organize what might otherwise be a random listing of attributes.

★ *Step 3: Making a preliminary concept map.* Begin the webbing process on an overhead transparency or a blank section of the board. Place "Canada" in the center; then add elements radiating outward as shown by the solid lines in Figure 7.6. Use branching to show related elements.

★ *Step 4: Adding new elements to the map.* Decide with students where new elements should be placed. In this example, the new elements come from the textbook passage noted earlier:

Canada is a country that now controls itself.
Canada got its freedom gradually.
Canada gained its independence from Great Britain in 1949.
Canada was partially independent before 1949.
The people of Canada select their leaders.

Many students will treat each fact as a separate item until they see a need or reason to organize or cluster them in a different way. To stimulate clustering, ask, "Is there any pattern to these new elements?" or "Do they fit together somehow?" Multiple categories that could accommodate these elements include history, political organization, and independence. There is no best way to organize the new items, but one way needs to be agreed upon and then added to the concept map. Our treatment is shown by the broken lines in Figure 7.6.

★ *Step 5 (Closure): Debriefing and reflection.* This step helps students reflect on what they have done and how they did it. The idea is to get students to think about how they dealt with the problem—to think about thinking. Ask questions such as these: "How did we deal with this?" "Is there a better way we could have done this?" "What have we learned from doing this?" Responses will vary.

Thinking about thinking Perhaps it is excessive to go to so much trouble with a four-sentence passage about Canada. In one respect, it would be simpler to ask children to remember the facts within that passage and to leave it at that. However, doing so would place the burden on the students, who *might* store the information in their short-term memory—perhaps long enough to take a test—but in six months or less it will assuredly be forgotten. Even having done all this, students are still likely to forget some specifics, such as the date of Canada's independence. Whether they should

FIGURE 7.6 A Concept Map of Canada

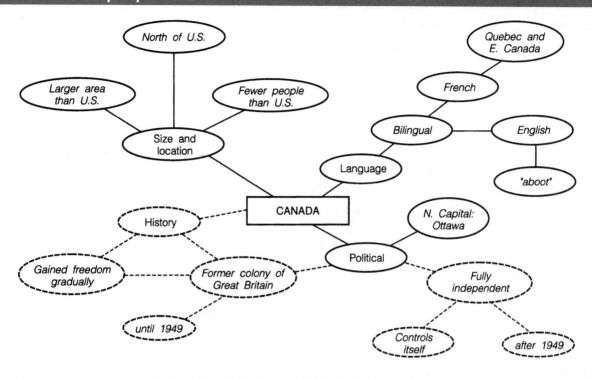

be expected to remember such information to begin with is debatable. What they should learn from this activity is a process for organizing and dealing with information in ways that are personally meaningful. Without meaning, the activity would be an academic exercise.

Somebody-Wanted-But-So Summary/Review Charts. To use a Somebody-Wanted-But-So summary/review chart with students, the teacher enters only the headings for the four columns, illustrated in Figure 7.7, on large paper or an overhead transparency. Working interactively with students, the teacher then fills in the columns, from left to right, for one or more topics that the class has studied.

Summary review charts

To illustrate the utility of this technique, both social studies and language arts topics are shown in Figure 7.7. However, this summary/review activity can only be done *after* learning experiences that provide students with the information they must have to complete the chart. This necessarily means that summary/review charting does not lend itself to initial teaching activities.

"Somebody," "Wanted", "But," and "So" are everyday terms that even very young children understand. However, middle-school teachers may wish to substitute the

FIGURE 7.7 Sample Summary/Review Chart

SOMEBODY	WANTED	BUT	SO
The South (1861)	States' rights (slavery)	The North opposes slavery	Civil War breaks out
John Wilkes Boothe	To keep slavery and support the Confederacy	Lincoln (and the North) abolish slavery	He shoots Pres. Lincoln
Cinderella's Stepmother	A good life for her daughters, but not Cinderella	Fairy godmother intervenes	Drats, foiled again!
Mr. MacGregor	A nice garden	Peter Rabbit eats his vegetables	He chases Peter with a hoe

somewhat more abstract terms: "Character," "Motive," "Conflict," and "Resolution." Nonetheless, even some adults will prefer the terms "Somebody," "Wanted," "But," and "So," apparently because they are less complex and bring everything down one level of abstractness.

SUMMARY

This chapter has focused on helping children gain meaning from spoken or written words. The first premise is that in the absence of meaning, literacy is an impossibility. Meaning depends largely on the extent to which children can make connections between new ideas and their existing base of experiences. Helping children to make those connections is one of the most important roles a teacher plays.

Language literacy refers to the ability to use language—to read, write, speak, and listen—fluently and effectively in different situations. Recent research has indicated that children require opportunities to talk and play with standard English, the language of textbooks and the school, in ways that mimic how they learned their language in the first place: by listening, observing, and sometimes by testing theories about how language operates in realistic and purposeful situations. Too often, children in traditional classrooms had few opportunities to practice or demonstrate their oral language skills. When researchers discovered that children with poor oral language facility also tended to be poor readers and writers, things began to change—although slowly at first. It has become increasingly apparent that the basis for literacy is the child's facility with oral language. In slightly different terms, this means that if children cannot understand the spoken word, they will be not be able to understand those ideas when they try to read them, nor will they be able to convey those ideas in written form.

SUGGESTED ACTIVITIES

1. Select two social studies texts (from different publishers) for the same grade level. Select at least two topics common to both books—there will be many—and compare the two texts in terms of their concept loading.

2. Using one of the texts from the preceding activity, select one chapter at random. On a separate paper, create a two-column list with the overall heading "Potentially Troublesome Concepts." The subhead for one column

should be "Concepts that lack real-world referents," which will include figurative expressions and other abstract concepts described in this chapter. The subhead for the second column should be "Concepts observable in the real world." After reading the first ten pages of the chapter, place any potentially troublesome concepts in the appropriate category. Then select one of the concepts from those that lack real-world referents and design a teaching activity that might help children build meaning for that idea.

3. Some teachers contend that the only way children will learn to use standard English correctly is by writing and speaking correctly in classroom discussions and writing activities. Other teachers accept dialectal usages in oral communication but insist on correct English in the children's written work. Still other teachers allow children to use whatever language they feel most comfortable with, so long as it is appropriate (no cursing, etc.). Determine where you stand on this issue.

SUGGESTED READINGS

Print Resources

Lucy McCormick Calkins. (1994). *The art of teaching writing.* Portsmouth, NH: Heinemann. A book with this title *must* be well written; this one is superb.

_____. (2000). *The art of teaching reading.* New York: Longman Group. Another excellent work by this talented writer.

J. D. Cooper. (1993). *Improving reading comprehension.* 2nd ed. Boston: Houghton Mifflin.

_____. (2000). *Literacy: Helping children construct meaning* (4th ed.). Boston: Houghton Mifflin. An excellent resource on developing literacy skills.

Linda Christiansen. (1994). Whose standard? Teaching standard English. *Rethinking our classrooms: Teaching for equity and justice.* Milwaukee, WI: Rethinking Schools Ltd. This touching and thought-provoking article by a teacher who grew up speaking nonstandard English, describes what she went through as she learned to adapt her own language patterns to the prevailing standard in our culture today.

Leslie W. Crawford. (1993). *Language and literacy learning in multicultural classrooms.* Needham Heights, MA: Allyn & Bacon. This book is especially useful because of its focus on multicultural classrooms.

Donald Graves. (1994). *A fresh look at writing.* Portsmouth, NH: Heinemann. This work is by the person who started the writing revolution in the United States.

Internet Resources

Introductory Note: Web sites sometimes change Internet addresses or cease operating entirely. All the addresses supplied here were operating when this book was printed, but should any of them they fail to work properly, try entering the desired topic or organization in any standard search engine.

Constructivist Learning

http://netra/exploratorium.mcgill.ca/fedwww/wac/ intedpsych/students/lgraha/paper.html

This insightful article explains the basis for constructivist teaching and learning.

National Reading Styles Institute

http://www.nrsi.com/homepage.html

This site focuses on helping children who display different reading and learning styles: auditory, visual, analytical, tactile, and kinesthetic.

Visualizing Verbs

http://www.cypress.ne.jp/schwindt/tesol/vtnvs.htm

This site describes a technique for using colored index cards to help students, especially ESL students, visualize the complexities of the English verb system.

Reading and Writing Across the Curriculum

http://www.indiana.edu/~eric_rec/bks/wac.html

This site is sponsored by the ERIC Clearinghouse on Reading, English, and Communication and provides links to sites and materials for teaching reading and writing across the curriculum.

What Is a Thinking Curriculum?

http://www.ncrel.org/sdrs/areas/rpl_esys/thinking/html

This article focuses on metacognitive teaching and curriculum design for engaging students with content.

Instruction

Part 3 presents the "nuts and bolts" of teaching social studies. Chapter 8, Planning and Orchestrating Instruction, and Chapter 9, Assessing Learning, address these most basic elements of instruction. Chapter 10, Strategies for Effective Teaching, examines aspects of teacher- and student-directed instruction, both of which should be part of every teacher's repertoire. Also integral to Part 3 are the group-management skills and teaching strategies relating to small-group instruction, which are examined in Chapter 11, Strategies for Active Learning.

Chapter 12, Nurturing Critical and Reflective Thinking, examines teaching activities and skills that can enable children to analyze, interpret, and otherwise deal with various kinds of social studies information. Although critical thinking has long been a part of teaching social studies, it is currently being reemphasized because of its inclusion on many state-mandated tests. The title for Chapter 13, Helping Students Use Maps, Globes, and Graphics, provides a clear indication of its focus, as does the title of Chapter 14, Using Instructional Tools: Print, Multimedia, and Community Resources.

Planning and Orchestrating Instruction

Key Questions

- How does one plan (compose) social studies lessons and units?
- What are the major components of instructional planning?
- How do teachers manage the planning process?
- How do goals and objectives differ?

Key Ideas

- Planning is a systematic process, as opposed to a series of discrete steps, in which each aspect interacts with every other aspect of instruction.
- Planning is complex only because of the number of elements that must be considered; it is not inherently complicated.
- Effective planning hinges on two elements: (1) determining what students should know and be able to do *after* instruction, and (2) orchestrating instructional activities that enable them to reach those goals.
- Learning outcomes are stated with varying levels of specificity.

Introduction: On Composing and Orchestrating

Teachers play both roles

In the musical world, there's a clear distinction between composers, who write the music, and arrangers, who adapt the piece for particular settings. Seldom do the same people do both tasks. In the instructional world, however, teachers are regularly expected to do both—although not simultaneously. Teachers are responsible for planning (composing) instructional sequences and then orchestrating them during the actual teaching. Teachers don't often use such imposing terminology, but you should get the idea.

In the process of composing this chapter, I considered reprinting published unit and lesson plans, of which there are thousands in the literature and on the

Internet. Because completed plans do not reflect the processes their developers used to create them, this option was rejected. Neither do they indicate what the developers thought about but excluded from their final plans. In many respects, deciding what *not* to include in a teaching unit or lesson plan is just as important as deciding what to include, especially if you are the one doing the including.

Considerations

Instead of finished plans, this chapter takes you through the process of planning a sample third-grade teaching unit and the lesson plans associated with it. It also considers some other planning-related elements, such as how you might involve students in determining what they will study, and how state and national standards have affected teachers' planning. In the next chapter, the focus is on the reciprocal of planning: assessment—which determines how well students have reached the outcomes created during the planning process described in this chapter.

The next section focuses on a subtle but vitally important consideration in planning; that is, determining how you will involve children in *using* social studies content. You undoubtedly recall hearing teachers say things like, "read this page in the text and learn it." Such teachers obviously regard social studies content as something to teach, and as something students need to learn. Yet there is another equally valid perspective: approaching social studies content as something teachers use to teach. If these seem like word games, the next section should clarify things considerably.

Involving students

A Perspective on Using Social Studies Content

You probably remember that delightful children's classic *Mike Mulligan and His Steam Shovel* (Burton, 1939), in which Mike's steam-powered shovel, Mary Anne, is nearly sent to steam-shovel heaven because the new, engine-powered shovels are getting most of the jobs. In Burton's story, Mike and Mary Anne agree to dig the cellar for the new Popperville town hall. They also agree to complete the job in just one day; otherwise they won't get paid. By digging furiously for the entire day, Mike and Mary Anne manage to finish the job—except for one thing. In their haste, Mike forgets to leave a way to get Mary Anne out of the cellar (see Figure 8.1). So there she sits, quietly belching smoke, at the bottom of the huge hole.

Creative thinking

Henry B. Swap, a member of the Popperville town council, arrives at the construction site and argues that because Mary Anne is stuck in the cellar, the job wasn't finished within the agreed-upon time and Mike should not be paid. The day is saved when a little boy, who has been watching the whole episode, suggests that they build the new town hall around Mary Anne and make her its new furnace. And Mike? He could become the new janitor.

Structure and function

Mike Mulligan and His Steam Shovel is not the kind of content that you would normally associate with social studies. Nevertheless, a teacher could use the story to introduce the idea of structure and function. That idea reflects the fact that certain structures—like steam-powered shovels—could be used for several functions (such as a hole digger, a *very* slow form of transportation, or even a furnace). Some of those functions, such as digging, are obviously more appropriate than others, yet all are potential functions for a steam-powered shovel.

FIGURE 8.1   Children's Book Illustration

Serving multiple purposes

Many teachers approach social studies subject matter as if it had only one major function, as something that "teachers teach and students are expected to know." This section shows how content can serve a variety of instructional purposes and how it can become something that teachers and students *use,* not simply something that students are expected to know.

Using content as a vehicle

Content utilization refers to the notion of using content (subject matter) as a *vehicle,* as a way to help teachers and students move toward educational destinations. Using content as a vehicle is not restricted to social studies, but the main focus here is on using content in teaching social studies.

Throughout this section the terms *content* and *subject matter*—the "stuff" of instruction—are used synonymously. It matters not whether you are using excerpts from a biography of Martin Luther King or Thomas Jefferson, or a textbook passage dealing with vital services in a community. A teacher could use the ideas inherent in social studies content as the "stuff" children are supposed to know, or as a vehicle to help students identify and test hypotheses, or to distinguish between

Multiple uses

facts and opinions, or to teach countless other critical thinking skills. Students could also use the ideas inherent in social studies content as a basis for looking for recurring patterns in the human experience, to test previously identified hypotheses, as a springboard for further inquiry and research, and for many other purposes. In other words, social studies content can have a multitude of uses.

The Model Student Activity, "Who Is Qualified for the Presidency?" (from Chapter 1) reflects content utilization in action. In that activity, the biographical information served as a vehicle to help students identify factors such as age, education, marital status, and the like, that might influence the selection and election of a president. It was *not* intended to teach information that students would be expected to remember about the candidates themselves. The point here is the reciprocal relationship between the teachers' purposes and the kind of content they use with their students:

Purpose determines use

Purposes ⟷ Content

If a teacher's purpose is to involve children in identifying factors that influence the selection of a president, the teacher could use the "Presidency" activity to do that. However, instead of using the "Presidency" activity, other teachers might wish to have students debate the importance of a previously prepared list of factors that can influence presidential elections. Either approach is equally valid, although not necessarily equally effective.

The content can suggest potential uses

The first point here is that the relationship between purposes and content is reciprocal, or nearly so. A teacher's purposes can dictate the content she or he needs, just as certain content, like the "Presidency" activity, can suggest some purposes for which you could use it. The second point is that major curriculum goals are the dominant element in the purpose-content relationship. The "Presidency" activity (and every other Model Student Activity in this book) must fit into a larger picture. At the risk of stating the obvious, teachers should not use the "Presidency" activity in the middle of a unit on the geography of Australia if they want to maintain any sense of curricular continuity. Content vehicles can *suggest* purposes for which they can be used, but they do not *determine* what those purposes should be.

● Using Unconventional Content to Teach Social Studies

Education has such a long tradition of using written or printed materials as content sources that it's easy to overlook other materials that can serve the same purposes. In this section, we illustrate how two cans of Green Giant Niblets corn might serve as a content vehicle for social studies (and other subject areas).

Why corn? Why not something more conventional? First, using corn as a content vehicle avoids the "it's something that all children should know" syndrome.

Purposes clarified

There is probably nothing about two cans of corn that students must know (see Figure 8.2). The second purpose is to illustrate how it's possible to identify and teach legitimate skills by using neutral content. A third related purpose is to illustrate that this content vehicle, mundane as it is, can also be used in subject areas other than social studies. Whether you ever elect to use this "corny" curriculum with students would depend on your purposes, of course.

The immediate task here is to use the canned corn as a vehicle for potential questions and teaching activities. Besides posing possible research questions, you could identify potential instructional activities, such as "Design a new label" or "Try to figure out a more appealing color scheme for the existing label." Or you could

FIGURE 8.2   The Basis for the Corn Curriculum

NUTRITION INFORMATION PER SERVING
Serving Size: ½ cup (solids and liquid)
Servings Per Container: 2

Calories . . . . 90 Fat 0g
Protein . . . . 2g Sodium** . . . 230mg
Carbohydrate . . 20g Potassium . . 170mg
**Nutrition is calculated for liquids and solids together. If the liquid is removed, there will be 180mg sodium.

PERCENTAGE OF U.S. RECOMMENDED DAILY ALLOWANCES (U.S. RDA) PER SERVING:

Protein . . . . . 2 Thiamine (B₁) .2 Calcium . . . . .*
Vitamin A . . . 2 Riboflavin (B₂) .4 Iron . . . .*
Vitamin C . . . 10 Niacin . . . . . . 4 Phosphorus . .6
*Contains less than 2% of the U.S. RDA of these nutrients.

Ingredients: Golden Whole Kernel Corn, Water, Sugar, Salt.

Distributed by Green Giant Co., The Pillsbury Company, Minneapolis, MN 55402

††Weight of corn means weight before addition of liquid necessary for processing.

NUTRITION INFORMATION PER SERVING
Serving Size: ½ cup (solids & liquid)
Servings Per Container: 4

Calories . . . . 80 Fat 0g
Protein . . . . 2g Sodium** . . . 290mg
Carbohydrate . . 18g Potassium . . 170mg
**Nutrition is calculated for liquids and solids together. If the liquid is removed, there will be 230mg of sodium.

PERCENTAGE OF U.S. RECOMMENDED DAILY ALLOWANCES (U.S. RDA) PER SERVING:

Protein . . . . . 2 Thiamine (B₁) . * Calcium . . . . .*
Vitamin A . . . 8 Riboflavin (B₂) .2 Iron 2
Vitamin C . . . 8 Niacin . . . . . . 4 Phosphorus . .4
*Contains less than 2% of the U.S. RDA of these nutrients.

Ingredients: Golden Whole Kernel Corn, Water, Sugar, Salt.

Distributed by Green Giant Co., The Pillsbury Company, Minneapolis, MN 55402

Source: Green Giant®, Niblets®, and the Giant figure are registered trademarks of The Pillsbury Company. Used by permission. All rights reserved.

do both. It is useful to begin with a combination of questions and potential teaching activities because they provide a focus for possible lessons. A question such as "How many words can be made from the word *niblets*?," for example, clearly implies a language-related activity. In presenting the task to students, it's not essential that the teacher pose the question directly. Rather, the teacher can say something such as "Let's see how many words we can make from the letters in *niblets.*" If you use such an activity, you could present it either as a task or as a question.

Brainstorming

Try your hand at brainstorming three or four potential research questions or teaching activities in each of the major subject areas: language arts (including reading), mathematics, science, and social studies. Some potential questions and activities are suggested to get you started. Note that as you identify potential research questions, it is *not* essential that you be able to answer them in advance. Some of your best and most interesting questions will be those you can't answer immediately. For example, questions like "Why do most cans have ridges (or rings)?" or "Is there any tin in a tin can?" can serve as things to research or inquire about. Concern for answers to those questions can come after your students (or you) have inquired.

Language Arts

Possible activities

* Is *niblets* a real word? How could we find out?
* Write a story in which the Green Giant comes to life.
* Classify the words on the label beginning with *G* as naming words, action words, or describing words. Star the words that fit into more than one category. Then use at least some words from your list to create a cinquain poem.

Other Language Arts Questions/Activities

_____

_____

_____

Mathematics

* Identify three ways to figure out the number of kernels in the large can. Then determine which way is the most accurate.

Possible activities

* Determine how you could measure the length of the label without taking it off the can.
* When would purchasing the large can be a bad buy?
* Figure out three different-shaped cans that would hold the same amount of corn.

Other Math Questions/Activities

_____

_____

_____

Science

* What else is in these cans besides corn? How could we find out? Why would this be important to know?

Possible activities

* Does "net weight" include the liquid the corn is packed in? How could we find out?
* Are tin cans really made from tin? How could we find out?
* Will the canned corn grow if we plant it? How could we find out?

Other Science Questions/Activities

_____

_____

_____

Social Studies

Possible activities

* Do most people in this class prefer canned corn or frozen corn? How could we find out?
* What information on the label is there by law? When did labeling laws come into effect? Why?
* What ingredients (resources) went into growing the corn and producing the can and label?
* What role does corn play in our diet? How could we find out?
* What occupations are involved in getting corn from the Green Giant's valley to us?

Other Social Studies Questions/Activities

_____

_____

_____

Shiting to a process focus

A question such as "How could we find out?" shifts the focus of an activity from a concern for the answers to a concern for *finding* answers. Realistically, the answers to many of these questions, such as "What else is in these cans besides corn?" (water, salt, etc.), have little utility in a child's day-to-day life. However, their transfer value often lies in the processes that students use to arrive at their answers—processes that students can use to investigate other problems they encounter. Indeed, how can you find out what is in these cans besides corn?

Separating the grain from the chaff

The potential questions and activities identified here are a nebulous collection, nothing more. And simply because potential questions and activities have been identified doesn't mean they are worth using with students; some may have very limited instructional value and should be discarded. The point is that content—even seemingly unconventional content like canned corn—can be used for a variety of teaching purposes and in different subject areas. It's all a matter of how you perceive it.

Managing Multiple Planning Elements

Students who have studied social studies are typically expected (1) to *know* something about the facts, concepts, and generalizations of social studies; (2) to apply *skills* that enable them to use the knowledge they have acquired; and (3) to have acquired certain *attitudes* and *values* that our society feels are important for all citizens to share. These expectations are seldom as separate as they appear here, because the three areas (knowledge, skills, and attitudes) often overlap.

The composing tasks of planning

Determining what children should know at the end of an instructional episode and determining what skills, attitudes, and values they should acquire along the way are the basic composing tasks of planning. Almost immediately thereafter come the tasks of identifying and designing instructional activities and then orchestrating them in ways that make sense to you and to children. All of this should ultimately lead to the outcomes identified in the composing phase. That's the simplified version of how planning is supposed to work, but other elements enter the picture.

Grade-level planning teams are becoming increasingly popular, even in departmentalized settings. *(© Elizabeth Crews)*

These include your students' abilities, which will influence the kinds of activities you can use with them, as well as state-mandated requirements and national standards. Each of these elements is considered as they affect the various phases of planning.

Composing a Sample Unit: Part 1

Planning a teaching unit is like lesson planning, only on a broader scale. Instead of focusing on one lesson, unit planning focuses on creating a series of related lessons. Because teaching units have a broader focus than individual lessons, they can attend to broader learning outcomes than is possible with most lessons. In addition, unit planning offers a way of ensuring that the lessons you teach today will relate to the lessons you taught yesterday, and to those you will teach tomorrow. This simply means there is a flow to how students learn.

Making certain that things relate

● Identifying a Unit Focus

To determine what our sample unit will be about, we could simply pick a topic and "go for it." The traditional content focus of third-grade social studies is "communities," so we would surely be safe in developing one or more units on that topic. Or we might select other topics, like "transportation" or "Native Americans," especially if we have lots of teaching materials on those topics. However, few teachers today are free to teach anything they want to. They may be able to sneak in one or two units on their favorite topics over the course of a year, but most of what they

STANDARDS

teach needs to be compatible with state-mandated essential elements and national standards. Of course, teachers could ignore state mandates entirely, but no one needs to tell you that in this age of accountability doing so is ill advised. We'll come back to the impact of state and national standards momentarily.

Using corn as a vehicle

In this instance we want portions of our sample unit to reflect the "Can of Corn" curriculum development activity presented earlier. Doing so illustrates that it's possible to design a legitimate teaching unit based on something as mundane as a can of corn. Obviously, there is nothing about canned corn that every student needs to know, but then this unit is not going to teach *about* canned corn per se. Rather, the intent is to *use* the corn as a content vehicle, as a tangible point of departure that allows us (and our students) to consider the kinds of decisions that went into producing it and other products. Why, for example, would a farmer decide to grow corn instead of another crop, such as wheat or soybeans? Land is an obvious resource for farmers, but what other factors enter into their decisions to grow one crop instead of another? And what other resources besides land would a farmer need to grow corn? Then too, what resources are used to produce the can that the corn (or any vegetable) comes in, to make and print the label, and to get the corn from the field where it was grown to the supermarket? Finally, are there some human resources (in addition to natural resources) that come into play here?

Using Questions in Planning.   Most curriculum guides and published units provide (1) a statement of the unit theme or topic, (2) a list of desired learning outcomes (goals and objectives) (3) a list of suggested student activities, (4) a list of resources and materials essential to teaching this unit, (5) assessment procedures or other evaluation activities, and (6) a listing of additional resources. The sequence of presentation sometimes leads prospective teachers to believe that instructional planning follows the same sequence, although in most instances it probably does not. For example, some elements here, such as some of the questions developed earlier, may not appear in the final unit. Nevertheless, key questions such as "Why do farmers decide to grow corn instead of cotton, soybeans, wheat, or other crops?" and "What human resources are involved in producing canned vegetables?" suggest what students could be expected to know at the completion of the unit.

The process may differ from final presentation

After identifying the unit topic, how humans use resources, consider identifying some key questions that students *could* answer at the end of the unit. The questions will lend specificity and clarity to your lessons and, perhaps more importantly, can easily be converted into learning outcomes. For example, "Why do farmers decide to grow corn instead of cotton, soybeans, wheat, or other crops?" can be restated as "Students will explain the factors that farmers consider in de-

Questions simplify the identification of outcomes

Progress Report

Using the "can of corn" as an entry point, we have identified a unit focus, "How People Use Resources," as well as some questions and activities that are associated with that topic.

FIGURE 8.3 Preliminary Web for Canned Corn

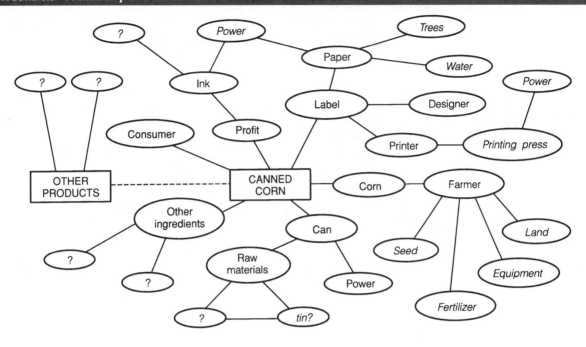

ciding which crops to produce." The absence of questions makes it more difficult to identify specific learning outcomes. In addition, in the initial stages of instructional planning (which is where we are), everything is tentative. As we get further into our planning, we may generate more key questions and topics to pursue, but we are just as likely to discard some questions (and the topics they are associated with), especially if we cannot create reasonable teaching activities that are geared to them. An example of this is provided shortly.

Keeping some elements and discarding others

Using Webbing as a Planning Tool.   Because the relationship between canned corn and how people use resources is still fairly amorphous at this point, you could elect to use a webbing technique to get a better handle on the topic. The *webbing* process produces a kind of semantic map similar to the one for Canada in Chapter 7, which shows the range and scope of relationships among related elements.

Building a web for corn

There are several ways to begin the webbing process. One is to brainstorm (free-associate) by listing anything you can think of related to the theme or topic (canned corn). A second technique is to identify questions and possible teaching activities, a process that we began earlier. Or you could do either of these. Because we've already explored some aspects of our corny curriculum we'll follow up on that here. Figure 8.3 shows a web that is based on and expanded from the questions and activities we developed earlier. The web and everything else noted thus far seems to confirm that the notion of resources—natural and human—offers a potentially workable direction or theme for this unit. Next we need to make sure that our proposed unit will be compatible with state-mandated essential elements and/or national standards.

● How State and National Standards Affect Planning

STANDARDS

In the days before states got into the business of mandating curriculum standards, which was followed almost immediately by statewide testing programs, teachers could follow their instincts in selecting content to teach. More recently, the creation of national standards has added an additional element that teachers must consider.

The Impact of State-Mandated Standards. When the states first began mandating curriculum standards, most of the standards followed a similar format. The goals were stated as general outcomes, such as "Students will understand the interplay of economics in their daily lives." Objectives associated with each of the goals were stated more explicitly, such as "[The students will] identify the relationship between supply and demand and its effect on the price of a product," and "[The student will] identify the natural resources that determine the types of jobs in your community in the past, present, and future." These sample goals and

Most state programs have similar expectations

objectives are derived from one state's core curriculum document for third-grade social studies, but they could just as easily have been from another state because the requirements are very similar, in some cases almost identical.

State mandates would not be the imposing force they have become if the states had not created testing programs that are keyed to them. Test results are almost always released to the local media, and certain schools may be singled out as "exemplary" or, the more feared designation, "low performing." The pressures that such devices can place on teachers are significant indeed.

A change in emphasis

Over the last decade, there has been a significant change in how most states pose their curriculum mandates. Instead of narrowly defined content objectives, such as "Does the student know who fought whom in the War of 1812?" the shift has been toward more generic topics and skills, such as the student's ability to apply reflective thinking skills to various kinds of information.

STANDARDS

Determining Compatibility with State Mandates. After identifying the key concept for this unit—"The allocation of resources, both natural and human, results from human decisions"—the next task is to determine whether it is compatible with state mandates. For illustrative purposes, here are one state's essential elements for third-grade social studies:

Sample state mandates

Goal 01—The students will practice a variety of listening, speaking, writing, and reading skills in completing social studies activities. [This goal appears in all elementary grades, but the objectives become more complex at the higher grade levels.]
Goal 02—The students will understand the cultural and historical development of their local community.

Goals

Goal 03—The students will understand that people use natural resources to meet their basic needs and these resources must be protected and conserved.

Goal 04—The students will understand geographic concepts.

Goal 05—The students will understand the interplay of economics in their daily lives.

Goal 06—The students will understand that the purpose of government is to protect and serve the needs of citizens in their community.

For brevity, the objectives portion for only one goal statement (05) are reproduced.

Objectives (for Goal 05)

Students should be able to:

Objectives

0501—Define wages, prices, producer, consumer, specialization, division of labor, profit, loss, and productivity.

0502—Explain reasons for spending and saving money.

0503—Identify relationships between supply and demand and its effect on the price of a product.

STANDARDS

0504—Identify an advantage of division of labor job specialization which increases productivity and creates interdependence.

0505—Identify the natural resources that determine the types of jobs in your community in the past, present, and future.

0506—Identify the role of profits as being the primary reason for production.

0507—Identify how inventions influence change in society.

The scope of these state mandates is broader than can be dealt with in this unit, or any single unit for that matter. However, there seems to be a "fit" between this unit and Goal 03 and Objective 0505 (of Goal 05) of the state's essential elements. The mandates may also suggest additional elements to include, which will be determined as planning progresses.

The Impact of National Standards. There is a kind of "chicken-egg" question of whether state standards have had an impact on the creation of national standards, or vice versa. The outcomes and terminology used in the state standards are often similar to the national standards. This means that instead of assessing whether students know the combatants in the War of 1812, state testing programs are more likely to focus on behaviors such as those found in the national standards for history, geography, and the other social science disciplines.

National standards are overarching expectations

The Standards for Historical Thinking, proposed in 1995 by the National Center for History in the School, are presented in the Resource Handbook. The Essential Elements (Standards) for Geography (1994), are presented in Chapter 2. One of six geography standards is reproduced below, first, because it reflects the expectations common to the standards documents, and second, because our sample unit will address this standard directly.

STANDARDS

The Fifth Essential Element of Geography: Environment and Society

The physical environment is modified by human activities, largely as a consequence of the ways in which human societies value and use the earth's natural resources. Human activities are also influenced by the earth's physical features

You can proceed inductively or deductively

and processes. The geographically informed person knows and understands the following:

* How human actions modify the physical environment
* How physical systems affect human systems
* The changes that occur in the meaning, use, distribution, and importance of resources

A Perspective on Learning Outcomes

Outcomes should fit the time span

As teachers plan their courses, units, and lessons, the time span they are dealing with affects how they create and state their learning outcomes. For example, it's doubtful that any teacher can attain the goal of "producing effective citizens," because this is a desired outcome for an entire school experience. As such, it would represent the collective effort of teachers over a period of years. Still other outcomes, such as having students "understand the geography of the Western Hemisphere" or "understand the Civil War" will cover shorter periods, possibly a course, semester, or a unit of study. Daily lessons, on the other hand, almost always have even more specific outcomes or objectives than units or courses.

The levels of specificity for educational outcomes are shown below:

Goals

Level 4: Very General. Example: The student will be able to cope with the problems of life. (School or Lifelong Goal)

Objectives

Level 3: General. The student will understand how technology has influenced our way of life. (Course Goal)

Level 2: Specific. Given a limited amount of information about unknown nations, students will be able to identify two or more plausible hypotheses that describe life in those nations. (Unit or Course Objective)

Level 1: Very Explicit. Example: Given a state highway map, the student will be able to use the index to locate five towns or villages. (Specific Lesson Objective)

Objectives are stated specifically

Broadly stated goals, such as helping students "to understand the geography of the Western Hemisphere" or "to understand how humans use resources" indicate the overall direction that teaching should take. However, these outcomes are not specific enough to indicate what students who understand "the geography of the Western Hemisphere" or "how humans use resources" should know or be able to do. This is where more specifically stated outcomes, often called objectives, (or learner objectives) enter the picture. An objective, such as "name forty-five of the fifty state capitals," indicates exactly what students should know and thus lends precision and direction to what could otherwise be very general expectations. There are problems with an objective like "name forty-five of the fifty state capitals," which are considered shortly, but the overall point is that although goals and objectives play a role in teaching social studies, they serve different functions.

Goals and objectives serve different functions

Stating Outcomes in Performance Terms

Stating expectations for units or lessons often depends on the specificity of the words you use. Of the two lists of phrases shown below, determine which one uses terminology more appropriate for units and courses, and which is more applicable to daily lessons.

Goals vs. objectives

List 1	*List 2*
To grasp the significance of	To write or list
To understand	To illustrate
To recognize	To define
To appreciate or to enjoy	To predict or to suggest
To believe or to have faith in	To name or identify
To comprehend or to understand	To locate or to rate
To know (or to know thoroughly)	To restate or to tell why
To be aware of	To distinguish between or to discuss

The terms in List 1 are more often associated with units or courses, whereas the more explicit terms in List 2 are typically associated with specific lessons. Learning outcomes that use the more specific format are sometimes called *performance objectives, behavioral objectives, criterion-referenced objectives,* or *learner objectives* and typically have four components:

Characteristics of performance outcomes

1. An *object* of instruction ("state capitals")
2. A *condition* under which the behavior will be demonstrated ("from memory")

3. A *standard* (*criterion or performance level*) that the student must demonstrate ("forty-five of fifty")
4. An identifiable *task* or *behavior* ("to name")

Judging the Appropriateness of Objectives

Criteria for judging appropriateness

Although the sample objective "Students will be able to name forty-five of the fifty state capitals from memory" reflects all the criteria for precisely stated objectives, it still has some problems. Every objective must be judged in terms of (1) whether students can realistically achieve it, which may depend on students' grade level and maturity, (2) whether it is logically consistent with the purpose(s) to which it relates, *and* (3) whether the goal or objective pertains to something that children *should* attempt to do. Given enough time, for example, most first graders could probably memorize forty-five of the fifty state capitals. But simply because children *could* achieve that objective does not mean it is something they *should* strive for.

The "who cares?" test is one technique for judging the appropriateness of learning outcomes. For an objective such as "Students will identify from memory the number of horses that pulled Cinderella's coach," you need simply ask "who cares?" If your answer is "nobody," the objective should probably be discarded.

Creating Intermediate-Level Outcomes

Intermediate level outcomes—a middle ground

Learning outcomes should be stated as precisely as possible, but this does not mean that *everything* must or can be stated in behavioral terms. For example, it's almost impossible to specify precise behavioral indicators for creative or open-ended group activities, especially when there are no right answers. The same situation can exist for objectives pertaining to attitudes or higher-level thinking skills, such as analysis and synthesis, and for works of children's literature. To accommodate situations like these, it is helpful to create somewhat intermediate-level goal statements, which, although they may lack the specificity of instructional objectives, are often explicit enough to guide instruction. For example, suppose you want to use a book like Bunting's (1991) *Fly Away Home* with your students. This is a moving story of a homeless boy and his father who live in an airport. Developing precise objectives for this story, such as "The student will from memory, identify at which gate the father and son most often slept" is possible, but some of them will probably be on the same level as "How many horses pulled Cinderella's coach?" Such objectives could ask students to focus on what is essentially trivia. After using a story such as *Fly Away Home,* some acceptable intermediate level goals might include (1) for students to appreciate what it feels like to be homeless, and (2) to be aware of the things that homeless people sometimes think about as they search for shelter. Intermediate-level goal statements can provide guidance for identifying instructional objectives, unit objectives, and even course objectives.

Goals and Objectives for Thinking and Feeling

Many elementary and middle-school classrooms have a semipermanent poster or bulletin board that states:

Knowledge
Comprehension
Application
Analysis
Synthesis
Evaluation

• •

These bulletin boards reflect the work that Benjamin Bloom and his associates did over forty years ago when they developed a system for organizing and classifying educational goals and objectives. Two major parts of this landmark work are the *Taxonomy of Educational Objectives: The Classification of Educational Goals, Handbook I: Cognitive Domain* (Bloom et al., 1956), and *Handbook II: Affective Domain* (Krathwohl et al., 1964). A *taxonomy* is simply a hierarchical classification scheme whereby each level builds upon and is more complex than the previous level.

The *cognitive domain* refers to activities that involve different kinds of thinking and remembering. The taxonomy for the cognitive domain is organized in terms of the complexity of the thinking skills involved, as shown on the sample poster above. Thus, when you hear people refer to "higher-level thinking skills," they are in all likelihood referring to skills at the higher and more complex levels of the *Taxonomy* (application, analysis, synthesis, and evaluation).

The *affective domain* includes attitudes and values, both of which involve feelings and emotions. For analytical and planning purposes, it's possible to treat the cognitive (knowing) and affective (feeling) domains separately, but in practice the two often merge together. You've seen this in instances where your teacher's attitudes and feelings about certain subject matter came across as strongly as the subject matter itself.

The part of social studies directed toward the affective domain is reflected by goals such as "Develops respect for the American way of life," "Develops an appreciation for American history," or "Becomes a responsible school citizen." It is one thing to state a desired attitude, such as "being a good classroom citizen," but it is another to identify specific behavioral indicators for that notion. Although everyone might agree that a "good school citizen" is someone who pays attention, turns in work on time and so on, it soon becomes difficult to avoid stating behaviors that students should not exhibit—does not interrupt, never gets out of seat. Unfortunately, when possible affective objectives are phrased as positive statements, such as "The student will stop interrupting the teacher whenever the teacher is talking," they can take on a "Have you stopped browbeating your spouse yet?" flavor. Our point is that developing affective objectives is a difficult task.

Content, Process, and Affective Outcomes. The reason for this detour through the various kinds of instructional outcomes is to indicate why our teaching unit will have three kinds of goals or objectives. The first type is knowledge or

The Taxonomies

Cognitive domain—thinking

Affective domain—feelings and attitudes

The challenge of affective objectives

content objectives, which indicate what we expect students to know from having studied this unit. For example, after studying a unit on resources, it is reasonable to expect students to know what resources are. Thus one of the content objectives will be that the student will describe the nature of a resource. The second type of outcome is skill or *process objectives,* which indicate how students will use data. Process objectives depend largely on the kinds of teaching activities we develop (and which we haven't done yet), but an illustrative objective is that students will generate and test three hypotheses that explain how farmers decide what crops to grow. The third type of outcome is attitudinal or *affective goals,* which indicate the attitudes and appreciations we would like students to develop from having studied this unit. There may not be many affective goals, but one example is that the student will appreciate the need to use resources wisely. We will identify additional outcomes for each category as our planning progresses.

Outcomes focus on different elements

TECHNOLOGY UPDATE

Teaching Units and Lesson Plans on the Internet

So many lesson plans and units are available on the Internet that some sites have their own minisearch engines. The following is a sampling of sites that have lesson plans and units available for downloading.

Academy Social Studies Curriculum Exchange for Elementary (K–5) or Intermediate (6–8) Schools. Two sites with 130 different lesson plans. The address for elementary plans is:

> http://ofcn.org/cyber.serv/academy/ace/soc/
> elem.html

The address for intermediate (6–8) plans is:

> http://ofcn.org/cyber.serv/academy/ace/soc/
> inter.html

Columbia Education Center in Portland, Oregon. This center offers a large assortment of lesson plans for Grades K–5 and 6–8. The address for K–5 plans is:

> http://www.col-ed.org/cur/#sst1

For intermediate plans, substitute "#sst2" for "#sst1" (do not type the quotation marks) in the K–5 address. Core Knowledge Lesson Plans and Units. All of the K–6 units and lessons available from this site correspond with the Core Knowledge program that we described in Chapter 3. Address:

> http://www.coreknowledge.org/

Education Station Lesson Plans. Uses a search engine for the 2,600 K–12 lesson plans at this site. Address:

> http://www.digicity.com/lesson/l_socstd.html

Publishers' plans and activities. Houghton Mifflin and McGraw-Hill are two of several publishers that have K–8 lesson plans available. The address for Houghton Mifflin is:

> http://www.hmco.com/school/search/
> activity.html

The address for McGraw-Hill is:

> http://www.mmhschool.com/teach/
> socialstud/socstu1.html

Lesson plans and activities that correspond with television programs. Three examples in this category are the History Channel Classroom Materials, at:

> http://www.historychannel.com/classroom/
> index.html

CNN (The Cable News Network) Lesson Plans and Multimedia Resources at:

> http://learning.turner.com/newroom/index.html

and the Discovery Channel School at:

> http://school.discovery.com

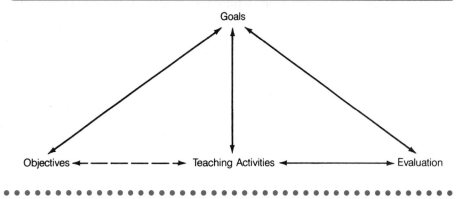

FIGURE 8.4 Planning: An Interactive Process

Goals

Objectives ← — — — — → Teaching Activities ← — — — — → Evaluation

Systematic Planning

An interactive process

As Figure 8.4 illustrates, determining your instructional intent, which means identifying your instructional goals, is the appropriate starting point in planning. Thereafter, planning usually becomes an interactive process or system in which the various elements mingle with each other. There is no predetermined order in which those elements must be considered. Sometimes you might focus on designing student activities for a particular goal or objective, after which you develop objectives and evaluation strategies to fit those activities. Once you are satisfied that you've covered your goals, you can then evaluate your plan in terms of its overall consistency. The key questions at this stage of unit development are "Does everything 'fit' together?" and "Will this plan do what I want it to do?" For the last question especially, the ultimate test will come when you use your plan with students.

Do all the elements "fit" together?

Composing a Sample Unit: Part 2

Identifying Learning Outcomes

STANDARDS

Keeping things manageable

Our next planning task is to identify a preliminary set of goals for this unit. We could pull these elements out of the blue, but for this unit we will use the state-mandated competencies noted earlier. We've done this because the competencies reflect topics common to third-grade social studies programs, state-mandated or otherwise.

Briefly, the mandated goals involve (1) communication skills, (2) the local community, (3) use of natural resources, (4) geographic concepts, (5) economics, and (6) government. Trying to deal with all of these at once could be overwhelming for children, to say nothing of adults, so the next decision is to narrow them down to the point that they are more manageable.

Organizing or Key Questions.   Identifying key or organizing questions can be a useful intermediate step in identifying additional learning outcomes. Those questions, some of which derive from the web completed earlier, are as follows:

Guiding questions

1. What are resources, and where do they come from?
2. What resources (and occupations) were involved in producing the two cans of corn?
3. What resources are used to produce other common products?
4. What other products could be produced from those same resources?
5. How do human and natural resources differ?
6. How do renewable and nonrenewable resources differ?
7. How are resources allocated?
8. How do goods and services differ?

These questions are not necessarily in their final order, nor is it essential to deal with all of them.

Relationship to Mandated Goals.   If it seems that we keep moving back and forth, we are. This reflects the systematic nature of planning, where it is necessary to balance several elements simultaneously. That's why we have gone back to our state-mandated goals once again. However, this time our focus is on only the goals that pertain to this unit (which is why Goals 02 and 06 do not appear here) and identify possible activities associated with each of them.

Correlating mandates and activities

STANDARDS

Goal 01—The students will practice a variety of listening, speaking, writing, and reading skills in completing social studies activities.

Activities.   Some teaching activities in this unit will have language arts–related extensions that address components of Goal 01. In one activity, for example, each child will select a simple product, such as a telephone pole, a hammer, or a wooden ruler. After he or she researches how the product is made, the child will present the results of the research in the form of an illustrated, first-person diary, for example, "Hi, I'm Teddy Telephone Pole, and I grew up on the slopes of Mount Helen. . . . " This activity will correlate with an ongoing language arts and reading activity in which the children are reading real biographies.

Goal 03—The students will understand that people use natural resources to meet their basic needs and these resources must be protected and conserved.

Activities.   Activities that involve identifying the occupations and resources that went into producing the canned corn—including the label, the corn, and the can itself—pertain to this goal and Goal 05. More specifically, we will create a "family tree" for a can of corn (which is described shortly).

Goal 04—The students will understand geographic concepts.

Activities.   This is not a major focus of this unit, but activities pertaining to crops that farmers grow will involve elements related to terrain, weather conditions, and so on. In addition, because the canned corn can represent products produced in certain geographic regions of the country, we will undoubtedly deal with additional elements of geography.

Goal 05—The students will understand the interplay of economics in their daily lives.

Activities. This will be a major area of this unit. In addition, the fact that corn and other products are produced, bought, sold, and consumed can lead to some of the following objectives.

Objective 0501: Define wages, prices, producer, consumer, specialization, division of labor, profit, loss, and productivity.

Objective 0503: Identify the relationship between supply and demand and its effect on the price of a product.

Objective 0505: Identify the natural resources that determine the types of jobs in your community in the past, present, and future.

Objective 0506: Identify the role of profits as being a primary reason for production.

● Other Elements

Assessing the unit's elements

One element we could include in our emerging unit could deal with the different forms of transportation involved in producing and transporting canned corn. Such a topic would be within the scope of Objective 0501, and it would also add an appealing focus to the unit, especially if we could create some interesting non-reading activities dealing with trucks, trains, and other forms of transport. On the other hand, most third graders are already aware of trucks, trains, and so on, so unless we are careful we could find ourselves conducting a lesson about how milk trucks carry milk.

To pursue the transportation focus, we need to determine what *prior knowledge* children must have before they can deal with the role that transportation plays in any kind of trade. An obvious prerequisite is the need to understand the notion of trade as the exchange of goods and services. The students must also understand the notion of transportation in terms of its function—the movement of goods and people. In addition, to understand why things are transported, students must also understand why goods are traded, which involves concepts related to self-sufficiency, interdependence, and profit.

Is this becoming too complex?

If this topic seems to have become very complex, you're right. The potential ideas include *trade, transportation, self-sufficiency, interdependence, goods and services, exchange,* and *communication.* Separately, none of these is beyond the grasp of third graders, but when it comes to helping them understand how these topics are interrelated, we have tackled something much more complicated than we bargained for, something unnecessarily complex for exemplary purposes. Thus, transportation will not be included as a significant element in this unit, for some of the reasons noted earlier. This decision illustrates a common planning phenomenon: the need to back up and either go in a different direction or, in some cases, delete or even start over. If everything went well on the first try, planning would be less exciting and less time consuming.

Backing up is not unusual

After considering many alternatives, we have finally laid the foundation for our unit. Our planning is far from complete, but the progress report on page 224 shows the elements identified thus far.

Identifying and Sequencing Teaching Activities

The basic structure for this unit is identified, but it still lacks clearly defined teaching activities (and some other components). There isn't necessarily one best way to proceed from this point. One option is to follow up on the earlier brainstorming by using the following technique.

One technique

Strategy for Identifying Instructional Activities.   The following technique for identifying potential teaching activities employs a modified brainstorming format. The number of entries per category can be expanded or reduced to fit the situation. Also, this activity can be treated like a grocery list, as something you can return to whenever you get a good idea.

Another technique

An Alternate Technique for Identifying Teaching Activities.   The preceding technique creates a pool of potential activities to select among. Another way to begin is by identifying a way to initiate the unit, preferably a way that grabs students' attention and establishes a direction for the activities that follow. Then you can go back to the activity pool and sequence things in ways that seem to make sense.

Creating an Initiating Activity.   Among the possible ways to initiate this unit, the first decision is not to begin with the usual defining of terms. Definitions will eventually need to be dealt with, of course, but beginning with them at the outset is not something that will grab students' attention. Beginning the unit by identifying the resources that went into producing the cans of corn—resources that we are fairly sure of, like metal for the can, and those we think we know, like fertilizer for growing the corn—seems to have some potential. (Note that we're using adult language here, not necessarily what we'd use with students.) Presenting a list of "things" (resources) that went into producing the canned corn is one alternative; or we could develop a kind of "family tree" for canned corn, as illustrated in Figure 8.5.

Factors to consider

Choosing between beginning the unit with a list of resources, a family tree activity, or something else is just one of the countless decisions that planning demands. In this instance, the family tree activity is appealing because it illustrates both the resources used in producing canned corn and their sequence of use. Also, it can be an appealing format for presenting data. Finally, developing a family tree for canned corn in a whole-class setting could serve as a model for follow-up activities in which small groups of students could create similar charts for other familiar products—furniture, clothing, agricultural products, or almost anything else.

Weighing alternatives

The detail provided here is to indicate some of the factors to consider in arriving at a decision. If the notion of a family tree is foreign to students, a preliminary activity in which students learn to create their own family trees may be advisable. This decision necessarily hinges on an awareness of students' previous experiences with family trees, which is something teachers gain simply by working with their classes.

Identifying Potential Learning Activities

Students could *read:* [List potential reading materials/activities, e.g., original source materials, etc.]

a. _____

b. _____

c. _____

Students could *view:* [List potential viewing activities, e.g., videos, CD-ROMs, etc.]

a. _____

b. _____

c. _____

Students could *listen to:* [List potential listening materials/activities, e.g. books for read-alouds, etc.]

a. _____

b. _____

c. _____

Students could *write:* [List potential writing activities, e.g., imaginary diaries, reports, etc.]

a. _____

b. _____

c. _____

Students might *construct:* [List potential modeling or construction activities (including art-related activities), e.g., collages, etc.]

a. _____

b. _____

c. _____

Students could *discuss* or *debate:* [List potential discussion or debate topics.]

a. _____

b. _____

c. _____

Students could *research/investigate:* [List potential research activities, e.g., how steel is made, etc.]

a. _____

b. _____

c. _____

Students could *complete:* [List other potential activities not included above, e.g., worksheets, etc.]

a. _____

b. _____

c. _____

Brainstorming potential learning activities that appeal to different modalities

You may have more than three activities in some areas and fewer in others

Planning: Progress Report

Unit Development

Unit title: How We Use Resources
Grade level: Primary (third)
Unit focus: Resource utilization
Generalization: The allocation and use of human and natural resources is based on decisions.
Major vehicle: Canned corn
Unit goals (partial listing):

Cognitive

* The child will understand what makes something a resource, either natural or human.
* The child will understand that the use of resources always involves choices and decisions. (For brevity, we have not repeated the additional goals shown earlier.)

Affective

* The child will appreciate the scarcity of resources, our widespread dependency on them, and the need to use resources wisely.

Topics: Resources, natural resources, human resources, wants, needs, allocation, scarcity
Objectives (tentative):

* The student will identify, from memory, three examples of natural resources.
* The student will distinguish between a human resource and a natural resource.
* The student will identify at least three alternative uses for a particular resource. (For brevity, we have not repeated the additional objectives shown earlier.)

Skill focus: To be determined in activities
Learning activities: Yet to be decided

Since the students' prior experiences are unknown to us here, we are forced to make assumptions. If we assume incorrectly or don't make provisions for instances where we have assumed improperly, we may find ourselves in serious trouble.

Sequencing potential activities

After students have identified some natural resources used to manufacture various products, they could compare their charts to decide which, if any, resources are common among the products. They could then produce pictorial charts (pictures cut from magazines or downloaded from the Internet) or murals showing the different products produced from a particular resource, with titles such as "Things

FIGURE 8.5   A Family Tree for a Can of Corn

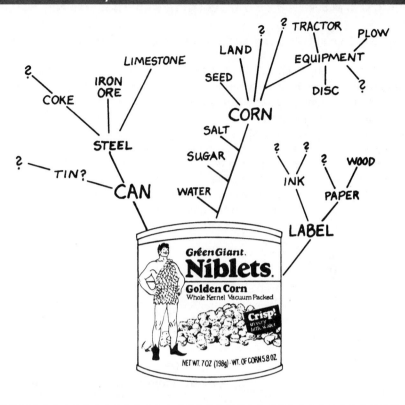

Made from Wood." So that children would not need to rely solely on their prior experiences for this, we would use some of the vast array of videos, with titles such as *The Story of . . . (Bread, Wood, Steel),* that focus on how we use natural resources.

Developing and sequencing learning activities is neither more nor less important than any other aspect of planning, but unfortunately, there is no formula or procedure to help do it. Many times it is simply a matter of what makes the most sense.

Determining a Culminating Activity.   This stage is something teachers may think about throughout the entire planning process. In this instance, we were sensitive to Brophy and Alleman's comments about end-of-unit activities that take considerable time but fail to engage students' thinking processes (see Commentary). Culminating activities should also provide opportunities to apply and extend some ideas previously dealt with in different contexts. By initiating the unit using canned corn as a vehicle, we can return to it in the culminating activity in

Deciding how to end the unit

Brophy and Alleman (1991) have suggested an important criterion for selecting teaching activities, which they call an activity's *cognitive engagement potential*. This refers to the extent to which a teaching activity has the potential to engage the student cognitively—that is, the degree to which it gets students thinking actively.

Brophy and Alleman argue that many teaching activities have only a limited potential to engage children intellectually. Notable among these is much of the "seatwork" that students encounter—the page after page of workbook-like questions that students must complete. Such activities are sometimes called "check-ups" or "skill-builders" or some other beneficial-sounding name, but it would probably be more honest to call them what they usually are: tests or merely busywork. Seldom will students "build a skill" simply by answering questions that test their prior knowledge.

Brophy and Alleman contend that the educational value of some long-term projects, including some hands-on activities and end-of-unit or end-of-semester activities, is also suspect. Likewise, some end-of-unit pageants or the construction of complex displays—like scale-model colonial villages—can consume vast amounts of time but have very limited instructional payoff. Students sometimes enjoy such long-term projects and may even look forward to them, but often their enjoyment may stem from the chance to avoid more seatwork.

a slightly different context. Returning to the master family tree chart for corn, we can ask the children to identify the main decision makers and to identify at least one alternative decision that each individual might have made in determining how he or she would use the available resources. Then, small groups of children will be given pictures of someone in a particular occupation (a machinist, a diary farmer, etc.), which will serve as the centerpiece of a collage in which students pictorially identify (1) the goods and services being provided and (2) the natural resources being used.

Ending activity   It is not essential to return to the canned corn in the culminating activity, but it seems to round things out rather nicely. It is also helpful, though not essential, if the culminating activity provides a bridge to the next unit, which might focus on conservation (the use and abuse of resources), the role of tools in using resources to produce goods and services, or perhaps the role of money as a medium for allocating resources.

Determining Ongoing Activities.   This aspect of planning is not essential unless you will have some activities that carry on throughout the entire unit. We intend to have two ongoing activities: (1) student journals and (2) the award-winning, computer-based simulation *DinoPark Tycoon* (1995), which is available

Ongoing activities   from MECC. In this engaging simulation, students must plan and operate a dinosaur theme park. In addition to meeting the needs their dinosaurs will have, such as land, fencing, and food, students must also decide how they will staff the park and make provisions for maintenance and daily operations.

FIGURE 8.6 Unit Plan Checklist

General Elements

Yes	No	Goals
_____	_____	Does it identify what students should know at the end of this unit?
_____	_____	Does it identify the skills that students should be able to demonstrate at the end of this unit?
_____	_____	Does it identify affective goals for this unit?
_____	_____	Does it identify what should be done for students who cannot demonstrate what is indicated above?
_____	_____	Does it identify cognitive and affective objectives for this unit?

Specific Elements

Yes	No	
_____	_____	Does it identify a vehicle or focus for the unit?
_____	_____	Does it identify a main idea or generalization for the unit?
_____	_____	Does it task-analyze the elements of this unit in terms of prerequisite understandings?
_____	_____	Does it state instructional objectives in performance terms?
_____	_____	Does it identify and sequence learning activities?
_____	_____	Does it identify guiding (key) questions?
_____	_____	a. For planning purposes?
_____	_____	b. For instructional use with students?
_____	_____	Does it identify teaching materials and resources?
_____	_____	Does it identify a way to initiate the unit?
_____	_____	Does it identify the means for student evaluation?
_____	_____	Does it identify a way to bring closure to the unit?
_____	_____	Does it devise a means for evaluating the unit for internal and external consistency (such as this checklist)?
_____	_____	a. Do the various sections of the unit "fit together" — for example, no "hidden objectives" (internal consistency)?
_____	_____	b. Is the unit, as a whole, justifiable? Can it be defended as worthy of being studied (external consistency)?

⬤ Reviewing the Unit for Completeness and Consistency

In planning this unit, several stages were left partially completed. Once the unit has taken on a clearer form and direction, it is time to go back and fill in the holes. A Unit Plan Checklist that can be useful for this task is shown in Figure 8.6.

The final test of any unit plan comes when you teach it with students. In the process, you will discover those activities that work well and those that don't and will make the necessary adaptations for the next time you teach it.

A Sample Unit Plan: Using Resources Wisely

Grade Level: Third Grade

Introductory Note: Because we have already discussed many elements of this unit plan, we have elected to refer you to relevant pages rather than repeat them again here. In addition, the following activities are described in adult terms, not necessarily as we would present them to children. In developing your units, you may wish to include key questions in the language you would use with students.

Introduction: As described on pages 222–224.

Curriculum Standards:

* **Benchmark Standard:** The Fifth Essential Element of Geography. See page RH-7.

* **Mandated Outcomes:** See pages 212–213.

Key Learning Outcomes: See pages 220–221.

Ongoing Activities: (1) Journals; (2) *DynoPark Tycoon* (MECC) simulation

Activity 1: Initiating Activity

Objective: Working in small groups, students will identify the components of canned corn.

Description: Phase One: Divide the class into small groups and, if possible, provide each with an identical can of corn. Ask each group to identify as many "things" as possible that went into making the corn, can, and label. Gauge the time spent on this portion of the activity by the students' interest. Five minutes or less may be sufficient.

Phase Two: Have the various groups report their findings. List the components on the chalkboard as each group reports. Probe, cajole, and stimulate as necessary. After the groups have gone as far as they seem able, ask if any of the items seem to go together (following the Taba concept-building procedure, pages 224, 226). Note that some items may go into more than one category.

Skill Areas: Observing, analyzing, inferring, classifying.

Activity 2: Building a Family Tree

Overview: The teacher and students will develop a model "family tree" for canned corn.

Objective: The child will explain the process for making a family tree (pedigree) chart.

Description: Working with the list of "things" previously identified, the teacher and students will locate components on a family tree chart similar to the one illustrated in Figure 8.5. As a group, students will identify all the "things" (not yet identified as resources) they can think of that were involved in producing the cans of corn. Have one student read the label. Items the students identify should be listed on the board and may include such things as farmer, metal, paper, and ink. Don't push too far here. For example, accept paper without going into paper's components (wood, etc.) unless the children insist on it. This will be picked up again in Activity 3.

Skill Areas: Recording data.

Optional Initiating Activity: If students are unfamiliar with a family tree chart, the unit could begin by having students make family tree charts of their own using snapshots if available or simply names of relatives.

Activity 3: Paper

Activities 3, 4, and 5 each follow a similar format. The children should tentatively identify the resources and processes that go into producing the various components of the cans of corn—paper, metal, and others. Their suggestions should be treated as hypotheses that will then be tested against data (on paper making, etc.) provided through films, filmstrips, or other media.

The exact nature of these activities and the length of time they take will depend on the materials and resources available.

Objectives:

* The student will identify a natural resource as something from our environment that people may use.

* The student will describe the process for making paper.

Description: The intent of this activity is to test and then validate the children's ideas about the resources used in making paper. Key question: What do you think paper is made from?

Phase One: List responses to the key question on the chalkboard.

Phase Two: Make paper following the instructions in the Resource Handbook.

Phase Three: Review the elements the children hypothesized originally. Add the resources to the master family tree chart.

Skill Areas: Hypothesizing, hypothesis testing.

Activity 4: Tin Cans

Objective: The student will identify the major components in metal cans.
Description: Follows the same format as Activity 3. Key question: What are tin cans made from?
  Possible materials include the following:

*   Films: *Tin from the Malayan Jungle* (International Film Bureau); *Steel & America* (Disney Productions)

*   Filmstrip: *Rocks, Minerals, and Mining* (Encyclopaedia Britannica Films)

*   *Explorapedia,* a children's interactive encyclopedia (Microsoft)

*   Other encyclopedia articles

Skill Areas: Hypothesizing, hypothesis testing.

Activity 5: Corn

Objectives:
*   The student will identify the major steps in the production of corn.

*   The child will name at least five resources used in the production of canned corn (for Activities 3, 4, and 5 collectively).

Description: Follows same format as Activities 3 and 4. Key question: What elements are involved in producing corn?
Possible materials include the following:

*   Filmstrips: *Farming in Indiana* (Jam Handy); *Where Food Comes From* (Encyclopaedia Britannica Films);

The Corn Belt (Society for Visual Education)

*   *Explorapedia,* a children's interactive encyclopedia (Microsoft)

*   Other encyclopedia articles

Skill Areas: Hypothesizing, hypothesis testing.
Optional Activities: Children can consider and investigate the nature of salt, ink, or any other component as interest warrants. Follow same format as Activities 3 and 4.

Activity 6: Where Do Things Come From?

Objective: Given a common object or article, the student will identify either (1) the components (resources) that were used to produce it or (2) the steps involved in its production.
Description: Each child (or small group) will select a common object or article and make a family tree chart for it (similar to the one done for the corn). For some materials, such as articles of clothing, this may involve identifying the steps in its production.
  Children should explain and display their charts.
Skill Areas: Observing, inferring.

Activity 7: Minisynthesis

Objectives:
*   The student will identify at least five resources originating in the land.

*   The student will distinguish between a human resource and a natural resource.

*   The student will distinguish between wants and needs.

Description: Using the corn chart and the materials the children constructed for Activity 6, develop a discussion-oriented activity that will help the children recognize that (1) the "things" (materials) that went into making the canned corn all ultimately originated in the land, (2) all goods ultimately have their origin in the land, and (3) people are involved at every step along the way. If the occasion has not arisen previously, the term *resources* can be identified as a label for "things," and the term *goods* can be associated with objects or products produced from natural resources.

  Key questions include the following: (1) Do you notice anything about those "things" that our cans of corn were made from? (2) Can you think of anything that does not come from the land?

Skill Areas: Classifying and labeling, inferring.

Activity 8: What Would Happen If?

Objective: Students will speculate on how things might be different if certain products were not available.

Description: This discussion activity is based on the key question, "What would happen if we didn't have any wood? electricity? water? bicycles? corn?"

Skill Areas: Hypothesizing, speculating.

Activity 9: Alternative Uses for Existing Resources

Objective: Given a picture of one product or basic natural resource, the student will identify at least seven other pictures of that resource being used in different ways.

Description: The intent of this activity, which may take several days, is to extend the idea that goods and basic resources are used in different ways. For example, a tree, while reflecting the use of the land in a particular way, can itself be used in different ways.

Provide individual students or groups with labeled pictures (cut from magazines, etc.) of various resources—land, a tree, water, and so on. The students are then asked to make a collage of pictures that illustrate different ways in which the product or resource might be used. The teacher should also make a collage showing land being used in different ways—for a playground, for growing crops, for housing, for parks, for parking lots.

Instruct students *not* to include their original picture in their collage until after the class has had an opportunity to identify what resource each collage depicts.

Skill Areas: Observing, interpreting, inferring.

Activity 10: What Could We Do with the Playground?

Objective: The students will identify at least three factors that might influence the ways in which resources are used.

Description: This activity is intended to illustrate that people have decided to use a particular piece of land,

the school playground, in a certain way. In other words, if oil were discovered beneath the playground, the land might be used for other purposes—in this case, to hold an oil well. How the playground is used is subject to certain limitations, including the presence of mineral resources.

Certain value issues also enter the picture. For example, if gold or oil were discovered on the school playground, it could be turned into a gold mine or an oil field, but *should* it? Any physical determinants—climate, for example—should be dealt with first through questions such as "Could our playground be used as an orange grove? a tree farm?"

Value considerations can then be introduced through role-playing. For example, the following situation could be presented to students.

Gold Discovered on School Playground

Gold has been discovered on the <u>(Name)</u> School playground. The Acme Mining Company wants to buy the playground and build a gold mine there. They are willing to pay a lot of money for the property.

The key question is, What should the school do?

Skill Areas: Inferring, identifying alternative explanations.

Culminating Activities

Objectives:

* The student will, from memory, (1) identify the primary decision makers (the farmer, the lumberman, etc.) involved in the production of the canned corn and (2) identify at least one alternative decision that those individuals might have made in terms of the way they used the resources available to them.

* Given a series of pictures of people in different occupations (a machinist, a dairy farmer, a baker, etc.), the student will identify (1) the goods or services being provided and (2) the natural resources being used.

Description: As described on page 226.

Detailed unit plans usually decrease the need for separate daily lesson plans. However, many prospective teachers' lesson plans are vehicles to communicate with cooperating teachers, college supervisors, and sometimes even principals (some of whom collect weekly lesson plans). As a result, your daily lesson plans may be more detailed than they would otherwise need to be for effective teaching. Thus the length and scope of your lesson plans may be a function of the dual purpose they serve: (1) as a plan for the students you teach and (2) to convey your intent to those who observe you.

Figure 8.7 shows a template you can use to write daily lesson plans.

FIGURE 8.7 Template for Daily Lesson Plans

Put the title of the lesson here

I.   **Introduction/Overview**

Write a brief overview of the lesson, including why it is something students should experience or learn. Also indicate how you intend to introduce (or set the stage) for the lesson.

II. **Entry-Level Knowledge/Skills**

Briefly describe what learners will need to know prior to this lesson (that they cannot pick up in the course of the lesson).

III. **State the Task (Objectives)**

Describe clearly what the end result of the learners' activities will be — answer a series of questions, solve a problem, summarize what they have learned, etc.

IV. **Resources/Advanced Preparation**

List the specific physical resources you need to teach this lesson. Do not include materials common to classrooms, such as chalkboard, overhead projector, etc. Attach copies of worksheets, charts, or other materials you plan to use with students.

V.   **The Process**

Describe the basic steps the learners will experience as they go through the lesson. These may include the following:

1. How you will make connections with the students' previous learning (review)
2. How you will make students aware of the objectives for the lesson
3. How you will introduce and/or model the content/skills
4. How you will provide guided practice (if applicable)

VI. **Assessment/Evaluation**

Describe how you will assess or evaluate students' performance or understanding.

VII. **Conclusion/Closure**

Briefly describe how you will bring this lesson to a close.

VIII. **Follow-up Activities**

Briefly describe other activities or lessons that logically follow from this lesson, or how you would integrate the "big ideas" from this lesson into other subject areas.

SUMMARY

For most teachers, planning is a never-ending process. It continues even as teachers are teaching, usually in the form of day-to-day adjustments. Additional planning often occurs after instruction as teachers decide what should be changed, deleted, and added to the unit when (and if) they teach it again.

This chapter identified the components of planning and illustrated how those components fit together. Goals are statements of intent that show the general direction teaching should take. A sample goal for the affective domain, which pertains to feelings and attitudes, is: "Students will appreciate the contribution of American patriots." A sample goal for the cognitive domain, which pertains to different types of thinking, is: "Students will understand the impact of technology on contemporary life." Objectives, on the other hand, describe specific behaviors that students are expected to demonstrate at the end of an instructional activity. Outcomes such as "The student will, from memory, identify three factors that led to the Civil War" and "Given a list of statements, the stu-dent will tell which are facts and which reflect opinions" reflect instructional (behaviorally stated or performance) objectives.

Simply because objectives are phrased in performance terms does not necessarily mean that they are good and worthy of instruction. Rather, teachers must evaluate potential objectives—no matter how they are stated—in terms of (1) their students' ability to achieve them, (2) the goals to which they relate, and (3) their appropriateness.

After you have identified your purpose and your instructional intent, instructional planning becomes a systematic, interactive process—as opposed to a sequence of discrete steps that one must follow. For example, objectives may imply or suggest certain teaching activities, just as activities may suggest or imply certain objectives. In most instances, the unit planning process moves from the "whole," the unit, to one or more of the specific "parts,"—the resources, the teaching activities, or assessment—and then moves back to the "whole."

SUGGESTED ACTIVITIES

1. Most colleges of education maintain collections of social studies curriculum guides and textbook series. If yours does not, the local school system might loan you copies. Where possible, get two different curriculum guides or texts (preferably the teacher's editions) *for the same grade level.* Compare and contrast them in terms of the following:

   a. the nature and clarity of their goals and objectives

   b. the relationship of suggested activities to the stated goals and objectives

   c. the similarities and differences in format, suggested topics, and suggested teaching approaches

2. Use the Brophy-Alleman framework for instructional activities that appears in the Resource Handbook to analyze the teaching activities that were included in the sample unit in this chapter. Determine whether any, some, or all of the activities should be replaced.

SUGGESTED READINGS AND RESOURCES

Print Resources

Linda L. Levstick & Keith C. Barton. (1997). *Doing history: Investigating with children in elementary and middle schools.* Mahwa, NJ: Lawrence Erlbaum. This book provides detailed examples of activities that engage children in historically related activities.

Stephanie Steffy & Wendy Hood. (1994). *If this is social studies, why isn't it boring?* York, ME: Stenhouse. This collection of first-person vignettes details how fourteen teachers were able to depart from traditional text-based teaching.

Internet Resources

Introductory Note: Web sites sometimes change their Internet addresses or cease operating entirely. All the addresses supplied here were operating when this book was printed, but if any of them fails to work properly, try entering the name of the target organization in any standard search engine.

AskERIC Lesson Plans

http://ericir.syr.edu/Virtual/Lessons

This highly recommended site provides an array of detailed lesson plans that are organized by school subjects, including social studies. It also has links to other Web sites that feature lesson plans.

Connections+

http://www.mcrel.com

This site is maintained by the Mid-continent Regional Education Laboratory and focuses mainly on standards and benchmarks, and associated lesson plans. Lesson plans are listed by subject/topic, and each contains a link that details a related content standard. This site offers excellent resources for connecting lessons to standards and benchmarks.

The Copernicus Education Gateway

http://www.edgate.com.

This highly recommended site is maintained by the Learning Channel with the cooperation of, and with links to, other prominent organizations including Encyclopaedia Britannica. With continuous updating and an amazing variety of resources, to say nothing of lesson plans that are linked to standards, this should be among the top ten sites on your Internet list. **Bookmark quality.**

Education World

http://www.education-world.com

This highly recommended site contains an astounding array of resources for teachers, including lesson plans. If you are an Internet novice, this is an excellent place to begin—it links to everything!

Lesson Plans Library

http://ed.info.apple.com/education/techlearn/ lessonmenu.htm

This site links to lesson plans prepared by the Apple K–12 education program. You first select your area of interest—elementary, middle school, or high school—and then select the desired subject area.

SCORE History/Social Science Online Resources

http://score.rims.k12.ca.us

This site is maintained by SCORE, the acronym for Schools of California Online Resources for Educators. Although geared primarily to California's curriculum and standards, it offers resources and lesson plans that are useful to teachers anywhere.

Teacher Explorer Center

http://ss.uno.edu/SS/homePages/SSLib.html

This site was created by the University of New Orleans and offers links to resources in the following five categories: content resources, lesson plans, teaching with technology, teacher resources, and research theory.

The New York Times Learning Network

http://www.nytimes.com/learning

If you are seeking lesson plans that are oriented toward current events, this is a recommended site for you. In addition to summaries of current (and past) news events, the site offers standards-based lesson plans, a lesson plan archive, and ideas for interdisciplinary lessons.

Social Studies Lesson Plans

http://ericir.syr.edu/plweb-cgi/lfastweb?search

This is an excellent site for social studies lesson plans designed for elementary and middle school classrooms.

Assessing Learning

Key Questions

- Where does assessment fit into the instructional cycle?
- How do norm-referenced and criterion-referenced evaluation differ?
- What is authentic assessment?
- How does one evaluate higher-level cognitive skills?
- What is the relationship between objectives and test questions?

Key Ideas

- Assessment is the reciprocal of planning.
- Authentic assessment is intended to more closely reflect the tasks that students might encounter in real life, as opposed to paper-and-pencil activities.
- Subjectivity is inherent in all assessment; the goal is to limit and control its influence.
- Every test question has an underlying objective, either implicit or explicit.
- The materials and strategies used to assess higher-level thinking skills may closely resemble the materials and strategies used to teach those skills initially.

Introduction: An Alternative Assessment Strategy

For twenty-six years, Janet Jacobsen has been teaching fifth grade in the same classroom in the Yakima Valley in south central Washington State. When she began teaching, the building was a K–8 elementary. It then became a K–6 elementary and is now a departmentalized 5–8 middle school. Mrs. Jacobsen is the head teacher for the fifth-grade teaching team and the building coordinator for social studies.

Upon meeting Mrs. Jacobsen for the first time, we asked her to explain how she approaches teaching social studies. "When I began," she said, "I went pretty

234

much by the book. But it always seemed that we were rushing to finish one chapter so we could get to the next one. That got 'old' after a while, for both the kids and me, so I began to cut out things—things we'd skip. I wasn't sure how I'd like it, or how the kids would react, but I've become a believer in studying fewer things in more depth."

"What did you leave out?" we asked.

"The War of 1812 was the first thing to go, because the kids can never understand who we were fighting and what we were fighting for. I also began to leave out the Mexican War, the Spanish American War . . . and things like the Depression of the 1930s.

"But I think the biggest change," Janet continued, "was when I decided to modify my role as teacher and help my kids become more responsible for their own learning. How do you say it—I shifted from being a 'sage on the stage'—the person with all the information—to a 'guide by the side.' "

Basically, Mrs. Jacobsen shifted to a modified cooperative-group investigation approach that is similar to how Tarry Lindquist organized her students as they created their cooperative biographies of Abraham Lincoln (as described in Chapter 1). The main difference between the two approaches is that in Ms. Lindquist's class, each group worked on the same topic—their biography of Lincoln—whereas in Mrs. Jacobsen's class, individuals and groups work on different topics.

The teaching strategies we observed on our first visit to Mrs. Jacobsen's classroom appear at the beginning of Chapter 10. If you don't mind skipping ahead to Chapter 10 now, you'll have a better context for understanding why Mrs. Jacobsen had to develop an alternative approach to assessment, which is the focus here. In a classroom where no two students are necessarily doing or learning the same thing, it could be very unfair if Mrs. Jacobsen tried to use traditional paper-and-pencil tests. So she created an approach to assessment that fit her new situation.

Mrs. Jacobsen began to explain her assessment techniques by walking over to a bookshelf and picking up a quarter-inch-thick booklet in an orange binder. "This is Jamie Button's report," she said proudly. "Take a look at it."

On the title page, in large bold type, it read: "How to Make (Mint) Money by Jamie Button." The next page, half-filled with print, was a combination dedication/copyright page. A portion of it said: "This book is dedicated with pride to my father, Craig Button, who helped me with some of the graphics and illustrations; to my sister Katy, who gave me time on the computer so I could finish this report; to my grandfather, Benton J. (B. J.) Burns (he's my mom's father), who showed me his collection of old coins; and . . ." It was as if Jamie had thanked half the people in the area! We looked quizzically at Janet, who said, "My kids feel this is one of the most important pages in their report, and I'm not about to argue with them." We weren't about to dispute the point, either.

"Sometimes my students work in pairs, and occasionally I have one or two threesomes, but no larger—bigger groups spend too much time figuring out who is going to do what," Janet noted, "and all of them produced creditable reports, not something they copied out of an encyclopedia." She then added, "The children's reports were on topics like: 'Pirates in Puritan Times,' 'A Comparison of Hawthorne's Written Works,' 'How Do You Make Change in Old English Money?' [where a shilling is one-twentieth of a pound sterling, and a shilling contains twelve pence], and a bunch of others. Everybody did visually based presentations, too. The kids were excited and involved, and they learned more from this activity than I ever imagined. And then," Janet added somewhat dispiritedly, "comes evaluation and grading."

In some cases, grading seems to drive everything else

"In a lot of schools, grading seems to overwhelm everything, we indicated."

"I know," Janet said, nodding in agreement. "Assessment and grading were the hardest things I had to deal with." Then she added, "And I have both extremes in this class: kids who won't do anything unless it's for a grade, and kids whom grades don't motivate in the least."

"Yeah," we responded. "We've been there."

"One of the first things I had to deal with was the school district's policy. It mandated that all teachers must have at least two grades each week in every subject for each grading period. That policy was O.K. when we used those 'skill builder' worksheets, which we graded and recorded as if they were tests, but that policy is still based on a lot of simplistic assumptions about how learning occurs. Learning is incremental, it doesn't always inch upward, bit by bit; sometimes it grows by leaps and bounds—like when you can see a light bulb go on in a child's expression that tells you, 'Yeah, I understand this!' The policy also forced me to spend a lot of time on testing and grading that I could have used for teaching."

Dealing with district policies

"So what did you do?"

Doubling up

Janet responded, "Well, sometimes if we did an activity that involved both social studies and language arts, for example, I would record the same grade twice, once in each subject area, but these were coping strategies for what I think was a questionable policy to begin with."

"So what did you do?" we asked.

"I began working to get the district's grading policy changed," Janet responded. "I got my colleagues to begin talking about the policy in their grade-level meetings. Most of them agreed that the policy was often difficult to comply with and that it seemed geared to helping administrators and teachers cover themselves if questions were raised. My seniority in this district probably helped my cause—some of my current students are children of my former students. Anyway, they couldn't dismiss me out of hand."

Policy changes

"Were you successful?"

Her response was, "Yes . . . and no." What they did was permit exceptions to the policy for teachers who filed an alternative evaluation and grading plan. That was fine with me, except that I had to figure out exactly how I would assess the kids— and this was new territory for me. But then I decided that if I couldn't defend what I wanted to do, and if I couldn't assess my students fairly, I probably shouldn't be doing it.

"With the kids studying different aspects of events like the 'Pine Tree Shillings' incident, I couldn't very well give them a knowledge-based test—most of the kids were learning different things. And then, it wasn't just knowledge that I was after. I wanted the children to begin taking some responsibility for their own learning, to learn how to inquire about things—to become experienced in using the inquiry process. And I wanted them to become skillful in organizing, interpreting, and presenting information. And I wanted to reward the kids who showed progress in developing those skills, not just give good grades to the kids who already had well-developed skills."

Goals

FIGURE 9.1 Social Studies Assessment/Progress Report

		Unsatisfactory	Satisfactory	Excellent

1. **Responsibility for Learning:**
   1.1 Demonstrates responsibility for learning.
   1.2 Progress in taking responsibility for learning.

Comments: _____

_____

2. **Subject Matter Knowledge:**
   2.1 Demonstrates subject matter knowledge.
   2.2 Progress in mastering subject matter.

Comments: _____

_____

3. **The Inquiry Process:**
   3.1 Ability to use the inquiry process.
   3.2 Progress in using the inquiry process.

Comments: _____

_____

4. **Organizing and Interpreting Information:**
   4.1 Ability to organize and interpret information.
   4.2 Progress in organizing and interpreting information.

Comments: _____

_____

5. **Sharing/Presentation Skills:**
   5.1 Ability to present information.
   5.2 Progress in presenting information.

Comments: _____

_____

• •

"That's an imposing agenda," we said.

"The more I thought about it, the more I began to wonder what I was getting into," Janet continued. "It's a lot easier to give kids the prepared tests that come with the textbooks series, and let it go at that . . . but I was determined."

A revised strategy   "So then . . .?" we asked.

"I decided to follow my instincts and develop an assessment strategy that reflected my goals." Janet opened a file folder and said, "Remember I'm a novice at this," and gave us a one-page form (shown in Figure 9.1).

"How do you use this?" we asked.

"At the beginning of the year I give the kids a copy, and we talk about what it means. Then at the end of each grading period, I have a five- or six-minute assessment conference with each student. They complete a copy of the form that they bring to our conference, along with everything they've done in social studies for the period—what I loosely refer to as 'their portfolio.' If they've lost stuff—and some of them always do—that's too bad. I also bring a preliminary copy of the form that I've filled in, based on my anecdotal notes on each child, and then we talk. Together, we complete the form and agree on a grade. The district uses computerized, fill-in-the-bubble grading forms that I fill out for the report cards, but also I send the assessment forms home with the students."

Conferences

"Do you weight each of the elements equally?"

"No," Janet answered. "I almost never give equal weight to the presentation skills, because some kids are naturally shy and some of them are less verbal than others. And sometimes the weightings change based on what we are doing. For example, during the six-week period just before we give the Iowa Test of Basic Skills [a standardized achievement test] we drop the inquiry format and do a teacher-directed overview of the parts of history that we won't get to. It's pretty much awareness-level stuff, but the kids need to be aware of it to do well on the tests. I even give old-fashioned tests, just like I used to. During that period, we use only the 'Subject-Matter Knowledge' criterion, because, well, that's all we focus on."

Weightings change depending on activities

"Doesn't it take forever to have conferences with every child?" we asked.

"Sometimes it seems like it," she responded, "but it only takes three class sessions to do everyone in each of my four classes. But," she continued, "I *really* have to watch my time—five or six minutes per student, no more, otherwise I'd be conferencing all the time."

Time considerations

"What do your other students do while you are conferencing?" we asked.

"Usually I try to schedule them so students are in the research phase of an activity," Janet indicated, "but it almost never works out right. So I give the kids options. While some of us are conferencing they can work on their projects, go to one of the centers I set up around the room, or they can read almost anything their hearts desire. Historical biographies and books like Jean Fritz's *Shh! We're Writing the Constitution* (1987) are really popular. But I will not give my students busywork activities, because that would violate my rule of doing something productive with their time."

Optional activities

"It sounds like you're happy with your assessment system," we observed.

"It's not perfect," Janet responded, "but it's better than what I used to use. And I keep fiddling with it every year to improve it."

An imperfect system

"What impresses us about your system is the way you've blended objective and subjective elements and involved your students in the conferencing process. Have you thought about writing this up for a journal article?" we asked.

Janet Jacobsen looked at us a little sheepishly and said, "Maybe when it's perfect."

There is no perfect assessment and grading system, at least none we know of. Yet, Mrs. Jacobsen's assessment system includes some notable aspects: (1) she uses a variety of different (nontest) data forms, including her anecdotal notes and the students' "portfolios," and (2) her assessment process is ongoing, even though the conference itself occurs near the end of the grading period. Too many people

Mistaken assumptions hold the mistaken notions that (1) assessment is something that occurs only at the end of the instructional cycle, and (2) the terms *evaluation, testing,* and *grading* are synonymous. Although evaluation, testing, and grading often go hand in hand, they are separate processes—at least in theory—as explained in this chapter.

Apparently because so many people lump *evaluation* and *grading* together in practice, some educators sought out a term that referred to "judging quality" but that did not also convey the notion of grading—as *evaluation* so often does. A term that reflects this notion and is being used increasingly is *assessment.* We will use both terms (evaluation and assessment) interchangeably throughout this chapter.

The first part of this chapter considers the roles that assessment can play in the instructional cycle. This is followed by several strategies you might use for gathering assessment information.

Assessment and the Instructional Cycle

Assessment is a natural part of the instructional cycle, which is shown in Figure 9.2. In Phase One of the instructional cycle, you decide where you want to go, instructionally speaking, by identifying learning outcomes. In Phase Two, you actually use the teaching activities and experiences with your students, helping them move toward the outcomes you established in Phase One. In the assessment phase of the instructional cycle (Phase Three), the focus shifts to students' performance. The key question in Phase Three is, How well have your students (and you) gotten to where you wanted to get to?

Phases of the instructional cycle interact The instructional cycle is a series of overlapping and interacting categories, not discrete steps; that is, you can't deal with one phase in isolation from the other phases. The area of the instructional cycle where things sometimes get confusing is shown by the broken arrow in Figure 9.2. That confusion is reflected

FIGURE 9.2   The Instructional Cycle

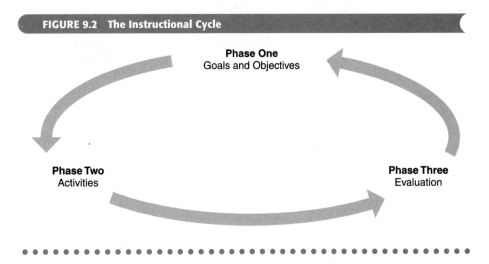

Phase One
Goals and Objectives

Phase Two
Activities

Phase Three
Evaluation

by two responses to the question, What happens after evaluation? One common response is, "Students receive a grade and then move on to something else." A less common response is, "Students continue to work on unmet objectives until they can demonstrate mastery of them." How you respond will depend on whether you are using mastery learning part of the time, some of the time, or never.

Assessment is a three-part process that consists of (1) identifying criteria or standards (determining what students will be expected to do), (2) gathering data on students' performance with respect to those standards, and then (3) making judgments about the individual's performance (based on the information you have gathered). The first component of assessment—determining what students will be expected to do—occurs during planning. The goals and objectives that you identify during planning should reflect the criteria (or standards) that students will be expected to demonstrate during assessment. For example, if your objectives indicate that you expect students to identify four of the five Great Lakes, or to distinguish statements of fact from statements of opinion with at least 80 percent accuracy, your assessment criteria are already established. You need only pose the evaluation task to students in an appropriate form.

STANDARDS

State-mandated tests are almost always based on corresponding curriculum standards that lay out with considerable specificity what students at each grade are expected to know. This means that most teachers do not need to create performance standards entirely on their own. At the same time, state-mandated materials usually reflect minimums, which means that teachers must identify performance expectations in areas where they go beyond state standards.

The second and third elements of assessment can occur during or after instruction. If students seem to be encountering problems during instruction, or even if they are not, it's simply common sense to stop periodically to evaluate how things are going. Evaluating students' progress as learning is "forming up" during instruction, instead of waiting until the end of an instructional episode, is known as *formative evaluation.*

What distinguishes formative evaluation from the commonsense assessment that often occurs spontaneously during teaching is its planned nature. In using formative evaluation, teachers (1) consciously plan to pause periodically to assess how things are going and then (2) use the criteria provided by their objectives to evaluate the situation. In this way, formative evaluation can provide useful information to supplement your intuitive sense of how things are going.

Formative evaluation is one of several forms of assessment, each of which serves a different purpose. The appropriate type of assessment is determined by the kind of information, and the kinds of questions, that you want answers to. The types and phases of assessment are reflected in Table 9.1.

Criterion-Referenced Evaluation

Criterion-referenced evaluation is "referenced," or keyed, to specified knowledge or skills, each of which serves as a criterion that students are expected to demonstrate. If you have decided that each of your students should be able to identify

TABLE 9.1 Types and Phases of Assessment as Reflected by Teachers/ Questions

Information Desired (Teachers' Questions)	Type of Programs	Phase of Instruction When Used	Typical Form of Assessment	Comments
"Can the student perform a designated task? Demonstrate a desired behavior?"	Criterion-referenced	Anytime	Teacher-made tests Standardized tests Observations Portfolios	Used to determine a student's skill proficiency. Sole focus is on individual performance.
"How does this student's performance compare with the class's performance as a whole?" or: "How does the performance of my students compare with that of similar students across the state or country?"	Norm-referenced	Anytime	Standardized tests	Used to compare an individual's performance with that of a group, or one group's performance with that of another group.
"How well are students moving toward our goals and objectives?" (How are we doing?)	Formative	During	Observations Journals Student comments	Used to determine progress during instruction.
"How am I doing as a teacher? As a student?"	Self-evaluation	Anytime	Varies	Criteria and results are usually private.
"All things considered, how does the student's overall performance rate?"	Summative	After	Varied measures	May be norm-referenced, criterion-referenced, specific or global, or some combination of all elements.
"Can the student exhibit mastery of important understandings as they apply to real-life problems or challenges?"	Authentic (Applied)	After	Demonstrated performances	Used to demonstrate performance in tasks related to real-life problems or expectations.

the location of the United States on a world map, for example, that becomes a referencing criterion. But what happens if some of your students are unable to meet that objective? If you use *mastery learning* in your classroom, students who do not meet the criterion must work through additional instructional activities until they can demonstrate mastery. Once your students meet the objective, they (and you) can move on to other objectives and teaching activities. In instances where mastery learning is not used, the student will probably receive a lower grade and then move on to other things.

Evaluation and mastery learning

Criterion-referenced evaluation can be used at any point in the instructional cycle. It can be used (1) as a pretest prior to instruction, (2) to determine student progress during instruction, and (3) to find out whether students have mastered the expected behaviors after instruction. Based on your students' performance on a criterion-referenced pretest, for example, neither you nor your students would need to waste time going over what they already know, and you could then devote your attention to areas where students need additional instruction.

If mastery learning were adhered to in its purest form, students would be expected to answer every question on a test correctly. By doing so, they would be demonstrating mastery of the desired behaviors. However, when several desired competencies are clustered together on a test, the performance standard or criterion is often established as a percentage of questions that must be answered correctly. Thus, to demonstrate mastery, students might be expected to complete at least 80 percent (or another percentage) of the test items correctly.

Alternative criteria

Every question on every test should reflect a corresponding learning outcome. For example, if you expect students to identify the year in which the Magna Carta was signed (1215), you need to have a test question or use some other means to assess that they know that information. Common sense suggests that if a teacher doesn't care whether students know when the Magna Carta was signed, a test question to that effect should not be on the test. However, students sometimes don't discover what they are supposed to know until they actually take the test. This situation may occur because some teachers wait until the night before the test to pore over the textbook or some other source, looking for test questions. Only then, *after* they've made the test, do the teachers' real expectations (objectives) become known—to themselves and, later, to students. Testing is not necessarily the preferred way to evaluate one's objectives, but by identifying clear objectives in the planning phase of instruction, teachers can reduce much of the mystique that is often associated with testing and evaluation.

Every objective should have a corresponding assessment, and vice versa

Vagueness about a teacher's expectations may explain why some students ask that proverbial question, "Will this be on the test?" At other times, the question is simply part of the grading game. In either case, the unfortunate implication is that if something isn't going to be on the test, it's not worth learning. In theory, *testing* is simply a technique for gathering evaluative information, nothing more. Yet no one needs to tell you that, in practice, testing is often a much more potent force.

Testing defined

Let's return for a moment to Janet Jacobsen's assessment strategy. Does she use criterion-referenced assessment? Because each of her students was investigating different aspects of the "Pine Tree Shillings" incident (see Chapter 10), and thus was learning different things, Janet did not establish knowledge objectives that applied to everyone. Then too, subject-matter knowledge was only one of five goals that Janet and her students were working toward. Although each of her goals serves as a kind of criterion, each was stated too globally to meet the strict definition of criterion-referenced evaluation.

Norm-Referenced Evaluation

Norm referenced: comparing students against a norm

Norm-referenced evaluation focuses on comparing one student's performance in relation to that of other students. The *norm* in norm-referenced evaluation is usually the average of students' performance—the class average—or, in the case of standardized tests, the performance of students across the school district, the state, or the country. Regardless of how the norm is determined, the purpose is to rate a student's performance relative to the norm.

Norm-referenced evaluation permits you to say, for instance, that "Johnny did better than 31 percent of the third graders who took this test on map skills." In this instance, Johnny's performance probably isn't very good—indeed, it may be awful—but unless you shifted to criterion-referenced evaluation and analyzed Johnny's performance on each test item, it's doubtful whether you could determine what problems caused Johnny to perform as he did.

Caution

The results of norm-referenced assessment are always stated comparatively—that is, in relation to whatever norm is being used. Thus, to learn that Maria got a 95 on her test might seem impressive at first, especially if you assume it was a 100-item test. However, if it was a 200-item test and the average score was 161, your impression of Maria's performance will probably change considerably. Your impression might change even more when you find that Maria is an average eight-year-old whose native language is Spanish, who has been in this country less than a year, and whose score of 95 was on a test of English vocabulary (or American history). Unless the group that Maria is being compared with (the norm) shares Maria's characteristics (age, linguistic background, etc.), the results of normative evaluation could be misleading.

DIVERSITY

Different ends and different means

Norm-referenced evaluation and criterion-referenced evaluation serve different purposes, so it is pointless to say that one is better than the other. In many respects, the comparative nature of norm-referenced evaluation has become one of the conventions of American schooling. But from a purely instructional point of view, criterion-referenced assessment can provide the information that teachers must have to target instruction toward the specific needs of individual students.

Summative Evaluation and Grading

Grading defined

For all practical purposes, *summative evaluation* and *grading* are synonymous. Summative evaluation, which always occurs at the end of an instructional episode, "summarizes" the changes that have occurred as a result of instruction, usually in the form of a grade. Grading, in its technical sense, refers to the process of judging whether someone (or something) belongs in a particular category. The key elements of grading are (1) determining the characteristics of the categories to be used for reporting purposes and then (2) deciding whether the person or object reflects those characteristics. Yet the basic question in both summative evaluation and grading is: All things considered, how would you judge the quality of a student's performance (or product)?

You already know that in most schools summative evaluation and grading are usually reflected by letters (A, B, C, D, F), numbers, descriptive expressions ("Satisfactory," "Excellent," etc.), or some combination of these. The labels we've got! What we lack are consistent descriptions of the categories to which they apply. As a result, almost everyone knows that one teacher's A can be another teacher's B, C, or even worse.

Some teachers use norm-referenced evaluation for grading purposes; that is, the student's grade is based on the individual's performance relative to the class's performance as a whole. That procedure is commonly called "grading on the curve" and is well known to most college students. Other teachers identify grading categories by using a criterion-referenced format. In those instances, the standards—such as "scores of 90 or more are an A"—are commonly established in advance. Things usually work out adequately *if* the preestablished standards are appropriate and *if* there are a limited number of elements that grades are based on. But when teachers say things like "In determining your grade, I'm going to 'count' your test scores, homework, class participation, and group work," expectations can become fuzzy. Other teachers use mathematical formulas (e.g., "Class participation counts one-fifth") in an apparent effort to make grading more objective. However, the mathematical manipulation of scores does not necessarily make grading more objective and teachers who use such devices may be doing little more than objectively manipulating subjectively selected data.

Judgment and subjectivity are currently an integral part of summative evaluation and grading. Subjectivity can be controlled, of course, which explains much of the emphasis on performance outcomes and on establishing clear expectations for students (as well as for teachers, who are also subject to periodic evalu-

Grading on the curve

Elaborate formulas do not make grading objective

● ——— **COMMENTARY** **Self-Evaluation and Grading**

I have not dealt with self-evaluation in this chapter because it is among the most private forms of evaluation; the criteria are usually private, as are the results—unless, of course, you choose to make them public.

Self-evaluation demands a considerable degree of self-awareness and self-direction. To help my students develop these qualities, I decided on one occasion to permit them to give themselves their citizenship grades. To be certain that everyone used similar grading criteria, I spent much time talking about what constituted "good citizenship." However, when the children turned in their grades, almost without exception, their grades were one to two grades lower than I would have given. Upon more investigation, I discovered that what I had considered trivial incidents, such as the failure to complete a homework paper on time, were blown out of proportion, and students had downgraded themselves accordingly. I ended up spending even

more time helping the children to examine their conduct in a broader perspective and trying to convince them that they were being overly harsh on themselves.

On another occasion I permitted college students to use self-evaluation as one element for determining their course grade. Once again, we attempted to identify mutually agreeable criteria. This time the results were very different; all thirty-four students gave themselves an A.

My elementary students had taken self-evaluation more seriously than I had anticipated, but by the college level the connection between grading and self-evaluation had apparently become tenuous at best. Interestingly, some students at both levels objected vehemently to basing their grades on self-evaluation. They claimed that grading was the teacher's responsibility, whereas self-evaluation was a private matter—one that should remain private.

ations). To make assessment and grading even more reliable, and thus avoid the wide discrepancies in grading from one teacher to the next, more and more schools are developing assessment rubrics. These are devices that more clearly and consistently identify the characteristics of performances that fit into existing grading categories. The development of rubrics is part of the movement toward authentic assessment, the focus of the next section.

Authentic Assessment

Are American schools "test driven"?

A retired British educator of our acquaintance is fond of chiding us that American schools are "test-driven." "Everything in your schools," he claims, "is geared to testing—weekly tests, six-week tests, final examinations; and then there is standardized testing at least once or twice a year. You Americans spend so much time on testing, it's a wonder the students ever have time to learn anything."

There's no question that testing in American schools is a time-consuming business. However, there is also growing recognition that many tests fail to measure learning in important and authentic ways. The problem, as Wiggins (1989) suggests, is that many tests are standardized, but they are not *standard setting*—that is, much of the learning that tests supposedly measure is neither realistic nor is it necessarily worth striving for. Rather, much testing is a perfunctory, bureaucratic checkup designed to put marks in a gradebook instead of posing authentic, challenging tasks that are related to real-life problems and expectations (Parker, 1991).

If much of the testing in schools today is inauthentic, even trivial, it's reasonable to ask what authentic assessment, or what is sometimes called "performance assessment" (Wiggins, 1989), would look like. Most authorities suggest that students engage in periodic performances (hence the term *performance assessment*) that reflect important understandings and abilities (Spady, 1994). Parker (1991, p. 88) recommends the following as attributes of authentic assessments:

Characteristics of authentic assessment tasks

1. Tasks that go to the heart of essential learnings; that is, they ask for exhibitions of understandings and abilities that matter.
2. Tasks that resemble interdisciplinary real-life challenges, not schoolish busywork that is artificially neat, fragmented, and easy to grade.
3. Tasks that are standard setting and that point students toward higher, richer levels of knowing.
4. Tasks that are worth striving toward and practicing for.
5. Tasks that are few in number and known to students well in advance.
6. Tasks that strike teachers as worthwhile.
7. Tasks that generally involve higher-order challenges and that ask students to go beyond the routine use of previously learned information.
8. Tasks that are attempted by all students.

Benchmarks

Parker (1991) argues that authentic assessment should be incorporated in benchmarks that occur at major academic transition points, such as the end of elementary school and the end of middle or junior high school. Parker (pp. 24–25) cites the following as examples of authentic benchmark assessment activities:

At the End of Elementary School

Assessment benchmarks

* Writing/Civics/History: Students write a summary of a current public controversy drawn from school life and tell how a courageous and civic-minded person they have studied (e.g., Sojourner Truth, James Madison) might decide to act on the issue.

* Geography: Students sketch a physical map of North America from memory and locate (given coordinates) five cities.

At the End of Middle/Junior High School

* Writing/Civics/History: Students write an analysis of a current public controversy facing their community and draw a historical comparison.

* Geography: Students sketch a world landform map from memory with continents labeled and locate (given coordinates) eleven capital cities.

The movement toward more authentic assessment is increasingly working its way into schools. For example, Larry Lewin, a teacher in Eugene, Oregon, described how he uses performance tasks to help students in his U.S. History/English class understand the events of 1492 (O'Neil, 1996). Larry's students spend several weeks preparing for and writing a short story from the point of view of either a Spanish sailor or a Taino Indian. The story, although fictional, must reveal the student's understanding of historical events.

Preparation

The target audience for the stories that Larry's students write is fifth graders, who are also studying 1492. The students' stories are judged on how realistically they present their fictional characters, the setting, and the other events that occur. In preparation for their assignment, students in Larry's class read several selections of historical fiction to help them understand the genre. Before beginning their final story, they must also write a short expository piece on "A Sailor's Life." The point is that students are not given a performance task and then turned loose to "sink or swim"; several miniperformances serve as building blocks for their final story.

The Use of Rubrics. When Larry Lewin assesses his students' final stories, he uses a rubric similar to the one shown in Figure 9.3. A *rubric* is a device that permits teachers to rate the characteristics of students' performances at various proficiency levels (see also O'Neil, 1994). The sample rubric shown in Figure 9.3 was designed to assess students' writing ability.

Rubrics are an assessment tool

A rubric itself does not eliminate teacher bias. For example, some teachers have difficulty giving a "4" rating to students' stories that contain only one or two mechanical problems, even though the criterion states "Grammatical or mechanical errors are hardly noticeable." Everyone knows that what is "hardly noticeable" to one teacher can be a major problem to another.

Rubrics can serve as diagnostic tools

The development of assessment rubrics reflects a movement to describe students' performance with more precision than is common to traditional letter grading. In addition, giving students the rubric in advance and then using it as the basis for a student-teacher conference can indicate where students are encountering problems and can serve as the basis for additional instruction. In other words, rubrics can sometimes serve as diagnostic tools, not simply grading devices.

FIGURE 9.3   Rubric for Assessing Students' Writing

Rating 4 = Excellent Response

Organization: Well-organized paper with a clear beginning and ending. Transitions are smooth and clear. Content is logically structured.

Clarity: All information is clearly explained.

Content: Information is thorough enough to provide a clear explanation.

Mechanics: Grammatical or mechanical errors are slight and hardly noticeable.

Rating 3 = Adequate Response

Organization: Paper is organized with a beginning and ending. The structure is logical, and there are no major problems in reading.

Clarity: Most of the information is clearly explained.

Content: There is sufficient information to explain the subject.

Mechanics: The grammatical and mechanical errors that may exist do not detract from the explanation.

Rating 2 = Less Than Adequate Response

Organization: Paper is not organized. It may lack a clear beginning and ending. The reader has difficulty moving from one idea to another.

Clarity: Parts of the paper are difficult to understand.

Content: Information is insufficient to provide a clear explanation; some unnecessary information is included.

Mechanics: Grammatical and mechanical errors are frequent enough to create problems for the reader.

Rating 1 = Inadequate Response

Organization: Paper has very little sense of organization. It has no clear beginning and ending. The reader has major difficulties following the explanation.

Clarity: Most of the information is difficult to understand.

Content: Information does not explain the topic. Much irrelevant information is included.

Mechanics: Numerous grammatical and mechanical errors make the information difficult to understand.

• •

Designing assessment rubrics can be a challenging task. Danielson (cited in ASCD, 1996) suggests the following standards:

Rubric design recommendations

1. Use a four-point scale, as shown in our sample, as opposed to a five- or six-point scale. A five-point scale corresponds more closely to the A-B-C-D-F grading system, but the larger number of points can make it more difficult for people to distinguish between the different levels.

Technology affords opportunities for multimedia presentations by teachers and students. © *Michael Zide*

2. Use equal distances between levels, as opposed to giant leaps.

3. Use examples of student work at each level. These provide concrete examples of performances at each level.

Proposals for more authentic assessment—and less testing—are consistent with the renewed emphases on active participation in social studies and on being certain that students can perform the tasks required of informed citizens. We believe that authentic assessment should replace much of the norm-referenced testing that goes on in schools today, and not become simply another layer that is added on to, and possibly dwarfed by, existing testing programs.

In place of, not on top of

Gathering Assessment Information

The keys to gathering useful assessment information are, first, identifying the kind of information you want and, second, using an appropriate means to gather that information. The kind of information needed to evaluate social studies usually relates to (1) what children know and are able to do (cognitive domain) and (2) what children believe and how they respond to what they believe and feel (affective domain). Assessment in the cognitive and affective domains is examined in the following sections.

Assessing Cognitive Knowledge and Skills

The most common technique for evaluating cognitive knowledge and skills involves a teacher's oral questions. The second most common technique involves paper-and-pencil testing. In this section we examine questions posed in test form.

Evaluation instruments

Instrument is the technical name for an evaluation technique or scale. There are three major categories of instruments: (1) nationally standardized tests and scales; (2) achievement tests developed by local, regional, or state agencies; and (3) tests constructed by teachers themselves.

Standardized Tests.   Standardized achievement tests are often used as part of statewide or schoolwide testing programs. For examples of standardized test items, see the graph for population growth of two cities in this chapter (p. 258), and the Pleasure Island Activity (Figure 13.6), which assesses map skills. The key element about standardized test items is that they almost always provide information for children to work with, a principle that should also be reflected in teacher-made tests for higher-level thinking skills. Consider how you would respond if you were asked to draw a graph of the corn production in Iowa between 1987 and 1997. Drawing a graph is not too difficult, but asking you to memorize Iowa's corn production for a ten-year period would probably elicit justifiable howls of protest. The example may seem extreme, but the point is that, when testing a student's ability to process information, the necessary data should be provided.

Provide data for students to work with

"Standardizing Authentic Assessment."   Efforts to combine elements of authentic assessment and traditional standardized testing seem to have met with mixed results. Instead of mainly multiple-choice questions—the format for traditional standardized tests—the "more authentic" tests typically present fewer questions and more varied tasks. This phenomenon is evident on the sample performance assessment of fifth-grade students' knowledge about the European origins of exploration, a familiar topic in American history courses, as shown in Figure 9.4.

Fewer questions, more varied tasks

ANALYSIS

Part I of the sample assessment asks students to provide open-ended definitions for vocabulary related to exploration. On a typical standardized test, students would be asked to select a multiple-choice item that best describes a "smallpox epidemic" or any of the other items. The students' answer sheets would typically be run through a test-scoring scanner very quickly. However, the open-ended-question format, as in this example, means that an evaluator must read each response to determine if it is acceptable. A similar situation exists for Parts II and III. There are multiple possible relationships between the elements for both of these questions, and the only way these can be evaluated accurately is by having someone analyze the child's thinking. The concern here is not that the sample questions are "bad"—for most of them may be an improvement over traditional assessment instruments—but rather in the time it takes to evaluate the answers. If classroom teachers were to pose assessment tasks like these to their students, they would anticipate evaluating their students' responses, regardless of how long it takes. But assessing students'

Machine scoring is problematic

FIGURE 9.4   Selected Examples of Authentic Standardized Test Questions

All of the following questions pertain to European exploration of the New World.

I. Short Answer

Directions: Write a short answer that explains what each of the following words mean and why the word was important in history. Try to write something for each word.

Vocabulary items

1. Colony

_____

_____

2. Christopher Columbus

_____

_____

Other words that follow this format (with spaces provided to respond) include: 3, New World, 4. Slavery, 5. Smallpox epidemic, 6. Trans-Atlantic route to Asia. 7. Indentured servant.

Demonstrating understanding

II. Comprehension

Directions: Your teacher has asked that you teach what you know about European exploration to some new students in your class. Think about everything you know about European exploration, including things you've learned from your friends and family, TV, and other sources. Then on the lines below, write what you will tell the new students. You can make drawings to help explain your ideas if you wish. [Several pages of lined paper follow.]

III. Problem Solving (Creative Thinking)

Directions: Imagine that it is the year 2020, and the earth is overcrowded. There is a shortage of food and energy resources (such as oil). The United States wants to send astronauts to distant planets to explore for new resources. Scientists think one of the distant planets may have valuable resources, and that some unknown kind of "beings" have homes there.

As an expert on exploration, the President asks you to advise her planning team. She understands that there are some similarities between what the astronauts will try to do and what happened when European explorers like Columbus explored the New World. Your knowledge of what happened in the past will be useful in planning what to do in the future.

Answer the following questions to prepare for advising the President.

Identifying similarities

1. What are some of the *similarities* (things that are the same) between this situation and what you know about what happened when European explorers like Columbus came to the New World? Describe at least two similarities, but write more if you can think of them. Use specific facts or events from history to support your ideas.

   _____

   _____

[Additional lines are provided for this and subsequent questions].

Identifying differences

2. **What are some of the *differences* between this situation and European exploration of the New World? Describe at least two differences, but write more if you can think of them.**

_____

_____

Identifying possible goals

3. **What are the *main goals or positive things* the explorers should be trying to accomplish on this mission? Describe at least two goals for Earth and two that could benefit the other planet, but write more if you can think of them.**

_____

_____

Identifying possible problems

4. **What are some possible *problems* that the explorers should try to avoid or minimize? Describe at least two problems for Earth and two for the other planet, but write more if you can think of them. If possible, give specific facts or events from history that support why you think these problems are likely.**

_____

_____

Identifying other elements

5. **What are some other *ideas or other things to consider* in making a good plan?**

_____

_____

Identifying a course of action

6. **Keeping in mind what you know about Columbus and other explorers in history, what do you think the president and astronauts *should plan or do* to make this new exploration as successful as possible?**

_____

_____

responses to standardized tests is a different animal. As Herman (1997) notes, the cost of preparing, administering, and evaluating the more authentic standardized assessment tests can be as much as 400 to 500 percent higher than traditional tests. Such increased costs are certain to cause schools to reflect on whether they can afford to use large-scale authentic testing.

Writing good questions is more difficult than it may appear

Teacher-Made Tests.   Developing good test questions may seem easy enough, but appearances can be deceptive. For example, it is not at all difficult to write a question such as "Abraham Lincoln was born in ___," but this apparently straightforward question places an unfair burden on students, who must figure out which of a multitude of possible answers (place? month? year?) the teacher has in mind. In such cases they may not be able to demonstrate what they know about Lincoln's birth.

VALIDITY

Validity refers to the extent to which test questions measure what they are intended to measure. If there is any doubt, the validity of our Lincoln question is very low.

Clarifying your intent

The validity of questionable test items can often be improved by adding information that clarifies the teacher's intent. To do this, teachers must first eliminate any fuzziness (from their original objectives) about what they expect of students. Thus an objective such as "From memory, the student will identify something about Abraham Lincoln" won't do, because the word *something* is too vague. Depending on what the teacher really expects students to know, the objective could be "From memory, the student will identify the place (state) in which Lincoln was born." In this instance, a short-answer test item could then be stated as follows: "Abraham Lincoln was born in the state of _____."

Changing the form of the question

The clarity of test questions can sometimes be improved by changing the form of the question itself. For example, instead of using a short-answer format, the sample Lincoln item could be presented as a multiple-choice or true-false question. In multiple-choice form, the question could be stated as follows:

_____ Abraham Lincoln was born in
   a. Illinois
*b. Kentucky
   c. Indiana
   d. Washington, D.C.

As a true-false item, the question could be phrased as

_____ Abraham Lincoln was born in Indiana. (F)

Considerations

Both examples clearly reflect the underlying objective, which pertains to identifying the state in which Lincoln was born. At the same time, changing to a multiple-choice or true-false format can also compromise validity somewhat because it introduces a larger "chance" (or guessing) factor than was true for the short-answer (completion) format. For true-false questions, students have a fifty-fifty chance of guessing the correct answer. This doesn't mean that you should forgo using true-false or multiple-choice test questions but that you cannot be as confident that they validly measure what you are trying to measure.

APPROPRIATENESS

Regardless of the form in which our Lincoln test item is asked, a crucial question remains: Should students be expected to recall such information from memory? Is it a worthwhile question that everyone should be expected to answer, or does it deal with trivia?

Is it worth knowing?

A test question such as "List the fifty states in order of their admission to the Union" can be perfectly valid, but it (and the underlying objective it reflects) must be judged in terms of its appropriateness—by whether it tests something that is worth knowing. Unless test items (and the objectives they reflect) are reasonable, appropriate, and worth knowing, validity doesn't even enter the picture. To avoid such problems and to be certain that your evaluation is consistent with your objectives, consider identifying potential test questions during planning, even if you don't plan to use testing as an evaluation technique. The test questions offer a way for you to crosscheck the clarity of your objectives, and your students may be impressed that you know what you want them to know.

● Sample Test Items

The sample test items that follow illustrate some of the common problems teachers encounter in writing test questions. After each "poor" question we suggest ways in which it might be improved.

A Fifth Grade Nontest—European Exploration of the Americas
Completion/Short Answer

Fill in the blanks with the correct answer.

Place blank at the end
of the sentence . . . .

1. *Poor:* The _____ _____ were among the first people to trade with the _____ inhabitants of the Caribbean islands. (Spanish/explorers/native [or orginal])
   Better: The first people to trade with the native inhabitants on the Caribbean islands were the _____ _____. Or: The first people to trade with the native inhabitants of the Caribbean islands were explorers from what country? _____
   Analysis: Ordinarily only one or two key words should be omitted, and ordinarily the omitted words should be near the end of the sentence, so that students need not continually reread the sentence to figure out the subject. In addition, the blank lines where students write their responses should be of approximately equal length so as not to provide clues to the desired answer.

Or use a question

Short-answer test items are often clearer if they are phrased as direct questions instead of as sentence-completion items. This is particularly true if the questions contain multiple elements. Thus an alternative short-answer format for this test item is:

What was the nationality of the first explorers to trade with the original inhabitants of the Caribbean islands? _____

2. *Poor:* The Spanish explorers landed on _____ _____ on _____ _____, _____. (Santa Domingo) (October 11, 1492)
   Better: None.
   Analysis: This test item has at least five problems. The first of these concerns whether children will understand that the desired responses include the name of the island and the date, which is not otherwise indicated. The second problem concerns the appropriateness of the underlying objective; that is, of expecting children to remember the name of the island and the month, day, and year of Columbus's landing. Third, the question resembles a sentence you might find in a social studies textbook, and from which a few words were deleted. Omitting key words from sentences in a textbook and then using them as test questions encourages memorization, not understanding. The fourth problem involves the number of blanks; there are so many that students are likely to spend a lot of time trying to figure out what the question is really asking. Finally, the form of the question answers the previous question.

Omitting words from textbooks
encourages memorization

Does one question
answer another?

One school of thought believes that if children can answer a test question correctly, they should get credit for it. We agree, except in instances where one question provides the answer to other questions. Whenever this occurs, the validity of the item is highly questionable. An equally important concern relates to the underlying objective. How precisely must students remember the date of Columbus's landfall? In other words, does asking students to remember the month, date, and year of Columbus's landfall amount to trivia? If you believe the objective is valid, consider asking two short-answer questions: On what island did Columbus land? And on what date did Columbus land?

True-False (Alternative Response)

Use + for true and 0 for false unless directed otherwise. (Capital T's and capital F's can look very much alike—sometimes intentionally so.)

3. *Poor:* _____ The Catholic religion was best suited to the lands that Columbus explored.
   Better: None.

Avoid opinions

   Analysis: The question asks the student to make a value judgment in the absence of clearly defined criteria. Avoid absolute terms wherever possible.

4. *Poor:* _____ The original inhabitants never helped Columbus or his crew.
   Better: None.

Use absolute terms cautiously

   Analysis: Absolute terms such as *none, never,* and *always,* which tend to be associated with false statements, should be avoided in true-false questions *unless you are dealing with situations where they are appropriate*—for example, "Evaluation always requires the identification of criteria."

5. *Poor:* _____ When Columbus first journeyed to the New World in 1491, his ships were the *Nina, Pinta,* and the *Santa Maria.*
   Better: _____ Columbus first journeyed to the New World in 1491.

Be sure that the intent of the question is clear

   Analysis: The "poor" question is misleading because the false element, the date, is subordinate to the main thrust of the question. True-false questions should avoid statements where false items are buried in an otherwise true statement.

An alternative (and probably better) technique for handling true-false questions that involve multiple elements is illustrated below:

Columbus's ships included

1. (+) the *Nina*
2. (0) the *Titanic*
3. (+) the *Santa Maria*
4. (+) the *Pinta*
5. (0) *Old Ironsides*

Multiple-Choice Questions

Select the best answer and write the letter in the space provided.

6. *Poor:* _____ A red-orange root plant grown by the native inhabitants was (a) corn, (b) yam, (c) bananas, (d) mangoes.
   Better: As multiple choice, none; if used at all, the question could be asked in a completion or true-false format.

The distractors should be plausible

   Analysis: All distractors for multiple-choice items must be plausible. In this instance, only one root plant is listed. In addition, this item could discriminate against children who may have never seen a mango or mango tree, or who do not know that corn is indigenous to continental North America.

7. *Poor:* Explorers to the New World _____ .
   a. were seeking places to avoid religious persecution.
   b. were seeking a new route to the Far East.
   c. were hoping to claim new lands for their sponsors, including King Ferdinand and Queen Isabella of Spain, King George of England, and King Louis of France.
   d. were hoping to become involved in fur trading.

Better: Explorers to the New World _____ .
a. were seeking places to avoid religious persecution.
b. were seeking a new route to the Far East.
c. were hoping to claim new lands for their sponsors.
d. All of the above
e. None of the above

Distractors should be similar in
style and length

Analysis: Where possible, most of the statement should be presented in the introduction, or stem, of the question. In addition, all answers should be plausible, and in the same style and of approximately the same length as the correct answer, and, most of all, include the correct answer. The poor question does not meet these criteria, especially response c, which adds three elements that could further confound this question. Note also that this question would be inappropriate unless children have studied the exploration of North America in some depth.

8. *Poor:* _____ Which of the following explorers sailed for Spain?
a. Jacques La Salle b. Henry Hudson c. Montreal
Better: _____ Which of the following explorers did not sail for Spain?
a. Ponce De Leon. b. Christopher Columbus c. Henry Hudson d. De Soto
Analysis: Multiple-choice questions should have a minimum of three and preferably four or five alternative answers, which are called foils. The fewer the foils, the higher is the probability that students may guess the right answer. More important, the correct alternative response must be provided (it is not provided in the "poor" form of this question). Further, alternative answers should be of the same general type—the names of people, the names of places, statements, and so on. Mixing different types of alternative responses or providing obviously false foils should be avoided. Also to be avoided are multiple-choice questions in which the correct answer is revealed by clues in the item itself, such as "Many colonial families used a (a) axe, (b) apple peeler, (c) candle mold, (d) ox." Only item c is grammatically correct. Such questions should be reserved for grammar tests.

Don't use the same
answer too often

You may have noted that for our sample multiple-choice questions the correct answer was usually item c. Because test-wise students often look for such a pattern, the position of correct responses should be distributed randomly throughout the test.

Matching

Write the letter from Column II in the space provided in front of the correct term in Column I.

9. *Poor:*

Column I	Column II
_____ 1. Patroon	a. the Native American word for corn
_____ 2. Maize	b. a Dutch system for landholding along the Hudson River
_____ 3. Mayflower	c. one of the middle colonies
_____ 4. Delaware	d. a ship

Better: Instructions: In the space provided, write the letter for the occupation (described in Column II) in the space provided in front of the term associated with that occupation (Column I).

	Column I	Column II
1.	_____ blacksmith	a. barrelmaker
2.	_____ chandler	b. hatmaker
3.	_____ cooper	c. wheelmaker
4.	_____ deacon	d. iron worker
5.	_____ teamster	e. ship's supplier
6.	_____ wheelwright	f. wagon driver
		g. church official

Matching questions should not "match" perfectly

Analysis: The items in the "poor" example are so few and so dissimilar that almost anyone could complete the exercise, even if they know nothing about "patroons." In addition, guessing is facilitated because Columns I and II have the same number of items. Guessing on matching questions is minimized if one column contains more items than are required or contains responses that are used more than once.

Matching categories

A fundamental problem in developing good matching questions lies in identifying enough similar items to place in the respective columns without resorting to trivia. Some of the following examples, adapted from Gronlund (1985), could be used for matching purposes. Separate questions would ask students to match a list of people with a list of their achievements, a list of inventors with their inventions, and so forth.

Column I	Column II
People	Achievements
Inventors	Inventions
Dates	Historical events
Objects	Names of objects
Places	Geographical locations
Rules	Examples
Principles	Illustrations

Whenever your tests begin to look like the "poor" examples, you've got problems. Not only will the form of your test items be questionable, but you may also be guilty of emphasizing the kind of trivia that has given social studies a bad reputation—one that in this case is justly deserved.

● Evaluating Critical Thinking Skills

Usually requires fewer items

Assessing a student's information-processing skills is not inherently more difficult than knowledge-level evaluation, but it is different. For example, assessing critical thinking typically requires fewer evaluation questions or tasks. Instead of a fifty-item test, for example, two or three skill-oriented questions are often sufficient.

Essay Questions. Essay testing can permit teachers to gain insight into how students think and process information. Students and teachers alike know that on essay tests it is nearly impossible to "fake it." At the same time, essay testing is an impossibility if students are not mature enough to express themselves effectively in writing. Because of this limitation, essay tests are not widely used in the primary grades. Some problems associated with essay test items are shown next.

Sample Essay Test Items

Write a good essay on one of the following questions.

1. *Poor:* What islands did Columbus's expedition visit?
   Better: None.
   Analysis: Essay questions should ask students to do more than simply reproduce information. In this instance, the question lends itself to a list, not an essay. A short-answer (completion) question would probably be better (e.g., "List three of the islands Columbus visited), but the appropriateness of the underlying objective is still questionable.

2. *Poor:* Discuss the explorers.
   Better: Describe, with examples, three ways in which the explorers to the New World were similar.
   Analysis: "Discuss the explorers" is so broad that it is difficult to know (a) where to begin and (b) what the intent of the question is. The improved question clearly conveys what the student is to do and also implies criteria by which the response will be judged.

3. *Poor:* Tell all you know about why people should always be brave and thankful.
   Better: None.
   Analysis: The task in the "poor" question is clear enough, but establishing valid criteria for evaluating students' responses would be almost impossible. This is a common problem in attempting to evaluate students' attitudes, which is what this question seems geared toward. Of course, teachers could gain insight into their students' attitudes by asking them to respond to questions such as "Why do you think some people are thankful?" But using those responses for grading purposes would be inappropriate. Some of the observational techniques suggested later in this chapter may prove to be more valid indicators of students' attitudes than direct or written questions like the ones illustrated here.

As noted earlier, another difference that separates thinking-skill test items from their knowledge-level cousins is their presentation of information to be interpreted and analyzed. In assessing critical thinking skills, the key element is the student's ability to transfer a process for manipulating information from whatever data they have worked with previously to the information presented on a test.

The following are examples of what we are talking about. Note that in Example 1 the information from *The Works of James I* was rewritten at a lower reading level.

Example 1

Skill Area: Analysis and interpretation of data.

Instructions: Read the following quotations. Explain what they show about the responsibility of individuals and how they control themselves.

Sample 1

Kings are like God. If you think of what God can do, you can think of what a king can do. For example, a king can do anything with his people. He can make them a success or make them a failure. He can judge whether or not what people do is right. But no person shall judge the king. A king's people are like chess pieces and the king is like a chess player. He decides the moves. He decides what the pieces will do. The people should serve the king. No person is to change the government. The government is the king's responsibility.

(Adapted from *The Works of James I* [1603])

Questions should lend themselves to an essay

Clear criteria for correct responses are required

Provide data for children to use

Population Growth of Two Cities Between 1875 and 1975		
Date	City A	City B
1875	111	72
1900	192	220
1925	1,621	400
1950	11,006	1,890
1975	24,000	2,773

Sample 2

Having taken this trip for the glory of God and to help the Christian faith, we agree to work together for the Glory and the Faith.

(From *The Mayflower Compact* [1620])

Example 2

This example shows how a portion of the previous question can be tested in multiple-choice format.

Skill Area: Translation and comprehension.

Comprehension

Which of the following statements best shows the main idea of Sample 1 (in the preceding question)? _____

a. People in a democracy have the right to participate in the government.
b. Kings rely on the people's support for everything they do.
c. The people keep a king in power.
d. Kings can do almost anything they want to.*

Example 3

Question 1. Skill area: Interpreting data.

Interpreting data

Instructions: Use the data in the table about population growth to answer the following questions. (True-False: Use + for true, 0 for false.)

1. _____ City A has always been larger than City B. (0)
2. _____ City A has grown faster than City B. (+)
3. _____ City A was larger than City B in 1975. (+)
4. _____ City A is likely to have more city employees than City B. (+)
5. _____ City B is likely to have more schools than City A. (0)

Alternative Assessment Strategies

Testing too often overshadows other equally useful assessment techniques that are dealt with in this section.

● "I Learned" Statements

An obvious and commonsense way to find out what students have learned is to ask them. Parents have done this for years. Unfortunately, parents often get less-than-satisfactory answers from children who have learned that a response like "Nothin'" can avoid the additional questions that are sure to follow.

Limit the focus to something manageable

Teachers who use "I learned" statements usually have much better results. The key is to limit the focus that students must deal with. Instead of asking about an entire day or week, teachers can pose the "I learned" question after a single lesson or series of lessons. The question "What did you learn?" forces students to reflect on their experience, and it permits them to self-select the elements of the lesson they think are important.

Children can respond to "I learned" statements in either oral or written form. Teachers of younger children can summarize "I learned" responses on the board or on large chart paper, or they can simply respond to children orally. Teachers of older children may request "I learned" statements in writing or make them a part of ongoing journal-writing activities or what are sometimes called "learning logs." Consider the following example taken from a child's journal:

> Now I understand why Great-Grampa thought ice cream was so special. His ice box was not cold enough to keep the ice cream from melting, so they had to make it fresh.

No matter how teachers gather "I learned" statements, asking students to pause and reflect on a lesson is clearly superior to the common alternative: "Okay, children, put away your books and get ready to go to lunch," and so on.

● Portfolios

The work of artists, photographers, and architects cannot be judged solely by objective criteria. So when those individuals apply for new commissions, they typically take a portfolio of their previous work with them. The samples in the portfolio show the variety and quality of their work—usually their best work—as well as how that work has changed over time. Samples of their poorer work are left behind in the studio, probably chalked up to experience.

Putting your best foot forward

When you think about it, a fundamental purpose of teaching is to help students grow and change, socially and intellectually, over time. Grades are one way to reflect growth and change, but grades are only generalized symbols. When a student's grades improve, the area of performance where the improvement occurred is seldom apparent, even to the teacher.

Consider using a portfolio, as Janet Jacobsen (from our earlier example) does, that contains representative samples of the student's best work as a basis for assessment. Every student develops a portfolio, which could include projects, papers, homework, tests, assignments, or anything representative of the quality of the student's work. The overall quality of their "best work" would vary from student to student, of course. Each student must also decide which material to include in the portfolio, and be prepared to explain why it is best.

Portfolios use real work, not symbols

From time to time, the teacher and student (and parents) can review the portfolio together, discussing the quality of the latest work and how it may be different from earlier work. Portfolio reviews are based on tangible samples, not on abstract symbols. Instead of making vague exhortations such as "You need to work on your grades," a teacher might point to several sample assignments and say "Sarah, you seem to have trouble with the last part of your assignments, like you're rushing to get them finished and don't care what you put down. Tell me about it." Portfolios need not replace the grading ritual so common in schools today but they would certainly be effective complements to it.

Permit specific feedback

──● Interviewing and Observing

Finding out what students know or are able to do by talking with them or watching them is hardly a new idea. Even Socrates did more than just ask questions! But observing and talking with students has traditionally been a casual affair. When students were obviously having difficulty, for example, teachers just as obviously walked over and talked with them about the problem. What distinguishes interviewing and observing from their more casual cousins is their systematic quality. An interview is systematic, though not rigidly so, and it is conducted for a particular purpose: to find out what students know about something and how they feel about it. In other words, the interview, like testing, is an information-gathering technique. The interview is not an opportunity to correct children's misconceptions or to teach them something.

Interviews and conferences are systematic

A major deterrent to interviewing is the amount of time it can take, as Janet Jacobsen's conferencing illustrated in the introduction to this chapter. A clear and sometimes preferable alternative to individual interviews is group interviews. Group sessions permit several students to share the teacher's attention.

Time demands

Suggested interview procedures include the following:

Recommended procedures

* Identify sets of similar questions on whatever it is you want to find out so that you don't always ask exactly the same questions.
* Keep your facial expression as "interested" but as unevaluative as possible.
* Do not be put off by an immediate response such as "I don't know." Often it's just the way children gain time while they think about something. Give them time to think; then probe.

Assessing Attitudes and Values

To assess students' cognitive skills, they must do something to demonstrate their ability. This could involve taking a test, participating in an interview, or otherwise proving what they can do. Students' attitudes and values, on the other hand, are typically expressed in the course of their day-to-day activities. Simply by observing students' activities over time, it is possible to infer what their attitudes and values are. This means that setting aside a special time for assessing attitudes and values is usually not required. Evaluators need to know what they are looking for, but attitudinal evaluation usually doesn't require any special behavior on the student's part. In many instances, students' behaviors may more accurately reflect their underlying beliefs and values if students *don't* know they are being observed; that way they're less likely to behave in ways they think are expected of them. The point is that observation is an excellent technique for gathering information on students' (or anyone's) attitudes and values.

Special strategies are usually not needed

As my wife and I were selecting a name for our first child, I suggested Michael. My wife, a former teacher, responded with an immediate "No." Inexperienced as I was, I soon discovered that name choosing is not an entirely rational process.

"What's wrong with Michael?" I asked.

"Well (emphatically), when I was teaching fourth grade, I had a student whose name was Michael. He picked his nose, smelled of garlic, and always needed a bath. There's no way that we're going to name our son Michael!"

It goes without saying that none of our three sons is named Michael. I mention this incident because it illustrates the *halo effect,* a common phenomenon that can influence a teacher's observation of students. Just as my wife's feeling about the name Michael was biased by her former student, it's not unusual for teachers to generalize from a few behaviors to all of a student's actions. In other words, a teacher may base a uniformly negative or positive (but not both) opinion of a student on just a few behaviors. That opinion can extend to almost everything the student does, which is why those with positive halos can sometimes get away with almost anything—the proverbial "teacher's pet"—whereas children with negative halos may be always suspect, even when they are completely innocent.

A major difficulty in assessing students' attitudes and values lies in identifying precise behavioral indicators for tolerance, respect, or whatever attitudes and values you want to focus on. It is equally difficult to identify attitudinal indicators that do not tread on people's personal liberties. For example, as long as someone's behavior doesn't interfere with another person's rights, the individual has the right to believe whatever he or she wants to believe and to like or dislike whatever (or whomever) he or she chooses.

The difficulties involved in identifying and stating precise behavioral indicators for an attitude or value, combined with an unwillingness to infringe on personal liberties, may explain why attitudes and values are usually expressed as goals (instead of as behavioral objectives). This lack of precision may also account for the absence of formal instruments to measure the development of attitudes and values. Despite this limitation, when attitudinal measures are used in conjunction with other techniques, they can provide information and a point of departure that would otherwise be denied the teacher. The following sections examine several techniques for assessing attitudes and values.

No precise behavioral indicators

● Attitude Scales

Conventional tests usually have correct answers; attitude scales do not. An *attitude scale* is composed of a set of questions or statements, such as "Students should willingly share ideas and materials with others" or "I think cats are smarter than dogs," to which individuals are then asked to respond in terms of their beliefs or preferences. Because those beliefs are personal, even if not always "politically correct," there are no previously established "right" answers on most attitude scales.

Attitude scales usually include several items that pertain to a particular attitude or belief. The individual responds to the items using a scale such as "Strongly Agree," "Agree," "Undecided," "Disagree," and "Strongly Disagree." By analyzing the pattern of responses, it becomes possible to infer the individual's attitude or

How will you use the
information and for what
purposes?

belief toward the topic in question. The key decision in dealing with attitude scales occurs before you administer one, namely, deciding what you intend to do with the information once you've gathered it.

● Questionnaires and Inventories

Questionnaires often deal with a wide range of topics, whereas interest inventories are usually restricted to what an individual likes or dislikes. Questions like "What do you like to do in your spare time?" or the familiar "What subjects do you like best (or least) in school?" are typical.

Questionnaires and inventories are easy to develop. You simply identify open-ended questions to which the respondent supplies a response. In interview settings, the students' responses are oral. Regardless of how you administer the questionnaire or interest inventory, you once again need to determine what you intend to do with the information after you've obtained it. Determining what your students do in their spare time, for example, can provide insight into your students and the activities they pursue. But only you can decide whether such information will affect the kind of teaching you provide, and whether collecting it is worth the time it takes.

● Checklists and Rating Scales

Checklists consist of a series of descriptive statements, such as "Works willingly with others" or "Participates in class discussions," next to which an evaluator makes a check mark to reflect the frequency of how often an item is observed. On rating scales, the evaluator typically writes a number or some other indicator to reflect the frequency or quality of the student's performance on the behavior in question. There are no restrictions on who should use a checklist or rating scale; it could be the teacher, other students, or, as in self-assessment, individual students themselves.

Checklists and rating scales often have very similar formats, as shown in Figure 9.5. The difference between the two formats usually lies in the kind of marking system employed. On a checklist, the evaluator marks a category to indicate how often the characteristic is observed, usually using descriptors such as *often, sometimes,* or *almost never.* On a rating scale, the evaluator usually writes a qualitative rating in the space provided to indicate the individual's performance.

Figure 9.5 illustrates how rating scales and checklists can be used either by external evaluators or by students and requires only minor modifications, primarily in terms of how the criterion behaviors are phrased, to fit either circumstance. Rating scales and checklists designed for external evaluators tend to use pronouns such as *he* or *she,* whereas materials designed for self-assessment are more likely to use the personal pronoun *I.*

Once the target behaviors are identified, checklists and rating scales are fairly easy to develop and use. If problems arise, it is more likely to be in interpreting the results. For example, if a checklist or rating scale shows that certain children do not contribute regularly in class discussions, this may simply validate what you already suspect—that certain children do not participate in class discussions. It is rare for checklists or rating scales to identify the underlying causes for that behavior. A shy child's lack of participation in group discussions, for example, may

Focus: How well does he or she (do I) work with peers?	Rating	Checklist Criteria		
		Always	Usually	Seldom
He or she cooperates with others as they work toward group goals. (I cooperate with others as we work toward our group's goals.)				
He or she keeps on task. (I keep on task.)				
He or she contributes new ideas. (I contribute new ideas.)				
He or she makes constructive suggestions when asked for help. (I make constructive suggestions when asked for help.) He or she encourages others. (I give others encouragement.)				

For rating scale, use: Outstanding = 4; Above Average = 3; Satisfactory = 2; and Needs Improvement = 1.

Note: Items in parentheses are phrased for self-assessment. Indicators are adapted from J. Alleman & J. Brophy. (1998). Assessment in a social constructivist classroom. *Social Education,* 62, 34.

• •

be based on factors far removed from the evaluation itself. The point here is that while checklists and rating scales can sometimes confirm what an observant teacher already suspects, they are unlikely to indicate why children behave as they do. Remember, too, that what observers report may be colored by their perceptions, and by the fact that students' responses may reflect what they think you want to hear, not how they really feel about a topic or issue. And, finally, remember that assessing students' attitudes and values, or even their class participation, can be more involved than it appears.

SUMMARY

Teachers have long used evaluation as more than just a basis for grading. However, grading is such a powerful phenomenon it can overshadow everything else. Most teachers know that *evaluation* and *testing* are not synonymous with *grading,* but they don't always act that way. Quite unintentionally, they may find themselves stressing "a very important test on Friday," thereby perpetuating the evaluation-grading mystique.

Assessment, like planning, is an ongoing process. Just as teachers' goals and objectives help to identify *what* they are attempting to do, assessment and evaluation helps them identify *how well* they (and their students) are actually doing it. Testing sometimes becomes a confounding variable, even though simply an information-gathering process, nothing more. Testing, like observations, interviews, checklists, portfolios, attitude scales, interest inventories, and rating scales, is a way of gathering information.

The assessment process consists of (1) identifying (or accepting) assessment criteria, the standards against which evaluative judgments are made; (2) measuring an individual's performance, behavior, or products in relation to those standards; and (3) making judgments about the individual's performance. The form that evaluation takes is largely determined by the teacher's purpose. If you wish to assess whether a student can demonstrate a certain skill or knowledge, you will undoubtedly turn to *criterion-referenced assessment*. However, if you wish to compare your students' performance with that of another group, you will turn to *norm-referenced evaluation*. In in-

stances when you are interested in determining how things are going during an instructional episode, you may turn to *formative evaluation*. If you are interested in determining the overall quality of a student's performance or product at the end of an instructional period, you will turn to *summative evaluation*. Finally, if your purpose is to figure out how well you are doing, you will undoubtedly turn to *self-evaluation*.

The growing interest in using portfolios for assessment purposes is, we think, a reflection of the broader move toward authentic assessment. Although much of the evaluation in schools today pertains to the knowledge and skills required to get through school, it often has little bearing on what it takes to be successful in life beyond schools. Authentic assessment does that; it seeks to assess performance through worthwhile and realistic activities that students will encounter in real life.

SUGGESTED ACTIVITIES

1. Obtain a copy of one of the standardized tests that deals with elementary social studies (your psychology department should have copies if your education department doesn't). First, take the test so that your attention is not distracted by the content of the questions. Then analyze the items in terms of the skills they are really testing.

2. Assume that the students in your fifth-grade class need help in developing the following skills: (a) classification, (b) inductive reasoning, (c) question posing, and (d) hypothesis development. Using social studies con-

tent, develop at least two activities designed to promote skill development in each of those areas. Then, using the same activity format but substituting data different from the data used in the learning activities, develop a way to evaluate student performance in those skill areas.

3. It has been argued that creativity, evaluation, and grading are incompatible, that you can't have one as long as you have any of the others. What do you think? Is it possible to reconcile creativity, evaluation, and grading?

SUGGESTED READINGS AND RESOURCES

Print Resources

J. Alleman & J. Brophy. (1998). Assessment in a social constructivist classroom. *Social Education, 62,* 32–42. This excellent article by two leading authorities in the field includes useful examples of rating scales and checklists.

D. Adams & M. Hamm. (1992). Portfolio assessment and social studies: Collection, selecting, and reflecting on what is significant. *Social Education* 56, 103–105. This article is noteworthy in this special issue of *Social Education* devoted to assessment.

P. Nickell. (Ed.) (1999). Authentic assessment in social studies. *Social Education, 63.* This theme issue of *Social Education* approaches authentic assessment from a variety of perspectives.

G. Wiggins. (1990). A true test: Toward more equitable assessment. *Phi Delta Kappan,* 70, 703–713. Wiggins argues that not only do we spend excessive time testing students, we seldom do much with the results of all that testing.

Internet Resources

Introductory Note: Web sites sometimes change their Internet addresses or cease operating entirely. All the addresses supplied here were operating when this book was printed, but if any of them fails to work properly, enter the name of the target organization in any standard search engine.

ERIC Clearinghouse on Assessment and Evaluation

http://ericae.net/main.htm

We spent hours on this site just getting ready to update this chapter. It contains an amazing variety of resources. Highly recommended.

Alternative Assessment in the Social Sciences

http://www.coe.ilstu.edu/jabraun/socialstudies/assess/

This site is loaded with examples of authentic assessment activities associated with the Illinois Goal Assessment Program for geography and social science. Among its most useful elements are sample evaluation rubrics and examples of students' work.

Authentic Assessment

http://www.nwrel.org/

This site, supported by the Northwest Regional Laboratory, offers links to Web sites and materials that focus on authentic assessment. Topics of interest include electronic portfolios, evaluating problem-solving processes, and creating assessment rubrics.

Alternative Assessment

http://cresst96.cse.ucla.edu/

This site is supported by the Center for the Study of Evaluation at the University of California at Los Angeles and provides excellent examples of alternative assessment strategies.

10

Strategies for Effective Teaching

Key Questions

- What teaching strategies work best for which objectives?
- What's the difference between teacher-directed and student-centered teaching strategies—in action, that is?
- How do teachers manage small-group activities?

Key Ideas

- Teaching techniques—lectures, discussions, and so on—are the building blocks from which teaching strategies are created.
- Teacher-centered strategies tend to be more appropriate for conveying information; student-centered strategies tend to be more appropriate for developing information-processing skills.
- Teaching strategies reflect a system of interacting behaviors purposely designed to achieve learning goals.
- Teachers may use several teaching techniques in a single lesson.

Introduction: The "Pine Tree Shillings" Activity

Janet Jacobsen is the fifth-grade teacher from the apple-growing region of Washington State whom you met in Chapter 9. You may recall from that visit that Mrs. Jacobsen gradually shifted from a traditional "coverage" approach to American history (the focus of most fifth-grade social studies programs) to a "less is more" approach. This means that she focuses on studying fewer topics but in greater depth. She also shifted from a heavily teacher-directed to a much more student-centered approach to social studies.

Changing roles

Mrs. Jacobsen continued to explain how she teaches social studies, by saying, "I use a modified cooperative-group investigation approach where the kids focus on researching and answering questions they've raised." She then walked over to her filing cabinet and pulled out a one-page handout. "Here's an example of how I get things started," she said. "This is about the 'Pine Tree Shillings' incident that

I took from an old reader." Janet pointed to an obviously old book, *Stories of Our Country* (Johonnot, 1887). "I got it for 50 cents at the Salvation Army store. This is my springboard."

Pine Tree Shillings

A springboard for inquiry

The Puritan colony of Massachusetts assigned John Hull to be the mint master. Using silver from old tableware, buccaneer bullion, and old European coins, he cast thousands of shillings, sixpence, and threepence. Each coin had an image of a pine tree on one side and the date 1652 on the other.

Sometime after Captain Hull had made his fortune minting coins, his plump daughter, Betsy, attracted a suitor, the young Sam Sewell. Captain Hull, recognizing that Sewell sought love and not a dowry, granted Betsy's hand in marriage.

Just after the wedding, Captain Hull instructed his servants to bring in a large set of scales. He directed his daughter to get on one side and then instructed his men to balance the scale. The servants scooped up handfuls of bright silver Pine Tree shillings into the other pan.

"There, son Sewell!" cried the honest mint master. "Take these shillings for my daughter's portion. Use her kindly, and thank Heaven for her. It is not every wife that's worth her weight in silver!"

—Hawthorne

(Johonnot, p. 81, cited in Lauritzen & Jaeger, 1994, p. 582)

Cognitive dissonance

The term *buccaneer bullion* in the second line immediately caught my attention. Buccaneers were pirates, of course, but pirates in New England? This was puzzling, but after deciding to pursue it later I said, "This just says 'Hawthorne.' Is this *the* Nathaniel Hawthorne?"

"That's a question the kids ask," Janet responded, "except most of them don't know about Nathaniel Hawthorne, so they ask, 'Who was Hawthorne?' After we've read the vignette, I invite questions about it. Look," she said, as she pulled three overhead transparencies from the file. "I save these from year to year to remind me what I'm getting into. The kids have literally hundreds of questions."

A few of the children's questions are shown here.

Children's questions

What is a mint master?
Were some mint masters dishonest?
How did a mint master make coins?
How did Captain Hull get the silver to make coins?
Did people donate old silverware? Why?
What is bullion? What is buccaneer bullion?
What is a shilling? A sixpence? A threepence? A pence?
Why was 1652 on the coins?
What did the scales look like?
How "plump" was Betsy?
What was Betsy really worth?
Is this a true story? Are the people real?
Who was Hawthorne?
What is a dowry? Do we still have dowries today? Were they common in Puritan times?

"I invite students to follow up on their most compelling questions," Janet added. "I forewarn the librarian before we get into this, and she gets a lot of books

TECHNOLOGY

ready for us. As a matter of fact, she's purchased a lot of books on coinage and Nathaniel Hawthorne because she knows the kids are going to ask for them."

"Even more than the books," Janet continued, "my kids love to get on the Internet. I can't tell you how impressed they are when they get an E-mail answer to one of their questions. When some of them deal with English money, like shillings and pence, they sometimes get E-mail responses from England; it's fabulous."

I told Janet, "Whenever I tried this kind of inquiry approach, there were always a few kids who wouldn't get involved. They'd say there was nothing they wanted to investigate. Do you ever encounter this?"

Computers as motivators

"Sure," Janet replied. "I always have a couple of students who need some prodding, but I never realized how powerful computers are as motivational tools. Few students can resist the prospect of receiving a personal E-mail from someone somewhere in the world. Anyhow, for the kids who still won't get involved, I tell them that they must be doing something productive; they can't just sit there and do nothing."

Investigating different facets of the incident

"Most of my students," Janet continued, "read books on colonial times to research the personalities; some of them go to the coin shop in the mall and look at examples of colonial coinage; some of them study the literature of Nathaniel Hawthorne to determine if it is similar to the 'Pine Tree' story; and some of them experiment with different models for testing how many coins Sam Sewell received in the dowry. The kids also record their findings in their journals, including the feelings that this inquiry evokes."

Sharing findings

"It usually takes a week or more to deal with this activity, usually more like two to three weeks when you add in the sharing time, because some of the kids really get into it. And because everyone's following a different line of inquiry, the sharing aspect of this unit is *really* important. I have one, and only one, rule for sharing: show us, don't just tell us. Every student makes some kind of visual presentation that describes his or her investigation. To eliminate duplicate reports, we sometimes team up for the sharing time. Most of the kids use the [Microsoft] *Works* program for word-processing and *Hyperstudio* for developing graphics for their presentations. To show the similarities between Hawthorne's writing style in the 'Pine Tree Shillings' piece and his other works, they used to copy pages from Hawthorne's works onto butcher paper. But now they use the scanner in the computer lab to transfer portions of the book directly into the computer. Then they make printouts for everyone. I'm thankful the language arts teacher also buys into this because she begins a unit on style at the same time I start this activity, and she uses Hawthorne as one of her examples."

TECHNOLOGY

"O.K., you've hooked me," I said. "Did any of the 'Pine Tree Shillings' stuff really happen?"

The real story

"Oh, yes," Janet replied. "Captain John Hull minted Pine Tree shillings in Massachusetts Bay colony in the mid- to late-1600s. However, all the Pine Tree shillings made after 1652 carried the same date. That was because when Charles II was restored to the English throne in 1652, the Massachusetts Bay colony lost the right to mint its own coins. Despite the new regulations, the Bay colony continued to mint its own coins for the next twenty years or so, and to avoid raising Charles II's suspicions, every coin was dated 1652. A clever ploy, don't you think?"

I agreed.

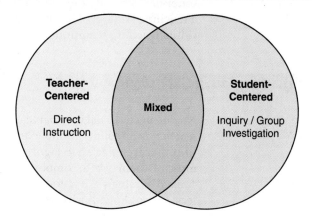

FIGURE 10.1   A Range of Teaching Strategies

Teacher-
Centered

Direct
Instruction

Mixed

Student-
Centered

Inquiry / Group
Investigation

This chapter focuses on teaching strategies, those patterns of daily lessons and activities that teachers design to enable their students to reach desired learning outcomes. At one time Mrs. Jacobsen supplemented the textbook with additional activities. However, she began moving toward a more student-centered, small-group investigative approach to instruction. Mrs. Jacobsen also told us (as described in the introduction to Chapter 9) that during the six-week period just before her students take standardized tests, she moves back to a very teacher-directed approach. During that time, she covers a large body of information that her students will be responsible for on the test. The point here is that Mrs. Jacobsen, and all teachers, have a range of teaching strategies at their disposal, as shown in Figure 10.1.

Using different strategies for different purposes

When Mrs. Jacobsen is working with her students on an activity like the "Pine Tree Shillings," her basic orientation is toward the right-hand side of the range. Then, when she moves into her pretest review mode, she shifts toward the left-hand side of the range. Some of the options and activities associated with each of these teaching orientations are examined in the first part of this chapter. We then turn to the skills necessary for working successfully with small groups. And finally, because teacher-centered and student-centered teachers often hold different views on how children should deal with social studies content, those dimensions are considered in the last section of this chapter.

Chapter organization

Teaching Strategies Defined

Strategy defined

Although the term *strategy* can sometimes have manipulative overtones, a teaching strategy is simply a series of activities designed to help students reach desired learning outcomes. Individual teaching techniques—such as lecturing, modeling, role-playing, conducting group discussions, videos, possibly computer-based simulations, and others—must somehow fit together to constitute a teaching strategy. The relationship between a teaching strategy and the individual teaching techniques is shown in Figure 10.2.

Identifying Teaching Strategies

No one needs to tell you that teaching strategies may range from almost complete teacher domination at one extreme to almost complete student involvement at the other (refer again to Figure 10.1). Few teachers are at either extreme, because most of them use a combination of teaching techniques and thus fall into a "mixed" strategy. Then, too, every classroom is teacher-directed to some extent at least, because that's what teachers are paid to do.

● Teacher-Centered Instruction

Teacher-centered instruction is usually characterized by a "telling" or "explaining" orientation. Many teacher-centered strategies are variations on a Read-Recite-Lecture-Test format. The recitation phase, which is typically an oral test of retained information, is sometimes omitted, especially at the college level. Occasionally the teacher may reverse the format and talk about material prior to having students read it. And on other occasions, additional elements may be added, such as videos, discussions, demonstrations, student reports, or current events periods. Despite such variations, the goal of most teacher-centered strategies is to present information to students as quickly and as efficiently as possible.

Goal: to present information

When teachers conduct question-and-answer sessions to determine how well students have retained information, they sometimes mistakenly refer to those sessions as discussions. *Discussion* may sound less formal and imposing than the correct term, *recitation,* but the two terms are not synonymous. The distinction between *discussion* and *recitation* is based on the purpose of the activity. Discussions can serve multiple purposes, including sharing different points of view on an issue, motivating students or developing interest in a topic, generating ideas, synthesizing ideas, or providing closure to an activity. The purpose of recitation is to test (orally) how well students have understood and retained prior information.

The difference between discussion and recitation

Despite the bad reputation sometimes associated with teacher-centered strategies, at times lecturing (or telling or explaining) and especially teacher modeling are both desirable and useful. This is often referred to as *direct instruction,* because teachers are doing something directly to students. When students are not fully aware of the issues associated with a topic, a so-called discussion can become a futile exercise in shared ignorance. At other times, students may find themselves floundering hopelessly because their teachers— who favor a student-centered approach to teaching—mistakenly believe that students can discover *everything* on their own, including the information that

Direct instruction

In some educational circles a notion prevails that lectures are inherently bad and that, should you ever lecture to your students, you will be committing a grievous sin. At the same time, you've undoubtedly witnessed some extremely good lectures during your career as a student, some of which made eight-o'clock classes worth getting up for. How then can it be that lecturing is such an evil?

Experience suggests that the quality of a lecture depends heavily on the lecturer's ability. Good lecturers demonstrate the following characteristics:

1. *They must be well versed in their subject.* Good lecturers stand at the opposite end of the continuum from students, whose reports to the class often reflect the total scope of their knowledge on a topic. Subject-matter expertise is just one qualification, however, because we've heard nationally known specialists in their fields deliver some abominable lectures.

2. *They must be master communicators.* Good lecturers must be sensitive to timing, pacing, and the form and style of expression—when to raise their eyebrow, change their tone of voice, use humor, or ask a question. The importance of these so-called show-biz aspects of lecturing was illustrated in what has been called "The Doctor Fox Effect." To determine whether the way a lecture was presented made any difference in how students reacted to it, two researchers hired a professional actor, whom they called Dr. Fox, to present six different types of lectures. The actor first memorized the scripts for three different lectures on the same topic. Each lecture differed in the amount of information it contained; one had a very high content, another had some content, and the third contained a lot of verbiage but little information. The actor then presented each lecture to different students in one of two ways. For one presentation of each type of lecture, Dr. Fox really hammed it up, using gestures, humor, movement, vocal inflection, and considerable enthusiasm. For the second set of lectures, all of the expressive embellishments were omitted and the actor virtually read from the prepared script.

What happened? According to Williams and Ware (1977), students who experienced the highly expressive presentations did significantly better on achievement tests that did students who experienced the less expressive presentations. In addition, the students almost always rated expressive presentations as "more effective" than the less expressive lectures, regardless of their content. The implication, then, is that even if you have little to say on a topic, you should say it with gusto!

FIGURE 10.2 Components of a Teaching Strategy

A teaching strategy is created from various combinations of short-term techniques, such as

- discussion
- modeling
- role-playing
- lecturing
- group projects
- individual reports
- case studies
- simulations
- decision making
- mapping
- etc.

is essential for students to know. Given enough time, for example, students might discover how to determine the distance between two cities on a map. But it is often more efficient and effective if the teacher gives an explicit demonstration and explanation in which she or he models that process for students. Likewise, through a minilecture or short presentation, teachers can also bring fresh information to bear on points in question. A daily diet of half-hour speeches would be excessive, but there are countless instances where minilectures are appropriate teaching activities.

Discovery vs. direct instruction

A Model for Effective Instruction. Over the last twenty years, researchers have focused intense interest on the relationship between teachers' strategies and students' academic achievement. One of the most consistently successful instructional sequences for dealing with *certain kinds of subject matter* was described by Rosenshine and Stevens (1986). This model is similar to what is sometimes referred to as the "Madeline Hunter" model, which is named after its creator. Both the Rosenshine and Stevens model, which is described next, and the Madeline Hunter model are highly sequenced, teacher-centered approaches to "direct instruction."

The direct instruction model

Begin the lesson with a short review of the previous day's work, reteaching if necessary.

Provide an overview and a short statement of objectives for the lesson.

Present new content/skills, usually in small steps and at a rapid pace; provide opportunities for student practice after each step.

Give clear and detailed instructions and explanations.

To check for comprehension, ask a lot of questions and try to obtain responses from all students.

Provide opportunities for students to practice under the teacher's guidance.

Provide systematic feedback and correctives, reteaching if necessary.

Provide independent practice until students' responses are firm, quick, and automatic.

Provide weekly and monthly reviews. (pp. 377, 379)

Sequence of activities

Rosenshine and Stevens indicate that this model is most appropriate for subjects that they call "well structured," that is, subjects that have a learning hierarchy and in which later learning depends on earlier learning (p. 377). As noted earlier, few areas of social studies (except for map skills) have the hierarchical structure with which this model might work well.

Appropriate for well-structured subjects

MAJOR TEACHER-CENTERED TECHNIQUES AND PURPOSES SUMMARIZED

Technique	Purpose(s)
Lecture	To present information
Recitation	To test, orally, retained information

Technique	Purpose(s)
Discussion	Multiple purposes: To motivate or generate interest To share points of view on an issue To generate ideas or identify new applications for ideas To synthesize ideas To bring closure to an activity

● Mixed Instruction

A blend of techniques

Mixed teaching strategies reflect a blend of teacher-centered and student-centered teaching techniques. Just how those techniques are blended often varies from teacher to teacher and, often, from topic to topic.

The further that teachers move away from the more clearly defined roles of the teacher-centered strategy, the more difficult it becomes to describe their behavior precisely. When the focus shifts to a student-centered teaching strategy, discussed next, the attention necessarily shifts to the teacher *and* the students, and to what the students will be doing.

● Student-Centered Instruction

Goal: to process information

Student-centered teaching strategies typically have a problem-solving or inquiry orientation. The goal of these teaching strategies is to help students develop the ability to manipulate and process information from various sources—academic, social, and experiential. To do this, teachers act as guides to assist students in identifying problems, generating possible answers, testing those answers in the light of available data, and applying their conclusions to new data, new problems, or new situations. In other words, the focus is on the skills of inquiring and processing information. This means that student-centered teaching strategies are usually more appropriate for helping students develop information-processing skills, whereas teacher-centered strategies are more appropriate for transmitting information.

Three formats

Individual and Group Investigation. Group investigations can be conducted in one of three ways: (1) the entire class acts as a research group in which everyone investigates aspects of the same problem simultaneously; (2) individuals or small research groups investigate one aspect or dimension of a classwide problem; or (3) individual or small research groups investigate separate problems. Mrs. Jacobsen's class used the second approach to investigate different dimensions of the "Pine Tree Shillings" incident. The following Model Student Activity, "The Wearin' of the Green," shows a whole-class approach to group investigation.

The Inquiry Process. The procedures Ms. Fleury (see the Model Student Activity) and her students followed are common to many individual or group investigations. For example, after Ms. Fleury remarked that more intermediate than primary students would wear green the following day, this struck a discordant

"The Wearin' of the Green"—
A Group Investigation

It was March, a time when winter seems to stretch out longer and longer. It was also the day before St. Patrick's Day.

Ms. Fleury, a fourth-grade teacher, commented to her class that although some families don't celebrate St. Patrick's Day, many students were likely to wear green clothing the following day. She added that students in the intermediate grades were more likely to wear green than primary-grade children. Her comment prompted a curious "why?" from one student, Stephen.

Ms. Fleury responded by saying that intermediate students were older and more likely to wear green clothing because many other intermediate students would be wearing green. Stephen suggested that primary children wear the clothes that their mothers lay out for them and that many of those mothers would see that their children wore something green; therefore primary children would be more likely to wear green. In other words, there were two competing views, one based on peer pressure and the other based on parental influence.

Ms. Fleury recognized that the question—who was more likely to wear green—was an opportunity for the class to gather data and to determine which view was correct.

The students decided that they would observe each classroom in the building. Some students would be observers and others would stay in their classroom—the "control room"—to process the results. As their planning progressed, the principal came into the room. She asked how much green someone needed to wear to be counted and whether it needed to be solid green. The students decided that someone had to have at least a sweater, shirt, blouse, skirt, slacks, scarf, or ribbon to be counted and that the dominant color had to be green. When everything seemed in place, the observers went to the different classrooms to ask permission to visit that room the next morning. The students agreed in advance to tell the teachers why they wanted to visit, but they knew that if they told each class what they were doing, it could change their results.

The next morning, the students observed their assigned classrooms and then gave the data to the student-tabulators. As Ms. Fleury had predicted, more intermediate students wore green than did primary level students. Ms. Fleury was going to let it go at that, but one student, Christie, said she thought that there were more fourth, fifth, and sixth graders than there were students in the primary grades. This meant that there were more intermediate students who *could* wear green, and naturally they would win.

This was something Ms. Fleury hadn't anticipated. The issue involved percentages, which was something the students had not worked with yet. The talliers provided the total number of primary- and intermediate-level students and the numbers at each level who wore green, which Ms. Fleury then used to find the percentage. The new results: 76 percent of the primary children wore green clothing, compared with 64 percent of the intermediate-level children. Ms. Fleury admitted that Stephen's hypothesis seemed to be true.

• •

note with Stephen, who politely disagreed by asking his question, "Why?" The difference between Stephen's views and Ms. Fleury's was a discrepant event that ultimately became the problem that the entire class investigated. The other phases of the inquiry process are discussed next.

Cognitive dissonance   1. *Awareness of a Possible Problem.* One's awareness of a discrepant event results from a kind of mental "disturbance" called *cognitive dissonance.* This happened to us when we were visiting with Mrs. Jacobsen and encountered the phrase *buccaneer bullion*, which didn't "fit" our existing view of American history.

The awareness of the problem is critical to the inquiry process. Likewise, when students don't sense dissonance—something that doesn't fit—they have nothing to explain, and nothing to research. Therefore, teachers who wish to use investigation-oriented teaching strategies may sometimes need to structure activities in which they intentionally create cognitive dissonance that provides students with a motive for inquiry. The "Pine Tree Shillings" incident served this purpose in Mrs. Jacobsen's class.

2. *Defining the Problem.* Based on the discrepancy between Ms. Fleury's and Stephen's views, the problem was: Will more or fewer primary-level students wear green clothing than intermediate-grade students?

3. *Hypothesizing.* Stephen's contention that primary children were more likely to wear green on St. Patrick's Day because their mothers usually laid their clothing out for them was a hypothesis. Likewise, Ms. Fleury's contention that intermediate children would wear green because they were more sensitive to peer pressure was a second hypothesis.

4. *Testing Modified Hypotheses.* An interesting aspect of this investigation is that it did not investigate the validity of either Stephen's or Ms. Fleury's explanations for *why* one age level was more or less likely to wear green clothing. Rather, it was restricted to the more basic problem: the age level of children who actually wore green clothing.

5. *Gathering Data.* Ms. Fleury and her students agreed on a process for collecting the information they needed—observing in other classrooms. They also defined their terms so that everyone knew what "wearing green" meant.

6. *Concluding, Tentatively.* Based on the preliminary data, it appeared that more intermediate students had worn green clothing than had primary students. Thus, Ms. Fleury was apparently correct, at least in terms of absolute numbers (though not in terms of the students' motivation).

7. *Testing the Conclusion.* Had there been no questions about the tentative conclusion, there would have been no need to test its applicability and it might have been accepted without further consideration. However, Christie raised the question about the number of students at each level who might potentially wear green, so it became necessary to reanalyze the data. That analysis showed that proportionately more primary students wore green than did intermediate students.

Based on this investigation, who was correct: Stephen or Ms. Fleury?

On-the-Spot Decision Making.   "The Wearin' of the Green" Model Activity reflects one teacher's decision to explore an unplanned problematic situation in more detail. Ms. Fleury clearly took advantage of an opportunity that arose from her offhand remark, but in doing so she obviously had to put her planned program aside for a day or so. Ms. Fleury had to make some quick decisions: Was this difference of opinion worth pursuing? And would the time that students spent doing it result in something that was educationally beneficial? It's difficult to predict outcomes in advance—and this activity could very well "bomb"—but Ms. Fleury obviously decided to go with it.

Another issue Ms. Fleury had to deal with sooner or later pertains to how this activity relates to the standards for social studies. In this instance, she would be

Inquiry, Discovery, and Problem Solving

When teachers talk about student-centered instructional strategies, they sometimes say, "I use a discovery approach"; others say, "I prefer a problem-solving approach." Because universally accepted definitions for inquiry, discovery, and problem solving don't exist, you would need to visit these teachers to find out how they actually teach. Despite the different terminology, these teachers' strategies are apt to be more similar than different.

One similarity among these approaches is their emphasis on thinking processes and skills. Literally, *discovery* refers to the moment that a student perceives a relationship among various data—when the student says "Aha, I've got it!" The teacher's role in discovery teaching is creating situations and environments where students are en-

couraged to discover and test their ideas. In many respects, discovery is part of a larger process that is similar to the inquiry processes that we outlined earlier.

Problem solving can be confusing because the expression is used to refer to several different types of activities. One of these, probably the most common, refers to what students do as they complete the exercises in a math text, most of which have a right or desired answer. A second type of problem solving involves genuine investigative inquiry, such as Ms. Fleury's students experienced in the "Wearin' of the Green" activity. Ms. Fleury's students were investigating a real problem and no one, including Ms. Fleury, knew what they would find in advance.

forced into making an after-the-fact (as opposed to preplanned) decision. Be advised that as long as instructional activities are educationally defensible, you can usually identify one or more standards that will encompass them. In this instance, the activity would fall within the scope of Middle Grades Exemplar E of the NCSS Theme of Individuals, Groups, and Institutions: "identify and describe examples of tensions between expressions of individuality and groups or institutional efforts to promote social conformity" (NCSS, 1994).

Inquiry Process Summarized. The phases of the inquiry/investigation process are summarized as follows:

The inquiry process

Phase 1. Becoming aware of a discrepant event, which leads to a problem to be solved.
Phase 2. Identifying hypotheses (possible explanations or tentative answers).
Phase 3. Testing the hypotheses in light of the data.
    3.1. If a hypothesis is rejected, the problem may be restated for clarity, before returning to Phase 2.
    3.2. If the hypothesis is accepted (not rejected), the inquirer proceeds to Phase 4.
Phase 4. Modifying the hypothesis, which has become a tentative conclusion, in light of additional data until satisfied that it is a plausible explanation.
Phase 5. Testing the tentative conclusion (Does it fit? Does it explain the discrepant event?).
Phase 6. Knowing your limitations; becoming aware of what you don't know.

The Dynamics of Group Investigation. Not all group investigations work out

Deciding on a hands-on activity

as well as the "Wearin' of the Green" activity. For example, consider what can happen when, in the course of studying the Inuit (Eskimos), you wrack your brain for some hands-on activities that students might do. You reject the idea of written reports because students have already written about the Inuit in their journals. You also decide against building harpoons because of the potential dangers associated with overly enthusiastic role-playing. You finally settle on the apparently safe idea of constructing model igloos from sugar cubes.

When you announce the igloo activity to the class, not everyone is thrilled with the prospect of model building. So you decide to make it an option, not a requirement. Next, Clarisa wants to know what kind of glue they should use to stick the sugar cubes together. Will plain paste work? Robert asks if he can use model airplane cement, the kind you use for plastic models. Or should he use Elmer's?

Resolving the glue problem

You have visions of half-constructed igloos collapsing if you give the wrong information, but you really don't know what will work. So you pose the question, "How do you suppose we can find out?"

Shamus claims that Elmer's works best because, well, he just *knows* it will. Shamus is usually right about such things and you are tempted to believe him this time, but Janet poses the obvious answer: "Everyone bring in the kind of glue they want to use and we'll test them." You agree, willingly and thankfully.

Other problems

Once the glue crisis is resolved, still other questions are likely to arise. For example, will you permit your students to glue their sugar cubes to Styrofoam balls (cut in half) and then fill in the gaps with granulated sugar? Or will you have them cut off one edge of each cube so that it will lean inward properly to form the igloo's "roof"? Real igloos are hollow in the middle, not filled with Styrofoam, so cutting the sugar cubes to fit properly would be more realistic. On the other hand, cutting sugar cubes isn't easy, and you begin to wonder if this activity is any safer than the harpoon project you discarded.

Reassessing the purpose of the activity

Thus far the igloo-building project has generated more nitpicking problems than you ever anticipated, and you begin to wonder whether it is really worth it. You may also find yourself rethinking how you had originally justified the project—that by building model igloos, your students would learn about what it was like to find shelter in a land of scarce resources. You may also wonder if this activity has anything to do with life in the Arctic, or whether it is simply a lesson in construction—in learning how to cut sugar cubes without crumbling them, and in finding what kind of glue sticks them together best.

Is the activity worthwhile?

The igloo-building episode is an example of what Brophy and Alleman (1990) refer to as activities that occupy students' time but that often lack substance and fail to engage students intellectually. The moral? When you are considering group activities, such as presenting a play on Mexico or holding a Greek Olympic Day, be certain that the mechanics of collecting sombreros and serapes, making the scenery, or building chariots does not overshadow everything else.

Inquiry versus Activity. The "Wearin' of the Green" and the igloo-building activity illustrate a key difference between genuine investigations and simple activities. In the "Wearin' of the Green," the children identified questions they wanted answered, and then did the research necessary to answer their questions. In other words, the inquiry process that the children followed was *purposeful and*

WebQuest: Tapping the Internet's Resources

A WebQuest [which is sometimes written as two words—Web Quest] is an increasingly popular, inquiry-oriented activity in which most or all of the information that students use is drawn from the Internet. Most WebQuests are based on a model developed in 1995 by Bernie Dodge at the San Diego State University.

A WebQuest usually begins with a brief introduction followed closely by the presentation of an engaging and highly doable task. In the hundreds, perhaps even thousands, of WebQuests available on the Internet, the tasks vary widely. They include such things as illustrating the process of making a mummy, journeying back in time to the colonial days, trekking the Santa Fe Trail, or planning for your survival on (or escape from) an isolated island. This is followed by (1) a description of steps (a process) for students to follow as they begin working on the task, and (2) links to predetermined resources that the student can use to complete the tasks. The intent in using predetermined links is to make sure students' time is well spent in using information as opposed to looking for it. Finally, there is an evaluation component, usually involving a rubric, and then a brief conclusion.

One of the best ways to become familiar with WebQuests is to get on the Internet and sample a few. You will find countless examples if you enter "WebQuests" or "Web Quests" into any search engine. The two key words above lead to separate listings, so try both of them. A WebQuest titled *A Perilous Journey,* which involves a group of Irish immigrants who join the Gold Rush in 1850, is available at the web site for this book at **college.hmco.com** (select "Education").

For information on designing WebQuests and additional sample WebQuests for different content areas and grade levels, the mother lode of WebQuest information is The WebQuest Page at: **http://edweb.sdsu.edu/webquest/webquest.html**

Process vs. product

systematic. For the igloo-building activity, however, the final product became the overriding concern, and the inquiry process got lost in the shuffle. An investigation is purposeful and systematic, whereas in a simple activity, the behavior is often not so systematic and organized.

The irony of inquiries and activities is that students often "feel good" about both. The students who conducted the "Wearin' of the Green" inquiry probably felt good about what they had accomplished. But the students who made model igloos probably felt good about their efforts too, even though they didn't learn much about their topic. Understand that feeling good, by itself, is not a sufficient criterion for judging the quality of a learning experience.

The Challenge of Student-Centered Teaching.   Involving students in the inquiry process is not without some practical problems. This is especially true for primary students. Even very young children can become aware of discrepant events, but apparently because there are so many discrepant events in young children's lives, they may either become so interested that they insist on sticking with a question until it's resolved to their satisfaction, or they dismiss it immediately and for no apparent reason. Unlike some adults, young children do not feel compelled to explain everything and apparently can live quite happily with things that they don't understand.

Practical problems

Older students, on the other hand, sometimes jump on the first explanation (hypothesis) they create and cling so tenaciously to it that they ignore other possibilities or data to the contrary. It sometimes becomes a case of "I've already made up my mind, so don't bother me with information!" In a child's world, where things are often clearly "right" or "wrong," the idea of rejecting a tentative answer because the data do not support it can be construed as being *wrong* (when it is actually *right* to reject it).

Children's perceptions of what it means to teach

Another more subtle but equally important consideration in moving toward student-centered instruction is students' perceptions of what it means to teach. Many children believe that teachers are actually "teaching" only when they stand in front of the entire class and do their thing—explaining, modeling, conducting a discussion, or whatever. Based on those prior experiences, children are apt to believe that teachers who use cooperative learning and small groups extensively are, as students put it, "not teaching very much."

Encouraging parental involvement

Such opinions are based primarily on the child's expectations (and often their parents' expectations) of teachers in general. Most children typically divorce how much they are learning, if they are even aware of it, from what student-centered teachers do to see that such learnings occur. Thus, it's wise to get parents involved from the outset—at least let them know what you are up to—before students' comments create negative perceptions that are difficult to overcome.

Managing group investigation

In terms of classroom management, involving an entire class in a single investigation, as Ms. Fleury did in the "Wearin' of the Green" activity, is a difficult task. However, because the activity occurred over a short (two-day) period, it was manageable. On the other hand, keeping an entire class involved with a single problem over a period of a week or more is difficult. Mrs. Jacobsen manages small-group investigations over a long period by having students self-select the problems they investigate. This procedure creates smaller groups that are inherently more manageable. However, having many small groups operating simultaneously also calls for some group-management skills on Mrs. Jacobsen's part, skills that would be far less important had she opted for a more teacher-centered strategy. Some of those group-management skills are examined in the following section.

Managing Small-Group Instruction

Helping children learn to work productively in small groups is directly related to the overall goal of social studies teaching: promoting citizenship education. It is difficult, perhaps even impossible for students to learn to work cooperatively with others if all they experience is large-group instruction. Likewise, it's almost impossible for students to demonstrate their willingness to respect the rights and opinions of others if they seldom get the opportunity to express their opinions.

Large versus small group activities

Almost everything you can do with large groups (of twenty to thirty students) can also be done in small groups; you can even lecture to two students if you want to. But the reverse is not true: what you can do with small groups is not always possible with large groups. Discussions that involve twenty or more students, for example, are less likely to be successful than discussions involving groups of five to seven students, simply because participants in the larger groups must wait so long before they get a chance to speak. On the other hand, good small-group discussions don't happen just because you create small groups in your class. Some special structuring is usually required, as noted later in this section.

The perils of group work

You may remember times in the past when your small group spent thirty minutes getting organized when you could have completed the group's task yourself in half the time. Or when everyone in your group got the same grade but only one or two individuals did all the work. Or when group activities didn't make any difference because your grades were based solely on tests and individual projects. All of these experiences reflect decisions that need to be made before you undertake group work as a teacher. For example, will students' small-group work be graded and, if so, on what basis? You also need to decide how the groups will be created. Will you let children choose whom they will work with, or will you do the selecting? If you do the selecting, will you put two students who dislike each other on the same committee? Will you put a low-social-status child in the same group with high-social-status children (or vice versa)? High- and low-status children can often work successfully in the same group, but the relationship between two children who actively dislike each other is unlikely to improve if they are in the same small group, primarily because most groups don't deal with the causes of their disenchantment.

● The Dynamics of Small Groups

From the moment you divide your class into small groups, the proportion of each student's responsibility to the group increases dramatically. Instead of representing one twenty-fourth of a class (of twenty-four), for example, a student could represent one-fourth of a group of four. The formula for determining the number of possible interactions (Ni) in small groups is $(NP - 1) \times NP = Ni$ (the number of persons in the group minus 1 times the number of persons in the group). This means that a group of four can have twelve possible interactions: $(4 - 1) \times 4 = 12$. If you were to create eight-person groups, the number of potential interactions increases to fifty-six: $(8 - 1) \times 8 = 56$. However, an eight-person group doing library research will probably spend as much time checking among themselves (and duplicating their efforts) as they will in doing the research itself. Thus the question of group size must be considered in relation to its purpose.

Formula for group interactions

As a general rule, smaller groups have fewer problems than larger groups. But then small groups can also encounter problems. Groups of two, for example, often have a high exchange of information, but they also tend to have high tension. Likewise, one individual in a two-person group tends to be seen as the active initiator, while the other person acts as a passive controller (with a veto). In groups of three, you need to be careful that two stronger members do not overwhelm the weaker member, whereas four-person groups can easily deadlock, two against two. Groups of five seem to be the most personally satisfying, because they are small enough for participation yet large enough for stimulation. In addition, the possibility of a three-two split among members of a five-person group provides an ally for minority members.

Characteristics of small groups

Small groups offer opportunities for hands-on experiences and increased involvement and participation. *(© Joel Gordon)*

Groups and Purposes

Purposes for small groups

You can establish small groups for any number of purposes, but four of the most common to social studies instruction are (1) to discuss issues or events, (2) to engage in decision-making exercises, (3) to provide small-group instruction, either remedial or enriched, and (4) to research or investigate problems or questions. Characteristics of these groups are summarized below.

DISCUSSION GROUPS

Purpose.   To provide children with opportunities to express and clarify their points of view on issues pertinent to their interests.

Size.   Two to six (enough children to stimulate interaction but not so many as to overwhelm or restrict the flow of discussion).

Establish clear and manageable tasks

Comment.   Because discussion groups can easily degenerate into rap sessions, consider establishing a task for the group, such as a conclusion, a verbal report, or a summary, that will be presented after the group's deliberations. Preprinted questions or other guides to help groups structure their discussion can also be useful. Consider appointing a student discussion leader and selecting group members instead of allowing children to form their own groups.

DECISION-MAKING GROUPS

Purpose.   To provide children with experience in group consensus and in considering alternatives and arriving at a decision.

Size.   Three to seven.

Short duration

Comment.   The life of most decision-making groups is short, seldom exceeding an hour and typically shorter than that. Consequently, the social status of discussion-group members is less critical than it is in longer-range tutorial or research groups. Students can form their own decision-making groups, or members can be selected at random. Also be certain that you have realistic activities or other established procedures for the early finishers.

TUTORIAL GROUPS

Purpose.   To provide individual help or advanced work to a small group that might most need or benefit from it.

Size.   Two to nine.

Opportunities for feedback

Comment.   Tutorial groups provide opportunities for more immediate, direct feedback than is possible in large-group settings. However, the rest of the class will need meaningful activities while you work with a tutorial group.

RESEARCH GROUPS (INVESTIGATIVE)

Purpose.   To provide students with opportunities to solve problems, research questions, pursue lines of inquiry, or prepare projects.

Organization is the key

Size.   Two to four.

Comment.   The limitation on group size should be observed. Also, you may need to spend considerable time providing explicit instructions and helping the group organize itself.

● Social Skills and Feedback

Some people claim that when children work together in small groups, they are learning social skills—how to cooperate, how to get along with one another, and so on. Whether placing children in situations that require cooperation will necessarily teach them anything about cooperation per se is debatable. It may mean that students cooperated only because they were placed in a situation that demanded it.

    When problems arise within small groups, it is sometimes difficult to know how to respond appropriately. For example, consider how a teacher might deal with

Beware of unwarranted assumptions

an uncooperative student, in this instance, a student named Jamie. The first impulse is usually to say something like "Jamie, you are not cooperating," or "The next time you work in a group, I want you to cooperate." The problem with such global statements is their lack of specificity. They assume that Jamie (1) is aware of how and when he has failed to cooperate and (2) is able (and wants) to do something about his apparent problem. If either of these assumptions is not valid, then simply telling Jamie to cooperate in the future is likely to be futile.

Dealing effectively with students who refuse to cooperate, who dominate groups, who don't respect the rights and opinions of others (both of which also reflect a form of noncooperation), or who refuse to accept their fair share of the work will depend in large measure on the kinds of messages you provide to them. In general, your feedback must be in a form that they, either individually or as groups, can do something with (or about).

● Characteristics of Effective Teacher Feedback

Specificity. Effective feedback should identify specific behaviors that the child can modify or do something about. Statements such as "You're not smart enough to be in this group" or "You two don't care about this group" are judgments, not descriptions. Besides being unnecessarily cruel, neither statement indicates what the child should do to correct the problem. On the other hand, a statement such as "Before you proceed, you need to recheck your source of information" provides information that the child can act on.

Positive feedback, such as "That was a good report" or "This group is really working well together," can be music to the ears of anyone—even if it is more judgmental than descriptive. However, negative feedback is another matter entirely. To say to Jamie (from the earlier example), "You are not a good group member," for example, is likely to evoke Jamie's ego-defense mechanisms, especially if you state it publicly. Perhaps the only time that such a statement will *not* cause problems is if Jamie values the fact that he is *not* a good group member. To avoid such consequences, feedback should be presented descriptively, nonjudgmentally, and as your reaction. Examples:

Poor: Jamie, you are not cooperating.
Better: You did not seem to listen to what the others were saying.

Poor: This group does not work well together.
Better: This group seems to be having difficulty deciding what information is important enough to include in the presentation.

Timing. The most useful feedback is provided immediately after the behavior in question takes place. Sometimes, of course, you may need to delay feedback until you can deal with a student individually. For example, if Jamie or another student is obviously upset about something—perhaps the death of a grandparent, or almost any of a thousand other things—it is probably not the time to criticize his unwillingness to cooperate; he's got other things on his mind. Likewise, if you are upset about something, the form of your feedback may serve your needs but not the student's. A sharp "Jamie, you should go along with the majority" may let you vent your feelings, but it could compound Jamie's problem.

Clarity. From time to time, it may be necessary to determine whether students are receiving the messages that you think you are sending: what you intend as

Be as descriptive as possible

When in doubt, add description

When to give feedback

descriptive feedback could or may be regarded by the children as criticism. At other times, a student may interpret a teacher's description of a group problem as if it were the student's own fault (when it is indeed a group problem). To determine that the communication is clear, the teacher can simply ask the receiver to rephrase the feedback.

Have students rephrase the feedback

Feedback that exhibits the characteristics identified here is appropriate for both small-group work and handling discipline problems in large-group settings (see, e.g., Schmidt & Friedman, 1987). In other words, a statement such as "Jamie, stop misbehaving" might be more effective if it were phrased like this: "Jamie, your persistent talking is bothering me and the people around you. Please stop." The rephrased statement identifies (1) the specific behavior in question, (2) the effects that behavior is producing in others, and (3) an appropriate course of action ("stop talking") that can eliminate the problem. Such a statement is specific, descriptive, clear, and delivered with appropriate timing—all elements of effective teacher feedback.

● Small-Group Management Practices Summarized

As you consider cooperative group work, consider the following recommendations:

Begin with short-range tasks

1. Begin long-term group work only when you feel confident that (a) you can manage several groups operating simultaneously and (b) the individuals in each group can work together with minimal problems. You can get some idea of how individuals can work together by beginning with short-range group assignments.

Preliminary decisions

2. Decide how you plan to evaluate the group work before you begin, and then make this information known to students. If you plan to grade their reports or presentations, tell them the criteria you intend to use. They will listen intently.

Clearly defined tasks

3. Identify clearly defined tasks and products (a report, a display, etc.) for each group. It may be necessary from time to time to remind the groups to focus on their tasks, and not on the final product.

4. Present common group tasks in a whole-class format. Presenting tasks to individual groups may invite problems among groups that have nothing to do until you get around to them.

Reasonable alternatives

5. Consider alternative ways in which groups can present the results of their efforts—videos, murals, skits, plays, charts, pictures, film. Long oral reports can leave much to be desired.

6. Make it clear that both group-process and content-related (but not interpersonal) problems are "fair game" for discussion in small groups or by the class as a whole, and allow time accordingly. Obviously, immediate intervention is recommended *before* a group begins to flounder.

Reasonable deadlines

7. Establish reasonable deadlines; you can always extend them if necessary. Without deadlines, groups working on even the simplest tasks can drag on forever. Similarly, have something prepared for groups that finish early.

SUMMARY

Teaching strategies are the ways in which teachers orchestrate a variety of day-to-day teaching techniques—such as discussions, lectures, case studies, and student projects—to achieve desired learning goals. How teachers do this will vary according to their philosophy of teaching and their instructional purposes. Teachers who see their role as primarily that of conveying information to students are most likely to adopt a teacher-directed "telling" or expository orientation, whereas teachers who want to foster their students' ability to engage in independent inquiry are more likely to adopt a student-centered orientation. However, many teachers adopt a mixed orientation: sometimes they play the primary role, and at other times the students play the active role.

The distinction between teacher-directed and student-directed teaching strategies is designed to highlight two different teaching orientations. Unfortunately, some people mistakenly assume that the term *student-centered* means that the teacher designs a few activities and then lets students take over. Students in a student-centered classroom usually have considerable responsibility for what they are learning, and in some cases, not all students will be learning the same things (as was evident in Janet Jacobsen's classroom at the beginning of this chapter). However, all teachers have overall responsibility for their students' activities and what they learn, regardless of their personal orientation. The skills demanded of a teacher to use a student-centered orientation successfully are equal to and often exceed the skills needed to operate a teacher-directed classroom.

When a purely teacher-centered teacher looks at a social studies textbook, he or she may regard it as four hundred pages or so of subject matter to impart to the students. However, when student-centered teachers look at the same textbook, they may say to themselves, "How can I use this information with my students?" The distinction they are making reflects the subtle yet vitally important distinction between "teaching content" and "using content to teach." In one instance, teachers may approach content as something students must know, but in other instances the content can serve as a vehicle to achieve other instructional purposes.

When students use social studies content for particular purposes—as a data source for testing hypotheses, for example—they are learning to use social studies content. Students learn to analyze social studies content by analyzing social studies content—hopefully in the presence of competent modeling and teaching. Students also learn how to generate hypotheses by generating hypotheses, and to distinguish between facts and opinions by doing so.

The essence of teaching social studies does not lie solely in *what* one knows, but also in how one *uses* what one knows. No teacher can be sure that as students use social studies content in the classroom they will automatically transfer this use to their outside activities, since factors beyond teachers' control will influence that action. However, the hope is that teachers will have provided students with the skills that enable them to make that transfer.

SUGGESTED ACTIVITIES

1. In a small group, address the question of whether children's participation in group activities should be part of their grade. In other words, should group work "count"? If you think it should, recommend some guidelines for incorporating group work in the grading procedure. If you think it should not, suggest why.

2. While students are engaged in group work many teachers find themselves confronted with an interminable line of students waiting to talk with them. How do you account for this?

3. Observe a children's television program, such as *Sesame Street,* and determine what teaching strategies are used most often.

SUGGESTED READINGS AND RESOURCES

Print Resources

Linda Albert. (1989). *A teacher's guide to cooperative discipline.* Circle Pines, MN: American Guidance Service. This book provides a clear, step-by-step approach to cooperative discipline.

Bruce Joyce & Marsha Weil. (1992). *Models of teaching* (3rd ed.). Englewood Cliffs, NJ: Prentice-Hall. This volume ranks among the landmark texts in education because it was one of the first to reduce the mountain of literature dealing with teaching strategies to manageable terms.

Stephanie Steffy & Wendy J. Hood (Eds.). (1994). *If this is social studies, why isn't it boring?* York, ME: Stenhouse. The fifteen, first-person vignettes in this book describe how teachers and others modified the ways in which they taught social studies to make it more student-centered.

Internet Resources

Introductory Note: Web sites sometimes change their Internet addresses or cease operating entirely. All the addresses supplied here were operating when this book was printed, but if any of them fails to work properly, enter the desired topic into any standard search engine.

Teaching Strategies

http://www.ca.sandia.gov/outreach/2020/2020Tstrat.html

This site is maintained by the Mid-Atlantic Association for Cooperation in Education and offers everything you ever wanted to know about cooperative learning and other student-centered teaching strategies. **Bookmark quality.**

AskERIC

http://ericir.syr.edu

This site contains thousands of lesson plans and other resources on a variety of topics.

Constructivist Project Guide

http://www.ilt.columbia.edu/k12/1ivetextnf/webcurr.html

This site, based at Columbia University, offers assistance on developing cooperative learning units.

Teachers Helping Teachers

http://www.pacificnet.net/~mandel/

Although this site focuses on teachers sharing their insights with others, it also offers resources and information on a variety of topics.

Maximizing Learning in Small Groups

http://www.cs.ukc.ac.uk/national/CSDN/html/EDUres/small-group-learning.html

This British site offers useful guidelines for using small-group instruction.

11 Strategies for Active Learning

Key Questions

- What is dramatic play?
- Why involve students in role-playing?
- What are simulations, and how do they differ from games?

Key Ideas

- Active learning often involves bringing the real world into the classroom.
- Group-based activities provide students with common experiences that can then be analyzed.
- Most teaching techniques can be adapted to fit certain teaching objectives.
- The debriefings that should follow group activities are often as important as the activities themselves.

Introduction: The Empty-Chair and Author's Chair Techniques

● Context One

Mr. Chris Huber's fifth-grade class has been studying Abraham Lincoln and his involvement in the Civil War. For this activity, Mr. Huber has placed an armchair in the front of the classroom facing the class.

MR. HUBER: Let's pretend that this chair is President Abraham Lincoln. He is a tall, bearded man with many interests and lots of problems. How might he be dressed?

CHILDREN: . . . [Fill in how you think children might respond.]

Role-playing: Example one   MR. HUBER: What do you think he is like? And with the war dragging on, how might he be feeling?

CHILDREN: . . .

MR. HUBER: Well, let's pretend that Jefferson Davis has just walked into the room.

287

He has heard that Mr. Lincoln, here [pointing to the chair], is going to free the slaves. Does anyone want to be Mr. Davis? Okay, Gerry, you be Jefferson Davis. I'll play Mr. Lincoln's part.

ALLISON: . . .

MR. HUBER: Okay, Allison. You play Mr. Lincoln.

ALLISON: Welcome, Mr. Davis. I wish we were meeting under happier times.

GERRY: Thank you, Mr. Lincoln. I do too.

ALLISON: . . .

GERRY: . . .

● Context Two

An empty armchair, designated as the "author's chair," is placed in the front of Janet Jacobsen's middle-school classroom. Sometimes student authors sit in the chair when they share their writings with the class. At other times, students who have studied the works of a particular author sit in the chair and role-play the author as other students interview them. On this day a fifth grader, Becky Rodgers [alias Nathaniel Hawthorne], is sitting in the chair.

Role-playing: Example two

BECKY: I'm pleased to be with you today.

MRS. JACOBSEN [interrupting Jason who was about to speak]: On behalf of our entire class I want to welcome you here today, Mr. Hawthorne.

JASON: Yeah. And are you the one who wrote our "Pine Tree Shillings" thing?

BECKY: What makes you ask that, sir?

JASON: 'Cuz that sheet Mrs. Jacobsen gave us said "Hawthorne" on it.

BECKY: Well, I've written many things, like *The Scarlet Letter, Twice Told Tales, The House of Seven Gables,* and lots of others. And yes, the "Pine Tree Shillings" is from something I wrote.

AARON: Did you really see them put Becky Hull on the scales and match her weight in silver?

BECKY: No, that happened 150 years before I was born. When I was a student at Bowdoin College, I used to write articles that I sold to newspapers and magazines. That's how I got my spending money. And that's when I wrote the "Pine Tree Shillings" article.

AARON: Oh!

CINDI: You mean people back then really paid people to marry their daughters?

BECKY: Yes, ma'am. Some traditions the Puritans brought with them from England continued while they were here.

CINDI: I thought that those people came here to have . . . what do you call it, religious freedom?

BECKY (patronizingly): I think you may be confusing the Puritans and the Pilgrims, my dear.

CINDI: Oh!

The first vignette illustrates the introductory moments from a role-playing episode that uses the "auxiliary-chair technique" originally developed by Rosemary Lippitt (1958). The second vignette illustrates the "author's chair" technique, as described by Graves and Hansen (1983). For both techniques, a chair is placed at the front of the classroom. In the first instance, the chair remains empty but is assigned human characteristics. Students then interact with the chair as they might interact with a person who has those characteristics. In the author's chair example, students who know something about whatever author they are role-playing sit in the chair and interact with other students accordingly. In cases where student authors sit in the chair (to discuss their written works with the class), there obviously is no role-playing.

A chair can serve many functions

The empty-chair technique focuses children's attention on the chair, not on the person playing the character in the chair. This helps to protect the "player" from the nervousness that occasionally accompanies drama-oriented activities. It also avoids another problem common to role-playing episodes, such as when a girl plays what may be perceived as a male role or vice versa. However, in the author's chair example, where students actually role-play a real person, advance preparation is obviously essential.

Post-role-playing activities

Not illustrated in the examples here are the post-role-playing discussion, analysis, and debriefing of what took place. In the Lincoln activity, the discussion would continue with a consideration of both the portrayal itself and how the role players felt and what they were thinking at various points in the enactment. The follow-up activities may also include one or more reenactments involving different players and revised roles. That kind of follow-up is probably not as essential in author's chair activities, but role-playing activities are not complete without appropriate debriefing and follow-up.

Re-creating reality in the classroom

Role-playing and the other activities considered in this chapter are intended to re-create reality—or a slice of reality—in the classroom. They also provide children with opportunities to "walk in someone else's shoes." Once that reality has been established, the children can then examine, analyze, and, ultimately get a handle on the "real" reality they will face outside the classroom.

This chapter begins with an examination of a dramatic-play activity and then moves to a variety of role-playing and decision-making activities. It also looks at games and simulations, and, finally, at expressive and enactive experiences, activities through which children express themselves through drama, and so on, or projects where students construct or build things.

Dramatic Play

Dramatic play involves the spontaneous acting out of real-life situations in structured settings. The settings can involve ships in a harbor, pioneers moving westward in the 1800s, or almost any other situation. Dramatic play differs from the play that children normally engage in because it (1) occurs in a structured setting and (2) is designed to lead to educational outcomes. These elements are illustrated in the following Model Student Activity, which describes a dramatic-play activity dealing with ships and ports. Note the amount of attention, detail, and especially the time that was devoted to structuring the dramatic-play environment.

The author of the Model Student Activity illustrates how dramatic play can be a stimulus for raising questions. Of course, in the lower primary grades, children's reading and research skills may require that you provide some answers for them. In fact, sometimes you may need to raise *and* answer some of the questions associated with dramatic-play activities.

Occasionally dramatic play can unintentionally convey incorrect or distorted ideas. Certain historical reenactments, for example, can be susceptible to distortion. Re-creating an 1849 westward journey in a covered wagon is unlikely to sensitize children to the problems encountered by pioneers, primarily because most classrooms are a far cry from the rugged terrain the pioneers had to cross. Far better for that purpose is a computer-based simulation, *The Oregon Trail* (MECC), or the updated and retitled version of that simulation, *Wagon Train 1848,* which is designed for a local area network of computers. In *Wagon Train 1848,* several teams interact simultaneously as they move westward. Other dramatic-play activities involving Mexican fiestas or re-creating Native American villages can also lead to some of the complications discussed in Chapter 4. Thus, dramatic-play activities must be handled cautiously lest they be of questionable instructional value.

Dramatic-play activities are best suited to children who also engage in real-play activities, which means these activities are restricted largely to the lower elementary grades. If you try the ships and harbor activity with fifth or sixth graders, most of them will feel they are being treated like babies. However, dramatic activities minus the "play" components often work well with older students, as described later in this chapter. Structuring the classroom environment, as was done for the ships and harbor activity, can also be done in ways appropriate in the intermediate and middle-school grades.

Dramatic play often requires extensive preplanning and a lot of materials. In summary, well-planned dramatic play can have the following outcomes:

Cautions

TECHNOLOGY

Outcomes

* Stimulate questions that children can then research
* Provide a means for children to use and understand concepts and symbols
* Reveal needs that can be addressed in subsequent instruction
* Stimulate other expressive activities (painting, models, etc.)
* Reveal new information and understandings the children have gained

Role-Playing

In both dramatic play and role-playing, one child might play a father or mother, another child might play a store owner, someone else might play a ship's captain or an airline pilot, and so forth. The difference between the two types of activities lies in three factors: (1) *intent,* (2) teacher *structuring,* which can range from loosely organized (unstructured) to more tightly controlled (structured), and (3) *student involvement.*

Three differentiating factors

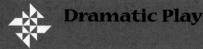
Arranging the Environment

After the class leaves on a Friday afternoon, you set about creating an arranged room environment where everything will be related to ships and ports. One bulletin board is filled with pictures of ships. Underneath goes a strip of tagboard on which you have printed "What do these ships carry?"

Another, but smaller, bulletin board is covered with a chart showing signal flags. Across the bottom of the chart hang four or five flags you have made from scraps of cloth. On a small table below the flags are small heaps of scrap cloth.

You cover the library table with books. In each are two or three colored markers, each inserted at a colorful picture or an exciting passage.

You set a large fish tank on the sink counter and fill it with water. You toss in a small wooden ship. Next to it you leave two metal ships (one must be large enough so that its displacement of water can be observed). You add a sign, "Why do metal boats float?" You drop a ruler and grease pencil next to the sign.

In one corner of the room you pin up, just above floor level, 6 feet of paper that will take tempera paint. Cans of paint and brushes sit nearby. Above the paper is an accurate picture of a port. In front of the paper you drop enough scraps of lumber so breakwaters and docks can be built.

Above the science table goes a picture of a lighthouse. On the table goes a set of instructions on how to build a lighthouse. Next to the instructions are batteries, wire, wood, tacks, bulbs—everything needed to build a lighthouse.

You use masking tape to hang a display. It shows men and women at work on ships and around the port. The caption asks, "What are these workers doing?"

You drop some more scraps of wood in the construction corner. Next to them go three small, dull saws, three small hammers, and an assortment of nails. You also leave a small ship that you made.

You put a song of the sea in the tape player, slip on your coat, and head for home. The trap has been baited. The quarry is the interest of your pupils.

Play, Discussion, and Research

On Monday morning your class can't miss the changes in the classroom. When school begins, tell the class they may spend a little time wandering around the room, looking at things, and playing with the objects.

Give them enough time to prowl, but not enough time to satisfy their curiosity. (The interrupted pleasure is sure to be returned to eagerly.) Then ask, "Well, what do you think this is all about?"

"Boats!"

"Sailing!"

"The ocean!"

You ask, "What did you see that you liked most?"

"The boats!"

"The lighthouse!"

"The tools!"

Pick out from one-third to one-half of the class (depending on the size of the class, the amount of free space you have, and the number of toy ships available). Say, "OK, each of you get a ship or boat, and you can play with it."

They play. You watch. The other pupils watch. You circulate among the watchers and ask quiet questions.

"What is Billy doing?"

"Why is Mary running her boat up the wall?"

"How would you do that?"

Then you shift the groups until everyone has had his chance to play with the toy ships. The class has finished its first session of *dramatic play*.

The next step is discussion of what went on during play. You will probably pursue several ideas that occurred to you as you observed the play, but I'll just use one example.

TEACHER: Billy, why were you and Kathy hitting your ships together?

BILLY: Because, I was sailing along, and she ran into me.

TEACHER: Why'd you run into his ship, Kathy?

KATHY: Because he was in my way. He should have let me by. He's a boy and I'm a girl, and boys are supposed to be polite to girls.

TEACHER: What happens if two ships smash into each other out in the ocean?

BILLY: They sink.

KATHY: The policeman comes out in a rowboat and gives them a ticket.

TEACHER: What policeman?

KATHY: Oh, you know. It was a joke.

TEACHER: Do ships smash into each other on the ocean?

BILLY: Sure, and some of them smash into ice cubes . . . uh, icebergers and sink.

TEACHER: Do all the ships that are on the ocean smash into each other all the time?

BILLY: . . . No.

TEACHER: Why not?

BILLY: I dunno.

TEACHER: How can you find out?

BILLY: Look it up.

TEACHER: Where?

BILLY: In the books.

TEACHER: How else?

BILLY: Ask somebody.

BILLY: Who?

BILLY: My dad.

KATHY: A sailor.

BILLY: A sixth-grader.

KATHY: The principal.

TEACHER: OK. Who wants to work with Billy and Kathy on this question?

And so it goes. A small research group is formed. You move on to another mistake or question or problem.

"Now, about that policeman in a rowboat. Do you really believe . . . ?"

And so on.

When children play, they reflect what they know. They do some things correctly, and they make some mistakes. The mistakes are used to stimulate discussion that leads to questions that can be researched.

You do not say, "Billy, you are doing that wrong. Someone show him the right way." What you want is for the pupil to find the right way by his own (or his research group's) efforts.

You keep at these questions until everyone has elected a research group. The next day, you review, with each group, what they are trying to find out. Don't tell them! Ask them.

"Everybody set? OK, how much time do you need?"

And off they go, some to the library table, some to the library. They will waste time this first time. Why not? They have to become acquainted with many new books. They have to find what will be useful. They skim and finger and look at pictures. You visit each group, praising and prodding. Research takes time. And you must be willing to let them take time.

Your responsibility is to be certain that they can find out. You have to be sure the answers are in materials available to them. Why else did you do your research and write that resource unit?

Of course, someone always comes up with a question you didn't, and couldn't, anticipate. Then you have to dig out the answer. If third-graders can't read your source, then you rewrite it as simply as you can. I don't think I ever taught a unit of any kind where I didn't have to do some rewriting for the class.

Then, after one day or three days—however long it takes to find answers or partial answers—each group makes its report. When all are armed with this new knowledge, you go back to a play session.

Let's review for a moment. You create an environment. The class explores that environment. You let the class play with the ships. You observe the mistakes in the play. The class discusses the mistakes. Research groups are formed. Research takes place. The results of research are reported. The class plays again.

Source: Abridged and reprinted with the permission of The Free Press, a division of Simon & Schuster from *Teaching Social Studies in the Elementary School* by John R. Lee. Copyright © 1974 by John R. Lee.

Sarah Ancell teaches third grade at Bozeman Elementary School in a city in the Southwest. She's part of a three-teacher team, who plan together, correlate their units, and occasionally trade classes for various activities.

All teachers on the team—Kippy Broderson, Sharon Newsom, and Sarah—agree that third grade is the upper limit for dramatic-play activities, and even then it's borderline. Some third graders take well to dramatic play, but often the children who don't like it make fun of those who do. As Kippy says, "At this grade level, we don't think it's worth the risk." "But," Sarah adds quickly, "we think the classroom environment is *really* important, regardless of how old the kids are."

It's impossible to describe all the different ways that Sarah and the Bozeman team arrange their classroom environments, so one example will have to suffice. When the students come down the hallway one morning, they find a huge tree—made from brown and tan colored paper and covering what used to be a pillar—its branches extending most of the way across the hallway ceiling. You can tell the tree is made from paper but it is still fairly realistic.

At first the tree's branches are bare, but a couple of days later, the branches are covered with pink blossoms. The children aren't too surprised because they made the flowers in art class. A few days later, green leaves appear among the blossoms; then the blossoms disappear and

only the leaves remain. The "branches" that hang down from the classroom ceilings mimic the changes in the tree in the hallway. Soon, tiny green apples appear, then larger green apples, and finally red apples. After a day when everyone has had an apple for a snack, both the apples and the green leaves disappear, replaced by yellow, gold, and red leaves. A few days later, the colored leaves disappear, and the tree returns to its original barren state.

As the tree and the classroom go through their various stages, children record the events in their journals. The students also do an assortment of activities related to plants, trees, and apples. They determine the average number of seeds in an apple in math; they make applesauce—after which they write the directions for "How to Make Applesauce"; they read the story of Johnny Appleseed (Kellogg, 1988) and plot his travels on a map; they study—what kinds of trees grow where, what kinds of trees lose their leaves, and what kinds keep their leaves in winter; they study products made from wood; and they read Shel Silverstein's *The Giving Tree* (1964).

Lest there be any question about it, the social environment in those classrooms is as warm and supportive as the physical environment is spectacular. But are all the decorations worth the tremendous amount of time and the considerable expense they require? Are they really necessary? Obviously, Sarah Ancell and her colleagues think so.

The intent in dramatic play is to re-create an experience so that as the children play they will get a vicarious feel for that experience and raise questions that lead to further research and investigation. The intent in role-playing is to provide children with opportunities to experience and *analyze a problem situation*. There is not much of a problematic nature associated with ships in a harbor, for example, as opposed to, say, a situation in which a pioneer family is moving west and, because of space restrictions, must decide between taking the family Bible or a set of heirloom china. The Bible-china question *might* arise during a dramatic play involving pioneers moving westward, but as a rule, role-playing situations are more narrowly defined. To this extent, role-playing is somewhat more structured and teacher directed than dramatic play.

Analyzing alternatives

In role-playing activities a few students re-enact a situation while the rest of the class acts as observers. In dramatic play, there is usually no audience and everyone is involved in the "play." How a role-playing group resolves a problem becomes the focus for discussion and analysis after the enactment is

Role of the audience

completed. However, unlike plays in which the actors follow a script, role-playing situations are open-ended, and the role players must decide how to resolve the situation.

Role-playing activities are sometimes used to help students develop a sense of social consciousness—to help them experience what it is like to "walk in another person's moccasins," that is, to view an issue or problem from another person's perspective (see Berman, 1990). Role-playing can also help sensitize students to the idea that maintaining a win-lose posture, one in which "I am right and they are wrong," often serves only to perpetuate a problem. For example, helping children understand that the police officer in the example at the opening of this chapter is expected to act in certain ways can provide a perspective that may explain some of his or her actions. The purpose here is neither to condemn nor to exonerate certain actions but to help children say, "This is where he or she seems to be coming from." When that is said, the basis for consensus building and resolving problems may have been laid.

In *Role Playing in the Curriculum*, Shaftel and Shaftel (1982) recommend the following procedure for handling role-playing activities:

Role-playing procedures

1. "Warming up" the group (problem confrontation)
2. Selecting the participants (the role players)
3. Preparing the audience to participate as observers
4. Setting the stage
5. Role-playing (an enactment)
6. Discussing the enactment
7. Further enactment (replaying revised roles, suggested next steps, exploring alternative possibilities)
8. Further discussion (which may be followed by more enactments)
9. Sharing experiences (relating the role-playing to one's life experiences) and further debriefing.

● Role-Playing and Decision-Making

Role-playing is often a part of decision-making activities. Depending on the way you arrange the activity, you can emphasize either the role-playing dimension or the decision-making dimension. The format for role-playing and decision-making activities is illustrated in the Model Student Activity entitled "The Lunch Policy." It involves (1) an open-ended problematic situation and (2) roles for the students to play.

Options

For "The Lunch Policy" and other activities like it, you could select either the role-playing or the decision-making option. Several factors might influence that decision. For example, if you think a group could handle this activity in five to ten minutes, you might select either option or both options. If it might take longer than five to ten minutes or the role-playing enactments might drag, you might lose the observers' attention. In that event, you might select the decision-making option in which all students are involved (in small groups) in the same situation simultaneously.

MODEL STUDENT ACTIVITY

The Lunch Policy

Provide the following information to students.

A fast-food restaurant (e.g., McDonald's or Burger King) is to open next week across the street from Meridian Elementary School. Some students have requested permission to eat lunch there. Currently students must eat at school, or they may go home for lunch if they bring a signed permission slip from their parents. The principal has called a meeting with the following people:

A parent

A student

A cafeteria director

A teacher

Tell students that the group must decide what to do.

Procedure

Role-Playing Option

Identify students to play each of the roles, and have them try to arrive at a decision agreeable to everyone. The rest of the class should discuss and evaluate both their decision and the procedures they used in arriving at it.

Decision-Making Option

Divide the class into small groups with each student taking a role. When all groups have made their decisions, they should be reported and evaluated by the class as a whole.

● Unstructured Role-Playing

In all role-playing activities, students must deal with a problematic situation. Teachers must identify the role players and be certain that everyone understands the situation. In other words, there is a certain amount of teacher direction in all role-playing activities, as well as a certain amount of spontaneity.

Unstructured: Limited teacher direction

Most of the role-playing examples presented thus far are unstructured; that is, the role players define their roles without specific teacher direction. In "The Lunch Policy," the teacher may have no idea how the situation will be resolved or whether the role players will become aware of all the factors that might influence the decision. In unstructured role-playing, teachers cannot be certain that a specific issue (such as safety in crossing the street) will emerge from the role-playing enactment. Of course, a teacher could introduce a neglected issue (such as the safety element) in the follow-up discussion, but teachers who want to be certain that specific issues are considered in the role-playing enactment can use a structured role-playing format.

● Structured Role-Playing

Structured: Includes roles and sample positions

The element that distinguishes structured from unstructured role-playing is the addition of positions or points of view that the role players must incorporate into their enactments. For example, if you are concerned that students will not know how a cafeteria director might feel about the lunch policy question, you could structure the activity by adding position statements to the roles in the previous Model Student Activity, as illustrated below:

1. A parent wants her children eating well-balanced meals, not hamburgers every day.
2. A student feels that the school should not dictate eating habits.
3. The cafeteria director needs a full cafeteria to meet operating expenses.
4. The teacher doesn't want to be bothered with permission slips and feels it is up to the parents and children to decide where lunch will be eaten.

Modified model The modified model for structured role-playing activities reflects the following elements:

1. an open-ended problematic situation,
2. roles for the individuals involved, and
3. position statements for each role player.

You are obviously free to add other roles or positions. Or you might use a mixture of each, specifying positions for some roles while leaving others open so that players can operate according to their convictions. Your procedure should be dictated by your objectives. If you wish to heighten the sense of drama and add an element of mystery, you can distribute the role positions on separate slips of paper so that, initially, only the role players know who they are. This approach tends to heighten interest at the outset of role-playing.

Providing Background Information. For structured role-playing activities such as "The Lunch Policy," providing simple position statements is usually adequate. In other instances, however, and especially in historical situations such as the Abraham Lincoln–Jefferson Davis conversation in the empty-chair example at the beginning of this chapter, students who play the Davis and Lincoln roles must have enough background information to understand why Davis supported slavery (and Lincoln opposed it). This is not the kind of matter that you would leave to the children's imaginations. The same provision would hold true if you wanted your class to role-play a negotiating session between the American colonists and the British to avoid the Revolutionary War. In both instances, the role players will need enough information to enable them to address the situation intelligently and accurately.

Historical settings

There are basically two ways to handle the background-information requirement for structured role-playing activities. One option is to treat the role-playing as a culminating activity that occurs *after* the class has studied the historical period or situation. Even then, some intensive review may be necessary, perhaps using a "Somebody-Want-But-So" summary chart described at the end of Chapter 7. A second option is to provide role players with background information that you have written or otherwise duplicated from a suitable source for them. The second option can be time-consuming, especially when you consider that the role players need sufficient time, perhaps even overnight, to digest the information you give them. The main point here is that the amount of advanced preparation nec-

Options

essary for structured role-playing activities will vary with the complexity of the situations your students will be focusing on.

Handling Conflict. If you choose to use role-playing activities with conflicting role positions, you must be prepared to help the group cope with the disputes that are almost guaranteed to occur. Many of us have been taught that conflict is bad, something to be avoided, yet in many real-life situations, conflict is unavoidable. Acting as if conflict does not exist does not make it disappear. Students need to view conflict as a reality of human life. However, they also need to understand that conflict can be managed if it is addressed directly, and the process of doing that can often yield creative and mutually agreeable solutions to problems. In other words, part of the purpose of some role-playing activities can be to explore ways in which conflict-based win-lose situations can be converted into consensus-building win-win situations.

Helping students deal with conflict

Simulation and Gaming

Simulations, which often involve elements of role-playing and decision-making, are a comparatively recent innovation in education. Games, which rarely involve role-playing, have been around much longer.

Simulating reality

Simulations are instructional activities in which elements from the real world are re-created (or simulated) in the classroom. For example, after an experience in which the classroom is turned into a miniature factory to mass-produce valentine cards (see Resource Handbook), students have an opportunity to discuss what it is like to perform a task over and over again, as one would on a real assembly line. Likewise, in the computer simulation *Oregon Trail,* students have an opportunity to experience the tribulations of traveling west in a covered wagon during the nineteenth century. If students playing *Oregon Trail* do not plan properly, they may die before reaching their destination—as real pioneers sometimes did. If death occurs, they can try to do better in the next round.

Reality is complex

In a simulation such as *Democracy,* students play the role of legislators who are seeking reelection. By negotiating with their colleagues for the passage or defeat of legislation in keeping with their constituents' interests, the student legislators may be able to win reelection. In the course of playing *Democracy,* students learn about factors that can influence the passage or defeat of legislation. In reality, however, the legislative process is so complex that were you to attempt to re-create it in a classroom, your students would be overwhelmed by the sheer number of things to consider (e.g., legislative procedure, parliamentary procedure, political parties, and lobbyists). About the only place you will find a totally realistic legislative process is in a real legislature, and that, unfortunately, cannot exist very practically in most classrooms. Thus *Democracy* and all other simulations necessarily simplify whatever real-world equivalent they represent.

Simplifying reality

Because all simulations simplify the reality they deal with, it becomes possible to analyze a situation without a lot of other elements clouding the picture. For example, students playing the first stages of *Democracy* are able to analyze the negotiation phase of the legislative process without the confounding influence of political parties or other factors. In later stages of the simulation, the legislator's convictions and the influence of political parties are added, so it more nearly reflects the real legislative process. (*Democracy* was originally developed by James S. Coleman for the 4-H Foundation and is available from Western Publishing Company, 850 Third Avenue, New York, NY 10022.)

Real-world models

The real world provides the model on which almost all simulations and many games are based. If you drive around Atlantic City, New Jersey, you will encounter street names such as Baltic Avenue, St. James Place, and Park Place, and the Boardwalk. Even the socioeconomic levels of the various neighborhoods roughly parallel the property values on a Monopoly board—or they did when the game of Monopoly was developed in the 1920s. That's because the model for Monopoly is based on real estate transactions in Atlantic City, New Jersey. But, to make a game of it, the Monopoly developers had to take some liberties with reality by adding more chance factors than are found in the real world. For example, you cannot buy property in Monopoly unless you land on the property, and where you land depends on the roll of the dice. Other chance factors include "Community Chest" and "Chance" cards, "Go to Jail," "Luxury Tax," and "Income Tax." All these make Monopoly fun to play, because you never know what will happen next, but the chance factor in Monopoly so exceeds reality that you can't use the game to teach the principles of real estate investment and development.

Simulations usually have outcomes, but not winners

Many games are simply contests in which winning is determined by a combination of prior knowledge, luck, and skill. These include those old classroom standbys, spelling bees and Twenty Questions, and the takeoffs on TV game shows like *Jeopardy!* and *Password*. Most simulations, on the other hand, lack the contest quality of games. All simulations have an outcome—a result—but these usually lack the clear flavor of winning or losing that is typical of most games. In addition, because the chance or luck factor in simulations is usually lower than in most games, simulations tend to be more realistic. These and the other characteristics of simulations and games are shown in Table 11.1.

● Computer-Based Simulations

Computer-based simulations consider many variables

Computer-based simulations usually have the ability to reflect more real-world complexities than are possible through nontechnological means. For example, as pioneers journeyed westward during the nineteenth century, they encountered one set of problems as they crossed the plains and different problems as they crossed the deserts and the mountains. In the *Oregon Trail* simulation that was noted earlier, microcomputers make it possible to replicate conditions that pioneers faced at various points on their journey. A somewhat similar situation prevails for the computer-based simulation *The Golden Spike* (National Geographic Society), in which players are involved in building the transcontinental railroad. If players spend too much money purchasing rails and ties and don't allocate enough money for food and wages for workers, they too must beware. Thus computer-based simulations can take information from a player's prior decisions and incorporate it into the next decision that the player must make.

TECHNOLOGY

Some computer-based simulations provide excellent opportunities for children to use map skills. In the simulation *Geography Search* (McGraw-Hill), players must make

TABLE 11.1 Differences Between Simulations and Games

Characteristics	Simulations Tend To:	Games Tend To:
Size	Involve more students, often the entire class	Be limited to fewer players, typically four, seldom more than eight
Length	Be of longer duration (more than one period)	Be of shorter duration (one period or less)
Chance	More realistically reflect the real world	Contain a "chance" factor that exceeds reality
Result	Produce an outcome usually without winners or losers	Have defined winners and losers
Preparation and materials	Require considerable advance preparation and materials	Require minimal preparation and materials

navigation decisions as they sail to the New World. The computer then provides them with the precise location of their ship. Likewise, in the simulation *SimCity 2000*, players must become the planner, designer, and mayor of one or more cities.

Limitations. Although the number of computer-based simulations for social studies is increasing, there are still very few for primary-level children. The fact that children must be able to read the instructions on the monitor is often a limitation for very young students. In addition, some programs may require knowledge that students do not have. For example, the simulation *Rails West* is about building the transcontinental railroad. It requires prior knowledge about financial markets (stocks, bonds, and debentures) that even adults can find taxing. Far less difficult is the simulation *Railroad Tycoon,* in which students can watch their locomotives chugging across the landscape.

May require prior knowledge

Many simulations (noncomputer-based) are designed or can be adapted for an entire class. However, unless you have access to a local area network, computer-based simulations are usually limited to one or two participants. The length of time it takes for an entire class to experience a particular simulation depends on the number of computers available, of course, but restrictions on the number of players are sometimes another limitation.

Limited number of players at one time

Building Simulations. Commercially produced simulations and games are available from a variety of sources, such as The Social Studies School Service (10000 Culver City Blvd., Culver City, CA 90232). However, some teachers develop their own simulations.

Using Interactive CD-ROMs

The year is 1492. Your monitor is displaying an animation of Queen Isabella and King Ferdinand's throne room in Spain. The king and queen are there, along with Queen Isabella's confessor, a brown-robed Franciscan monk named Francisco Jimenez de Cisneros, and a young adventurer, Christopher Columbus, who is pleading with Ferdinand and Isabella to allow him to find a new route to the Orient. After Ferdinand and Isabella agree to fund Columbus's voyage, the scene shifts to a view from a ship just offshore from a Caribbean island. Occasionally the scene also shifts to Columbus talking with one of his officers about what they might find on the island. If you move the cursor to the brush along the island's shoreline, you can view a closeup of what Columbus and his crew will encounter when they come ashore. Depending on where you place the cursor, you may see more junglelike terrain, and sometimes you will discover natives huddled in the underbrush. If you don't place the cursor on the different locations, you will simply follow Columbus as he lands on the island. The materials on this CD-ROM are called "interactive" because they permit viewers to examine elements they want to look at in more detail.

The above scenario is a segment from a CD-ROM called "Explorers of the New World" (Learning Company, $49). Christopher Columbus is one of several fifteenth- through seventeenth-century explorers, including Magellan, De Soto, and Henry Hudson, whose voyages are chronicled on this software. The explorers are fully animated, and some of them occasionally share their hopes and concerns with viewers. The actor who portrays Columbus reads accounts from the real journals of Columbus's voyages to the New World.

Just as impressive as "Explorers" is the CD-ROM "The Alamo: Victory or Death" (Archimedia Interactive, $140). Narrated by people like newscaster Dan Rather and with music of the period performed by contemporary country music stars like Johnny Cash and Mel Tellis, this two CD-ROM set presents more information than any teacher and class can possibly cover. Highlights include an interactive tour of the Alamo as it was before Santa Anna's attack, a recreation of the siege of the Alamo as seen from a bird's-eye view, and detailed views of weapons and materials from the period. One notable segment shows viewers how to load a flintlock musket, and then viewers practice shooting at a rabbit that runs across the screen. Because most muskets were not very accurate, the rabbit usually makes it across the screen safely.

Design principles

The first step in designing a simulation is deciding what aspects of the real world you wish to simulate. For your first effort, the rule of thumb is to keep it simple. Attempting to simulate the judicial system, for example, will prove overwhelming, but you could simulate one aspect of the judicial process, such as a jury's deliberation, as a starter. If you want to try your hand at some simulations, here are a few situations that can be used to generate simulation activities:

Possible simulations

1. *Zoning questions.* Should a gas station, liquor store, or high-rise low-income housing be permitted in a residential neighborhood?
2. *Community priorities.* What should a community spend its money on—sewers, parks, playgrounds, more police and firefighters?
3. *Deciding what is newsworthy.* Put together the front page of a newspaper, given an assortment of articles—news, sports, features—clipped from a local paper. Which stories should be given prominence? Why?
4. *School policy questions.* Should recess be abandoned? (Or should children be permitted to go to fast-food restaurants for lunch?)

Integrating simulations and decision-making

If some of these sound like decision-making activities, that's because they can be used in that form too. Decision-making and role-playing activities are often integrated into a simulation format.

Developing Board Games

Many elements of social studies, especially processes that result in products such as milk, bread, or steel, readily lend themselves to a board-game format. A sample board-game format is illustrated in Figure 11.1. The first step in designing this example, "The Milk Game," is to identify the stages of milk production: the dairy farm, transporting the milk from farm to dairy, the dairy itself, and so on. Segments of the game-board pathway were then outlined so that they corresponded,

FIGURE 11.1 Sample Board Game

in sequence, to the different stages of milk production. This game board uses straight pathways only because they are easy to draw neatly; curved trails would work equally well. The idea of this and similar board games is that as students move their tokens around the game board, they become familiar with the stages in the process—in this case, the process of milk production. It is possible to design much more complex and thought-provoking board games, of course, but this example is for illustrative purposes.

A simple example

Once the basic game board was laid out, it was necessary to find ways to make the game appealing and fun for students. Elements to consider here include determining

* how the winner will be decided (the first student to reach "Home").
* how the movement of tokens would be governed. A die (one of a set of dice) made from a three-inch cube of foam rubber cushion filler is one option although regular dice or playing cards (with the number of spaces indicated on them) could work equally well.

Adding chance factors

* how to add additional interest. One of the most common techniques is by using "Chance cards." In this example, players draw a chance card when they land on a square marked with a tiny milk carton. The chance element can also be added by marking directly on the squares, but chance cards can provide additional variety. To make this game even more realistic, the "Chance cards" were keyed to events that might occur as milk is produced. These included statements such as, "Your dairy farm is struck by a power failure, and you must milk the cows by hand—miss one turn," and "The milk truck encounters very light traffic—move ahead two spaces."

Other board games

The design principles for "The Milk Game" would be equally appropriate for other kinds of board games, including those based on the history or geography of a region. Instead of drawing the pathway on plain posterboard or oak tag, you could use a map of the region as the background, glued or dry-mounted to poster board. The trail (or pathway) can be drawn for something like "Sherman's March Game" on a road map of Georgia or the southeastern United States. "The Santa Fe Trail" game could be done on a map of the southwestern United States.

Steps for Designing a Simulation or Game

Helpful procedures

Designing a simulation or game begins with an idea. After that, it requires some materials, a little creativity, and often more time than you might imagine. The steps for designing a simulation or game are as follows:

1. Identify the process or system that you want to simulate.
2. Identify the specific characteristics of the system or process. These include the various stages in the process or system and any human components that are involved. It may be necessary to narrow your focus; for example, simulating only part of the nineteenth-century factory system, not the entire system.
3. Decide which characteristics of the system or process you wish to emphasize and which you are willing to omit.
4. Decide which format—simulation or game—is best suited to the topic.

5. Decide what the players will be doing. Will they be making something, playing a role, moving tokens around a board, or what?

6. Decide on an outcome. When will the simulation or game end—after the players have reached a decision, been reelected, reached "home," made the most points, or after time expires?

7. Decide how you will introduce the chance element (to make the activity more interesting). Make certain that negative and positive chance factors are equally balanced.

8. Simulations only: Decide how you will get information to the players. Will each player get different roles? Separate instructions?

9. Decide if everything you have decided on thus far "fits" together. If it does, begin developing or collecting whatever materials you will need.

10. Prepare a preliminary set of written rules or directions.

11. Try out the simulation or game on a small group of "guinea pigs." (This is one of the most essential steps in the entire process—you'll be amazed at what you forgot to consider.)

12. Make necessary adjustments as indicated by the field test.

Expressive and Enactive Experiences

Terms defined

Expressive experiences are activities in which children have an opportunity to express themselves through drama—plays, skits, pageants, and so on—or through dramatic play, music, role-playing, or other forms of sociodrama. *Enactive experiences,* which are sometimes called *projects,* are activities in which students build or create something, such as models or murals. Opportunities for children to express their creative or artistic talents are common to both experiences.

The role of problem solving

Most worthwhile enactive experiences incorporate a *research* or *problem-solving* dimension. For example, before boiling the first grain of rice for a Japanese meal, students should have identified what might be served at such a meal, what ingredients are used in the various dishes, how the foods are prepared and served, and on what occasions they are eaten. In other words, the guiding question here is, What are the components of a typical Japanese meal? Similarly, before building a model dairy farm, students should have compared a series of pictures of dairy farms (or visited dairy farms, if that is feasible) to identify their common characteristics. And before cooking that pioneer meal, students should have researched the foods available to the pioneers—for example, see *The Little House Cookbook* (Walker, 1979).

Don't ignore the research component

A research component is an essential part of enactive experiences. Often students are so eager to begin construction that they are reluctant to take the time needed to complete the necessary research. Failing to do that can produce countless problems, both for students and you as the teacher. If there is any question about this, refer back to the igloo-building activity described in Chapter 10.

Enactive experiences often have a dimension that cannot be measured in precise educational terms. Likewise hands-on activities can permit students to contribute to class activities in ways that are denied them in more formal, reading-oriented

Many hands-on activities require that students apply what they know in problem-solving situations. *(© Bob Daremmrich/The Image Works)*

Balancing assets and liabilities — activities. Thus the appropriate use of expressive and enactive experiences probably lies somewhere between two extremes—between teachers who are always building something or getting ready for another play or pageant and teachers who rarely use any of these experiences. Use expressive and enactive experiences as long as they (1) are integral to whatever you are studying, (2) involve a significant inquiry or research component that engages children intellectually, and (3) are done "right"— that is, they are a genuine reflection of the culture, period, or phenomenon.

SUMMARY

The teaching activities described in this chapter range from dramatic play, in which you establish a setting and then let the students' creativity come forth, to those in which the children follow precise, step-by-step directions, as in a simulation. The basic rule here is the more teachers structure an activity, the more they may lose spontaneity and creativity. The associated tradeoff is that what is lost in spontaneity may be offset by greater assurance that students will consider the issues and questions that have been built into a more structured activity. Whichever kind of group-based strategy you use—structured or unstructured, expressive or enactive—will ultimately depend on your purposes for developing the activity in the first place. Yet regardless of which type of activity you use, a key element in all of them is debriefing students afterwards.

SUGGESTED ACTIVITIES

1. Design a board game following the suggestions in this chapter. It may take time, but your students will love it.

2. Design a dramatic-play activity following John Lee's format but involving a different content area.

3. Design an unstructured role-playing activity. Then identify the techniques you could use to add greater structure to the experience.

4. Suppose a teacher informs you that he or she plans to serve raw fish to a class so that the students will have better appreciation of Inuit life. Identify the positive and negative learning outcomes that might result from this experience.

5. The Commentary described the elaborate physical environment that Sarah Ancell and her colleagues established in their classrooms. Decide the extent to which such attention to the environment is necessary, desirable, or is a frill.

SUGGESTED READINGS AND RESOURCES

Print Resources

Bill Bigelow. (1994). Role plays: Show, don't tell. In *Rethinking our classrooms: Teaching for equity and justice*. Milwaukee, WI: Rethinking Schools, 114–115. In this brief article on developing role-playing activities, Bigelow suggests that this strategy consistently brings students to life.

Fannie R. Shaftel & George Shaftel. (1982). *Role playing in the curriculum*. Englewood Cliffs, NJ: Prentice-Hall. The name Shaftel has become almost synonymous with role-playing and other group activities. This remains the most complete and authoritative source on role-playing.

Internet Resources

Introductory Note: Web sites sometimes change their Internet addresses or cease operating entirely. All the addresses supplied here were operating when this book was printed, but if any of them fails to work properly, enter the desired topic or organization in any standard search engine.

Role Playing: Tea at The White House

http://ericir.syr.edu/Virtual/Lessons/Social_St/ US_history/USH0003.html

This site offers detailed lesson plans that use role-playing techniques.

American Revolution Simulation

http://ericir.syr.edu/Virtual/Lessons/Social_St/ US_history/USH0027.html

This entry reflects one of the middle-grade lesson plans available at this site that uses simulation techniques to help students understand why the American colonies declared their independence.

Applications of Role Playing

http://www.nova.edu/~aed/horizons/vol9n1

and

http://gis.joensuu.fi/research/openuniv/openuniv2.html

These sites illustrate how role-playing strategies have been applied to distance learning and international education.

12

Nurturing Critical and Reflective Thinking

Key Questions

- How does one teach students to process information critically and reflectively?
- What kinds of materials and activities do teachers use to teach reflective thinking?
- What is decision making, and how does it relate to reflective thinking?
- How do teachers decide which questions to ask, and when to ask them?

Key Ideas

- Critical and reflective thinking skills are part of an interactive system of mental activities that we use to interpret and assess different kinds of information and experience.
- Teachers and students can model their thinking processes by talking out loud with each other.
- Metacognition involves thinking about one's thinking processes.
- Underlying every question that teachers ask is a purpose for asking it. These purposes may be as varied as the questions.

Introduction: Reading Between the Lines

Going beyond the printed word

"Reading between the lines" sounds innocent enough, but explaining it to young children can be challenging. Part of the problem is that even beginning readers know that the spaces between the lines on a page are blank. The situation is complicated further because "reading between the lines" is a figurative expression, like "it's raining cats and dogs." Even children who realize that you are speaking figuratively may still have no idea what you are talking about. Of course, you could explain that "reading between the lines" involves taking two or more pieces of information and then relating them in some way to produce a third idea that goes beyond the original information, but don't be surprised if your students still look puzzled.

Despite the complexity of its definition, "reading between the lines" is not that difficult to do, especially if the children have some previous experiences with it. However, instead of beginning with questions like "What is the author really saying?" or "What does the author really mean?," you could begin by saying something like "Let's see if we can figure out what this author is really saying," and then systematically modeling (demonstrating) your thinking processes for the children. In other words, questioning alone does not teach children the process, since most questioning strategies are primarily a test of their existing ability. In addition, most authorities (see Beyer, 1987) agree that reading between the lines and most other reflective thinking skills are best taught through modeling and by providing guided practice, not by questioning.

Experience precedes analysis

The premise throughout this chapter is that experience should precede analysis. This premise reflects a constructivist approach to learning wherein children (and adults) construct meaning by acting on and analyzing their earlier experiences. For example, it is doubtful whether many people know that a *quark* is the product of a collision between two electrons. You could memorize this definition, of course, but even then it is doubtful that quarks would be meaningful unless we had more experiences with physics, the properties of electrons, the reasons they collide, and what happens when they do. In more practical terms, this suggests that "reading between the lines" and other reflective thinking skills are best taught by (1) modeling the desired behaviors, including talking out loud as you think through the problem, (2) accompanying the modeling with clear explanations, (3) working with students as they practice the skills on related information, and then (4) talking (reflecting) with students about these experiences.

Goals

This chapter also is designed to address three goals. The first is to help you identify the thinking skills that students should develop, including metacognition, or thinking about thinking. The second is to illustrate how reflective thinking skills are part of a family of interrelated skills, and the third is to present some exemplary teaching activities that can help students process information efficiently and effectively.

How Critical Thinking Differs from Other Kinds of Thinking:

Terminology Clarified

When people talk about thinking—that largely unseen process that goes on in a person's mind—they risk encountering a morass of confusing terminology. Some people talk about critical thinking, others talk about creative thinking, some talk about problem solving and decision-making, and still others may talk about memorizing, remembering, hypothesizing, generalizing, or other related terms. Because these are not different terms for the same thing, this section clarifies such terminology.

Making sense of the terminology and mental processes related to thinking was a problem that Benjamin Bloom and his colleagues (Bloom et al. 1956) tackled almost fifty years ago. As described in Chapter 8, the result of their efforts was a six-stage hierarchy or Taxonomy of Cognitive (Thinking) Skills, often referred to as the *Taxonomy*. The *Taxonomy* is often posted, in an abbreviated form, in many classrooms across the country. Briefly, the major classifications of the *Taxonomy*, in order, are (1) Knowledge, (2) Comprehension, (3) Application, (4) Analysis, (5) Synthesis, and (6) Evaluation.

Lower-level thinking

The first two levels of the *Taxonomy*, Knowledge and Comprehension, are fairly straightforward. Knowledge refers to remembering previously learned material, whereas comprehension refers to grasping the meaning of (or understanding) certain material. The distinction between these categories is illustrated by young children who can recite the Pledge of Allegiance perfectly, but who have no idea what "one nation, indivisible" means.

Levels Three through Six of the *Taxonomy* become increasingly complex, as do the examples. Application, Level Three, refers to the ability to apply previously learned material in new situations. For example: Los Angeles is located (approximately) 60 degrees west of Boston. When it is noon in Boston, what time is it in Los Angeles? The student must remember that the earth rotates about fifteen degrees in an hour, and then apply that information to the problem. Level Four, Analysis, refers to the ability to break material down into its component parts so as to identify possible relationships between and among the various parts. For example, consider two statements such as "Judy has not eaten for over a day. She must be hungry." Upon analyzing these statements, the person should be able to distinguish between the fact (Judy not eating) and the inference (being hungry). The person should also be able to determine whether a third fact, such as the height of the world's tallest building, is relevant to the two prior statements (No—unless Judy happens to be trapped on the 107th floor!).

Higher-level thinking

Levels Five and Six of the *Taxonomy*, Synthesis and Evaluation, are more complex than the lower levels and thus resist simple examples such as those provided thus far. Synthesis refers to the ability to take existing parts and put them together in ways that create a new whole. Examples at this level include: writing a well-organized theme or speech, and creating a new scheme for classifying objects (events, or ideas). Consider the possibility of creating (or asking students to create) a scheme for classifying the various actions that have preceded the outbreak of war over the last three centuries. Certain actions, such as the Boston Tea Party, for example, might be considered antagonistic. Other actions could well be conciliatory.

Level Six, Evaluation, is the most complex level of the *Taxonomy*, but ironically it is also one of the easiest to misinterpret. Evaluation refers to making judgments about the value of certain materials in relation to *definite and previously identified criteria*. The criteria may be either internal, as in judging the organization of a speech or theme, or external, as in judging whether a speech or theme is relevant to a proposed topic or position. At this level, the evaluator must describe the relationship between the speech, theme, or whatever, and the previously identified criteria. Thus, for an evaluator to say, for example, "I liked it," is *not* acceptable at this level. To be acceptable, the evaluator must explain the explicit and previously identified criteria that he or she used to arrive at the decision. Everyone is entitled to their personal opinion, of course, but feelings and impressions based on private (personal) criteria are not acceptable according to the standards for this category. It is a matter of private versus public criteria. To fit this category, the evaluation criteria must be both public and identified beforehand, which necessarily excludes personal opinions.

Evaluation is <u>not</u> a matter of . . . personal opinion

In the next section, the foregoing explanation of the *Taxonomy* is used as a basis for examining thinking, creative thinking, critical thinking, and problem solving.

● Thinking

"Thinking" is a global term

Many of us may recall hearing our teachers say, "O.K. boys and girls, Let's put our 'thinking caps' on." Although you could debate whether anyone can take their "thinking cap" off, such requests are more likely to reflect efforts to forewarn children that a "tough one"—a question, problem, or whatever—is coming. Thinking encompasses such a wide range of cognitive activities, as reflected by the *Taxonomy,* that asking children "to put their thinking caps on" is probably meaningless to most of them. On the other hand, such requests may reflect a subtle way of saying "pay attention." Other global requests, such as "I want you to think about this one," probably have the same effect. Such requests probably do little to influence a child's ability to think, but then they probably do no harm either.

● Creative Thinking

Focuses on new or novel approaches

When teachers ask students to think creatively, they are in effect asking children to create new or novel approaches to a problem. In other words, the teachers are asking children to create, devise, plan or generate—all terms associated with Level Five, Synthesis, of the *Taxonomy*—ways to combat a problem. Hunger, for example, is obviously a very real problem in some areas around the world, so asking children to identify ways to combat world hunger would be an appropriate focus for creative thinking. The process of identifying such possibilities is usually referred to as *brainstorming*. Brainstorming generates a pool of possible solutions to a problem, but without evaluating individual recommendations until the pool has been created. That is, all ideas are accepted, without judgment, until the entire pool has been created.

Shifts from synthesis to evaluation

After suggestions for new ideas for combating world hunger have slowed down considerably (but before students become bored), the focus of creative thinking shifts from Synthesis—the creation of novel ideas—to Level Six, Evaluation. The ultimate question at this level is "Which of these suggestions is best?" However, the more basic question, consistent with the *Taxonomy,* is "How should we evaluate these suggestions?" The purpose here is to identify the criteria for separating workable suggestions from the unworkable and whimsical, a key element in Level Six, Evaluation. In other words, before deciding whether sending additional food to the needy is a good solution to the problem of world hunger, criteria must be identified for distinguishing between more workable and less workable solutions.

● Critical Thinking

Critical thinking differs from its other thinking cousins by its focus on working with information, especially primary source or uninterpreted information. The main elements of critical thinking include *analyzing and interpreting information (data) in ways that lead to* one or more of the following:

Critical thinking

* Hypothesizing about differences and similarities across examples
* Evaluating explanatory hypotheses in light of additional data or examples
* Making plausible inferences that can be tested with additional data or examples, and/or
* Drawing conclusions and/or generalizing based on the data or examples.

The "Nation X" Model Student Activity that appears later in this chapter illustrates the elements of critical thinking, as does The American Farmer Fact Sheet that appears on page 354. Critical thinking activities typically involve elements from Levels Three through Six of the *Taxonomy*.

● Problem Solving

There are essentially two types of problem solving. The first and probably most common is what students do in math class when they work through sets of problems to identify the right (or correct) answer. The second type of problem solving involves situations (not usually found in math classes) where there are "best," "more appropriate," or even multiple solutions. The "Where Would You Locate Your City?" Model Student Activity, which appears on pages 351 to 352, is an example of the second type of problem solving. Briefly, students are provided with different kinds of maps (topographical, rainfall, vegetation, etc.) of an area that they use to identify where (in the area) they will locate their city. Because different factors can influence their decision, there is not a single "right" answer, but rather several "better" answers, all equally defensible. The "Who Is Qualified for the Presidency?" Model Student Activity in Chapter 1 also reflects the second type of problem solving. As you may recall, in that activity the student's "problem" is determining which candidates are best and least qualified to hold that office. Once again, different groups of students may arrive at different solutions.

The first type of problem solving typically involves cognitive activities at the Application level (Three) of the *Taxonomy*. The second, broader form of problem solving can involve elements from Levels Three through Six.

What kind of problem is it?

Metacognition: Thinking About Thinking

Helping students become proficient thinkers and decision makers involves providing them with opportunities to process various kinds of information and experience. However, teaching students how to think critically will not necessarily make them self-directed, independent thinkers. The information-processing skills dealt with in this chapter will certainly provide the basis for independent, self-directed thinking and decision making, but actually helping students to consciously direct their thinking requires going a step further.

The goal is to help students reach the highest and most sophisticated level of thinking—consciously controlling and directing their own thinking. This means that individuals must think about *how* they are thinking while they think. For example, when you are considering a problem and you say to yourself something like, "I really ought to consider some alternative solutions," you are monitoring

Helping students become conscious of what thinking involves

or exercising control over how you are thinking. Doing this—thinking about how one is thinking—is called *metacognition.*

Most authorities (Beyer, 1987; Bonny, 1984; Costa, 1984) agree that metacognition develops slowly, apparently paralleling students' ability to think abstractly. Although Beyer suggests that "it is doubtful that most older students will engage in metacognition by the time they leave school" (p. 195), there are still things teachers can do to foster readiness for metacognition. These include maintaining a learning environment where thinking (as opposed to memorization and rote learning) is encouraged and valued. Also important is directing explicit attention to the components of thinking and problem solving as you model and use them with children. For example, asking "Does it look like we are getting anywhere?" or saying "Let's think about some other possibilities" can stimulate students' awareness of metacognitive behavior.

Other activities to stimulate readiness for metacognition, cited by Beyer (1985, pp. 196–197), include the following:

Activities to stimulate metacognition

1. *Conscious choosing.* Whenever students have an opportunity to make a choice—determining what to do next in class or what to do for recess, and so on—have them identify at least two options and then identify some possible consequences of each option. By reflecting aloud on the consequences, students can articulate criteria for making the choice and extend their thinking beyond the here and now to the anticipation of future events or ideas.

2. *Categorizing with multiple criteria.* Whenever students have an opportunity to discuss their actions or choices, have them make at least two categories, such as useful/not useful or like/not like or fun/not fun, and so on. Like the preceding activity, this activity extends student thinking and requires thinking about another thinking act.

Paraphrasing

3. *Paraphrasing what is heard.* Have students restate, put in their own words, or elaborate one another's plans and actions as they engage in them or observe their peers engaging in them. This may take the form of having students state goals, suggest ways to accomplish them, and try to outline exactly what would have to be done to carry out their "plan." They can also restate or paraphrase directions, or rate and discuss their own understanding of something. [Author's note: This activity and those that follow can be done orally, but they are also excellent topics for students to include in their journals.]

4. *Reflecting on how an answer was derived.* Have the students, on occasion, stop in the middle of a thinking task to discuss whether they are doing it correctly, exactly where they are in the process, whether they skipped anything and/or what to do next (and why) once they resume the process. Students can also predict the results of a thinking task and, when finished with it, reflect on and discuss the extent to which their prediction was accurate, whether or not anything occurred to alter it, and so on.

"I think" activities

5. *Engaging in "I think" activities.* After or before engaging in a thinking task, students can write a short paragraph describing how they were thinking about it. At first, such writing may be a disjointed stream of consciousness, but students can focus eventually on reporting how and why they did or planned to do a task in a specific way.

6. *Making plans.* Students can plan classroom activities and assignments in terms of goals, sequence of activities, and anticipated obstacles; list the plan on the

board; and refer to it as they execute it. Upon concluding the activity or assignment, they can evaluate their plan as well as the success of their activity.

To Beyer's list we are inclined to add a seventh element: "Limitation: Despite everything that we think we know, we also recognize that there are things we need to know more about, and that we might also be wrong somewhere along the way."

Modeling attitudes of reflective thinking

Modeling the desired behaviors is the key to teaching readiness for metacognition or any critical thinking skill. Among those behaviors are the beliefs and attitudes that help to create the environment within which any kind of thinking takes place. For example, teachers who try to provide positive reinforcement by always responding to correct answers with an immediate "That's right! Great answer!" may unwittingly be creating an environment that actually undermines reflective thinking. A simple "Thank you, let's think about that" could still provide the desired reinforcement, but without the negative side effect. The point is that attitudes and dispositions such as the willingness to suspend judgment, to consider alternative solutions or points of view, and to revise one's opinions in light of new evidence are as essential to teaching rational thinking and decision making as are the thinking skills themselves.

Teaching Reflective Thinking

When confronted with a genuine problem, most of us follow some variation of the inquiry/problem-solving process described in Chapter 10. Briefly, we identify and clarify the problem, identify and gather the necessary data, identify possible solutions (hypotheses), evaluate the alternative solutions to decide which one best fits the situation, and then act appropriately. During that process, we may employ one or more of the following skills:

Information-processing skills

1. describing
2. estimating
3. classifying/categorizing
4. evaluating (judging)
5. interpreting
6. inferring
7. deducing
8. hypothesizing (predicting)
9. analyzing
10. experimenting
11. planning and designing
12. generalizing

The preceding list of thinking skills may seem imposing, but all of them can be taught in some form to elementary and middle-school children. It is not unusual to find children who lack the vocabulary or prior experiences to handle complex forms of analysis, synthesis, or evaluation, yet most children can indicate, for example, if something in a story "fits" or if "something seems wrong."

Using language that fits children

The key often lies in how you present the task to them, and more specifically, in the language you use.

Skills that involve measuring, observing, and describing seldom pose unusual problems for students, but you will probably need to translate other skills into simpler language. Your exact translation will depend on the kind of data or experiences you're using, of course, but some examples are illustrated in Table 12.1.

TABLE 12.1 Translating Tasks into Children's Language

Task	Adult's Language	Child's Language
Classifying	Classify these into two categories.	Let's see if some of these go together.
	Can you classify these in different ways?	Can we group these together in different ways?
Hypothesizing and inferring	Develop two hypotheses that might explain this.	How can we explain this? Let's look for some other reasons why this happens.
	Given data, develop three hypotheses.	What is _____ really like?
Analyzing	Given two sources of data, identify possible contradictions.	Let's see if we can find anything "wrong" or unusual (about these data).
		Is there anything here that doesn't seem to "fit" right?
	Identify relevant or irrelevant information.	Is there information here that we don't need?
		Which information is most helpful?
Inductive reasoning	Given two or more data sources, develop an inductive generalization.	Let's find an idea that "fits" all these examples.
Deductive reasoning	Given an idea, can you test its validity?	Given this idea, let's think of other examples that it applies to, or examples where it does not apply.
Evaluating	Identify criteria to support your judgment.	Let's figure out why we think one criterion is better than another.

● COMMENTARY   **What We Know About Thinking**

Some of the research on thinking suggests the following:

* Students' performance in classrooms is often more dependent on the strategies they use to get and use information than on IQ.

* Novice thinkers often try to memorize and recall isolated bits of information, whereas more proficient thinkers tend to look for larger patterns and relationships within the information.

* Learning thinking skills often involves repetition and practice as well as reworking, organizing, and elaborating on the information.

* Thinking involves intuitive, inductive, inferential, and sometimes even illogical components.

* A key element of thinking involves learning how to apply and use what is known.

The balance of this section is organized to reflect the holistic ways in which we use thinking skills—that is, in relation to the inquiry (problem-solving) process. For example, before students "do" anything with information, they must sense the existence of a problem; they must have something to inquire about. Thus we first examine how teachers can help students identify problems. Following this are techniques for helping students identify hypotheses and make inferences, for helping students gather information and then do something with it, and, finally, for helping students to generalize beyond their immediate experience.

● Identifying Problems

Fact: When the story of Hansel and Gretel is told in some parts of Africa, the witch's house is made of salt, not candy.

When American children hear about how the tale of Hansel and Gretel is told in Africa, they may sense that somebody has been messing around with a story they know well. For some children at least, the change in the witch's house from candy to salt can be a *discrepant event* that leads to cognitive dissonance—that is, something that doesn't "fit" the world as they've come to know it.

Sensing that a problem exists is the first stage of problem solving. If children choose not to pursue the matter, the process can end there—with an awareness of a possible problem. The turning point comes when a child is sufficiently concerned to say something such as "I wonder why they changed the story of Hansel and Gretel." At that point, the child's awareness of a possible problem is converted into a *real* problem for which they want an answer.

If you are sufficiently interested in why some people in Africa use a different version of "Hansel and Gretel," you've probably moved to the next step of problem solving: speculating (hypothesizing) on possible reasons for an action. Lest we get ahead of ourselves here, consider that among some groups in Africa, wealth is measured by the number of cattle or wives or the amount of salt one has (or some combination thereof).

To reach the hypothesizing stage, you may need to provide activities in which you intentionally create cognitive dissonance among your students, thus providing them with motives for further inquiry. Unfortunately, it is often difficult to translate traditional social studies content into problems that really engage students. Traditional requests such as "Identify the capitals of the Middle Atlantic states" or "Trace the sequence of Roman emperors" are usually teachers' problems that may or may not become the students' problems.

Even within a fixed curriculum, teachers can use some techniques to enhance their students' involvement and create the feeling that they are dealing with *their* problems. These techniques include (1) creating mystery-type situations, where students must work with unknown elements, (2) providing only limited information at the outset of an activity, from which students try to "fill in the holes," and (3) using speculative-heuristic questions, such as "What if you were the fire chief?" or "What if you were a member of the Indian Parliament and were facing a request to . . . ?"

Creating mystery-type situations that evoke a sense of "problem" often involves limiting the amount of information available to students *at the beginning of an ac-*

This limitation on information holds for all statistical data, regardless of what kind of situation you are trying to establish. Most children can deal with only limited amounts of statistical data at one time—seven to ten pieces or less—whereas a page or even a half-page filled with statistics can easily overwhelm them (and most adults). The limitation on information is intended to prevent information overload at the outset of a lesson, but once an activity is under way, students should obviously have access to as much information as they want or need.

Limiting the information available

The following Model Student Activity (see page 316) is based on a teaching device called a *fact sheet.* A fact sheet is a sheet you provide to students that contains a few selected but uninterpreted facts. To enhance the children's interests, we've elected to add some mystery elements by concealing the name of the real country and identifying it only as "Nation X." Providing the name of Nation X, which we eventually will of course, would eliminate all traces of mystery from the problem, and students would simply rely on their prior knowledge about it. In this activity, students must use the uninterpreted facts to make inferences that describe Nation X. A minor problem here is keeping students' attention focused on *describing* Nation X, because they will want to guess which real nation Nation X is. Permitting students to make activities like this one into guessing games will restrict their usefulness.

Fact sheets

Data Suitable for Fact Sheets. Not all "facts" are suitable for fact sheets. On one occasion, for example, some teachers modified the "Nation X" format to apply to states. Their "State X" fact sheets included data such as the state bird, the state tree, the state motto (in Latin), a picture of the state flag, the date of the state's admission to the Union, and sometimes the state insect. This kind of information was so unique and so tied to the individual states that little could be said about it. To be told that the state bird of X is the cardinal or that the state tree is the buckeye tells you that the state has birds and trees, but then all states have birds and trees. The point is that the data on a fact sheet should permit comparisons but should not reflect unique, one-of-a-kind information.

Must use generalizable data

Fact sheets are devices for presenting information that the children then use, and we emphasize *use*—in this case to make inferences about Nation X. The purpose of the fact sheet is *not* to present factual information for children to memorize. Expecting students to understand that India has health care problems is one thing, but expecting them to remember that India has one doctor or nurse for every two thousand people violates the appropriateness criterion noted earlier.

Must focus on using data

Don't let your prior experiences with statistical information stand in the way of trying the fact sheet approach. Students often respond very positively to fact sheets. This is not a sales pitch for fact sheets; just consider not ruling them out until you've tried them.

You will be pleasantly surprised

● Culture Cards

The thought of cutting the pictures from a *National Geographic* is more than some people can bear. As a result, many teachers leave one of their most potent instructional resources sitting on the classroom shelf. Since almost every school library has a complete set of *National Geographic* that can be used for reference purposes, there's little reason not to use your copies for teaching purposes.

Nation X—Using a Fact Sheet

Overview

Using the following data, students are asked to describe Nation X. Like most inferences, these may be modified with additional information. How this activity ends depends on how far you wish to take it. We would follow up with culture cards (see following chapter text) that permit students to validate their inferences and provide additional information.

Procedure

1. Establishing set: "Today we are going to use just a few facts to describe a real nation. Some of our descriptions may be correct and some may be wrong; we'll know that after we get more information. So, let's see what we can tell about Nation X."

2. Display Fact Sheet 1 and pose the following task: "Using just this information, let's describe what Nation X is like. What can we tell about the people who live there?"

Fact Sheet 1

	U.S.A.	Nation X
Doctors and nurses (per 2,000 people)	15	1
Literacy (people over 15)		
Males (per 100 people)	92	55
Females (per 100 people)	92	28
Radios per 1,000 inhabitants	750	2
People living in cities (per 100 people)	66	18
Rooms in each dwelling (average number)	5	2

3. List inferences (in terms of key descriptors) on the board or overhead, or have small groups list their inferences on chart paper.

4. Summarize inferences, pointing out those that may be contradictory. For example, the data on doctors could suggest either that Nation X has poor health conditions or that Nation X needs only a few doctors.

5. You may wish to raise some questions such as, How is literacy defined? How big must a city be to be considered a city? Is it fair to say that Nation X is poor?

6. Present the class with the information in Fact Sheet 2 (on an overhead projector).

Fact Sheet 2

Life Expectancy for Males (in years)

USA 72
X 57

Consider whether this information confirms any hypotheses about health care or the way of life in Nation X.

7. After assessing whether the inferences follow from the data, ask students what other information they think they might want. (Be prepared for a long list.)

8. Present the following information (on an overhead transparency).

Fact Sheet 3

Nation	Population	Percentage of World Population
China	1,175 million	21
Nation X	931 million	15
United States	260 million	7
Russia	148 million	6
Japan	131 million	3

Some students will use the information from Fact Sheet 3 to guess the identity of Nation X. Or they can check population figures in the atlases found at the back of most social studies texts. In any event, trying to maintain the mystery much longer could prove frustrating, so you can tell the class that Nation X is India. (Knowing that, you can now assess your *own* inferences.)

9. At this point you have the option of pursuing the India study in one of several ways. You might wish to do two things simultaneously: (a) have students use their inferences as research questions to be answered, using whatever resources or references they can garner, and (b) pursue an inference that children often make about Nation X, namely, that it is poor. If they don't infer this, you can always build a case for it. Among reasons that will be suggested for India's poverty are its health and population problems.

10. You can pursue the poverty issue by raising questions such as: If most of the people in a country are poor, what does being poor mean? Is being poor an average condition? If so, would the average Indian be likely to define himself or herself as poor? The following information can then be presented to the class (again, using an overhead transparency may be easiest).

Fact Sheet 4

In many rural villages in India, the poorest families are those in which there are no children.

What does this statement suggest about the Indian value structure?

11. Closure: Using the original list of inferences, determine those about which students are fairly confident and those for which they need more information.

12. Follow up in future lessons with textbook-based passages or culture cards.

Source: Adapted from John T. Mallan and Richard Hersh. *NO G.O.D.s in the Classroom: Inquiry and Elementary Social Studies.* Philadelphia: W. B. Saunders, 1972.

- - -

What you are after in magazines such as *National Geographic* and *Smithsonian* are their spectacular photographs. If you have access to the necessary technology, equally good photographs can be downloaded from the Internet. Whatever source you use, uncaptioned photographs can provide the basis for remarkably involving information-processing activities.

Captionless photos present uninterpreted data

Captionless photographs can be used with students of any age or grade level, early childhood through graduate school (and not just with students who have reading problems). You could create an alternate activity by mounting the captions on a separate "caption card" and having students match the captions with the appropriate photos.

When pictures or photographs of a particular culture are clustered together, you have what we call *culture cards.* If you organize the photographs on some other basis, such as similar occupations or similar types of homes, you could just as well call them *picture cards.*

Techniques for Using Picture and Culture Cards

Possible activities

1. Prior to studying a culture or area, provide the class with a set of uncaptioned pictures of the people (Inuit, the Japanese, etc.) or the region (the Ukraine, Switzerland, etc.). Using just the pictures, ask students to describe the people or region as best they can. The object is not to guess who the people are or what the region is. You can reduce students' tendency to do that by simply telling the class, "Here are some pictures of "X" that we want to describe as best we can. How do the people live? What kind of area do they live in?"

Some descriptions (and inferences) that the students provide will be inaccurate because they are working with limited information. Inaccurate descriptions will be corrected as the students move into other materials—the texts, videos, and databases—that describe the culture or region. The students' inferences and descriptions should be treated as hypotheses to be tested as they obtain additional information.

Classifying pictures

2. After studying a culture, provide students with a set of uncaptioned cards intermingling photographs from two or three cultures. The students' task is to separate the pictures of the culture just studied from pictures of other cultures.

3. Provide students with a set of randomly assorted culture cards, and ask them to group the cards according to (a) criteria that you supply (family activities, seasons, etc.) or to (b) criteria of their choosing. This type of classifying activity is an integral part of concept building.

4. As a small-group activity, students can write their own captions for the pictures. They can then compare their captions with the original captions (which are mounted on a separate "caption card").

● Determining Researchable Problems

During most social studies activities, students will generate some questions that no amount of research can ever answer. In the previous Model Student Activity, for example, an inference that India is poor because the people are lazy will un-

T E C H N O L O G Y   U P D A T E

Pictures Are Worth a Thousand Words

Somewhere among the Library of Congress's (LOC) 13.6 million images (photographs, pamphlets, paintings, etc.) you can surely find something that would be useful for whatever topic your students are studying. If the prospect of searching through several million images seems a little daunting, be advised that the LOC has a keyword search index that will narrow your choices considerably. Moreover, only a few thousand of the LOC's images are available for downloading on line at:

http://lcweb.loc.gov/coll/print/guide/

Many printers can make passable copies of downloaded images, but if you would rather have photo-quality prints, these are available at reasonable cost from the Library's Photo Reproduction Division.

The Library of Congress is only one source of downloadable images. If your topic is more subject-specific, check out one or more of the following:

The Louvre, at:
http://www.paris.org/Musees/Louvre/

The National Museum of the American Indian, at:
http://www.si.edu/nmai/

The Gallary of the Open Frontier, at:
http://www.unl.edu/UP/gof/home.html

The U.S. Holocaust Museum, at:
http://www.ushmm.org/

The Museum of Fine Arts, at:
http://www.mfa.org/

The Library of Congress's American Memory Page, at:
http://lcweb2.loc.gov/ammem/ammemhome. html

If you are still unable to find what you are looking for, visit the Smithsonian Institution at:
http://www.si.edu/

doubtedly lead to frustration and discontent should your students attempt to research it. It's simply not a researchable question as long as *poor* and *lazy* are left undefined. The teaching implication in such cases should be evident: you will need to help children examine the researchability of possible problems. To do otherwise could send them on a wild-goose chase.

Help students determine a problem's researchability

Some of the following statements and problems are based on Model Student Activities considered thus far. Others are not. Decide which of the following statements, as presented here, lend themselves to further student research or study:

Test yourself

Yes/No   *Problems/Statements*

_____ 1. Identify the constitutional requirements for the office of president of the United States.

_____ 2. Bill Clinton and Franklin D. Roosevelt were two of the best presidents the United States ever had.

_____ 3. The Dutch are an industrious and friendly people.

_____ 4. The introduction of new technology into a culture is likely to lead to other changes.

_____ 5. American farmers today produce more food on larger, more specialized farms than did farmers ten or twenty years ago.

_____ 6. Yuppies are more patriotic than retired people.

_____ 7. Most students in *this* class like Italian food.

Vague terminology poses problems

Remember Ms. Fleury's class from the "Wearin' of the Green" activity, where the students discovered they had to decide how much green clothing someone had to wear to be considered "wearing green"? Somewhat the same problem influences the researchability of the problems listed here. Researchable problems (hypotheses, inferences, and questions) cannot use vague terms, yet they must be specific enough that one need not spend a lifetime in the quest. As such, Statements 1, 4, 5, and 7 are researchable, but Statements 2, 3, and 6 need to be specified more precisely before students can deal with them. For Statement 3, for example, it might be possible to define *industrious* and *friendly*, but how do you define *the Dutch*? Are the Dutch only those people who live in the Netherlands? Or do they include all people of Dutch descent?

● Hypothesizing and Inferring

Based on the "Help Wanted" cartoon shown in Figure 12.1, which of the following might you reasonably infer?

Yes/No

_____ 1. Business seems to be good.

_____ 2. The cartoon depicts a scene in the United States.

_____ 3. The employer has a bias against women.

_____ 4. Women are not good workers.

_____ 5. The sign reflects a basic societal belief that a woman's place is in the home.

_____ 6. The cartoon depicts a scene that might take place today.

It's reasonable to infer that business is good; otherwise there would not be a "Help Wanted" sign. On the other hand, perhaps working conditions in the plant

FIGURE 12.1 **Cartoon for Inferencing**

are so bad that employees quit after only a few days. If that were true, the management would continually need additional help just to maintain normal operations. But then perhaps all of the current employees are now women, and they want males so as to satisfy a quota. All of these are plausible inferences.

From inferences to hypotheses

If you have no intention of testing which of these inferences is valid, your inference would remain just that—a plausible inference. But when you set out to test whether business is good, at least as depicted in the cartoon, your inference then functions as a hypothesis. That is, your inference is a testable proposition: the reason the plant displays a "Help Wanted" sign is that business is good and the company therefore needs additional employees. To test your hypothesis, you clearly would need more data about the events depicted in the cartoon.

Formal hypotheses testing is public

All of us make inferences as we attempt to explain and understand events around us. Because we infer and hypothesize anyway, why then should there be such concern for formal hypothesis testing? The answer is that what we do in informal situations has application in many more formal situations and with many kinds of data sources. In informal situations we might be satisfied using impressionistic data—a hunch, a whim, or a feeling—but formal hypothesis testing requires that all elements of the process be *public*. In other words, in face-to-face relations, we can use whatever information we wish, but in more formal data-validating situations, we are expected to follow the rules of science—hence our distinction between inferences and hypotheses.

Knowns and Unknowns.   When something is known, there's not much left to hypothesize about. A statement such as "Milk comes from cows," for example, isn't likely to lead to any speculation. But if you ask, "Where does milk come from?" you can get some interesting hypotheses:

* From trucks
* From dairies
* From the supermarket

The accuracy of these responses is clearly testable, but you must also assess whether students will gain enough from testing them to make the effort worthwhile. We can test the accuracy of knowns, but we must hypothesize about things that are unknown or that can be explained only in part.

Using physical objects for hypothesizing

Physical objects can often serve as excellent vehicles for hypothesizing activities, especially when the object and its uses are unknown to students. A colonial bootjack—a forked board used to help remove one's boots—or even a butter churn can lead to creative hypothesizing activities.

Coins, stamps, buttons—almost any physical object—can provide the basis for hypothesizing and inferring activities. For coins, for example, the student's task can be stated as follows: "Given a half-dollar, a quarter, a dime, a nickel, and a penny, what do you know about the people who made them, the world they live in, and what things they seem to value?"

"Buildings seem to be important, as well as eagles."
"Except for one, all the coins have a man on them."
"They have a letter and number system."
"They have a god in whom they trust."
"They have a language we don't understand, *E Pluribus Unum*."

Dealing with unknowns

In summary, hypothesizing and inferring activities require something that is unknown to students, because otherwise there may be nothing for children to explain. To help children hypothesize and infer, teachers can provide them with unexplained events—unknowns that, through inferring, hypothesizing, and hypothesis testing, can become knowns.

● Gathering and Interpreting Data

Before anyone bothers to gather and process data, it's only common sense to have previously identified a purpose for that information. Gathering data is something we do in response to a problem, although in school settings the problems are often imposed on us.

Because students and teachers may perceive data gathering differently, teachers need to ask themselves two questions: What's my motive (as a teacher) for having students study this? and What are my students' motives for dealing with this information? Motivation, then, is a process of identifying the best possible match between your motives as a teacher and the motives of your students.

Conditions for data gathering

Successful data gathering depends on three interacting elements: (1) a precisely stated problem, (2) an awareness of the specific information needed, and (3) the ability to deal with data that are presented in different forms (narratives, charts, graphs, etc.). Among the most important of these is stating the problem precisely. This was driven home to me on one occasion when I made my sixth-grade students "ambassadors" and asked each of them to do a written report on a foreign nation. At the time, I failed to consider that a precisely stated problem provides the criteria for determining what information should be included—*and excluded*. Without those criteria, students put anything even remotely related to the country into their reports. The student who "did" Scotland, for example, brought her report to class in a huge carton. Reading the reports was a nightmare and, like it or not, grading was based on a subjective mixture of quality and weight. My students were proud of the huge stacks of information they had gathered, most of which I suspect they never read. The next year I spent considerable time narrowing the topics down to a more manageable size.

Criteria for inclusion
and exclusion

Teachers sometimes equate data gathering with "library research," as we did, and thus neglect data that can grow out of students' experiences. Even primary children can get involved in data-gathering procedures. Conducting surveys to determine children's favorite TV shows or the time at which most students go to bed, for example, are possible topics for data collection.

Using children's experiences

Using Data from Primary and Secondary Sources.   Some kinds of information (or data) better lend themselves to information processing than do other forms of data. You may recall the earlier comments about information such as the state tree, state flower, and so on. When your purpose is to help children process information, your main focus should be on providing them with unprocessed information—raw data—that they can work with. As a rule that information should be presented in uninterpreted form so that students can do the interpreting.

Raw data is uninterpreted

Social studies programs that emphasize helping students work with information from primary sources often lean heavily on uninterpreted information, some of which (as for surveys) the students may gather firsthand. Note that *primary* in this sense refers to firsthand accounts, whereas *secondary* accounts relate to already interpreted information.

As a kind of self-check, decide which of the following sources are most likely to provide primary (firsthand) accounts (use a P) and which are most likely to contain secondary (previously interpreted) accounts (use an S). Use ? if you are not sure.

Data sources

_____ Aerial photographs	_____ Lectures
_____ Advertisements	_____ Letters (personal)
_____ Artifacts	_____ Magazine articles
_____ Atlases	_____ Maps
_____ Census reports	_____ Paintings
_____ Diaries	_____ Documentary photographs
_____ Directories	_____ Reports
_____ Documents	_____ Survey reports
_____ Encyclopedias	_____ Textbooks
_____ Interviews	_____ Journal articles

The secondary sources on this list include encyclopedias, lectures, magazine articles (and *some* journal articles), reports, and textbooks. Some sources, such as advertisements, may be questionable, especially since the way data are used in advertisements is often questionable. Interviews might also be questionable, because interviewees sometimes give the answer they think the interviewer is anticipating. Maps could also fall into the questionable category, because someone had to transform (i.e., process) data into map form. However, for all practical purposes, it is safe to regard most maps (and the balance of the items on this list) as primary sources. You can turn to them as some of your best resources for process-based activities.

Using Data Banks.   The problem of keeping track of skills-based teaching materials need not become overwhelming, especially if you either have access to a computer or are willing to develop a data bank. A data bank can take a variety of forms. Some teachers store the information on their personal computers, whereas others prefer 5- by 8-inch index cards, like the one illustrated in Figure 12.2. The data bank should include two elements: (1) sets of data for students to work with, which may include extrapolated raw data, charts, graphs, tables, figures, maps, and, if necessary, hypothetical data; and (2) notations regarding different ways in which students can use the data.

Potential data-based activities

When potential teaching materials are organized in data-bank form, the following things should become apparent:

* You need not use all the data at one time. Rather, you can select the kind and amount of data to be included in an activity.
* When you provide the data for students to work with, students tend to spend less time on data gathering and significantly more time on developing reflective thinking skills.

FIGURE 12.2   Sample Data-Bank Card (5 × 8 Format)

Skill: Generalizing from data

Data	Possible Activities
Boston is on the Charles River.	1. Check accuracy of each statement.
Moscow is on the Volga River.	2. Identify two variables at work in each statement.
London is on the Thames River.	3. Make a general statement, about both variables, that would include all statements given.
Cincinnati is on the Ohio River.	4. Identify/locate three other cities that would fit under the broad general statement.
Paris is on the Seine River.	5. Identify one "major" city that appears to be an exception.
	6. Formulate three possible explanations for the exception in number 5.

Generalizing

One of the more challenging aspects of teaching is helping students identify patterns or relationships among otherwise unconnected events or pieces of data. That challenge, expressed in a word, is *generalizing*.

Looking for patterns in the data

The process of making generalizations requires that students move into the realm of abstraction. Yet many students and even some adults may get so wrapped up in the specific details or the content of situations that they tend to consider those details separately. We are not talking about the need to generalize here, for that clearly exists. The concern is with some people's unwillingness to move into the realm of abstraction, which is something that adults are sometimes reluctant to do.

Working with classes of behavior

Generalizing reduces the disorder and confusion of otherwise isolated bits of experience. That reduction is achieved by organizing data or experiences into classes and categories. Generalizing, then, involves making statements about classes or categories of objects or events. Examples of how you can help children do this are provided in the next section.

Strategies for Teaching Critical Thinking Skills

Teaching strategies for helping children think reflectively typically involve (1) the teacher modeling the desired behaviors, or (2) posing a sequence of questions to the whole class or to cooperative learning groups, or a combination of the two, which is (3) followed by a period of reflection on the activity itself—on what worked and what didn't. After providing children with data to interpret, the basic teaching strategy follows a three-element pattern based on What?, Why?, and What does it mean?

Question 1: What?

To call the What-Why-What does it mean? sequence a questioning pattern could be misleading. Each element (What?, Why?, etc.) could be posed as a question, of course, but consider posing the elements in the sequence as tasks, using them as guides as you model the process. By using the sequence as a general guideline, you can then tailor specific questions that correspond to the data you are using. As an example, consider the information on the sample data-bank card shown in Figure 12.2. The "What?" task is intended to elicit what students notice about the data, including things that are common or anything unusual. However, if your students lack the prior knowledge to identify Boston, Moscow, London, etc. (as shown on the data card) as large cities, you will need to point this out to them. Young students often have problems distinguishing between the names of cities, states, and countries—they think that London and Paris are countries—so some brief detours may be needed here. Before students can look for patterns among data, they need to understand the data they are dealing with.

Question 2: Why?

Once your students understand that many cities are located along large rivers, you can then move to Phase 2: "Why do you suppose this happened?" The purpose of the "Why?" phase of the sequence is to elicit explanations or inferences that might explain the phenomenon. Accept all reasonable hypotheses. Every community needs a reliable water supply, of course, but large rivers also offer avenues for trade and commerce. Still, the availability of water alone may not explain why some communities are smaller than those on the data card.

After children have explored possible inferences and explanations (about the relationship between cities and rivers), you can move to Phase 3, "What does this mean?" Students often want to generalize hastily and make statements such as "All big cities are located near large rivers because they [the rivers] offer reliable water supplies and opportunities for trading." Accurate as their generalization might seem, they are not finished yet. This is where the issue of probability mentioned in Chapter 2 enters the picture. This is also where they will certainly need more data about large cities. Consider that at least two of the ten largest cities in the United States—Atlanta, Georgia, and San Antonio, Texas—are not located on large rivers. The San Antonio River, for example, averages only 2 to 3 feet deep, and certainly cannot support large river craft.

The points here are several. First, to help children identify patterns among data that will then permit them to develop generalizations, they should deal with a very limited amount of information at first, such as the five statements on our sample data-bank card. At the same time, the tradeoff comes with helping children to understand that they cannot make generalizations based on limited information alone. Teachers need to be ready to provide additional data that may or may not be consistent with the original information and that students can then use to confirm the accuracy of the general statements they make. Taking exceptions into account is part of that process, and students need to understand that failing to accommodate exceptions can cast the shadow of doubt on their overgeneralizations. It is true, for example, that many major cities are located along large rivers, but saying that "all major cities are located along major rivers" is not

true. To take the exceptions into account, students need to alter their original generalization by using "many" or "most" instead of "all." Closure for this activity can come when the teacher says, "Are we accurate if we say that 'many major cities grew up along large rivers because of the reliable water supplies and opportunities for trade and commerce that the rivers offered'?" In the next section some of the other purposes that questions can serve are examined.

● COMMENTARY   *On Avoiding "Queen Bee" Questions*

From time to time, all of us have encountered teachers who ask questions such as "Who can tell me the capital of Alabama?" or "Who can tell me what a body of land surrounded by water is called?" The problem with questions like these is their phrasing; that is, both begin with "Who can tell me . . . ?" These can be referred to as "Queen Bee" questions, because they implicitly suggest that whoever answers them will impress the teacher by doing so. Both

"Who can tell me the capital of Alabama?" and "What is the capital of Alabama?" lead to the same answer: Birmingham. However, "Queen Bee" questioning tends to make impressing "me," the teacher, the focal point of the activity. The "Who can tell me?" question format may seem innocuous enough, but using it repeatedly could send powerful messages about the kind of classroom environment you are trying to maintain.

Everybody knows that questions are a teacher's stock in trade. Theoretically, a teacher's questions are supposed to lead to something, but this mission sometimes goes astray. For example, some teachers ask a question like "Has anyone ever been to Disneyland?," which they hope will motivate students and pique their interest. But if you are leading into an activity that you are going to do regardless of how your students respond, such questions could be irrelevant. Whether such questions actually engage young students is questionable, and unless students' responses (about Disneyland) are relevant to the lesson that follows, you should consider moving into the activity immediately by saying something such as "Now, we're going to do an activity that . . ."

Is the question really relevant?

For Every Question There Is a Purpose

For every question teachers ask, there is (or should be) an underlying purpose, something the teacher is trying to get at. In many respects, deciding what questions to ask, deciding how to ask them, and deciding what answers you anticipate is part of every teaching strategy. The reverse of this statement is equally true—for every purpose there is a question. To illustrate this, let's use the information presented on the data card shown in Figure 12.2, which we used previously.

If students are not aware that the names listed on the data card (London, Boston, Moscow, etc.) are major cities, the activity could become an exercise in futility. To determine whether students already have this or any other prior knowledge in their possession, you could ask a *memory-recall* question, such as "What major city is located along the Thames River?" The main purpose of memory-recall questions is to determine if students can recall specific, factual information.

Memory-recall questions

If your purpose is to determine whether students can identify patterns among data, you might ask students a *descriptive-interpretive* question. This category of questions asks students to describe, interpret, or otherwise explain what the cities listed on the data card have in common. Asking this question was part of the "Why?" phase of the sequence described earlier. In this instance, students' description or interpretation must be in their own words, not a memorized rehash of someone else's description (otherwise it becomes a memory-recall question).

Descriptive-interpretive questions

Once students have concluded that the large cities shown on the data card are located along major rivers, you could follow up by asking them to speculate on why this is the case. Was it simply the availability of water, or did other elements play a role? Although you might be asking another "Why?" question, in this instance it would be an *application-synthesis* question that requires students to identify possible relationships and draw conclusions, bringing in other information as needed. Application-synthesis questions require that students put things together (synthesize) so as to identify relationships or generalizations that go beyond specific events. Note, however, that unless application-synthesis questions are preceded by several lower-level questions, they may seem to come from nowhere.

Application-synthesis questions

If you are interested in determining whether students have internalized the data-card lesson, you might ask an *evaluative-judgmental* question such as "How would you advise colonists as to the best places to locate their settlements?"

Evaluative-judgmental questions

Evaluative-judgmental questions always contain a "good-bad" or "better-best" element, which is what makes them judgmental. These questions require students to produce an evaluation or render a judgment. A distinguishing characteristic of evaluative-judgmental questions is that students must identify the *criteria* they will use in reaching their evaluation. Thus, an evaluative-judgmental question might be phrased more accurately as follows: "What criteria would you use to decide whether colonists had established their settlements to ensure possible growth?" Although this might seem a long-winded way to pose a question, the intent is to emphasize the need to specify clearly and in advance the criteria by which something is being judged. In the absence of such criteria, students' responses will be purely personal opinion.

Other potential questions could ask your students to speculate in a hypothetical mode. Examples of such *speculative-heuristic* questions based on our data card include "What might have happened if Boston (London, Paris, etc.) were located 100 miles upstream from its present locations?" The "what-if" form illustrated in this example is characteristic of speculative-heuristic questions. Speculative-heuristic questions are excellent for generating inquiry, promoting divergent thinking, and getting students to speculate on and analyze alternative courses of action, but be cautious here; asking three "what-if" questions in a row may be enough to confuse even your most sophisticated students.

The various types of questions are summarized in Table 12.2.

Speculative-heuristic questions

TABLE 12.2 Types of Questions by Category and Purpose

Type of Question	Purpose
Memory-recall	To determine whether students can recall previously learned information
Descriptive-interpretive	To describe, interpret, and/or explain events or actions in the student's own words, including reasons (nonspeculative) for why individuals acted as they did
Application-synthesis	To identify relationships and to form and draw reasonable conclusions that go beyond the particular action or event
Evaluative-judgmental	To render an evaluation or judgment as to actions or events in light of explicit, previously identified criteria
Speculative-heuristic	To encourage divergent thinking and to speculate on and analyze alternative courses of action

Student involvement can be enhanced if teachers increase their "wait time."
(© Susie Fitzhugh)

Wait Time

"Whenever we have a discussion, the same kids participate all of the time and the rest of the class just sits there. Sometimes the students who talk don't have much to say, and it is all very superficial. I don't know. I'm about ready to give up on discussions."

Frustrated teachers have been echoing complaints like this for years, yet they often overlook a potential solution to their problem. The solution takes no special skills and has achieved dramatic results where it's been employed. It is: Doing nothing. Well, almost nothing.

In some now-classic research, Mary Bodd Rowe (1969) examined the relationship between a teacher's wait time and the quality of classroom discussions. Wait time refers to the period of silence between the end of a teacher's question and the teacher's next statement or question. Rowe found that many teachers apparently have difficulty tolerating silence during a discussion; their average wait time was only nine-tenths of a second. No wonder students didn't participate! They didn't have time to think before the teacher went on with another comment or question.

After Rowe informed teachers how short their wait time was, they decided to double it—at least to two seconds. Awkwardly at first, the teachers waited the allotted two seconds, even though it sometimes seemed like an eternity. The results? The number of students participating in class discussions improved dramatically, as did the quality of their contributions. When teachers also lengthened the period of silence between a student's response and the teacher's next com-

Avoid responding too quickly

What two seconds of silence can yield

ment or question—what Rowe called "Wait Time II"—the results were even more impressive. Even more students responded, including some who almost never participated, and the quality of discussions also improved.

The implication is clear: if your discussions don't go well and the same students participate all the time, try lengthening your wait time. If you do that and your discussions still don't go well, you may need to reexamine the kinds of questions you are asking.

Decision-Making

Choosing among alternatives

Decision-making is the process of making reasoned choices from among alternatives. In social studies, decision-making often has two meanings, one of them broad and the other narrow. In the broad sense, *decision-making* describes a total approach to social studies, one that incorporates all the process skills that we deal with in this book. In its narrower sense, *decision-making* describes instructional activities that ask students to apply decision-making skills. The concern in this section is with decision-making in the narrower, "activities" sense of the term.

The Model Student Activity, "Returning from the Crusades," (see pages 330–331) illustrates a common model for decision-making activities. A heuristic (what if?) question is posed in the introduction, and students are then asked to select among the various choices provided. This is essentially the same format used in the "Who Is Qualified for Presidency?" Activity in Chapter 1, although in this case there are more possible choices. In this and many other decision-making activities, participants must first make decisions individually and then reach consensus in small groups. In addition, and because many decision-making activities do not have previously identified "correct" answers, teachers usually identify the common ground, or the most common choices selected by all the groups.

──● Developing and Using Decision-Making Activities

Applications

Decision-making activities often work well as introductions to areas with which children are unfamiliar, particularly because the activities help to raise questions about what an area is (or was) like. Decision-making problems can be shifted to almost any area or historical period. For example, "If you were Marco Polo . . ." or "If your family was going from Connecticut to California in 1849 . . . what would you bring with you?"

Decision-making activities must be limited to problems that are both real and manageable for students; otherwise they'll have no basis for considering the alternatives. This means that for most elementary students, a question such as "Which had a better organizational basis, the League of Nations or the United Nations?" isn't a manageable problem for a decision-making format. As a rule, decision-making activities for elementary and middle-school students should afford immediate access to the information on which their decisions will be based.

Maintain a clear focus

Decision-making activities can serve as a focus for information-processing skills, but unless teachers continually stress rational information processing, these activities can degenerate into arguments of "My opinion is as good as

MODEL STUDENT ACTIVITY

Returning from the Crusades

Introduction

The year is 1291. You are a knight who has been fighting to win back the Holy Lands—the Middle East—from the Moslems for your king and country, England. After months of fighting, you learn that the battle to win Jerusalem was lost. It has been a long and hard journey, but it is time for crusaders, like yourself, to leave the Moslem lands.

Weary and unhappy because of losing the battle, your thoughts turn toward seeing your family and loved ones once again. However, as you begin your journey back to England, you notice some abandoned Turkish villages that have different things lying about. You lost everything except the clothes on your back, so you decide to pick up some of the things the Turks have abandoned. However, between your backpack and horse you can carry only an additional 50 pounds. Even if you put some things into your pockets (instead of the backpack), your horse may not be able to carry the extra weight.

Below is a list of things you find in the foreign lands. Select the ones you would want to take back to England with you. When you have decided which items to take, rank-order these, with 1 being the most important. But remember, you can carry only 50 pounds.

Group Rank	Your Rank	
____	____	Large pouch of Turkish coins (8 lb.)
____	____	Small barrel of flour (30 lb.)
____	____	Pouch of water—2 gallons (6 lb.)
____	____	Your bow and arrows (4 lb.)
____	____	A small, live Mulberry tree (9 lb.)
____	____	Large, 4-person tent (18 lb.)
____	____	20 yards of silk cloth (8 lb.)
____	____	One iron cooking pot (13 lb.)
____	____	Shovel (4 lb.)
____	____	One jar of silk worms (3 lb.)
____	____	One camel (No weight, can be led)
____	____	Persian rug (24 lb.)

Group Rank	Your Rank	
____	____	Arabian math books (20 lb. for all of them)
____	____	10 Arabian toys (10 lb. @ 1 lb. each)
____	____	Food to last for the journey (33 lb.)
____	____	Small pouches of spices (6 lb.)
____	____	An elegant silk dress (4 lb.)
____	____	Stray puppy (6 lb.)
____	____	10 blown glass goblets (5 lb. @ 1/2 lb. each)
____	____	Fishing pole (4 lb.)
____	____	Small package of apricots (3 lb.)
____	____	Arabian artwork—1 piece (9 lb.)
____	____	Soap, 1 bar (1/2 lb.)
____	____	Other _____
		(Weight will vary)

Source: This activity was designed by and is reprinted by permission of Ms. Dena Hawley.

Procedure

1. *Individual selections:* Students should rank-order their choices of the goods they propose to take back to England.

2. *Group selections:* If you have not already done so, create small groups of about five members each. Ask each group to create a single list of items they will be taking back to England.

3. *Determining the common ground.* Ask each group to list their items on the chalkboard. Ask groups to explain their rationale for selecting the items they did, and then circle the goods that were common to all groups.

4. *Exploring the exceptions.* Explore items that were selected by only one or two groups and ask them why they selected those items.

5. *Realities:* Display (on the overhead) the following list of items that Europeans actually brought from the Middle East. These items included:

Silk cloth and silk worms

Mulberry trees (to feed the silk worms) [Note: a jar of silkworms would die en route without mulberry leaves for food.]

Blown glass objects

Apricot trees

Arabic system of numbering

Assorted spices for preserving food and for seasoning

Camels

Persian rugs

Translations of Latin and Arabic literary works

Middle Eastern styles of clothing

Nice-smelling soap

Analysis

This activity asks students to make decisions similar to those made by people over 700 years ago. At the conclusion of this activity, students should be able to see the influence that Middle Eastern nations, especially Turkey, ultimately had on Medieval European cultures. Students should also be able to consider the extent to which their decision might have "changed history," as well as explain the extent to which interchange with nations in the Middle East led to changes in what is sometimes called "the Dark Ages."

Content utilization revisited

yours." Attention should also be focused on the processes that students use in arriving at their decisions, not just on the decisions themselves.

Decision-making activities require students to *use* information, as do other process-oriented activities such as fact sheets, surveys, and problem situations. Decision-making activities can be incorporated into social studies programs at every grade level on a regular basis and should not be relegated to a trivial role—as something "neat" to do on a Friday afternoon or during a rainy recess. As for all critical thinking and decision-making activities, the focus on *using* information and on rational decision-making should be maintained.

SUMMARY

This chapter has focused on activities that can help you manage skill-oriented instruction. It was noted that reflective thinking skills are part of a family of skills that cannot be held in isolation for very long. Hypothesizing, for example, cannot end there; once students have hypothesized, they must then do something with those hypotheses. Otherwise they—the students and the hypotheses—will be left hanging.

One key to developing information-processing and decision-making activities lies in limiting the amount of information available to students at the outset of the activity to avoid information overload. After students understand the original information, additional data can (and should) be supplied. Paralleling the limitation on

the amount of information, it was also suggested that students are not likely to do much thinking about information that already has been interpreted. Thus a second key factor in creating critical thinking activities involves selecting uninterpreted information with which students can work. Finally, it was suggested that some process-oriented and decision-making activities can be misused or become gimmicky if a focus on information processing is not maintained.

Throughout this chapter, I've suggested that asking questions may actually be a test of your students' prior knowledge. My concern is not for the students who can answer the questions you pose, but for the students who sit silently, praying that you will not call on them. The questions and tasks that teachers pose will often determine the way their students use social studies content. The five types of questions that teachers might ask—memory-recall, descriptive-interpretive, application-synthesis, evaluative-judgmental, and speculative-heuristic—are keyed to the thinking skills a student must employ to answer them.

Teachers who ask higher-level questions—that is, higher in terms of their level on the *Taxonomy of Educa-tional Objectives*—are more likely to demand that their students use content. This doesn't make knowledge-level questions "bad," however, because they can be used to determine if students have essential prior information in their possession. However, the goal in most instances is to help children move beyond the knowledge level.

SUGGESTED ACTIVITIES

1. Design a forced-choice format decision-making activity following the guidelines suggested in this chapter.

2. Following the guidelines suggested in this chapter, develop either a fact sheet that contrasts two states or two countries, or create a set of culture cards.

SUGGESTED READINGS AND RESOURCES

Print Resources

Barry K. Beyer. (1991). *Teaching thinking skills: A handbook for elementary teachers*. Boston: Allyn & Bacon. This handbook provides an excellent overview of thinking skills as well as exemplary lessons to teach those skills. Companion volumes by Beyer include *Practical strategies for the teaching of thinking* (1987) and *Developing a thinking skills program* (1988).

Internet Resources

Introductory Note: Web sites sometimes change their Internet addresses or cease operating entirely. All the addresses supplied here were operating when this book was printed, but if any of them fails to work properly, enter the desired topic or organization in any standard search engine.

The Center for Critical Thinking

http://www.criticalthinking.org/

This site is sponsored by several nonprofit organizations and offers a wealth of resources and materials for teaching critical thinking. Some sample lesson plans show excellent ways to use children's literature to foster critical thinking.

Critical Thinking on the Web

http://www.philosophy.unimelb.edu.au/reason/critical/

This Australian site offers a remarkable array of resources that are arranged into twenty-four categories. These range from on-line tutorials through language and thought, great critical thinkers, textbooks, software, and links for teachers. An excellent starting point.

Case Studies and Problem Solving

http://www.cba.neu.edu/~ewertheim/introd/cases.html

This site offers a six-step approach for using problem-solving strategies on case study materials.

Teaching Thinking Skills

http://www.nwrel.org/scpd/sirs/6/cull.html

This site, which is maintained by the Northwest Regional Educational Laboratory, offers summaries and an extensive bibliography of recent research related to thinking skills and problem solving.

13

Helping Students Use Maps, Globes, and Graphics

Key Questions

- How can students use maps, charts, and other forms of social studies information?
- How can mathematics be used in social studies?

Key Ideas

- Maps, globes, graphs, and charts are specialized forms in which information is presented.
- All maps omit certain information; if they didn't, the information they do present would be lost in a fog of detail (which is also true of other data forms).
- When students have difficulty gaining access to specialized forms of information, part of the problem may be their lack of understanding about how the information got into that form in the first place.
- Some map and globe skills—specifically, latitude, longitude, and scale—are founded in mathematics and should be treated accordingly.

Introduction: Basic Premises

Whenever someone says "social studies," many people think first of history and geography, followed closely by maps and globes. There's no question that maps, globes, and, to a lesser extent, charts and tables are integral to social studies, yet there is nothing inherently "social" about any of them. They are simply specialized ways for presenting information.

Specialized ways for presenting information

The information presented on most maps, globes, graphs, charts, and tables can almost always be presented in other forms. Aerial photographs, for example, can convey at least as much (and probably more) information as many landform maps. Likewise, the information on a chart or table could be presented in a written description. Although a narrative of the income tax tables would probably be hopelessly confusing, it could be done.

Decoding maps, charts, and graphics

Reading a map, chart, or graph demands decoding skills not unlike those required to read information presented in narrative form—as you are doing now. True, the symbols are different: the dots and squares on a map, for example, usually stand for different things. Yet the process of bringing meaning to these symbols is a form of decoding.

Reading plays such an important role in gaining access to the information on maps, graphs, charts, and tables that the approach in this chapter is borrowed from the language-experience approach to teaching reading. That approach reflects the premise that if children can see their speech being encoded into written form, they will be better able to read those symbols.

How encoding and decoding are related

This chapter is also based on the premise that one reason students sometimes have difficulty reading maps or tables is that they don't understand how the information got *into* that form. In other words, students may not understand what the information on a map is supposed to represent. Likewise, when children have difficulty decoding charts and tables, the problem may lie in their inability to understand how information was encoded into the chart or table in the first place. This may explain why there is so much emphasis on providing encoding experiences—mapmaking, table making, and chart making—as a necessary balance for the decoding experiences—map reading, table reading, chart reading—that traditionally play important roles in social studies programs.

The first section of this chapter examines map- and globe-related skills and identifies exemplary activities you might use to teach those skills. The following sections consider experiences with tables, charts, and other graphic forms.

Maps and Globes

No one needs to tell you that maps are among the more abstract devices used in teaching social studies. As Monmonier (1991) noted, we live in a three-dimensional world that is too rich in details to be presented on a complete and yet uncluttered two-dimensional map. As a result, many maps distort the reality they depict by leaving out more information than they include and by using a variety of symbols to describe the information that is included.

Why maps omit details

The abstract nature of maps is illustrated in Figure 13.1. What to us may look like a random collection of sticks and shells can make perfect sense to mariners from the Marshall Islands. The sticks represent wave patterns, and the shells mark reefs and islands. With maps like this one, the Marshall Islanders navigated their way across empty stretches of the Pacific.

Large-area maps can pose special problems for children, who have probably never seen the real-world elements those maps depict. That many adults may have difficulty interpreting Figure 13.1 reflects the fact that some maps are models of things we have never seen and in many cases never will.

Maps as models

The abstract nature of maps is often compounded by the rapidity with which they lose one-to-one correspondence. For example, many things that children see and know to exist in their immediate environment do not appear on most maps of the area. Trees and buildings are among the first real-life elements to disap-

FIGURE 13.1   A Mariner's Map

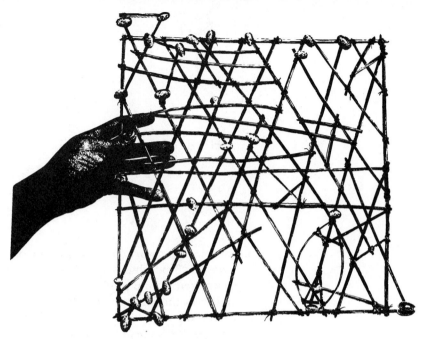

Source: Illustration by Paul M. Breeden, © National Geographic Society.

• •

pear. And as the map scale grows larger, cities often become dots or squares that look nothing like the areas they represent.

Maps also demand that we look at things from a different perspective. Except for astronauts, few of us have had the luxury of viewing the world while suspended in space. (Landsat maps made from satellite photographs have helped considerably in this respect—see p. 342.) Maps require that we assume the perspective of "looking down on" or what, in children's terms, can be described as a bird's-eye view. Because that perspective is not one that most children have experienced in their daily lives, you could provide activities in which young children look at objects from a bird's-eye view. Here are some suggestions:

The perspective of maps: bird's-eye view

1. Draw a picture of your shoe. (If the heel is visible, it's not a bird's-eye view.)
2. Hold a "bird's-eye view contest." Place small objects in a paper bag, where they cannot be seen by others, and have students draw and identify pictures of the objects as they would be seen from a bird's-eye view. Note that doll house furniture works well for this activity.
3. Follow the activity above by having students draw larger objects from their environment from a bird's-eye view. Some examples are pictured in Figure 13.2.

Map-related activities

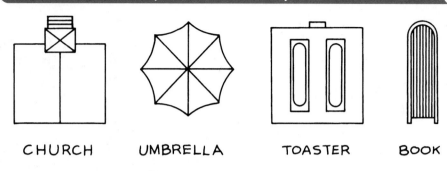

FIGURE 13.2 Common Objects Seen from a Bird's-Eye View

CHURCH   UMBRELLA   TOASTER   BOOK

4. Have students work with an interdisciplinary computer program, such as *The Backyard* (Brøderbund). By clicking on an assortment of objects, the child may be whisked to faraway places. Other scenarios involve locating buried treasure and reassembling animal skeletons.
5. In working with children's stories, draw hypothetical bird's-eye view maps of the area. For a story like Robert McCloskey's (1941) *Make Way for Ducklings*, for example, you could make a map of the area as seen from a duck's-eye view.

Mapmaking

Mapmaking refers to activities in which children actually produce a map. This excludes a variety of map-copying activities (even though they are sometimes called "mapmaking") in which children color in and correctly label outline maps. Copying existing maps may be useful in helping to fix areas in a child's mind, but it teaches little about what maps are or the purposes they serve. In addition, map-copying lessons too often focus on the artistic dimensions of mapping, especially if students use colored glitter or other unusual materials to depict the different areas. Such maps should probably be judged as works of art rather than as ways for displaying certain types of information.

Map copying is not mapmaking

Mapmaking in the encoding sense requires an area to be mapped. Beginning with bird's-eye views of various objects, students can move to increasingly larger areas, such as their living room or bedroom, their classroom, the school building, the neighborhood around the school, or other areas of the community. Figure 13.3 shows a third grader's map of his home and yard. The map is detailed and accurate, except that the cardinal directions are incorrect (the front of the house faces to the east). The back yard, which looks like a swimming pool, is really grass surrounded by a concrete walkway—to keep the grass from going into the shrubbery. The child has maintained a high level of one-to-one correspondence by showing things that he knows are present in the environment, including the piano keys, the boat in the side yard, and the jungle gym/swing set, which is made from ladders, in the back

Children seldom omit any details

FIGURE 13.3   Third-Grader's Map of His House and Yard

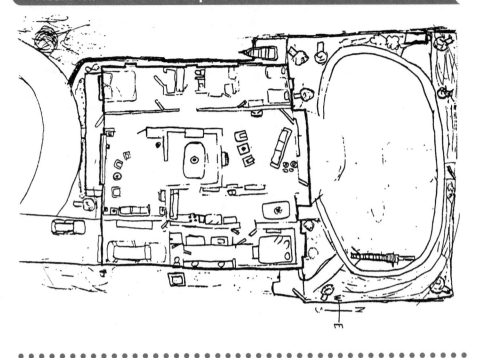

yard. About the only things not drawn strictly from a bird's-eye view are the trees, which is wholly expected for children of this age. Note that students who live in multistory houses are usually baffled by the prospect of showing several floors simultaneously; they should map each floor separately.

Specific objectives

Objectives for initial mapmaking activities include (1) helping children to visualize their immediate environment from a bird's-eye (or spatial) perspective and (2) helping them to understand that when anything is reduced in size—as maps are in relation to the areas they depict—some things must be omitted. Children should consider on what basis some things are kept in and others left out.

Relief Maps.   If your school is located on the plains of west Texas, making a relief map of the area is probably pointless; much of the terrain is as flat as a table-

Moving from two dimension to three

top. In other areas of the country, relief maps can show hills and valleys, thus illustrating yet another type of mapmaking. But beware! Making accurate relief maps can be a time-consuming and often messy process.

Making Relief Maps.   To build relief maps of small areas such as the neighborhood around a school, you might have students actually measure the changes in elevation. However, because doing that is more difficult than it may seem, consider using topographical maps from the U.S. Geological Survey, or downloaded from **www.topzone.com,** which offers maps in three scales. Topographical maps can be less abstract than other maps because they show buildings and other features in addition to changes in elevation.

Relief maps can be constructed from a variety of materials. The least messy but most costly is clay—pound after pound of clay. Several recipes for other relief-map making materials are included in the Resource Handbook.

Computer-Based Maps.   Instead of constructing relief maps, you may wish to draw on the maps included in computer database programs such as *PC-Globe, PC-USA,* and *Encarta World Atlas.* Most such programs contain a variety of maps and other data for any given area: relief maps, political maps, landform maps, population distribution maps, major cities, highways, rainfall—you name it. Most programs also permit you to print the maps.

The *Atlas* software is notable for its ability to focus on small areas of a larger map, creating exploded views. Used with a computer projection system, it permits students to see map details that were previously difficult to see even on large wall maps.

Scale.   In most mapmaking activities, the question often arises as to whether maps should be drawn to scale. For primary-grade children, the answer is generally no; neatly drawn but not-to-scale drawings will usually suffice. For the intermediate grades, the answer depends on the math program your students are using. The notion of scale, like latitude and longitude, is mathematically based. And scale, perhaps better than anything else, reflects the zenith of representational thought. In this case, one thing is said to equal something else. For younger elementary students, the notion that one inch can equal one foot (or one mile or ten miles) can present some of the same difficulties that algebra students encounter when they find that *x* can equal anything.

Scale is so integral to maps and mapmaking that it cannot be dealt with casually. By the end of the intermediate grades, for example, Hanna and his colleagues suggest that children have experienced some of the following ideas related to scale (Hanna et al., 1966, p. 25):

* Scale is the relation of distance on the map to the distance the map represents on the ground.
* The scale of a map is large or small in relation to the object the map represents.
* Maps that use a large scale can show many details about a small area.
* Maps that use a small scale can show large areas but with fewer details.
* Scale permits the measurement of the distance between any two points on the earth's surface.
* The scale on one part of a map may be different from the scale on another part (an inset map, for instance).

You may have to be satisfied when most of your students can use the scale on a map to calculate the distance between two points. However, many math programs introduce representational thought, and even the notion of scale, much earlier than they used to. Therefore, consider correlating your mapmaking activities with your math program.

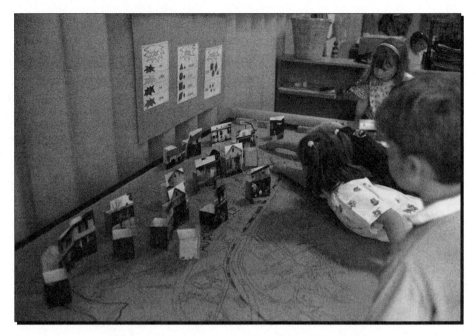

Adding three-dimensional models may help children better understand two-dimensional maps. *(© Mary Lang/Positive Images)*

Translation Mapping. *Translation* is a major subdivision of the comprehension category of the *Taxonomy of Educational Objectives* and is defined as changing data from one form to another. This is, in fact, what mapmaking is all about—depicting three-dimensional reality in a two-dimensional map form. The following map-related activities involve different kinds of translation. Although some of them may not seem especially thrilling, they are educational.

Scope and sequence

* Produce a written description of information contained on a chart or table (educational, but not too thrilling).

* Produce a map of a nation, such as Japan, from a written or oral description. (This activity is more interesting than it may seem and produces some very interesting maps—inaccurate but interesting.)

* Produce and translate a map. (In this activity, one group of students produces a map and another group uses it to locate an object—interesting, though the instructions are more complex than the activity.) The class is divided into teams of two. Each team places an object somewhere around the school grounds (lavatories are off-limits), returns to the classroom, and provides an oral description to the second team, which produces a map from that description. Finally, the maps are given to yet a third team, which must retrieve the object. As a follow-up, share the various problems the teams encountered in either making or using the maps.

When Should Map and Globe Skills Be Taught?

There is no single established sequence for map and globe skills for the elementary and middle-school grades. Sometimes first graders are expected to know and locate the major continents and oceans, for example, but in other instances, this may not be covered until Grade 2 or later.

From time to time, various individuals and groups have identified a desirable scope and sequence for teaching map and globe skills. A sample scope and sequence for map and globe skills developed by the Joint Committee on Geographic Education of the National Council for Geographic Education and the Association of American Geographers (1984) appears in Table 13.1.

TABLE 13.1 Suggested Scope and Sequence for Elementary Map and Globe Skills

Grade Level	Recommended Learning Outcomes
Kindergarten	1. Knows and uses terms related to location, direction, and distance (*up/down, left/right, here/there, near/far*). 2. Recognizes a globe as a model of the earth. 3. Recognizes and uses terms that express relative size and shape (*big/little, large/small, round/square*). 4. Identifies school and local community by name. 5. Recognizes and uses models and symbols to represent real things.
Grade 1	1. Knows geographic location of home in relation to school and neighborhood. 2. Knows the layout of the school campus. 3. Uses simple classroom maps to locate objects. 4. Identifies state and nation by name. 5. Follows and gives verbal directions (*here/there, left/right*). 6. Distinguishes between land and water symbols on globes and maps. 7. Relates locations on maps and globes to locations on Earth. 8. Observes, describes, and builds simple models and maps of the local environment.
Grade 2	1. Makes and uses simple maps of school and home neighborhoods. 2. Interprets map symbols using a legend. 3. Knows and uses cardinal directions. 4. Locates one's community, state, and nation on maps and globes. 5. Identifies local landforms. 6. Differentiates between maps and globes. 7. Locates other neighborhoods studied on maps. 8. Traces routes within and between neighborhoods using a variety of maps and models. 9. Compares pictures and maps of the same area.

TABLE 13.1 Suggested Scope and Sequence for Elementary Map and Globe Skills *(continued)*

Grade Level	Recommended Learning Outcomes
Grade 3	1. Uses distance, direction, scale, and map symbols.
	2. Compares own community with other communities.
	3. Compares urban and rural environments.
Grade 4	1. Interprets pictures, graphs, charts, and tables.
	2. Works with distance, direction, scale, and map symbols.
	3. Relates similarities and differences between maps and globes.
	4. Uses maps of different scales and themes.
	5. Recognizes the common characteristics of map grid systems (map projections).
	6. Compares and contrasts regions on a state, national, or world basis.
Grade 5	1. Recognizes distance, direction, scale, map symbols, and the relationship of maps and globes.
	2. Works with longitude and latitude.
	3. Uses maps, charts, graphs, and tables to display data.
	4. Discusses location in terms of *where* and *why.*
	5. Maps the correspondence between resources and industry.
	6. Maps physical and cultural regions in North America.
Grade 6	1. Improves understanding of location, relative location, and the importance of location.
	2. Uses maps, globes, charts, and graphs.
	3. Readily uses latitude, longitude, map symbols, time zones, and basic Earth-Sun relationships.
	4. Gains insight about the interaction of climate, landforms, natural vegetation, and other interactions in physical regions.
	5. Maps trade routes, particularly those connecting developed and developing nations.
	6. Plots distributions of population and key resources on regional maps.

Source: Abridged and adapted from Joint Committee on Geographic Education (1984).

Using Maps and Globes

Landsat Maps. Satellite photography has made it possible to illustrate the earth in a manner previously possible only with a globe. Landsat satellites have circled the earth and sent back color photographs of remarkable clarity. The landsat map shown in Figure 13.4 is of New York City, Long Island, and the New Jersey coast. The sample is reproduced in black and white, but it should give you some idea of the potential

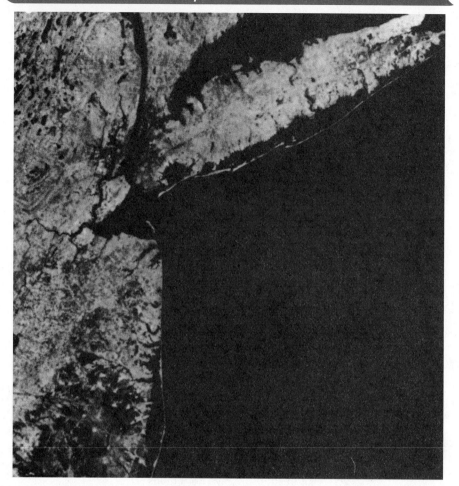

Source: Courtesy of Community and Education Services Branch, Public Affairs Division,
National Aeronautics and Space Administration.

• •

this innovation has for map-related instruction. Landsat maps are available from the
Educational Programs Office, NASA Goddard Flight Center, Greenbelt, MD 20771.

The merits of globes   **Globes.**   Landsat maps notwithstanding, the globe is still one of the most accurate tools for helping children orient themselves to the earth. It can help them
distinguish between land and water areas, and it can also help to correct the common notion that "up" on a map is north and "down" is south. Students may still
use those expressions, but at least they will understand that up is away from the
center of the earth and down is the reverse. With a globe, they can also learn that
north is toward the North Pole and south is toward the South Pole, something almost impossible to illustrate clearly on a wall map.

FIGURE 13.5 Distortions Created by Different Map Projections

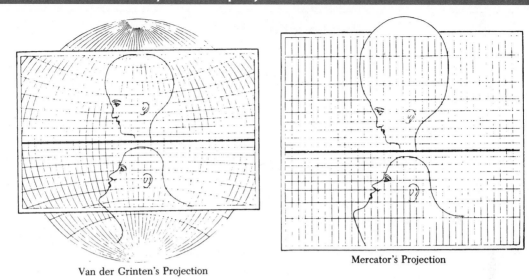

Van der Grinten's Projection

Mercator's Projection

When it comes to locating specific places on the globe, two problems usually emerge. To avoid the problem of having students line up and file past the globe, some schools purchase classroom sets of eight- to twelve-inch globes, which are often kept on a cart and wheeled from classroom to classroom as needed. The second problem is a function of the size of the globe. On a twelve-inch globe, for example, the United States measures approximately four inches from west to east. The average wall map of the United States measures approximately four feet from west to east, thus permitting the presentation of much more detail. Some schools have purchased very large, thirty-six-inch globes—which often serve as focal points for libraries or learning centers—but even such large globes are limited in the amount of detail they can present. The globe is an excellent geographic tool, but when it comes to detail, you'll probably need to turn to a wall map.

Size limits the amount of detail

Wall Maps. Getting a round Earth to fit onto a flat map has perplexed cartographers for centuries. The classic example of peeling an orange and then trying to make the peel lie flat illustrates the essence of the problem. In cartographic terms, it is a question of "projection." Projecting rounded surfaces onto a flat map in different ways can yield the images shown in Figure 13.5.

Misleading impressions

The distortion on most wall maps is greatest at the high latitudes and is largely responsible for the question children commonly ask: "Why is Australia a continent but Greenland isn't?" It's a logical question, because on many maps, such as the Mereator projection shown on page 345, Greenland appears to be two to three times the size of Australia. Using a globe, students will find that Australia is three times larger than Greenland—Australia has 2,975,000 square miles versus Greenland's 840,000 square miles. Explaining to students how some maps make small things appear larger than they really are is no small feat! For very small areas, the

Plotting Earthquakes

Everyone knows that during the 1990s some of the worst earthquakes in the United States occurred in California. What many people do not know is that earthquakes of varying magnitudes are daily events around the globe. Some earthquakes are so weak you can barely feel them, and others are so powerful they cause widespread destruction. The key questions are: (1) Are some places in the world more prone to earthquakes than others, and (2) if so, where?

Overview: This problem-solving activity uses latitude and longitude to plot the location of recent earthquakes on an oversized map of the world. The completed map should resemble the one shown in Exhibit B.

Materials:

1. A *really* large outline map of the world. (Suggestion: Make an overhead transparency of an appropriate world map by (a) mounting large paper on the wall and then (b) projecting the enlarged image onto the paper. Then (c) have children trace the outlines of continents and countries with markers. They should (d) use small dots to locate the location of parallels of latitude and meridians of longitude. After they (e) remove the map from the wall and lay it on the floor, students can use yardsticks and fine-point markers to draw in the latitude and longitude. Once this is done, they can (f) label the completed map and remount it on the wall.)

2. Earthquake locators. These are 1- by 1-inch squares of clear overhead transparency material with an X drawn on them. (Suggestion: Make a sheet of neatly drawn Xs, and then make three or four transparencies. Cut the individual Xs apart. Since there are many earthquakes, you will need many Xs; start with at least fifty).

3. Download the earthquake locations from the Internet at either:

   http://home.synapse.ru/cgi-bin/eq/
   http://wwwneic.cr.usgs.gov/neis/bulletin

   The data will be similar to the data in Exhibit A.

Exhibit A

Introductory Note: There are often six to nine earthquakes every day that are above 3.5 on the Richter scale, and countless more tremors of lesser magnitude (Mag). The selected earthquakes shown below were in excess of 5 magnitude and often caused significant damage and deaths. Because of the large number of earthquakes each day, consider mapping only those that exceed a threshold of 3.5 or 4 on the Richter scale; otherwise your map will become cluttered very quickly.

	Date	Time	Latitude	Longitude	Mag.	Region/Comments
1997	May 10	07:57	33.83 N	59.81 E	7.3	Northern Iran: Over 1,500 deaths, 2,300 injured, and 10,500 homes destroyed.
	May 13	05:38	31.82 N	130.28 E	5.7	Kyushu, Japan: 34 injured.
	June 23	19:13	47.60 N	122.57 W	5.0	Washington, Puget Sound Region: Slight damage.
	July 9	19:24	10.59 N	63.48 W	6.6	Near the Coast of Venezuela: Over 80 deaths and 500 injured; extensive damage.
	Oct. 14	09:53	22.10S	176.77 W	6.7	South of Fuji Islands
	Oct. 15	01:03	30.93 S	71.22 W	6.8	Off the Coast of Chile: Over six deaths, 300 injured, and 5,000 homes destroyed.
	Nov. 21	11:23	22.21 N	92.70 E	5.9	India-Bangladesh Border Region: 23 deaths and 200 injured.
1998	Jan. 30	16:09	23.51 S	69.83 W	6.4	Northern Chile
	Feb. 4	14:33	37.07 N	70.20 E	6.1	Afghanistan-Tajikistan Border Region: 3,000 to 5,000 deaths and thousands injured and homeless.

4. Attach the earthquake locators on the map at the correct locations by using small loops of clear Scotch tape.

5. Identify patterns of the earthquake-prone areas around the world. Follow up with research on what sets these areas apart from other areas.

Exhibit B

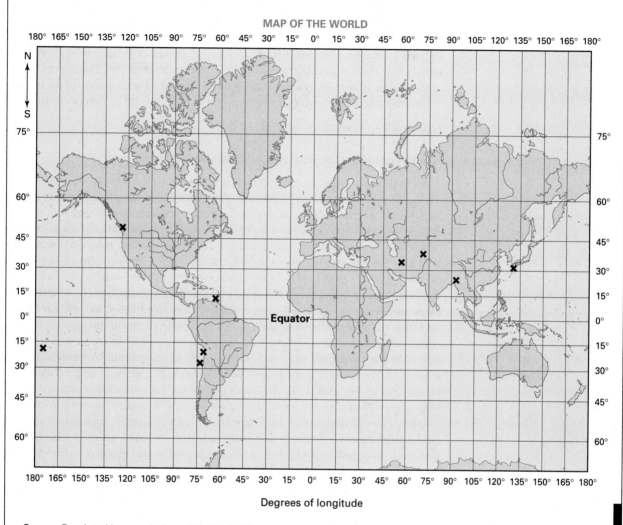

MAP OF THE WORLD

Degrees of longitude

Source: Reprinted by permission of Mr. Denis Mishin.

distortion created by different map projections is usually negligible, but for large land masses, consider using a globe in conjunction with wall maps.

To avoid the "north is up" phenomenon, you might occasionally lay wall maps on the floor. Some schools have gone even further; they paint huge outline maps on the school parking lot or playground. Such large-scale maps should be accurate in direction and as accurate as possible in scale.

Large-scale maps

Latitude, Longitude, and Other Grid Systems

Latitude and longitude

Most map and globe skill programs from fourth grade upward call for instruction in latitude and longitude. Among the more difficult ideas for children to grasp is the fact that although most parallels of latitude are imaginary lines that appear only on a map, 90 north latitude and 90 south latitude are not lines but are points (or, in mathematical terms, poles). Also difficult is the idea that although the meridians of longitude are of equal length, the parallels of latitude get shorter as one moves away from the equator. One reason that children may find these ideas so hard to grasp is because latitude and longitude are often taught as arbitrary systems rather than as part of circular or spherical measurement. The Model Student Activity, "Pumpkin Geography," shows one way to deal with this difficult topic.

Teaching latitude and longitude can be reduced to three components:

1. Use of a grid system (any grid system)
2. Use of the grid system (longitude and latitude)
3. Understanding the basis for longitude and latitude

Grid-based map games

Even primary children can become adept at using a grid system, especially one involving a combination of letters and numbers. Math texts frequently include an assortment of grid-related activities, sometimes more than social studies texts. Also, many gridding activities can be converted into games that kids love to play. A classic is Battleship, in which a student locates his or her navy on a simple grid and then another student tries to sink the navy by calling out the various squares on the grid. You could also obtain classroom sets of state road maps from one of the petroleum companies or the state highway department and create a version of Cops and Robbers. In small groups, the robbers identify a quadrant on the map and then the rest of the students ask them questions that can be answered only by yes or no, such as "Are you in a square near a large city?" In other words, it is the detective game adapted to a map. This activity serves several purposes: it provides experience in using a grid system for locational purposes; it helps children formulate questions; and it also provides familiarity with state geography. The road map game will prove very popular even after the skills you're teaching are learned.

After your students have had experience using a simple grid system, you can explain the basis for latitude and longitude and its relationship to the globe. In this case, your task will become one of applying to the globe a system that children have already worked with. If you opt to present latitude and longitude through an expository teaching strategy, you will find yourself explaining two things at once: both the system and its application to the globe. Whatever approach you finally use, correlate latitude and longitude with whatever math program you are using.

Map Reading (Decoding Maps)

Encoding complements decoding

Students who have had rich and varied mapmaking (encoding) experiences are likely to find that map reading is considerably easier to cope with. Realistically, however, children will be expected to read a wider range of maps than most of them will have had experience making.

Pumpkin Geography

The following illustrations show how you can use pumpkins to teach geography.

Set A: Shows hemispheres, the equator, and the prime meridian.

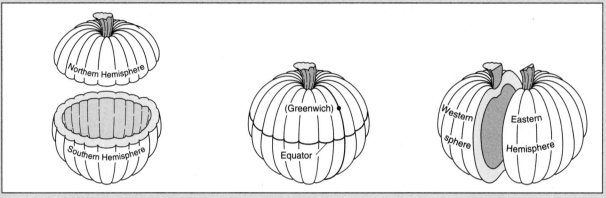

Set B: Shows how circular measurement is translated into latitude and longitude.

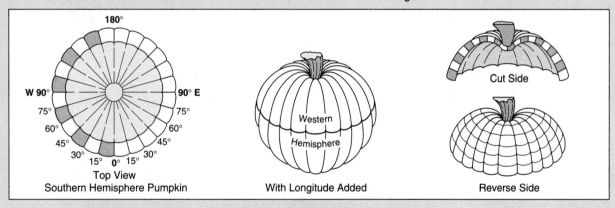

Set C: A pumpkin globe with latitude, longitude, and continental shapes drawn on.

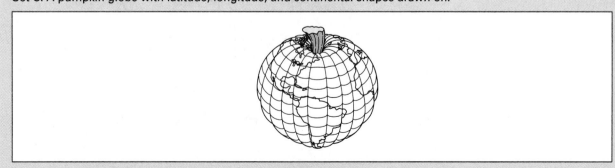

Note: Use fine-point permanent markers to draw features on the pumpkin.

By the time students leave elementary or middle school, they generally are expected to be able to answer the questions on page 349, which are based on the map shown in Figure 13.6. The questions are similar to those found on standardized achievement tests. This is doing two things: (1) illustrating how map and globe skills are likely to be tested and (2) identifying what those skills are. Accordingly, you should (1) try to answer the questions and (2) identify, in the space provided, the skill or skills required to answer the questions. You may want to use the scope and sequence presented in Table 13.1 as a guide for identifying the skills needed.

Questions

1. What is the northernmost city on Pleasure Island?

   A. Beta   B. Alpha   C. Gamma   D. Zeta

   Skill: _____

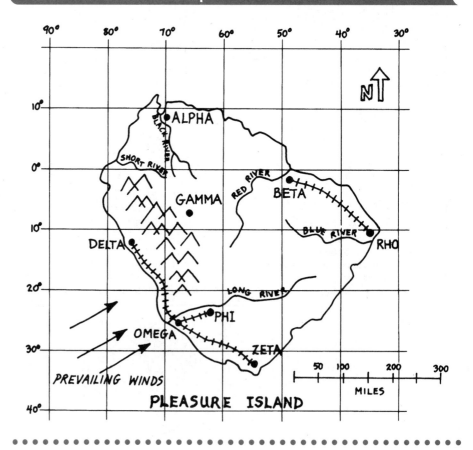

FIGURE 13.6   Pleasure Island Map

2. How far is it from Delta to Rho?
   A. 250 miles   B. 550 miles   D. 900 miles
   Skill: _____

3. Which river flows toward the northeast?
   A. Long River   B. Blue River   C. Black River   D. Red River
   Skill: _____

4. What is the busiest port city on Pleasure Island?
   A. Beta   B. Gamma   C. Omega   D. Phi
   Skill: _____

5. What city probably gets the least rainfall?
   A. Beta   B. Gamma   C. Delta   D. Can't tell
   Skill: _____

6. What city lies closest to the equator?
   A. Beta   B. Alpha   C. Rho   D. Can't tell
   Skill: _____

7. In what hemisphere is most of Pleasure Island located?
   A. Northern   B. Eastern   C. Southern   D. Can't tell
   Skill: _____

(*Answers:* 1. B; 2. B; 3. D; 4. C; 5. B; 6. A; 7. C)

Task Analysis.   Most map skills are complex chains of steps that must be fol-

Most skills are a sequence of steps

lowed in sequence. For example, to identify the hemisphere in which Pleasure Island is located (see preceding Question 7), the student must know that the equator is at 0° latitude, and that as one moves southward the degrees of latitude increase in number until one reaches 90° south latitude at the South Pole. The student must then apply this knowledge to the information provided on the map. As a further example of this, identify what you must know to determine whether Pleasure Island is in the Eastern or Western Hemisphere.

The mathlike nature of map skills makes it possible to determine precisely what students must know and do to achieve success. For example, to determine the distance from Delta to Rho (Question 2), the student must know that (1) all maps have a scale; (2) the scale indicates real distances in shortened form; (3) by using a measuring device (a ruler, etc.), one can convert the distance on a map to the real distance; and so forth. All of these elements must be brought to bear on the problem in the correct sequence; otherwise, failure is almost guaranteed.

Students who have used symbols, scale, and directions to make maps are likely to have fewer problems when they encounter these elements in map reading. But when students encounter problems, consider planning lessons in which you model the use of the skill in question. For example, to help students find the distance from

Model the process

Delta to Rho, make an overhead transparency of Figure 13.6, and then model the process in a simple, step-by-step fashion. No elaborate questioning procedure is necessary. Because most map and globe skills yield a single correct answer (such as the distance between two cities), showing your students an efficient process for finding that answer will not inhibit their creativity in the least.

●━ Map-Related Activities

Some effective and interesting map-related student activities begin with a heuristic question such as "If you were the town council, where would you build the new incinerator (or park, or shopping center, or apartment complex)?" and use maps as the main data source.

Another type of map-based activity involves presenting students with a sequence of maps, each of which adds specialized information. In the following Model Student Activity, students are asked where they would locate a city on a mythical island. Then, in succession, additional information on terrain (landforms), vegetation, and rainfall is provided, each on a separate map.

Literary Mapping.   Remember reading Mark Twain's *The Adventures of Huckleberry Finn,* in which Huck and his comrades travel to various places along the Mississippi? Most of the places Huck visits are real, and most can be located on a map of the area. While reading *Huck Finn* wouldn't it make sense to trace Huck's travels on a map? Such an activity need not be a major undertaking. In fact, it is probably best done almost incidentally to reading the story, yet the activity will show a functional use for map skills.

Mapping hypothetical areas

There is a wealth of children's literature in which the settings are real places and, thus, locatable on a map. There is still more literature in which the settings are fictional but are described in enough detail that it's possible to create a map of the area. Think about Beatrix Potter's *Peter Rabbit* for a moment. The cardinal directions might be amiss, but it is possible to map the relative location of major elements in *Peter Rabbit*—the tool shed, Mr. McGregor's garden, the fence, the watering can in which Peter hides, and so forth. Each child's map might be different, but the idea is to create a tangible map of an idealized literary location. Other children's literature that lends itself to mapmaking includes *Little Black Bear Goes for a Walk,* by Beatrice Freschet (1977); *Rosie's Walk,* by Pat Hutchins (1968); Robert McCloskey's (1941) classic *Make Way for Ducklings,* which was referred to earlier, and *Henry Explores the Jungle,* by Mark Taylor (1968).

Sandra Pritchard (1989) expanded on the notion of using children's literature for teaching geography and map skills by identifying story-related activities that correlate with the five themes for geographic education (Joint Committee on Geographic Education, 1984) that was presented in detail in Chapter 2. Following is an abridgement of some of Pritchard's recommended geography-related activities for Virginia Lee Burton's (1943) *Katy and the Big Snow.*

Location: Position on the Earth's Surface

Activities correlating literature and the five geography themes

* Locate buildings and streets on a map.
* Identify and locate cardinal directions.
* Determine in which direction Katy went from the school to the railroad station, from the police station to the fire station, etc.
* Describe the location of buildings in relation to other buildings and streets.

Place: Physical and Human Characteristics

★ Discuss seasonal changes in the little town, and how those changes affect people.
★ Describe a walk along First or Third Street.

Relationships Within Places: Human-Environment Interaction

★ Tell how the snow affects the lives of people in the town.
★ Tell what might happen if Katy had not been able to plow out the town.

MODEL STUDENT ACTIVITY

Where Would You Locate Your City?

Overview

The object of this activity is to determine whether students will change their original decision in light of new information.

Procedure

Provide students with a copy of Map 1. Ask where, with just the information they have, they would locate a city if they were prospective settlers. Assume that the area is otherwise uninhabited. Permit students to discuss their choices in small groups, and then have each group present its choice to the entire class. Then provide each group with copies of Maps 2, 3, and 4 (see page 352), one at a time, permitting discussion and explanations (as warranted) after each map is distributed.

Sources/Variation

Making the maps for this activity used to be a major undertaking. However, for any teacher with access to the computer programs referred to earlier (*PC-Globe, PC-USA, USA Atlas, World Atlas,* and *Microsoft Encarta*), it is now a simple process, and the areas that students deal with are real. The computer programs will usually print whichever maps you need. However, it is usually necessary to remove the name of the area manually, using typewriter white-out, tape, or some other method, if you wish it to remain anonymous. After students have decided where to locate their cities, you can provide them with a computer-generated map showing the actual location of major cities.

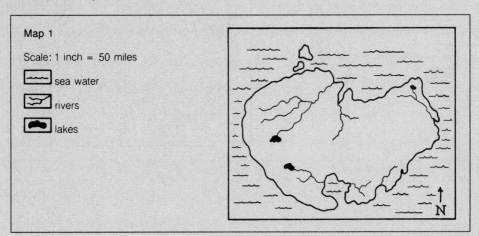

Map 1

Scale: 1 inch = 50 miles

▱ sea water

▱ rivers

▱ lakes

(continues on next page)

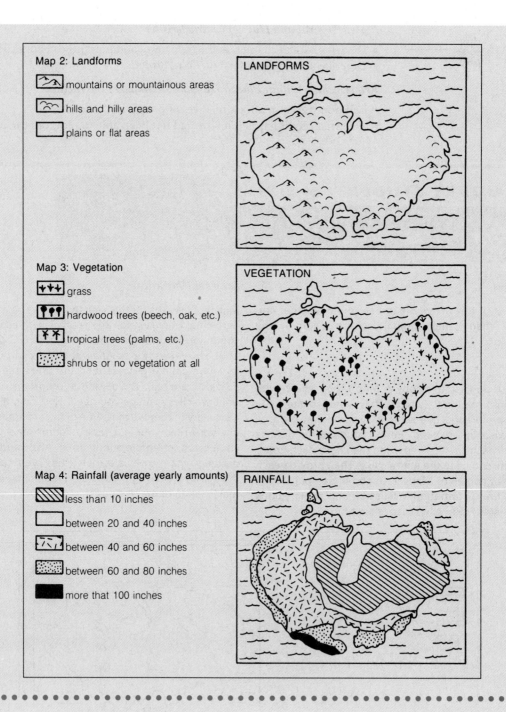

Map 2: Landforms

mountains or mountainous areas

hills and hilly areas

plains or flat areas

LANDFORMS

Map 3: Vegetation

grass

hardwood trees (beech, oak, etc.)

tropical trees (palms, etc.)

shrubs or no vegetation at all

VEGETATION

Map 4: Rainfall (average yearly amounts)

less than 10 inches

between 20 and 40 inches

between 40 and 60 inches

between 60 and 80 inches

more that 100 inches

RAINFALL

Movement: Humans Interacting on the Earth

* Identify and describe the various forms of transportation in the story and on the map.
* Identify and describe the various forms of communication.
* Find symbols for buildings, roads, and airports on various maps.

Region/Neighborhoods: How They Form and Change

* Identify different kinds of neighborhoods in the little town.

Making maps of idealized locations from children's literature may help sensitize students to the ways in which authors describe the physical setting in which stories are set, especially if you call attention to it. Such a purpose may lack clear relevance to social studies, of course, but by giving tangible meaning to a literary element such as "the setting of the story," it could show up in subsequent stories that children write.

Working with Other Graphic Forms

Some teachers and students seem to regard graphs, tables, and charts as one of the "bad breath" areas of social studies. However, quantitative data are not difficult to deal with if they are approached from a "use" perspective—that is, if students actually do something with the information on a chart, graph, or table.

One instructionally troublesome aspect of graphs, tables, and charts is their efficiency in presenting information. They can present so much information in so little space that students can quickly suffer from information overload. Thus the earlier suggestion to limit the information you provide children at the beginning of an activity prevails here.

Avoiding information overload— limit the amount of data

A second consideration involves the way you present the numbers for statistical information. For example, there were 7,527,152,000 bushels of corn and 2,035,818,000 bushels of wheat grown in the United States in 1990. You probably had to count the number of places in numbers this large, which have been rounded some to begin with. Because large numbers can overwhelm children, consider rounding them even more—to 7.5 billion bushels of corn, for example. The idea is that the numbers provide the basis for identifying trends and relationships, such as that the United States grows about three times more corn than wheat. It isn't necessary to have numbers accurate to the last possible bushel to identify such relationships. And certainly the numbers are not something you would expect children to memorize.

Helping students deal with large numbers

Helping children deal with large numbers is largely a matter of making them as easy to understand as possible. In addition, because many children have no comprehension of how big a billion or how tremendous a trillion really is, consider using Schwartz's (1985) wonderful book, *How Much Is a Million?*, before you deal with large numbers.

●── Fact Sheets

The fact sheet illustrated in Figure 13.7 was produced by a fourth-grade teacher who was teaching a unit on farming in the United States. Although the information on it is limited, it still proved to be too much for her students to process at one time. She then had them fold the paper so that only Part I was visible.

FIGURE 13.7 Model Fact Sheet Format: The American Farmer

Part I

Corn Grown		Beef Produced	
1965	104 million tons	1965	17 million pounds
1995	246 million tons	1995 (est.)	24 million pounds

Wheat Grown		Eggs Produced	
1965	27 million tons	1965	5.5 million dozen
1995	72 million tons	1995 (est.)	5.9 million dozen

Part II

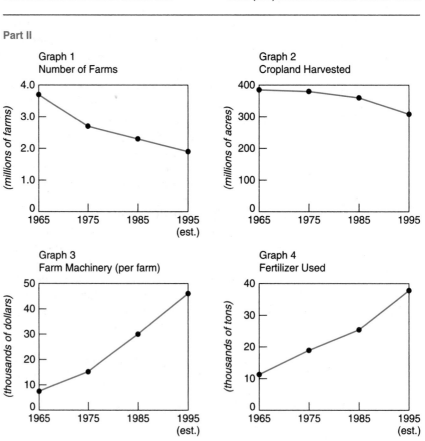

As she used the American Farmer Fact Sheet, the teacher alternated between modeling and questioning designed to help the children (1) read the charts and graphs and (2) determine what this information meant. For example, the teacher said, "Let's see if we can find out what has happened to the number of farms in this country." "They went down," was the chorus of responses. "Does anyone want to explain how we can figure that out?" After one student volunteered to explain the process for finding that information, the teacher then said, "To find out if the number of farms went down a lot or just a little, we have to look at the numbers." She then modeled the process for showing that the number of farms decreased by almost one-half (50%) and concluded that this seemed like a big decrease.

Working through all the information in a similar fashion, the students concluded that although there are fewer farms in the United States, the amount of food produced on those farms has increased. They also concluded that since fewer farmers (Graph 1) were farming almost the same number of acres as in the past (Graph 2), the average size of a farm is larger today than it was in the past. Furthermore, the students concluded that fewer farmers can grow more food because of the increased use of machinery (Graph 3) and fertilizer (Graph 4). They also suggested that there could be other reasons for this (better weather, etc.), but that they didn't have enough information to be certain of these causes.

Using just the information on the American Farmer Fact Sheet, students developed their own conclusions about the changing nature of American farming. Of course, a teacher could approach the topic by having students read a section in the textbook. That section, in all likelihood, would begin like this: "American farms today are larger than they used to be. Farmers also use more machinery and . . ." In this instance, however, students would be reading *someone else's conclusions* about farming instead of using information to build their own.

Encoding Quantitative Data

Before children can use the information on a graph, table, or chart, they must be able to handle that information at the literal level. For example, if children cannot read Graph 1 on the American Farmer Fact Sheet, then it may be necessary to back up and show them how the information was translated (or encoded) into graph form.

As a general rule, encoding experiences for primary-level students should involve simple examples and small quantities. They can be as simple as tallying the number of girls and boys in a classroom, as illustrated in Figure 13.8. Until students are able to think representationally, it is probably wisest to maintain one-to-one correspondence—that is, where one symbol on a table represents something the child can see in reality. In Figure 13.8, each symbol stands for one classmate. As students grow progressively more able to handle representational thought— as when one symbol equals five classmates, for example—their encoding experiences can become increasingly complex.

Simple surveys can provide a wealth of information for encoding activities. That's what one teacher used when her students had graph-reading problems. Small groups of students surveyed the traffic passing by the school at different times of day. They counted the number of cars and trucks, the number of pickup

FIGURE 13.8   Sample Table Encoded by Students

Boys and Girls in Ms. James's Classroom October, 1997		
Boys	♂♂♂♂♂♂♂♂♂♂♂	11
Girls	♀♀♀♀♀♀♀♀♀♀♀♀♀♀	14
♂ Boy ♀ Girl		25

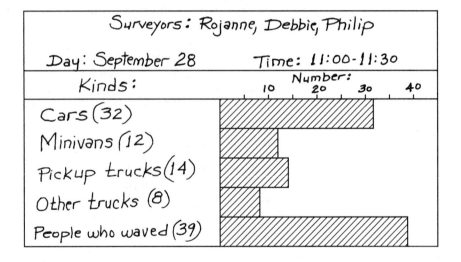

FIGURE 13.9   Summary of Traffic Survey

Surveyors: Rojanne, Debbie, Philip

Day: September 28   Time: 11:00-11:30

Kinds:	Number:
Cars (32)	
Minivans (12)	
Pickup trucks (14)	
Other trucks (8)	
People who waved (39)	

Graphing data from surveys

trucks and minivans, and the number of people who waved back at them. Then, with the teacher's help, the groups put their information onto bar graphs, which were hung around the room to provide a basis for comparison. The result of one group's efforts is illustrated in Figure 13.9.

Making Tables.   Once data have been gathered, they must be presented in a readily understandable form. One such form, a table, is intended to communicate the relationships between the data. General considerations for constructing tables (and graphs) include the following:

Four characteristics of tables

* Tables should be self-sufficient. That is, a table should give a complete and understandable message: what is being related, the form in which the relationship is established, the source of the information—everything needed to help readers make their own interpretations.
* All rows and columns must have clear headings that follow an identifiable pattern—for example, high to low, alphabetical, geographic—and, where appropriate, indicate the measure being used—percentages, thousands, square miles, and so on.
* The source of the data should be included in a footnote.
* The table title should make clear what information is being related and in what terms.

The Model Student Activity, "Constructing a Table," follows these guidelines for table (and graph) construction.

MODEL STUDENT ACTIVITY

Constructing a Table

Sample Data

Temperature and Snow Report, Week of January 9–15

* Monday's high temperature was 30°. Tuesday's high was 25°. Wednesday's high was 28°, followed by 32° on Thursday, 35° on Friday, 37° on Saturday, and 30° on Sunday. The average high temperature for the week was 31°.

* The snowfall for the week totaled 14 inches. It did not snow on Wednesday, Friday, or Saturday. It snowed 4 inches on Monday and 7 inches on Tuesday, for a total of 11 inches for the first two days. Average snowfall was 2 inches a day for the week.

These data were converted into table form, as shown in the next column.

Source: Personal measurements

Temperature and Snow Report, Week of January 9–15

Day	High Temperature (F)	Snow (Inches)
Monday	30	4
Tuesday	25	7
Wednesday	28	0
Thursday	32	1
Friday	35	0
Saturday	37	0
Sunday	30	2
Average high 31	Total snowfall 14	
	Average daily snowfall 2	

Decoding Graphs and Tables

Before children can do anything with the information on a graph or in a table, they must gain access to that information. Fortunately, the process of decoding information presented on a graph or in a table is amenable to task analysis. Probably the easiest way to go about this is to ask yourself two related questions: (1) what must the student know (and in what sequence) to gain access to the information? and (2) at what points might students experience problems?

Modeling is the key

We do not recommend using indirect or discovery strategies for teaching the procedures associated with table or graph reading. There are just too many points at which students might encounter problems. Thus this is another instance where modeling and step-by-step teacher-directed instruction, followed by guided practice, are wholly appropriate.

Charts

In the days before overhead projectors and copiers became widely available, chart making was probably more common than it is today. With current technology, it is a simple process to make an overhead transparency of a small chart that will be read-

MODEL STUDENT ACTIVITY

Linear Charting

This technique, called *linear charting,* consists of having students attach pictures or short descriptions of a process in the correct sequence on a piece of string or yarn. A linear chart for the production of bread is illustrated below.

This may not sound like an exciting activity, but actually doing it often proves otherwise. Consider that linear charting can also be used for more than just social studies activities. For example, instead of book reports, students might illustrate the significant scenes or events in a story and then attach those pictures, in the correct sequence, to a piece of yarn. When students present their reports, the rest of the class can refer to a visual representation of the book's events instead of listening to a strictly oral presentation.

   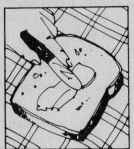

ily visible to everyone in the class. However, once the overhead projector is turned off, the image is gone, whereas a poster-size chart displayed somewhere in the classroom can be viewed repeatedly. An alternative is to use the magnification feature of most copying machines and make enough copies for everyone in the class.

Types of charts   An endless variety of things can be depicted in chart form. If you were to present a schematic drawing of the structure of an organization such as the U.S. Congress, you would have an *organizational chart.* If you were to outline the steps a bill passes through in Congress en route to becoming a law, you would have a *flow chart.* Virtually any process—the production of steel, bread, or whatever—can be illustrated in pictures, in a short narrative description, or in a combination of the two on a flow chart.

Charts, like maps, omit details   All charts summarize whatever they depict. They are like most maps and outlines in that they highlight major points or phrases while omitting details. However, the need to summarize information can be an asset when you have students engage in chart making, because summarizing forces them to identify the main ideas that they should put on their chart. In this context, chart making can be an effective culminating activity for small-group work.

Linear Charting.   An alternative form of charting that uses pictures attached to a piece of string or yarn is shown in the Model Student Activity on page 358. This procedure is also useful for highlighting the main elements of a story, in which case it is sometimes called "story mapping."

SUMMARY

This chapter has suggested several approaches for helping children gain access to specialized forms of information—namely, maps, globes, graphs, and tabular data. For each of these forms, encoding experiences—which include map, graph, table, and chart making—can help children understand how information gets into a particular form. Such encoding experiences may provide students with a good basis for decoding or gaining access to information displayed on maps, graphs, tables, and charts.

Unlike some of the other areas that social studies encompasses, map, table, and graph reading (decoding) involves an identifiable sequence of the knowledge and skills necessary for gaining access to information. If any

step is omitted, or if the sequence of steps is confused, the student is likely to fail. To avoid failure and the sense of frustration that can accompany it, "task-analyze" what the student is being asked to do by identifying the knowledge and skills required to complete the task. This analysis can provide the basis for step-by-step instruction as you guide your students through the decoding process.

Once students have gained access to information, the next phase is a "natural": they need to do something with it. It becomes almost a circular process when you recognize that what students do with information can provide a reason for them to get (and want) access to it.

SUGGESTED ACTIVITIES

1. Design a map-based decision-making activity that deals with a problem presently confronting the community you are living in, or, as an alternative, use a hypothetical community.

2. It is sometimes argued that much of the time devoted to instruction in longitude and latitude is wasted and could be better spent on something else. That argument is based on the claim that although *latitude* and *longitude* are concepts many Americans know, they rarely, if ever, use them. Develop a response to that argument.

3. Review the instructional activities presented in this chapter, and identify those that teach and those that test a student's preexisting skills.

4. Design a fact sheet that could serve as the basis for a lesson on any of the following topics: immigration, health care, education, community, industrialization.

5. Obtain two social studies textbooks *for the same grade level* but from different publishers (your curriculum library or learning-resource center should have copies available). Compare the two books in terms of the map-reading skills they require of students. Also compare them in terms of the quantitative-data skills they require, if any.

SUGGESTED READINGS AND RESOURCES

Print Resources

A. K. Ellis. (1997). *Teaching and learning elementary social studies* (6th ed.). Boston: Allyn & Bacon. This text contains an excellent chapter on making and interpreting maps.

Massachusetts Geographic Alliance. (1990). *Global geography: Activities for teaching the five themes of geography*. Boulder, CO: Social Science Education Consortium. I recommend this collection of activities, all of which come with the necessary teaching materials.

Mark Monmonier. (1991). *How to lie with maps*. Chicago: University of Chicago Press. Monmonier explains why "a good map tells a multitude of little white lies" (p. 25).

Internet Resources

Introductory Note: Web sites sometimes change their Internet addresses or cease operating entirely. All the addresses supplied here were operating when this book was printed, but if any of them fails to work properly, enter the desired topic or organization in any standard search engine.

Map Machine

http://www.nationalgeographic.com/resources/ngo/maps/

The National Geographic Society provides downloadable maps, information about each country in the world, and a variety of other map-related information.

Mapmaker, Mapmaker, Make Me a Map

http://ur.utenn.edu/ut2kids/maps/map.html

This University of Tennessee site provides a tutorial on map-making and links to a variety of other map-related sources.

Great Globe Gallery

http://www.fpsol.com/gems/geography.html

This site offers links to a variety of maps and globes including satellite views, weather maps, and medieval globes.

U.S. Geological Survey

http://www.usgs.gov/

This site contains an abundance of learning resources on working with maps.

Map Collection

http://www.lib.utexas.edu/Libs/PCL/Map_collection/ map_collection.html

This University of Texas collection is just one of many collections available on the Internet.

How Far Is It?

http://www.indo.com/distance/

This site calculates the latitude, longitude, and distance between any two cities. It also allows you to generate maps of the two places.

U.S. Bureau of the Census

http://www.census.gov/

This site offers more statistical information than you would believe, as well as TIGER maps that you can use for transparencies and overlays.

The World Wide Web Virtual Library: Geography

http://geography.pinetree.org

The site offers a variety of maps and map-related tools.

Topographic Maps

http://www.topozone.com

This wonderful site offers free and downloadable topographic maps, in color and your choice of three different scales, of any area in the United States or Puerto Rico. **Bookmark quality.**

14

Using Instructional Tools: Print, Multimedia, and Community Resources

Key Questions

- ❋ What resources are available for teaching social studies?
- ❋ What considerations are involved in using those resources?
- ❋ What do teachers do when schools lack the resources they want?

Key Ideas

- ❋ Instructional tools may lurk in unlikely places.
- ❋ Using instructional tools effectively depends on preplanning.
- ❋ Identifying community resources is often less difficult than using those resources effectively.
- ❋ Resources provide options for teachers in developing teaching activities, individualizing instruction, prompting student interest, achieving social studies goals and objectives, and allowing students to transfer skill and content learning to a variety of contexts.

Introduction: Teaching in the Electronic Age

An abstraction has become real

TECHNOLOGY

As more and more schools gain access to the Internet, the resources for teaching social studies have grown exponentially. For years everyone heard about how the reservoir of knowledge was growing by leaps and bounds, but because most of us had no way to tap into the vastness of that reservoir, the so-called information explosion was largely an abstraction. Today the Internet, combined with other forms of computer-based technology, provides access to more resources than most of us can ever use. The information explosion has become very real.

No longer must teachers rely solely on textbooks, maps, and almanacs, because computer-based resources have made life considerably easier. Many teachers also recognize that, although the Internet makes available a large amount of information, it does not teach children how to interpret and use that information.

Computerized resources for teaching social studies, along with some older resources like overhead projectors, share a common characteristic: they plug into electrical outlets. However, there is still a wide array of nonelectrical resources available, especially if you know what you are looking for. For example, something as mundane as the Yellow Pages of the telephone directory could provide the basis for a variety of social studies activities:

Activities based on a telephone directory

★ For identifying the government services available in the local community.

★ For identifying alternative ways in which the Yellow Pages could be organized, and then considering what those organizational patterns would mean for (1) users, (2) advertisers, and (3) the telephone company.

★ For finding out what it costs, if anything, to be listed in the Yellow Pages. Is it free? And if charges do apply, speculating on how they are determined and why businesses might pay to be listed. When schools are listed in the Yellow Pages, do you suppose they pay? Or are some listings free and others must be paid for?

★ For an activity in which students use the Yellow Pages from the 1960s or 1970s and a current directory to find the location of selected businesses, such as laundromats, florists, hardware stores, video rental outlets (which did not exist in the 1960s), and movie theaters. Plotting the location of each business on a city map, and determining if the number and locations of the businesses have changed over time.

The balance of this chapter is organized in an arbitrary and somewhat eclectic way; it covers print materials and computers, nonprint and visual resources, and finally community resources. Addresses for the teaching resources noted here are included in the Resource Handbook.

Textbooks

Almost all schools have textbooks, and some classes have access to several different texts. However, some schools—even those with ample financial resources—have elected not to use social studies textbooks. Still other schools may not have enough copies of a single text for all students in the class, but this is usually intentional. Sometimes the number of texts will be limited to no more than ten copies of a particular book. Because there may be as many as forty or fifty social studies texts in a given classroom, it's technically incorrect to say that teachers don't have any textbooks. Teachers in those schools are probably using a *multitext*

Some schools use a multi-text approach

approach, in which they select elements from different books as they need them. This approach reduces the pressure that teachers sometimes feel to cover every chapter in a book.

Generalizing about social studies textbooks can be risky, but here goes:

★ Social studies textbooks for elementary and middle schools today are more similar than they are different, especially in states that have mandated curriculums.

★ You can get usable teaching ideas from every social studies textbook or accompanying teacher's guide—no matter how old and decrepit.

* Textbooks have a way of becoming the basis for social studies programs, not a resource to be used with them.

Texts as tools

For teachers who wish to depart from textbook-dominated programs, the first step is to reflect on their perception of the textbook. When they come to regard a text as a tool, as something to use when it suits their purposes, they will have begun the transition from treating the text as a body of information to be learned to treating it as a resource to be used as it is needed.

The following are some alternative ways in which you might use textbooks:

Alternative uses for textbooks

* As a source of background information that students read either (1) prior to studying a topic or concept or (2) after the need for the information has been established.
* As something students read when they need additional information on a topic.
* As a source of potential in-class activities (or test questions).
* As a contrasting point of view or as a source of data for further analysis.
* As a means to confirm or challenge certain hypotheses after group discussion—for example, "India is a 'poor' nation."
* As a vehicle for identifying the main idea of several related paragraphs.
* As a source for establishing the meaning of various terms (so that they need not be dealt with in class).
* As a way of placating people who think that a course isn't worthwhile unless it has a textbook associated with it.
* As an object of study (to determine how the text was organized and constructed).

Supplementary Print Materials

The supplementary print materials available to social studies teachers range from periodicals and current events newspapers through an unbelievable assortment of trade books (children's books) to self-contained teaching kits on almost any topic you can name. Supplementary print materials are considered in terms of these categories.

● Current Events Publications

If your elementary school was like my elementary school, some of your teachers used a weekly or monthly affairs periodical. These include publications such as *My Weekly Reader, Let's Find Out* (kindergarten), *Scholastic News* (Grades 1–6), or *Junior Review* (Grades 6–9). These publications are still widely available.

Beware of articles selected at random

Instead of current events periodicals, which must be purchased separately, your teachers may have relied more heavily on daily newspapers. From time to time, they may have asked you to bring in a newspaper article to share with the class for current events time. But unless they put limitations on the kind of clipping you could bring in, a typical assortment might deal with topics such as last Saturday's Little League game or a bank robbery in northeastern Nevada. Seldom do child-selected articles focus on proposed constitutional amendments, changing views of morality, or the problems of international diplomacy—unless a teacher insists on it. Even then, many children will be unable to understand or interpret the significance of such events. Such an assignment reflects the current events problem: much as we might like children to be interested in and aware of events and issues going on around the world that may influence their lives, many of those events and issues can go beyond their current level of comprehension and concern. The fact that some teachers have difficulty explaining things such as inflation or why the Palestine Liberation Organization and Israel have traditionally been at odds illustrates another dimension of the problem. Helping children to understand what is going on in the world at any particular moment is only part of the problem; they also need to understand why these events are occurring.

Current Events or Current Affairs?   As a teacher, you have at least two options for keeping students abreast of happenings going on around them. One option is to maintain an ongoing current events program. In this context, an *event* is anything that has happened or is happening, either trivial or potentially significant. A second option is to establish a current *affairs* program that focuses on continuing issues or concerns. In the absence of realistic limitations, a current events approach can become a warmed-over version of the nightly news, in which case the purposes of the program might be better served if the class actually watched the news on television.

Current affairs programs focus on in-depth studies of ongoing issues—the environment, human rights, conflicts occurring in various parts of the world (the Middle East, Africa, or Bosnia), and so forth. Consequently, current affairs programs are less likely to reflect the piecemeal approach that can occur in current events programs. In a current affairs program, your focus might be on different dimensions of the farm crisis. Or you might use changes in the price (or weight) of bubble gum or candy bars as an entrée to the continuing study of rises in the cost of living. The idea of a current affairs program is to tie together the separate events of a continuing problem to help students understand the significance of problems that could remain beyond their comprehension if dealt with on an isolated events basis.

With the Internet and other modern technology, the world has been reduced to the global village of almost instantaneous communications. As a result, you may recall seeing television coverage of people, especially children, running for cover to avoid being shot or killed in hostilities somewhere around the world. Our concern is with the feelings, and sometimes fears, that these images can generate among young children. The purpose of current events and current affairs programs is to help children make sense of events occurring in the world around them, not to frighten them.

Weekly news periodicals, like *Weekly Reader* and *Scholastic,* can furnish the background information essential for interpreting current events. The broad range of events and happenings that the weekly periodicals include may compensate for their lack of in-depth coverage. Thus the basic decision you face in developing a current affairs or current events program (and in deciding whether to use one of the current events periodicals) is whether to aim for in-depth understanding of

The current events problem

Current affairs focus on ongoing issues

Seeking common elements among separate events

Depth versus breadth

In the aftermath of the tragic bombings of the World Trade Center building in New York City and the federal office building in Oklahoma City, it became apparent we can no longer tell children that "terrorism occurs in places that are far far away" and that "such events can't happen here." Adults can take consolation in knowing that their chances of being involved in a terrorist attack are less than one in 100 million (Ellerbee, 1995), but such information seldom offers much comfort to young children. So what, then, is a teacher to do? Ellerbee (1995) offers the following suggestions.

* Let children talk about the event, and let them know it is okay to feel sad or confused—or even scared. However, do so in ways that respect the child's privacy; some children cope by not talking.

* Remind children that it is unfair to judge large groups of people by the actions of a few. You may wish to use words like *cowardly, sneaky,* and *unacceptable,* to rein-

force the notion that violence is not the way to get what you want—something that good people already know.

* Understand that in the immediate aftermath of terrorist attacks, many children are more concerned about their parents' safety than their own. Where appropriate, encourage parents to spend extra time with their children.

* Help children to understand that most terrorist acts are isolated events; they do occur, but not often. Also point out the reassuring things that often happen in their aftermath: the rescuers who risk their lives to save others, the communities near and far who lend supplies and support, and the massive outpouring of sympathy for the victims and rage at the perpetrators. People do indeed care about others.

Source: Ellerbee, L. (1995). What shall we tell the kids? *Liberal Opinion Week,* 6 (May 1), p. 7.

relatively few continuing problems or to aim for awareness of a broader range of topical coverage.

In many instances, current affairs can be esoteric for elementary children, even if the events are reduced to their simplest dimensions. This is because it is extremely difficult, for example, to capture the reasons for the traditional animosity that exists between Arabs and Israelis in a single, easy-to-understand publication. Thus you may be better off opting for the broader coverage that you gain with an events approach, especially if you teach at the primary level. However, if you plan to teach at the intermediate or middle-school levels, the possibility of pursuing a current affairs approach becomes much more realistic. Or you can do both; you can use an affairs approach for some issues and settle for broad awareness for other issues.

Options

Newspapers. Daily newspapers provide what the current events periodicals don't, including coverage of local news. But teachers who look to newspapers solely as a source of local news are not looking far enough. In some schools, teachers base much of their instructional program—social studies, math, language arts, and reading—on daily newspapers. Students do comparison shopping using the grocery ads, compute batting averages (math) using the sports page, invest (mythically) in the stock market, examine weather patterns (using the weather map and forecast), realphabetize the newspaper's directory, put scrambled headlines back together again, compare the amount of space devoted

Using the newspaper to teach

to various categories of articles (international news, national news, etc.), use small sections of the paper to compare the amount of factual data (reporting) with the amount of opinion (editorials), or compare the amount of space devoted to ads with the space devoted to news.

Newspaper-based activities

You might give groups of students identical collections of stories clipped from several newspapers and ask them to compose a front page. They should be prepared to explain their reasons for including the articles they did. You could also remove the headlines from various articles and have children create their own based on the content of the story. They can then compare their headlines with the originals. Or they could take several days' accumulation of TV schedules and try to identify patterns in TV programming.

You could do other things with a daily newspaper, but the preceding examples should serve to illustrate the idea. For many newspaper-related activities, it is not necessary for children to be able to read or understand the articles in order to use the newspaper as a learning tool. As with most instructional resources, the essential idea is to consider the newspaper as a resource, as something you can teach *with*, not simply teach *about*.

● Trade Books

Criteria for selecting children's books

In the publishing world, a textbook is a book designed for classroom use. Fiction or nonfiction books intended for sale to the public are *trade books*. *Mike Mulligan and His Steam Shovel* (Burton, 1939) is a juvenile trade book, as are Kenneth Grahame's (1908) classic, *The Wind in the Willows,* and thousands of others.

Because so many trade books are available, the National Council for the Social Studies reviews only those books considered "most notable" during a given year. Thus, unless the book (1) is written primarily for children (K–8), (2) emphasizes human relations, (3) presents an original theme or a fresh slant on a traditional topic, (4) is highly readable, and (5) includes maps and illustrations where appropriate, it is not included in the listing that appears in each May issue of *Social Education.*

Historical fiction, nonfiction, biography—somewhere there's a trade book that applies to whatever your class is studying. To assess the quality of books for children, McGowan (1987) has recommended the following criteria:

1. Decide whether the book is *developmentally appropriate.* Can the prose be understood by its intended audience, and are the setting, plot, and themes familiar to young readers?

2. Determine whether the book has *literary value.* Is it meaningful and enjoyable to read, and has the author written with attention to character development, dialogue, plot, imagery, and message?

3. Determine whether the book presents *valid information.* Is the story told with reasonable accuracy and in a "true-to-life" fashion?

4. Determine whether the book has *a message of value.* Does the author examine an issue worthy of the reader's attention, or does the story involve values that the reader should eventually assimilate?

An area of children's fiction particularly appropriate to social studies is ethnic literature. For example, *The Big Push* by Betty Baker (1972), based on a historical incident that occurred when the Hopi Indian children were forced to go to school, is almost guaranteed to generate an active discussion. Likewise, children are likely to enjoy *The Hundred Penny Box* by Sharon Bell Mathis (1975), a poignant story about a young boy who convinces his mother not to throw out all the old things that belong to his great-great-great-aunt, who lives with them.

You might consider using trade books in one or more of the following ways:

* As supplementary reading for children
* As background reading for yourself
* As reference material for children to use
* As a springboard for writing activities
* As the vehicle for units or lessons
* As the basis for an individualized reading program that parallels whatever you are dealing with in social studies

● Teaching Kits

Teaching kits are self-contained packages of instructional materials. We have long been fascinated by David Macaulay's wonderful series of books: *Cathedral* (1973), *Pyramid* (1975), *Castle* (1979), *The Way Things Work* (1988), and others. PBS Video (1420 Braddock Place, Alexandria, VA 22314-1698) has now developed multimedia teaching kits based on Macaulay's books. The kits, "Middle Ages" (which combines *Cathedral* and *Castle*) and "Pyramid," cost approximately $200 and include videotapes, teaching modules, and related material. *The Way Things Work* is now available on CD-ROM.

Many museums and state departments of education offer specialized teaching kits on a loan or rental basis. The Institute for Texan Cultures in San Antonio, for example, offers rental kits on "The Indians of Texas." If that topic is not something your students might study, consider the "Mysteries in History" toolbox available from the Indianapolis Children's Museum. Or contact the education coordinator at the nearest historical museum of reconstructed settlement (e.g., Old Sturbridge Village in Massachusetts, Connor Prairie Settlement in Indiana) or your state department of education to find whether they have instructional materials available for loan or rent. Addresses for these sources are in the Resource Handbook.

Self-contained teaching kits can cost upward of $750. As a result, the lower cost of loan or rental kits (approximately $25 plus shipping) often makes them more attractive to cost-conscious administrators. On the other hand, most kits last for years. If four teachers at a grade level share a teaching kit and use it for five years, the per-use cost of a $750 kit would be $37.50, which is not much more than the rental costs.

● Workbooks

Most social studies textbook series have workbooks that are correlated with them, but these must be ordered separately each year; they don't just come with the texts. These materials are called *pupil study guides, activity guides,* or something similar, but they are *workbooks* nonetheless. If you teach in a program that demands the kind of reinforcement that workbooks offer, you may find them helpful.

Computer-Based Resources

Computer-based resources

Like many teachers, I use my computer extensively. All my course syllabi, most of my instructional materials (class handouts), and many of my examinations are now created and stored on the computer. If I were teaching in a school where I had to keep lots of student records, I would use a computer-based grade-book program. They can provide up-to-date analyses of students' progress and can provide almost instant grades at the end of the semester. Considering the amount of information and routine paperwork that teachers must deal with, computers have proven to be wonderful tools for managing classroom-related tasks.

TECHNOLOGY

● Instructional Applications

The six basic modes of computer-assisted instruction (CAI) are (1) tutorial, (2) drill and practice, (3) simulation, (4) integrated application programs, (5) problem solving, and (6) hypermedia environments (Braun, Fernlund, & White, 1998). Each of these is described next.

Tutorial Mode.   Tutorial programs were among the earliest forms of social studies software. They are designed to present information to students, usually step by step and in sequential chunks, and are often accompanied by colorful graphics. In a tutorial program, the computer takes the place of the teacher, the textbook, or another source as the provider of information. Most tutorial programs

Mastery learning

also use a form of branching or mastery learning. This means that when the students respond correctly to a series of questions the program will move them into new material. However, if students respond incorrectly, the computer will recycle them until they can demonstrate mastery.

Tutorial programs are available for a variety of topics, including basic economics, introductory history and geography, and, in some cases, nonsubject-related topics. For example, *Kids on Keys* (Spinnaker) is a tutorial program designed to familiarize young children with the computer keyboard.

Drill-and-Practice Mode.   Drill-and-practice programs are designed to reinforce prior learning through repetitive practice. If you wish your students to learn the states and capitals or to practice locating places using latitude or longitude, for example, there are several programs that can help them. In fact, most social studies software falls into the drill-and-practice mode.

Electronic workbook

Drill-and-practice programs have been likened to electronic workbooks. But unlike traditional workbooks, the material is often presented randomly rather than sequentially. This means that students do not interact with the same series of questions and activities each time they use the software. In addition, drill-and-

practice programs often use a gamelike format that, when combined with superb graphics, color, and sound, can make them appealing and almost painless.

A major asset of drill-and-practice programs is their ability to provide immediate feedback. For example, wherever students enter an incorrect answer, the program typically responds with an encouraging "Try again, Zack." Unfortunately, *Immediate feedback* most computer-based programs do not recognize or give credit for partially correct or misspelled answers, as human graders might. Some drill-and-practice programs avoid this limitation by asking questions in a multiple-choice format, so that students need enter only the letter (A, B, C, or D) for the correct response. Despite these limitations, the interactive nature of drill-and-practice programs can add life to what might otherwise be dull stuff.

Simulation Mode.   The simulation mode was described in some detail in Chapter 9, so we will say little more about it here. Using simulations, children can place themselves into lifelike situations in which they must make decisions similar to those that had to be made in whatever real-life situation the simulation depicts. Those decisions may relate to traveling westward on the *Oregon Trail* (or its newer siblings, *Yukon Trail* and *Amazon Trail*, MECC, 1996), building and operating a dinosaur theme park (*DinoPark Tycoon*, MECC, 1995), or operating a school store (*Classroom StoreWorks*, Tom Snyder, 1997).

Computer-based simulations are very popular but can also be very time con-*Beating the computer* suming. In addition, children sometimes approach simulations as they do video games, where their objective is to outwit the program so they can "win." Such situations may require human intervention—a teacher-led discussion, perhaps—that refocuses students' attention on the content being simulated, and not just the outcome.

Integrated Application Programs.   Databases, spreadsheets, and word-processing programs have been available for at least a decade, but integrated application programs incorporate these formerly separate entities into a single powerful program. Examples include *Appleworks* (Claris), *Microsoft Word* (Microsoft), *Clarisworks* (Claris), *Greatworks* (Symantec), and *Works for Windows* (Microsoft). *Integrated packages* Any one of these programs can be useful for developing and presenting data for teacher-developed instructional activities and for upper elementary and middle-school students' presentations. For example, Janet Jacobsen's students used the *Works* program to create their reports and the graphics associated with them. More appropriate for lower elementary students are programs like *Magic Slate* (Sunburst), *KidWriter* (Spinnaker), or FrEd Writer (Computer Using Educators). Because even most kindergarten children are able to use computers successfully, any hesitancy in this area probably reflects the teacher's misgivings and not the students' capabilities (cf., Bryant, 1992).

Problem-Solving Mode.   Integrated application programs can provide the basis for some fascinating problem-solving activities. For example, consider posing the following question to your students: "How do underdeveloped nations differ from developed nations?" The first step is helping students to decide what

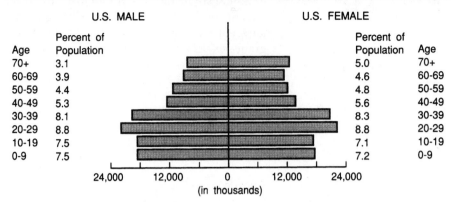

FIGURE 14.1 Age Distribution, United States of America (USA) and Bangladesh

U.S. MALE   U.S. FEMALE

Age	Percent of Population		Percent of Population	Age
70+	3.1		5.0	70+
60-69	3.9		4.6	60-69
50-59	4.4		4.8	50-59
40-49	5.3		5.6	40-49
30-39	8.1		8.3	30-39
20-29	8.8		8.8	20-29
10-19	7.5		7.1	10-19
0-9	7.5		7.2	0-9

24,000   12,000   0   12,000   24,000
(in thousands)

Total population: 248,231,000   Life expectancy (male): 72 years
Total male population: 120,640,000   Life expectancy (female): 79 years
Total female population: 127,591,000

BANGLADESH MALE   BANGLADESH FEMALE

Age	Percent of Population		Percent of Population	Age
70+	1.0		0.8	70+
60-69	1.7		1.4	60-69
50-59	2.6		2.3	50-59
40-49	4.0		3.6	40-49
30-39	5.6		5.1	30-39
20-29	7.9		7.6	20-29
10-19	13.2		12.0	10-19
0-9	15.6		15.6	0-9

20,000   10,000   0   10,000   20,000
(in thousands)

Total population: 114,718,000   Life expectancy (male): 54 years
Total male population: 59,194,000   Life expectancy (female): 53 years
Total female population: 55,524,000

Source: Copyright © 1990 PC Globe, Inc. Used by permission.

TECHNOLOGY

characteristics might separate underdeveloped and developed nations. Using a database program, you can easily provide per capita income information for different nations, which students can then use to determine which ones are "developed" or "undeveloped." Once that decision is made, students can use a database program to determine what characteristics are associated with "developed" and "undeveloped" countries.

Figure 14.1, which shows the age distribution data for the United States and Bangladesh, was generated by the *PC Globe* database program. Other programs offer similar capabilities. By comparing these data for the United States and

Bangladesh, students can identify at least one factor, the birth rate, that characterizes the difference between developed and undeveloped nations.

Hypermedia Environments.   There are basically two types of hypermedia programs: (1) Internet browsers, such as *Netscape* and *Microsoft Internet Explorer*, and (2) hypertext programs such as *Hypercard* and *Hyperstudio* (for Apple computers) and *Linkway* (for PCs). All of these programs permit users to navigate interactively through audio, video, and text modes. You must have a modem or be wired directly to a network server to use an Internet browser, but hypertext-based programs have no such requirements.

Interactive navigation

Hypertext programs are assembled much like a deck of index cards—each containing certain information—that can be arranged and rearranged in different ways. By pressing a button located on each card, you can move to the next card or, in some instances, start a CD-ROM or other audiovisual device. When a hypertext program is combined with audiovisual equipment, the result is a hypermedia environment, perhaps even a multimedia extravaganza!

Hypertext programs are especially well suited for presentations, either by teachers or students. This is because users can easily alter the sequence of presentation. Unfortunately, the description of hypertext programs is often more imposing than the programs themselves. Most middle-school students can learn to use *Hyperstudio* readily, whereas most primary students often feel more comfortable using a somewhat simpler version called *SlideShow*.

Programs for presentation

● Telecommunications

TECHNOLOGY

More and more elementary classrooms today have computers. However, far fewer classrooms have one or more computers, one or more modems, and one or more telephone lines. All three elements—computer, modem, and telephone line—are needed before your classroom computer can connect to the Internet and the on-line information services such as America Online, Compuserve, and Prodigy. The key and most costly element in connecting your classroom computer to the outside world is a dedicated telephone line.

Help is in sight

You may remember Janet Jacobsen from an earlier vignette, whose students use the on-line services (e.g., America Online, etc.) and communicate via E-mail with individuals around the world. By current standards, her classroom is exceptional, simply because it has its own telephone line. The federal initiative to wire all schools should one day make such facilities commonplace.

● Evaluating Software

The quality of social studies software varies tremendously. Sometimes a program's instructions are unclear; in other instances, a program may produce inaccurate stereotypes or require information that students don't have. Such flaws can make the programs unusable or, in the case of inaccurate stereotyping, inappropriate for use with children.

Recommended criteria for evaluating computer software are illustrated in Figure 14.2.

FIGURE 14.2 Computer Software Evaluation Form

Program (title) _____ Grade Level(s) _____

Producer _____ Cost _____

Hardware Required: _____
_____

I. Program Description (describe briefly):

II. General Considerations:
Does the program promote

1. active social studies learning?   Yes _____   No _____

2. meaningful social studies learning?   Yes _____   No _____

3. a pluralistic perspective on our society?   Yes _____   No _____

4. an integrative interdisciplinary perspective?   Yes _____   No _____

III. Instructional Design:
(Briefly summarize any of the following elements
that apply; note any problems):

1. Is the content accurate, appropriate, and   Yes _____   No _____
   worthwhile?

2. Is the content appropriately sequenced and   Yes _____   No _____
   free from stereotyping or biases?

3. Does the reading level fit the recommended   Yes _____   No _____
   audience?

4. Does the program make unusual demands   Yes _____   No _____
   of the student, e.g., excessive background
   knowledge, reading lengthy narratives, etc.?

IV. Technical Considerations:

1. Are the instructions/documentation well   Yes _____   No _____
   organized, clearly written, and complete?

2. Are all needed materials included?   Yes _____   No _____

3. Does the program operate as it is supposed to?   Yes _____   No _____

Overall Rating _____ *Evaluated by:* _____

Source: Part II is adapted from Rose & Fernlund, 1997.

Reading and the written word—the print media—have so dominated American schools that nonprint media—videotape, pictures, films, and the like—have a long way to go before they have the educational impact of the printed word. Nevertheless, there have been substantial increases in both the amount of nonprint media available and in the different kinds of nonreading-based materials designed for educational purposes.

Pictures, Films, and Videotapes

The largest and most obvious category of alternatives to the printed word is pictures—those things "worth a thousand words." They come in many forms: collections of study prints, films and filmstrips, videotapes, and paintings and other works of art. Or they can be nothing more than illustrations and advertisements that you have clipped from magazines, calendars, and other sources.

The beauty of photographs as teaching tools lies in their ability to present selected yet uninterpreted data (as described in the section on culture cards, pages 315 and 317–318). Yet educators too often tend to interpret the data for viewers almost immediately. Explanatory captions are provided for most photographs and illustrations, and a narration serves this purpose for films. The intent, traditionally, has been to use the narration or picture caption to convey information. However,

On removing captions and narrations

removing or eliminating the caption or narration increases viewers' involvement with the picture because it forces them to make their own interpretations.

Videos and films are available for almost any topic you can name. There is also a body of educational films and videos that have no narration, only the natural sound of whatever they depict. For example, more than six hours of nonnarrated film or video beautifully portray the life of the Netselik Eskimos (*Fishing at the Stone Weir, Caribou Hunting at the Crossing Place, Autumn River Camp, Parts I and II*, and *Winter Sea Ice Camp, Parts I and II*) and are available from libraries across the country.

Eliminating the narration automatically eliminates any vocabulary problems the narration could present. So the same nonnarrated film or video can sometimes be used by primary students, twelfth graders, and even adults, usually with a different emphasis at each level.

Video cassettes

Videotape cassettes have largely replaced traditional 16-mm films in most areas. This has come about largely because of the videotape's availability, lower cost, and, most important, convenience. Because schools or teachers usually own their videotapes, the hassle of scheduling films up to a year in advance is essentially eliminated.

Making your own videos

As the cost (and size) of videocamcorders has decreased, more teachers are making their own videotapes. This has been a boon in schools where field trips have been largely eliminated because of policy or budget considerations, or when it would be dangerous to take a large group of students to a site, such as a steel mill. Yet even where field trips are permitted, some teachers videotape them anyhow so that they can call attention to specific elements when they get back to their classroom.

TECHNOLOGY UPDATE

Virtual Touring on the Internet

Unless you teach in the vicinity of Plimoth Plantation in Massachusetts, or Colonial Williamsburg in Virginia, taking your class on a field trip to either place is probably out of the question. And if you are studying the Middle Ages, you probably don't even think about visiting a medieval castle or cathedral, both of which are in Europe. However, by connecting to the Internet, there are hundreds of places your class can visit via a "virtual tour." Some of these places include:

1. The Plimoth Plantation at:
   http://spirit.lib.uconn.edu/ArchNet/Topical/Historic/Plimoth/Plimoth.html

2. Colonial Williamsburg at:
   http://www.history.org

3. Old Philadelphia at:
   http://www.libertynet.org/iha/index/html

4. The Museum of Egyptian Antiquities in Cairo, Egypt, at:
   http://interoz.com/egypt/museum

5. The twelfth century Durham Castle and Cathedral in Durham, United Kingdom, at:
   http://www.dur.ac.uk/~dla0www/c_tour/tour.html

Virtual touring on the Internet is usually interactive. This means you can determine how quickly to progress through the tour and whether you wish to investigate additional areas of interest. For example, the diagram below is the floor plan of Durham Castle. By clicking your mouse on one of the numbers, you will get a photograph and a more detailed explanation of that area.

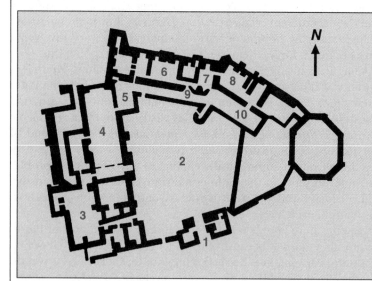

1. The Gatehouse
2. The Courtyard
3. The Entrance, Buttery and Kitchen
4. The Great Hall
5. The Black Staircase
6. The Norman Gallery
7. The Norman Chapel
8. The State Rooms
9. Bishop Tunstall's Gallery
10. Bishop Tunstall's Chapel

Durham Castle Plan

Source: Reprinted by permission of the University of Durham, Durham, UK.

If you are curious as to whether there is a virtual tour available for a topic that your class is studying, contact the on-line collection of virtual tours at:

http://www.dreamscape.com/frankvad/tours.html. You can also use an on-line search engine to locate similar sites.

Realia

Realia: the real thing

Remember when a fellow student brought in his "genuine" Indian arrowhead collection to share with the class? Or when someone's relatives had been to the Orient and brought back an authentic Japanese fan? These things—the arrowheads, the Japanese fan, and other real objects that might be associated with social studies teaching—are all encompassed by the term *realia.*

Most realia are adjuncts to social studies teaching, primarily because the objects are precious to their owners, often part of a collection, and as such the owner would rather not have them handled and possibly broken. Thus they often become things to be displayed—looked at but not used—during a teaching activity, and perhaps rightfully so. Some realia are probably best handled via display and in a passing fashion, such as when a student brings in a World War II bayonet during your study of colonial America.

Options

Using realia unrelated to whatever your class is studying is difficult to justify on almost any grounds. But assume, for a moment, that somewhere in your travels you have acquired a colonial candle mold and your class will be studying colonial America. What are your options? You have several. First, you could display the device and say, "This is a colonial candle mold." You could then describe how it was used.

Second, you might place the mold in a prominent location but say nothing about it. Questions are going to be asked about it, you can be sure. But to the question "What is it?" you could respond, "What do you think it is?" You might mount a large sheet of paper near the mold and ask the children to list what they think it is. At a convenient time, you might display an illustration of someone using a candle mold, again saying nothing about it. Someone will soon notice it, and you may not even need to say anything else at all. Or you might pose the question "How are candles made today?," which will initiate another adventure.

As springboards to inquiry

If the function of the realia is obvious, you might wish to take a different tack. For the Japanese fan mentioned earlier, you might want to ask who uses fans in Japan and why. Are they necessarily to keep Japanese women cool? If you pursue this line of questioning, identify—in advance—some sources the students can use to validate their answers. They may find that fans are a normal part of a Japanese dancer's equipment.

Community Resources

Every community everywhere has someone who has been somewhere or who knows something that can be useful in your social studies program. And almost every community also has places you can visit that will also be an asset to your program.

Resource Persons

Using resource people effectively

Identifying individuals in the community who have specialized knowledge or experience is not especially difficult. The list can go from authors to zookeepers. The more challenging task is using those resource people effectively.

Part of the problem occurs because resource people are, by definition, specialists. As such, they are familiar with the intricacies, the nuances, and the jargon of their specialization. Your students, however, may be at a level where their main concern is with the most fundamental aspects of a specialized area.

The local history buff who, for example, gets enmeshed in the minutiae of who married whom in the early 1840s can't count on keeping your students' interest for very long. Once their interest is lost, your students may begin to get restless, and your guest speaker may take their behavior as a personal affront. Therefore, even though it may seem an imposition, clarify in advance exactly what you want the speaker to cover to ensure a successful experience for both the resource person *and* your class.

A related problem arises because resource people are sometimes ill equipped to do more than talk to students. Unless they deal with young children regularly, they are unlikely to have audiovisual aids or other media to enliven their presentations. Even if they have such media, you will need to have worked with your class to establish a need or desire for whatever information the resource person can provide. One of the most helpful things you can do is provide the resource person with a list of questions or topics that your class has developed before the presentation. This helps ensure that (1) the class has at least a passing acquaintance with whatever the resource person will cover (otherwise students won't be able to frame intelligent questions) and (2) the resource person has an idea of the level of the class's concerns and can prepare accordingly.

A final suggestion about using resource people: be wary of people who *insist* on talking to your class. Among the people who willingly volunteer their services, there are always some who would use the schools as a platform for their special causes. Even if you are sympathetic to the cause, whatever it may be, you may risk your professional future by honoring their offer. Before issuing an invitation, be certain to check school policies and inform the appropriate administrative personnel (principal, etc.) of your intentions.

● Oral History

Oral history refers to written histories that are produced primarily from spoken (or oral) sources. When students get involved in oral history projects, they usually do so on a cooperative learning basis. Several students working together develop a written history using data they have gathered by interviewing individuals from the community who have firsthand knowledge of historically interesting events or ways of life. The interviews are tape-recorded and then converted into transcripts that provide the basis for the written history. The resulting document, probably the only one of its kind in existence, is usually placed in the school library.

Oral history is ideally suited to the study of recent local history. The key element is that there must be people around who know something about the period or topic in question and are willing to be interviewed. Grandparents and senior citizens are frequent and often willing subjects for oral history projects.

A key aspect of oral history activities involves helping students to plan and structure their interviews. If they don't plan carefully, they can easily end up with random conversations of little historic value. Student interviewers must be clear about

Margin notes:

Preliminary actions

Lay the necessary groundwork

Caution

Using community resources to create history

Plan interviews in advance

what information they are after, who is going to ask which questions, and so forth. Their purpose may be to get a local resident's account of the day the old courthouse burned down, someone's views on how population growth has affected the community, or almost anything else that might be of interest. The students' purpose is to conduct an interview *about something*. It doesn't matter so much what that "something" is as long as students understand what kind of information they are after.

Here are some guidelines for conducting oral history activities:

Suggested guidelines

1. The focus should be on one manageable topic, especially in the lower elementary grades.

2. Prepare carefully for the interview, including helping students to "bone up" on the topic by using other sources—wills, diaries, other accounts. On the other hand, don't do so much preparation that your students lose interest.

3. Equipment for the interview may include props like an old photograph or picture, but a tape recorder is essential.

4. Appointments for interviews should be made through official sources so that students don't face the burden of explaining the entire project. Interviews should be restricted to one hour or less.

5. Send students in interview teams of two or three.

6. Contact the computer teacher for possible assistance in putting the transcripts on a word processor.

The logistics of oral history combined with the mechanics of producing transcripts from several dozen tape-recorded interviews can sometimes become so cumbersome that the project may not seem worth the effort. At the same time, students involved in an oral history project are actually creating history. In the process, they can also be developing skills in listening, observing, and asking questions; organizing information; and distinguishing fact from opinion and relevant from irrelevant information. If they do nothing else, oral history activities may lead students to a better understanding and appreciation of the older generation. That alone may make oral history projects worth the effort.

——● Field Trips and Tours

Some teachers take their students on tours of museums, bakeries, fire stations, and the like, which can provide enriching, hands-on experiences that would be impossible to duplicate in a classroom. Other teachers, however, take their students on field trips to the same places. The distinction between *tours* and *field trips* is based on (1) the activities that take place in the classroom prior to the trip and (2) the students' perceptions about why they are going.

Before scientists "go out into the field," they usually identify their purpose for going. When archaeologists decide to dig at a particular site, for example, their decision is usually based on (1) prior research, (2) a clear sense of purpose (for digging), and (3) previously identified questions or problems that they hope to answer. Likewise, if your students were going on a field trip to a bakery, they should arrive armed with *previously identified* questions that they want answers for:

"Do bakeries grind their own flour?" "Do bakeries use the same kind of flour available in supermarkets?" In other words, because of the students' previous classroom experience, they arrive at the site with a clear sense of why they are there. Students will probably enjoy the experience and learn things they didn't have questions about, but this is simply extra frosting on the cake.

Logistics. Although tours and field trips can add immeasurable value to education, most experienced teachers can also tell horror stories about things that went wrong on a field trip or tour: kids who got lost, children who spent all their lunch money at the souvenir stand, and so forth. The logistical problems can have you tearing your hair out in short order.

In addition, students sometimes assume that rules for classroom conduct don't apply to outside-of-school activities, as on a field trip or tour, which then leads to discipline problems. Although there is certainly no guarantee, the clearer sense of purpose associated with field trips will probably result in fewer discipline problems. Likewise, preplanning can eliminate some of the logistical and discipline-related problems associated with field trips and tours. Consider the following suggestions:

* Obtain administrative approval before announcing the trip to students. (On the application form, always use "field trip," even if you're planning a tour to the zoo—it sounds better and may be easier for the administrator to justify.)

* Avoid going anywhere on Mondays and Fridays. Over the weekend (for a Monday trip), kids often forget to bring their lunches, spending money, and so on. Friday trips deny the opportunity for immediate follow-up.

* Recruit, screen, and instruct parent chaperons so that they can contribute significantly to the trip. Don't wait until just before leaving to tell parents what you expect of them. Send a note home beforehand that outlines (1) what you expect parents to do, (2) rules you have discussed with students, and (3) any other pertinent information.

* Create task groups with specific responsibilities before the trip takes place. For example, there can be recorders (keep records and journals), collectors (obtain necessary items for or from the trip), photographers, public relations people (thank-you-note writers), and maintenance people (clean up).

* If you are taking a tour, select an impressive place. If you were bored on your last trip to the sewage-treatment plant, your students probably will be bored too.

* Take everyone, including your troublemakers. Leaving them behind could lead to deep-seated resentment you can never overcome.

* Send parental permission slips home even if the school uses a blanket permission form covering all field trips for the year.

* Even with signed permission slips, you may be legally liable if you agree to supervise students in too large an area. We're not talking about the Superdome here. Trying to supervise students in two large halls of a museum could make you liable if something happened to someone. Err on the safe side, and *take one adult for each group of five children.* If you plan to videotape the trip, take along a parent to do that so you remain free to devote your complete attention to leading the expedition.

* Use name tags (including the school name). This is essential for young children; for older students it enables chaperons to call them by name.

* Avoid going in private cars whenever possible; the legal hazards (insurance coverage, etc.) are considerable.

* Be sure to take a first-aid kit, a summary of students' medical information, especially allergies, and a list of the children's home and emergency phone numbers.

* Prepare a guidesheet for students to complete while at the museum or other resource.

* Be certain to debrief the activity. As is true of most things educational, what happens after a field trip is as important as what takes place during or before it.

* Be sure to send thank-you notes to all parents who assist you.

Don't overlook walking field trips to nearby locations. Supermarkets, banks, bakeries, and those old standbys, the post office and fire station, often welcome visits from schoolchildren. Whether you walk or take a bus, the crucial element is that your students understand why they are going on the field trip. Otherwise, field trips and tours may be seen as a lark or just another day off from school.

● Using Community Resources

Using community resources—either resource persons or field trips—involves both a logistical and a substantive dimension. The logistical side includes such things as contacting individuals and arranging for buses (and rest stops, parental approval and assistance, etc.). The substantive dimension relates to the content that you and your class (and perhaps a resource person) will be studying.

Many school districts have specific guidelines for the logistical (and legal) considerations concerning resource persons and field trips. Sometimes they also cover substantive questions. Could you, for example, invite an avowed white supremacist to speak to your class? Could you take your students on a field trip to a slaughterhouse or a funeral home? Consider how you would respond if you were an elementary principal and a teacher came to you with such a request. If the teacher could show a clear relationship between the slaughterhouse (or the funeral home) and whatever the class was studying, would it make any difference to your decision? The issues here are far from simple.

Once you have gotten the necessary permissions, the success of the experience will probably depend on the preliminary work you do before a resource person enters your classroom or before your class leaves on the field trip. The basic questions you need to ask yourself include the following:

* Is a community resource appropriate for the purposes of my group?
* Have I planned preliminary activities that provide a context within which my class can interpret whatever they hear or see?
* Have I identified appropriate follow-up activities?
* Does my class have an identifiable need for the information that the resource can provide?
* Do my students understand what is expected of them—both in terms of their conduct and in terms of what they are to learn?

If you can answer these questions in the positive, you'll be on the way to making effective use of the resources that your community can provide. If you cannot, keep your aspirin handy.

Acquiring Instructional Resources

Determining what is available

Where do teachers get the things they teach with? Many school systems provide a budget from which teachers purchase teaching materials. Where such budgets exist, they are almost always small. In acquiring instructional resources, your first step is to identify what is available from commercial publishers or other sources. You can usually find catalogs of educational materials somewhere in the school—the library, the resource center, or the teachers' lounge. The names and addresses of the major teachers' magazines and social studies journals are located in the Resource Handbook.

Evaluate free materials carefully

Many school systems accept teachers' requests for materials in the spring and purchase the materials the following summer. This may mean that you don't have the opportunity to purchase materials during your first year of teaching. In that event, you will be forced to do what hundreds of other teachers do—buy materials yourself. But before doing that, you have a couple of other options. First, find out if there is something you can use that is free (or inexpensive). The quality of free and inexpensive materials can vary tremendously, however, so be selective. Evaluate why various concerns are willing to sell materials inexpensively or give them away. Many schools subscribe to one or more guides to free and inexpensive materials. Sources and addresses are listed in the Resource Handbook.

Second, consider making your own materials. Some of the best teaching resources are those that teachers have developed themselves. For example, teachers created most of the student activities in this book. Most of them went through some refining—that is, they were tried out with students and then revised—but once developed, they become a resource to be used in future years.

Procedure

The process of developing teaching materials is not as difficult as you might suspect (a large dose of common sense is about as helpful as anything). Typically, you do the following:

1. Identify (a) the major concept(s) you want to teach and (b) the major question(s), issue(s), or skill(s) you want the children to deal with. (Note: This is sometimes the most difficult step of all.)
2. Decide what kind of format you want to use—a fact sheet, role-playing, limited-choice decision-making, and so on.
3. Create the activity (and duplicate as needed).
4. Use the activity with your students.
5. Revise as needed, based on what you found in Step 4.

It's sometimes wise to add a Step 3(a): before you duplicate an activity for students, share it with someone you can rely on for honest feedback—a colleague, a fellow student teacher, or someone else. You are almost certain to find that something you thought was perfectly obvious isn't, and thus you will gain a chance to make appropriate adjustments before using the activity with your students.

SUMMARY

There are countless resources teachers can use for teaching social studies, including a can of corn, as noted earlier, a colonial candle mold perhaps, or even a telephone directory. Determining what is or is not a potential teaching resource is primarily a matter of perception, a matter of asking yourself what you could teach by using "that." The second key is one stressed throughout this book; that is, a resource is something you use to teach, as opposed to something you teach about.

The one resource available almost everywhere is the textbook. Using a textbook as your primary resource during your first year of teaching is understandable and, in some cases, politically expedient. But as you become more familiar with the terrain you are expected to cover, consider integrating some of the other resources available to you. These may include daily newspapers, children's books—both informational and fictional—and perhaps one of the current events publications. They may also include computer-based resources, such as tutorials, drill-and-practice programs, simulations, integrated application programs that incorporate databases, spread-sheets, and word-processing programs, and, if you have the necessary hardware, programs that allow your students to connect to the Internet or develop presentation materials using one of the hypertext-based programs.

Even if you do not have sophisticated computer equipment, there are other traditional resources that can add to your program. These include individuals in the community who can provide expertise on particular subjects, as well as field trips and tours to places that your students might not otherwise visit. However, the key to using community resource people, field trips, or tours successfully lies in the kind of preliminary work you do before the event occurs. Students who understand why they are listening to a resource person or visiting a particular site are much less likely to regard the event as a lark.

Regardless of what resources for teaching social studies you choose to use, the basic expectation is that they reflect accurate and unbiased, quality "stuff." In addition, the resources must be used in ways that capture the students' attention. Unless they can fulfill that requirement, the quality issue becomes irrelevant.

SUGGESTED ACTIVITIES

1. Congratulations! Your budget request has been approved and the board of education has authorized $250 per teacher for social studies teaching materials. You can really use some new materials; for example, your textbook carries a 1995 copyright. Your other materials consist of a wall map of the world and one of the United States, a sixteen-inch globe, and an almanac dated 1985. How will you (or your team) spend those funds?

2. In small groups, plan a field trip for an elementary or middle-school class. Then, as a group, go on the field trip you have planned, making certain someone brings a camera. Share your findings with the rest of the class: include your preliminary research, slides of the trip itself, and the way in which you would follow it up.

SUGGESTED READINGS AND RESOURCES

Print Resources

Michael J. Berson, Barbara C. Cruz, James A. Duplass, & J. Howard Johnson. (2001). *Social studies on the Internet.* Upper Saddle River, NJ: Prentice Hall. This little volume is filled with Internet addresses along with short descriptions of what each site offers. Its organization follows an eclectic but useful pattern—subjects commonly taught in social studies, planning and instruction, controversial issues, and so on.

J. A. Braun, Jr., P. Fernlund, & C. S. White. (1998). *Technology tools in the social studies curriculum.* Wilsonville, OR: Franklin-Beedle and Associates. This book provides an excellent overview of the latest technology-related options available to teachers. Also includes reprints of articles.

Mildred Knight Laughlin & Patricia Payne Kardaleff. (1991). *Literature-based social studies: Children's books & activities to enrich the K–5 curriculum.* Phoenix, AZ: Oryx Press. Although we have cited this volume previously, we repeat it here because it contains exemplary units that are based on children's books and that are keyed to topics common to many social studies programs.

Thomas M. McGowan & Meredith McGowan. (1986). *Children, literature, and social studies: Activities for the intermediate grades.* Omaha, NE: Special Literature Press. This excellent publication provides a wealth of information on basing social studies activities on children's fiction.

Internet Resources

Introductory Note: Web sites sometimes change their Internet addresses or cease operating entirely. All the addresses supplied here were operating when this book was printed, but if any of them fails to work properly, enter the desired topic or organization into any standard search engine.

SOFTWARE AND SOFTWARE REVIEWS

SuperKids Software Reviews

http://www.superkids.com/aweb/pages/reviews/socstudl/sw_sum 1.shtml

Parents, teachers, and children do reviews of social studies software at this site. Very useful.

Lexington (Mass.) Recommended Software

http://1ink.ci.lexington.ma.us/WWW/Shelley/recsoft/index.html

This site, maintained by the Lexington, Massachusetts Public Schools, has a large section on reviews of social studies software.

Technology and Learning Online

http://www.techlearning.com/

This highly recommended site is the home page of the journal *Technology and Learning*. A notable feature is its software review search engine, which permits you to search for reviews of software related to social studies or the other subjects taught in elementary and middle schools.

OTHER SOCIAL-STUDIES–RELATED MATERIALS

Sources

http://www.intel.com/intelleducate/teacher/links

This extremely useful site is maintained by the Intel Corporation and offers links to resources for classroom teachers. These include professional organizations, the ERIC Clearinghouses, specialty Internet publications, and numerous other areas that involve technology and education. **Bookmark quality.**

Software and Other Social Studies Materials

http://www.summit.k12.oh.us/site/Curriculum/socialstudies.htm

This site, maintained by the Summit County (Akron), Ohio, Education Service Center, includes links to a variety of materials and software for social studies teachers.

Social Studies Software

http://ed.info.apple.corn/education/techlearn/sp/socstsoft.html

Apple Computer maintains this site, which includes listings of social studies software titles that are organized by categories. These include: (1) simulation software, (2) historical software, and (3) reference software. Useful.

K–12 Software Catalog

http://www.wkbradford.com/subjsoci.htm

The internal search engine at this site permits you to seek out social studies materials for (1) elementary, (2) middle school, and (3) secondary schools programs that are available from the Bradford Publishing Company.

Epilogue

Remember when you:

- Couldn't understand why Australia was a continent but Greenland wasn't?
- Thought Paris, Boston, and Chicago were states?
- Memorized the Preamble to the Constitution, the Gettysburg Address, or the presidents of the United States in order?
- Were taught that "mail carriers deliver the mail" when you already knew it? . . .

Introduction: Reflecting on Things Past

This book began by asking whether you remembered some of the things listed above. It ends with the hope that you have a better context for explaining and interpreting those things you remembered. Hopefully, you understand that the perspective from which some maps are drawn makes Australia appear smaller than Greenland (even though it is actually about three times larger) and that young children often have difficulty distinguishing among cities, states, and countries until they gain more experience with their world.

Many changes occur in social studies education over the years, ranging from efforts to teach "history as history" and "geography as geography," through attempts to teach children to use the social and behavioral sciences as they deal with the worlds in which they live. To whatever extent I have an opportunity to influence the direction that social studies education in the future may take, I wish to suggest the following as possible emphases that can take us into the twenty-first century.

Instructional Premises for the Twenty-First Century

- Observation and listening should receive increased emphasis as access skills.
- There should be increased emphasis on helping students become more aware of the thinking processes they use.

383

* There should be increased awareness of the extent to which mathematics can be a tool for communicating social information.

* There should be an increased use of literature, both fiction and nonfiction, in teaching social studies.

* There should be increased recognition of the power of technology to place a world of data at students' fingertips.

* From the primary grades onward, students should be increasingly involved in designing and conducting their own investigations (their own "social studies," if you will).

* Social studies programs and teaching should emphasize systems of relationships among social phenomena rather than the learning of isolated pieces of information.

* In social studies teaching, increased emphasis should be on helping students become skillful in making and testing social ideas.

* The assessment of students' performance will be increasingly based on portfolios and specific examples of student achievement.

* The trend toward "less is more"—that is, helping students to develop indepth understanding of fewer significant topics, with correspondingly less superficial coverage—should continue.

From time to time, various individuals and organizations release reports intent on showing what students don't know. Most of those reports are accompanied by claims that we need to teach more of "this" and more of "that" to rectify the apparent crisis. I am not trying to excuse the many problems in schools today, but *so long as the reservoir of available information continues to grow, there will always be things that students don't know.*

Efforts to teach children everything they might ever be expected to know may have contributed to the problem. The time available for teaching has not increased significantly over the last century, whereas the reservoir of knowledge grows larger with each passing day. By trying to cram everything into the limited time available, many social studies (and other school) programs have opted for breadth—for covering large amounts of information in a comparatively short time—instead of focusing in depth on significant understandings, ideas, and skills. The superficial skimming that occurs in "trying to cover everything" has too often resulted in mere exposure and the knowledge of a few facts and names, but at the cost of in-depth understanding.

Clearly all students should know certain basics, certain fundamental ideas and skills. How you identify *which* fundamentals those are depends on the view of the world for which you are educating children. Sometimes this may mean placing more emphasis on information like "Columbus voyaged to America" and "New Delhi is the capital of India," assuming, of course, that social studies programs have ceased emphasizing such information. But also we need to ask ourselves how such information will help students today to function in an increasingly information-rich world—a world of computers and other electronic media. In other cases, the fundamentals can include powerful questions and ideas that are drawn from the human experience—questions like "What makes us human?"

and "How did we get this way?" and ideas like "Change begets change" and "All people define the world from their own frame of reference." In still other cases, the fundamentals can include skills—the process (critical thinking) skills identified earlier.

To deal with either the content or process to the exclusion of the other is to deal with neither well. Skills taught in isolation can be forgotten as quickly as facts taught in isolation. Teaching social studies should not be a matter of teaching content *or* teaching process skills, for the two are reciprocal and inseparable. As we move into this century, social studies teaching must reflect content *with* process, and process *with* content, for these, I think, are children's keys to their world.

As a kind of benediction, here is an old proverb that has served well over those years:

A proverb

> Give a man a fish
> and you feed him for one day.
> Teach him how to fish, and
> he feeds himself for a lifetime.

In many respects, teaching social studies is indeed like teaching children how "to fish." I hope that this book will serve as your guide to opening the fascinating world of social studies to the children you teach. Best wishes!

D. A. W.

Contents
Introduction

Introduction

One morning when I first began teaching, the principal (the late Warren Immel) came into my classroom and announced that the class would be getting the newspaper (the *Cleveland Plain Dealer*) free of charge for the next two months. This would be great, I thought, because now all of the students could keep up to the minute on current events. I quickly discovered that spending fifteen to twenty minutes of a forty-five-minute class reading the morning newspaper leaves little time to discuss current events, much less deal with the regular curriculum. As I got further and further behind, I began to wonder whether newspapers were the wonderful resource they were supposed to be. I would have given almost anything for a little booklet called "Using Newspapers in the Classroom," which I didn't know at the time was (and still is) available without cost from the newspaper.

This handbook has been designed to help you address the kinds of problems that I faced when we began using the daily newspaper in our classroom. We have done so from the perspective that a *resource* is useful only when you really need or want it. The Resource Handbook is also designed as something you can turn to when you want or need additional information on a social studies–related topic.

The Resource Handbook has four parts. Part 1 includes materials that are detailed extensions of topics that we discuss in the text itself. If you are interested in the answers to some of the activities in the text, or if you want to examine the national standards for social studies, look in Part 1 of the Handbook.

Part 2 of the Handbook includes (1) an annotated lesson planning guide, and (2) Alleman and Brophy's guidelines for designing teaching activities. Part 3 of the Handbook provides listings of sources for a variety of teaching and resource materials. If you are interested in looking for living history sites or sources for inexpensive instructional materials, for example, look for these in Part 3.

Part 4 of the Handbook provides annotated bibliographies of children's literature. This section has four parts: (1) children's books that are useful for teaching character and selected morals and values, (2) children's historical fiction and folk literature for common social studies topics, (3) nonfiction books you might use to teach about topics commonly taught in social studies, and (4) children's books for teaching about women's roles throughout history. With the multitude of children's literature available for teaching social studies, and considering the broad range of topics that social studies encompasses, I trust that you will find these bibliographies useful.

Part 1

Materials Related to Activities in the Text

1.1 Data Cards for the "Presidency" Activity

Card 1

Data About Benedict Arnold, as of 1801. Before he joined the British in their attempt to defeat the rebels during the American Revolution, Arnold had served George Washington with distinction during military campaigns from 1776 to 1779. Distressed with financial worries and feeling that he was not receiving adequate recognition from the Continental Congress for his services, he abandoned the American cause and became one of the best-known traitors in American history.

Card 2

Data About Franklin D. Roosevelt, as of 1945. The American people elected Roosevelt president four times. Because of his New Deal programs designed to combat the severe financial depression of the 1930s and his leadership during World War II, many historians have classified him as one of the most effective chief executives ever to hold the office. Some of Roosevelt's critics, however, have felt that he misused the power of the presidency by exerting extensive political pressure on Congress to secure passage of the New Deal legislation. He served as president from 1933 until his death in 1945. An attack of polio in the early 1920s left Roosevelt's legs partially paralyzed for the remainder of his life.

Card 3

Data About Martin Luther King, Jr., as of 1968. Before he was assassinated in 1968, the Reverend Martin Luther King, Jr., had become one of the most active champions of the nonviolent civil rights movement. Beginning with his successful boycott of segregated city buses in Birmingham, Alabama, King rose to become leader of the Southern Christian Leadership Conference, one of the most effective organizations to lobby for federal civil rights legislation during the 1960s.

Card 4

Data About Alexander Hamilton, as of 1804. Until his death in a duel with Aaron Burr, Hamilton served his country as an adviser to George Washington. His arguments for adoption of the federal Constitution were instrumental in its final approval. His financial genius helped to establish the United States on a firm financial footing during its early years.

Card 5

Data About Eleanor Roosevelt, as of 1949. Eleanor Roosevelt, wife of Franklin D. Roosevelt, became one of America's most active champions of the poor, minority groups, women's labor unions, and civil rights. As Franklin Roosevelt's wife, she was an unofficial adviser for many of his New Deal domestic policies. After her husband's death in 1945, Mrs. Roosevelt was appointed a U.S. delegate to the United Nations.

Card 6

Data About Cesar Chavez, as of 1974. Chavez, the son of poor migrant-worker parents, is the founder and leader of the National Farm Workers Organization (NFWO). He has been especially active in unionizing the Mexican-American farm workers of Southern California. His most notable success occurred with the NFWO's nationwide boycott of nonunion-picked lettuce.

Card 7

Data About Abraham Lincoln, as of 1865. With the exception of George Washington and Franklin D. Roosevelt, probably no other president ever entered office facing such immense problems as did Abraham Lincoln. Historians of Lincoln's life generally agree that he did as much as any chief executive could have done to lead the Union to victory in the Civil War and to attempt to heal the wounds of that conflict in both the North and the South. On numerous occasions before and during his presidency, Lincoln suffered periods of severe mental depression. His untimely assassination occurred in 1865.

Source: Adapted from Marsha Hobin, "Clarifying What Is Important," In Allan O. Kownslar, Ed., *Teaching American History: The Quest for Relevancy.* © National Council for the Social Studies. Reprinted by permission.

1.2 NCSS Standards for Social Studies (Abridged)

The NCSS standards are organized around ten thematic strands that correspond with one or more relevant disciplines and that span the educational levels from the early and middle grades to high school. The standards are expressed in statements that begin with "Social studies programs should include experiences that provide for the study of"—for instance, culture. The thematic strands are as follows.

Culture

The study of culture prepares students to answer questions such as: What are the common characteristics of different cultures? How do belief systems, such as religion or political ideals, influence other parts of the culture? How does the culture change to accommodate different ideas and beliefs? What does language tell us about the culture? Relevant courses and disciplines include geography, history, sociology, and anthropology, as well as multicultural topics across the curriculum.

Time, Continuity, and Change

Human beings seek to understand their historical roots and to locate themselves in time. Knowing how to read and reconstruct the past allows one to develop a historical perspective and to answer questions such as: Who am I? What happened in the past? How am I connected to those in the past? How has the world changed, and how might it change in the future? Why does our personal sense of relatedness to the past change? Relevant courses and disciplines include history.

People, Places, and Environment

The study of people, places, and human-environment interactions assists students as they create their spatial views and geographic perspectives of the world beyond their personal locations. Students need the knowledge, skills, and understanding to answer questions such as: Where are things located? Why are they located where they are? What do we mean by "region"? How do landforms change? What implications do these changes have for people? Relevant courses and disciplines include geography and areas studies.

Individual Development and Identity

Personal identity is shaped by one's culture, by groups, and by institutional influences. Students should consider such questions as: How do people learn? Why do people behave as they do? What influences how people learn, perceive, and grow? How do people meet their basic needs in a variety of contexts? How do individuals develop from youth to adulthood? Relevant courses and disciplines include psychology and anthropology.

Individuals, Groups, and Institutions

Institutions such as schools, churches, families, government agencies, and the courts play an integral role in people's lives. It is important that students learn how institutions are formed, what controls and influences them, how they influence individuals and culture, and how they are maintained or changed. Students may address questions such as: What is the role of institutions in this and other societies? How am I influenced by institutions? How do institutions change? What is my role in institutional change? Relevant courses and disciplines include sociology, anthropology, psychology, political science, and history.

Power, Authority, and Governance

Understanding the historical development of structures of power, authority, and governance and their evolving functions in contemporary U.S. society and other parts of the world is essential for developing civic competence. In exploring this theme, students confront questions such as: What is power? What forms does it take? Who holds it? How is it gained, used, and justified? What is legitimate authority? How are governments created, structured, maintained, and changed? How can individual rights be protected within the context of majority rule? Relevant courses and disciplines include government, politics, political science, history, law, and other social sciences.

Production, Distribution, and Consumption

Because people have wants that often exceed the resources available to them, a variety of ways have evolved to answer such questions as: What is to be produced? How is production to be organized? How are goods and services to be distributed? What is the most effective allocation of the factors of production (land, labor, capital, and management)? Relevant courses and disciplines include economics.

Science, Technology, and Society

Modern life as we know it would be impossible without technology and the science that supports it. But technology brings with it many questions: Is new technology always better than old? What can we learn from the past about how new technologies result in broader social change, some of which is unanticipated? How can we cope with the ever-increasing pace of change? How can we manage technology so that the greatest number of people benefit from it? How can we preserve our fundamental values and beliefs in the midst of technological change? This theme draws upon the natural and physical sciences, social sciences, and the humanities. Relevant courses and disciplines include history, geography, economics, civics, and government.

Global Connections

The realities of global interdependence require understanding the increasingly important and diverse global connections among world societies and the frequent tension between national interests and global priorities. Students will need to be able to address such international issues as health care, the environment, human rights, economic competition and interdependence, age-old ethnic enmities, and political and military alliances. Relevant courses and disciplines include geography, culture, and economics; may also draw upon the natural and physical sciences and the humanities.

Civic Ideals and Practices

An understanding of civic ideals and practices of citizenship is critical to full participation in society and is a central purpose of social studies. Students confront such questions as: What is civic participation and how can I be involved? How has the meaning of citizenship evolved? What is the balance between rights and responsibilities? What is the role of the citizen in the community and the nation, and as a member of the world community? How can I make a positive difference? Relevant courses and disciplines include history, political science, cultural anthropology, and fields such as global studies, law-related education, and the humanities.

Abridged from the Executive Summary of *Expect Excellence: Curriculum Standards for Social Studies Electronic Edition* (1996), 2–4.

1.3 K–4 Standards for Historical Thinking

Standard 1. Chronological Thinking, which includes the following performance indicators: (a) distinguishing between past, present, and future time, (b) identifying in historical narratives the temporal structure of a historical narrative or story, (c) establishing temporal order in constructing their [students'] own historical narratives, (d) measuring and calculating calendar time, (e) interpreting data presented in time lines, (f) creating time lines, and (g) explaining change and continuity over time.

Standard 2. Historical Comprehension, which includes (a) reconstructing the literal meaning of a historical passage, (b) identifying the central question(s) the historical narrative addresses, (c) reading historical narratives imaginatively, (d) providing evidence of historical perspectives, (e) drawing upon the data in historical maps, (f) drawing upon visual and mathematical data presented in graphics, and (g) drawing upon the visual data presented in photographs, paintings, cartoons, and architectural drawings.

Standard 3. **Historical Analysis and Interpretation,** which includes (a) formulating questions to focus their inquiry or analysis, (b) identifying the author or source of the historical document or narrative, (c) comparing and contrasting differing sets of ideas, values, personalities, behaviors, and institutions, (d) analyzing historical fiction, (e) distinguishing between fact and fiction, (f) comparing different stories about a historical figure, era, or event, (g) analyzing illustrations in historical stories, (h) considering multiple perspectives, (i) explaining causes in analyzing historical actions, (j) challenging arguments of historical inevitability, and (k) hypothesizing influences of the past.

Standard 4. **Historical Research Capabilities,** which include the following performance indicators: (a) formulating historical questions, (b) obtaining historical data, (c) interrogating historical data, and (d) marshaling needed knowledge of the time and place and constructing a story, explanation, or historical narrative.

Standard 5. **Historical Issues—Analysis and Decision-Making,** which includes the following performance indicators: (a) identifying issues and problems in the past, (b) comparing the interests and values of the various people involved, (c) suggesting alternative choices for addressing the problem, (d) evaluating alternative courses of action, (e) preparing a position or course of action on an issue, and (f) evaluating the consequences of a decision.

Source: K—4 Standards for Historical Thinking, National Center for History in the Schools (1995). Reprinted by permission.

1.4 The Essential Elements of Geography

The following are the six "essential elements" and eighteen related standards developed by the Geography Education Standards Project (1994).

Element One: The World in Spatial Terms

Geography focuses on the relationships between people, places, and environments by mapping information about them in a spatial context. The geographically informed person knows and understands:

1. How to use maps and other geographic representations, tools, and technologies to acquire, process, and report information from a spatial perspective.
2. How to use mental maps to organize information about people, places, and environments in a spatial context.
3. How to analyze the spatial organization of people, places, and environments on the earth's surface.

Element Two: Places and Regions

The identities and lives of people are rooted in particular places, and in those human constructs called regions. The geographically informed person knows and understands:

4. The physical and human characteristics of place.
5. That people create regions to interpret the earth's complexity.
6. How culture and experience influence people's perceptions of places and regions.

Element Three: Physical Systems

Physical processes shape the earth's surface and interact with plant and animal life to create, sustain, and modify ecosystems. The geographically informed person knows and understands:

7. The physical processes that shape the patterns of the earth's surface.
8. The characteristics and spatial distribution of ecosystems on the earth's surface.

Element Four: Human Systems

People are central to geography in that human activities help to shape the earth's surface. Human settlements and structures are also part of the earth's surfaces that human beings compete to control. The geographically informed person knows and understands:

9. The characteristics, distribution, and migration of human populations on the earth's surface.
10. The characteristics, distribution, and complexity of the earth's cultural mosaics.
11. The patterns and networks of economic interdependence on the earth's surface.
12. The processes, patterns, and functions of human settlements.
13. How the forces of cooperation and conflict among people influence the division and control of the earth's surface.

Element Five: Environment and Society

The physical environment is modified by human activities, largely as a consequence of the ways in which human societies value and use the earth's natural resources. Human activities are also influenced by the earth's physical features and processes. The geographically informed person knows and understands:

14. How human actions modify the physical environment.
15. How physical systems affect human systems.
16. The changes that occur in the meaning, use, distribution, and importance of resources.

Element Six: The Uses of Geography

The knowledge of geography enables people to develop an understanding of the relationships between people, places, and environments over time—that is, of the earth as it was, is, and might be. The geographically informed person knows and understands:

17. How to apply geography to interpret the past.
18. How to apply geography to interpret the present and plan for the future.

Source: Geography Education Standards Project (1994). *Geography for Life: National Geography Standards 1994.* Washington, DC: National Geographic Society. Reprinted by permission.

1.5 Sample Learning Style Inventory

Place the letter that best reflects your preference in the blank provided.

_____ 1. When you really want to study something and learn it well, would you rather (a) work alone, (b) study with others having similar interests, (c) work by yourself but in a setting where there are other people around?

_____ 2. Assuming that each of the following modes is effective and that you have a choice, would you most prefer to learn something by (a) reading, (b) listening, (c) observing?

_____ 3. Learning situations that cause you the most concern are those that appear to be (a) ambiguous, (b) rather closely defined as to the desired outcome, (c) without guidelines, where you are completely on your own.

_____ 4. Do you have most trouble learning things that (a) use abstract symbols, (b) use diagrams and charts, (c) use mathematical numbers and figures?

_____ 5. When you are not really interested in something you are studying, do you find yourself (a) able to discipline yourself to study, (b) easily distracted by other things, (c) going through the motions to look as though you are studying?

_____ 6. When memorizing something, do you find yourself (a) developing a theme within which to relate the parts, (b) creating a pattern that cues the parts, (c) trying to picture the thing in your mind?

_____ 7. Would you prefer to study something that (a) involves some creative effort of your own, (b) calls for you to apply analytical and critical skills, (c) lays out all the points in front of you so you have a chance to understand it?

_____ 8. When do you find that you do your best learning? (a) in the early morning, (b) around midday, (c) in the afternoon, (d) during an "all nighter."

_____ 9. When studying, do you find that you (a) create relationships without being told, (b) understand the material but have some difficulty putting it together, (c) must be given the "whole" before the "parts" make sense?

____ 10. In most classes, would you rather be taught by someone who (a) knows the material and can tell it to you clearly and precisely, (b) knows the material and teases and leads you to conclusions, (c) knows the material but primarily raises questions?

____ 11. Do you feel most comfortable when asked (a) to analyze the material studied, (b) to report on the material studied, (c) to summarize the material studied?

____ 12. When studying something completely new, do you (a) need someone around to encourage your efforts, (b) prefer to figure it out for yourself, (c) tend to give up easily even if encouraged?

____ 13. Do you consider yourself as a student who (a) grasps new ideas quickly, (b) goes at a slightly slower pace, yet masters ideas well, (c) deals with new material so thoroughly that you are able to identify new ideas and/or relationships that extend beyond those explicit in the original materials?

____ 14. When studying with a particular instructor, are you (a) very conscious of the teacher's reaction to how you are doing, (b) indifferent to what the teacher thinks about your progress, (c) interested in the teacher's response but only after you have completed the task on your own?

____ 15. If taking a class in which there were no grades or other rewards, would you probably (a) work just as hard as you would if there were grades, (b) end up doing something else you really wanted to do, (c) exert minimal effort?

____ 16. Do you like taking courses where (a) both the objectives and procedures are clearly spelled out, (b) the procedures are fairly clear but the objectives are vague, (c) both the objectives and procedures are vague but there is a lot of excitement and drive on the part of the instructor?

____ 17. When studying something new, would you say your attention span is (a) continuous, (b) irregular, (c) short but concentrated, (d) without a particular pattern?

____ 18. Do you sense the most satisfaction when (a) you've been able to figure out and repair something using your hands and your mind, (b) you've been able to conceptualize or see some meaning in academic work, (c) other people say they think you've done a good piece of work, regardless of what that work is?

____ 19. When you find yourself in a situation determined by the clock, do you usually (a) start making all sorts of mistakes under pressure, (b) slow down and do what you can, (c) speed up and surprise yourself at how much you can do when the heat is on?

____ 20. If you asked those people who know you best, they would probably say that (a) you are usually level-headed and have a lot of common sense, (b) it takes you a long time to get an idea but when you do you hang on to it, (c) you are always coming up with far-out ideas that sometimes work?

____ 21. When bored in a class, do you usually (a) daydream, but of things related to what you are studying, (b) daydream of things seldom related to what you are studying, (c) pay attention even though it doesn't mean very much?

____ 22. Do you find that when something new comes up you (a) adapt rather easily, (b) fight it for a while but are willing, usually, to give it a try, (c) make darn well sure it makes sense and/or is right before making any effort to accept it?

____ 23. When in a classroom with other students and observing a teacher teaching, do you (a) think of other ways to present the material and to teach, (b) listen to what the teacher is saying rather than watch how he or she is teaching, (c) wonder what the teacher wants and how you can deliver?

____ 24. If you don't like the instructor, for whatever reason, do you (a) tend not to do well, (b) find reasons for not studying and learning, (c) not let it affect how hard you try?

____ 25. Do you get upset when studying something that (a) has no immediate and practical application, (b) appears to have some application but you are not sure just what, (c) is too darn practical and immediate?

____ 26. When a teacher fails to "come across," do you have a tendency to blame (a) the teacher who, after all, is responsible for the class, (b) the subject matter—especially if the teacher tries, (c) both the teacher and yourself for not making it worthwhile?

27. If you took a course in social studies, would you want it to (a) focus primarily upon the facts, (b) pose some insight into contemporary problems of society, (c) have some payoff in your daily life?

28. The problem with many teachers is that they (a) overkill, that is, teach too much of the same thing, (b) try to cover too much, (c) do not allow the student to really wrestle with the content.

29. Do you believe that most students gain confidence through (a) having rather well-established objectives and procedures, (b) being allowed to try different things, (c) psyching out the reward system and playing the game?

30. When studying, do you prefer (a) absolute silence, (b) low background noise, including music, (c) relative quiet, (d) loud conversation or music, etc., (e) sometimes one way, sometimes another?

31. Where do you prefer to study? (a) in your own room, (b) in a learning center, (c) at the library, (d) at a media center.

32. What types of assignments do you most prefer? (a) teacher-directed, (b) projects by contracts, (c) self-directed projects, (d) a combination of these.

33. How do you most prefer to be evaluated on something? (a) by formal tests, (b) through teacher conferences, (c) on research papers or other written projects, (d) on the amount of your class discussion.

34. Which of the following is most likely to bring forth your best performance? (a) self-satisfaction, (b) clearly defined teacher expectations and deadlines, (c) public recognition of your achievement, (d) working in a subject area with which you are quite comfortable and familiar.

Summary

Instructional modes. Determine your preferred instructional mode from responses to questions 2, 4, 7, 8, 11, 17, 19.

_____

_____

Structure. Determine the degree of structuring from responses to questions 3, 6, 9, 12, 13, 16, 20, 22, 23, and 32.

High	Medium	Low

Social context of learning. Determine the general expectations for the way in which teachers handle their authority from questions 1, 10, 19, and 24.

_____

_____

Group-related activities. Determine your preference for group-related activities from responses to questions 1, 12, 30, 31, and 34.

_____

_____

Physical context of learning. Determine your preferences regarding the physical environment from the responses to questions 8, 17, 30, and 31.

_____

_____

Reward/Praise. Determine preferences for reward/praise from responses to questions 14, 15, 26, 29, 33, and 34.

_____

_____

Goal preferences. Determine your general goal preferences from the responses to questions 5, 18, 25, and 27.

Longer range	Shorter range

1.6 Sources of Commercially Available Learning Style Measures Include:

* Learning Style Inventory, Price Systems, Box 1818, Lawrence, KS 66044-1818

* Learning Style Profile. National Association of Secondary School Principals, 1904 Association Dr., Reston, VA 22091-1598.

1.7 Recipes/Directions

1.7.1. Recipes for Relief Maps

Papier-Mâché. Tear newspapers into strips and soak in water overnight. Mix wheat paste (wallpaper paste) with warm water to the consistency of thin cream. Squeeze water out of the newspaper strips, dip into the paste, remove the excess, and then apply to the map form.

Salt and Flour. Mix four cups flour, two cups salt, and approximately two cups water. Knead thoroughly. Food coloring may be added to the water, or tempera paint can be kneaded into the mixture. The mixture may require from two to three days to dry completely.

Sawdust and Glue. Mix slightly thinned white glue with dampened, fine sawdust until it reaches a workable consistency.

Once the relief maps have dried, they can be coated with a thin mixture of plaster of Paris and water and then allowed to dry overnight. This coating will keep paint from soaking in as much as it otherwise would.

1.7.2 Directions for Making Paper

Introduction. This recipe produces a very rough paper similar to papyrus. Before you begin this activity, you might ask for parent volunteers who will make several, small wooden frames (open rectangles), about 6 by 9 inches, with old window screening attached to the bottom. Old picture frames also work well.

Materials List

One blender, to mix the ingredients
Several clean sponges
A tub or container large enough to hold the screened frames
Grass (or cattails—leaves only, no heads)
Water
One or two old bedsheets
Torn pieces of old, used, lightweight paper (not newsprint)
One bottle laundry starch

Procedure. Place equal amounts of torn paper and the grass or cattail leaves into the blender, and cover with water to make a pulp. Turn blender to high and mix thoroughly. Make several batches, adding about 1 tablespoon of laundry starch to each batch. Put the pulp into a tub that is large enough to accommodate the screen. Add as little water to the tub as necessary to create a fluid mixture, and stir. Insert the screen into the water until it is covered with a layer of the pulp mixture, then pull up and out. Lay the screen on the old bedsheet, and use sponges to soak up some of the excess water from the pulp, but do not let it get so dry that the pulp sticks to the screen. Place a dry area of the sheet over the screen, and then flip so the pulp falls out of the screen onto the sheet. Place on a flat surface, remove the screen, and let the paper dry overnight.

This paper that you produce will be rough, fragile, and difficult to write on. In addition, it may not be even at the edges. Help students to understand that the 8 1/2 × 11 paper we are all familiar with is a convention of modern life and is the result of advanced paper-making techniques.

Part 2 Planning Resources

2.1 Alternative Lesson Planning Guide

This planning guide is designed to serve different kinds of lessons. Therefore some elements, like motivation and establishing set, will apply to all lessons, but other components may not. At times, you may teach lessons that don't use guided practice or review, for example, or where there is no need to state assumptions. Skip the sections that don't apply to the kind of lesson you are teaching. Note also that because this guide is designed to communicate your lesson to someone else, such as a cooperating teacher or a university supervisor, it is necessarily more comprehensive and specific than the day-to-day plans that most teachers use. Most teachers will have usually thought about the following planning elements, even if they don't write them in their plan books.

I. *Overview/Rationale/Justification.* Provide a brief overview of this lesson *and* why it is something that students should experience or learn.

The key questions here are the following: What's going to happen in this lesson? What is the main idea(s) you are driving at? How will this lesson pertain to something your students will use in the future?

II. State *Objectives.* List at least two objectives for this lesson.

Objectives should be stated in terms of behaviors or knowledge that students will demonstrate at the end of the lesson.

III. *Assumptions.* Identify specific skills or knowledge that students must have *prior* to lesson.

This section of the planning guide pertains primarily to skill- and concept-oriented lessons and may not be relevant to other kinds of lessons. State prerequisite knowledge/skills specifically, such as the ability to count by fives or to identify the symbols used to show cities on a map. Do not identify global skills, such as reading, the ability to multiply, how to use a map, and so on.

IV. Review, Developing Motivation, and Setting the Focus.

In most cases, the following elements can be described in a sentence or two.

A. *Review.* Describe how you will relate this lesson to students' prior learning experiences.

Identify how you will make connections with previous learning in ways that have meaning for students.

B. Develop *Motivation and Setting the Focus* (Establishing Set). This planning element has three components: a description of (1) how you will get students interested in this lesson, (2) how you will introduce the content/skills, and (3) how you will make students aware of the objectives for the lesson.

Your introduction or beginning activity should be content centered and tied to the purpose of the lesson. Be especially cautious about using seemingly obvious questions for "motivational" purposes—that is, "Has anyone ever seen television? or an elephant? etc." (everyone has). Be equally careful about your terminology. For example, a "discussion" involves the identification and assessment of different points of view on an issue; it is not a random sharing of opinions or question-and-answer. Most children can readily tell you about the time they went to Disneyland, for example, but this is more likely to be recitation, not a discussion. Having children share their perspectives on abortion could provide a legitimate (though unlikely) basis for a discussion. The point is that having children share their prior experiences may be desirable—even if no one listens to them—but such activities should not be presented as discussions.

V. Develop the *Lesson.*

A. Provide *Instructional Input.* Outline and describe the content and skills included in the main body of the lesson and how you will present them.

In this part of the lesson you will present content, use manipulatives, give examples, explain, define, read, model, and provide directions for activities, and so on. You may wish to write a script for portions of this section as long

2

as you recognize that scripts can be confining and destroy spontaneity.

B. *Modeling* the Content and Skills. Describe how you will model or demonstrate the content and skills introduced in Part V-A.

Modeling is among the most important parts of the lesson and refers to doing, explicitly demonstrating, talking through, and thinking aloud. Modeling should afford students an opportunity to "see" your reasoning process, to see how you attack a problem. Note that showing the children a completed model, of a narrative story for example, is not modeling.

C. Check for Student Understanding (*Assessment*). Describe how you will assess students' understanding to make sure they have mastered the content and skills introduced in Part V-A.

Use oral, written, or signal responses to check for students' understanding before moving on to application or guided practice. Signal responses can include raising hands, crossing arms, putting a hand on the head, and so on.

VI. *Guided Practice*. Describe the guided practice you will provide relating to the content and skills developed in Part V-A.

This aspect of the lesson cycle is most appropriate, even essential, to certain subjects like mathematics and may be less appropriate to other subjects, like literature. Guided practice is usually called for if you ask students to apply something that you have taught.

VII. *Closure* (and Assign Individual Practice or Homework as Appropriate). Describe how you will close the lesson. Describe the individual practice or homework you will assign, if appropriate, to this lesson.

The purpose of closure is to "lock in" the learning experience. You might summarize the main points of the lesson, or have students do so, explain how the content and skills will be needed in the future, or have students do something "one more time." The closure should have substance; it cannot be a hasty review of the lesson or an administrative end, for example, "Close your books."

VIII. *Follow-up* Activities. Briefly describe other activities or lessons that logically follow from this lesson, or how you would integrate the "big ideas" from this lesson into other subject areas.

Few lessons contain elements that cannot be followed up on. Sometimes it may be the content of the lesson—what it is like to live in different climates, for example. At other times, the process that students used in this lesson can apply to other lessons—practice with a model for writing descriptive narratives, for example. In this section, you should indicate how you will tie this lesson into future lessons. The question to ask yourself here is, How does this lesson tie into other things I might teach?

2.2 Principles for the Design, Selection, and Evaluation of Instructional Activities (Abridged)

Criteria	Response		
A. Primary Principles	**Yes**	**No**	**NA**
A1. *Goal Relevance*			
A1.1 Does the activity address worthwhile curricular goals?	—	—	—
A1.1a Is the activity's primary goal an important one?	—	—	—
A1.1b Is there a clear relationship between what students will be doing and the activity's primary goal?	—	—	—
A1.2 Does the activity deal with (a) powerful ideas that are (b) represented accurately?	—	—	—
A1.3 Is the format of the activity clear and uncomplicated?	—	—	—
A2. *Appropriate Difficulty Level*			
A2.1 Is the activity difficult enough to challenge students but not so difficult that it confuses or frustrates them?	—	—	—
A2.2 Do students have the relevant prior knowledge or skills that the activity requires?	—	—	—

Criteria	Response			Criteria	Response		
A. Primary Principles (cont.)	Yes	No	NA	**B. Secondary Principles (cont.)**	Yes	No	NA

A. Primary Principles (cont.)   Yes No NA

A2.3 Does the activity provide enough structuring that students can complete it with reasonable effort? — — —

A2.4 Does the activity *not* combine difficult new processes and difficult new content? — — —

A3. *Feasibility*

A3.1 Is the activity feasible in terms of (a) normal constraints (space, time, equipment, etc.) (b) the possibility for students to carry out instructions unambiguously and complete the activity with a sense of closure and accomplishment? — — —

A4. *Cost Effectiveness*

A4.1 Does the activity justify its costs in time and trouble for both teachers and students? — — —

A4.2 Will the structure of the activity (e.g., closed vs. open-ended, etc.) accomplish the goal directly and without needless complications? — — —

A4.3 Can students who lack prior knowledge or skills be accommodated? — — —

A4.4 If the activity cuts across subject lines, does it (a) address major goals in those subjects, and (b) still reflect time allotments for those subjects? — — —

B. Secondary Principles   Yes No NA

The following are desirable but not essential.

B1. *Multiple Goals*

B1.1 Does the activity accommodate multiple goals (e.g., content and process, etc.) as opposed to just a few goals? — — —

B. Secondary Principles (cont.)   Yes No NA

B1.2 Does the activity call for integration across subjects or for inclusion of special topics? — — —

B2. *Motivational Value.* All things considered, is the activity one that students will enjoy or at least find meaningful and worthwhile? — — —

B3. *Topic Currency*

B3.1 Does the activity deal with recently taught major ideas (as opposed to minor details or isolated content)? — — —

B3.2 Are skills incorporated for authentically applying current knowledge (as opposed to isolated skill exercises)? — — —

B4. *Whole-Task Completion.* Does the activity provide for the completion of a meaningful task (as opposed to isolated skill practice)? — — —

B5. *Higher-Order Thinking*

B5.1 Does the activity provide opportunities to process information (interpret, analyze, etc.) (as opposed to just locating and reproducing information)? — — —

B5.2 Does the activity provide opportunities for genuine discourse and discussion (as opposed to recitation)? — — —

B5.3 If the activity involves writing, does it call for coherent written explanations or arguments (as opposed to filling in blanks or copying)? — — —

B6. *Adaptability.* Can the activity be adapted to accommodate individual differences among students? — — —

Source: Abridged from Jere Brophy and Janet Alleman, "Activities as Instructional Tools: A Framework for Analysis and Evaluation," *Educational Researcher,* Vol. 20, No. 4 (May 1991), pp. 15–19.

2

Part 3   Instructional Resources

3.1 Sources for Teaching Materials

1. Social Studies Journals

1. *Social Studies and the Young Learner,* which is available from the National Council for the Social Studies, 3501 Newark Street NW, Washington, DC 20016. This is the only journal that deals specifically with elementary and middle-school social studies.
2. *Social Education,* the K–12 journal of the National Council for the Social Studies. Address: 3501 Newark Street, NW, Washington, DC 20016.
3. *The Social Studies,* also a K–12 journal. Published by Heldref Publications, 1319 Eighteenth Street, NW, Washington, DC 20036-1802.

2. Social Studies Publications for Children

Write (or call) the publishers listed here for examination copies of these materials.

2.1 General

Calliope: World History for Young People
Cobblestone Publishing Inc.
7 School Street
Peterborough, NH 03458
(800) 821-0115

Calliope is published five times during the school year and is for students in Grades 4–8. Each issue features in-depth information and activities on a single topic.

Cobblestone: The History Magazine
    for Young People
Cobblestone Publishing Inc.
7 School Street
Peterborough, NH 03458
(800) 821-0115

Cobblestone is appropriate for students in Grades 4–8 and is published ten times a year. Each issue features an episode of historical interest, such as the Underground Railroad or the Roaring Twenties.

National Geographic World
National Geographic Society
Dept. 01090
17th and M Streets NW
Washington, DC 20036

This monthly magazine is appropriate for eight- to twelve-year-olds (or older). Each issue contains articles on a variety of social studies topics.

2.2 Current Events Publications

My Weekly Reader
American Education Publications
245 Long Hill Road, P.O. Box 360
Middletown, CT 06457

Let's Find Out (kindergarten) or *Scholastic News* (Grades 1–6)
Scholastic, Inc.
730 Broadway
New York, NY 10003-9538

Junior Review (Grades 6–9)
Civic Education Service
1733 K Street NW
Washington, DC 20006

3. Resources for Global Education

Two excellent sources of information about global education are:

1. The American Forum for Global Education, 45 John Street, New York, NY 10038, and
2. The Stanford Program on International and Cross-Cultural Education (SPICE), Littlefield Center, Room 15, 300 Lassen Street, Stanford, CA 94305-5013.

4. Resources for Law-Related Education

Center for Civic Education
5146 Douglas Fir Road
Calabasas, CA 91302

Materials include student books (e.g., *We the People,* and *With Liberty and Justice for All*), teachers' guides, and resource materials.

Constitutional Rights Foundation
6310 San Vincente Boulevard
Los Angeles, CA 90048

Materials, primarily for Grades 7–12, include simulations, lesson plans, student resources, a *Bill of Rights Newsletter,* and other materials.

American Bar Association
Special Committee on Youth Education for
    Citizenship
1155 East 60th Street
Chicago, IL 60637

Materials include a newsletter for teachers, *Update on Law-Related Education,* classroom materials, and a catalog of law-related audiovisual materials.

Law in a Free Society
606 Wilshire Boulevard
Santa Monica, CA 90101

Materials include case studies and lesson plans for Grades K–12, and inservice training.

Law in Action Units
West Publishing Company, Inc.
50 West Kellogg Boulevard
St. Paul, MN 55165

Materials include units and lesson plans for Grades 5–9.

National Institute for Citizen Education in the Law
605 G Street NW, Suite 401
Washington, D.C. 20001

Materials focus primarily on teacher training and the development of law-related curriculum materials.

Opposing Viewpoints Series
Greenhaven Press
Box 831
Anoka, MN 55303

Materials offer opposing points of view on a variety of law-related issues.

5. Resources for Character Education

American Institute for Character Education
    A nonprofit educational research foundation that offers a K–9 character education curriculum. Dimension II Building, 8918 Tesoro, Suite 220, San Antonio, TX 78217. Phone: (512) 829-1727 or (800) 284-0499.

Center for the Advancement of Ethics and Character
    Dedicated to helping schools recapture their role as moral educators, the Center has developed a model that emphasizes the curriculum as the primary vehicle for transmitting moral values to the young. The Center publicizes this model through its teacher academics for public school teachers and administrators. A similar program is directed toward college and university faculty responsible for the preparation of future teachers. The Center is also involved in researching and developing curricular materials for use by schools, teachers, and parents. Kevin Ryan, Boston University, School of Education, 605 Commonwealth Avenue, Boston, MA 02215. Phone: (617) 353-3262.

Center for Character Education
    An academic alliance of schools and universities that brings together educators interested in implementing the Integrated Character Model for moral education. This model reflects the view that knowledge, affect, and action are integrated in persons of mature character. Duquesne University, School of Education, 410 Canevin Hall, Pittsburgh, PA 15282. Phone: (412) 434-5191.

Center for Civic Education
    This Web site is sponsored by the Center for Civic Education, a nonpartisan corporation dedicated to fostering the development of responsible participation in civic life. The Center specializes in civic/citizenship education, law-related education, and international educational exchange programs for developing democracies. The CCE Web site has curriculum materials, sample lesson plans, and related children's literature bibliographies as well as a comprehensive on-line catalog, a good listing of available papers and articles on civic education, and a wonderful annotated list of Internet resources. **www.civiced.org**

The Character Counts Coalition
    This project of the Josephson Institute represents a national partnership of organizations and individuals involved in the education, training, or care of youth. It reflects a collaborative effort to improve the character of America's young people by focusing on the six pillars of character: trustworthiness, respect, responsibility, fairness, caring,

3

and citizenship. It aims to combat violence, dishonesty, and irresponsibility by strengthening the moral fiber of the next generation. 4640 Admiralty Way, Suite 1001, Marina del Rey, CA 90292. Phone: (310) 306-1868.

The Character Education Partnership

A nonpartisan coalition of organizations and individuals concerned about the moral crisis confronting America's youth and dedicated to developing moral character and civic virtue in young people as a way of promoting a more compassionate and responsible society. Activities include a national clearinghouse, community programs, school support, publications, annual and regional forums, and a national awards and media campaign. John A. Martin, Executive Director, The Character Education Partnership, 1250 North Pitt Street, Alexandria, VA 22314. Fax: (703) 739-4967. **www.character.org**

Ethics Resource Center

This center is working toward restoring our society's ethical foundations by strengthening the capacity of our institutions to foster integrity, encourage ethical conduct, and support basic values. Established in 1977 as a nonprofit, nonpartisan, and nonsectarian organization, the Ethics Resource Center has developed practical and effective programs that address the needs of the education, business, and government communities. Resources include research support, curricular materials, workshops, and conference sponsorship. 1120 G Street NW, Washington, DC 20005. Phone: (202) 737-2258.

Exploring Ethics Through Children's Literature

This organization offers a literature-based program for Grades 2–6. Critical Thinking Press, P.O. Box 448, Dept. 4, Pacific Grove, CA 93950-0448. Phone: (800) 458-4849. Fax: (408) 372-3230.

The Giraffe Project

This Is a nonprofit literature project devoted to spreading the word about people who "stick their necks out for the common good." Its various programs include The Giraffe Heroes Program, a story-based curriculum that teaches "courageous compassion and active citizenship"; the Giraffe Heroes Training Program; and a variety of public information and awareness programs. **www.giraffe.org**

International Center for Character Education

The International Center for Character Education (ICCE), housed at the University of San Diego, has as its purpose to "enable school personnel, parents, teacher educators, faith community members . . . to come together to study, discuss . . . the character education of children and youth." The ICCE offers the only Certificate and MA programs in character education and a variety of other services and awards. **www.teachvalues.org**

The Jefferson Center for Character Education

This organization was formed in 1963 to publish and promote programs for schools that teach sound character values and personal responsibility. 202 South Lake Avenue, #240, Pasadena, CA 91101. Phone: (818) 792-8130.

Project Wisdom

A for-profit organization that is "committed to providing schools with Character Education materials that encourage students to reflect" on values and their application. The centerpiece of the program is a collection of thought-provoking messages to be read over the PA system. The program also includes a reproducible set of weekly themes, weekly journals, classroom discussion guides, and a booklet of quotations for the classroom. **www.entech.com/projectwisdom**

WiseSkills

This organization offers a community-based character-building program for Grades K–8. Legacy Learning, P.O. Box 3213, South Pasadena, CA 91031-6213. Phone: (818) 441-7944.

Source Note: This listing is abridged and adapted from "The Bonner Center for Character Education Web Links," at the California State University, Fresno, and from "Character Education Organizations and Publications," maintained by the Center for the Fourth and Fifth Rs, Dr. Thomas Lickona, Director, Education Department, SUNY Cortland, Cortland, NY 13045. Used by permission.

3

6. Other Sources of Materials

Social Studies School Service Catalog (free)
10000 Culver Boulevard, P.O. Box 802
Culver City, CA 90230

Where to Find It Guide (published annually in a fall issue of *Scholastic Teacher*)
Scholastic Magazines, Inc., 50 W. 44th Street
New York, NY 10036.

6.1 Teachers' Magazines

1. *Teaching-PreK–8.* Address: P.O. Box 54805, Boulder, CO 80323-4805.
2. *Teacher.* Address: 4301 Connecticut Avenue NW, Suite 432, Washington, DC 20077-3522.
3. *Learning* (the year varies with the current year). Address: 1111 Bethlehem Pike, Springhouse, PA 19477.
4. *Instructor.* Address: 7 Bank Street, Dansville, NY 14437.

6.2 Guides to Free or Inexpensive Materials

Educator's Guide to Free Social Studies Materials, edited by Patricia H. Suttles and William H. Hartley. Educators Progress Service, Inc., Randolph, WI 53956. *Note:* Guides to other free and inexpensive material are also available.

Free and Inexpensive Materials on World Affairs, by Leonard S. Kenworthy. Teachers College Press, 1234 Amsterdam Avenue, New York, NY 10027.

Free and Inexpensive Teaching Aids, by Bruce Miller. Box 369, Riverside, CA 92502.

Free and Inexpensive Learning Materials (updated annually). George Peabody College of Vanderbilt University, Nashville, TN 37203.

Selected Free Materials for Classroom Teachers, by Ruth H. Aubrey. Fearon Publishers, 6 Davis Drive, Belmont, CA 94002.

6.3 Newspaper-Related Materials

Many local newspapers maintain a "Newspaper in Education" department that will provide teaching tips and other aids for integrating newspapers into the curriculum. If your local paper does not offer such a service, contact the American Newspaper Publishers Association Foundation (The Newspaper Center, Box 17407, Dulles International Airport, Washington, DC 20041) for information.

3.2 Directory of Living History Museums

Alabama

Constitution Hall Village
404 Madison Street
Huntsville, AL 35801
(800) 678-1819

Constitution Hall Village is located at the site of the drafting of Alabama's 1819 constitution. Both single-day and five-day educational programs are available.

Alaska

Eklutna Village Historical Park
510 L Street, Suite 200
Anchorage, AK 99501
(907) 276-5701

Eklutna is the oldest continuously inhabited Athapaskan site in Alaska. Its cemetery contains spirit houses that were built to protect the spirits of the deceased, and the park has two Russian Orthodox churches built by missionaries in the 1830s.

Native Village of Alaskaland
Fairbanks Native Association
201 First Avenue, 2nd Floor
Fairbanks, AK 99701
(907) 452-1648

This village contains a variety of different types of housing used by Native American Alaskans, including sod dwellings and plank houses.

Arizona

Pioneer Arizona
3901 West Pioneer Road
Phoenix, AZ 85027
(602) 993-0212

Descendants of the horses that Columbus brought to North America on his second voyage in 1493 are raised at Pioneer Arizona. The museum also includes more than twenty buildings that reflect the influences of Native American, Spanish, and Mexican cultures.

Arkansas

Arkansas Territorial Restoration
200 East 3rd Street
Little Rock, AR 72201
(501) 324-9351

This museum reflects frontier life in Arkansas from 1819 to 1870.

California

El Pueblo de Los Angeles Historic Monument
125 Paseo de la Plaza, Suite 400
Los Angeles, CA 90012
(213) 628-0605

This community, which later became known simply as Los Angeles, has twenty-seven reconstructed buildings.

Mission San Juan Capistrano
31882 Camino Capistrano #107
San Juan Capistrano, CA 92675
(714) 248-2048

Franciscan padres founded the Mission of San Juan Capistrano in 1776. The Serra Chapel is the oldest continuously inhabited building in the state of California. The mission is also famous for the annual migration of swallows each spring.

Colorado

Bent's Old Fort National Historic Site
35110 Highway 194 East
La Junta, CO 81050
(719) 384-2596

This reconstructed frontier fur trading post features blacksmithing and frontier medicine.

Connecticut

Mystic Seaport and Maritime Museum
50 Greenmanville Avenue
Mystic, CT 06355
(203) 572-0711

The Mystic Seaport and Preservation Shipyard is home to nineteenth-century tall ships and schooners. The maritime museum contains antique navigational equipment. The accompanying planetarium has programs explaining how sea captains relied on the stars to determine their location at sea.

Delaware

Delaware Agricultural Museum
866 North DuPont Highway
Dover, DE 19901
(302) 734-1618

Historic activities and demonstrations vary depending on the season. During the summer, children can experience schooling from that period of our history. Lessons are taught from the McGuffey Reader and Noah Webster's Blue Backed Speller with "ciphering" done on a slate. During July and August, children can dress in clothing of the period, churn butter, feed the chickens and cow, and enjoy a storyteller. During the winter months, guides provide interpretations of rural life in the 1850s.

Hagley Museum and Library
P.O. Box 3630
Wilmington, DE 19807
(302) 658-2400

The Hagley Museum and Library focuses on the E. I. du Pont family's role and history in the nineteenth century. Tours include the du Ponts' Georgian mansion and gardens, workers' quarters, and gunpowder mills.

Florida

Historic Saint Augustine Spanish Quarter
P.O. Box 1987
Saint Augustine, FL 32085
(904) 825-6830

Saint Augustine was founded more than 470 years ago and is the oldest continuously inhabited European settlement in North America. Life during the Spanish colonial period of the 1740s is portrayed in restored buildings and gardens.

Georgia

Agrirama
P.O. Box Q
Tifton, GA 31793
(912) 386-3344

This museum consists of almost forty restored buildings that illustrate traditional and progressive farming.

Idaho

Pioneer Village and Idaho Historical Museum
610 North Julia Davis Drive
Boise, ID 83702
(208) 334-2120

This museum village consists of restored and reconstructed log cabins and adobes that may be toured by school groups.

Illinois

Lincoln's New Salem State Historic Site
R.R. #1, Box 244A
Petersburg, IL 62675
(217) 632-4000

Abraham Lincoln first stopped at New Salem when he and a friend copiloted a flatboat down the Sangamon River to the Ohio and Mississippi Rivers. He later returned there to settle and study law. The re-created village provides demonstrations of activities common to daily living during Lincoln's lifetime.

Naper Settlement
210 West Porter
Naperville, IL 60540
(708) 420-6010

This mid- to late-nineteenth-century settlement features historic games and crafts, soap making, and open hearth cooking.

Indiana

Conner Prairie
13400 Allisonville Road
Fishers, IN 46038
(317) 776-6000

Conner Prairie presents three historically accurate areas, each with its own costumed interpreters. Prairietown is an 1836 Indiana village; the second area features the nineteenth-century home of William Conner, a land developer and politician; and the third area is a Pioneer Adventure Area where children are encouraged to participate in dipping candles, soap making, weaving, and wood carving.

Historic New Harmony
506 1/2 Main St.
P.O. Box 579
New Harmony, IN 47631
(812) 682-4488

The Harmonie Society fled Germany because of religious persecution and ultimately developed a utopian community that later failed.

Iowa

Living History Farms
2600 NW 111th Street
Urbandale, IA 50322
(515) 278-2400

This museum depicts agrarian culture from the sixteenth century through to the 1850s.

Amana Colonies
P.O. Box 303
Amana, IA 52203
(800) 245-5465

In 1855 a group of separatists from Germany settled on 27,000 acres in Amana. The community features three furniture factories and several craft shops.

Kansas

Old Cowtown Museum
1871 Sim Park Drive
Wichita, KS 67203
(316) 264-0671

This museum features thirty buildings from an authentic cow town of the Old West.

Kentucky

Shaker Village of Pleasant Hill
3500 Lexington Road
Harrodsburg, KY 40330
(606) 734-5411

This nineteenth-century Shaker village has more than thirty original buildings, each furnished with Shaker furniture.

Louisiana

Acadian Village
200 Greenleaf Road
Lafayette, LA 70506
(800) 962-9133

This museum features a general store and houses from nineteenth-century Acadiana.

Maine

Norlands Living History Center
R.R. #2 Box 3395
Livermore Falls, ME 04254
(207) 897-2236

This center has two programs, one that depicts the post–Revolutionary War period and the other that portrays the post–Civil War era.

Maryland

Baltimore City Life Museums
800 East Lombard Street
Baltimore, MD 21202
(410) 396-3279

Six different museums portray life in nineteenth-century Baltimore.

Massachusetts

Hancock Shaker Village
P.O. Box 898
Pittsfield, MA 01202
(413) 443-0188

The Hancock Shaker Village features more than twenty restored buildings, and demonstrations of furniture and textile making.

Plimoth Plantation
P.O. Box 1620
Plymouth, MA 02362
(508) 746-1622

The Plimoth Plantation features a reconstructed village and a replica of the Mayflower.

Michigan

Colonial Michilimackinac
P.O. Box 873
Mackinaw City, MI 49701
(616) 436-5563

This former military outpost and fur trading center has re-created a 1770s Native American encampment, complete with wigwams.

Troy Museum and Historic Village
60 West Wattles Road
Troy, MI 48098
(313) 524-3570

This museum presents a program in which children reenact chores that were common to pioneer families.

Minnesota

Oliver H. Kelley Farm
15788 Kelley Farm Road
Elk River, MN 55330
(612) 441-6896

This farm depicts life in 1860s Minnesota.

Missouri

Arrow Rock State Historic Site
P.O. Box 1
Arrow Rock, MO 65320
(816) 837-3330

Located near the beginning of the Santa Fe Trail, this nineteenth-century village includes a restored church, tavern, courthouse, and newspaper office.

Nebraska

Stuhr Museum of the Prairie Pioneer
3133 West Highway 34
Grand Island, NE 68801
(308) 381-5316

3

This museum features a Pawnee lodge (replica) and a collection of Native American and Old West artifacts.

New Hampshire

Strawbery Banke
P.O. Box 300
Portsmouth, NH 03802
(603) 433-1100

Strawbery Banke, which was once a colonial seaport, depicts four centuries of history and culture.

New Jersey

Historic Batso Village
Wharton State Forest
Route #9 Batso
Hammonton, NJ 08037
(609) 561-3262

Batso Village was a nineteenth-century ironworking and glassmaking center.

New Mexico

El Rancho de Las Golondrinus
Route 14, P.O. Box 214
Santa Fe, NM 87505
(505) 471-2261

This town was founded by the Spanish as an overnight stop on the Royal Road to Mexico City.

New York

Museum Village
Museum Village Road
Monroe, NY 10950
(914) 782-8247

This village depicts agrarian life in the 1880s.

Old Bethpage Village Restoration
Nassau County Department of Recreation
  and Parks
Round Swarp Road
Old Bethpage, NY 11804
(516) 572-8400

This reconstructed village reflects agricultural, domestic, and trade activities from the pre–Civil War period.

North Carolina

Oconaluftee Indian Village
P.O. Box 398
Cherokee, NC 28719
(704) 497-2111

This village, which is located on the Cherokee Reservation, shows the history and traditions of the Cherokee Nation.

Ohio

Hale Farm and Village
P.O. Box 296
Bath, OH 44210
(216) 666-3711

This living museum depicts life in the 1850s. Demonstrations include glassblowing, candlemaking, blacksmithing, and maple sugaring (in season).

Ohio Village
1982 Velma Ave.
Columbus, OH 43211
(614) 297-2439

This museum portrays problems encountered by African-Americans during the early 1800s.

Pennsylvania

Historic Fallsington
4 Yardley Ave.
Fallsington, PA 19054
(215) 295-6567

This 300-year-old village was founded as a haven for Quakers and features a garden containing plants common to colonial America.

South Carolina

Middleton Place
Ashley River Road
Charleston, SC 29414
(803) 556-6020

At this restored eighteenth-century plantation, guides demonstrate woodworking and blacksmithing.

3

Tennessee

Museum of Appalachia
P.O. Box 0318
Highway 61
Norris, TN 37828
(615) 494-7680

The best time to visit is during the Fall Homecoming, in October, when demonstrations of goat milking, molasses-making, and spinning dog hair into thread are featured.

Texas

Old City Park
1717 Gano Street
Dallas, TX 75215
(214) 421-5141

This city park contains thirty-five restored buildings, from a log cabin to an antebellum mansion.

The Ranching Heritage Center
4th & Indiana
Lubbock, TX 79409
(806) 742-2498

This facility traces the history of ranching from the days of dugout homes to the early 1900s. It features over twenty restored buildings and railroad facilities.

Utah

Ronald V. Jensen Living Historical Farm
4025 South Highway 89-91
Welssville, UT 84339
(801) 245-4064

Interpreters demonstrate how family members on a Mormon farm in the early 1900s did their daily chores.

Virginia

Colonial Williamsburg
P.O. Box 1776
Williamsburg, VA 23187
(804) 229-1000

Among the largest and most famous of the living history museums in the United States, Colonial Williamsburg contains more than 100 restored or reconstructed buildings. A variety of educational programs are available.

Washington

Fort Nisqually Historic Site
Point Defiance Park
5400 North Pearl
Tacoma, WA 98405
(206) 591-5339

This living museum re-creates a former fort and Hudson Bay Company trading post.

Rainier Legacy
Pioneer Farm/Ohop Indian Village
7716 Ohop Valley Road
Eatonville, WA 98328
(206) 832-6300

This museum, which is open between early March and late November, contrasts a Native American settlement with that of European pioneers.

Wisconsin

Old World Wisconsin
South 103 West 37890
Highway 67
Eagle, WI 53119
(414) 594-2116

This living history museum shows nineteenth- and twentieth-century farmsteads for a variety of Scandinavian cultures.

3

Part 4   Annotated Bibliographies of Selected Children's Books

4.1 Children's Books for Teaching Character, Morals, and Values

In the following bibliographies, the grade-level designation "P" means the book might be more valuable for the primary grades, kindergarten to Grade 3; the designation "I" means the intermediate grades, 3–8.

A. Self-Esteem

Adoff, Arnold. (1991). *Hard to Be Six.* Illus. by Cheryl Hanna. Lothrop, Lee & Shepard. P, 32 pages.

> On the occasion of his sister's tenth birthday, a six-year-old boy reflects on how tough it is to be just six.

Allinson, Beverley. (1990). *Elfie.* Scholastic. P, 32 pages.

> Elfie has the loudest voice of any ant you will ever meet, so loud, in fact, that all the other ants in the community run away from her. Elfie feels (and is) rejected for a voice that she can't seem to control. When an emergency arises, Elfie's bellowing voice saves the lives of the rest of her family, and they come to accept her for what she is.

Browner, Anthony. (1985). *Willie the Champ.* Knopf. P, 32 pages.

> Willie is a sensitive boy who likes to read, listen to music, and take walks in the park but isn't any good at activities like soccer, swimming, or bike racing. One day when Willie encounters the neighborhood bully, Buster Nose, he doesn't run away as the other kids do. Instead, he defends himself against Buster and is declared a hero by the other children.

Bryan, Ashley. (1989). *Turtle Knows Your Name.* Atheneum. P, I, 32 pages.

> This West Indian tale is about a boy with a very long name, Upsilimana Tumpalerado. He works dili-gently just to pronounce his name, and when he fi-nally succeeds, he and his grandmother celebrate. Unfortunately, only one of his friends, Turtle, can remember and pronounce his name, but Turtle's effort makes Upsilimana Tumpalerado feel good.

Cameron, Ann. (1988). *Most Beautiful Place in the World.* Knopf. I, 64 pages.

> Abandoned by his parents, Juan lives with his grandmother in San Pablo, Guatemala. During the day he works as a shoeshine boy to earn his keep. Eventually Juan learns to read and realizes that where he lives is the most beautiful place in the world.

Carle, Eric. (1984). *The Mixed-Up Chameleon.* Harper. P, 32 pages.

> Sometimes he is green and sometimes he's brown, but this poor chameleon doesn't know who he is or what color he ought to be.

Cohen, Barbara. (1991). *213 Valentines.* Illus. by Wit Clay. Holt. P, I, 55 pages.

> Wade is an African-American boy who has trans-ferred to Kennedy School to participate in its gifted and talented program. At the new school, Wade feels so unpopular that he is sure he will not receive any valentine cards—except from the one person who drew his name. To avoid this, Wade buys 200 valentines, which he sends to himself and a friend under the names of famous people.

Glenn, Maggie. (1990). *Ruby.* Putnam. P, 32 pages.

> Ruby, a teddy bear, thinks that the "S" stamped on her paw at the toy factory means "special." The other teddy bears tell her that it means "sec-ond" and that she is a mistake. To avoid being thrown out, Ruby escapes from the factory and makes her way to the best toy shop in town. A lit-tle girl then selects Ruby because she is different from all the others; Ruby has character.

Graham, Amanda. (1987). *Who Wants Arthur?* Gareth Stevens. P, 32 pages.

> Arthur, a dog who has been in the pet shop for what seems like forever, decides that for someone to want him, he will need to act like other popular animals. For example, when Arthur sees that fish are popular, he tries to act like a fish, but to no avail. Only after Arthur becomes himself does someone buy him.

Hooks, William H. (1989). *The Three Little Pigs and the Fox.* Illus. by S. D. Schindler. Macmillan. P, I, 32 pages.

> In this version of the classic tale, the smallest pig, the female runt of the litter, outwits the fox and saves her bigger brothers.

Klass, Sheila Solomon. (1991). *Kool Ada.* Scholastic. I, 176 pages.

> Ada is a strong-willed girl with adjustment problems. Not only is she new to her northern school, but she has recently moved from a home in the rural, southern mountains. A compassionate teacher finally helps Ada understand that her rough exterior and quick temper are only compounding her problems.

Lane, Megan Halsey. (1990). *Something to Crow About.* Dial. P, 32 pages.

> In this predictable book, Randall is a rooster who wants to lay eggs, and Cassie is a chicken who would like to cock-a-doodle-do. They both eventually realize that being different is what they should crow about.

Leaf, Munro. (1936). *The Story of Ferdinand.* Illus. by Robert Lawson. Viking. P, 48 pages.

> In this classic story, Ferdinand is a bull who would rather smell the flowers than butt horns with the other bulls. When it comes time to select new candidates for the bull ring, Ferdinand goes off by himself and sits next to some flowers. Unfortunately, Ferdinand sits on a bee, which results in a demonstration of jumping and wild movements that convinces the judges that he belongs in the bull ring. When Ferdinand finally enters the ring for his "big event," all he does is smell the flowers in the ladies' hats.

Levine, Ellen. (1989). *I Hate English.* Illus. by Steve Bjorkman. Scholastic. P, I, 32 pages.

> Every non-native speaker of English knows what a hard language it is to learn. This is the case in this story of a young girl who is being tutored in English but sees little need to learn it. Eventually she begins to feel better about speaking her native tongue and about acquiring a second language.

Lionni, Leo. (1969). *Alexander and the Wind-Up Mouse.* Random House. P, 32 pages.

> Alexander is a real mouse who meets Willie, a wind-up mouse. Alexander tries to transform himself into a mechanical mouse like Willie, who is loved by a human, only to find that Willie has been discarded by his owner. Alexander then realizes that being a real mouse isn't so bad after all.

Milhouse, Katherine, & Dalgiesh, Alice. (1990). *The Turnip, an Old Russian Tale.* Putnam. P, 32 pages.

> Mice are among the most powerful literary creatures, and so it is in this tale. Everyone who tries to pull a turnip from the ground is unsuccessful until the mouse finally lends a hand.

Peet, Bill. (1986). *Pamela Camel.* Houghton Mifflin. P, 48 pages.

> Poor Pamela Camel thinks that she is the dumbest animal in the circus. Pamela feels so bad that she runs away, but in the process she saves a train from destruction. For her heroism, she is given first place in the circus parade.

Polacco, Patricia. (1990). *Just Plain Fancy.* Bantam. P, 32 pages.

> Naomi is an Amish girl, one of the plain people. Amid all the plainness, Naomi complains to her little sister that just once she would like to have something fancy. One day as Naomi is collecting eggs, she notices one that is different and fancier than the rest. She places it under a hen, and when it hatches it produces an unusual looking bird. Naomi fears that her fancy bird, a peacock, will be shunned. Instead, the elders view Naomi's peacock as a miracle.

Rodgers, Frank. (1988). *Who's Afraid of the Ghost Train?* Harcourt Brace Jovanovich. P, 32 pages.

Robert is afraid of almost everything and gets teased by his friends accordingly. One day his grandpa, a former lion tamer, gives him an idea for handling his fears. He tells Robert to pretend that the lions are just big babies. Robert tries this technique when riding the Ghost Train at the carnival the next day.

Seuss, Dr. (1990). *Oh, The Places You'll Go!* Random House. P, I, 48 pages.

Like most Seuss books do, the delightful rhyming text of this book reflects optimism personified.

Thomas, Patricia. (1971/1990). *"Stand Back," Said the Elephant, "I'm Going to Sneeze!"* Illus. by Wallace Trip. Lothrop. P, 48 pages.

When an elephant sneezes, all kinds of unexpected things can happen—and do in this story. But once again, a mouse surprises the elephant and keeps him from sneezing, thus saving the other animals from their embarrassing responses to his sneeze. Unfortunately, the elephant ends up laughing, the effects of which are almost as bad as sneezing.

Waber, Bernard. (1972). *Ira Sleeps Over.* Houghton Mifflin. P, 48 pages.

Should Ira take his teddy bear, Tah Tah, when he is invited to stay over at his best friend Reggie's house? Will Reggie make fun of him for sleeping with a teddy bear? Ira decides against taking Tah Tah, but after they are settled in to sleep, Reggie quietly pulls his own teddy bear, Foo Foo, out of a dresser drawer. Ira then runs home to rescue Tah Tah and bring her to Reggie's for the night.

Yorinks, Arthur. (1988). *Bravo Minski.* Illus. by Richard Egielski. Farrar, Straus & Giroux. P, 32 pages.

It is difficult to be a scientific genius, especially when your father hauls you around Europe showing off your talents, but this is Minski's fate. But one day, when Minski hears an opera star, he determines to find a way to get the same kind of beautiful voice. Although his father thinks that Minski's musical intentions are impractical and unworthy of a scientific genius, Minski pursues his quest to become a musical performer.

Zolotow, Charlotte. (1972). *William's Doll.* Illus. by William Pene du Bois. Harper. P, I, 32 pages.

William has a basketball and a train set, but what he really wants is a doll. It doesn't matter that his brother thinks he is a creep, and the boy next door calls him a sissy; they just don't understand. William's grandmother is apparently the only person who understands how he feels and is willing to give him the doll he seeks.

B. Respect for Others

Anholt, Lawrence. (1991). *What I Like.* Illus. by Catherine Anholt. Putnam. P, 32 pages.

In simple rhyming text, six children share the different things they like to do. They eventually join hands and chant, "What we all like is . . . making a friend."

Brewster, Patience. (1991). *Rabbit Inn.* Little, Brown. P, I, 32 pages.

Some unexpected guests are coming to Rabbit Inn, so all the other animal guests cooperate to help the rabbit owners to clean up the place. On the last page of the book, they find out who the special guests are.

Damrell, Liz. (1991). *With the Wind.* Illus. by Stephen Marchesi. Orchard. P, 32 pages.

Much of this story focuses on a young boy's thrill of riding a horse. Not until the next-to-last page do the illustrations show that this child has a disability; he has a brace on his leg and is placed in a wheelchair after his ride.

Herman, Charlotte. (1991). *Max Malone Makes a Million.* Illus. by Cat Bowman Smith. Henry Holt. P, I, 64 pages.

After Max reads about a get-rich-quick scheme, he sets out on one of his own. A six-year-old neighbor volunteers to help him, but Max just scoffs at him. In this instance, the younger child (the six-year-old) is successful and Max is not.

4

Hoffman, Mary. (1991). *Amazing Grace.* Illus. by Caroline Binch. Dial. P, 32 pages.

This is one of the growing number of books, like Spinelli's *Maniac Magee,* that addresses prejudice and bias directly. In this case, Grace, a truly talented dancer, wants the role of Peter Pan in a school play. But because she is both a black and a female, her classmates decide it would be inappropriate for her to play that role. Fortunately, Grace's grandmother is able to help her deal with her disappointment.

Isadora, Rachel. (1991). *At the Crossroads.* Greenwillow. P, I, 32 pages.

This book is about the children from a segregated South African township who gather at a crossroads to await their father's return from ten months in the mines. The African experience on which this book is based is real, and the underlying emotion—jubilation at the return of a loved one—is universal.

Johnston, Tony. (1986). *Pages of Music.* Illus. by Tomie dePaola. Putnam. P, I, 32 pages.

An artist and her son visit the island of Sardinia, where the poor shepherds share their bread with them. The son, who never forgets the sound of shepherd's pipes, returns years later as a composer and conductor. With him he brings his entire orchestra and an orchestral piece he has composed especially for the shepherds of Sardinia.

Joseph, Lynn. (1990). *Coconut Kind of Day.* Lothrop, Lee & Shepard. P, 32 pages.

This is a collection of poems, told in dialect, about a day in the life of a Caribbean child. Differences between island life and life in the United States are obvious.

Kline, Suzy. (1991). *Mary Marony and the Snake.* Illus. by Blanche Sims. Putnam. P, I, 64 pages.

Mary Marony stutters and her second-grade classmates, especially Marvin Higgins, tease her. Mary earns the respect of her fellow students when Marvin's father brings a snake to school and Mary rescues it when it gets loose.

Morris, Ann. (1990). *On the Go.* Lothrop, Lee & Shepard. P, I, 32 pages.

The photographs in this nonfiction book show how people move themselves and things from one place to another in various parts of the world. Children learn that it is normal for people in some parts of the world to carry things on their heads or use various pack animals.

Ringgold, Faith. (1991). *Tar Beach.* Crown. P, 32 pages.

The "tar beach" is the tarred roof of a Harlem tenement on which residents place blankets to sunbathe. It is a special place where Cassie retreats to dream about life. This story was originally written by Faith Ringgold to accompany her story quilt, and a bit of the quilt is seen on each page until at the end you view the completed work.

Shelby, Anne. (1991). *Potluck.* Illus. by Irene Trivas. Orchard. P, 32 pages.

Potluck is an alphabet book. For each letter of the alphabet, a child whose name begins with that letter uses an action that begins with that letter to bring a food that begins with that letter to a potluck meal. The illustrations depict children of all racial and cultural backgrounds, and the foods they bring come from around the world.

Spinelli, Jerry. (1990). *Maniac Magee.* Little, Brown. I, 154 pages.

This Newbery Award winner involves a white, homeless school dropout who lives for a time with a black family, then teaches an illiterate former minor league baseball player how to read, and finally makes friends with Mars Bars, the "baddest" black kid in town. The human relationships and the caring are both touching and profound.

Stevenson, James. (1991). *The Worst Person's Christmas.* Greenwillow. P, I, 32 pages.

This book uses a cartoon format to show a Scrooge-like person who refuses to celebrate Christmas until some neighborhood children give him a present. He is ultimately forced to be jovial for the holidays.

4

Williams, Karen Lynn. (1991). *When Africa Was Home*. Orchard. P, I, 32 pages.

> Peter, a white child, was raised by an African nanny while his parents were working for the Peace Corps in Malawi. Peter has no desire to return to the United States, but he must say goodbye to his African extended family and friends. In the United States, he hates the cold snow and dreams of his former home in Africa. At the end of the story, the family returns to Africa and Peter is happy to be home again.

This bibliography is adapted from *Literature-Based Moral Education: Children's Books & Activities for Teaching Values, Responsibility, & Good Judgment in the Elementary School* by Linda Leonard Lamme, Suzanne Lowell Krogh, and Kathy A. Yachmetz. (1992). Used by permission of The Oryx Press, 4041 North Central at Indian School Road, Phoenix, AZ.

4.2 Historical Fiction and Folk Literature for Common Social Studies Topics

A. PRIMARY GRADES (K–3)

1. Prehistory through A.D. 1

Literature Reflecting African or Egyptian Perspectives

Araujo, F. P. (1994). *The Perfect Orange: A Tale from Ethiopia*. Illus. by Xiao Jun Li. Rayve.

> An orphan girl gives the King an orange and accepts a donkey in return; only then does she learn that its bags are full of riches.

Bryan, A. (1989). *Turtle Knows Your Name*. Atheneum.

> This folktale from the West Indies is about the importance of names to family members.

Jupo, F. (1967). *Atu, The Silent One*. Holiday.

> This story focuses on Atu, an African boy, and the way his people might have lived many years ago.

Kimmel, E. A. (1994). *Anansi and the Talking Melon*. Illus. by J. Stevens. Holiday.

Anansi, who has eaten Elephant's melon, tries to trick Elephant into believing it was a talking melon. Elephant shares his news with others, but King Monkey is insulted by the melon and disorder ensures.

Maddern, E. (1993). *The Fire Children: A West African Creation Tale*. Illus. by F. Lessac. Dial.

> This tale explains the origin of people who have different skin tones.

Mike, J. M. (1992). *Gift of the Nile: An Ancient Egyptian Legend*. Illus. by C. Reasoner. Troll.

> This is the story of Mutem Wia, whose father gives her to the Pharaoh as a gift.

Souhami, J. (1996). *The Leopard's Drum: An Ashante Tale from West Africa*. Illus. by author. Little, Brown.

> Osebo, the leopard, refuses to give Nyame, the Sky God, a drum that Nyame envies. Nyame offers to reward the animal that can bring it to him, and although many animals try, only Achicheri, the tortoise, succeeds.

Walsh, J. P. (1995). *Pepi and the Secret Names*. Illus. by F. French. Lothrop, Lee & Shepard.

> Pepi assists his father in decorating a royal tomb, makes friends with animals, guesses their secret names, and then gets them to pose for his father.

Literature Reflecting an Asian Perspective

Hong, L. T. (1995). *The Empress and the Silkworm*. Illus. by the author. Albert Whitman.

> Set in China nearly 5,000 years ago, Si Ling-chi, the Empress, unwinds the thread of a cocoon that falls from a mulberry tree. She creates the first silk material that becomes a robe for the Emperor.

Ishii, M. (1987). *The Tongue-Cut Sparrow*. Trans. by K. Paterson. Illus. by S. Akaba. Dutton.

> A kind husband and his selfish wife get different rewards.

Jaffe, N. (1995). *Older Brother, Younger Brother: A Korean Folktale*. Illus. by W. Ma. Viking.

> A young brother cares for an injured baby sparrow, which returns with a gift of wealth.

4

McDermott, G. (1981). *The Stone-Cutter: A Japanese Folk Tale.* Illus. by the author. Puffin Books.

> This tale from Japan is about a boy who wanted to be stronger than the sun and mightier than a cloud.

Mosel, A. (1972). *The Funny Little Woman.* Illus. by B. Lent. Dutton.

> A woman escapes from the wicked Oni and takes a magic cooking spoon.

Shute, L. (1986). *Momotaro, the Peach Boy: A Traditional Japanese Tale.* Lothrop, Lee & Shepard.

> A small boy, who was born inside a peach, grows to challenge the evil *oni* who threaten his community.

Van de Wetering, J. (1978). *Little Owl: An Eightfold Buddhist Admonition.* Houghton Mifflin.

> Stories about animal characters introduce different aspects of the Buddhist religion.

Wells, R. (1996). *The Farmer and the Poor God: A Folktale from Japan.* Illus. by Yoshi. Simon & Schuster.

> A farmer and his wife who have been impoverished by the Poor God, who lives in their attic, plan to escape their curse by running away. The god hears them and weaves sandals to follow them. The couple change their minds about going, and the sandals make them rich and happy.

Yep, L. (1993). *The Man Who Tricked a Ghost.* Bridgewater Books.

> Young Sung makes himself rich by learning the secret of a fierce warrior ghost, and then using this to defeat him.

Young, E. (1995). *Cat and Rat: The Legend of the Chinese Zodiac.* Illus. by the author. Holt, Rinehart & Winston.

> The Emperor announces that the winners of a race through the forest will have one of the years in the zodiac named after them.

Literature Reflecting European Perspectives

Turner, A. (1987). *Time of the Bison.* Illus. by B. Peck. Macmillan.

> This fictional tale is set in prehistoric times and tells about how Scar Boy wants to earn a new name.

Literature Reflecting Hispanic Perspectives

Blackmore, V. (1984). *Why Corn Is Golden: Stories about Plants.* Illus. by S. Martinez-Ostos. Little, Brown.

> This collection of folk stories is about corn and other plants.

Gershator, P. (1994). *Tukama Tootles the Flute: A Tale from the Antilles.* Illus. by S. Saint James. Orchard.

> The music from Tukama's flute helps him to escape the clutches of a two-headed giant.

Greger, C. S. (1994). *The Fifth and Final Sun: An Ancient Aztec Myth of the Sun's Origin.* Houghton Mifflin.

> This folktale tells why humans live in the Age of the Fifth Sun—the first four suns were destroyed by jealous gods.

Kurtz, J. (1996). *Miro in the Kingdom of the Sun.* Illus. by D. Frampton. Houghton Mifflin.

> This Incan folktale is the story of Miro, a girl who can run swiftly and understand the language of the birds. She is able to free her imprisoned brothers and find a cure for the ailing son of the Incan king.

Mora, P. (1995). *The Race of Toad and Deer.* Illus. by M. Itzna Brooks. Orchard.

> In this Guatemalan tale, a deer challenges a toad in a race similar to that of "The Tortoise and the Hare."

Pitre, F. (1995). *Paco and the Witch.* Illus. by C. Hale. Lodestar.

> A witch has cast a spell on a Puerto Rican boy that can be broken only if he can guess her name. A crab teaches Paco a song to remember the name and the boy is saved. The witch goes looking for the animal that betrayed her, so the crab hides whenever he see a human.

Literature Reflecting Greek, Mediterranean, or Middle Eastern Perspectives

Aesop (1985). *Aesop's Fables.* Illus. by M. Hague. Holt, Rinehart & Winston.

> This book includes thirteen fables.

Bahous, S. (1993). *Sitti and the Cats.* Illus. by N. Malick. Roberts Rinehart.

This Palestinian fairy tale focuses on the harshness of village life.

Hort, L. (1995). *The Goatherd and the Shepherdess: A Tale from Ancient Greece.* Illus. by L. Bloom. Dial.

In this classic Greek myth, a shepherdess, Chloe, saves her lover, Daphnis, from kidnappers by blowing on a dying cowherder's pipes.

Hutton, W. (1991). *The Trojan Horse.* McElderry.

This is the classic Greek tale about how Greek soldiers, hidden inside a huge horse, capture the city of Troy.

Kimmel, E. A. (1994). *The Three Princes: A Tale from the Middle East.* Illus. by L. E. Fisher. Holiday.

A princess says that she will marry whichever suitor returns from a quest with the most magnificent wonder. She marries the one who sacrifices his treasure for her.

Rockwell, A. (1996). *The One-Eyed Giant and Other Monsters from the Greek Myths.* Illus. by the author. Greenwillow.

This book presents ten myths about such monsters as Typhon, Echidna, Hydra, Cyclopes, and Medusa.

Literature Reflecting Native American Perspectives

Gates, F., reteller. (1994). *Owl Eyes.* Illus. by Y. Miyake. Lothrop.

This Mohawk legend tells how Raweno, the creator, gives each animal its traits. Because Owl pesters everyone as Raweno is trying to do this, he gives him big eyes and ears, to see only what is in front of him and hear what he is told.

Hausman, G., reteller. (1996). *Eagle Boy: A Traditional Navajo Legend.* Illus. by C. and B. Moser. HarperCollins.

Learning about the Eagle Way, which is culturally significant to the Navajo, is the focus of this legend about a young boy who dreams of eagles and is taken up to the clouds to meet Eagle Chief.

Orie, S. D. C. (1995). *Did You Hear Wind Sing Your Name? An Oneida Song of Spring.* Illus. by C. Canyon. Walker.

This poem explores the sensations and feelings related to spring, including dewdrops and new leaves.

Philip, N. (1995). *Songs Are Thoughts: Poems of the Inuit.* Illus. by M. Foa. Orchard.

The free-verse selections in this book, which were originally intended to be sung, reflect the wisdom and happiness of the Eskimo people.

Stevens, J. (1996). *Old Bag of Bones: A Coyote Tale.* Holiday.

This retelling of a Shoshoni tale is about the trials of Old Coyote when he asks Buffalo to share his strength, youth, and power.

Young, E. (1993). *Moon Mother: A Native American Creation Tale.* Illus. by the author. HarperCollins.

This tale explains how people and tribes came to be, and why newborn babies cry.

Literature Reflecting Pacific and Australian Perspectives

Maddern, E. (1993). *Rainbow Bird: An Aboriginal Folktale from Northern Australia.* Illus. by A. Kennaway. Little, Brown.

Bird Woman snatches fire from Crocodile Man and then flies around putting fire into the heart of every tree. Thereafter, people can make flames from dry wood.

Literature Involving Children with Disabilities

de Armond, D. (1988). *The Seal Oil Lamp.* Sierra/Little.

This ancient Inuit tale tells about Allugua, a child who is born blind and, at age seven, is going to be abandoned until the Mouse Woman intervenes to save him.

de Paola, T. (1988). *The Legend of the Indian Paintbrush.* Putnam's.

This is the story of Little Gopher, a child who cannot be like other children, and why the wildflowers bloom with such brilliant colors.

Literature Reflecting Religious Perspectives

Aroner, M. (1993). *The Kingdom of Singing Birds.* Kar-Ben.

This classic Hasidic tale is about making one's own choices. When the King calls Rabbi Zusya to make his silent birds sing, Zusya tells him that he must set the birds free.

Kuskin, K. (1993). *A Great Miracle Happened There: A Chanukah Story.* HarperCollins.

A mother tells her son about the origins of Chanukah.

MacGill-Callahan, S. (1995). *When Solomon Was King.* Illus. by S. T. Johnson. Dial.

King Solomon's life is saved by a lioness that Solomon had restored to health.

McDermott, G. (1974). *Arrow to the Sun.* Viking.

This Pueblo Indian tale tells about the people's beliefs about the sun.

Uchida, Y. (1986). *The Dancing Kettle.* Creative Arts Books.

The legends and myths in this Japanese collection all relate to the principles of Shintoism.

2. Early History A.D. 1 through A.D. 1700

Literature Reflecting African Perspectives

Aardema, V. (1995). *Anansi Finds a Fool: An Ashanti Tale.* Illus. by B. Waldman. Dial.

In this amusing folktale, Anansi is outfoxed while trying to trick someone else.

Bryan, A. (1986). *Lion and the Ostrich Chicks and Other African Folk Tales.* Atheneum.

This is a collection of Hausa folktales.

Wisniewski, D. (1992). *Sundiata: Lion King of Mali.* Clarion.

This biography relates the life of Sundiata, who overcomes the inability to speak or walk, to become the Lion King of the Mali Empire.

Literature Reflecting Asian Perspectives

Han, S. C. (1995). *The Rabbit's Escape.* Illus. by Y. Heo. Holt.

This Korean folktale is about Rabbit's escape from a turtle that intends to deliver him to the Dragon King of the East Sea.

Ho, M., & Ros, S. (1995). *The Two Brothers.* Illus. by J. and Mou-Sen Tseng. Lothrop, Lee & Shepard.

Sem and Kern are two orphaned brothers from Cambodia. They encounter an abbot in a Cambodian monastery who prophesies that Sem is destined for kingship and Kern for wealth.

Uchida, Y. (1993). *The Magic Purse.* Illus. by K. Narahashi. McElderry.

When a poor man does an errand for a beautiful woman he meets, she gives him a magic purse of gold coins that support him through his life. Each year, the man follows the woman's instructions and leaves one coin in the purse.

_____. (1995). *The Wise Old Woman.* Illus. by M. Springett. McElderry.

When a cruel lord in medieval Japan decrees that the elderly at age seventy must be abandoned in the mountains, a young farmer hides his elderly mother to protect her.

Early Life in the American Colonies

Bulla, C. (1981). *A Lion to Guard Us.* Crowell.

This is the touching story of how three motherless children keep their lion's head doorknocker as they sail from London to Jamestown to find their father in the new colony.

_____. (1988). *Squanto, Friend of the Pilgrims.* Scholastic.

This is the biography of Squanto, the Native American who befriended and offered immeasurable aid to the Pilgrims at the Plymouth Colony.

Good, M. (1993). *Reuben and the Fire.* Illus. by P. B. Moss. Good Books.

This is a fictionalized account of Amish life depicted through the activities of Reuben and his sisters. When Reuben sees his neighbor's barn burn down, the entire Amish community gathers for a barn raising.

Spier, P. (1979). *The Legend of New Amsterdam.* Doubleday.

This is a fictionalized account of a huge metropolis.

Walters, K. (1993). *Samuel Eaton's Day: A Day in the Life of a Pilgrim Boy*. Scholastic.

> This fictionalized account describes the daily life of seven-year-old Samuel Eaton in the Plimouth Colony.

Literature Reflecting European, Mediterranean, or Middle Eastern Perspectives

Adler, D. (1991). *A Picture Book of Christopher Columbus*. Illus. by J. Wallner & A. Wallner. Holiday.

> This biographical picture book focuses on the life and time of Columbus.

Conrad, P. (1991). *Pedro's Journal*. Illus. by P. Koeppen. Caroline House.

> This is the fictionalized diary of twelve-year-old Pedro, a ship's boy, who sails on Columbus's first voyage. Unfortunately, he is at the helm of the *Santa Maria* when he sails into a reef and sinks the ship.

Hodges, M. (1993). *The Hero of Bremen*. Holiday.

> In this tale, Roland, a legendary hero, assists the crippled Hans to get land needed by the town of Bremen.

Pushkin, A. (n.d.). *The Fisherman and the Goldfish*. Illus. by V. Konashevich. Trans. by P. Tempest. Moscow Progress Publishers.

> This is the Russian version of "The Fisherman and His Wife," in which an old man asks a goldfish for favors.

Talbott, H., reteller. (1995). *King Arthur and the Round Table*. Illus. by the reteller. Morrow.

> This story follows King Arthur and his establishment of the Round Table.

Literature Reflecting Hispanic Perspectives

Marzollo, J. (1991). *In 1492*. Illus. by S. Bjorkman. Scholastic.

> The rhyming text in this book depicts Columbus and his arrival in the new world.

Literature Reflecting Native American Perspectives

Brebeuf, Father Jean de. (1993). *The Huron Carol*. Dutton.

> This is the story of the birth of Christ as set in the Huron world. It was written in the 1600s by a missionary, Father Jean de Brebeufin.

Fradin, D. (1992). *Hiawatha: Messenger of Peace*. Margaret K. McElderry/Macmillan.

> This is the biography of Hiawatha, an Iroquois, who helped unite the seven Iroquois tribes into the Iroquois Confederacy.

Kessel, J. K. (1983). *Squanto and the First Thanksgiving*. Illus. by L. Donze. Carolrhoda.

> This is the biography of Squanto, the last of the Paatuxet Indians, who helps the Pilgrims survive the harsh winter of 1620.

Sage, J. (1995). *Coyote Makes Man*. Illus. by B. Techentrup. Simon & Schuster.

> In this Crow legend, a coyote creates a new creature.

Sewall, M. (1995). *King Philip's War*. Atheneum.

> This fictionalized story is told in two voices: the Wampanoag and Pilgrim. The different points of view explain how relations between the colonists and the Native People eventually led to King Philip's War and, ultimately, to the destruction of the Wampanoags and their allies.

Swamp, C. J. (1995). *Giving Thanks: A Native American Good Morning Message*. Illus. by E. Printup, Jr. Lee & Low.

> The words in this text, which give thanks to Mother Earth and the Great Spirit, are taken from Iroquois ceremonies.

Talashoema, H. (1991). *Coyote and Little Turtle: A Traditional Hopi Tale*. Trans. from Hopi by E. Sekaquaptewa and B. Pepper.

> In another of the Coyote legends, Little Turtle tricks Coyote into throwing him into the pond.

3. 1700 through 1900

Famous Americans

Adler, D. A. (1996). *A Picture Book of Davy Crockett*. Illus. by J. and A. Wallner. Holiday.

> This brief biography chronicles Crockett's life from his birth in Tennessee to his death at the Alamo.

Aliki. (1988). *A Weed Is a Flower: The Life of George Washington Carver*. Illus. by the author. Simon & Schuster.

> This biography relates the life and achievements of George Washington Carver.

Giblin, J. C. (1992). *George Washington: A Picture Book Biography*. Illus. by M. Dooling. Scholastic.

> This biography follows events in Washington's life from childhood onward.

_____. (1995). *Thomas Jefferson: A Picture Book Biography*. Illus. by M. Dooling. Scholastic.

> This pictorial biography chronicles events in Jefferson's life from childhood onward.

Walter, R. (1992). *The Story of Daniel Boone*. Dell.

> This biography highlights the exploits of this famous Kentucky frontiersman.

Literature with African or African-American Themes

Barrett, T. (1993). *Nat Turner and the Slave Revolt*. Millbrook.

> This is a fictionalized account of the rebellion that Nat Turner led against slave holders in Hampton, Virginia.

Bennett, E. (1992). *Frederick Douglass and the War Against Slavery*. Millbrook.

> This is a biography of Frederick Douglass, who was born into slavery, but who became one of the foremost writers and speakers in the abolitionist movement.

Johnson, D. (1994). *Seminole Diary: Remembrances of a Slave*. Macmillan.

> This fictional story is in a diary format and tells how Libbie and her family escape from slavery and join with the Seminole Indian tribe for safety.

Miller, W. (1995). *Frederick Douglass: The Last Days of Slavery*. Illus. by C. Lucas. Lee & Low.

> This biography focuses on Douglass and his actions, particularly his refusal to accept being a slave.

Wright, C. C. (1995). *Wagon Train: A Family Goes West in 1865*. Illus. by G. Griffith. Holiday.

> This fictional story portrays the hardships that an African-American family faces when they travel west.

Literature Reflecting Asian Perspectives

Coerr, E. (1988). *Chang's Paper Pony*. Illus. by D. K. Ray. Harper & Row.

> This is the fictional story of Chang, who works in the kitchen of a gold mining camp in California. Chang finds gold nuggets under the floor in a cabin, returns them to their owner, and is rewarded with the pony he has always wanted.

Conger, D. (1987). *Many Lands, Many Stories: Asian Folk Tales for Children*. Illus. by R. Ra. Tuttle.

> This is a collection of fifteen folktales from various countries in Asia.

Literature Reflecting European Perspectives

Conway, C. (1994). *Where Is Papa Now?* Illus. by author. Caroline House/Boyds Mills Press.

> The fictional story of the daughter of a New England ship's captain who wonders where he is as his ship travels around the world.

Penn, M. (1994). *The Miracle of the Potato Latkes: A Hanukkah Story*. Illus. by G. Carrni. Holiday.

> One potato that Tante Golda shares with an old beggar during a potato famine multiplies until she has enough to serve potato pancakes (latkes) to her guests.

Literature Reflecting Hispanic Perspectives

Gray, G. (1978). *How Far, Felipe?* Harper.

> This fictional story is about Felipe and his family as they move from Mexico to California with Colonel Juan de Anza's expedition in 1775.

Living in the Era 1700 to 1900

Hall, Donald. (1979). *Ox-Cart Man*. Illus. by B. Cooney. Viking.

> This story follows a New England family in the nineteenth century as the father takes their year's farm products to sell in the city.

Saunders, S. R. (1995). *The Floating House.* Illus. by H. Cogancherry. Macmillan.

> This is a fictional story about the McClure family's journey down the Ohio River en route to new land in Indiana.

Shelby, A. (1995). *Homeplace.* Illus. by W. A. Halperin. Orchard.

> This fictional story traces a family's history in the same house that began as a log cabin built by an ancestor in 1810.

Smiler, N. (1992). *Snowshoe Thompson.* Illus. by J. Sandin. HarperCollins.

> This is the fictionalized story of John Thompson, who moves to northern California from Scandinavia in the early 1850s and becomes a mailperson.

Smucker, B. (1996). *Selina and the Bear Paw Quilt.* Illus. by J. Wilson. Crown.

> When a Mennonite family decides to flee to Canada just before the Civil War, the grandmother gives her granddaughter a handmade bear-paw patterned quilt.

Life on the Frontier

Brenner, Barbara. (1978). *Wagon Wheels.* Illus. by D. Bolognese. Harper & Row.

> This is a fictionalized account of a true story of a black pioneer family who sought free land offered in Kansas.

Coerr, Eleanor. (1986). *The Josefina Story Quilt.* Illus. by B. Degen. Harper & Row.

> This story is about a young girl who makes quilt squares to record her travels west in a covered wagon.

Harvey, Brett. (1988). *Cassie's Journey.* Illus. by D. K. Ray. Holiday.

> Cassie describes the problems her family encounters traveling by covered wagon from Illinois to California in the 1860s.

Holling, Clancy. (1942). *Tree in the Trail.* Houghton Mifflin.

> This old but fascinating account describes events that occurred around a cottonwood tree in Kansas that eventually became a yoke for a team of oxen.

Hooks, William H. (1988). *Pioneer Cat.* Random House.

> The story of a young girl who smuggles a cat on a wagon train to Oregon.

Levinson, Nancy S. (1988). *Clara and the Bookwagon.* Illus. by C. Croll. Harper & Row.

> Clara learns to read after the first traveling library visits her father's farm.

Rounds, Glen. (1983). *Mr. Yowder and the Windwagon.* Holiday.

> This delightful book describes Mr. Yowder's fruitless attempt to use wind power to drive a prairie schooner.

4. 1900 to the present

Noted Americans

West, A. (1992). *Roberto Clemente: Baseball Legend.* Millbrook.

> This is a biography of Roberto Clemente, the Puerto Rican boy who became an outfielder for the Pittsburgh Pirates.

Literature Reflecting African or African-American Perspectives

Aardema, Verna. (1981). *Bringing the Rain to Kapiti Plain.* Illus. by B. Vidal. Dial.

> This African folktale tells how Ki-pat brings rain to end the drought.

Greenfield, Eloise. (1972). *Honey, I Love.* Illus. by D. and L. Dillon. Crowell.

> A young African-American girl shares poems of activities and people she loves and enjoys.

Hamilton, Virginia. (1985). *The People Could Fly.* Illus. by L. and D. Dillon. Knopf.

> This collection of African-American folktales is about animals, the supernatural, and striving for freedom.

4

Pomerantz, Charlotte. (1989). *The Chalk Doll*. Illus. by F. Lessac. Lippincott.

> Rosa's mother describes her life and childhood in Jamaica.

Literature Reflecting Asian Perspectives

Rattigan, J. K. (1993). *Dumpling Soup*. Illus. by L. Hsu-Flanders. Little, Brown.

> This is an account of seven-year-old Marisa, a Hawaiian girl who celebrates New Year's with her extended family.

Say, Allen. (1982). *The Bicycle Man*. Houghton Mifflin.

> In postwar-occupied Japan, a group of school-children are amazed by an American soldier's bicycle tricks.

Literature Reflecting European Perspectives

Ioosse, B. M. (1995). *The Morning Chair*. Illus. by M. Sewall. Clarion.

> When a young boy and his parents leave Holland for New York City, the boy is comforted by the fact that the family is bringing some of its rituals with them.

Polacco, P. (1990). *Thunder Cake*. Philomel.

> In this tale of Russian origin, a little girl's Babushka (grandmother) helps her to overcome her fear of thunderstorms by baking a Thunder Cake, which they eat during the storm.

Schwartz, D. M. (1991). *Supergrandpa*. Illus. by B. Dodson. Lothrop, Lee & Shepard.

> This is the fictionalized story of a sixty-three-year-old man who enters the Tour of Sweden, a 1,000-mile bicycle race.

Life in the Twentieth Century

Baker, S. A. (1995). *Grandpa Is a Flyer*. Illus. by B. Farnsworth. Albert Whitman.

> This is a fictionalized account of a grandfather who shares his love for flying with his grand-daughter.

Good, M. (1982). *Nicole Visits an Amish Farm*. Walker.

> This is a story of how a child from the city spends her summer on an Amish farm.

_____. (1995). *Reuben and the Blizzard*. Illus. by P. B. Moss. Good Books.

> This is a story of how Reuben and his Amish family are affected by a blizzard.

Harvey, B. (1987). *Immigrant Girl: Becky of Eldridge Street*. Holiday.

> This story about Russian immigrants living in New York City is based on a young girl's diary.

Schertle, A. (1995). *Maisie*. Illus. by L. Dabovich. Lothrop, Lee & Shepard.

> This is a fictional account of a farm girl who shares events from her life up to her ninetieth birthday.

Family Life/Problems

Aliki. (1979). *The Two of Them*. Greenwillow.

> A little girl's grandfather cares for her until she grows up; then she cares for him until he dies.

Blaine, Marge. (1975). *Terrible Thing That Happened at Our House*. Illus. by J. Wallner. Parents Magazine.

> Children may need to accept new responsibilities when Mother goes back to work.

Brown, Laurie Krashy, & Brown, Marc. (1986). *Dinosaurs Divorce*. Little, Brown.

> This account may help to offset some of the anxieties that children feel when their parents are going through a divorce.

Clifton, Lucille. (1983). *Everett Anderson's Goodbye*. Illus. by A. Grifalconi. Henry Holt.

> This is the story of a boy who goes through several stages in coming to accept his father's death.

Drescher, Joan. (1980). *Your Family, My Family*. Walker.

> This story shows how family units are often made up of different combinations of people.

Fisher, Iris. (1987). *Katie-Bo*. Illus. by M. Schaer. Adama.

> This is the story of an American family that adopts a Korean child.

Hazen, Barbara Shook. (1979). *Tight Times*. Illus. by T. Hyman. Viking.

A family living in poverty supports one another even though the father has lost his job.

Hutchins, Pat. (1985). *The Very Worst Monster.* William Morrow.

This account tells about Hazel's effort to overcome her jealousy when her baby brother arrives.

MacLachlan, Patricia. (1982). *Mama One, Mama Two.* Illus. by R. Bornstein. Harper & Row.

This is the story of a little girl who must live with foster parents while her mother recovers from a mental illness.

Roy, Ron. (1980). *Breakfast with My Father.* Illus. by T. Howell. Houghton Mifflin.

David is disappointed when his father, who is separated from his mother, does not take him to their usual Saturday breakfast.

Rylant, Cynthia. (1984). *This Year's Garden.* Illus. by M. Salagyi. Bradbury.

A family's responsibilities for caring for a garden change with the seasons.

Smith, Miriam. (1989). *Annie and Moon.* Illus. by L. Moyes. Gareth Stevens.

Moon, the cat, must adjust to living in new places, just as do Annie and her mother.

World War II

Ahlberg, J. and Ahlberg, A. (1981). *Peek-A-Boo!* Puffin.

This book offers a delightful account of a day in the life of a British toddler during World War II.

Bishop, Claire H. (1952). *Twenty and Ten.* Viking.

This is a story of how twenty Gentile children hide and protect ten Jewish children from the Nazis in occupied France.

Coerr, Eleanor. (1977). *Sadako and the Thousand Paper Crunch.* Dell.

Sadako is diagnosed with leukemia ten years after the Allies dropped the atom bomb on her home in Hiroshima.

Innocenti, Roberto. (1985). *Rose Blanche.* Creative Education.

This is the story of Rose Blanche, who lives in a small German town where the war doesn't seem to cause many changes in her life—until she discovers a concentration camp outside of town.

Leitner, Isabella. (1992). *The Big Lie.* Scholastic.

Isabella and her family are taken to Auschwitz, but not all of them survive the ordeal.

Spiegelman, Art. (1986). *Maus 1: A Survivor's Tale.* Scholastic.

This is a comic book with Polish mice and Nazi cats, in which an old Jewish mouse tells his son the story of his life during the war.

Tsuchya, Yukio. (1988). *Faithful Elephants: A True Story of Animals, People, and War,* translated by Tomoko Dykes. Trumpet.

This is the story of how the keepers at the Tokyo Zoo must kill the wild animals because the army fears that bombs may hit the zoo and permit the animals to escape.

Literature Reflecting Mediterranean or Middle Eastern Backgrounds

Heide, F. P., & Gilliland, J. H. (1990). *The Day of Ahmed's Secret.* Lothrop, Lee & Shepard.

This first-person story tells of one day in the life of a young boy, Ahmed, who lives in a Middle Eastern city.

Oberman, S. (1994). *The Always Prayer Shawl.* Illus. by T. Lewin. Caroline House/Boyds Mills.

This is the story of how a prayer shawl passes down through the generations.

Portnoy, M. A. (1994). *Matzah Ball: A Passover Story.* Illus. by K. J. Kahn. Kar-Ben.

At a baseball game, Aaron's mother reminds him that he cannot eat certain foods because it is Passover. Aaron is unhappy but an elderly man sitting beside him gives a special piece of matzah.

Segal, Sheila F. (1994). *Joshua's Dream: A Journey to the Land of Israel.* Illus. by J. Iskowitz. Roberts Rhinehart.

This is a fictionalized account of how Joshua and his family go to Israel and plant a tree in the desert.

Literature about Native American Peoples

Martin, Bill, Jr., & Archambault, John. (1987). *Knots on a Counting Rope.* Illus. by T. Rand. Henry Holt.

> A Native American boy and his grandfather recall his birth, his first horse, and an amazing race.

Rogers, Jean. (1988). *Runaway Mittens.* Illus. by Rio Munoz. Greenwillow.

> A young Eskimo boy continually loses his mittens until newborn puppies find a use for them.

Von Ahnen, K. (1994). *Charlie Young Bear.* Illus. by P. Livers Lambert. Council for Indian Education Series/ Roberts Rinehart.

> In this fictional account, Charlie, a young Mesquakie boy, dreams of buying a bicycle with money that his people will get for past treaty violations.

Whitehorse, B. (1994). *Sunpainters: Eclipse of the Navajo Sun.* Northland.

> A contemporary Native American listens to his grandfather's story about the little people who re-paint the world during an eclipse of the sun.

Literature Reflecting Hispanic Perspectives

Thomas, J. R. (1994). *Lights on the River.* Illus. by M. Dooling. Hyperion.

> Teresa and her family remember how they cele-brated Christmas in their village in Mexico before they left to become migrant workers.

Williams, V. B. (1984). *A Chair for My Mother.* Greenwillow.

> This is the story of a family saving money to buy a new chair after a fire in their apartment.

B. INTERMEDIATE GRADES (3–6)

1. Prehistory through A.D. 1

Living in the Times Before Christ

Fahs, S., & Spoerl, D. (1988). *Earth Sky Life Death.* Starr King Press.

> This collection includes some creation stories from various cultures, including Adam and Eve, the creation of humans by Prometheus, and Odin's ancestors.

Literature Reflecting African or Egyptian Perspectives

Anderson, D. A. (1993). *The Origin of Life on Earth: An African Creation Myth.* Sights Productions.

> This myth, which presents an African version of how life originated, emphasizes the sacredness of life, and the need for determination and generosity.

Giblin, J. C. (1990). *The Riddle of the Rosetta Stone: Key to Ancient Egypt.* Crowell.

> This is the story of how the Rosetta Stone's mes-sage was deciphered, and how it has influenced our knowledge of the Egyptian civilization.

Greger, C. S. (1996). *Cry of the Benu Bird: An Egyptian Creation Story.* Illus. by adapter/author. Houghton Mifflin.

> This story explains how the Benu bird arises from an ocean surrounded and starts time on earth while another being, Atum, creates life and order.

Nevin, T. (1996). *Zamani: African Tales from Long Ago.* Jacaranda.

> These folktales from various African countries in-volve humans talking with animals.

Stanley, D., & Vennema, P. (1994). *Cleopatra.* Illus. by D. Stanley. Morrow.

> This account portrays Cleopatra as a brilliant and daring ruler.

Literature Reflecting Asian Perspectives

Hong, L. T. (1995). *The Empress and the Silkworm.* Il-lus. by the author. Albert Whitman.

> Set in China nearly 5,000 years ago, Si Ling-chi, the Empress, unwinds the thread of a cocoon that falls from a mulberry tree. She then creates the first silk material that becomes a robe for the Emperor.

Tata, M. (1995). *The Geese and the Tortoise and Other Stories.* Illus. by H. Benton. Tata.

> The three stories in this volume were originally written in Sanskrit. "The Crows and the Snake" deals with peace, "The Four Friends" with friend-ship, and "The Geese and the Tortoise" with vanity.

Zhang, S. N. (1994). *Five Heavenly Emperors.* Tundra Books.

> Chinese myths of creation are depicted.

4

Literature Reflecting European Perspectives

Bilenko, A. (1974). *Ukranian Folk Tales.* Illus. by R. Adamovich. Dnipro Publishing of Kiev.

> This collection of twenty tales shows how good deeds are rewarded and wicked deeds are punished.

Chandler, R. (1980). *Russian Folktales.* Illus. by I. I. Bilibin. Random House.

> This is a collection of folktales from Eastern Europe.

Osborne, M. P. (1996). *Favorite Norse Myths.* Illus. by T. Howell. Scholastic.

> This collection includes myths such as "How Thor Got His Hammer" and "The Golden Apples."

Smimova, G. (1993). *Fairy-Tales of Siberian Folks.* Trans. from Russian by O. Myazina and G. Shchitnikova. Vital.

> The sixty animal fables in this collection represent fifteen ethnic groups in Siberia.

Literature Reflecting Hispanic Perspectives

Baquedano, E. (1993). *Aztec, Inca & Maya.* Knopf.

> This account contrasts three major civilizations.

Flor, A. A. (1989). *Feathers Like a Rainbow: An Amazon Indian Tale.* Harper.

> This tale, set in the Amazon rain forest, explains how the birds got their colors.

Gaudiano, A. (1972). *Azteca: The Story of a Jaguar Warrior.* Roberts Rinehart/Denver Museum of Natural History.

> This story about an Aztec warrior shows how his beliefs in the power of the jaguar influenced his life.

Literature Reflecting Greek, Mediterrean, or Middle Eastern Perspectives

Climo, S. (1995). *Atalanta's Race: A Greek Myth.* Illus. by A. Koshkin. Clarion.

> After Atalanta races her lover, Melanion, they face Aphrodite's revenge.

Coolidge, O. (1949). *Greek Myths.* Illus. by E. Sandoz. Houghton Mifflin.

> An excellent collection of Greek myths.

Eisler, C. (1992). *David's Songs; His Psalms and Their Story.* Illus. by J. Pinkney. Dial.

> A young shepherd, David, who eventually became King of Israel, wrote forty-two Psalms that have endured for over 2,000 years.

Hutton, W. (1991). *The Trojan Horse.* McElderry.

> This is the classic Greek tale about how Greek soldiers hidden inside a huge horse were able to capture the city of Troy.

Lasky, K. (1994). *The Librarian Who Measured the Earth.* Illus. by K. Hawkes. Little, Brown.

> This is the biography of Eratosthenes of Cyrene, a librarian and geographer who estimated the circumference of the earth.

Literature Reflecting Native American Perspectives

Ehlers, S. (1979). *The Bossy Hawaiian Moon.* Illus. by W. H. Kiyabu. Edward Enterprises of Honolulu.

> This is a tale of how the stars and clouds show the bossy moon that they too are supposed to live in the sky.

Hodges, M. (1972). *The Firebringer: A Paiute Indian Legend.* Little, Brown.

> This tale tells how the Native People first obtained fire.

Philip, N. (1995). *Songs Are Thoughts: Poems of the Inuit.* Illus. by M. Foa. Orchard.

> The free-verse selections in this book reflect the happiness and life of the Eskimo people.

2. Early history A.D. 1 through A.D. 1700

Perspective: Early Life in the American Colonies

Aliki. (1984). *The Story of William Penn.* Prentice-Hall.

> This is a biography of William Penn, the Quaker who established the colony of Pennsylvania as a refuge for religious nonconformists.

Fritz, I. (1980). *Who's That Stepping on Plymouth Rock?* Putnam's.

> This book portrays the history of early settlers landing on Plymouth Rock.

4

Kagan, M. (1989). *Vision in the Sky: New Haven's Early Years 1638–1783*. Linnet Press.

> This fictional account focuses on the strict Puritan values imposed on the early Colonists, and on their relations with the Native Americans.

Lobel, A. (1971). *On the Day Peter Stuyvesant Sailed into Town*. Illus. by author. Harper & Row.

> When Peter Stuyvesant lands in New Amsterdam (New York), the town is a mess. Stuyvesant leads a massive clean-up effort.

Stone, M. (1989). *Rebellion's Song*. Steck-Vaughn.

> This collection of stories focuses on the lives of six people living in Colonial times.

Van Leeuwen, I. (1996). *Across the Wide Dark Sea: The Mayflower Journey*. Illus. by T. B. Allen. Dial.

> This story is a fictionalized account of a young boy's journey on the Mayflower.

Literature Reflecting European Perspectives

Asimov, I. (1991). *Ferdinand Magellan: Opening the Door to World Exploration*. Illus. by J. R. Karpinski. Gareth Stevens.

> This biography details Magellan's childhood and life as the first explorer to sail around the world.

Asimov, I., & Kaplan, E. (1991). *Henry Hudson: Arctic Explorer and North American Adventurer*. Gareth Stevens.

> This book chronicles the problems that Henry Hudson encountered as he searched for the fabled Northwest passage.

Davis, M. G. (1979). *The Truce of the Wolf: A Legend of St. Francis of Assisi*. In *Anthology of Children's Literature* by Edna Johnson et al. Houghton Mifflin.

> This is the story of how Francis of Assisi, Italy, negotiates peace between a wolf and fearful villagers.

Fisher, L. E. (1992). *Galileo*. Macmillan.

> This is a biography of Galileo, whose astronomical observations were attacked by the Catholic Church and others. Despite the attacks, many of his observations about gravity, magnetism, and motion became the basis for modern scientific thought.

_____. (1993). *Gutenberg*. Illus. by the author. Macmillan.

> This biography focuses on the man whose invention (the printing press) changed the course of history.

Hunt, Jonathan. (1996). *Leif's Saga: A Viking Tale*. Simon & Schuster.

> Sigrid is a young Viking girl whose father tells her the story of Leif Ericson.

Materll, H. M. (1995). *Foods & Feasts with the Vikings*. Silver Burdett.

> This book explores the foods that the Vikings ate and what they drank.

Literature Reflecting Hispanic Perspectives

de Trevino, E. B. (1963). *Nacar, The White Deer*. Farrar, Straus & Giroux.

> A mute, Mexican shepherd boy protects a white deer and presents it to the King of Spain.

Foreman, M., & R. Seaver. (1992). *The Boy Who Sailed with Columbus*. Arcade.

> This is the fictional account of Leif, an orphan, who is left behind as punishment after he runs the *Santa Maria* aground.

Rohmer, H., Chow, O. & M. Vidauke. (1987). *The Invisible Hunters*. Children's Book Press.

> This is a fictionalized account of how the first European traders affected the life of the Miskiot Indians in seventeenth-century Nicaragua.

Schlein, M. (1991). *I Sailed with Columbus*. Illus. by T. Newsom. HarperCollins.

> Julio, a ship's boy, befriends a native boy who helps to calm the superstitious crew. Useful information on navigation and measuring distance.

Literature Reflecting Native American Perspectives

Bierhorst, J. (1987). *Doctor Coyote: Native American Aesop's Fables*. Illus. by W. Watson. Macmillan.

> This collection of brief fables has traveled from Aesop to Native Americans.

Nashone. (1988). *Grandmother Stories of the Northwest*. Sierra Oaks Press.

   Some of the stories in this collection show the Native Americans heritage in the west.

3. 1700 through 1900

Famous Americans

Adler, D. A. (1987). *Thomas Jefferson: Father of Our Democracy*. Holiday.

   This is a biography of Jefferson, his life and times.

Monjo, F. N. (1974). *Grand Papa and Ellen Aroon*. Dell.

   This fictional account is written from the perspective of Thomas Jefferson's nine-year-old granddaughter.

Vance, M. (1947). *Martha, Daughter of Virginia: The Story of Martha Washington*. Illus. by N. Walker. Dutton.

   This life story chronicles Martha's life from childhood to her widowhood.

Wade, M. D. (1995). *Benedict Arnold*. Watts.

   This biography chronicles the life of one of America's most famous traitors.

Literature Reflecting African or African-American Perspectives

Everett, G. (1992). *John Brown: One Man Against Slavery*. Illus. by J. Lawrence. Rizzoli.

   This biography of John Brown's raid on the arsenal at Harper's Ferry is written from the perspective of his teenage daughter.

Ferris, J. (1988). *Go Free or Die: A Story about Harriet Tubman*. Carolrhoda.

   This biography is a moving chronicle of the life of Harriet Tubman, an escaped slave who returned to the South to spy for the Union Army and lead people out of slavery.

Johnson, D. (1993). *Now Let Me Fly: The Story of a Slave Family*. Macmillan.

   This is a fictional story of Minna and her family's harsh life on a plantation.

Lester, J. (1987). *The Tale of Uncle Remus: The Adventure of Brer Rabbit*. Dial.

This collection has over forty tales that are retold in black English.

Lyons, M. E. (1994). *Master of Mahogany: Tom Day, Free Black Cabinetmaker*. Scribner's.

   This is the biography of Tom Day, who eventually becomes one of the largest furniture producers in North Carolina.

Pelz, R. (1990). *Black Heroes of the Wild West*. Open Yesterday and Today Hand Publishing.

   This is a collection of brief biographies about African-Americans and their journeys to the frontier.

Porter, C. (1992). *Meet Addy*. Pleasant Co.

   Addy Walker is an African-American girl who grows up during the Civil War.

Winter, J. (1989). *Follow the Drinking Gourd*. Knopf.

   This is a fictional account of Peg Leg Joe, a one-legged sailor who teaches slaves about the Underground Railroad. Includes the song and music he uses to do this.

Living in America (1700 to 1900)
Life on the Frontier

Lawlor, Laurie. (1986). *Addie Across the Prairie*. Illus. by G. Owens. Albert Whitman.

   Describes the adjustments that a young girl, Addie, must make when her family moves from Iowa to the Dakota territory.

MacLachlan, Patricia. (1985). *Sarah, Plain and Tall*. Harper & Row.

   This is the classic tale of a prairie farmer who orders a wife from New England by mail order.

Wilder, Laura Ingalls. (1953). *On the Banks of Plum Creek*. Illus. by G. Williams. Harper & Row.

   This story describes the life of a pioneer family along Plum Creek in Minnesota.

The Civil War Era

Beatty, Patricia. (1987). *Turn Homeward, Hannafee*. William Morrow.

   This book describes how the Union Army forced two children from Georgia to the north, and of their escape and return home.

4

_____. (1988). *Walking the Road to Freedom*. Illus. by P. Hanson. Carolrhoda.

> The story of a woman who speaks out against slavery and advocates women's rights.

Lester, Julius. (1968). *To Be a Slave*. Illus. by T. Feelings. Dial.

> This collection is based on interviews with former slaves.

MacLachlan, P. (1994) *Skylark*. HarperCollins.

> This is a sequel to MacLachlan's *Sarah, Plain and Tall* (1985, Harper & Row).

Nixon, Joan Lowery. (1987). *A Family Apart*. Bantam.

> This is the touching story of six children who are adopted by farm families in the Midwest because their mother cannot support them.

Reit, Seymour. (1988). *Behind Rebel Lines*. Harcourt Brace Jovanovich.

> This is a story of the exploits of Emma Edmonds, who spied for the Union Army.

Turner, Ann. (1987). *Nettie's Trip South*. Illus. by R. Himler. Macmillan.

> Nettie is a ten-year-old girl who travels to Richmond before the Civil War and is shocked by the aspects of slavery she has seen.

Literature Reflecting European Perspectives

Levinson, R. (1985). *Watch the Stars Come Out*. Dutton.

> This fictional story about crossing the Atlantic in the 1890s is told from a child's point of view.

Turner, B. (1991). *The Haunted Igloo*. Houghton Mifflin.

> This is the fictional story of Jean-Paul, a French Canadian who walks with a limp because of a birth defect. When the native Inuit boys tease him and exclude him from their activities, Jean-Paul learns to deal with his limitations.

Yoder, J. W. (1996). *Rosanna of the Amish*. Herald Press.

> This fictionalized story follows the life of an Irish orphan who was raised by the Amish in central Pennsylvania in the 1800s.

Literature Reflecting Hispanic Perspectives

Meyer, K. A. (1987). *Father Serra: Traveler on the Golden Chain*. Our Sunday Visitor Publishers.

> This is a biography of Father Serra, who spent almost thirty years helping to found the missions in California.

Literature Reflecting Mediterrean or Middle Eastern Perspectives

Shepard, A. (1995). *The Enchanted Storks*. Illus. by A. Dianov. Clarion.

> This tale set in ancient Baghdad tells about a ruler and his assistant, who are tricked by a magician.

Literature Reflecting Native American Perspectives

Young, R., & J. Dockery, editors. (1994). *Race with Buffalo: And Other Native American Stories for Young Readers*. Illus. by W. E. Hall. August House.

> This is a collection of over thirty tales, arranged by subjects, that go back to ancient times.

4. 1900 to the present

Noted Americans

Cedeno, M. E. (1993). *Cesar Chavez: Labor Leader*. Millbrook.

> This is the biography of Chavez's struggle to improve working conditions for the farm workers in California.

Gutman, B. (1973). *Hank Aaron*. Grosset.

> This is the biography of a baseball superstar.

Literature Reflecting African or African-American Perspectives

Rosen, M. I. (1995). *A School for Pompey Walker*. Illus. by A. B. L. Robinson. Harcourt.

> This is the fictionalized story of a free slave who sold himself into slavery to raise money for a school.

Literature Reflecting Asian Perspectives

Graff, N. (1993). *Where the River Runs: A Portrait of a Refugee Family.* Illus. by R. Howard. Little, Brown.

> This fictionalized story tells of the struggles of the Prek family as they escape the civil war in Cambodia and journey to the United States.

Life in Twentieth-Century America

Foster, S. (1987). *Where Time Stands Still.* Putnam.

> This book shows the life of Amish children today.

Lehrman, Robert. (1992). *The Store That Mama Built.* Macmillan.

> This is an account of how a Jewish immigrant woman operates a store in a small town in Pennsylvania at the turn of the nineteenth century.

Taylor, Mildred. (1990). *The Road to Memphis.* Dial.

> This story is part of the continuing saga of the Logans, a close-knit African-American family that must deal with white hatred and bigotry in the South. In this account, Stacy Logan is old enough to join the army, and the war is never far from anyone's mind.

West, T. (1993). *Fire in the Valley.* Silver Moon Press.

> Early in the twentieth century, eleven-year-old Sarah Jefferson and her family protest Los Angeles's desire to divert water from their valley.

Wyman, Andrea. (1991). *Red Sky at Morning.* Holiday.

> This is a fictional account of the struggles that a twelve-year-old girl, Callie Common, and her grandfather face trying to run a farm in Indiana by themselves.

World War II

Degens, T. (1974). *Transport 7-41-R.* Viking.

> This story describes a thirteen-year-old girl's journey from the Russian sector of defeated Germany to Cologne on a train carrying returning refugees in 1946.

Garrigue, Sheila. (1985). *The Eternal Spring of Mr. Ito.* Bradbury.

> This is the account of a young English girl who is sent to stay with relatives in Canada and learns about racism and hysteria toward Japanese citizens.

Levitin, Sonia. (1970). *Journey to America.* Atheneum.

> Lisa and her family leave Berlin to escape the Nazis in 1938. After many hardships they are reunited in America.

Lowry, Lois. (1989). *Number the Stars.* Dell.

> A ten-year-old girl and her family use courage and cunning to help their Jewish friends escape the Nazis in German-occupied Denmark.

Maruki, Toshi. (1980). *Hiroshima No Pika.* Lothrop.

> This work chronicles the ordeal of Young Mii, who is eating breakfast at home in Hiroshima when the atom bomb is dropped.

Yolen, Jane. (1988). *The Devil's Arithmetic.* Viking Kestrel.

> During one Passover celebration, Hannah opens the door and finds herself transported to a Polish village during the war. After she is placed in a concentration camp, she understands why no one should ever forget the Holocaust.

Literature Reflecting Mediterranean or Middle Eastern Perspectives

Heide, F. P., & Gilliland, I. H. (1992). *Sami and the Time of the Troubles.* Illus. by T. Lewin. Clarion.

> This fictionalized account is set in Beirut, Lebanon, and describes what it is like to live amid sporadic warfare.

Literature Reflecting Native American Perspectives

Chandonnet, A. (1993). *Chief Stephen's Parka.* Roberts Rinehart.

> Chief Stephen's wife is preparing to sew a parka for her husband, which will enable him to be a successful hunter and leader.

Cossi, O. (1994). *Fire Mate.* Roberts Rhinehart.

> This is an account of a Native American girl's search for her "Fire Mate," a tradition that is a part of her people's folklore.

4

George, J. C. (1995). *Everglades.* Illus. by W. Minor. HarperCollins.

> As they tour the Everglades in a dugout canoe, a Native American storyteller tells children about how people have affected the original inhabitants.

Gilliland, H. (1994). *Flint's Rock.* Roberts Rinehart.

> A young Cheyenne is devastated when he learns that he must leave his dog, his village, and his grandfather to live with his sister in the city.

C. MIDDLE SCHOOL GRADES (6–8)

1. Prehistory through A.D. 1

Literature Reflecting African or African-American Perspectives

Aardema, V., reteller. (1994). *Misoso: Once Upon a Time Tales from Africa.* Illus. by R. Ruffins. Knopf.

> This is a varied collection of folktales.

Literature about Early People of North America and Europe

Bruchac, J. (1995). *Gluskabe and the Four Wishes.* Illus. by C. Nyburg Shrader. Cobblehill.

> This Abenaki folktale is about four men who are given wishes, but with "strings" attached.

Dyer, T. A. (1981). *A Way of His Own.* Houghton Mifflin.

> A band of hunters and gatherers abandons Shutok because they believed his crippled back held an evil spirit that gave them bad luck.

Lopez, B. (1990). *Crow and Weasel.* North Point Press.

> A fictionalized account of the first meeting of humans.

Literature Reflecting European or Mediterranean Perspectives

Craig, R. (1995). *Malu's Wolf.* Orchard.

> This account focuses on the life, beliefs, and taboos of Malu, whose Cro-Magnon tribe lives in southern Europe.

Dillon, E. (1974). *Rome Under the Emperors.* Thomas Nelson.

> This is a fictional tale of four boys who live during the days of the Roman Empire.

Getz, D. (1994). *Frozen Man.* Illus. by P. McCarty. Holt.

> This is an illustrated account of the frozen body of a man who died 5,000 years ago.

Martell, H. M. (1992). *Over 6,000 Years Ago: In the Stone Age.* Macmillan.

> This account portrays Stone Age culture based on archaeological evidence found mainly in Europe.

Moessinger, P. (1994). *Socrates.* Creative Education.

> This account takes the form of a (fictional) letter from Socrates to his sons explaining his philosophy.

Walsh, J. P. (1922). *Crossing to Salamis.* Heinemann.

> This fictional story tells of a family's flight from Athens to Salamis to escape an invading army.

2. Early history A.D. 1 through 1700

Literature Reflecting African or African-American Perspectives

Hamilton, V. (1969). *The Time-Ago Tales of Jadhu.* Illus. by N. Hogrogian. Macmillan.

> This is a collection of folk literature.

Literature Reflecting Asian Perspectives

Haugaard, E. C. (1984) *The Samurai's Tale.* Houghton Mifflin.

> This fictional tale describes the life of the samurai, the professional soldiers of Japan.

Miller, L. (1987). *The Black Hat Dances: Two Buddhist Boys in the Himalayas.* Putnam's.

> This is a fictionalized account of a novice in a monastery in Sikkim whose lifestyle differs markedly from a typical person in that culture.

Namioka, L. (1992). *The Coming of the Bear.* HarperCollins.

> This is a fictionalized account from the 1600s about Japanese colonists, who were trying to settle the island of Ezo (Hokaido), and their problems with the original, Aimu inhabitants.

San Souci, R. D. (1992). *The Samurai's Daughter*. Illus. by S. T. Johnson. Dial.

> This fictional account of a Samurai's daughter's search for her banished father provides excellent insights into the life of the Samurai in Japan.

Literature Reflecting European or Mediterranean Perspectives

Fritz, J. (1980). *Where Do You Think You Are Going, Christopher Columbus?* Illus. by M. Tomes. Putnam's.

> This is a fictionalized biography of the famous explorer.

_____. (1994). *Around the World in a Hundred Years: From Henry the Navigator to Magellan*. Illus. by A. B. Venti. Putnam's.

> This is a fictionalized account of the explorer's voyages.

Hernandez, X., & Comes, P. (1990). *Barmi: A Mediterranean City Through the Ages*. Illus. by J. Ballonga. Trans. by K. Leverich. Houghton Mifflin.

> This account describes the growth of Barmi, a fourth-century, fictional city in southern Europe.

Haugaard, E. C. (1963). *Hakon of Rogen's Saga*. Illus. by L. and D. Dillion. Houghton Mifflin.

> This is the fictional story of Hakon who must flee from home when his island is invaded.

Hunter, M. (1981). *You Never Knew Her as I Did!* Harper.

> This is the fictionalized biography of Mary, Queen of Scots that is written by a page in her court.

O'Dell, S. (1981). *The Feathered Serpent*. Houghton Mifflin.

> This is the fictional story of the conflict that a young priest, who is working with the Mayan people, feels between his beliefs and the Mayan's beliefs in worshiping idols and offering sacrifices.

Early Life in the American Colonies

Bowen, G. (1994). *Stranded at Plimoth Plantation, 1626*. HarperCollins.

> This story of daily life in the Plimoth colony is based on the fictional diary of Christopher Sears, a young settler.

Levitin, S. (1973). *Roanoke: A Novel of the Lost Colony*. Atheneum.

> This fictionalized account describes relationships between the colonists and the Native People.

Petry, A. (1964). *Tituba of Salem Village*. Crowell.

> This is a fictional story about Tituba who, as an intelligent black slave, comes under suspicion by witch-hunters in Salem, Massachusetts.

Literature Reflecting Hispanic Perspectives

Rohmer, H., Chow, O., & Vidauke, M. (1987). *The Invisible Hunters*. Children's Book Press.

> This fictionalized account describes the impact that the first European traders had on the Miskiot Indians in seventeenth-century Nicaragua.

Marvin, I. R. (1993). *Shipwrecked on Padre Island*. Illus. by L. Miller. Hendrick-Long.

> In this fictional story, a young girl loses her bracelet on Padre Island in 1554; 400 years later it is found by another girl.

Literature Reflecting Native American Perspectives

Highwater, J. (1972). *Anpao: An American Indian Odyssey*. Lippincott.

> This is a Blackfoot legend of Scarface.

3. 1700 through 1900

Living in the Eighteenth and Nineteenth Centuries

Banim, L. (1994). A *Spy in the King's Colony*. Illus. by T. Yuditskaya. Silver Moon Press.

> This story, set in Boston in 1775, involves eleven-year-old Emily Parker, who suspects someone of being a spy for the Loyalists. She gets involved in delivering a secret-coded note to General Washington.

Fix, P. (1994). *Not So Very Long Ago: Life in a Small Country Village*. Dutton.

> This is a fictionalized account of daily life in a European village.

Haley, A. (1988). *A Different Kind of Christmas*. Doubleday.

> This fictional story relates to the Christmas season on the Underground Railroad.

Riskind, M. (1981). *Apple Is My Sign.* Houghton Mifflin.

> This is the fictionalized story of Harry Berger, nick-named "Apple" because his family tends orchards, who attends a school for the deaf.

West, T. (1994). *Mr. Peale's Bones.* Silver Moon Press.

> This is the fictionalized account of a young boy and his father who help to excavate mammoth bones in upstate New York.

Literature Reflecting Asian Perspectives

Fleischman, P. (1983). *Path of the Pale Horse.* Harper & Row.

> This is the fictional story of Lep, an apprentice doctor, whose faith in medicine is shaken during a Yellow Fever epidemic.

Yep, L. (1993). *Dragon's Gate.* HarperCollins.

> This is a fictionalized account of experiences of the Chinese immigrants who built the transcontinental railroad.

———. (1985). *Mountain's Light.* Harper.

> This is a fictionalized account of Chinese immigrants during the days of the California Gold Rush.

Literature Reflecting Hispanic Perspectives

Finley, M. P. (1993). *Soaring Eagle.* Simon & Schuster.

> This is an account of how rumors of war between Mexico and the United States affect a young boy and his father.

Krumgold, J. (1953). *And Now Miguel.* Illus. by J. Chariot. Crowell.

> This is a fictional story about how Miguel looks forward to the time when he is old enough to join the men who work on a ranch.

O' Dell, S. (1981). *Carlota.* Houghton Mifflin.

> This is a fictional tale of how Carlota and her father ambush settlers who are trying to annex California to the United States.

Literature Reflecting Native American Perspectives

Hudson, J. (1990). *Dawn Rider.* Putnam's.

> This is the fictional story of a teenage Blackfoot girl, Kit Fox, who, although forbidden to ride horses, disobeys and helps her people when their camp is attacked.

———. (1989). *Sweetgrass.* Philomel.

> This is a fictionalized account of how a fifteen-year-old Blackfoot girl dealt with the effects of smallpox in her family.

Wallin, L. (1984). *In the Shadow of the Wind.* Macmillan.

> This is the fictionalized story of a white boy and Native American girl who fall in love at a time when the Creek People were trying to save their lands from settlers.

4. 1900 to the present

Living in the Twentieth Century

Armstrong, W. (1969). *Sounder.* Illus. by J. Barkley. Harper.

> This is a fictional account of the hardships faced by a black sharecropper and his family.

Blue, R. (1979). *Cold Rain on the Water.* McGraw.

> This fictionalized story tells of a Jewish family's journey from Russia to the United States.

Kerr, R. (1994). *The Texas Orphans: A Story of the Orphan Train Children.* Eakin Press.

> This is a fictionalized account of orphans from New York City who are put on a train to Sequin, Texas, where they start new lives with new families.

World War II

Sook, N. C. (1991). *The Year of Impossible Goodbyes.* Houghton Mifflin.

> This fictionalized account describes how a family dealt with the Japanese occupation during World War II.

Literature Reflecting African or African-American Perspectives

Walter, M. P. (1982). *The Girl on the Outside.* Lothrop, Lee & Shepard.

4

This is a fictionalized story of two students who set out to desegregate Central High School in Little Rock, Arkansas.

Literature Reflecting Asian Perspectives

Huong, D. T. (1988). *Paradise of the Blind*. Morrow.

This fictionalized account describes life in Vietnam under Communist rule in the 1970s through the eyes of a teenage girl.

Yep, L. (1991). *The Star Fisher*. Morrow.

This is a fictional account of a Chinese-American teenager living in West Virginia, who quarrels with her parents about their adherence to Chinese traditions.

Literature Reflecting European or Mediterranean Perspectives

Skurynski, G. (1992). *Good-Bye, Billy Radish*. Bradbury Press.

This is the fictional story of two best friends, Hank Kerner and Billy Radish (really Bazyli Radichevych), who have different points of view about working in the steel mills.

4.3 Annotated Bibliography of Nonfiction Books for Common Social Studies Topics

A. PRIMARY GRADES (K–3)

Noted Americans, Legendary

Kellogg, Steven. (1984). *Paul Bunyan*. Morrow.
Presents incidents in the life of this legendary hero.

_____. (1986). *Pecos Bill*. Morrow.
Presents incidents in the life of this legendary Texas hero.

_____. (1988). *Johnny Appleseed*. Morrow.
Presents the real life and legends of Jonathan Chapman, alias Johnny Appleseed, who helped build the orchards of the Midwest.

Le Sueur, Meridel. (1947). *Little Brother of the Wilderness*. Knopf.

This is another of several biographies of Jonathan Chapman (Johnny Appleseed).

Noted Americans, Real

Adler, David A. (1989). *A Picture Book of Abraham Lincoln*. Illus. by John and Alexandra Wallner. Holiday.

Follows Lincoln from log cabin to the White House.

_____. (1989). *A Picture Book of George Washington*. Illus. by John and Alexandra Wallner. Holiday.

Follows Washington's rise to become the "Father of Our Country."

_____. (1989). *A Picture Book of Martin Luther King Jr.* Illus. by Robert Casilla. Holiday.

Follows King's contributions to civil rights.

Bertol, R. (1970). *Charles Drew*. Crowell.

This is a biography of the African-American doctor who became the first director of the Red Cross Blood Bank.

Blue, R., & Naden, C. (1991). *Colin Powell: Straight to the Top*. Millbrook.

This biography chronicles the life of Colin Powell.

Cavan, S. (1992). *W. E. B. Du Bois and Racial Relations*. Millbrook.

This account is about W. E. B. Du Bois, one of the founders of the NAACP.

_____. (1992). *Thurgood Marshall and Equal Rights*. Millbrook.

This biography is the life story of the first black justice to serve on the U.S. Supreme Court.

Freedman, Russell. (1987). *Lincoln, A Photobiography*. Clarion.

Presents the life of Abraham Lincoln in text and pictures.

Pinkney, A. D. (1993). *Alvin Ailey*. Illus. by B. Pinkney. Hyperion.

This biography is about a noted African-American dancer.

Roberts, N. (1988). *Henry Cisneros.* Children's Book Press.

> This biography chronicles the life of Henry Cisneros, a noted San Antonio mayor and former cabinet officer.

Smith, K. B. (1987). *Martin Luther King, Jr.* Messner.

> This account of King's life uses illustrations from the Smithsonian Institution and the National Portrait Gallery.

Literature Reflecting African or African-American Perspectives

Bradby, M. (1995). *More Than Anything Else.* Illus. by C. K. Soentpiet. Orchard.

> This is a fictionalized biography of Booker T. Washington, a former slave with an overwhelming desire to learn how to read and write.

Coles, R. (1995). *The Story of Ruby Bridges.* Illus. by A. Ford. Scholastic.

> This is a biography about a six-year-old who enters a whites-only school in New Orleans in 1960.

Cwiklik, R. (1992). *A. Phillip Randolph and the Labor Movement.* Millbrook.

> This account is about a civil rights crusader.

Musgrove, M. (1976). *Ashanti to Zulu.* Dial.

> This award-winning alphabet book shows customs from twenty-six African cultures.

Saint James, S. (1994). *The Gifts of Kwaanzaa.* Albert Whitman.

> A family's preparation for the African-American Harvest Festival is described through the eyes of a child.

Walker, A. (1974). *Langston Hughes, American Poet.* Illus. by D. Miller. Crowell.

> This biography chronicles the life of one of America's greatest African-American poets.

Archaeology

Dragonwagon, Crescent. (1990). *Home Place.* Macmillan.

> This story tells what it is like for an early family to live in modern times.

Pickering, R. B. (1987). *I Can Be an Archaeologist.* Children's Book Press.

> This book also suggests how children can use artifacts as clues to the past.

Pryor, B. (1992). *The House on Maple Street.* Mulberry.

> An arrowhead is lost hundreds of years ago but is found as the years go by.

Ancient Egypt

Courtalon, C. (1988). *On the Banks of the Pharaoh's Nile.* Young Discovery Library.

> This text introduces children to the culture through illustrations and a text that should be read aloud by an adult.

Maestro, B. (1991). *The Discovery of the Americas.* Lothrop.

> This text details the travels of the Stone Age people across the Bering Land bridge to North America.

Metropolitan Museum of Art. (1991). *The Giant Book of the Mummy.* New York, Metropolitan Museum.

> This huge book focuses on the discovery of the tomb of Tutankhamen, the Boy King.

Early Life in the American Colonies

Sewall, M. (1990). *People of the Breaking Day.* Atheneum.

> The book provides a detailed account of the daily life of the Wampanoag people prior to the arrival of the colonists.

Water, K. (1996). *Tapenum's Day: A Wampanoag Boy in Pilgrim Times.* Illus. by R. Kendall. Scholastic.

> A fictionalized person, Tapenum, describes the daily life of the Wampanoag people. Also includes photographs from the re-created Native American home site at the Plimouth Plantation.

Life in the Colonies

Costabel, E. D. (1988). *The Jews of New Amsterdam.* Atheneum.

> This is an account of Jews who journeyed to America during the Colonial period, and their dis-

covery that life in the colonies did not value equality for everyone.

Life in the Twentieth Century

Baer, E. (1984). *This Is the Way We Go To School.* Scholastic.

> Written in a simple rhyming pattern, this book depicts the modes of transportation that children around the world use to get to school.

Brandenberg, A. (1984). *Feelings.* Greenwillow.

> Different feelings generated by everyday situations are presented in a manner with which children can identify.

Gray, N. (1988). A *Country Far Away.* Orchard Books.

> Two young boys, one of whom lives in an American suburb and the other in a village by the ocean, share similar experiences.

Kandoian, E. (1989). *Is Anybody Up?* Putnam's.

> As Molly starts to prepare her breakfast, many people in other parts of the world are doing the same thing.

Morris, A. (1989). *Bread, Bread, Bread.* Lothrop, Lee & Shepard.

> The photographs in this book show that people all over the world eat bread or something similar to it.

Spier, P. (1980). *People.* Doubleday.

> This book describes the appearance, customs, food, traditions, and people from all areas of the world.

Life on the Frontier

Freedman, Russell. (1988). *Buffalo Hunt.* Holiday.

> This is an illustrated account of the life of Native Americans on the Great Plains, and the importance of the buffalo to their lives.

_____. (1985). *Cowboys of the Wild West.* Clarion.

> This account focuses on the day-to-day life of cowboys and the hardships they faced on a trail drive.

_____. (1987). *Indian Chiefs.* Holiday.

> This book presents the biographies of six Native American chiefs who resisted efforts to take their tribal lands.

Jakes, John. (1986). *Susanna of the Alamo.* Illus. by P. Bacon. Harcourt Brace Jovanovich.

> This account focuses on Susanna Dickinson, one of the few survivors of the Battle of the Alamo.

Literature Reflecting Asian Perspectives

Haskins, Jim. (1987). *Count Your Way Through Japan.* Illus. by Martin Skoro. Carolrhoda.

> Life in Japan is depicted using the Japanese words and symbols for numbers one through ten.

Weston, Reiko. *Cooking the Japanese Way.* Lerner.

> Describes Japanese food habits and recipes.

Literature Reflecting European Perspectives

Beirne, B. (1992). *Siobhand's Journey: A Belfast Girl Visits the United States.* Illus. First Avenue Ed.

> This photo essay is about a young Irish girl, Siobhand McNulty, who leaves the religious/political conflict of Northern Ireland to spend a summer with an American family.

Fisher, L. E. (1994). *Kinderdike.* Illus. by the author. Macmillan.

> This poem is a tribute to a Dutch town that rebuilt after a devastating flood.

Kalman, B. (1992). *We Celebrate Hanukkah.* Crabtree.

> This book explains the origins of Hanukkah.

Mitchell, B. (1993). *Down Buttermilk Lane.* Illus. by J. Sandford. Lothrop, Lee & Shepard.

> This account shows one day in the life of an Amish family.

Stanley, D. (1996). *The True Adventure of Daniel Hall.* Illus. by the author. Dial.

> This is the biography of Hall's four-year journey on a whaling ship.

4

Wildsmith, B. (1996). *Saint Francis*. Eerdmans.

This book focuses on the major events of the life of St. Francis of Assisi.

Literature About Native American Peoples

Costable, E. D. (1992). *The Early People of Florida*. Illus. by the author. Atheneum.

This book details the life of the indigenous people of Florida from prehistoric times to 1845 (statehood).

Driving Hawk, V. (1993). *The Sioux*. Illus. by R. Himler. Holiday.

This book describes the history, culture, and present-day life of the Sioux.

Gnese, A. (1995). *Anna's Athabaskan Summer*. Illus. by C. Ragins. Caroline House/Boyds Mills Press.

This is an account of the activities at a midsummer fish camp along a river in Alaska.

Hoyt-Goldsmith, D. (1992). *Arctic Hunter*. Holiday.

This account follows Reggie and his family from the Alaskan town north of the Arctic Circle, where they live in the winter, to the fishing and hunting camp where they go in the summer.

Sneve, V. D. H. (1996). *The Cherokees*. Illus. by R. Himler. Holiday.

This picture book history shows what has happened to the Oklahoma and North Carolina bands in the last 200 years since the Trail of Tears.

Literature Reflecting Hispanic Perspectives

Adler, D. A. (1992). *A Picture Book on Simon Bolivar*. Illus. by R. Casilia. Holiday.

This illustrated biography chronicles Bolivar's life and accomplishments.

Anderson, J. (1992). *Miguel Hidalgo Costilla: Father of Mexican Independence*. Milbrook.

This is the biography of Father Hidalgo, the Catholic priest who called his parishioners to rebel against the Spanish colonial government.

———. (1992). *Simon Bolivar: Latin American Liberator*. Milbrook.

This biography traces the life of Simon Bolivar, who was instrumental in overthrowing Spanish rule in Central and South America.

Jacobs, F. (1992). *The Tainos: The People Who Welcomed Columbus*. Putnam's.

This book describes the life of native people on a Bahamian island in the late fifteenth century.

Palacios, A. (1993). *Viva Mexico!: A Story of Benito Juarez and Cinco de Mayo*. Illus. by H. Berelson. Steck-Vaughn.

This biography follows the life of Benito Juarez until his presidency in 1816 and explains the Battle of Puebla, which was the basis for the annual, May 5th celebration.

Reed, L. R. (1995). *Pedro, His Perro, and the Alphabet Sombrero*. Illus. by the author. Hyperion.

In this modified alphabet book, Pedro celebrates his birthday by decorating a sombrero with objects from A (avion/airplane) to Z (zorillo/skunk). (Pronunciation guide included).

Literature Reflecting Mediterranean or Middle Eastern Perspectives

Fleetwood, J. (1992). *While the Shepherds Watched*. Illus. by P. Melnucsuk. Lothrop, Lee & Shepard.

A young boy participates in a night filled with wonder as he sees the birth of a lamb, is visited by an angel, and visits a stable in Bethlehem.

Matthews, M. (1996). *Magid Fasts for Ramadan*. Illus. by E. B. Lewis. Clarion.

Fasting is a common practice for Islamic families celebrating Ramadan, but eight-year-old Magid is considered too young.

Yolen, J. (1996). *O Jerusalem*. Illus. by J. Thompson. Scholastic.

This is the story of how Jerusalem has dealt with three religions.

B. INTERMEDIATE GRADES (3–6)

Noted Americans, Real

D'Aulaire, I., & D'Aulaire, E. P. (1952). *Buffalo Bill*. Doubleday.

This biography chronicles events in the life of Buffalo Bill.

Johnston, J. (1977). *Harriet and the Runaway Book: The Story of Harriet Beecher Stowe and Uncle Tom's Cabin.* Illus. by R. Himler. Harper.

This is a biography of Harriet Beecher Stowe, a New Englander, who writes one of the most famous books opposing slavery.

Murphy, J. (1995). *Into the Deep Forest with Henry David Thoreau.* Illus. by K. Kisler. Clarion.

This biography is based on entries in Thoreau's journal.

Stanley, D., & Vennema, P. (1993). *Charles Dickens: The Man Who Had Great Expectations.* Illus. by D. Stanley. Morrow.

This biography chronicles highlights from Dickens's life.

Rome

Cohen, D. (1992). *Ancient Rome.* Illus. by H. Bond. Bantam.

This book offers a concise overview of the history of ancient Rome. It includes the conflict with Carthage, the activities of Hannibal, gladiator contests, and the emperors, and the destruction of Pompeii.

MacDonald, F. (1993). *A Roman Fort.* Peter Bedrick.

This book uses drawings and diagrams to show how a Roman fort was constructed. It also includes living conditions and soldiers' weapons.

Literature Reflecting African or African-American Perspectives

Altman, S., & Lechner, S. (1993). *Many Voices, One Song, Followers of the North Star: Rhymes about African-American Heroes, Heroines, and Historical Times.* Children's Book Press.

This accounts presents a rhyming story about courageous African-Americans who sought a better life.

Ferris, J. (1988). *Go Free or Die.* Illus. by K. Ritz. Carolrhoda.

This is the biography of Harriet Tubman, the former slave who became a legendary figure on the Underground Railroad by helping almost 300 other slaves (including her parents) gain their freedom.

Lawrence, I. (1993). *The Great Migration: An American Story.* HarperCollins.

This pictorial account shows the migration of African-Americans from the South in 1916–1919.

Ritter, L. S. (1995). *Leagues Apart: The Men and Times of the Negro Baseball Leagues.* Illus. by R. Merkin. Morrow.

This is the story of baseball's Negro League and some of its stars.

Africa and Egypt

Giblin, J. C. (1990). *The Riddle of the Rosetta Stone: Key to Ancient Egypt.* Crowell.

This is the story of how the message of the Rosetta Stone was deciphered and how it has influenced our knowledge of the Egyptian civilization.

Harris, N. (1995). *Everyday Life in Ancient Egypt.* Illus. by K. Maddison. Watts.

This book offers an illustrated overview of the history of Egypt. Includes topics such as food, clothing, shelter, and religion.

Millard, A. (1979). *Ancient Egypt.* Illus. by A. McBridge and others. Warwick.

This book offers an overview of the ancient Egyptian civilization.

Archaeology

Hooper, M. (1996). *The Pebble in My Hand: A History of Our Earth.* Viking.

Finding a pebble on the ground leads a child to speculate on where it came from.

Hoopes, L. L. (1989) *Half a Button.* Harper & Row.

Suggests how artifacts serve as clues to the past.

Early Colonial Period

Anderson, I. (1984). *The First Thanksgiving Feast.* Illus. by G. Ancona. Clarion.

4

This book, with photographs from the Plimouth Plantation, offers a first-person account of life in 1620s.

Sewall, M. (1986). *The Pilgrims of Plimoth.* Atheneum.

This book, which describes the lives of people living in the Plymouth Colony, is based on the writings of Governor William Bradford.

China

Fisher, L. E. (1986). *The Great Wall of China.* Illus. by the author. Macmillan.

This account covers all facets of the building of the Great Wall of China.

Civil War

Johnson, Neil. (1989). *The Battle of Gettysburg.* Four Winds.

This account is based on photographs from the 125th anniversary reenactment of the Battle of Gettysburg.

Literature Reflecting Asian Perspectives

Brown, T. (1995). *Konnichiwa! I Am a Japanese American Girl.* Photographs by Kazuyoshi Arai. Holt.

This book describes a young girl's life in San Francisco.

Cha, D. (1996). *Dia's Story Cloth: The Hmong People's Journey of Freedom.* Illus. by C. Cha and N. T. Cha. Lee & Low.

This is the autobiography of a young girl and her family who flee from Laos in the 1960s, spend time in a refugee camp in Thailand, and then emigrate to the United States.

McMahon, P. (1993). *Chi-Hoon: A Korean Girl.* Illus. by M. O'Brien. Caroline House/Boyds Mills Press.

This is an account of an eight-year-old's life in modern Seoul.

Schmidt, J., & Wood, T. (1995). *Two Lands, One Heart: An American Boy's Journey to His Mother's Vietnam.* Illus. by T. Wood. Walker.

This is a touching story of how a refugee from Vietnam takes her son back for a visit to her homeland.

Literature Reflecting European Perspectives

Carrick, C. (1993). *Whaling Days.* Illus. by D. Frampton. Clarion.

This book traces whaling from twelfth-century Basque whalers through modern whaling methods.

Lauber, P. (1970). *Who Discovered America? Settlers and Explorers of the New World Before the Times of Columbus.* Random House.

This text is an overview of exploration in pre-Columbian times.

Moscinski, S. (1993). *Tracing Our Irish Roots.* John Muir.

This book describes the potato famine and other conditions in Ireland, as well as the prejudice the Irish encountered when they arrived in the United States.

Greece

Asimov, I., & Reddy, F. (1995). *Astronomy in Ancient Times.* Gareth Stevens.

This book focuses on astronomy at the time of the ancient Greeks.

Pearson, A. (1995). *Everyday Life in Ancient Greece.* Illus. by E. Dovey. Watts.

This book offers an illustrated overview of life in ancient Greece, including food, clothing, housing, and religion.

Literature Reflecting Hispanic Perspectives

Anderson J. (1989). *Spanish Pioneers of the Southwest.* Illus. by G. Ancona. Dutton.

This book portrays the life of a Spanish pioneer family in eighteenth-century New Mexico.

Lasky, K. (1994). *Days of the Dead.* Photographs by C. G. Knight. Hyperion.

This book shows how a rural family prepares for traditional Mexican celebrations.

Westridge Young Writers Workshop. (1992). *Kids Explore America's Hispanic Heritage.* John Muir.

This text presents the Mexican side of the Battle of the Alamo.

Living in America, 1700 to 1900

Ammon, R. (1989). *Growing Up Amish.* Atheneum.

This account explains the Amish movement and its associated lifestyle.

Bial, R. (1994). *Shaker Home.* Houghton Mifflin.

The text focuses on life in communal Shaker communities.

Rappaport, D. (1987). *Trouble at the Mines.* Crowell.

This is a fictionalized account of the coal strike in Pennsylvania in 1899, as recounted by a coal miner's daughter.

Life on the Frontier

Anderson, Joan. (1986). *Pioneer Children of Appalachia.* Illus. by G. Ancona. Clarion.

This photoessay of Appalachian pioneer life between 1790 and 1830 was made at a living history museum in West Virginia.

Cooper, Michael. (1989). *Klondike Fever.* Clarion.

This photoessay focuses on the founding of the city of Dawson during the Alaskan gold rush.

Fisher, Leonard E. (1987). *The Alamo.* Holiday.

This book presents the history of the Alamo, site of the famous battle in which Jim Bowie, Davey Crockett, and other famous frontier figures died.

World War II

Bergman, Tamar. (1991). *Along the Tracks.* Trans. from the Hebrew by Michael Swirsky. Houghton Mifflin.

This is the true story of a young Jewish boy who flees Nazi-occupied Poland but is separated from his family and becomes one of the thousands of abandoned children wandering through Russia.

Dahl, Roald. (1986). *Going Solo.* Penguin.

This is the story of Dahl's experience as a fighter pilot in Africa, Greece, and the Middle East.

Mochizuki, Ken. (1993). *Baseball Saved Us.* Lee & Low.

This is a touching account of how Japanese-Americans imprisoned in a desert internment camp build a baseball field to relieve the monotony of their imprisonment.

Uchida, Yoshiko. (1971). *Journey to Topaz: A Story of the Japanese-American Evacuation.* Scribner's.

This is a moving account of how Japanese-American families were moved to internment camps during World War II.

Literature Reflecting Mediterranean or Middle Eastern Perspectives

Fisher, L. E. (1989). *The Wailing Wall.* Illus. by the author. Macmillan.

The author traces the history of the Wailing Wall in Jerusalem, where Jews have long gathered before their Sabbath and Feast Days.

Lee, K. (1993). *Tracing Our Italian Roots.* John Muir.

This book describes the hardships of life in Italy, and the prejudice that people who emigrated to the United States faced when they got here.

Paris, A. (1995). *Jerusalem 3000: Kids Discover the City of Gold.* Pitspopany Press.

This is the story of the city of Jerusalem from its earliest days to the present time.

Schur, M. R. (1996). *When I Left My Village.* Illus. by B. Pinkney. Dial.

This is the account of a family of Ethiopian Jews who escape persecution and a drought by walking through the desert at night.

Mexico, Aztecs, Incas, and Mayans

Baquedano, E. (1993). *Aztec, Inca and Maya.* Knopf.

This text uses a compare and contrast approach to introduce the three civilizations—Aztec, Inca, and Mayan.

Glubok, S. (1968). *The Art of Ancient Mexico.* Harper.

This book focuses on Mexico prior to the arrival of the Spaniards. Includes pre-Columbian cultures such as the Aztec, Mixtec, Toltec, and Zapotec.

Martinez, G., & Edwards, J. (1973). *The Mexican Americans.* Houghton Mifflin.

> This book focuses on pre-Columbian Mexico but extends to the mission period in California and Mexican independence.

de Trevino, E. B. (1980). *Here Is Mexico.* Farrar, Straus & Giroux.

> This book traces Mexican history from pre-Columbian times to the colonial period.

Literature Reflecting Native American Perspectives

Arnold, C. (1992). *The Ancient Cliff Dwellers of Mesa Verde.* Illus. by R. Hewett. Clarion.

> This book describes the history of the Anasazi, who disappeared from southwest Colorado after they constructed magnificent cliff dwellings.

Freedman, R. (1987). *Indian Chiefs.* Holiday.

> This is a collection of brief biographical sketches of Native American leaders.

McLerran, A. (1995). *The Ghost Dance.* Illus. by P. Morin. Clarion.

> This book describes the impact that the westward expansion had on the resources needed by Native Americans.

Roop, P., & Roop, C. (1992). *Ahyoka and the Talking Leaves.* Illus. by Y. Miyake. Lothrop, Lee & Shepard.

> This is the biography of Ahyoka, a Cherokee girl, who discovers that letters relate to sounds. Ahyoka and her father create an alphabet and written language for their people.

Warren, S. (1992). *Cities in the Sand: The Ancient Cities of the Southwest.* Chronicle.

> This book explores life in the Anasazi cliff dwellings, the irrigation canals of the Hohokarn, and the pottery of the Mogollon.

C. MIDDLE SCHOOL GRADES (6–8)

Ancient Egypt

Macdonald, F. (1993). *Ancient Egyptians.* Barron's.

> This illustrated account covers most aspects of this civilization.

Literature Reflecting Asian Perspectives

Fagan, B. M. (1987). *The Great Journey: The Peopling of Ancient America.* Thames & Hudson.

> This account focuses on the arrival of peoples in North America.

Satder, H. R. (1992). *The Earliest Americans.* Illus. by J. D. Zallinger. Clarion.

> This account tells about the humans who came to North America across the land bridge between Siberia and Alaska.

Literature Reflecting Hispanic Perspectives

Bendick, J. (1993). *Tombs of the Ancient Americas.* Watts.

> This text, with photographs, focuses on the Incas.

Jimenez, C. M. (1993). *The Mexican American Heritage.* COSMEP.

> History from prehistoric times to present day.

Literature Reflecting Native American Perspectives

Ayeer, E. J. (1993). *The Anasazi.* Walker.

> The text focuses on the Anasazi Pueblo people, and the methods that archaeologists use to learn about their lifestyles.

Monroe, J. G., & Williamson, R. A. (1993). *First Houses: Native American Homes and Sacred Structures.* Houghton Mifflin.

> This text explores a variety of Native American dwellings—longhouses, hogans, earth lodges, tipis, and kivas.

Yue, C., & Yue, D. (1988). *The Igloo.* Houghton Mifflin.

> This account portrays the Thule People, the ancestors of the Inuit.

Life in the Twentieth Century
World War II

Forman, James. (1970). *Ceremony of Innocence.* Hawthorne.

> Until they were executed by the Gestapo, Hans and Sophie Scholl published the "White Rose" leaflets that denounced Nazism.

4

4.4 Annotated Bibliography of Children's Books for Teaching About Women and Women's Roles Throughout History

A. Prehistory to A.D. 1

1. Primary Grades (1–3)

Bernhard, E., reteller. (1994). *The Girl Who Wanted to Hunt: A Siberian Tale.* Holiday.

> Anga, a young girl, wants to be a hunter like her father, but she must somehow escape a demanding stepmother.

Gerson, M. (1994). *How Night Came from the Sea: A Story from Brazil.* Illus. by C. Golembe. Little, Brown.

> An African sea goddess, Jemanja, allows people to escape the scorching sun by bringing them the gift of night.

Gerspem. (1995). *People of the Corn: A Mayan Story.* Illus. by Carla Golembe. Little, Brown.

> This is a creation myth about the role of corn in the Mayan civilization.

Jiang, W. (1992). *La Heroina Hua Mulan: The Legend of Mu Lan.* Illus. by the author and Xing Gen. Victory Press T. R. Books.

> This story, which is set in ancient China, tells how Mu Lan fights for her country disguised as a boy.

Kimmel, E. (1995). *Rimonah of the Flashing Sword: A North African Tale.* Illus. by O. Rayan. Holiday.

> Princess Rimonah joins a band of forty thieves and rides with them against her jealous stepmother, the queen.

Yep, Lawrence. (1990). *The Shell Woman and the King.* Dial.

> This is the story of a young Chinese girl who outsmarts a selfish king.

2. Intermediate Grades (3–6)

Lee, J. M. (1995). *The Song of Mu Lan.* Illus. by the author. Front Street.

> Set in China around 400 B.C., this is the story of Mu Lan, who, for ten years, takes the place of her father in battle.

3. Middle-School Grades (6–8)

Brennan, J. H. (1992). *Shiva's Challenge: An Adventure of the Ice Age.* HarperCollins.

> In this fictional account, Shiva, who lived around 14,000 B.C., finds her way home from an icebound wasteland.

McGraw, E. J. (1990). *Mara, Daughter of the Nile.* Coward.

> This is the fictional story of Mara, a slave whose mixed loyalties allow her to spy for both the king and queen.

B. Early history A.D. 1 through A.D. 1700

1. Primary Grades (K–3)

Accorsi, W. (1992). *My Name Is Pocahontas.* Illus. by the author. Holiday.

> This is a fascinating biography of Pocahontas, the daughter of the Native American chief Powhatan.

Raphael, E., & Bolognese, D. (1993). *Pocahontas: Princess of the River Tribes.* Illus. by the authors. Scholastic.

> This is a brief biography of selected events in the life of Pocahontas.

Van Woerkom, D. (1975). *Becky and the Bear.* Illus. by M. Tomes. Putnam's.

> This is a fictionalized account about Becky, a young girl who lives in Maine, whose father and brother refuse to allow her to hunt with them. When Becky encounters a bear, she feeds it molasses and rum to make it fall asleep; then she and her grandmother tie the bear to a tree.

2. Intermediate Grades (3–6)

Christian, M. B. (1990). *Goody Sherman's Pig.* Macmillan.

> This is a fictionalized account of Goody Sherman's 1636 battle with church elders and the courts over

her runaway pig. This battle is said to have caused the colony to create two legislative branches of government.

Fisher, A. (1970). *Jeanne d'Arc.* Illus. by A. Fortenberg. Crowell.

This biography depicts the life of Joan of Arc, the nineteen-year-old girl who led the French Army, and became the national heroine of France. (Read aloud to young children).

Fradin, D. B. (1990). *Anne Hutchinson.* Enslow.

This is a biography of Anne Hutchinson, who preached that people with true religion would follow God's guidance through an "Inner Light." Brought to court, Anne is found guilty of "traducing" the ministers and ordered to leave the colony. She ultimately founds a settlement at Portsmouth that offers religious freedom.

Fritz, E. I. (1991). *Anne Hutchinson.* Chelsea.

This biography also traces events in the life of Anne Hutchinson, who was banished from the colony in New England.

Garden, N. (1995). *Dove and Sword: A Novel of Joan of Arc.* Illus. by the author. Farrar, Straus & Giroux.

This is the fictionalized story of Gabrielle, a young girl who goes to war. (Read excerpts aloud to young children).

3. Middle-School Grades (6–8)

Brooks, P. S. (1983). *Queen Eleanor: Independent Spirit of the Medieval World.* Lippincott.

This is a biography of the twelfth-century queen, Eleanor of Aquitane.

Burch, J. J. (1991). *Isabella of Castile: Queen on Horseback.* Watts.

This biography tells the story of the Queen of Spain who, with her husband, Ferdinand, financed Columbus's voyages to the New World.

Churchill, W. (1969). *Joan of Arc: Her Life as Told by Winston Churchill.* Dodd.

This is the biography of Joan of Arc, the heroine of France, who was eventually condemned and burned at the stake.

Duran, G. (1992). *Malinche. Slave Princess of Cortez.* Linnet/Shoe String Press.

This is the biography of Malinali/La Malinche, an Aztec princess who was a slave and interpreter for Cortez during his conquest of Mexico.

Nichols, J. K. (1993). *A Matter of Conscience: The Trial of Anne Hutchinson.* Illus. by D. Krovatin. Steck-Vaughn.

This biography describes the religious climate in Salem, Massachusetts.

C. 1700 through 1900

1. Primary Grades (1–3)

Adler, D. A. (1995). *A Picture Book of Sojourner Truth.* Holiday.

This is the story of Sojourner Truth, a former slave who becomes a passionate advocate against slavery.

Blumberg, R. (1993). *Bloomers!* Bradbury.

In this fictionalized story, Libby intrigues her cousin, Elizabeth Cady Stanton, when she comes to town wearing an outrageous costume for the times—bloomers. The costume soon becomes the uniform of the women's movement.

McCully, E. A. (1996). *The Bobbin Girl.* Illus. by the author. Dial.

This is the fictionalized story of Harriet Hanson Robinson, whose home becomes a meeting place for women who walk out from their jobs in textile mills in protest of a pay cut.

McKissack, P. and F. (1993). *Sojourner Truth, Ain't I a Woman?* Scholastic.

This biography describes Sojourner Truth's trial when she sues in court to regain her son.

Miller, R. H. (1995). *The Story of Stagecoach Mary.* Illus. by C. Hanna. Silver Burdett Press.

This is a fictionalized account of Mary Fields, the first African-American woman to drive a stagecoach that carries the mail.

Raphael, E., & Bolognese, D. (1994). *Sacajawea: The Journey West.* Scholastic.

This biography is about the Native American girl who accompanied the Lewis and Clark expedition.

Roop, P., & Roop, C. (1987). *Keep the Lights Burning, Abbie.* Illus. by P. Hanson. Lathrop, Lee & Shepard.

> This is a fictionalized story of Abbie, the daughter of a lighthouse keeper in Maine, who must take over during a storm when her father leaves and her mother becomes ill.

St. George, J. (1989). *By George, Bloomers!* Shoe Tree.

> This is a fictionalized story of how bloomers came to be a symbol of the women's rights movement.

2. Intermediate Grades (3–6)

Berleth, R. (1994). *Mary Patten's Voyage.* Albert Whitman.

> This is a fictionalized account of how a ship captain's eighteen-year-old wife took over and sailed the ship around Cape Horn.

Dalgliesh, A. (1987). *The Courage of Sarah Noble.* Macmillan.

> This fictionalized account is based on the true story of eight-year-old Sarah Noble, who goes into the wilderness with her father to cook and care for him.

Fritz, J. (1995). *You Want Women to Vote, Lizzie Stanton?* Illus. by D. Disalvo-Ryan. Putnam's.

> This biography depicts Elizabeth Cady Stanton's efforts for women's rights.

McGovern, A. (1975). *Secret Soldier: The Story of Deborah Sampson.* Scholastic.

> This is a biography of a young woman who disguises herself as a boy and joins the army in the Revolutionary War.

Jordan, D. (1994). *Susie King Taylor: Destined to be Free.* Illus. by H. Bond. Just Us Books.

> This is a biography of a slave who learns to read and write, escapes from slavery, and becomes a teacher of black children and adults. She then becomes a nurse in the Union Army.

San Souci, R. (1993). *Cut from the Same Cloth: American Women of Myth, Legend, and Tall Tale.* Philomel.

> This book is a collection of stories about women from different cultures whose heroic actions and deeds often saved themselves, and their families and friends.

3. Middle School Grades (6–8)

Atkinson, L. (1978). *Mary Jones: The Most Dangerous Woman in America.* Crown.

> This biography is about an early supporter of the labor movement.

DePauw, L. G. (1975). *Founding Mothers: Women in America in the Revolutionary Era.* Houghton Mifflin.

> This account focuses on women's contributions to the Revolutionary War.

Hoople, C. G. (1978). *As I Saw It: Women Who Loved the American Adventure.* Dial.

> This account describes the struggles and contributions of colonial and pioneer women.

Levenson, D. (1973). *Women of the West.* Watts.

> This is a collection of brief biographies about the lives of Native American, African-American, and European-American women.

Markham, L. (1992). *Helen Keller.* Watts.

> This is a biography of Helen Keller.

Meade, M. (1976). *Free Woman: The Life and Times of Victoria Woodhull.* Knopf.

> This is the biography of the first woman to run for president of the United States.

Meigs, C. L. (1970). *Jane Addams: Pioneer for Social Justice.* Little.

> This is the biography of social reformer Jane Addams, the founder of Hull House.

D. 1900 to the present

1. Primary Grades (1–3)

Gonzalez, F. (1992). *Gloria Estefan: Cuban-American Singing Star.* Millbrook.

> This is a biography of Gloria Estefan, who enters the United States as a Cuban exile and becomes an international star in the music world.

Hawxhurst, I. C. (1993). *Antonia Novello: U.S. Surgeon General.* Millbrook.

> This is the biography of the Puerto Rican girl who became the Surgeon General of the United States.

2. Intermediate Grades (3–6)

Giblin, J. C. (1992). *Edith Wilson: The Woman Who Ran the United States.* Viking.

> This is the biography of the life of Edith, who supported President Wilson when he became ill during World War I.

Igus, T. (1991). *Great Women in the Struggle.* Just Us Books.

> This is a collection of brief profiles of eighty-plus African-American women.

Kerby, M. (1990). *Amelia Earhart: Courage in the Sky.* Illus. by E. McKeating. Puffin.

> This is the biography of the noted aviator, Amelia Earhart, who disappeared on an around-the-world flight.

Ransom, C. F. *Listening to the Crickets: A Story about Rachel Carson.* Carolrhoda.

> This is the biography of the biologist whose book, *Silent Spring,* played a major role in banning the use of the insecticide DDT.

Veglahn, N. (1977). *The Mysterious Rays: Marie Curie's World.* Illus. by V. Juhasz. Coward.

> This biography chronicles the later life of Marie Curie, the French chemist who discovered radium.

3. Middle-School Grades (6–8)

Fisher, M. P. (1989). *Women in the Third World.* Watts.

> This account provides profiles of women involved in contemporary issues.

Freedman, R. (1993). *Eleanor Roosevelt: A Life of Discovery.* Clarion.

> This is a biography of Eleanor Roosevelt.

Hull, M. (1994). *Rosa Parks: Civil Rights Leader.* Chelsea.

> This biography describes how Parks's refusal to give up her bus seat sparked the Montgomery Boycott and led to subsequent civil rights actions.

Roosevelt, E. (1984) *Eleanor Roosevelt, with Love: A Centenary Remembrance.* Dutton/Lodestar.

> This biography is by Roosevelt's son, Eliot.

Schneider, D. (1993). *American Women in the Progressive Era, 1900–1920.* Facts on File.

> This account, which includes primary sources, describes women's struggle for equality.

Stanley, S. C. (1993). *Women in the Military.* Messner.

> This account describes women who have served in wartime as well as the establishment of women's branches of the armed forces.

References

Prologue: Reflecting on What's Ahead, p.1

Alter, J., & Denworth, L. (1990). A (vague) sense of history. *Newsweek*, Special Issue, 31–33.

Newmann, F. M. (1988). Can depth replace coverage in the high school curriculum? *Phi Delta Kappan*, 69, 346.

Parker, W. C. (1990). Assessing citizenship. *Educational Leadership*, 48, 17–22.

Schaps, E., & Solomon, D. (1990). Schools and classrooms as caring communities. *Educational Leadership*, 48, 38–42.

1. The Dynamics of Social Studies, p.8

Arendt, H. (1961). *Between past and future*. New York: Viking.

Asante, M. K., & Ravitch, D. (1991). Multiculturalism: An exchange. *The American Scholar* 60 (Spring), 267–276.

Banks, J. A. (1989). Approaches to multicultural curriculum reform. In J. Banks & C. McGee Banks (Eds.), *Multicultural education: Issues and perspectives* (pp. 189–207). Boston: Allyn & Bacon.

———. (1997). *Educating citizens in a multicultural society*. New York: Teachers College Press.

Barnicle, M. (1994). Dropping our eyes at true evil. *The Boston Globe*, 25 February, C1.

Bell, D. (1990). Resolving the contradictions of modernity and modernism (Part II). *Society* 27, 66–75.

Dewey, John. (1938). What is social study? *Progressive Education*, 15 (May), 367–369.

Gross, R., & Dynesson, T. (1991). *Social science perspectives on citizenship education*. New York: Teachers College Press.

MacIntyre, A. (1990). How to be a North American. In J. Quay & J. Veninga (Eds.), *Making connections: The humanities, culture, and community* (pp. 1–25). Occasional Paper No. 1. American Council of Learned Societies and the Federation of State Humanities Councils.

Martin, J. R. (1995). A philosophy of education for the year 2000. *Phi Delta Kappan*, 76(5), 355–359.

National Council for the Social Studies. (1994). *Expect excellence: Curriculum standards for social studies*. Executive Summary. Washington, DC.

Ravitch, D. (1990). New York education chief seeks new stress on nonwhite cultures. *The New York Times*, 7 February, B4.

Salinas, P. D. (1997). *Assimilation, American style*. New York: Basic Books.

Tocqueville, Alexis de. (1947). *Democracy in America*, ed. Henry Steele Commager, tr. H. Reeve. Oxford: Oxford University Press.

Wiggins, G. (1989). The futility of trying to teach everything of importance. *Educational Leadership* 47 (November), 44–49.

2. History and the Social Sciences: The Knowledge Base for Social Studies, p.42

Arendt, H. (1961). *Between past and future*. New York: Viking Press.

Bednarz, S. (1997). Using the geographic perspective to enrich history. *Social Education*, 61, 139–145.

Brody, R. A. (1989). Why study politics? In National Commission, *Charting a course: Social studies for the 21st century* (pp. 59–63). Washington, DC: National Commission on Social Studies in the Schools.

Brophy, J. E., & VanSledright, B. A. (1997). *Teaching and learning history in elementary schools*. New York: Teachers College Press.

Bruer, J. (1993). *Schools for thought: A science of learning in the classroom*. Cambridge: Harvard University Press.

Bruner, J. (1986). *Actual minds, possible worlds*. Cambridge: Harvard University Press.

Caine, R. N., & Caine, G. (1994). *Making connections: Teaching and the human brain*. New York: Addison-Wesley.

Commager, H. S., & Muessig, R. (1980). *The nature and study of history*. Columbus, OH: Merrill.

Dawson, E. (1929). *Teaching the social studies*. New York: Macmillan.

Egan, K. (1979). What children know best. *Social Education,* 43, 130–134.

Elkind, D. (1982). *The hurried child.* Reading, MA: Addison-Wesley.

Gardner, H. (1991). *The unschooled mind: How children think and schools should teach.* New York: Basic Books.

Good, T. L., & Brophy, J. E. (1994). *Looking in classrooms* (6th ed.). New York: HarperCollins.

Henry, T. (1994). Mapping out geography plan. *USA Today,* 21 October, 4D.

Joint Committee on Geographic Education. (1984). *Guidelines for Geographic Education.* Washington, DC: National Council for Geographic Education and the Association of American Geographers.

Levstik, L., & Barton, K. (1997). *Doing history: Investigating with children in elementary and middle schools.* Mahwah, NJ: Lawrence Erlbaum Associates.

———— & Pappas, C. (1987). Exploring the development of historical understanding. *Journal of Research and Development in Education,* 21, 1–15.

Momigliano, A. (1982). History in an age of ideologies. *The American Scholar,* 51, 495–507.

Piaget, J. (1950). *The psychology of intelligence.* New York: Harcourt Brace.

Postman, N., & Weingartner, C. (1969). *Teaching as a subversive activity.* New York: Dell.

Theroux, P. (1997). Letter from Hong Kong. *New Yorker,* 12 May, 54–65.

Thornton, S. J., & Vukelich, R. (1988). Effects of children's understanding of time concepts on historical understanding. *Theory and Research in Social Education,* 15, 69–82.

3. How Social Studies Programs Are Organized, p. 68

Apple, M. (1993). *Official knowledge: Democratic education in a conservative age.* New York: Routledge.

Cornbleth, C., & Waugh, D. (1995). *The great speckled bird: Multicultural politics and educational policymaking.* New York: St. Martin's Press.

Hirsch, E. D. (1988). *Cultural literacy.* New York: Vintage Books.

————. (1991–1993). *What your kindergarten [through sixth] grader needs to know.* New York: Doubleday.

Johansen, B. (1982). *Forgotten fathers.* Cambridge, MA: Harvard Common Press.

Joyce, W. W., Little, T. H., & Wronski, S. P. (1991). Scope and sequence, goals, and objectives: Effects on social studies. In J. P. Shaver (Ed.), *Handbook of social studies teaching and learning* (pp. 321–331). New York: Macmillan.

Larkins, G., Hawkins, M. L., & Gilmore, A. (1987). Trivial and noninformative content of elementary social studies: A review of primary texts in four series. *Theory and Research in Social Education,* 15 (Fall), 299–311.

Marshall, M. (1996). Disadvantaged students narrow gap. *Common Knowledge,* 9, 3 & 5.

National Council for the Social Studies (NCSS), Task Force on Scope and Sequence. (1989). In search of a scope and sequence for social studies. *Social Education,* 53, 380–382.

Pappas, C. C., Keifer, B., & Levstik, L. (1995). *An integrated language perspective in elementary school: Theory into action.* White Plains, NY: Longman.

Peterson, B. (1995). What should children learn? A teacher looks at E. D. Hirsch. In D. Levine, R. Lowe, B. Peterson, & R. Tenorio (Eds.), *Rethinking schools: An agenda for change* (pp. 74–88). New York: New Press.

Starna, W. (1990). Letters to the editor. *The New York Times,* 7 March.

Taba, H. (1967). *Teacher's handbook for elementary social studies* (introductory ed.). Menlo Park, CA: Addison-Wesley.

Weatherford, J. (1988). *Indian givers: How the Indians of America transformed the world.* New York: Crown.

Whitmire, R. (2000). Core knowledge boosts scores. *USA Today,* 30 May, 8D.

4. The Dimensions of Cultural Diversity, p. 96

Banks, J. (1989). Approaches to multicultural curriculum reform. In J. Banks & C. McGee Banks (Eds.), *Multicultural education: Issues and perspectives* (pp. 189–207). Boston: Allyn & Bacon.

Barber, B. R. (1992). *An aristocracy for everyone: The politics of education and the future of America.* New York: Ballantine Books.

Bigelow, B. (1996). On the road to cultural bias: A critique of the Oregon Trail CD-ROM. *Rethinking Schools.* 10, Milwaukee, WI: Rethinking Schools.

Christensen, L. (1994). Unlearning the myths that bind us. In B. Bigelow, L. Christensen, S. Karp, B. Miner, & B. Petersen (Eds.), *Rethinking our classrooms: Teaching for equity and justice.* Milwaukee, WI: Rethinking Schools.

Delpit, L. (1995). *Other people's children.* New York: New Press.

Elrich, M. (1994). The stereotype within. *Educational Leadership,* 51, 12–15.

Flynn, V., & Chambers, R. D. (1994). Promoting gender equity: What you can do? *Learning 94,* 22 (5), 58–59.

Gay, G. (1991). Culturally diverse students and social studies. In J. Shaver (Ed.), *Handbook of research on social studies teaching and learning* (pp. 154–174). New York: Macmillan.

————. (1997). Educational equity for students of color. In J. A. Banks & C. A. M. Banks (Eds.), *Multicultural education: Issues and perspectives* (pp. 171–194). Boston: Allyn & Bacon.

Grant, C. A., & Sleeter, C. E. (1989). *Turning on learning.* New York: Merrill.

Kames, M. (2000). Girls can be president. *Middle-Level Learning.* An occasional publication of the National Council for the Social Studies. January/February 2000, M5–M8.

Lee, E. (1994). Taking multicultural, anti-racist education seriously. In B. Bigelow et al. (Eds.), *Rethinking our classrooms: Teaching for equity and justice.* Milwaukee, WI: Rethinking Schools.

Sadker, M., & Sadker, D. (1994). *Failing at fairness: How America's schools cheat girls.* New York: Macmillan.

Shade, B. J., & New, C. A. (1993). Cultural influences on learning: Teaching implications. In J. A. Banks & C. A. Banks (Eds.), *Multicultural education: Issues and perspectives* (pp. 317–331). Boston: Allyn & Bacon.

Stokes, S. S. (1997). Curriculum for Native American students: Using Native American values. *The Reading Teacher,* 50, 576–584.

Children's Literature

Mochizuki, K. (1993). *Baseball saved us.* New York: Lee & Lowe.

Uchida, Y. (1971). *Journey to Topaz: A story of the Japanese-American evacuation.* New York: Scribners.

5. The Dimensions of Instructional Diversity, p. 125

Bigelow, B. (1994). Getting off the track. *Rethinking our classrooms: Teaching for equity and justice.* Milwaukee, WI: Rethinking Schools.

Campbell, L. (1997). How teachers interpret MI theory. *Educational Leadership,* 55, 14–19.

Dunn, R., & Dunn, K. (1992). *Teaching elementary school students through their individual learning styles.* Boston: Allyn & Bacon.

Gardner, H. (1993). *Frames of mind.* New York: HarperCollins Basic Books.

————. (1993). *Multiple intelligences: The theory in practice.* New York: Basic Books.

———— & Checkley, K. (1997). The first seven . . . and the eighth. *Educational Leadership,* 55, 8–13.

Good, T., & Brophy, J. (2000). *Looking in classrooms* (8th ed.). New York: Longman.

Henning, D. (1994). *Communication in action.* Boston: Houghton Mifflin.

Kohl, Herbert. (1994). I won't learn from you! In B. Bigelow et al. (Eds.), *Rethinking our classrooms: Teaching for equity and justice.* Milwaukee, WI: Rethinking Schools.

Kraus, R. (1998). Aruegho, J. (illus.) (1998). *Leo the late bloomer.* New York: HarperCollins Juvenile Books.

Mooney, J., & Cole, D. (2000). *Learning outside the lines.* New York: Simon & Schuster.

Rosenthal, B. (1971). *The images of man.* New York: Basic Books.

Schwabe, M. (1994). The pigs: When tracking takes its toll. *Rethinking our classrooms: Teaching for equity and justice.* Milwaukee, WI: Rethinking Schools.

Temple, L. (2000). Disputed health duties injected into teaching of disabled. *USA Today,* 15 February, 9D.

Turnbull, A., Turnbull, R., Shank, M., & Leal, D. (1999). *Exceptional lives: Special education in today's schools* (2nd ed.), Upper Saddle River, NJ: Merrill/Prentice Hall.

Children's Literature

Lyon, G. (1994). *Mama is a miner.* New York: Orchard Books.

Priceman, M. (1994). *How to make an apple pie and see the world.* New York: Alfred Knopf.

6. Developing Character and Values, p. 144

Bennett, W. J. (1994). *The book of virtues.* New York: Simon & Schuster.

Berreth, D., & Scherer, M. (1993). On transmitting values: A conversation with Amitai Etzioni. *Educational Leadership,* 51, 12–15.

Brogmann, A. (1992). *Crossing the postmodern divide.* Chicago: University of Chicago Press.

Canter, L. (September, 1989). Assertive discipline: More than names on the board and marbles in a jar. *Phi Delta Kappan,* 70, 57–60.

Doyle, D. P. (February, 1997). Education and character. *Phi Delta Kappan,* 78, 440–443.

Fabes, R. A., et al. (1989). Effective rewards on children's prosocial motivation: A socialization study. *Developmental Psychology, 25,* 509–515.

Gilligan, C. C. (1977). In a different voice: Women's conceptions of the self and morality. *Harvard Educational Review, 49,* 481–517.

———. (1982). *In a different voice: Psychological theory and women's development.* Cambridge, MA: Harvard University Press, 25–32.

Glasser, W. (1990). *The quality school.* New York: Harper & Row.

Grusec, J. (1991). Socializing concerns for others in the home. *Developmental Psychology, 27,* 338–342.

Hersh, R. H., Miller, J. P., & Fielding, G. D. (1980). *Models of moral education: An appraisal.* New York: Longman.

Himmelfarb, G. (1995). *The demoralization of society.* New York: Knopf.

Kilpatrick, W. (1992). *Why Johnny can't tell right from wrong.* New York: Simon and Schuster.

Kohn, A. (February, 1997). How not to teach values. *Phi Delta Kappan, 78,* 429–439.

Leming, J. S. (1985). Research on social studies curriculum and instruction: Interventions and outcomes in the socio-moral domain. In William B. Stanley (Ed.), *Review of research in social studies education, 1976–1983.* Washington, DC: National Council for the Social Studies, and the Boulder, CO: ERIC Clearinghouse for Social Studies/Social Science Education, and the Social Science Education Consortium, 123–213.

———. (November, 1993). In search of effective character education. *Educational Leadership, 51,* 63–71.

Lickona, T. (March, 1977). How to encourage moral development. *Learning, 5,* 37–43.

———. (November, 1993). The return of character education. *Educational Leadership, 51,* 6–11.

Lockwood, A. L. (May, 1977). What's wrong with values clarification. *Social Education, 41,* 399–401.

———. (1993). A letter to character educators. *Instructional Leadership, 51,* 72–75.

Mussen, P., & Eisenberg-Berg, N. (1977). *Roots of caring, sharing, and helping: The development of prosocial behavior in children.* New York: Freeman.

Raths, L. E., Harmin, M., & Simon, S. B. (1978). *Values and teaching* (2nd ed.). Columbus, OH: Charles E. Merrill.

Rogers, C., & Frieberg, H. G. (1994). *Freedom to learn* (3rd. ed.). Englewood Cliffs, NJ: Merrill/Prentice-Hall.

Ryan, K. (1993). Doing half the job. *Houghton Mifflin/Educators' Forum,* Fall, 12.

———. (1986). The new moral education. *Phi Delta Kappan, 68* (November), 228–233.

Scott, K. C. (1987). Missing developmental perspectives in moral education. *Theory and Research in Social Education, 15* (Fall), 257–273.

Sizer, T. (1985). *Horace's compromise.* Boston: Houghton Mifflin.

Williams, M. M. (1992). *How a value is treated in middle schools: The early adolescents.* Michigan: University Microfilms International.

Woolever, R., & Scott, K. P. (1988). *Active learning in social studies.* Glenview, IL: Scott, Foresman.

7. Social Studies: Gateway to Literacy, p. 168

Button, K., Johnson, M., & Furgeson, P. (1996). Interactive writing in a primary classroom. *The Reading Teacher, 49,* 2–10.

Chall, J. S., & Conard, S. (1991). *Should textbooks challenge students?* New York: Teachers College Press.

Christiansen, L. (1994). Whose standard? Teaching standard English. *Rethinking our classrooms: Teaching for equity and justice.* Milwaukee, WI: Rethinking Schools.

Clay, M. (1993). *The early literacy observation survey.* Portsmouth, NH: Heinemann.

Cooper, J. D. (2000). *Literacy: Helping children construct meaning* (4th ed.). Boston: Houghton Mifflin.

———. (1993). *Helping students construct meaning.* Boston: Houghton Mifflin.

Dickinson, D. (1987). Oral language, literacy skills, and responses to literature. In J. Squires (Ed.), *Dynamics of language learning.* Urbana, IL: National Council of Teachers of English.

Flood, J., & Lapp, D. (1987). Reading and writing relations: Assumptions and directions. In J. Squires (Ed.), *Dynamics of language learning.* Urbana, IL: National Council of Teachers of English.

Henning, D. (1994). *Communication in action.* Boston: Houghton Mifflin.

Hymes, L., & Hymes, J. (1960). *Hooray for chocolate.* Reading, MA: Addison-Wesley.

Irvin, J. L., Lunstrum, J. P., Lynch-Brown, C., & Shepard, M. F. (1995). *Enhancing social studies through literacy strategies.* Washington, DC: National Council for the Social Studies.

Langer, J. A. (1981). From theory to practice: A pre-reading plan. *Journal of Reading, 25,* 106–110.

McAuley, K., & Wilson, R. H. (1985). *The United States past to present.* Lexington, MA: Heath.

Morrow, L. M. (1989). *Literacy development in the early years: Helping children read and write.* Englewood Cliffs, NJ: Prentice-Hall.

Olge, D. D. (1989). The know, want to know, learn strategy. In K. D. Muth (Ed.), *Children's comprehension of text: Research into practice* (pp. 205–223). Newark, DE: International Reading Association.

Pinnell, G. S., & McCarrier, A. (1994). Interactive writing: A transition tool for assisting children in learning to read and write. In E. Hiebert & B. Taylor (Eds.), *Getting reading right from the start: Effective early literacy interventions* (pp. 149–170). Needham, MA: Allyn & Bacon.

Robinson, F. (1962). *Effective study.* New York: Harper & Row.

Routman, R. (1996). *Literacy at the crossroads.* Portsmouth, NH: Heinemann.

Sewall, G. T. (1988). American history textbooks: Where do we go from here? *Phi Delta Kappan,* 69, 552–558.

Taba, H., Durkin, M., Frankel, J. R., & McNaughton, A. (1967). *Teacher's handbook for elementary social studies* (introductory ed.). Reading, MA: Addison-Wesley.

Welton, D. A. (1982). Expository writing, pseudowriting, and social studies. *Social Education,* 46 (October), 444–448.

ASCD. (1996). Designing rubrics for authentic assessment. *ASCD Education Update,* 38 (December), 7.

Gronlund, N. E. (1985). *Measurement and evaluation in teaching* (5th ed.). New York: Macmillan.

Herman, J. L. (1997). Large-scale assessment in support of school reforms: Lessons in the search for alternative measures. (CSE technical report 446). Los Angeles, CA: University of California, Los Angeles, Center for the Study of Evaluation.

O'Neil, J. (1994). Making assessment meaningful. *ASCD Curriculum Update,* 36, 3–5.

———. (1996). Teaching for performance. *ASCD Education Update,* 38, 8, 1, 6.

Parker, W. C. (1991). *Renewing the social studies curriculum.* Alexandria, VA: Association for Supervision and Curriculum Development.

Spady, W. G. (1994). Choosing outcomes of significance. *Educational Leadership,* 51 (6), 18–22.

Wiggins, G. (1989). Teaching to the authentic test. *Educational Leadership,* 46 (April), 41–47.

Children's Literature

Fritz, J. (1987). *Shh! We're writing the constitution.* Illustrated by Tomie de Paola. New York: G. Putnam's Sons.

8. Planning and Orchestrating Instruction, p. 202

Bloom, B. S., et al. (1956). *Taxonomy of educational objectives: The classification of educational goals, handbook I: Cognitive domain.* New York: Longman.

Brophy, J., & Alleman, J. (1991). Activities as instructional tools: A framework for analysis and evaluation. *Educational Research,* 20 (May), 9–22.

Krathwohl, D. R., et al. (1964). *Taxonomy of educational objectives: The classification of educational goals, handbook II: Affective domain.* New York: Longman.

Children's Literature

Bunting, E. (1991). *Fly away home.* Boston: Houghton Mifflin.

Burton, V. L. (1939). *Mike Mulligan and his steam shovel.* Boston: Houghton Mifflin.

9. Assessing Learning, p. 234

Alleman, J., & Brophy, J. (1998). Assessment in a social constructivist classroom. *Social Education,* 62, 32–42.

10. Strategies for Effective Teaching, p. 266

Brophy, J., & Alleman, J. (1990). Activities as instructional tools: A framework for analysis and evaluation. Occasional Paper No. 132. East Lansing: Michigan State University, Institute for Research on Teaching.

Hawthorne, N. (1870). *Twice told tales.* Boston: James R. Osgood.

Johonnot, J. (1887). *Stories of our country.* New York: D. Appleton.

Lauritzen, C., & Jaeger, M. (1994). Language arts teacher education within a transdisciplinary curriculum. *Language Arts,* 71 (8), 581–587.

National Council for the Social Studies. (1994). *Expectations of excellence: Curriculum standards for social studies.* Washington, DC: National Council for the Social Studies.

Rosenshine, B., & Stevens, R. (1986). Teaching functions. In Merlin C. Wittrock (Ed.), *Handbook of research on teaching* (3rd ed., pp. 376–391). New York: Macmillan.

Schmidt, F., & Friedman, A. (1987). Strategies for resolving classroom conflicts. *Learning 87,* 15 (February), 40–42.

Williams, R. G., & Ware, J. E. (1977). An extended visit with Dr. Fox: Validity of student satisfaction with instructional ratings after repeated exposures to a lecturer. *American Educational Research Journal,* 41 (Fall), 449–457.

11. Strategies for Active Learning, p. 287

Berman, Sheldon. (1990). Educating for social responsibility. *Educational Leadership,* 48 (November), 75–83.

Graves, D., & Hansen, J. (1983). The author's chair. *Language Arts,* 60 (February), 176–183.

Kellogg, S. (1988). *Johnny Appleseed.* New York: Morrow.

Lee, J. R. (1974). *Teaching social studies in the elementary school.* New York: Macmillan.

Lippitt, R. (1958). The auxiliary chair technique. *Group Psychotherapy,* 11 (January), 8–23.

Shaftel, F. R., & Shaftel, G. (1982). *Role playing in the curriculum.* Englewood Cliffs, NJ: Prentice-Hall.

Silverstein, S. (1964). *The giving tree.* New York: Harper & Row.

Walker, B. M. (1979). *The little house cookbook.* New York: Harper & Row.

12. Nurturing Critical and Reflective Thinking, p. 306

Beyer, B. K. (Ed.). (1987). *Practical strategies for the teaching of thinking.* Boston: Allyn & Bacon.

Bloom, B. S., et al. (1956). *Taxonomy of educational objectives: The classification of educational goals, handbook I: Cognitive domain.* New York: Longman.

Bonny, E. (1984). Thinking about thinking. *Educational Leadership,* 42 (March/April), 234–238.

Costa, A. L. (1984). Mediating the metacognitive. *Educational Leadership,* 42 (November), 57–62.

Rowe, Mary Bodd. (1969). Science, silence, and sanctions. *Science and Children,* 6, 11–13.

13. Helping Students Use Maps, Globes, and Graphics, p. 303

Hanna, P. R., et al. (1966). *Geography in the teaching of the social studies: Concepts and skills.* Boston: Houghton Mifflin.

Joint Committee on Geographic Education. (1984). *Guidelines for geographic education.* Washington, DC: National Council for Geographic Education and the Association of American Geographers.

Monmonier, M. (1991). *How to lie with maps.* Chicago: University of Chicago Press.

Pritchard, S. F. (1989). Using picture books to teach geography in the primary grades. *Journal of Geography,* 88, 126–136.

Children's Literature

Burton, V. L. (1943). *Katy and the big snow.* Boston: Houghton Mifflin.

Freschet, B. (1977). *Little black bear goes for a walk.* New York: Scribners.

Hutchins, P. (1968). *Rosie's walk.* New York: Macmillan.

McCloskey, R. (1941). *Make way for ducklings.* New York: Viking.

Potter, Beatrix. (1995). *Peter rabbit.* Dover.

Schwartz, D. M. (1985). *How much is a million?* Illustrations by S. Kellogg. New York: Lothrop, Lee & Shepard.

Taylor, M. (1968). *Henry explores the jungle.* New York: Atheneum.

14. Using Instructional Tools: Print, Multimedia, and Community Resources, p. 361

Braun, J. A., Jr., Fernlund, P., & White, C. S. (1998). *Technology tools in the social studies curriculum.* Wilsonville, OR: Franklin, Beedle & Associates.

Bryant, K. (1992, September). Apply early language connections. *The explorer.* 1–2.

Ellerbee, L. (1995). What shall we tell the kids? *Liberal Opinion Week,* 6 (May 1), p. 7.

Macaulay, D. (1973). *Cathedral.* Boston: Houghton Mifflin.

McGowan, T. M. (1987). Children's fiction as a source for social studies skill-building. *ERIC Digest* (No. 37). Bloomington, IN: Clearinghouse for Social Studies/Social Science Education.

Rose, S. A., & Fernlund, P. M. (1997). Using technology for powerful social studies learning. *Social Education,* 61, 160–166.

Children's Literature

Baker, B. (1972). *The big push.* New York: Coward, McCann & Geoghegan.

Burton, V. L. (1939). *Mike Mulligan and his steam shovel.* Boston: Houghton Mifflin.

Grahame, K. (1954). *The wind in the willows.* New York: Scribners. (Originally published in 1908.)

Mathis, S. B. (1975). *The hundred penny box.* New York: Viking Press.

Name Index

Subject Index

About the Author

David A. Welton is a native Ohioan, who, after teaching briefly at Syracuse University, has been a Professor of Social Studies Education at Texas Tech University for the past 25 years. He holds bachelors degrees from Western Reserve and Kent State universities, and a masters and doctorate from Ohio University (Athens, Ohio, not Columbus!). Dr. Welton has been active in the National Council for the Social Studies and is a former editor of the Elementary Education section of its journal, *Social Education*. He has also authored numerous articles on the teaching of social studies.

Dr. Welton and his wife, Kathleen, are the parents of three boys—now young men—all of whom have left the high desert of West Texas for the mountains of Colorado and New Mexico. In their absence, their parents are once again enjoying the unhindered use of their automobiles and telephone.